Fodor's **07**

NEW YORK CITY

**Where to Stay and Eat
for All Budgets**

**Must-See Sights
and Local Secrets**

Ratings You Can Trust

Fodor's Travel Publications   New York, Toronto, London, Sydney, Auckland
www.fodors.com

FODOR'S NEW YORK CITY 2007

Editor: William Travis

Editorial Contributors: Lynne Arany, Michelle Delio, Kevin Doughten, Paul Eisenberg, Sarah Gold, Melissa Klurman, Christina Knight, Adam Kowit, Sara Marcus, Diane Mehta, Stasha Mills, Michael Nalepa, Jennifer Paull, Meryl D. Pearlstein, Sandra Ramani, John Rambow, Tom Steele, Jackie Terrebone

Editorial Production: Tom Holton

Maps and Illustrations: David Lindroth, *cartographer;* William Wu; with additional cartography provided by Henry Columb, Mark Stroud, and Ali Baird, Moon Street Cartography, and Adam Cohen, Earth Data Solutions; Bob Blake and Rebecca Baer, *map editors*

Design: Fabrizio La Rocca, *creative director;* Guido Caroti, Chie Ushio, Tina Malaney; Moon Sun Kim, *cover designer;* Melanie Marin, *senior photo editor*

Production/Manufacturing: Robert B. Shields

Cover Photo (Brooklyn Bridge): Andy Caulfield

ISBN-10: 1–4000–1680–0

ISBN-13: 978–1–4000–1680–8

ISSN: 0736–9395

SPECIAL SALES

This book is available for special discounts for bulk purchases for sales promotions or premiums. Special editions, including personalized covers, excerpts of existing books, and corporate imprints, can be created in large quantities for special needs. For more information, write to Special Markets/Premium Sales, 1745 Broadway, MD 6-2, New York, New York 10019, or e-mail specialmarkets@randomhouse.com.

AN IMPORTANT TIP & AN INVITATION

Although all prices, opening times, and other details in this book are based on information supplied to us at press time, changes occur all the time in the travel world, and Fodor's cannot accept responsibility for facts that become outdated or for inadvertent errors or omissions. So **confirm information when it matters,** especially if you're making a detour to visit a specific place. Your experiences—positive and negative—matter to us. If we have missed or misstated something, **please write to us.** We follow up on all suggestions. Contact the New York City editor at editors@fodors.com or c/o Fodor's at 1745 Broadway, New York, NY 10019.

PRINTED IN THE UNITED STATES OF AMERICA

10 9 8 7 6 5 4 3 2 1

Be a Fodor's Correspondent

Your opinion matters. It matters to us. It matters to your fellow Fodor's travelers, too. And we'd like to hear it. In fact, we *need* to hear it.

When you share your experiences and opinions, you become an active member of the Fodor's community. That means we'll not only use your feedback to make our books better, but we'll publish your names and comments whenever possible. Throughout our guides, look for "Word of Mouth," excerpts of your unvarnished feedback.

Here's how you can help improve Fodor's for all of us.

Tell us when we're right. We rely on local writers to give you an insider's perspective. But our writers and staff editors—who are the best in the business—depend on you. Your positive feedback is a vote to renew our recommendations for the next edition.

Tell us when we're wrong. We're proud that we update most of our guides every year. But we're not perfect. Things change. Hotels cut services. Museums change hours. Charming cafés lose charm. If our writer didn't quite capture the essence of a place, tell us how you'd do it differently. If any of our descriptions are inaccurate or inadequate, we'll incorporate your changes in the next edition and will correct factual errors at fodors.com *immediately*.

Tell us what to include. You probably have had fantastic travel experiences that aren't yet in Fodor's. Why not share them with a community of like-minded travelers? Maybe you chanced upon a beach or bistro or B&B that you don't want to keep to yourself. Tell us why we should include it. And share your discoveries and experiences with everyone directly at fodors.com. Your input may lead us to add a new listing or highlight a place we cover with a "Highly Recommended" star or with our highest rating, "Fodor's Choice."

Send your nominations, comments, and complaints by mail to the New York City Editor, Fodor's, 1745 Broadway, New York, NY 10019. Or e-mail editors@fodors.com with the subject line "New York City Editor." You and travelers like you are the heart of the Fodor's community. Make our community richer by sharing your experiences. Be a Fodor's correspondent.

Happy traveling!

Tim Jarrell, Publisher

CONTENTS

MAPS

NEW YORK CITY IN FOCUS

CLOSEUPS

ABOUT THIS BOOK

Our Ratings

Sometimes you find terrific travel experiences and sometimes they just find you. But usually the burden is on you to select the right combination of experiences. That's where our ratings come in.

As travelers we've all discovered a place so wonderful that its worthiness is obvious. And sometimes that place is so experiential that superlatives don't do it justice: you just have to be there to know. These sights, properties, and experiences get our highest rating, **Fodor's Choice**, indicated by orange stars throughout this book.

Black stars highlight sights and properties we deem **Highly Recommended,** places that our writers, editors, and readers praise again and again for consistency and excellence.

By default, there's another category: any place we include in this book is by definition worth your time, unless we say otherwise. And we will.

Disagree with any of our choices? Care to nominate a place or suggest that we rate one more highly? Visit our feedback center at www. fodors.com/feedback.

Budget Well

Hotel and restaurant price categories from ¢ to $$$$ are defined in the opening pages of the respective chapters. For attractions, we always give standard adult admission fees; reductions are usually available for children, students, and senior citizens. Want to pay with plastic? **AE, D, DC, MC, V** following restaurant and hotel listings indicate if American Express, Discover, Diners Club, MasterCard, and Visa are accepted.

Restaurants

Unless we state otherwise, restaurants are open for lunch and dinner daily. We mention dress only when there's a specific requirement and reservations only when they're essential or not accepted—it's always best to book ahead.

Hotels

Hotels have private bath, phone, TV, and air-conditioning and operate on the European Plan (a.k.a. EP, meaning without meals), unless we specify that they use the Continental Plan (CP, with a Continental breakfast), Breakfast Plan (BP, with a full breakfast), or Modified American Plan (MAP, with breakfast and dinner) or are all-inclusive (including all meals and most activities). We always

list facilities but not whether you'll be charged an extra fee to use them, so when pricing accommodations, find out what's included.

Many Listings

★	Fodor's Choice
★	Highly recommended
⊠	Physical address
↔	Directions
⌖	Mailing address
☎	Telephone
🖷	Fax
⊕	On the Web
✍	E-mail
🎟	Admission fee
☉	Open/closed times
▶	Start of walk/itinerary
Ⓜ	Metro stations
⊟	Credit cards

Hotels & Restaurants

🏨	Hotel
⤡	Number of rooms
⚬	Facilities
⅙	Meal plans
✕	Restaurant
⌂	Reservations
🏛	Dress code
⤬	Smoking
⚇	BYOB
✕🏨	Hotel with restaurant that warrants a visit

Outdoors

🏌	Golf
⛺	Camping

Other

☺	Family-friendly
ⓕ	Contact information
⇨	See also
⊠	Branch address
☞	Take note

NEW YORK THEN AND NOW

The Dutch Arrive

When the Dutch founded the settlement that would become New York City in the early 1600s, they valued what many locals today still hold dear: freedom, self-expression, excitement, progressive politics, and profit. Before that, the area was controlled by its original owners, the Lenape Indians. The first Europeans to arrive were primarily an assortment of eager entrepreneurs and crooked politicians. Pirate Captain Kidd had a house near the wharves, and he and his colleagues' business activities were enthusiastically supported by a succession of director-generals more concerned with making money than governing. Eventually even the tolerant Dutch became disgusted. Peter Stuyvesant, a particularly resolute man, was made director-general and charged with controlling the wild colony. He closed taverns and brothels and made everyone attend church on Sunday. All seemed to be going well until Charles II of England made a present of New Amsterdam to his brother the Duke of York. The duke sent a fleet to claim his gift. Stuyvesant, with no local military force, surrendered. In September of 1664, New Amsterdam became New York.

Peace & War

The city prospered under English rule until the 1760s, when the British imposed crushing taxes on the colonies. Protests were staged, and tea was flung into the Hudson River. On April 23, 1775, a messenger from Boston arrived with news that the American Revolution had begun. New Yorkers seized control of City Hall and the customhouse. On July 9, 1776, in what is now City Hall Park, President George Washington read the Declaration of Independence aloud: "When in the course of human events, it becomes necessary for one people to dissolve the political bands which have connected them with another . . ." The crowd went wild. A mob raced down Broadway and ripped down a statue of King George III. His head was placed on a stake, his body melted down to make bullets. But within two months the city was under British martial law and remained so until the end of the war. On November 25, 1783, George Washington led his army into Manhattan in triumph, and the war was over. For the next two years, New York would serve as the new nation's capital.

TIMELINE

1626	Dutch acquire Manhattan Island from the Lenape Indians.
1664	Dutch surrender to English, New Amsterdam is renamed New York.
1784	New York City is (briefly) the capital of the United States of America.
1789	George Washington inaugurated as president in Federal Hall on Wall Street.
1811	Street grid system is adopted.
1820	New York becomes nation's largest city.
1850	First issue of the *New York Times* is published.
1857	Landscaping starts in what will become Central Park.
1869	American Museum of Natural History opens.
1880	The Metropolitan Museum of Art opens.
1883	Brooklyn Bridge opens.

NEW YORK THEN AND NOW

Gangs & Riots

In the 1800s New York was a city divided. Fifth Avenue was dotted with magnificent mansions and dubbed "Millionaires Row." But home was a dark, dank tenement for many of the more than 1.1 million residents. Epidemics ravaged the slums and street gangs with names like the Dead Rabbits and Plug Uglies roamed the city. The latter got their name because they "protected" fire hydrants (plugs). The city's several firefighting forces competed for work and paid gang members to restrict hydrant access. The police didn't get along either. In the 1850s the state government restricted membership in the Metropolitan police force to native-born Americans. Mayor Fernando Wood and the city's émigré population promptly established the Municipal Police Department, manned mostly by immigrants. The two forces engaged in frequent battles for control of the city's police stations. Criminals arrested by one force were often freed by the other. It took two decades for New York's pugnacious police to make peace with each other. The police were ineffective during the Draft Riots in July of 1863, but in their defense the riots are commonly considered to be the worst case of civil unrest in U.S. history. The riots were a protest against Abraham Lincoln's "Enrollment Act of Conscription" drafting men to fight in the Civil War. Thousands took fierce exception to the fact that the rich could dodge the draft by paying the government $300. By the time the insurrection ended, four days later and only after federal troops were brought in from the battlefield of Gettysburg to contain the mayhem, hundreds were wounded, dozens were dead, and property valued at more than $1,500,000 (approximately $30 million in today's money) had been destroyed.

Modern Times

In 1898 Manhattan, the Bronx, Brooklyn, Queens, and Staten Island joined together to form Greater New York. The first subway was built in 1904, and Grand Central Terminal opened seven years later. Electricity turned Broadway into the Great White Way. The Chrysler Building, at that time the world's biggest skyscraper at 1,000 feet high, opened for business on May 27, 1930. Within a year the Empire State Building, 1,250 feet high, stole the tallest title. But these engineering landmarks were overshadowed by the October 1929 stock market crash, which ushered

1886	Statue of Liberty dedication ceremony on Bedloe's Island.
1892	U.S. Immigration Center opens on Ellis Island.
1898	"The Five Boroughs"—Brooklyn, the Bronx, Manhattan, Queens, and Staten Island—consolidate into Greater New York City.
1911	Triangle Factory Fire in Greenwich Village kills 145 female garment workers, leading to sweeping changes in fire department, workplace safety regulations, and building codes.

1904	First New York subway company, the Interborough Rapid Transit, begins operations.
1925	New York City becomes the most populous city in the world.
1931	The Empire State Building opens.
1951	United Nations relocates from Flushing Meadows Park, Queens, headquarters to East Side of Manhattan.
1970	McSorley's Old Ale House forced to admit female customers.
1973	Twin Towers commence one-year reign as the world's tallest buildings.

in the Great Depression. The economy limped along until World War II, when NYC emerged as the center of America's economic power. But life in the city wasn't pretty. Crime again became a problem in the decades following WWII, businesses moved from the city, and politicians did little to stem the rising tide of discontent.

In the 1970s, it all fell apart. The city was bankrupt and requested financial help from the federal government. President Gerald R. Ford refused. Locals still remember that October 30, 1975, *Daily News* headline: "Ford to City: Drop Dead." Eventually, the White House approved federal loan guarantees. But mass looting during the infamous 1977 blackout, soaring crime, and strikes by seemingly every essential service provider—garbage collectors, doctors, even the police—made the city feel almost inhabitable. Happily, economic boom times combined with strong efforts by business owners and Mayors Koch and Guiliani led to dramatic reductions in crime rates and improvements in infrastructure and quality of life. By the 1990s New York was cleaner and safer than it had ever been. As the world knows, the city was the site of the worst terrorist attack in U.S. history on September 11, 2001; thousands were killed when two hijacked planes slammed into the Twin Towers. Residents vowed that the city would come back better and stronger.

Mission accomplished: New York City is thriving as never before and remains one of the world's greatest—locals would say THE greatest—and most fascinating cities.

1980	John Lennon gunned down by Mark Chapman.
1993	World Trade Center terrorist bombing kills six.
2000	NYC population tops 8 million.
Sept. 11, 2001	Terrorists demolish the Twin Towers.
July 6, 2004	Cornerstone laid for the "Freedom Tower," which will be built over the former location of the Twin Towers.

WHAT'S
WHERE

To get a genuine insider's view of Manhattan, walk, as often as possible, along the city's narrow, densely packed streets and watch the city unfold. You'll see food purveyors unloading trucks in Chinatown, seamstresses rolling racks of clothes along streets in the Garment District, artists putting up installations in Chelsea galleries, and chefs sifting through produce at the city's green markets. Some areas, like Midtown and Lower Manhattan, resemble a *Blade Runner* set, with tiny, specialized shops squeezed between neoclassical or Gothic-Revival buildings and sleek glass-faced high-rises. Residential neighborhoods uptown consist of leafy wide streets accented by glittery designer boutiques and high-end grocers, doormen fronting entranceways, and ritzy carriage houses replete with private driveways. Unusually, Manhattan's character shifts every few blocks. Pocket parks, small swaths of greenery, pop up every dozen blocks, and street vendors populate the sidewalks. Downtown, the vibe is more relaxed, with dusty thrift shops and used book stores, swanky-chic cocktail lounges that inhabit the storefronts of soot-smudged warehouses, and, in the West Village and Tribeca, cobblestone streets lined with antiques and wine stores, and cafés spilling out, in good weather, onto the street.

Neighborhoods define the character of this sometimes unwieldy but always engrossing town. Some, like the Lower East Side, are defined by a landmark like the Eldridge Street Synagogue and the conservative and Hasidic Jews who live and work there. Others, like artsy-chic Soho, barely resemble their original form—Soho was once seedy and filled with sweatshops, then reinvigorated and gentrified. This guide checks into all the boroughs of the Big Apple, but naturally focuses on the commercial hub of Manhattan. Its long, thin stretch is covered here from south to north, from Wall Street and the East Village to Morningside Heights and Harlem.

LOWER MANHATTAN

The Dutch began the colony of Nieuw Amsterdam on these narrow streets, and a century and a half later, George Washington was sworn in on Wall Street as the United States' first president. Luckily, the destruction that leveled the nearby World Trade Center did not physically damage the area. The area that defines Lower Manhattan stretches from the island's southern tip at leafy Battery Park, up through the financial district (including Wall Street) and to the majestic court build-

WHAT'S WHERE

	ings of the City Hall area, and east to the retail extravaganza of the South Street Seaport at the East River.
CHINATOWN & LITTLE ITALY	As you head east from Broadway along Canal Street, Chinese discount stalls and jewelry stores seem to multiply. Along this main drag and the side streets winding south you'll find houseware dealers, martial arts studios, herbal grocers, noodle shops, and knickknack stores. Chinatown has grown north of its original boundary of Canal Street, spilling into much of what was once Little Italy, now confined to a touristy stretch of Mulberry Street between Canal and Broome streets. Still, Italian food purveyors, largely along Grand Street, keep traditions alive. September's San Gennaro street fair sponsors a cannoli-eating contest and a parade.
SOHO, NOLITA & TRIBECA	A fashionable neighborhood of cast-iron buildings and a few Belgian brick streets, SoHo (*South of Houston* Street) is bounded on its other three sides by Lafayette Street, Canal Street, and 6th Avenue. Artists transformed SoHo's late-19th-century factories into loft studios in the 1960s, and many galleries that followed have been replaced by trendy stores. To the south and west are the broader, cobblestone streets of TriBeCa (the *Triangle Below Canal* Street), which extends to Murray Street and east to West Broadway. A-list fashionistas hang out in NoLIta (*North of Little Italy*), with one-of-a-kind boutiques and cafés, and bounded by Houston, Canal, Broadway, and Allen streets.
THE EAST VILLAGE & THE LOWER EAST SIDE	The East Village, an edgy neighborhood of artists and punks, was gentrified in the 1990s, when NYU students and young executives joined the mélange that frequented the coffee shops, black-box theaters, and St. Marks Place—a raggedy stretch of vintage stores, fetish shops, and sidewalk vendors. The area is bounded by 14th Street, 4th Avenue or the Bowery on the west, Houston Street, and the East River. Southeast, below Houston and along Orchard and Delancey streets, is the Lower East Side, where the legacy of Jewish immigrants remains strongest. A handful of synagogues remain, as do discount clothing and fabric stores. Young design shops, bars, and restaurants prevail, but you can still find a corset or a Stetson hat.

GREENWICH VILLAGE & THE MEATPACKING DISTRICT	The collection of narrow, tree-lined streets known to New Yorkers simply as "the Village"—from 14th Street south to Houston Street and from the Hudson River east to 5th Avenue—remains true to its 19th-century heritage as a haven for bohemians, artists, actors, and carousers. Jazz clubs and piano bars line Grove Street; literary legends have left their mark at speakeasies and taverns. Christopher Street and Sheridan Square are the stomping grounds for the city's gay population. Farther west at 14th Street is the once blue-collar Meatpacking District, now occupied by haute designer showrooms and see-and-be-seen clubs and restaurants.
CHELSEA	Like its London district namesake, New York's Chelsea has a small-town personality, with quiet streets graced by renovated town houses. The neighborhood, from 6th Avenue to the Hudson River, and from 14th Street to the upper 20s, has always been congenial to writers and artists, and has supplanted the Village as the center of gay life. The Chelsea Hotel on 23rd is known for long-term bohemian residents, such as Allen Ginsberg, Stanley Kubrick, Jimi Hendrix, and Robert Crumb. The contemporary art scene thrives in galleries west of 10th Avenue from West 20th to West 29th streets.
UNION SQUARE, MURRAY HILL & GRAMERCY	The unofficial center of activism and youthful excitement is Union Square, a park bounded by 17th and 14th streets, Broadway, and Park Avenue. It supports the city's best green market, where top chefs sift through artisanal produce for that night's dinner menu. North, up Broadway, the much-loved Flatiron Building is wedged into the tight triangle created by 5th Avenue, Broadway, and 23rd Street. Within walking distance are the brownstone mansions and town houses of ritzy Gramercy in the East 20s, and of Murray Hill in the East 30s. Moneyed families such as the Roosevelts and Morgans made their homes here in the mid-19th century.
TIMES SQUARE & MIDTOWN WEST	Once profoundly seedy, Times Square is now New York's exemplar of tacky razzle-dazzle, glaringly bright every day of the year, with fashion ads and tickers wrapped around buildings. Thirty or so major Broadway theaters and Radio City Music Hall are nearby, between West 41st and 53rd streets and 6th and 9th avenues. Before and after the show, industry and audience members dine on Restaurant Row (46th Street between 8th and 9th avenues) and along 9th Avenue in Hell's Kitchen. Music aficionados of different bandwidths

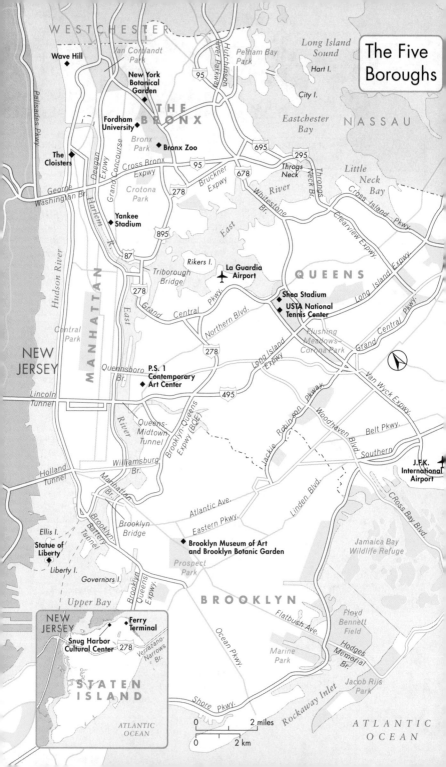

	make their way to West 57th Street for Carnegie Hall or the Hard Rock Cafe.
ROCKEFELLER CENTER & MIDTOWN EAST	The 19-building Rockefeller Center complex inhabits 22 acres of prime real estate between 5th and 7th avenues and 47th and 52nd streets. The center is full of photo ops, such as the ice-skating rink and towering Christmas tree, and the fan-staging area outside NBC's *Today Show*. North along 5th are the biggest names in New York retailing: Saks, Tiffany's, Bendel's, Bergdorf Goodman, Takashimaya. The pews inside St. Patrick's Cathedral are a good place to unwind; so is the New York Public Library and Bryant Park, behind it on 42nd Street. To the east is Grand Central Terminal, the Chrysler Building, and United Nations headquarters, flanked by colorful flags.
THE UPPER EAST SIDE	North of 59th Street, from 5th to Park avenues, are New York's toniest residences, where the wealthiest of Old Money grows old (or tries not to). The area is home to more million-aires—and billionaires—than any other part of the city. His-toric district designation has ensured that much of the area won't stray from its turn-of-the-20th-century good taste. This stretch of 5th Avenue has earned its nickname Museum Mile for the world-class collections of art and artifacts scattered along its length. Over on Madison Avenue, steel yourself for the clash of desire and resources when viewing the wares at the many haute couture boutiques.
THE UPPER WEST SIDE	Ornate prewar buildings line the residential boulevards that make up the Upper West Side, a stately backdrop to the baby strollers, aspiring actors, and Juilliard students strolling across Broadway and other avenues. Students pack the American Museum of Natural History by day; at night, Lincoln Center for the Performing Arts is the cultural hub. A few dozen blocks north, Morningside Heights famously houses the ivied build-ings of Columbia University, one of the nation's oldest, and the magnificent French Gothic Cathedral of St. John the Di-vine. Two of the most visited buildings alongside Riverside Park are here: Grant's Tomb and Riverside Church.
HARLEM	For nearly a century, from the Harlem Renaissance literary and cultural movement onward, Harlem has been a hotbed of African-American and Hispanic-American arts and life. Music is a part of the draw, from gospel services at Baptist churches to amateur night at the Apollo Theatre. The collection of the

WHAT'S WHERE

Schomburg Center for Research in Black Culture includes early jazz and blues recordings. The legendary Cotton Club and Lenox Lounge, both on 125th Street, are still hot. The Studio Museum of Harlem hosts exhibits by and about black artists and local culture. Harlem extends north from 110th Street to about 145th Street.

BROOKLYN & THE OUTER BOROUGHS	The largest of the five boroughs, Brooklyn is known for the Dodgers, Coney Island, Prospect Park and Grand Army Plaza, the Brooklyn Museum, and the Brooklyn Botanic Gardens. Each of its neighborhoods has a distinct character, from Italian-Americans in Bensonhurst to Orthodox Jews in Borough Park. Many artists have launched Brooklyn into the public imagination, from filmmaker Spike Lee to novelists Bernard Malamud and Jonathan Letham. Beyond Brooklyn is Staten Island, whose claims to fame are its commuter-transporting ferry, and Historic Richmondtown. Queens, also a borough of immigrants, has pocket communities and the Noguchi Museum, Shea Stadium, P.S. 1 Contemporary Art Center, and the Museum of the Moving Image. The Bronx, Manhattan's northern extension, is best known for Yankee Stadium. Also celebrated are Arthur Avenue's Italian food, the New York Botanical Garden, and the Bronx Zoo. Off-coast but part of the Bronx is City Island, a small fishing community.

Experience
New York City

WORD OF MOUTH

"What an amazing place. The artwork, the architecture, and the attention to detail had me awestruck. We ended up spending quite a bit of time inside and outside the building just looking and admiring. Art Deco rules! We went to the Top of the Rock the first night . . . Once there, we were treated to a full-on view of the Empire State Building and an impressive light show."

—Iamq, about Rockefeller Center

NEW YORK CITY PLANNER

How's the Weather?

Although there's an occasional bone-chilling winter day, with winds blasting off the Hudson River, snow only occasionally accumulates in the city. Late summer is the only really unpleasant time of year, especially the humid, hot days of August (when the temperature can reach 100°F). Air-conditioned stores, restaurants, theaters, and museums provide respite from the heat, as do the many green expanses of parks. Subways and buses are usually air-conditioned, but subway stations can be as hot as saunas. When September arrives—with its dry "champagne-like" weather—the city shakes off its summer sluggishness. Mild and comfortable, autumn shows the city off at its best, with yellow-and-bronze foliage displays in the parks.

Best Time to Go?

New York City is a year-round city. The months between October and May are when most Broadway shows open, museums mount major exhibitions, and formal seasons for opera, ballet, and concerts hold sway. In late spring and summer, the streets and parks are filled with ethnic parades, impromptu sidewalk concerts, and free performances under the stars. Also in summer, a number of touring orchestras and opera and ballet companies visit the city. Except for regular closing days and a few major holidays, the city's museums are open year-round.

Getting Around

In almost every neighborhood, you'll have your pick of transportation. The subway and bus networks are thorough, although getting across town on a bus can take an eternity. Still, if you're not in a rush, public buses are great because they allow you to see the city as you travel. Yellow cabs are abundant, except at the rush hour of 4:30–5 PM, when many are off duty (shift-change time). Like a taxi ride, the subway is a true New York City experience and usually the quickest way to get around. But New York is a walking town. So depending on the time of day and your destination, hoofing it could be the easiest and most enjoyable option.

The map of Manhattan is, for the most part, easy to follow. Above 14th Street the streets form a regular grid pattern. Numbered streets run east and west (crosstown), and broad avenues, most of them also numbered, run north (uptown) and south (downtown). The chief exceptions are Broadway and the thoroughfares that hug the shores of the Hudson and East rivers. Broadway runs the entire length of Manhattan. At its southernmost end it follows the city's north–south grid; at East 10th Street it turns and runs on a diagonal to West 86th Street, then at a lesser angle until West 107th Street, where it merges with West End Avenue.

Below 14th Street, Manhattan street patterns are more chaotic. They may be aligned with the shoreline, or they may twist along the route of an ancient cow path. Below 14th Street you'll find West 4th Street intersecting West 11th Street, Greenwich Street running roughly parallel to Greenwich Avenue, and Leroy Street turning into St. Luke's Place for one block and then becoming Leroy again. There's an East Broadway and a West Broadway, both of which run north–south and neither of which is an extension of plain old Broadway. Logic won't help you below 14th Street; only a good street map and good directions will.

New York City Hours

New York is very much a 24-hour city. Its subways and buses run around-the-clock, and plenty of services are available at all hours and on all days of the week. Many restaurants stay open between lunch and dinner, some offer late-night seating, and others serve around-the-clock. Bars generally close at 4 AM, clubs may stay open later. Note that smoking is prohibited in all enclosed places, including restaurants, bars, and clubs. Stores are generally open Monday–Saturday from 10 AM to 6 PM or 7 PM, but neighborhood peculiarities do exist and many retailers remain open until 8 PM or even later. Sunday hours are common in most areas of the city.

SAFETY TIPS

New York City is one of the safest large cities in the country. However, do not let yourself be lulled into a false sense of security. As in any large city, travelers in New York remain particularly easy marks for pickpockets and hustlers. After 9/11, security was heightened throughout the city.

■ Never leave any bags unattended, and expect to have you and your possessions inspected thoroughly in such places as airports, sports stadiums, museums, and city buildings.

■ Ignore the panhandlers on the streets and subways, people who offer to hail you a cab (they often appear at Penn Station, the Port Authority, and Grand Central), and limousine and gypsy cab drivers who (illegally) offer you a ride.

■ Keep jewelry out of sight on the street; better yet, leave valuables at home. Don't wear gold chains or gaudy jewelry, even if it's fake. Men should carry their wallets in their front pants pocket rather than in their back pockets. When in bars or restaurants, never hang your purse or bag on the back of a chair or put it underneath the table.

■ Avoid deserted blocks in unfamiliar neighborhoods. A brisk, purposeful pace helps deter trouble wherever you go.

Discounts

Consider purchasing a CityPass, a group of tickets to six top-notch attractions in New York—the Empire State Building, the Guggenheim Museum, the American Museum of Natural History, the Museum of Modern Art, Circle Line Cruises, and the *Intrepid* Sea-Air-Space Museum. The $53 pass, which saves you half the cost of each individual ticket, is good for nine days from first use. It also allows you to beat long ticket lines at some attractions. You can buy a CityPass online (www.citypass.com) or at any of the participants' ticket offices.

Visitor Centers

Contact NYC & Company (810 7th Ave., between W. 52nd and W. 53rd Sts., 3rd fl., Midtown West, 212/484-1222, www.nycvisit.com) for brochures, subway and bus maps, discount coupons to theaters and attractions, and multilingual information counselors. In addition to its main center near Times Square on 7th Avenue between West 52nd and West 53rd streets, the bureau also runs kiosks at the south tip of City Hall Park, in Chinatown at the intersection of Canal, Walker, and Baxter streets, and in Harlem at 163 West 125th Street, near Adam Clayton Powell Jr. Boulevard.

NEW YORK CITY'S TOP ATTRACTIONS

Metropolitan Museum of Art

(A) One of the world's greatest museums, the Met is also the largest art museum in the Western Hemisphere. Works of art from all over the world and every era of human creativity are part of this elegant and expansive treasure chest. When canvas and marble overwhelm you, turn to the temples, courtyard gardens, and silky dresses that also make up the collections.

Times Square

(B) Whirling in a chaos of flashing lights, honking horns, and shoulder-to-shoulder crowds, Times Square is the most frenetic part of New York City. With huge billboards of underwear models, superfast digital displays of world news and stock quotes, on-location broadcasts at television studios, and countless other technologically sophisticated allurements, you'll be mesmerized by its usual high-wattage thunder.

Empire State Building

(C) Atop the 86th-floor observatory (1,050 feet high) of this definitive New York icon, you can see up to 80 mi on a clear day. But at night the city's lights are dazzling. The French architect Le Corbusier said, "It is a Milky Way come down to earth." The building is equally stunning from afar. Its pencil-slim silhouette is an art-deco monument to progress, a symbol for New York City, and a star in some great romantic scenes, on- and off-screen.

Museum of Modern Art

(D) A "modernist dream world" is how critics described the museum after its $425 million face-lift. Yoshio Taniguchi, the Japanese architect responsible for the six-story structure, said he wanted to "create an environment rather than simply making a building." Indeed, soaring galleries suffused with natural light hold

such masterpieces as Monet's *Water Lilies,* Picasso's *Les Demoiselles d'Avignon, and* Van Gogh's *Starry Night.* But it's the museum itself that is the attraction.

Brooklyn Bridge

(E) "A drive-through cathedral" is how the critic James Wolcott describes one of New York's noblest and most recognized landmarks. Spanning the East River, the Brooklyn Bridge connects Manhattan island to the once-independent city of Brooklyn. A leisurely hour's stroll on the Brooklyn Bridge's boardwalk is an essential New York experience. Traffic is beneath you, and the views along the East River and harbor are wide open.

Statue of Liberty

(F) Presented to the United States in 1886 as a gift from France, Lady Liberty has become a near-universal symbol of freedom and democracy, standing a proud 152 feet high, on top of an 89-foot pedestal (executed by Richard Morris Hunt), on Liberty Island. You get a taste of the thrill millions of immigrants must have experienced as you approach Liberty Island on the ferry from Battery Park.

American Museum of Natural History

(G) The spectacular dinosaur halls alone make for a thrilling visit. Add the Rose Center for Earth and Space, a 94-foot blue whale, and the Hall of Mammals, and you've only scratched the surface of the millions of artifacts and specimens here at the world's largest and most important museum of natural history.

NEW YORK CITY'S TOP ATTRACTIONS

Central Park

(H) Amid its 843 acres of meandering paths, tranquil lakes, ponds, and open meadows, Central Park plays host to equestrians, softball players, ice-skaters, roller skaters, rock climbers, bird-watchers, boaters, chess and checkers aficionados, theater- and concert-goers, skateboarders, and more. But nearly everyone occasionally takes the time to escape the rumble of traffic, walk through the trees, and feel, at least for a moment, far from the urban frenzy.

Bronx Zoo

(I) One urban jungle deserves another. Only at the world's largest urban zoo is there room for gorillas to lumber around a 6½-acre simulated rain forest, or tigers and elephants to roam nearly 40 acres of open meadows.

SoHo

(J) The elegant cast-iron buildings, occasional cobblestone street, art galleries, chic boutiques, and swanky hotels make this a wonderful area in which to shop, drink, and dream of a more glamorous life.

GATEWAY TO THE NEW WORLD

A quintessential part of a visit to New York, a trip to the Statue of Liberty and Ellis Island takes up the better part of a day. It involves a ferry ride, long lines, security checks, and ultimately, the rare opportunity to stand within the single most powerful symbol of American ideals, not to mention one of the world's great monumental sculptures. It's worth the effort. It's no overstatement to say that these two sights have played defining roles in American culture.

THE STATUE OF LIBERTY

Impressive from the shore, the Statue of Liberty is majestic in person and up close. For millions of immigrants, the first glimpse of America was the Statue of Liberty. You get a taste of the thrill they must have experienced as you approach Liberty Island on the ferry from Battery Park and witness the statue grow from a vaguely defined figure on the horizon into a towering, stately colossus.

What's Here

The statue itself stands atop an 89-foot pedestal designed by American Richard Morris Hunt, with Emma Lazarus's sonnet "The New Colossus" ("Give me your tired, your poor, your huddled masses yearning to breathe free . . ."). This massive pedestal section is now the only area to which visitors have access, and only with timed tickets and after an extensive security check.

Inside the pedestal is an informative and entertaining museum. Highlights include the torch's original glass flame that was replaced because of water damage (the current flame is 24-karat gold and lit at night by floodlights), full-scale copper replicas of Lady Liberty's face and one of her feet, Bartholdi's alternative designs for the statue, and a model of Eiffel's intricate framework.

The observatory platform is a great place for a photo op; you're 16 stories high with all of Lower Manhattan spread out in front of you. You'll then descend to the promenade at the bottom of the base, where you're still four stories high. Be aware that to reach the platform you'll need to walk up 26 steps from the elevator drop-off point.

Liberty Island has a pleasant outdoor café for refueling as well as a large cafeteria. The gift shop sells trinkets little better than those available from street vendors.

Know Before You Go

You're allowed access to the museum only as part of one of the free tours of the promenade (which surrounds the base of the pedestal) or the observatory (at the pedestal's top). The tours are limited to 3,000 participants a day. To guarantee a spot on one of the tours, you must order tickets ahead of time—they can be reserved up to 180 days in advance, by phone or over the Internet. There are a limited amount of same-day standby tickets available at the Castle Clinton and Liberty State Park ticket offices.

Once you reach the island, there are no tickets available. And without a ticket, there is absolutely no admittance into the museum or observatory. Note that there has been no access to the torch since 1916 (so you didn't just miss your chance) and the narrow, double helix stairs leading to the statue's crown have been closed to visitors since 9/11. You will, however, get a good look at the statue's inner structure on the observatory tour through glass viewing windows that look straight into the statue. Be sure to try the view from several different viewing spots to get the whole interior.

Liberty Highlights

■ The surreal chance to stand next to, and be dwarfed by, the original glass torch and the copper cast of Lady Liberty's foot.

■ The vistas of New York from the observatory platform.

■ The rare opportunity to look up the skirt of a national monument.

Statue Basics

☎ 212/363-3200, 212/269-5755 ferry information; 866/782-8834 ticket reservations

🌐 www.statuereservations.com

🎫 Free; ferry $11.50 round-trip

🕐 Daily 8:30–5; extended hours in summer.

Liberty helicopters

VIEWS OF THE CROWN

Some unique ways to see Lady Liberty:

Rise in the Ritz-Carlton Battery Park: A swank cocktail lounge 14 stories high with straight sight lines to the statue.

Liberty Helicopter: Sightseeing tours that fly over the crown and torch (⇨ Chapter 1, Sightseeing Tours).

Kayak: Free kayak tours of the harbor depart from the NYC Downtown Boathouse (See Smart Travel Tips, Sports & the Outdoors).

FAST FACT: To move the Statue of Liberty from its initial home on a Paris rooftop to its final home in the New York Harbor, the statue was broken down into 350 individual pieces and packed in 214 crates. It took four months to reassemble it.

FAST FACT: The face of Lady Liberty is actually a likeness of sculptor Frederic-Auguste Bartholdi's mother—quite a tribute.

FAST FACT: *Liberty Enlightening the World*, as the statue is officially named, was presented to the United States in 1886 as a gift from France to celebrate the centennial of the United States, a symbol of unity and friendship between the two countries. The 152-foot-tall figure was sculpted by Frederic-Auguste Bartholdi and erected around an iron skeleton engineered by Gustav Eiffel (the same Eiffel who would later create the Eiffel Tower).

Foundation of the pedestal to torch: 305'6"

Heel to top head: 111'6"

GATEWAY TO THE NEW WORLD

1

ELLIS ISLAND

Chances are you'll be with a crowd of international tourists as you disembark at Ellis Island. Close your eyes for a moment and imagine the jostling crowd 100 times larger. Now picture that your journey has lasted weeks at sea and that your daypack contains all your worldly possessions, including all your money. You're hungry, tired, jobless, and homeless. This scenario just begins to set the stage for the story of the millions of poor immigrants who passed through Ellis Island at the turn of the 20th century. Between 1892 and 1924, approximately 12 million men, women, and children first set foot on U.S. soil at the Ellis Island federal immigration facility. By the time the facility closed in 1954, it had processed ancestors of more than 40% of Americans living today.

What's Here

The island's main building, now a national monument, reopened in 1990 as the Ellis Island Immigration Museum, containing more than 30 galleries of artifacts, photographs, and taped oral histories. The centerpiece of the museum is the white-tile Registry Room (also known as the Great Hall). It feels dignified and cavernous today, but photographs show that it took on a multitude of configurations through the years, always packed with humanity undergoing one form of screening or another. While you're there, take a look out the Registry Room's tall, arched windows and try to imagine what passed through immigrants' minds as they viewed lower Manhattan's skyline to one side and the Statue of Liberty to the other.

Along with the Registry Room, the museum's features include the ground-level Railroad Ticket Office, which has several interactive exhibits and a three-dimensional graphic representation of American immigration patterns; the American Family Immigration Center, where for a fee you can search Ellis Island's records for your own ancestors; and, outside, the American Immigrant Wall of Honor, where the names of more than 600,000 immigrant Americans are inscribed along a promenade facing the Manhattan skyline.

The gift shop has a selection of international dolls, candies, and crafts. You can also personalize a number of registry items here as well.

Making the Most of Your Visit

Because there's so much to take in, it's a good idea to make use of the museum's interpretive tools. Check at the visitor desk for free film tickets, ranger tour times, and special programs.

Consider starting your visit with a viewing of the free film *Island of Hope, Island of Tears*. A park ranger starts off with a short introduction, then the 25-minute film takes you through an immigrant's journey from the troubled conditions of European life (especially true for ethnic and religious minorities), to their nervous arrival at Ellis Island, and their introduction into American cities. The film is a primer into all the exhibits and will deeply enhance your experience.

The audio tour ($6) is also worthwhile: it takes you through the exhibits, providing thorough, engaging commentary interspersed with recordings of immigrants themselves recalling their experiences.

Ellis Island Highlights

- Surveying the Great Hall.

- The moving film *Island of Hope, Island of Tears*.

- Listening to the voices of actual immigrants who risked their lives to come to America.

- Reading the names on the American Immigrant Wall of Honor.

- Researching your own family's history.

Ellis Island Basics

☎ 212/363-3200 Ellis Island; 212/883-1986 Wall of Honor information

🌐 www.ellisisland.org

🎫 Free; ferry $11.50 round-trip

🕐 Daily 8:30-5:15; extended hours in summer.

Ellis Island: New arrivals line up to have their papers examined. ca. 1880 - 1910.

IMMIGRANT HISTORY TIMELINE

Starting in the 1880s, troubled conditions throughout Europe persuaded both the poor and the persecuted to leave their family and homes to embark on what were often gruesome journeys to come to the golden shores of America.

1880s 5.7 million immigrants arrive in U.S.

1892 Federal immigration station opens on Ellis Island in January.

1901–1910 8.8 million immigrants arrive in U.S.; 6 million processed at Ellis Island.

1907 Highest number of immigrants (860,000) arrives in one year, including a record 11,747 on April 17.

1910 75% of the residents of New York, Chicago, Detroit, Cleveland, and Boston are now immigrants or children of immigrants.

1920s Federal laws set immigration quotas based on national origin.

1954 Ellis Island immigration station is closed.

FAST FACT: Some immigrants who passed through Ellis Island later became household names. A few include Charles Atlas (1903, Italy); Irving Berlin (1893, Russia); Frank Capra (1903, Italy); Bob Hope (1908, England); Knute Rockne (1893, Norway); and Baron Von Trapp and his family (1938, Germany).

FAST FACT: In 1897, a fire destroyed the original pine immigration structure on Ellis Island, including all immigration records dating back to 1855.

FAST FACT: Only third-class, or "steerage," passengers were sent to Ellis Island. Affluent first- and second-class passengers, who were less likely to be ill or become wards of the state, were processed on board and allowed to disembark in Manhattan.

Four immigrants and their belongings, on a dock, look out over the water; view from behind.

PLANNING

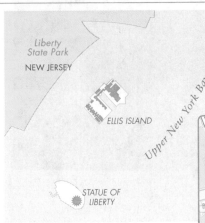

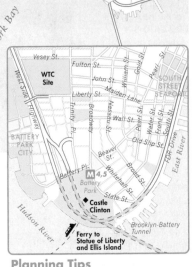

Admission

There's no admission fee for either sight, but the ferry ride, run by Circle Line, costs $11.50. Ferries leaving from **Battery Park** (See Chapter 2) every half hour take you to both islands. (Note that large packages and oversize bags and backpacks aren't permitted on board.) Pay the additional $1.75 charge to reserve tickets in advance—you'll still have to wait in line, both to pick up the tickets and to board the ferry, but you'll have a spot on the Statue of Liberty observatory tour, which will make your experience significantly richer. Without a reserved-in-advance ticket, you will not have access to the actual statue, no exceptions.

Where to Catch the Ferry

Broadway and Battery Pl., Lower Manhattan Ⓜ Subway: 4, 5 to Bowling Green.

When in New Jersey

Directly on the other side of the Hudson River from Battery Park, Liberty State Park is an impressive stretch of green with ample parking and quick ferries to the monuments. Lines are almost never an issue here, something that can't be said about the New York side.

Planning Tips

Buy tickets in advance. This is the only way to assure that you'll have tickets to actually enter the Statue of Liberty museum and observatory platform.

Be prepared for intense security. At the ferry security check, you will need to remove your coat; at the statue, you will need to remove your coat as well as your belt, watch, and any metal accessories. No strollers or backpacks are allowed in the statue (lockers are available).

Check ferry schedules in advance. Before you go, check www.statuereservations.com.

Keep in mind that even though the monuments close at 5 PM, **the last ferry to the Statue of Liberty and Ellis Island is at 3:30 PM.** You need to arrive by at least 3 PM (to allow for security checks and lines) if you want to make the last ferry of the day.

FREE NEW YORK

They say you can't get anything for free. Not so in New York, where you can enjoy some of the very best music, dance, theater, and film the city has to offer and pay absolutely nothing. The best part is that most of the free events are in summer, and usually outside. The Metropolitan Opera and the New York Philharmonic give free concerts in parks scattered around all five boroughs. And look for exciting events like the Downtown NYC River to River Festival, the Hudson River Festival, and the South Street Seaport Music Festival. Below are our Top 25 free New York experiences.

1. Walk across the Brooklyn Bridge

2. Gaze up at the ceiling of the New York City Public Library's Reading Room

3. Marvel at the bustle of Grand Central Terminal

4. Ride the Staten Island Ferry for awesome views of the city and the Statue of Liberty

5. Listen in on a choir rehearsal at St. Thomas Church

6. Browse the art galleries in Chelsea and Soho

7. Check out famous film sites

8. Visit the Bronx Zoo (free on Wednesdays; donation suggested)

9. Be entertained by Washington Square Park's street performers

10. Walk Somewhere and Everywhere

11. Whitney Museum of American Art (Friday 6–9 pm; pay what you wish)

12. Play in Central Park

13. Museum of Modern Art (Free Fridays 4–8 pm)

14. Smell the flowers at the New York Botanical Garden (free Sat. 10–noon; Wed.)

15. Check out the sculptures in Madison Square Park

16. Catch Shakespeare in the Park

17. Metropolitan Museum of Art ($15 suggested donation)

18. Kayak on the Hudson at the Downtown Boathouse (free)

19. Attend a reading at one of the city's many bookstores

20. Watch a free flick during the summer in Bryant Park

21. Catch a free show at the Apple store in Soho

22. See what's moored at Pier 63

23. Watch the sunset from Riverside Park

24. Check out music and dance peformances at Lincoln Center Out-of-Doors festival

25. Enjoy Free Wi-Fi: Bryant Park, Battery Park, Union Square Park

CITY
ITINERARIES

New York Icons

Begin a day dedicated to New York icons with a bird's-eye view atop the Empire State Building. Stroll up 5th Avenue past the leonine guardians of the New York Public Library and step inside to behold the gleaming Main Reading Room. Forty-second Street takes you east to the Beaux-Arts Grand Central Terminal, a hub of frenetic activity and architectural wonder. Move on to the Chrysler Building, an art deco stunner, and continue east to the United Nations. Make your way west across 49th Street to the triumvirate of Saks Fifth Avenue, Rockefeller Center, and St. Patrick's Cathedral. Shopping, ice-skating at the Rockefeller rink, or visiting a nearby museum could fill your day until dusk, a good time to walk south on 7th Avenue toward the bright lights of Times Square.

⊙ Rush hour is a contact sport in Grand Central Terminal and Wednesday's foot traffic through Times Square can grind nearly to a standstill as audiences pour in and out of Broadway matinees.

A Day in Little Italy & Chinatown

Even though Little Italy no longer resembles its 19th-century heyday, when the area around Mulberry Street between Canal and Grand streets was flush with immigrants, the small enclave still resonates with flavor. Authentic grocers line Grand Street, where you can get fresh mozzarella and other cheese at Di Palo's (206 Grand) cheese and sausage shop or Alleva Dairy (188 Grand), hearty sandwiches at the Italian Food Center (186 Grand), and fresh pasta at Piemonte Ravioli (190 Grand). It's worth stopping for an espresso and cannoli at Ferrara, at 195 Grand. If you must eat pasta in Little Italy, now known for its generic red-sauce eateries, try Rocky's at 45 Spring.

After your jaunt in Little Italy, head one block east of Mulberry to Mott Street, which has the highest concentration of restaurants and just about everything else, from dumpling shops to Southeast Asian grocers. While meandering around, if you smell a buttery vanilla aroma wafting from a cart nearby, stop and buy a pack of fresh-cooked egg cakes. Chinatown's hub, Canal Street, runs east–west, and is packed with street vendors hawking watches, toys, jewelry, and luggage.

Branching off on side streets north and south of Canal are shops with everything from tchotchkes and Asian home furnishings to pungent fish and pork buns. Some of the most unlikely places serve the most soul-warming meals: steamed soup dumplings at Joe's Shanghai (9 Pell), Korean food at Li Hua (171 Grand), Hong Kong–style noodles at NY Noodle Town (28½ Bowery), and excellent seafood at Oriental Garden (14 Elizabeth)—a place frequented by local chefs. Get some litchi or green-tea ice cream for dessert at the Chinatown Ice Cream Factory at 65 Bayard, or soothe yourself with an after-dinner drink at Chinatown's hippest, swanky-kitsch hangouts: Double Happiness (173 Mott) or Happy Ending (302 Broome).

Wander Around

Do what many New Yorkers like to do on their days off—wander. Make your way to Chinatown for a dim sum breakfast or tapioca-filled soft drink. From here head north to SoHo and NoLita for galleries and chic boutiques and restaurants. Farther east, the Lower East Side is a former immigrant enclave where you'll find the Lower

East Side Tenement Museum and bargain shopping on Orchard Street. If you haven't eaten by now, hit a café a few blocks north in the happening East Village, home to yet more shops and vintage stores. From Union Square, walk up Broadway to the fashionable Flatiron District with its inimitable Flatiron Building. Have dinner in one of the neighborhood's noted restaurants.

A Day in Brooklyn

For a breath of fresh air, take the 2 or 3 train to Park Slope's Grand Army Plaza or the Q to 7th Ave.–Flatbush. On Saturdays you'll exit the subway at Grand Army Plaza in the middle of a bustling farmer's market, with artisanal produce and, in warmer weather, cooking demonstrations by Brooklyn chefs. Just east of the Plaza on Eastern Parkway is the Beaux-Arts Brooklyn Museum, with a world-class collection from American art to Egyptian antiquities. Stroll around the halls for an hour, then venture east another block to the entrance of the Brooklyn Botanical Garden, known for its shady wooded areas, more than 1,200 varieties of roses, and its idyllic Japanese garden and pond. After a few hours of wandering, your appetite should be kicking in: continue your stroll southward into the 585-acre Frederick Olmsted–designed Prospect Park, Brooklyn's recreational center.

Finally, head west through Prospect Park into Park Slope for some lunch. Brooklyn's top-tier neighborhood has European-style mansions, wide leafy blocks, and elegant brownstone apartment houses. When you hit 7th Avenue, you'll find modish boutiques and scores of restaurants. The best of the bunch is Sette Enoteca, a casual but high-quality wine bar and restaurant at the corner of 7th Avenue and 3rd Street.

Continue north along 7th Avenue or down to 5th Avenue for more restaurants and boutiques, then head back to Flatbush to catch the train to Manhattan.

The Art Experience

The Metropolitan, Guggenheim, and Whitney museums, the city's triumvirate of fine-art institutions, are good for years of browsing, but you can easily see all three in a day, with well-calculated snack stops and a respite in Central Park. Get a mellow, inspiring start at the Guggenheim, Frank Lloyd Wright's playfully inverted ziggurat, completed in 1959. It showcases serious and populist art, from Brancusi to Matthew Barney, on six gently sloping ramps; two annexes contain the permanent collection of 19th- and 20th-century paintings. Only a few steps south is the world-famous Metropolitan Museum. Don't attempt to see everything here—choose a few exhibits or galleries, trek around a bit, then escape to Central Park, behind the museum, for a rest. For lunch, April through November, you can hit the Boathouse-72nd St., mid-park, and overlooking a lake. In winter, slip into any of the bistros, cafés, or sandwich shops lining Madison Avenue. Along Madison, try the rustic-chic Le Pain Quotidien at 83rd St. or E.A.T. Café at 81st, or, for picnic materials, Dean & Deluca at 85th. Once nourished, consider heading back into the Met to see a few more galleries, or head over to the galleries at the Whitney to see the lively collection of 20th-century American art—from conceptual artists like Andrea Zittel to everyone's favorite, Edward Hopper.

SIGHTSEEING
NEW YORK CITY

A guided tour can be a good way to get a handle on this sometimes overwhelming city, to explore out-of-the-way areas to which you might not want to venture on your own, or get in-depth exposure to a particular facet of the city's history, inhabitants, or architecture.

Boat Tours

In good weather, a Circle Line Cruise (Pier 83 at W. 42nd St., Midtown West, 212/563–3200, www.circleline42.com) is one of the best ways to get oriented. Once you've finished the three-hour, 35-mi circumnavigation of Manhattan, you'll have a good idea of where things are and what you want to see next. Narrations are as interesting and individual as the guides who deliver them. The Circle Line operates daily, and the price is $28. Semi-Circle cruises, more limited tours of two hours, also run daily; they cost $23.

NY Waterway (Pier 16 at South St. Seaport, Lower Manhattan, 212/269–5755, www.circlelinedowntown.com) runs two-hour harbor cruises for $26. Dates and times vary, but the cruises run year-round. The 90-minute Twilight Cruise ($21) operates from early May through early November; the Harbor Cruise, which covers the same territory during the day, operates year-round.

Several cruises leave from South Street Seaport's Pier 16. The cargo schooner *Pioneer* (Pier 16 at South St. Seaport, Lower Manhattan, 212/748–8786, www.southstseaport.org), owned by the South Street Seaport Museum, makes two-hour voyages Tuesday through Sunday, from after Memorial Day through mid-September. Reservations, which can be made no more than two weeks in advance, are a good idea. The fare is $25.

Bus Tours

Gray Line New York (Port Authority Bus Terminal, 625 8th Ave., at W. 42nd St., Midtown West, 800/669–0051, www.graylinenewyork.com) runs a number of "hop-on, hop-off" double-decker bus tours in various languages, including a downtown Manhattan loop, upper Manhattan loop, Harlem gospel tour, and evening tours of the city. Packages include entrance fees to attractions and one-day Metro-Cards. The company also books sightseeing cruises, as well as day trips to Atlantic City, Hyde Park, the Woodbury Common outlet mall, and other locations in the New York area.

Guided Tours

The wisecracking PhD candidates of Big Onion Walking Tours (212/439–1090, www.bigonion.com) lead themed tours such as "Revolutionary New York" and its famous "multiethnic eating tours" in addition to neighborhood eating walks. The Downtown Alliance (212/606–4064, www.downtownny.com) conducts free, history-rich tours of the Wall Street area on Thursday and Saturday at noon. Meet on the steps of the U.S. Custom House at Bowling Green. For tours of the City Hall area, meet at the New York City Heritage Tourism Center on Broadway between Vesey and Barclay streets, Tuesday at noon.

The Municipal Art Society (212/935–3960, 212/439–1049 recorded information, www.mas.org) conducts a series of walking tours on weekdays and both bus and walking tours on weekends. Tours emphasize the architecture and history of particular neighborhoods. New York City Cultural Walking Tours (212/979–2388, www.nycwalk.com) have covered such sundry topics as buildings' gargoyles and

the old Yiddish theaters of the East Village. Tours are run every Sunday from March to December; private tours can be scheduled throughout the week.

The Urban Park Rangers (311 in New York City, 212/639–9675 outside of New York, www.nycparks.org) conducts free weekend walks and workshops in city parks. The knowledgeable Joyce Gold (212/242–5762, www.nyctours.com) has been conducting tours since 1976. Regular historical walks include Harlem, Gramercy Park, and the Lower East Side. The contributions of immigrants and artists to various neighborhoods are often highlighted in other tours.

Arthur Marks (212/673–0477) creates customized tours on which he sings show tunes about the city. Private tours start at $500; you may wish to inquire about group tours, which Marks gives from May through November. Walk of the Town (212/222–5343) tailors tours to your interests; special themes include "Cops, Crooks, and the Courts," "When Harlem Was Jewish," and "The Lullaby of Broadway." Tours are available by appointment only; most start at $300.

Special Interest Tours

Central Park Walking Tours (212/721–0874, www.centralparkwalkingtours.com) covers the park daily but mostly on the weekends. Its two-hour tours are thematic, investigating such features as prominent trees and the park's unique bridges and arches.

The Times Square Alliance (7th Ave. between W. 46th and W. 47th Sts., Midtown West, 212/768–1560, www.timessquarenyc. org) runs a free tour of the Times Square area that takes you to theaters and other sights in the area. Tours leave Friday at noon from the Times Square Information Center.

Self-Guided Tours

Talking Street's (212/586–8687, www. talkingstreet.com) two audio tours of New York City are delivered to you via a number you call on your cell phone. Comedian Jerry Stiller's coverage of the Lower East Side emphasizes the turbulent period around 1900; a walking tour of Lower Manhattan and the World Trade Center site is narrated by actress Sigourney Weaver. Both tours cost $5.95 and take less than two hours to complete; you can buy them, using a credit card, over the phone or on the company's Web site.

The SoundWalk (SoundWalk, www. soundwalk.com) line of audio tours covers unusual sights in a nonstuffy way. They get you off the main drags and on to the nonobvious parts of such areas as the Bronx, Times Square, and DUMBO. The tours sell for around $25 and are available as downloadable audio files as well as CDs.

AUTHENTIC NEW YORK CITY

It's easy to lose yourself in one section of New York City and forget that there are a myriad of places to explore where the locals go. Beyond the well-known museums like the Metropolitan Museum of Art and the Guggenheim, or popular restaurants like Tavern on the Green and Per Se, there are others that command attention in unusual ways. There's also the outdoorsy world, which astonishes out-of-towners who think that New York City is only a city of concrete, skyscrapers, and nonstop traffic. You can spend many weeks in New York and discover something new and amazing each day. Here's a taster below.

Explore Museums in Queens

Some of Manhattan's most interesting museums are located in the funkiest of places. P.S. 1, a contemporary-art museum, is in an old school house in Long Island City, Queens. An outdoor showcase, with changing and highly experimental exhibits, the nearby Socrates Sculpture Park is across the street from the Isamu Noguchi Garden Museum. This atmospheric museum has both indoor and outdoor exhibits and is set in a converted factory building, the former working studio of the famous Japanese-American sculptor.

Eat Like a Local

You can emulate the tendency of New Yorkers to ignore their kitchens and eat out at some of the city's more intriguing ethnic cafes, taking a tour of the world, neighborhood by neighborhood. Try Russian borscht on the Boardwalk in Brighton Beach (Brooklyn), Indian tandoori on East 6th Street, Korean barbecue in Little Korea in the West 30s, some of the best coal-oven pizza in the world, and New York's famous bagels and nova. You can also take to the streets for some great quick options that go beyond pretzels or hot dogs.

Try the stands selling kebabs or falafel, or even fruit smoothies—there's a ton of them set up around Rockefeller Center near 6th Avenue. New Yorkers' love affair with food is also evident at the Greenmarket at Union Square, where vendors bring seasonal produce, cheeses, and other local offerings that also show up on restaurant menus throughout the city.

On the Lower East Side, having a bialy from Kossar's is a must, followed by a pickle at Gus's and an ice-cream tasting at Il Laboratorio del Gelato—they're all within a few blocks of each other. If you can still move, there's also Yonah Schimmel's for a knish or Orwasher's Bakery uptown for the most heavenly rye, pumpernickel, and Irish soda breads.

Ride the Subway

To see a real cross section of working-class New York, do what 3.5 million people do daily: take a ride on a New York subway. By taking the 7 train from Times Square to Flushing, Queens, you'll cross a wide variety of ethnic neighborhoods. In fact, this train is designated a National Millennium Trail and has been dubbed "the international express," a living heritage experience. Or grab the L train from Union Square and go three stops to Brooklyn to join all the hipsters walking along Williamsburg's Bedford Avenue, an area viewed by some as the "new Manhattan." You never know, you might see Mayor Michael Bloomberg on the subway—that's how he commutes to work.

FABULOUS
FESTIVALS

NYC & Company–Convention and Visitors Bureau (212/ 484–1222, www.nycvisit.com) has exact dates and times for many of the events listed below, and the bureau's Web site has more information on all sorts of activities.

WINTER

The Lunar New Year, celebrated over two weeks, includes extravagant banquets, a flower market, and a colorful paper-dragon dance that snakes through Chinatown. New York's first St. Patrick's Day Parade took place in 1766, making this boisterous tradition one of the city's oldest annual events. The parade heads up 5th Avenue, from 44th Street to 86th Street.

SPRING

At the International Asian Art Fair, 50 dealers from around the world exhibit furniture, sculptures, bronzes, ceramics, carpets, jewelry, and more from the Middle East, Southeast Asia, and the Far East. Prices begin at $1,000. The week before Easter, the Macy's Flower Show creates lush displays in its flagship emporium and sets its Broadway windows abloom. Exquisite flower arrangements are also on display in Rockefeller Center.

As in the classic Fred Astaire movie *Easter Parade,* you (or even your pet) can don an extravagant hat and strut up 5th Avenue in the Easter Promenade. The parade centers around St. Patrick's Cathedral, at 51st Street.

The Cherry Blossom Festival at the Brooklyn Botanic Garden takes place during the trees' peak flowering and includes Taiko drumming groups, traditional Japanese dance and arts, and bento box lunches for picnicking.

The International Fine Art Fair brings dealers from all over the country to the Seventh Regiment Armory, where they show off exceptional paintings, drawings, and sculptures from the Renaissance to the 20th century. On the second or third Saturday in May, booths of the Ninth Avenue Food Festival line 20 blocks of 9th Avenue (from West 37th to West 57th Street) and cook up every conceivable type of food. Most of 9th Avenue's many food stores and restaurants participate, selling samples of their wares as well as specially prepared delicacies.

Ships from the armed forces of the United States and from other countries join up with Coast Guard ships during Fleet Week for a parade up the Hudson River. After the ships dock, they are open to the public. The center of this event, which is held the week before Memorial Day, is the *Intrepid* Sea-Air-Space Museum. Since 1931,

FABULOUS
FESTIVALS

Memorial Day has marked the start of the Washington Square Outdoor Art Exhibit, an open-air arts-and-crafts fair with some 600 exhibitors who set up along the park and on surrounding streets. The action continues for two weekends, from noon to sundown.

Nine of the major museums lining 5th Avenue from 82nd up to 104th Street waive their admission and have special late hours for the Museum Mile Festival, held the second Tuesday in June. Fifth Avenue is closed to traffic, and entertainers perform in the streets.

SUMMER

JVC Jazz Festival New York brings giants of jazz and new faces alike to Carnegie Hall, Lincoln Center, Birdland, Bryant Park, and other venues around town. Lesbian & Gay Pride Week includes a film festival, concerts aplenty, and many other events. It culminates with the world's biggest annual gay pride parade, which heads down 5th Avenue and then to Greenwich Village on the last Sunday of June.

Celebrate Brooklyn Performing Arts Festival brings pop, jazz, rock, classical, klezmer, African, Latin, and Caribbean multicultural music, as well as spoken-word and theatrical performances, to Prospect Park's Bandshell. The streets around Brooklyn's Our Lady of Mt. Carmel Church are full of Italian festivities for two weeks, beginning the first Thursday in July.

The Washington Square Music Festival is a series of Tuesday evening free outdoor classical, jazz, and big-band concerts. Lower Manhattan celebrates Independence Day with the Great 4th of July Festival, which includes arts, crafts, ethnic food, and live entertainment. South Street Seaport also puts on a celebration.

Macy's 4th of July Fireworks fill the night sky over the East River. The best viewing points are FDR Drive from East 14th to East 41st streets (access via E. 23rd, E. 34th, and E. 48th streets) and the Brooklyn Heights Promenade. The FDR Drive is closed to traffic, but arrive early, as police sometimes restrict even pedestrian traffic. Harlem Week, the world's largest black and Hispanic festival, runs throughout the month. Come for the food, concerts, gospel events, a film festival, children's festival, an auto show, and a bike tour.

The 10-day Howl! Festival, named in honor of the famous poem by beat poet (and East Village resident) Allen Ginsburg, includes more than 250 music, art, and theatrical performances. One highlight is Wigstock, a show of drag queen performances held in Tompkins Square Park.

A Caribbean revel modeled after the harvest carnival of Trinidad and Tobago, the West Indian American Day Carnival, in Brooklyn, is the centerpiece of a week's worth of festivities. Celebrations include salsa, reggae, and calypso music performances, as well as Monday's gigantic parade of floats, elaborately costumed dancers, stilt walkers, and West Indian food and music.

Garlands and lights bedeck Little Italy's Mulberry Street and environs for the Feast of San Gennaro, the city's oldest, grandest, largest, and most crowded *festa*, held in honor of the patron saint of Naples.

FALL

Some 200 publishers set up displays along 5th Avenue from 42nd to 57th streets for New York Is Book Country, where you can buy new fall releases and unusual old books, meet authors, admire beautiful book jackets, and enjoy live entertainment and bookbinding demonstrations. Bring the kids.

Begun in 1963, the New York Film Festival is the city's most prestigious annual film event. Cinephiles pack various Lincoln Center venues—advance tickets to afternoon and evening screenings are essential to guarantee a seat.

The Brooklyn Academy of Music (BAM) Next Wave Festival attracts artsy crowds with its program of local and international cutting-edge dance, opera, theater, and music. You can see such "regulars" as Phillip Glass, John Cale, Lou Reed, and the German dance-theater troupe of Pina Bausch.

Thousands of revelers, many in bizarre but brilliant costumes or manipulating huge puppets, march up 6th Avenue (from Spring to West 23rd streets) in the rowdy Greenwich Village Halloween Parade.

The New York City Marathon, the world's largest, begins on the Staten Island side of the Verrazano-Narrows Bridge and snakes through all five boroughs before finishing in front of Tavern on the Green in Central Park. New Yorkers turn out in droves to cheer on the runners.

The Macy's Thanksgiving Day Parade is a New York tradition. The huge balloons float down Central Park West from West 77th Street to Broadway and Herald Square. The parade begins at 9 AM; when it comes to getting a good spot, the earlier the better.

On New Year's Eve, the famous ball drop in Times Square is televised all over the world. Arrive early, and dress warmly!

NEW YORK CITY WITH KIDS

Even though much of New York is focused on the adult pursuits of making money and then spending it, kids can run riot in this city, too. Below are our Top 10 kids' favorite attractions.

American Museum of Natural History. This museum contains more than 30 million specimens and cultural artifacts. Exhibits range from dinosaurs to gems and minerals, from life in the sea to cultures from around the world to the ends of the cosmos.

The Bronx Zoo. The Bronx Zoo is the country's largest metropolitan wildlife park, home to more than 4,500 animals, including endangered and threatened species. Kids can peek at a subterranean naked mole rat colony or watch big and beautiful endangered cats through the glass at Tiger Mountain, a not-to-be-missed exhibit.

Central Park. Central Park is to New York as the sun is to the solar system. Need to let the kids burn off some steam? Head to 67th Street and 5th Avenue for the tree house playground. A playground at 99th Street (east side) accommodates children with disabilities. Other playgrounds are on the east side at 71st, 77th, 85th, 95th, 108th, and 110th streets and on the west side at 68th, 81st, 85th, 89th, 91st, 93rd, 96th, 100th, and 110th streets.

Central Park Zoo. A perfect destination for little ones, the zoo is walkable and stroller-friendly, and even the youngest tot can see the animals from low-lying or low-sitting carriages. Three climatic regions—the Rain Forest, Temperate Territory, and Polar Circle—form the focal points.

Children's Museum of Manhattan. Exhibits in the five floors of exhibition space change

frequently. You can follow the dream-adventure of Alice in Wonderland or bring literacy to life with Clifford the Big Red Dog and his friend Emily Elizabeth. The fun continues with a special Dr. Seuss celebration, where your child's imagination can run wild.

Museum of Modern Art. Nicknamed MoMA, this museum maintains the world's foremost collection of 20th-century art: more than 135,000 paintings, sculptures, drawings, prints, photographs, architectural models and drawings, and design objects.

New York Aquarium. Alongside the cotton candy and amusements of Coney Island, this aquarium is home to more than 10,000 species of marine life, including beluga whales, giant sea turtles, sand-tiger sharks, and sea otters.

New York Botanical Garden. Nearly 50 gardens and plant collections make up this landmark. Its hands-on activities, imaginative exhibits, and fanciful gardens are exciting and inviting.

Sony Wonder Technology Lab. You're not just going to just see technology here; you will become part of it during an adventure through four floors of hands-on educational fun. Don't despair if you and your kids are not techno-whizzes; helpful guides throughout the lab will answer your questions and offer assistance.

South Street Seaport Museum. Whether it's a concert, a show by street performers, guided tours, or family programs, there's always something happening at the museum. Family Gallery Guides direct you around the world's largest collection of items related to New York's port.

Lower Manhattan

WORD OF MOUTH

"Museums, ferries, and the view from the Empire State building all cost you—[the Brooklyn Bridge] doesn't. And the views are spectacular on a clear day. Takes about 45–50 minutes to walk across, depending on how many pictures you stop to take."   —jdavis

"If you're in NYC mid-September, you've GOT TO go to the San Gennaro Feast in Little Italy. Go hungry and just eat your way through all the yummy Italian food."   —sailorgirl

Sightseeing
★ ★ ★ ★ ★
Nightlife
★
Dining
★ ★
Lodging
★ ★
Shopping
★

New York was born on the southern tip of Manhattan, and a visit here provides a glimpse of the city both past and present. From the 19th-century brick facades of South Street Seaport to the skyscraper-lined canyons of Wall Street and lower Broadway, this is an area you can fully appreciate only by walking its streets. Look sharp: the history and culture lie beneath your feet and tower over your head. The neighborhood is also a testament to change, and taking it all in involves not only seeing what's here but also noticing the absences, most notably the empty gulf among the skyscrapers, where on a sunny autumn morning in 2001, the landscape changed brutally, redefining New York, and America's position in the world.

What's Here

Jutting out into New York Harbor as if it were Manhattan's green toe is verdant **Battery Park.** It's filled with sculptures and monuments (some more impressive than others) and commands fine views of Staten Island, the Statue of Liberty, and Ellis Island. The park's primary structure is **Castle Clinton National Monument,** a circular red-stone fortress built during the War of 1812 on what was then an island outcropping to help defend the city from the British. At the west end of Battery Park, ferries depart for Ellis Island and the Statue of Liberty. East of the park along the waterfront is the terminal for the **Staten Island Ferry,** a not-to-be-missed free ride across New York Harbor. Just north of the terminal, dwarfed by high-rises, is the white columned 1793 **Shrine of St. Elizabeth Ann Seton at Our Lady of the Rosary,** one of the many mansions that once lined State Street and the former home of the first American-born saint.

The north tip of Battery Park touches **Bowling Green,** an oval greensward at the foot of Broadway that in 1733 became New York's first public park. The space provides an excellent view up Broadway of the formidable Canyon of Heroes, where icons like Amelia Earhart and Joe DiMaggio were honored in ticker-tape parades. You can see some vintage ticker-tape machines just steps away at the small but richly packed **Museum of American Financial History.** On Bowling Green's south side is the Beaux-Arts **Alexander Hamilton U.S. Custom House,** home to the National Museum of the American Indian, whose collection ranges from Mayan artifacts to contemporary Native American art. The warren of blocks east of here, centered on Pearl Street, contain remnants of New York's colonial history, including the stately 1719 **Fraunces Tavern.** Running alongside Pearl Street is Stone Street, the city's oldest paved street. A small alley off Stone Street is Mill Lane, where New York's first Sephardic Jewish community was forced to worship secretly in a mill during the mid-1600s.

Cutting through Lower Manhattan's financial district, **Wall Street** is arguably the most famous thoroughfare in the world. The epicenter of Wall Street is the **New York Stock Exchange,** at the intersection of Broad Street. The exchange isn't open to visitors, but there is a related museum at the **Federal Hall National Memorial.** Marking Wall Street's west end is **Trinity Church,** where Alexander Hamilton is buried. Two blocks north of Wall Street nests the bulwark **Federal Reserve Bank of New York,** storehouse of a third of the world's gold reserves. Head west of Wall Street and the skyscrapers open up to the gaping 16 acres of Ground Zero, the **World Trade Center site.** Displays along its western side (Church Street) list the names of those who were lost on September 11, and tell the history of the towers. Abutting the site at its northeast corner is **St. Paul's Chapel,** which served as a refuge for rescue and recovery workers in the year following September 11 and now hosts an exhibit recalling their efforts.

Battery Park City skirts the WTC site on the west, impressively constructed out of rock excavated during the construction of the twin towers. It's mostly residential, but noteworthy for the lovely waterfront esplanade and several parks. Also here are the **World Financial Center**—whose open Winter Garden atrium often hosts performances and contains architectural plans for the WTC site—and the hexagonal **Museum of Jewish Heritage,** which utilizes documentary footage and period personal objects to give an intimate perspective to the 20th-century Jewish experience.

Extending to the river from the corner of Water and Fulton streets is the 11-block **South Street Seaport Historic District,** a charming, cobblestone corner of New York filled with 18th-,19th-, and early-20th-century architecture and port details. Front Street has especially well-preserved brick buildings that date back to the 1700s. South Street Pier 16, where a number of historic ships are docked, also serves as a departure point for various cruises. To the north is Pier 17, a multilevel dockside shopping mall of national chain retailers. Its weathered-wood rear decks make a splendid spot from which to sit and contemplate the river.

GETTING ORIENTED

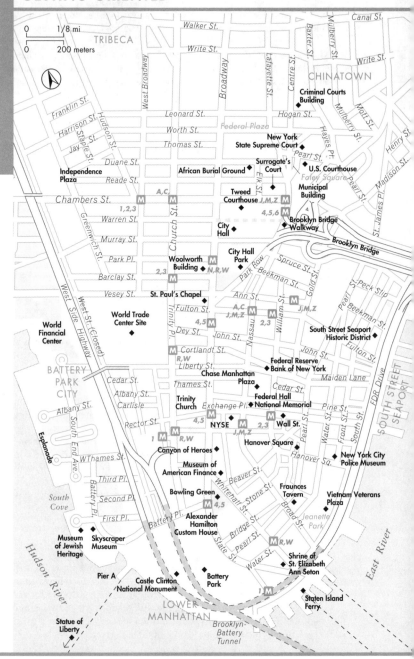

TRIBECA

CHINATOWN

Walker St.

Write St.

Canal St.

Write St.

Broadway

West Broadway

Leonard St.

Worth St.

Thomas St.

Federal Plaza

Hogan St.

Franklin St.

Harrison St.

Staple St.

Jay St.

Hudson St.

Duane St.

Reade St.

Chambers St.

Warren St.

Murray St.

Park Pl.

Barclay St.

Vesey St.

Greenwich St.

Church St.

Independence Plaza

African Burial Ground

New York State Supreme Court

Surrogate's Court

U.S. Courthouse

Criminal Courts Building

Municipal Building

Tweed Courthouse

City Hall

Brooklyn Bridge Walkway

Brooklyn Bridge

Woolworth Building

City Hall Park

St. Paul's Chapel

World Trade Center Site

World Financial Center

BATTERY PARK CITY

Albany St.

Esplanade

South End Ave.

W.Thames St.

Third Pl.

Second Pl.

First Pl.

South Cove

Battery Pl.

Museum of Jewish Heritage

Skyscraper Museum

Pier A

Castle Clinton National Monument

Battery Park

LOWER MANHATTAN

Brooklyn–Battery Tunnel

Statue of Liberty

Hudson River

Fulton St.

Ann St.

Dey St.

John St.

Cortlandt St.

Liberty St.

Cedar St.

Albany St.

Carlisle

Rector St.

Thames St.

Trinity Church

Chase Manhattan Plaza

Federal Hall National Memorial

NYSE

Wall St.

Exchange Pl.

Canyon of Heroes

Museum of American Finance

Bowling Green

Alexander Hamilton Custom House

Federal Reserve Bank of New York

South Street Seaport Historic District

Maiden Lane

Hanover Square

Hanover Sq.

Beaver St.

Stone St.

Whitehall St.

Bridge St.

State St.

Pearl St.

Water St.

Fraunces Tavern

Vietnam Veterans Plaza

New York City Police Museum

Shrine of St. Elizabeth Ann Seton

Staten Island Ferry

Jeanette Park

Broad St.

South Street Seaport

FDR Drive

East River

Trinity Pl.

Nassau St.

William St.

Beekman St.

Spruce St.

Gold St.

Park Row

Peck Slip

Pearl St.

Foley Square

Centre St.

Lafayette St.

Baxter St.

Mulberry St.

Mott St.

Henry St.

Madison St.

St. James Pl.

0   1/8 mi
0   200 meters

TOP 5

- A pilgrimage to the World Trade Center site

- The Ionic columns of the buildings on Wall Street

- Strolling the leafy walkways of Battery Park

- Watching the sunset on a walk across the Brooklyn Bridge

- Taking a free ride across New York Harbor on the Staten Island Ferry

MAKING THE MOST OF YOUR TIME

Visit lower Manhattan on weekday to capture the district's true vitality—but expect to be jostled on the crowded sidewalks if you stand still too long. On weekends you could feel like a lone explorer in a canyon of buildings. The neighborhood shuts down at evening; conclude your visit by watching the sunset on the Hudson River.

GETTING HERE

You can reach the area via countless subway lines, after which you should walk to get around. A useful starting place is the Fulton Street Broadway–Nassau, serviced by nine different subway lines, which lands you within walking distance of the World Trade Center site, City Hall, and South Street Seaport. If you want to make the World Trade Center site your first stop, take R or W train to Cortlandt Street; it puts you on the perimeter of the site.

QUICK BITES

If you want to forgo the ubiquitous Starbucks, head to **Financier Patisserie** (62 Stone St. 212/344–5600), on a handsome cobblestone lane just off Hanover Square, for pastries, soups, and sandwiches.

The cuisine at South Street Seaport may be run-of-the-mill, but it's worthwhile to stop off at the **Promenade Food Court** on the third floor of Pier 17 for the spectacular view. To get away from the crowds, grab a drink at **Bridge Café** (279 Water St., 212/227–3344), just a hop from the seaport, nestled at the base of the Brooklyn Bridge. The space in this 1794 bar is small but serves more than 100 domestic wines and 75 single-malt scotches.

A GOOD WALK

From Battery Park, walk north up State Street to Bowling Green, catching the view up Broadway's Canyon of Heroes, then right down the eastern fork of Broadway (Whitehall Street) to Bridge Street. Turn left and walk up Bridge Street, which will become Pearl Street, and continue up to tiny Hanover Square (stop for a delicious bite at Financier Patisserie and check out Stone Street on the other side of the café). Continue up Pearl, turn left onto Wall Street, and head west to Wall Street's endpoint at Trinity Chapel. On the other side of the church, turn right and walk up Trinity Place to the World Trade Center site.

Toward Lower Manhattan's northern border, Broadway and Park Row fork to enclose the grassy colonial-era **City Hall Park,** in the center of which sits the diminutive structure of **City Hall.** In and above the park are some of the country's most famous courthouses, their front steps familiar backdrops for coverage of both sensational and significant trials. On Foley Square are the **U.S. Courthouse,** where Julius and Ethel Rosenberg were tried for espionage, and the stately **New York County Courthouse.** Farther up at 100 Centre Street is the **Criminal Courts Buildings,** a forbidding structure whose grim art deco tower connects to the detention center by a skywalk known as New York's Bridge of Sighs. Also in the area are two of the city's finest old skyscrapers: the **Municipal Building,** which towers above the surrounding courts, topped with a 25-foot-high gilt statue of Civic Fame; and the white terra-cotta **Woolworth Building,** with an extravagant Gothic-style lobby. Two blocks north of the park at Federal Plaza is the **African Burial Ground,** part of the area once used to inter an estimated 20,000 African-Americans until the cemetery was closed in 1794. Just steps south of the Municipal Building, a ramp curves up into the pedestrian walkway over the **Brooklyn Bridge.** The river-and-four-borough views from the bridge are wondrous.

Places to Explore

African Burial Ground. This grassy corner is part of the original area used for burial of the city's colonial-period African-Americans who were not allowed to be buried at a church. An estimated 20,000 were interred here from the late 1600s through 1795. By the early 1800s, the site had been subsumed into the city. The site was discovered during a 1991 construction project, and by an act of Congress it was made into a National Historic Landmark, dedicated to the people who were enslaved in the city between 1626 and Emancipation Day in New York, July 4, 1827. ⌧ *Duane and Elk Sts., at 290 Broadway, Lower Manhattan* ☎ *212–637–2039, Weekdays 9–4* ⊕ *www.africanburialground.gov* Ⓜ *Subway: 1, 2, 3, J, M, Z to Chambers St.; 4, 5, 6 to Brooklyn Bridge/City Hall,.*

Battery Park. Jutting out at the southernmost point of Manhattan, leafy Battery Park provides plenty of places to sit and rest, including two tiers of wood benches that line the promenade facing the New York Harbor. From here, you can see Governors Island, a former Coast Guard installation now managed by the National Park Service; a hilly Staten Island in the distance; the Statue of Liberty; Ellis Island; and the old railway terminal in Liberty State Park, on the mainland in Jersey City, New Jersey. On crystal-clear days you can see all the way to Port Elizabeth's cranes, which seem to mimic Lady Liberty's stance.

The park's main structure is **Castle Clinton National Monument,** the takeoff point for ferries to the Statue of Liberty and Ellis Island. The monument was once known as Castle Garden, when from 1855 to 1890 it served as America's first official immigration center (Ellis Island opened in 1892). The interior of the park is loaded with monuments and statues, including *The Sphere,* which for three decades stood on the plaza at the World Trade Center as a symbol of peace. Damaged but still intact after the collapse of the towers, it serves as a temporary memorial to those who lost their lives the year before. In 2005, the Bosque gardens by landscape artist Piet Oudulf were opened, as was the Spiral Fountain, with 35 illuminated and interactive jets. Adjoining Battery Park on this western side is Robert F. Wagner Jr. Park, which has public bathrooms and a restaurant-café.

The southern link in a chain of parks connecting Battery Park north to Chambers Street, **Robert F. Wagner Jr. Park** has a flat, tidy lawn and wide benches from which to view the harbor or the stream of runners and rollerbladers on the promenade. A brick structure that holds public bathrooms and a restaurant provides additional views from its flat roof. ⊠ *Between Battery Pl. and Hudson River, Lower Manhattan.*

⊠ *Broadway and Battery Pl., Lower Manhattan* Ⓜ *Subway: 4, 5 to Bowling Green.*

DID YOU KNOW?

Now in the middle of Battery Park, Castle Clinton was once 200 feet off the southern tip of the island. Originally called the Southwest Battery, it was erected during the War of 1812 to defend the city. (The East Battery sits across the harbor on Governors Island.) As dirt and debris from construction were dumped into the harbor, the island expanded, eventually engulfing the landmark.

Bowling Green. This oval greensward at the foot of Broadway became New York's first public park in 1733. On July 9, 1776, a few hours after citizens learned about the signing of the Declaration of Independence, rioters toppled a statue of British king George III that had occupied the spot for 11 years; much of the statue's lead was melted down into bullets. In 1783, when the occupying British forces fled the city, they defiantly hoisted a Union Jack on a greased, uncleated flagpole so it couldn't be lowered; patriot John Van Arsdale drove his own cleats into the pole to replace the flag with the Stars and Stripes. The copper-top subway entrance here is the original one, built in 1904–05. Free 90-minute walking tours meet every Thursday and Saturday at noon at the front steps of the U.S. Customs House, opposite Bowling Green.

★ **Brooklyn Bridge.** "A drive-through cathedral" is how the critic James Wolcott describes one of New York's noblest and most recognized landmarks. Spanning the East River, the Brooklyn Bridge connects Manhattan island to the once-independent city of Brooklyn. Before the bridge opened, Brooklynites had only the Fulton Street Ferry to shuttle them across the river. A walk across the bridge's promenade—a boardwalk elevated above the roadway and shared by pedestrians, in-line skaters, and bicyclists— takes about 40 minutes, from Manhattan's civic center to the heart of Brooklyn Heights. It's well worth traversing for the astounding views. Midtown's jumble of spires and the Manhattan Bridge loom to the north. Mostly modern skyscrapers crowd Lower Manhattan, and the tall ships docked at their feet, at South Street Seaport, appear to have sailed in straight from the 19th century. Governors Island sits forlornly in the middle of the harbor, which dramatically sweeps open toward Lady Liberty and, off in the distance, the Verrazano-Narrows Bridge (its towers are more than twice as tall as those of the Brooklyn Bridge). Its twin Gothic-arch towers, with a span of 1,595½ feet, rise 272 feet from the river below; the bridge's overall length of 6,016 feet made it four times longer than the longest suspension bridge of its day. From roadway to water is about 133 feet, high enough to allow the tallest ships to pass. The roadway is supported by a web of steel cables, hung from the towers and attached to block-long anchorages on either shore. Ⓜ *Subway: 4, 5, 6 to Brooklyn Bridge/City Hall; J, M, Z to Chambers St.*

▌ NEW YORK MINUTE

One of the best ways to see the city's southern tip is to stroll across the board-walk on the Brooklyn Bridge. You can start in Manhattan at the Brooklyn Bridge/City Hall subway stop, or in Brooklyn Heights at the High Street subway stop (a better option, as the skyline is ahead of you the entire time). Whichever you choose, budget about 40 minutes.

City Hall. Reflecting the classical refinement and civility of Enlightenment Europe, New York's decorous City Hall is a three-story palace with a facade punctuated by arches and columns and a cupola crowned by a copper statue of Justice. Built between 1803 and 1812, the federal-style structure with French influences was originally clad in white Massachusetts marble on its front and sides only; the back was faced in more modest brownstone because city fathers assumed the city would never grow farther north than this. Alabama limestone over a granite base now covers all four sides. A sweeping marble double staircase leads from the soaring domed rotunda to the second-floor public rooms. The small, Victorian-style **City Council Chamber** in the east wing has mahogany detailing and ornate gilding; the **Board of Estimate Chamber,** to the west, has colonial paintings and church-pew-style seating; and the **Governor's Room** at the head of the stairs, a museum and reception room, is filled with historic portraits and furniture, including a writing table that George Washington used in 1789 when New York was the U.S. capital. The **Blue Room,** which was traditionally the mayor's office, is on the ground floor and is now used for mayoral press conferences.

Although the building looks genteel, the City Hall politicking that goes on there can be rough and tumble. News crews can often be seen jockeying on the front steps as they attempt to interview city officials. City Hall is open to the public for tours. ✉ *City Hall Park, Lower Manhattan* ☎ *212/639–9675* ✆ *Free* ☉ *Tours weekdays; reservations required 2 wks in advance* Ⓜ *Subway: 4, 5, 6 to Brooklyn Bridge/City Hall.*

Criminal Courts Building. Fans of crime fiction, whether on television, in the movies, or in novels, may recognize this rather grim art deco tower, which is connected by a skywalk (New York's Bridge of Sighs) to the detention center known as the Tombs. In *The Bonfire of the Vanities,* Tom Wolfe wrote a chilling description of this court's menacing atmosphere. ✉ *100 Centre St., at Hogan Pl., Lower Manhattan.*

Federal Hall National Memorial. The site of this memorial is rich with both the country's and the city's history. The City Hall here hosted the 1765 Stamp Act Congress and, beginning in 1789, served as the Federal Hall of the new nation. On its balcony, George Washington took his oath as the country's first president. After the capital moved from New York to Philadelphia in 1790, the Federal Hall reverted to New York's City Hall, then was demolished in 1812 when the present City Hall was completed. The current Greek Revival building, built as a U.S. customhouse in 1842, was modeled on the Parthenon. On the steps stands an 1883 statue of George Washington. His likeness was rendered by noted sculptor and presidential kin John Quincy Adams Ward. The hall's interior, which holds a museum with exhibits on New York and Wall Street, is scheduled to reopen in September 2006 following extensive renovations. ✉ *26 Wall St., at Nassau St., Lower Manhattan* ☎ *212-825-6870* ✍ *Free* ☉ *Weekdays 9–5* Ⓜ *Subway: 2, 3, 4, 5 to Wall St.; A, C to Broadway-Nassau; J, M to Broad St.*

Federal Reserve Bank of New York. Built in 1924 and enlarged in 1935, this neo-Renaissance structure made of sandstone, limestone, and ironwork looks the way a bank ought to: strong and impregnable. The gold ingots in the subterranean vaults here are worth roughly $140 billion—reputedly a third of the world's gold reserves. Hour-long tours of the bank are conducted five times a day and require reservations made at least five days in advance. They include the gold vault, the trading desk, and "FedWorks," an interactive multimedia exhibit center where you can make and track hypothetical trades. Computer terminals and displays provide almost as much information as an Economics 101 course—explaining such points as what the Federal Reserve Bank does (besides store gold), what the money supply is, and what causes inflation. ✉ *33 Liberty St., between William and Nassau Sts., Lower Manhattan* ☎ *212/ 720–6130* ⊕ *www.newyorkfed.org* ✍ *Free* ☉ *1-hr tour by advance reservation, weekdays 9:30–2:30* Ⓜ *Subway: A, C to Broadway/Nassau; R to Rector St.; J, M, Z, 2, 3, 4, 5 to Fulton St.*

Whoever named the streets in Lower Manhattan didn't have much of an imagination. Bridge Street once had a bridge that crossed Broad Street, which was broad enough to have a canal running down its center. Stone Street was the first to get cobblestones, and Pearl Street was paved with mother-of-pearl shells. And yes, Wall Street had a wall that was erected to keep out invaders.

🕭 **Fraunces Tavern.** This tavern, with a white-marble portico and coffered frieze, is a rare remnant of New York's colonial-era existence. Built in 1719 and converted to a tavern in 1763, it was the meeting place for the Sons of Liberty until the Revolutionary War, and in 1783 George Washington delivered a farewell address here to his officers celebrating the British evacuation of New York. Today a museum occupies the two floors above a restaurant and bar. It contains two fully furnished period rooms—including the Long Room, site of Washington's address—and other modest displays of 18th- and 19th-century American history. The museum also hosts family programs (such as crafts workshops), lectures, and concerts. ✉ *54 Pearl St., at Broad St., Lower Manhattan* ☎ *212/ 425–1778* ⊕ *www.frauncestavernmuseum.org* ✍ *$4* ☉ *Sept.–June, Tues.–Fri. noon–5, Sat. 10–5; July and Aug., Tues.–Sat. 10–5* Ⓜ *Subway: R, W to Whitehall St.; 4, 5 to Bowling Green; 1 to South Ferry; 2,3, to Wall St.; J, M, Z to Broad St.*

Municipal Building. Who else but the venerable architecture firm McKim, Mead & White would the city government trust to build its first sky-

Continued on page 39

GROUND ZERO
THE WORLD TRADE CENTER SITE

Every New Yorker has a story about September 11th: what they saw, where they were when it happened, who they worried about, who they lost.

In its perpetual aftermath, no two people look at the tragedy the same way. Perhaps the only thing that elicits unanimous agreement, then and now, is the sentiment voiced that day by then-Mayor Rudolph Giuliani: "The number of casualties will be more than any of us can bear, ultimately."

What will you experience when you visit Ground Zero? Quite simply, we can't tell you. Perhaps more so than anything we've tried to describe in our guides, you just have to be there to know.

But here's what we can tell you.

■ Approximately 50,000 people worked in the north tower (1 World Trade Center) and south tower (2 World Trade Center), and another 40,000 visited the 16-acre complex every day. Beneath the towers was a mall with nearly 100 stores and restaurants. The entire complex—hosting more than 430 companies from 28 countries—was so large it had its own zip code—10048.

■ Each 110 stories tall (though at 1,368 feet, the north tower was six feet taller), the towers were triumphs of mid-20th-century engineering. Their construction began in 1968, and they officially opened in 1973. Avoiding the thick interior columns typically used at the time, the architects gave each building an exterior skeleton made up of 244 slim steel columns and an inner "core" tube that supported the weight of the tower and housed its elevators and stairwells.

■ On September 11, 2001, terrorist hijackers steered two jets into the World Trade Center's twin towers, demolishing them and five outlying buildings and killing 2,973 people.

■ Both planes were Boeing 767s. American Airlines Flight 11 hit the north tower at 494 mph. United Airlines Flight 175 hit the south tower at 586 mph. Researchers speculate that the higher speed of United 175 may have caused the south tower to fall first, even though it was hit second.

■ Why *did* the towers fall? A three-year federal study revealed several reasons. The airplanes damaged the exterior columns, destroying core supports for at least three of the north tower's floors and up to six of the south tower's floors. Ensuing fires, fed by tens of thousands of gallons of fuel, further weakened the buildings. The collapse of the most heavily damaged floors then triggered a domino effect, causing the towers to crumple at an estimated speed of about 125 mph. The collapse of the towers released dust clouds filled with toxins, including jet fuel, cement, glass, fiberglass, and asbestos.

■ Dubbed Ground Zero, the fenced-in 16-acre work site that emerged from the rubble has come to symbolize the personal and historical impact of the attack. A steel "viewing wall" now encircles the site, bound on the north and south by Vesey and Liberty streets, and on the east and west by Church and West streets. Along the east wall are panels that detail the history of lower Manhattan and the WTC site before, during, and after September 11. There are also panels bearing the names of those who perished on 9/11/01 and during the 1993 World Trade Center attack.

Left: Ground Zero today. Center: Pedestrians flee as the south tower falls. Right: Views of the World Trade Center before the September 11 attacks.

■ Controversy has swirled around the site's future. As of this writing, the plan is to build five buildings on the World Trade Center site. Its centerpiece, if realized, will be the tallest building in the world: the 1,776-foot "Freedom Tower," due for completion in 2009. A park with a memorial to the victims and heroes of 9/11, a cultural center, a performing-arts venue, and a new PATH terminal are also planned.

UNDERSTANDING THE DEVASTATION

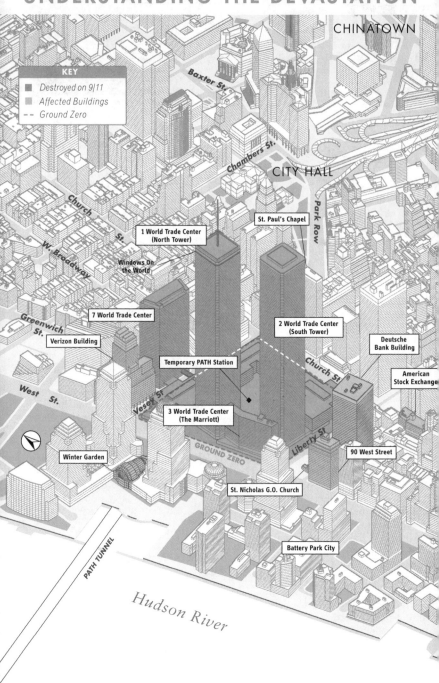

CHINATOWN

KEY
- Destroyed on 9/11
- Affected Buildings
- -- Ground Zero

Baxter St.

Chambers St.

CITY HALL

Church St.

Park Row

St. Paul's Chapel

1 World Trade Center
(North Tower)

W. Broadway

Windows On
the World

7 World Trade Center

2 World Trade Center
(South Tower)

Greenwich
St.

Verizon Building

Deutsche
Bank Building

Temporary PATH Station

Church St.

American
Stock Exchange

West
St.

Vesey St.

3 World Trade Center
(The Marriott)

Liberty St.

GROUND ZERO

90 West Street

Winter Garden

St. Nicholas G.O. Church

Battery Park City

PATH TUNNEL

Hudson River

In the days after 9/11, police barricades permitted only residents and emergency personnel to go south of 14th Street. A second line of barriers blocked access below Houston Street to all but residents, and only emergency workers were permitted south of a National Guard perimeter running from Chambers Street to the Brooklyn Bridge.

1 WORLD TRADE CENTER
(The North Tower)

The first hijacked jet, American Airlines Flight 11, crashed into the north tower at 8:46 AM, cutting through floors 93 to 99. Evidence suggests that all three building stairwells became impassable from the 92nd floor up. The tower collapsed at 10:28 AM. Cantor Fitzgerald, a brokerage firm headquartered between the 101st and 105th floors, lost 658 of its 1,050 employees. At the Windows on the World restaurant (floors 106 and 107), 100 patrons and 72 staff members perished.

2 WORLD TRADE CENTER
(The South Tower)

The second hijacked jet, United Airlines Flight 175, hit the south tower at 9:03 AM, crashing through the 77th to 85th floors. The plane banked as it hit, so portions of the building remained undamaged on impact floors. Consequently, one stairwell initially remained passable from at least the 91st floor down. The tower collapsed at 9:58 AM.

3 WORLD TRADE CENTER
(The Marriott)

Located between the north and south towers, the New York Marriott World Trade Center was completely destroyed in the attacks. Before the towers fell, hundreds of people evacuated through the hotel's lobby. The building had an ominous history, stretching back to 1981 when a fire broke out two days before its first guests checked in. In 1993, damage from the first World Trade Center bombing shut the hotel down for a year and a half. Part of the World Trade Center Site Memorial will cover the area previously occupied by the hotel.

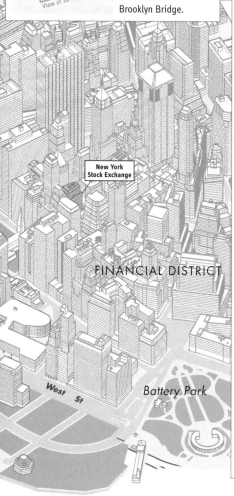

FINANCIAL DISTRICT

New York Stock Exchange

West St

Battery Park

7 WORLD TRADE CENTER

This 47-story building was struck by large chunks of falling debris from the north and south towers. Mayor Giuliani's emergency command center—which he would never get to use on 9/11—was on the 23rd floor. The building remained standing despite suffering structural damage, but fires broke out and burned unchecked for seven hours, eventually causing the building to collapse at 5:20 PM. The new 52-story 7 World Trade Center opened in May 2006.

VERIZON BUILDING

As 7 World Trade Center collapsed, a 60-foot-tall pile of its rubble fell against the Verizon Building, severely damaging the switching center and cutting off phone service to Lower Manhattan. The impact also took a heavy toll on the art deco building's east facade, south-facing wall, foundation walls, and two structural columns; repair workers have replaced 1,800 windows, 520,000 exterior bricks, and 22,500 cinder blocks—many by hand.

NEW YORK STOCK EXCHANGE AND AMERICAN STOCK EXCHANGE

The New York Stock Exchange (NYSE) remained closed for six days after the attacks (including 9/11). When trading resumed on September 17, the Dow Jones industrial average dropped 684.81 points. The American Stock Exchange (Amex) was damaged on September 11, and for two weeks Amex stocks and exchange-traded funds were traded on the NYSE floor. During that time, Amex options were traded on the floor of the Philadelphia Stock Exchange.

ST. PAUL'S CHAPEL

Though it's directly across from the World Trade Center site, St. Paul's sustained no major damage in the attacks. After September 11, the chapel was host to an eight-month volunteer relief effort for Ground Zero recovery workers, providing food, shelter, and medical care. St. Paul's has long been a sanctuary for those with heavy burdens—George Washington worshipped here on his inauguration day.

WINTER GARDEN

The 10-story glass-domed Winter Garden, home to the World Financial Center's Arts & Events Program, was severely damaged in the attacks. The atrium reopened in September 2002 after extensive repairs, which included the installation of 2,000 windows and 1.2 million pounds of stone. The venue hosts a year-round series of free exhibitions, festivals, and performances.

2

GROUND ZERO THE WORLD TRADE CENTER SITE

DEUTSCHE BANK BUILDING

Falling World Trade Center debris cut a 15-story gash in the north facade of the Deutsche Bank Building, which has been unoccupied since 9/11. Various negotiations delayed deconstruction of the badly damaged and contaminated building until March 2006. The complex demolition plan calls for removing World Trade Center dust and contaminants from the building, gutting it, and then disassembling it.

90 WEST STREET

The terra-cotta and limestone exterior of this Cass Gilbert–designed 1907 office building, one block away from the south tower, was damaged by fire and falling debris. Now renovated and restored, 90 West Street has been converted into apartments.

ST. NICHOLAS GREEK ORTHODOX CHURCH

Tiny St. Nicholas Greek Orthodox Church was buried in rubble and completely destroyed. The church will be rebuilt on a site near its former location.

PATH/SUBWAY LINE

About 1,000 feet of the tunnels used by the Metropolitan Transit Authority's 1 and (now defunct) 9 subway trains collapsed after the towers fell, closing Cortlandt Street station (slated to reopen spring 2007). The Port Authority of New York and New Jersey's World Trade Center PATH train station was also damaged in the attacks. After the first plane hit, PATH workers began evacuating the WTC station and rerouting inbound trains. The last train to unload was reloaded and backed out of the station; after the evacuation, an empty train picked up the remaining station workers and carried them to safety. The entire evacuation was completed 48 minutes

From left to right: View of the burning towers from Washington Square Park. (Top) One of two pedestrian bridges that connected the World Financial Center to the WTC. (Bottom) Firefighters search the WTC rubble on September 12, 2001. Part of the facade of one of the towers rises above the Ground Zero debris. (Top) A November 11, 2001, peace vigil near Ground Zero. (Bottom) Protesters demonstrate against military retaliation in the days following September 11.

before the first tower fell. In November 2003, PATH opened a temporary station at the World Trade Center. The best way to view the WTC site is by riding the PATH from Hoboken.

BATTERY PARK CITY

Many people fled across the Hudson River to New Jersey on boats commanded by volunteer captains. One ferry line alone reported evacuating nearly 30,000 people. The community's 9,000 residents were left homeless, and almost half of the renters never returned.

RUDY'S REACTION

Shortly after the north tower was hit, New York City Mayor Rudolph Giuliani rushed to the scene and conferred with fire commanders—one of whom, Chief of Department Peter Ganci, would be killed just moments later. When 7 World Trade Center—the site of the mayor's emergency command center—was deemed unsafe, he went across the street to 75 Barclay, but fled to underground tunnels as debris from the north tower hit the building.

The mayor emerged at 100 Church Street and was walking north on Church when the south tower fell. Like many others, he began running for his life. Giuliani stayed in the fray in the ensuing hours, saying at one point that day: "We've undergone tremendous losses, and we're going to grieve for them horribly, but New York is going to be here tomorrow morning, and it's going to be here forever."

(Left to right) New York Gov. George Pataki, New York City Mayor Rudolph Giuliani, and Sen. Hillary Rodham Clinton (D-N.Y.) tour Ground Zero on September 12, 2001.

CLEANUP AND RECOVERY

■ Within 24 hours of the 9/11 attacks, trucks and tractor trailers began hauling debris to barges that made their way to the Fresh Kills landfill on Staten Island. In total, 1.8 million tons of debris were moved to the landfill over eight months, three months sooner than expected.

■ Fires in the World Trade Center debris pile were not completely extinguished until December 19, 2001, more than three months after the towers collapsed.

■ The Salvation Army served 3,320,935 free meals at Ground Zero.

■ Cleanup officially ended May 28, 2002, at a Ground Zero ceremony led by New York City Mayor Michael Bloomberg, when the final girder from the World Trade Center was removed.

■ The cleanup cost $750 million (it was expected to cost $7 billion).

Health warnings posted on the doors of a restaurant near the World Trade Center site.

VISITING THE SITE

WHEN TO GO: There are no special viewing hours and the site seldom feels crowded, even though more than 25,000 people visit each day. Early weekday mornings, when many tourists and locals are still working on their first cups of coffee, are good times to go.

HOW TO GET HERE: Subway: R, W to Rector St.; 2, 3, 4, 5, A, C, J, M, Z to Fulton St./Broadway-Nassau; E to World Trade Center.

TOURS: Every Saturday and Sunday, escorted walking tours of Lower Manhattan, including a stop at Ground Zero, are conducted by **New York City**

Vacation Packages (888/692-8701, www.nycvp.com, $19). **Talking Street** tours (212/262-8687, www.talkingstreet.com, $5.95) converts your cell phone into a tour guide, calling out 16 stops at and around Ground Zero. Portions of the profits go to the World Trade Center Memorial Foundation.

scraper in 1914, a building intended to house both administrative offices and a subway system? The roof section alone is 10 stories high, bristling with towers and peaks and topped by a 25-foot-high gilt statue of Civic Fame. New Yorkers come here to pay parking fines and get marriage licenses (and to get married, in a civil chapel on the second floor). An immense arch straddles Chambers Street (traffic used to flow through here). The subway station at the south end of the building lies under an arcaded plaza with vaults of Guastavino tile construction. A gift shop at the left side of the main entrance sells NYC maps, history books, and other souvenirs. ⊠ *1 Centre St., at Chambers St., Lower Manhattan* Ⓜ *Subway: J, M, Z, 4, 5, 6 to Chambers St.*

New York State Supreme Court. With its stately columns, pediments, and 100-foot-wide steps, this 1927 granite-faced courthouse was designed in a classical Roman style, reminiscent of Rome's Pantheon. It deviates from its classical parent in its hexagonal rotunda, shaped to fit an irregular plot of land. The 1957 courtroom drama *Twelve Angry Men* was filmed here. Viewers of *Law and Order* will recognize the outdoor steps. The courthouse also hosts thousands of marriages a year. ⊠ *60 Centre St., at Foley Sq., Lower Manhattan.*

St. Paul's Chapel. St. Paul's, oldest (1766) public building in continuous use in Manhattan, and its 18th-century cemetery abut the World Trade Center site. For more than a year following the disaster, the chapel fence served as a shrine for visitors seeking solace. People from around the world left tokens of grief and support, or signed one of the large drop cloths that hung from the fence. After having served as a 24-hour refuge where rescue and recovery workers could eat, pray, rest, and receive counseling, the chapel, which amazingly suffered no damage, reopened to the public in fall 2002 with an ongoing exhibit titled "Unwavering Spirit: Hope & Healing at Ground Zero," honoring the workers and recalling their efforts in the months following September 11. ⊠ *209 Broadway at Fulton St., Lower Manhattan* ☎ *212/233–4164* ⊕ *www. saintpaulschapel.org* ☉ *Mon.–Sat. 10–5:45, Sun. 8–3:45* Ⓜ *Subway: 2, 3, 4, 5, A, C, J, M, Z to Fulton St.*

Shrine of St. Elizabeth Ann Seton at Our Lady of the Rosary. This redbrick federal-style town house near the Staten Island Ferry terminal provides a rare glimpse at Lower Manhattan architecture from an earlier day. With its distinctive colonnade, shaped to fit the curving street, it exemplifies the mansions that once lined the street. The house was built in 1793 as the home of the wealthy Watson family. Mother Seton lived here with her family from 1801 until the death of her husband in 1803. She joined the Catholic Church in 1805 and went on to found the Sisters of Charity, the first American order of nuns. In 1975 she became the first American-born saint. Masses are held here daily. ⊠ *7 State St., near Whitehall St., Lower Manhattan* ☎ *212/269–6865* ⊕ *www.setonshrine.com* Ⓜ *Subway: R, W to Whitehall St.*

South Street Seaport Historic District. Had it not been declared a historic district in 1977, this charming, cobblestone corner of New York with the city's largest concentration of early-19th-century commercial buildings would likely have been gobbled up by skyscrapers. In the early 1980s the Rouse Company, which had already created Boston's Quincy Market and Baltimore's Harborplace, leased the real estate from the city to restore and adapt the existing buildings, preserving the commercial feel of centuries past. The result is a hybrid of historical district and shopping mall. Many of its streets' 18th-, 19th-, and early-20th-century architectural details re-create the city's historic seafaring era.

At the intersection of Fulton and Water streets, the gateway to the Seaport, stands the **_Titanic_ Memorial,** a small white lighthouse that commemorates the sinking of the RMS _Titanic_ in 1912. Beyond it, Fulton Street, cobbled in blocks of Belgian granite, turns into a busy pedestrian mall. Just to the left of Fulton, at 211 Water Street, is **Bowne & Co. Stationers,** a reconstructed working 19th-century printing and museum gift shop. Continue down Fulton Street to Front Street, which has wonderfully preserved brick buildings—some dating from the 1700s. On the south side of Fulton Street is the seaport's architectural centerpiece, **Schermerhorn Row,** a redbrick terrace of Georgian- and federal-style warehouses and counting houses built from 1811 to 1812. Some upper floors house gallery space, and the ground floors are occupied by upscale shops, bars, and restaurants. Also here at 12 Fulton Street is the main lobby of the **South Street Seaport Museum** (☎ 212/748–8600 ⊕ www.southstseaport. org ☯ Apr.–Oct., Tues.–Sun. 10–6; Nov.–Mar., Fri.–Mon. 10–5), which hosts walking tours, hands-on exhibits, and fantastic creative programs for children, all with a nautical theme. You can purchase tickets ($8) at either 12 Fulton Street or Pier 16 Visitors Center.

Cross South Street, once known as the Street of Ships, under an elevated stretch of the FDR Drive to **Pier 16,** where historic ships are docked, including the _Pioneer,_ a 102-foot schooner built in 1885; the _Peking,_ the second-largest sailing bark in existence; the iron-hulled _Wavertree_; and the lightship _Ambrose._ The Pier 16 ticket booth provides information and sells tickets to the museum, ships, tours, and exhibits. Pier 16 is the departure point for various seasonal cruises. To the north is **Pier 17,** a multi-level dockside shopping mall that houses national chain retailers such as Express and Victoria's Secret, among others. Its weathered-wood rear decks make a splendid spot from which to sit and contemplate the river, with views as far north as midtown Manhattan and as far south as the Verrazano-Narrows Bridge.·⊠ _South Street Seaport_ ☎ _212/732–7678 events and shopping information_ ⊕ _www. southstreetseaport.com_ ☞ _$5 to ships, galleries, walking tours, Maritime Crafts Center, films, and other seaport events_ Ⓜ _Subway: A, C, 2, 3, 4, 5 to Fulton St./Broadway Nassau._

▎FRUGAL
FUN

About 70,000 people ride the Staten Island Ferry every day, and you should be one of them. Without having to pay a cent, you get great views of the Statue of Liberty, Ellis Island, and the southern tip of Manhattan. You'll pass tug boats, freighters, and cruise ships—a reminder that this is still a working harbor.

Tweed Courthouse. Under the corrupt management of notorious Tammany Hall politician William Marcy "Boss" Tweed, this Italianate gem with a medieval-inspired south wing, took some $12 million and 20 years to build (it was finally finished in 1872, but the ensuing public outrage drove Tweed from office). Today, its imposing marble structure, with its columned classical pediment outside and seven-story octagonal rotunda inside, serves as headquarters of the New York City Department of Education; it has also served as a location for several films, most notably *The Verdict*. Tours are offered weekdays. Free. Reservations should be made two weeks in advance. 212/NEW-YORK. ⊠ *52 Chambers St., between Broadway and Centre St., Lower Manhattan* ☎ *212/639–9675* ☜ *Free* ☉ *Tours weekdays; reservations required 2 wks in advance* Ⓜ *Subway: 4, 5, 6 to Brooklyn Bridge/City Hall; J, M, Z to Chambers St.; R, W to City Hall.*

U.S. Courthouse. Cass Gilbert built this courthouse in 1936, convinced that it complemented the much finer nearby Woolworth Building, which he had designed nearly three decades earlier. Granite steps climb to a massive columned portico; above this rises a 32-story tower topped by a gilded pyramid, not unlike that with which Gilbert crowned the New York Life Insurance building uptown. Julius and Ethel Rosenberg were tried for espionage at this courthouse, and hotel queen Leona Helmsley went on trial here for tax evasion. The courthouse is under renovation, with 500 Pearl Street currently functioning in its place. ⊠ *40 Centre St., at Pearl St., 1 Foley Sq., Lower Manhattan* Ⓜ *Subway: 4, 5, 6 to Brooklyn Bridge/City Hall.*

Vietnam Veterans Memorial. At the center of a triangular plaza sits this 14-foot-high, 70-foot-long rectangular memorial, on which passages from news dispatches from the wartime period and the letters of military service people are etched into its wall of greenish glass. ⊠ *End of Coenties Slip between Water and South Sts, adjacent to 125 Broad St., Lower Manhattan.*

Wall Street. Named after a wooden wall built across the island in 1653 to defend the Dutch colony against the Native Americans (mostly Algonquins), ⅓-mi-long Wall Street is arguably the most famous thoroughfare in the world—shorthand for the vast, powerful financial community that clusters around the New York and American stock exchanges. "The Street," as it's also widely known, began its financial career with stock traders conducting business along the sidewalks or at tables beneath a sheltering buttonwood tree. Today it's a dizzyingly narrow canyon—look to the east and you'll glimpse a sliver of East River waterfront; look to the west and you'll see the spire of Trinity Church, tightly framed by skyscrapers.

At the intersection with Broad Street stands the New York Stock Exchange, Wall Street's epicenter. The largest securities exchange in the world, it nearly bursts from its neoclassical 1903 building with six Corinthian columns supporting a pediment with a sculpture entitled *Integrity Protecting the Words of Man* designed by John Quincy Adams Ward—a fitting temple to the almighty dollar. Today's "Big Board" can handle a trillion shares of stock per day. Unfortunately, the exchange isn't open to visitors.

Down by the Riverside

NEW YORK IS A CITY OF ISLANDS, surrounded by ocean, bay, river, and sound. The entire waterfront of the five boroughs measures 578 mi, making it the longest and most diverse of any municipality in the country. Down by the water, the air is salty and fresh, the views are exhilarating, and the mood is peaceful and quiet. The thin ribbon of park currently runs from Battery Park as far north as 59th Street, and is full of joggers, cyclists, and rollerbladers. A trio of piers off Greenwich Village (45 and 46 at Charles Street, and 51 at Jane Street) provide grassy lawns for napping, fields for playing, and a water-theme playground. Greenspace advocates have also spruced up the Empire-Fulton Ferry State Park in Brooklyn's industrial DUMBO neighborhood, which has incredible views of the East River between the Brooklyn and Manhattan bridges.

Though New Yorkers are now spending leisure time by the water, New York grew up as a shipping and shipbuilding town. The Port of New York was first centered near the South Street Seaport on the East River, where the 18th-century streetscape and historic sailing vessels recall the clipper-ship era. Street names suggest the contours of Manhattan before settlers filled in the wetlands: Pearl Street, where mother-of-pearl shells were collected; Water Street; and Front Street. The port then moved to the wider, less turbulent Hudson River, where Robert Fulton launched the first steamboat in 1807. After the opening of the Erie Canal in 1825, which connected it to the Great Lakes and the West for trade, the city became the preeminent port in the country, the gateway to the continent

for exports and imports, the "golden door" for immigrants. In the late 1800s, New York Harbor, crisscrossed with ferries, barges, tugs, canal boats, freighters, and passenger liners, was the busiest in the world. Until the Brooklyn Bridge was completed in 1883, even Manhattanites and Brooklynites couldn't visit each other except by ferries that landed at Fulton Street in lower Manhattan and Fulton Ferry Landing in DUMBO.

On the Hudson River, where older generations once boarded grand ocean liners to make a two-week journey across the Atlantic, New Yorkers are once again using boat travel—this time to commute within their own city. Ferry service provides commuters a transportation method that harkens back to the 1800s. In addition to the 200-plus-capacity boats of New York Waterways, the small, 54-seat New York Water Taxis are serving both rush-hour travelers and tourists.

At the West Side Highway and Christopher Street, walk out on Greenwich Village's popular pier to take in the view back toward the fading vestiges of a Victorian-era waterfront: a panorama of warehouses (many converted to apartments and clubs) and smaller buildings that house cheap hotels and seedy bars. At 14th Street, remember Herman Melville, who worked as a customs inspector nearby. Just south of the Chelsea Piers complex, note the remains of the pier house where the *Titanic* was scheduled to conclude its maiden voyage. In summer, check out the piers that spring to life with public events—movies, dances, and food festivals.

For a clear lesson in the difference between Ionic and Corinthian columns, look at 55 Wall Street. The lower stories were part of an earlier U.S. customhouse, built in 1836–42; it was literally a bullish day on Wall Street when oxen hauled its 16 granite Ionic columns up to the site. When the National City Bank took over the building in 1899, it hired architects McKim, Mead & White to redesign the building and in 1909 added the second tier of columns but made them Corinthian. ⊠ *Lower Manhattan* Ⓜ *Subway: 4, 5 to Wall St.*

Wall Street Rising Downtown Information Center. One block south of the NYSE, this nonprofit organization, dedicated to restoring the vibrancy and vitality that existed in Lower Manhattan before the World Trade Center tragedy, is combination information and neighborhood civic center. ⊠ *25 Broad St., at Exchange Pl., Lower Manhattan* ☎ *212/425-4636* ⊕ *www.downtowninfocenter.org* ☉ *Weekdays 11–7* Ⓜ *Subway: 2, 3, 4, 5 to Wall St.; J, M, Z to Broad St.; R, W to Rector St.*

Woolworth Building. Called the Cathedral of Commerce, this ornate neo-Gothic edifice—originally faced almost entirely in white terra-cotta—was, at 792 feet, the world's tallest building when it opened in 1913. The symmetrically planned lobby's rich details include a stained-glass skylight and sculptures set into the portals to the left and right: one represents an elderly F. W. Woolworth counting his nickels and dimes, another depicts the architect, Cass Gilbert, cradling in his arms a model of his creation. Glittering mosaic tiles fill the dome and archways. ⊠ *233 Broadway, between Park Pl. and Barclay St., Lower Manhattan* Ⓜ *Subway: 2, 3 to Park Pl.; N, Q, R, W to City Hall.*

World Financial Center (WFC). The four towers of this complex, 34–51 stories high and topped with different geometric ornaments, were designed by Cesar Pelli and serve as company headquarters for the likes of American Express and Dow Jones. The sides of the buildings facing the World Trade Center towers were damaged during the September 11 attacks but have been fully restored. The glass-domed Winter Garden atrium is the main attraction here; it's a pleasant open space that's the site of music and dance performances, as well as a display of architectural plans for the WTC site and a selection of stores and restaurants. At the south end of the WFC complex, the South Bridge footbridge connects One WFC to the intersection of Liberty and Washington streets. The windows on the north side of the footbridge provide a view of the World Trade Center site. ⊠ *West St. between Vesey and Liberty Sts., Lower Manhattan* ⊕ *www.worldfinancialcenter.com.*

Lower Manhattan At a Glance

SIGHTS
African Burial Ground
Brooklyn Bridge
Castle Clinton National
  Monument
City Hall
Criminal Courts Building
Federal Hall National
  Memorial
Federal Reserve Bank of
  New York
Fraunces Tavern
Ground Zero (the World
  Trade Center Site)
Municipal Building
New York State Supreme
  Court
St. Paul's Chapel
Shrine of St. Elizabeth Ann
  Seton at Our Lady of the
  Rosary
South Street Seaport
  Historic District
Staten Island Ferry
Tweed Courthouse
U.S. Courthouse
Vietnam Veterans
  Memorial
Wall Street
Wall Street Rising
  Downtown Information
  Center

Woolworth Building
World Financial Center
  (WFC)

MUSEUMS & GALLERIES
(⇨ Ch. 14)
Alexander Hamilton U.S.
  Custom House/National
  Museum of the American
  Indian
Museum of American
  Finance
New York City Police
  Museum
Skyscraper Museum

PARKS & GARDENS
Battery Park
Bowling Green
City Hall Park
Robert F. Wagner Jr. Park

WHERE TO EAT
(⇨ Ch. 18)

BUDGET DINING
Financier, *Café*

MODERATE DINING
Delmonico's, *American*
Roy's New York, *Pan-Asian*

EXPENSIVE DINING
Bayard's, *Contemporary*

WHERE TO STAY
(⇨ Ch. 19)

BUDGET LODGING
Best Western Seaport Inn
Holiday Inn Wall Street

MODERATE LODGING
Embassy Suites Hotel New
  York
Millennium Hilton

EXPENSIVE LODGING
Ritz-Carlton New York,
  Battery Park

BARS & NIGHTLIFE
(⇨ Ch. 16)
Rise, *bar*
Bridge Café, *bar*

ARTS & ENTERTAINMENT
(⇨ Ch. 15)
Winter Garden,
  performance venue

SHOPPING (⇨ Ch. 17)

DEPARTMENT STORES
Century 21

MUSIC
J&R Music World

SOUVENIRS
City Store

SoHo & Chinatown

INCLUDING TRIBECA & LITTLE ITALY

WORD OF MOUTH

"[For a taste of Chinatown], I would recommend crossing Bowery and exploring the area along and northeast of East Broadway; under the Manhattan Bridge overpass is an agglomeration of both Fujianese and Vietnamese places including a couple of multistory shopping/eating arcades. You will see very few tourists in this area but you can taste some great food."

—ekscrunchy

www.fodors.com/forums

Sightseeing
★ ★ ★

Nightlife
★ ★ ★

Dining
★ ★ ★

Lodging
★ ★

Shopping
★ ★ ★ ★ ★

Shopping is the main draw to SoHo (*South of Hou*ston Street) these days, although gallery hopping, people-watching at a sidewalk café, and nighttime foraging for hip hangouts are not far behind. A quieter version of SoHo, TriBeCa (the *Tri*angle *Be*low *Ca*nal Street) lies south of Canal Street and owes much of its fame to Robert De Niro, who has invested substantial resources in the community, including the non-profit TriBeCa Film Center. Unlike the similarly trendy SoHo district, which became a mecca of designer boutiques, TriBeCa keeps more to itself, with relatively quiet streets even at peak hours. The money is hidden away here be-hind the grand industrial facades, but you can get a taste of it at one of the posh "neighborhood" restaurants.

East of Broadway, busloads of tourists eat, shop, and explore their way through the tangle of streets that make up Little Italy and Chinatown, New York's most famous immigrant neighborhoods. A few nostalgic blocks of Mulberry Street nestled between chic NoLIta and Canal Street are all that remains of the vast Italian community that once dominated the area—which makes the few old-time grocers and shops still in busi-ness all the more special. Chinatown, by contrast, is more than a tourist attraction: a quarter of the city's 400,000 Chinese residents live here above storefronts crammed with souvenir shops and restaurants serv-ing every imaginable regional Chinese cuisine, from modest dumplings to sumptuous Hong Kong feasts. Restaurants proudly display their wares: if America's motto is "A chicken in every pot," then Chinatown's must be "A roast duck in every window."

What's Here

SoHo, Tribeca & NoLita

The strip of Broadway between Houston and Broome streets is an outdoor mall with mass market stores like H & M, Banana Republic, and Victoria's Secret. Head off the main drag either west for well-known designer outposts like Emporio Armani and Ralph Lauren or east to NoLita to walk slowly past the blink-and-you'll-miss-them low-attitude stores on Elizabeth, Mulberry, and Mott streets displaying custom-designed jewelry, hand-sewn dresses, lovingly crafted blown glass, and high-concept lighting.

A fire in early 2006 damaged the 23,000-square-foot **Prada.** It has since reopened and is worth a stop to check out the design, even if you're not in the market for a $1,000 skirt. A showcase of everything modern and wired, the **Apple Store** is a destination for technology lovers. Edgy in the '70s and '80s, SoHo was populated with artists and bohemians of every stripe. And though many of the galleries for which the neighborhood was known moved uptown, a concentration of galleries still remains. Several of SoHo's better exhibition spaces are clustered on the south end of Greene and Wooster streets near Grand and Canal streets. These include **Deitch Projects,** the **Drawing Center,** and **Spencer Brownstone.**

Architecture buffs will take notice of the world's greatest concentration of cast-iron buildings. Many styles—Italianate, Victorian Gothic, Greek Revival—are visible. The block between Spring and Broome is gorgeous and that between Canal and Grand streets has the longest row of cast-iron buildings anywhere. Greene Street has cast-iron architecture at its finest. Two standout buildings are the **Queen of Greene Street** and the **King of Greene Street.** Even the lampposts are architectural gems: note their turn-of-the-20th-century bishop's-crook style, adorned with various cast-iron curlicues from their bases to their curved tops. If you can take a minute to look up and not get run over by the shopping hordes, Broadway has some architectural gems such as the Beaux-Arts **Little Singer Building** and the **Haughwout Building.** The 1885 Romanesque Revival **Puck Building** is a well-known event space, with more than 5 acres to rent. This elegant brick building was named for *Puck* magazine, published here 1887–1916. To the east, amid the chic boutiques of NoLIta, stands **St. Patrick's Old Cathedral,** the first Catholic cathedral in New York City and the seat of the Roman Catholic Archdiocese in New York until the current St. Patrick's opened on 5th Avenue in 1879.

If you are visiting with kids, check out the **Children's Museum of the Arts** for its exhibitions and imaginative programs, activities, and events; and the **Scholastic Store,** for their brands, such as Harry Potter and Clifford the Big Red Dog, in an interactive, multimedia environment, as well as a full schedule of programming.

There is no dearth of bars and restaurants here, some of the most popular in the three trendy hotels that have emerged in the last decade. The **Mercer Hotel** has a restaurant (Mercer Kitchen) operated by celebrity chef Jean-Georges Vongerichten, and its bar (both subterranean) is

GETTING ORIENTED

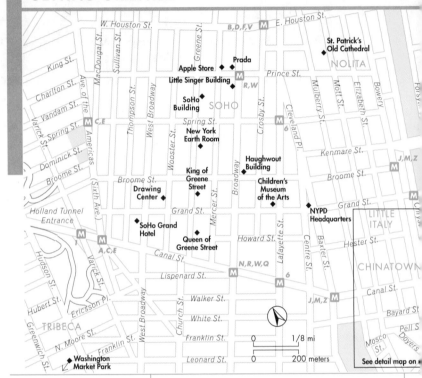

TOP 5

- ■ Browsing the Prada Store

- ■ Window shopping SoHo's designer boutiques

- ■ The authentic Italian grocers on Grand Street

- ■ Exploring Chinatown's sidewalk food markets

- ■ The San Gennaro Festival

MAKING THE MOST OF YOUR TIME

If you're coming to shop in SoHo and NoLIta, plan to arrive no earlier than 11 AM and try to avoid Monday, as some shops are closed. SoHo can be a madhouse any time of the day, any day of the week, especially on Saturday and Sunday. But that's part of the fun. TriBeCa is quiet any time, but that's part of the charm. Since the sights here are few but the great restaurants many, consider stopping here for dinner or kick the day off with a weekend brunch.

Little Italy and the main drag of Chinatown together represent a very small area. You could transverse Mulberry and Mott streets in half an hour if you wanted; or you could occupy hours browsing the shops and exploring side streets. If your goal is a good meal, dinner here can be a delicious way to conclude a visit.

Keep in mind the main streets are packed almost every day, and especially clogged on weekend afternoons. But this makes excellent people-watching from outdoor cafés.

3

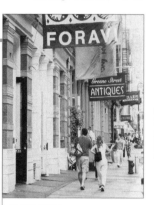

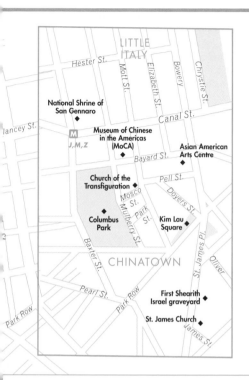

GETTING HERE

SoHo is roughly bounded by Houston Street, Canal Street, Avenue of the Americas, and Broadway and NoLIta between Houston, Broome, Crosby, and Bowery. There are plenty of options to reach the area via both east and west side trains: the 6 (east side) or A, C, E (west side) to Spring Street; R, W to Prince Street; B, D, F, V to Broadway-Lafayette. The 1 subway line stops in the heart of TriBeCa (Franklin St.).

Chinatown's tiny streets and heavy congestion make this a bad place to arrive by car. Conversely, plenty of subway lines service the neighborhood. If you're heading to Little Italy, the 6 (Spring St.) or the R, W (Prince St.) will get you to Soho and then it's a short walk southeast. The N, R, Q, W (Canal St.), 6 (Canal St.), J, M, Z (Canal St.), and the B, D (Grand St.) will land you on the west and east sides of Chinatown.

QUICK BITES

Snack (⊠ 105 Thompson St., between Prince and Spring Sts., SoHo ☎ 212/925-1040) serves cheap and tasty Greek-inspired fare. Duck into **Odeon** (⊠ 145 West Broadway, TriBeCa ☎ 212/233-0507), a slick art deco restaurant-bar, for bistro-type food like skirt steak and *frisée aux lardoons*, or a drink and snack at the bar anytime from noon to 2 AM.

Consistently voted one of the city's best pizza places, **Lombardi's** (⊠ 32 Spring St., between Mott and Mulberry, Little Italy ☎ 212/941-7994) can get you fed and on your way in under 45 minutes. For a quick snack, sample the crispy pastries, rice dumplings wrapped in banana leaves, yam cakes, and other intriguing treats at **May May Chinese Gourmet Bakery** (⊠ 35 Pell St., Chinatown ☎ 212/267-0733). A colorful flag hangs outside the entrance of **Chinatown Ice Cream Factory** (⊠ 5 Bayard St., Chinatown ☎ 212/608-4170), where the flavors range from litchi to almond cookie to green tea.

also a draw. Named for its address, **60 Thompson** has a swanky new in 2004 modern Thai restaurant on the ground floor called **Kittichai,** a comfortable outdoor seating area, a lounge one flight up (Thom Bar), and a rooftop bar (A60) that's open only to hotel guests and by invitation. Down a strip of West Broadway that is lined with small, always-lively restaurants, the **SoHo Grand** has a great meeting place on the second floor called the **Grand Bar & Lounge,** The Gallery restaurant, and a small outdoor area in summer cheekily called The Yard. The most well-known of all SoHo restaurants might be **Balthazar,** a popular brasserie that has a bakery next door where you can get sandwiches, salads, tarts, and a smorgasbord of sticky sweet crossaints, brioche, and other delights, all for takeaway.

Chinatown & Little Italy

You know you're in Chinatown when you reach the traffic-clogged Canal Street. Its sidewalks are lined with street vendors, and on weekends the crowds move at a snail's pace. A good place to get oriented is the **Museum of Chinese in the Americas.** Catercorner from the museum is **Columbus Park.** This gathering spot occupies the area once known as the Five Points, the tough 19th-century slum ruled by Irish gangs that provided the backdrop for Martin Scorsese's film *Gangs of New York.*

For a quick taste of Chinatown, head one block east of Mulberry Street to Mott Street, Chinatown's main thoroughfare. This area is where the first Chinese immigrants (mostly men) settled in tenements in the late 1880s. Today the street is dense with restaurants, bakeries, tea parlors, and souvenir shops, most of them lying below Canal Street. The few blocks above Canal overflow with food markets selling vegetables and fish (some still alive and swimming). In addition to food, the street is the site of the **Church of the Transfiguration.**

Just north of the church is Pell Street, a narrow lane of wall-to-wall restaurants whose neon signs stretch halfway across the thoroughfare. To the right off Pell is alley-size **Doyers Street,** the site of early-20th-century gang wars and today a favorite location for film shoots. At the end of Doyers is the **Bowery.** Once a grand boulevard lined with theaters and taverns, it earned a reputation as the city's skid row that lasted more than a century, from the late 1800s until recent decades, when revival efforts cleaned up its nefarious aspects. Today, it is a commercial thoroughfare.

■ TIP→ Safety: Even Chinatown's side streets remain highly trafficked until most restaurants close, at around 11 PM. Late at night you may want to stick to major streets and avoid walking alone.

Across the Bowery is **Kim Lau Square,** a crazy intersection of 10 streets converging at odd angles, in the center of which stands a graceful arch honoring Chinese casualties in the American wars. North of the square along the Bowery is the **Asian American Arts Centre,** which displays recent works by Asian-American artists. South of the square, heading past Park Row down St. James Place, are two remnants of this neighborhood's more distant past: the **First Shearith Israel Graveyard,** the first Jewish cemetery in the United States, and **St. James Church,** a stately 1837 Greek revival edifice where former New York govenor Al Smith once served as altar boy.

Crowded with restaurants, cafés, bakeries, imported-food shops, and souvenir stores, the few blocks of Mulberry Street between Canal and Broome streets is where Little Italy still lives and breathes. A block west stands the **San Gennaro Church,** with a jewel-box-like interior dating from 1892.

■ TIP→ **Every September the church sponsors the Feast of San Gennaro. About 1 million people turn out for the 11-day festival that sizzles with the smell of sausages and onions. Held under a canopy of red, white, and green lights strung along Mulberry Street, this is by far the city's largest annual street fair.**

Where Grand Street intersects Mulberry are a number of fine Italian grocers, including the fourth-generation family-run **DiPalo's Fine Foods** and **E. Rossi Co.,** established in 1902, an antiquated shop selling espresso makers and other essential items for Italian homes. At the corner of Hester and Mulberry streets stands what was once **Umberto's Clam House** (now Ristorante Da Gennaro), where in 1973 mobster Joey Gallo was munching scungilli when he was fatally surprised by mob hit men.

One block west of Mulberry at Broome Street is the **New York City Police Headquarters,** an opulent Renaissance Revival structure with baroque embellishments and a striking copper dome, which served as the city's police department headquarters until 1973. It's now a high-price condominium; big-name residents have included Cindy Crawford and Winona Ryder.

Places to Explore

SoHo, NoLIta & TriBeCa

Charlton Street. The city's longest stretch of federal-style redbrick row houses preserved from the 1820s and 1830s runs along the north side of this street, which is west of 6th Avenue and south of West Houston Street. The high stoops, paneled front doors, leaded-glass windows, and narrow dormer windows are all intact. Also part of this historic district, King and Vandam streets have more federal-style and Greek Revival houses. This quiet enclave was once the site of a mansion called Richmond Hill, which served variously as George Washington's headquarters and the home of Abigail Adams, and Aaron Burr.

Haughwout Building. Nicknamed the Parthenon of Cast Iron, this five-story, Venetian palazzo–style structure was built in 1857 to house E. V. Haughwout's china, silver, and glassware business. Each window is framed by Corinthian columns and rounded arches. Inside, the building once contained the world's first commercial passenger elevator, a steam-powered device invented by Elisha Graves Otis. Otis went on to found an elevator empire and made high-rises practical possibilities. ⊠ *488–492 Broadway, at Broome St., SoHo* Ⓜ *Subway: N, Q, R, W to Canal St.*

King of Greene Street. This five-story Renaissance-style 1873 building has a magnificent projecting porch of Corinthian columns and pilasters. Today

Gangs of Five Points

DEBAUCHERY HAS MADE the very houses prematurely old," novelist Charles Dickens wrote in 1842 after visiting Five Points. Although his prose was a bit purple, historians agree that the description of this former Lower Manhattan neighborhood was accurate.

In the mid-19th century, Five Points was perhaps the city's most notorious neighborhood. This intersection of five streets—Mulberry, Anthony (now Worth), Cross (now Park), Orange (now Baxter), and Little Water (no longer in existence)—had been built over a drainage pond that had been filled in the 1820s. When the buildings began to sink into the mosquito-filled muck, middle-class residents abandoned their homes. Buildings were chopped into tiny apartments that were rented to the poorest of the poor, who at this point happened to be newly emancipated slaves and Irish immigrants fleeing famine.

There's no doubt that Five Points was a dangerous place to live. Newspaper accounts at the time tell of robberies and other violent crimes on a daily basis. And with ward leaders like William Marcy Tweed—better known as "Boss" for his stranglehold on local politics—more concerned with lining their pockets than patrolling the streets, keeping order was left to the club-wielding hooligans portrayed in Martin Scorsese's *Gangs of New York*.

But the neighborhood, finally razed in the 1880s to make way for Chinatown's Columbus Park, has left a lasting legacy. In the music halls where different ethnic groups begrudgingly met, the Irish jig and the African-American shuffle combined to form a new type of fancy footwork called tap dancing.

the King is painted a brilliant shade of ivory. ✉ *72–76 Greene St., between Spring and Broome Sts., SoHo* Ⓜ *Subway: C, E to Spring St.*

Little Singer Building. Ernest Flagg's 1904 masterpiece reveals the final flower of the cast-iron style with a delicate facade covered with curlicues of wrought iron. The central bay windows are recessed, allowing the top floor to arch over like a proscenium. Don't miss the L-shape building's second facade on Prince Street. Its sibling, the Singer Tower, was at one time the tallest building in the world. That structure, at 165 Broadway, was, unfortunately, razed in 1967. ✉ *561 Broadway, SoHo* Ⓜ *Subway: R, W to Prince St.*

Queen of Greene Street. The regal grace of this 1873 cast-iron beauty is exemplified by its dormers, columns, window arches, projecting central bays, and Second Empire–style roof. ✉ *28–30 Greene St., between Grand and Canal Sts., SoHo* Ⓜ *Subway: N, R, Q, W to Canal St.*

Ⓒ **Washington Market Park.** This much-needed recreation space was named after the great food market that once sprawled over the area. It's now a green, landscaped stretch with a playground and a gazebo across from a public elementary school. At the corner, a stout little red tower resembles a lighthouse, and iron ship figures are worked into the playground fence—reminders of the neighborhood's long-gone dockside past. ⊠ *Greenwich St. between Chambers and Duane Sts., TriBeCa* Ⓜ *Subway: 1, 2, 3 to Chambers St.*

Chinatown

Church of the Transfiguration. Built as the English Lutheran Church of Zion in 1801, this imposing Georgian Gothic structure changed its name and denomination nine years later, becoming the Zion Protestant Episcopal Church. It became a Roman Catholic church in 1853, when many of its members moved away from the slums of Five Points. Today, in what is the largest Chinese Catholic community in the country, the church is distinguished by its trilingualism: mass is said in Cantonese, Mandarin, and English. ⊠ *29 Mott St., at Mosco St., Chinatown* ☎ *212/962–5157* ⊕ *www.transfigurationnyc.org* ☉ *Masses weekdays 8 AM and 12:10 PM, Sat. 6 PM, Sun. 9 AM, 10:15 AM, 11:30 AM, 12:45 PM* Ⓜ *Subway: N, Q, R, W, 6 to Canal St.; 4, 5, 6 to Brooklyn Bridge/City Hall.*

HERE'S WHERE

It may not look like a movie set, and that may be why the corner where Doyers Street spills into Pell Street is irresistible for filmmakers. Tobey McGuire and Kirsten Dunst had a heart-to-heart talk here in *Spider-Man 2*. Woody Allen used it as a location for two of his films, *Alice* and *Small Time Crooks*. It's also seen in *The Believer* and *King of New York*.

Columbus Park. In the morning, groups of elderly Chinese practice the graceful movements of tai chi in this shady park that received major renovations in 2005, including the historic pavilion. During the afternoons the tables fill for heated games of mah-jongg. In the mid-19th century, the swampy area was known as the **Five Points**—after the intersection of Mulberry Street, Anthony (now Worth) Street, Cross (now Park) Street, Orange (now Baxter) Street, and Little Water Street (no longer in existence)—and was notoriously ruled by dangerous Irish gangs. In the 1880s a neighborhood-improvement campaign brought about the park's creation. Ⓜ *Subway: N, Q, R, W, 6 to Canal St.*

First Shearith Israel Graveyard. Consecrated in 1656 by North America's oldest Jewish congregation, this small burial ground bears the remains of Sephardic Jews (of Spanish-Portuguese extraction) who emigrated from Brazil in the mid-17th century. You can peek through the gates at the ancient headstones here and at the second and third Shearith Israel graveyards on West 11th Street in Greenwich Village and West 21st Street in Chelsea, respectively. ⊠ *55 St. James Pl., Chinatown* Ⓜ *Subway: 4, 5, 6 to Brooklyn Bridge/City Hall.*

Kim Lau Square. Ten streets converge at this labyrinthine intersection crisscrossed at odd angles by pedestrian walkways. Standing on an island in this busy area is the **Kim Lau Arch,** honoring Chinese casualties in American wars. A statue on the square's eastern edge pays tribute to a Quin Dynasty official named Lin Zexu. The 18-foot, 5-inch-tall granite statue reflects Chinatown's growing population of mainland immigrants and their particular national pride: the Fujianese minister is noted for his role in sparking the Opium War by banning the drug. The base of his statue reads: PIONEER IN THE WAR AGAINST DRUGS. On the far end of the square, at the corner of Catherine Street and East Broadway (Chatham Square), stands a building that was built to resemble a pagoda. Ⓜ *Subway: 4, 5, 6 to Brooklyn Bridge/City Hall.*

Little Italy

National Shrine of San Gennaro. Every September this church—officially known as the Most Precious Blood Church—sponsors the Feast of San Gennaro, the biggest annual event in Little Italy. Dating from 1892, the church's richly painted, jewel-box-like interior is worth a glance, especially for the replica of the grotto at Lourdes. The church is open for services on weekends. For a visit during the week, see the rector at 109 Mulberry Street. ✉ *113 Baxter St., near Canal St., Little Italy* ☎ *212/768–9320 festival information, 212/226–6427 church* ⊙ *Masses Sat. noon, 5:30; Sun. 9, noon, 2 (Vietnamese)* Ⓜ *Subway: N, Q, R, W, 6 to Canal St.*

NEW YORK MOMENT

About 1 million people turn out each year for September's Feast of San Gennaro, an 11-day festival that sizzles with the smell of sausage and onions. Held under a canopy of red, white, and green lights strung across Mulberry Street, this is by far the largest of the city's annual street fairs.

New York City Police Headquarters. This magnificent Edwardian baroque structure with a striking copper dome served as the headquarters of the New York City Police Department from the building's construction in 1909 until 1973. The five-story limestone structure was designed to "impress both the officer and the prisoner with the majesty of the law." In 1988 it was converted into a luxury condominium complex and is known today as the Police Building Apartments. Big-name residents have included Cindy Crawford, Winona Ryder, and Steffi Graf, among others. ✉ *240 Centre St., between Broome and Grand Sts., Little Italy* Ⓜ *Subway: N, Q, R, W, 6 to Canal St.*

SoHo & Chinatown At a Glance

SIGHTS
Charlton Street
Church of the
  Transfiguration
First Shearith Israel
  Graveyard
Haughwout Building
Kim Lau Square
King of Greene Street
Little Singer Building
National Shrine of San
  Gennaro
New York City Police
  Headquarters
Queen of Greene Street

MUSEUMS & GALLERIES
(⇨ Ch. 14)
Asian American Arts Centre
Children's Museum of the
  Arts
Deitch Projects
Drawing Center
Museum of Chinese in the
  Americas (MoCA)
Nancy Hoffman
New York City Fire
  Museum
New York Earth Room
OK Harris Works of Art
Ronald Feldman Fine
  Arts

PARKS & GARDENS
Columbus Park
Washington Market Park

WHERE TO EAT
(⇨ Ch. 18)

BUDGET DINING
Aquagrill
Bread
Bubby's
Café Habana
Dos Caminos SoHo
Ghenet
Great New York
  Noodletown
Honmura An
Jazzi Wok
Jing Fong
Joe's Shanghai
Kitchenette
Le Pain Quotidien

Lombardi's
MarieBelle
Nha Trang
Pepe Rosso to Go
Petite Abeille
Rialto
Rice
Saint's Alp Teahouse
Sanur
Snack
Sweet 'n' Tart Restaurant &
  Café
Woo Lae Oak
XO Kitchen

MODERATE DINING
Balthazar
Blue Ribbon
Blue Ribbon Sushi
Dylan Prime
Fresh
The Harrison
The Mercer Kitchen
Montrachet
Nobu
Odeon
Peasant
Ping's Seafood
Savoy
Tribeca Grill

EXPENSIVE DINING
Bouley
Chanterelle

WHERE TO STAY
(⇨ Ch. 19)

BUDGET LODGING
Cosmopolitan
Holiday Inn Downtown

MODERATE LODGING
60 Thompson
Mercer Hotel
SoHo Grand
Tribeca Grand

BARS & NIGHTLIFE
(⇨ Ch. 16)
Bar 89, *bar*
Brandy Library, *bar*
Broome Street Bar, *bar*
Canal Room, *dance club*
Culture Club, *dance club*
Don Hill's, *rock club*
Double Happiness, *bar*

Fanelli's, *bar*
Knitting Factory, *jazz, rock
  club*
Lucky Strike, *bar*
MercBar, *bar*
Naked Lunch, *bar*
Pegu Club, *bar*
Pravda, *bar*
Raoul's, *bar*
The Room, *bar*
S.O.B.'s, *world music
  venue*
Thom Bar, *bar*

ARTS & ENTERTAINMENT
(⇨ Ch. 15)
HERE Arts Center, *theater*
Joyce SoHo, *dance*
Drawing Center, *readings*
Housing Works Used Book
  Café, *readings*
Tribeca Performing Arts
  Center, *jazz*
When, *film*

SHOPPING (⇨ Ch. 17)

DEPARTMENT STORE
Pearl River Mart

ANTIQUES
Jacques Carcangues, Inc

BOOKS
Housing Works Used Book
  Café
McNally Robinson

CHOCOLATE
Jacques Torres Chocolate
  Haven
Kee's Chocolates
Lunettes et Chocolat
Marie Belle
Vosges Haut Chocolat

CLOTHING
A Bathing Ape
A.P.C
Agnès b
American Apparel
Anna Sui
Anne Fontaine
A/X: Armani Exchange
Barbara Bui
BCBG/Max Azria
Betsey Johnson

3

Bu and the Duck
Calypso
Calypso Enfant et Bébé
Catherine Malandrino
Chanel
Christopher Fischer
Club Monaco
Costume National
Duncan Quinn
Find Outlet
Guess?
H By Hilfiger
INA
J. Crew
John Varvatos
Kirna Zabête
Les Petits Chapelais
Lilliput
Lyell
Malia Mills
Marc Jacobs
Marni
Mayle
Miu Miu
Nanette Lepore
New York Firefighter's
    Friend
Patricia Field
Paul Frank
Phat Farm/Baby Phat
Philosophy di Alberta
    Ferretti
Polo Sport
R by 45rpm
Rebecca Taylor
Reiss
Resurrection

Sean
Seize sur Vingt
Shoofly
Tory Burch
Tracy Feith
Vivienne Tam
What Comes Around
    Goes Around
Yohji Yamamoto

ELECTRONICS
Apple Store SoHo

HOME DECOR
Armani Casa
Bellora
c.i.t.e
Cath Kidston
Clio
De Vera
Jonathan Adler
Mood Indigo
Moss
Pylones
Shabby Chic
Troy

JEWELRY
Dinosaur Designs
Femmegems
Fragments
Me + Ro
Objets du Désir
Robert Lee Morris
Stuart Moore
Versani

LEATHER GOODS
High Way
Jack Spade

Jamin Puech
Kate Spade
Manhattan Portage
Sigerson Morrison
    Handbags

LINGERIE
37 = 1 Atelier
Agent Provocateur
Le Corset
Mixona

PERFUME/COSMETICS
Fresh
L'Artisan Parfumeur
L'Occitane
M.A.C
Make Up For Ever
Ricky's
Santa Maria Novella
SCO
Sephora
Shu Uemura

SHOES
Camper
Hollywould
John Fluevog Shoes
Otto Tootsi Plohound
Sigerson Morrison

STATIONERY
Industries Stationery
Kate's Paperie
Untitled

TOYS
Kid Robot

WINE
Vintage New York

East Village & the Lower East Side

WORD OF MOUTH

"The research into the real families had clearly been extensive, with census information and photographs to illustrate that these people had really existed. All in all it was excellently done. A really thought-provoking museum, and especially good to visit to supplement a trip to Ellis Island and give more insight into the history of the city and its people."

—guiUK, about the Lower East Side Tenement Museum

Sightseeing
★ ★

Nightlife
★ ★ ★ ★ ★

Dining
★ ★ ★ ★ ★

Lodging
★ ★

Shopping
★ ★ ★ ★

Houston Street divides the area south of 14th Street and east of 4th Avenue and the Bowery into the East Village (above) and the Lower East Side (below), two neighborhoods that contain some of the city's funkiest nightlife, restaurants, and shops, all backed up with loads of cultural history. The East Village, best known as the birthplace of American punk and the refuge of artists, activists, and other social dissenters, is also home to a pastiche of ethnic enclaves, whose imprints are visible in the area's churches, restaurants, shops, and—of course—residents. The grittier Lower East Side has seen waves of immigration of European Jews, then Hispanics and Chinese, a legacy excellently captured in the neighborhood's soul, the Lower East Side Tenement Museum.

Although there are great sites here, these neighborhoods are for exploring, so put on your walking shoes. So many communities converge that each block can seem like a new neighborhood. And while the daytime's great for sites and shopping, it's the evening when the area really comes alive. Whether it's wine and cheese at 'inoteca or a burlesque show at The Slipper Room, venues cater to every interest and orientation. Style cavorts with grunge, and you'll find twenty-somethings in perfectly distressed jeans eating some of New York's finest food at wd-50, Bond Street, and The Tasting Room.

What's Here

A good place to orient yourself in the East Village is Astor Place, the triangle formed by the intersections of East 8th Street, Lafayette Street, Astor Place, and 4th Avenue. The area swarms with youthful foot traffic, from film students shooting a scene to political groups soliciting signatures. Dominating the location is the **Sculpture for Living,** a curvaceous glass-and-steel tower of million-dollar apartments. The building's name and shape seem to ironically reference what had previously been Astor Place's focal point, **the Alamo,** a giant spinning cube on the central traffic island. New York City's first public abstract sculpture, the cube defiantly remains a hangout for skateboarders and studded youth. A few yards away is another piece of history: the entrance to the **Astor Place Subway Station,** a cast-iron replica of the 1904 Beaux-Arts kiosks that covered most subway entrances during the early years of the Interborough Rapid Transit (IRT).

Running east of Astor Place are three of the East Village's most distinctive blocks. East 7th Street between 2nd and 3rd avenues is dominated by **St. George's Ukrainian Catholic Church,** the meeting place for the local Ukrainian community and the site of an annual Ukrainian folk festival in the spring. The block is also known by some as "Beer Row" for its odd assortment of brewpubs, including **McSorley's Old Ale House.** The mahogany bar, gas lamps, and potbelly stove all hark back to decades past, though it's hard to tell which one.

One block north is **St. Marks Place,** as 8th Street between 3rd Avenue and Avenue A is called. Over the years, beatniks, artists, and punk rockers have congregated at this hub of the East Village scene. Today, the block between 2nd and 3rd avenues is something of a teenage goth scene crammed with vendors selling jewelry, incense, and vinyl clothing; it's also home to a number of Japanese bars and noodle houses.

■ TIP→ Historical documents notwithstanding, many claim that the New York egg cream hatched at Gem Spa (131 2nd Ave., 212/995–1866), a 24-hour newsstand just off St. Marks Place. Cold milk, seltzer, and chocolate syrup combine to make the historically rich beverage, which comes in two sizes: $1.50 for a small, $2 for a large.

One more block north and a world away is Stuyvesant Street, a strip of historic redbrick row houses and the oldest street in Manhattan laid out precisely along an east–west axis (unlike the surrounding street grid, which follows the island's geographic orientation). At its northern end is **St. Mark's-in-the-Bowery Church,** a charming 1799 fieldstone country church that occupies the former site of Dutch governor Peter Stuyvesant's family chapel. Nearby is the **Strand,** an enormous secondhand bookstore where you can pass hours among its 2 million volumes.

At the southeast corner of Astor Place is one of the country's leading art schools, **Cooper Union** housed in an impressive Italianate freestanding brownstone. South of Astor Place along Lafayette Street is **Colonnade Row.** Marble Corinthian columns front this grand sweep of four 1833 Greek Revival mansions that once served as residences to millionaires John Jacob Astor and Cornelius Vanderbilt. Now their lower levels house restaurants and theater spaces. Across the street is **Joseph Papp Public Theater,** known for hosting bold and innovative theater, including the openings of *Hair* and *A Chorus Line.* Next door, **Joe's Pub** brings such A-list performing artists as Mos Def and Sandra Bernhard

GETTING ORIENTED

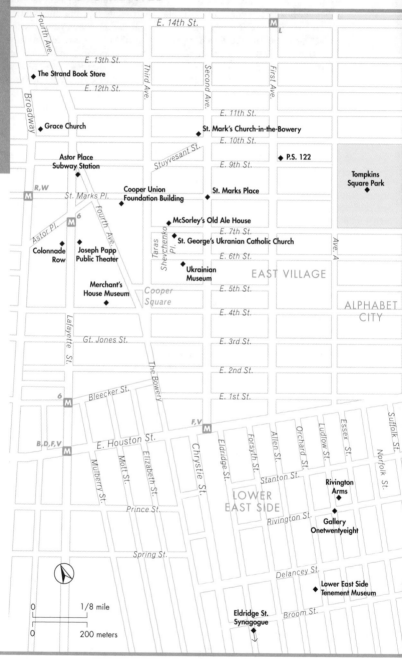

E. 14th St.

Fourth Ave.

E. 13th St.

Third Ave.

Second Ave.

First Ave.

M   L

◆ The Strand Book Store

E. 12th St.

Broadway

◆ Grace Church

E. 11th St.

◆ St. Mark's Church-in-the-Bowery

E. 10th St.

Stuyvesant St.

E. 9th St.

◆ P.S. 122

Astor Place
Subway Station

Tompkins
Square Park
◆

R,W

M

St. Marks Pl.

Cooper Union
Foundation Building

St. Marks Place

Ave. A

Astor Pl.

M   6

Fourth Ave.

◆ McSorley's Old Ale House

E. 7th St.

◆ Colonnade
Row

◆ Joseph Papp
Public Theater

Taras Shevchenko Pl.

◆ St. George's Ukranian Catholic Church

E. 6th St.

EAST VILLAGE

◆ Merchant's
House Museum

◆ Ukrainian
Museum

E. 5th St.

Cooper
Square

ALPHABET
CITY

E. 4th St.

Lafayette St.

Gt. Jones St.

E. 3rd St.

The Bowery

E. 2nd St.

6

M

Bleecker St.

E. 1st St.

F,V

M

B,D,F,V

M

E. Houston St.

Chrystie St.

Eldridge St.

Forsyth St.

Allen St.

Orchard St.

Ludlow St.

Essex St.

Suffolk St.

Mulberry St.

Mott St.

Elizabeth St.

Stanton St.

Norfolk St.

Rivington
Arms
◆

LOWER
EAST SIDE

Prince St.

Rivington St.

◆ Gallery
Onetwentyeight

Spring St.

Delancey St.

◆ Lower East Side
Tenement Museum

0   1/8 mile

Eldridge St.
Synagogue
◆

Broom St.

0   200 meters

4

TOP 5

◼ Shopping for books at the Strand
◼ Walking on St. Marks Place
◼ Stopping for a beer (or two) at McSorley's
◼ A pastrami sandwich and cheesecake at Katz's Delicatessen
◼ Visiting the Lower East Side Tenement Museum

MAKING THE MOST OF YOUR TIME

Although the East Village seems never to shut down, it really lets loose on weekend nights, when reservation books fill up and crowds of bar-hoppers converge. Visiting on weekdays make for a more low-key experience, when establishments attract mostly locals. During the daytime, Saturday is when you'll catch the street life at its most vibrant, while on Sunday the neighborhood experiences a collective hangover.

The Lower East Side is not an early riser any day of the week. Although there's plenty to see during the day, return after nightfall for a totally different vision: blocks that had previously been empty rows of pulled-down gratings will have transformed into clusters of throbbing bars. When shopping, be aware that a number of traditional establishments close on Saturday to observe the Jewish Sabbath, and on Sunday, the three blocks of Orchard below Houston become a pedestrian-only strip where street vendors set up their stands.

GETTING HERE

Streets are generally clogged with traffic here, but if you must drive, look for parking on Broadway, west of Astor Place. A far better choice is to take the R or W subway line to 8th Street or the 6 to Astor Place. To reach Alphabet City, take the L to First Avenue or the F or V to Second Avenue. Head southeast from the same stop on the F or V and you're on the Lower East Side.

SAFETY

This area has become quite safe in recent years, and crime is not significantly more common than in other parts of the city. You may not want to walk alone at night, especially east of 1st Avenue or on the Lower East Side, although on Friday and Saturday nights most main streets will be well trafficked until past 2 AM.

QUICK BITES

Bright and bustling 24-hour **Veselka** (✉ 144 2nd Ave., East Village ☎ 212/228–9682), an East Village staple, serves diner classics alongside traditional Ukrainian fare such as borscht and pierogies. If your sweet tooth is calling, **Veniero's Pasticceria and Café** (✉ 342 E. 11th St., East Village ☎ 212/674–7264), opened in 1894, has rows of fresh cannoli, cookies, and other desserts.

Take in the bohemian Alphabet City scene over coffee and biscotti at **Café Pick Me Up** (✉ 145 Avenue A, East Village ☎ 212/673–7231), whose open-air front looks onto Tompkins Square Park.

Nosh your way through Jewish history at **Russ & Daughters** (✉ 179 E. Houston St., Lower East Side ☎ 212/475–4880), a fourth-generation destination for smoked fish since 1914. **Katz's Delicatessen** (✉ 205 E. Houston St., Lower East Side ☎ 212/254–2246), opened in 1888, is where the pastrami is still sliced by hand.

to its cabaret-style space. Around the corner on E. 4th Street is the **Merchant House Museum.**

Lovers of punk rock should head south to **CBGB**, the birthplace of American punk, where the Ramones, Blondie, and the Talking Heads laid the groundwork for a generation of music. The club is seriously scruffy, but even if that's not your thing the T-shirts make a great souvenir, and you can get them at **CB's 313 Gallery** next door.

The area east of 1st Avenue is nicknamed **Alphabet City**, as the avenues are labeled with letters, not numbers. Alphabet City was once a burned-out area of slums and drug haunts, but has gentrified and is mostly safe today. Still, the area holds on to its bohemian roots—captured in the hit musical *Rent*—and the tiny bars and restaurants that seem to spring up daily on avenues A, B, and C and the streets in between attract all kinds. The focal point of Alphabet City is the leafy **Tompkins Square Park**, a respite amid the crowded tenements. On the park's east side at 151 Avenue B stands a brownstone where jazz musician Charlie Parker lived from 1950 to 1954.

Directly south of the East Village, on the other side of Houston Street, begins the Lower East Side, a juxtaposition of old and new worlds, where one of the city's hottest nightlife spots is growing amid aged businesses that hark back to the neighborhood's immigrant heritage. The historic heart of the Lower East Side is Orchard Street, the center of New York's garment district at the turn of the 20th century. Some of the old facades remain, as do dated clothing shops, but a younger generation of fashion-furious boutiques are moving in. Farther south on Orchard Street is the **Lower East Side Tenement Museum**, one of the city's most underrated and overlooked museums. Several historic synagogues, their gorgeous facades squeezed among the tenements, are still in use. **The Eldridge Street Synagogue** was the first Orthodox synagogue erected by the large number of Eastern European Jews who settled on the Lower East Side in the mid- to late 19th century. The only Romaniote (Greek Jewish) synagogue in the Western Hemisphere, **Kehila Kedosha Janina** doubly functions as a museum to this obscure branch of Judaism. The city's oldest synagogue, dating to 1850, is now the **Angel Orensanz Center for the Arts**, named for the sculptor who purchased the synagogue when it fell into disrepair.

The epicenter of the hip, gentrified Lower East Side falls along the parallel-running Rivington and Stanton streets, between Orchard and Essex streets, and the section of Ludlow Street that crosses them. Among the restaurants and bars that fill the storefronts are vintage boutiques and cutting-edge art galleries. Two unique shops are **Toys in Babeland**, a sex shop for women, and **Economy Candy**, jam-packed with barrels of sugary treats. Across the street from it, jutting out incongruently from the surrounding tenements, is the **Hotel on Rivington.**

Places to Explore

Alphabet City. The north–south avenues beyond 1st Avenue are all labeled with letters, not numbers, which give this area its nickname. Alphabet City

A Good Walk

IT'S HARD TO HAVE A BAD WALK in this area, as almost any block will turn up an interesting shop, café, or piece of architecture. That said, you could encapsulate much of the East Village in the four blocks from Astor Place to Tompkins Square Park, walking either along 7th Street, St. Marks Place (8th Street), or Stuyvesant Street followed by 10th Street, depending on your tastes (see What's Here). To continue to the Lower East

Side, turn south at the park and head down Avenue A to Houston Street. From here, culture mavens should walk south down Ludlow Street, turning to explore the intersecting Stanton and Rivington streets, and the historically curious should instead walk south down Orchard Street to see the vestiges of the immigrant Jewish neighborhood, including the Tenement Museum.

4

was once a burned-out area of slums and drug haunts, but some blocks and buildings were gentrified during the height of the East Village art scene in the mid-1980s and again in the late '90s. The reasonably priced restaurants with their bohemian atmosphere on Avenues A, B, and C and the cross streets between them, attract all kinds. A close-knit Puerto Rican community lies east of Avenue A, but amid the Latin shops and groceries Avenue B is now a sort of far-out restaurant row. From the whiff of things, Avenue C looks not far behind. ⊠ *Alphabet City extends from Ave. A to East River, between 14th and E. Houston Sts., East Village.*

Astor Place Subway Station. At the beginning of the 20th century, almost every Interborough Rapid Transit (IRT) subway entrance resembled the ornate cast-iron replica of a Beaux-Arts kiosk that covers the stairway leading to the uptown No. 6 train. Inside, tiles of beavers line the station walls, a reference to the fur trade that contributed to John Jacob Astor's fortune. Milton Glaser, a Cooper Union graduate, designed the station's attractive abstract murals. ⊠ *On traffic island at E. 8th St. and 4th Ave., East Village* Ⓜ *Subway: 6 to Astor Pl.*

Colonnade Row. Marble Corinthian columns front this grand sweep of four Greek Revival mansions (originally nine) constructed in 1833, with stonework by Sing Sing penitentiary prisoners. These once-elegant homes served as residences to millionaires John Jacob Astor and Cornelius Vanderbilt until they moved uptown. Today they house apartments and restaurants, and the northernmost building is the home of the Astor Place Theatre and *Blue Man Group.* ⊠ *428–434 Lafayette St., between Astor Pl. and E. 4th St., East Village* Ⓜ *Subway: 6 to Astor Pl.*

Cooper Union Foundation Building. This impressive eight-story Italianate brownstone structure overlooks humble Cooper Square, where 3rd and 4th avenues merge into the Bowery. A statue of industrialist Peter Cooper, by Augustus Saint-Gaudens, presides here. Cooper founded this college in 1859 to provide a forum for public opinion—Abraham Lincoln, Mark Twain, and Susan B. Anthony have all delivered speeches here—and free technical education for the working class. The foundation still offers tuition-free education in architecture, art, and engineering. Cooper Union was among the first structures to employ iron beams—rolled in Cooper's own foundry—and a design that accommodated an elevator. The Great Hall Gallery is open to the public and presents changing exhibitions during the academic year. A few steps down from the Public Theater near Cooper Union sits one of Manhattan's newest residential skyscrapers, **Astor Place.** An anomaly among the predominantly low-rise architecture of this neighborhood of storefronts, student-frequented stores and schools, Astor Place gives residents birdlike views on four sides from its luxury lofts. Designed by illustrious post-modern architect Charles Gwathmey (known for his addition to the Guggenheim Museum) to optimize Manhattan's last triangular site (formerly a parking lot), the "undulating" shape of the glass building sits in bold contrast with its more traditional neighbors. ⊠ *7 E. 7th St., at 3rd Ave., East Village* ☎ *212/353–4100 exhibition information, 212/353–4195 events* ✉ *Free* ☉ *Weekdays 11–7, Sat. noon–5* Ⓜ *Subway: 6 to Astor Pl.; R, W to 8th St./Broadway.*

DID YOU KNOW?

Second Avenue was called the **Yiddish Rialto** in the early part of the 20th century. Eight theaters between Houston and 14th streets showed Yiddish-language musicals, revues, and melodramas. Embedded in the sidewalk in front of the Second Avenue Deli (156 2nd Ave., at 10th St.) are Hollywood-style squares that commemorate the Yiddish stage luminaries.

Eldridge Street Synagogue. This was the first Orthodox synagogue erected by the large number of Eastern European Jews who settled on the Lower East Side in the late 19th century. The lavish Moorish Revival–style building is undergoing a major restoration. Inside is an exceptional hand-carved ark of Italian walnut, a sculptured wooden balcony, jewel-tone stained-glass windows, and an enormous brass chandelier. Once the largest Jewish house of worship, it is now the Congregation K'hal Adath Jeshurun and Anshe Lubz. ⊠ *12 Eldridge St., between Canal and Division Sts., Lower East Side* ☎ *212/219–0888* ⊕ *www.eldridgestreet.org* ✉ *$5* ☉ *Sun., Tues., Wed., Thurs., 11–4; Tours on the hr 11–3* Ⓜ *Subway: F to E. Broadway; B, D to Grand St.*

Joseph Papp Public Theater. In 1854, through a bequest from John Jacob Astor, the city opened its first public library in this expansive redbrick and brownstone Italian Renaissance–style building. It was renovated in 1967 as the Public Theater to serve as the New York Shakespeare Festival's permanent home. The theater opened its doors with the popular rock musical *Hair.* Under the leadership of the late Joseph Papp, the Public's five stages built a reputation for bold and innovative performances; the long-running hit *A Chorus Line* had its first performances here, as have many less commercial plays. Today, the theater hosts controversial modern works and imaginative Shakespeare productions here and at Central Park's Delacorte Theater for free during the summer as part of Shakespeare in the Park. **Joe's Pub** (☎ 212/539–8777) next door brings such A-list musical and performing artists as Mos Def, Macy Gray, and Sandra Bernhard to its cabaret-style space. ⊠ *425*

Rock-and-Roll Tour

FROM GLAM TO PUNK, the East Village is rock music's beating heart. Start at the northeast corner of St. Marks and 2nd Avenue, where, at the **Gem Spa** newsstand (131 2nd Ave.), the groundbreaking New York Dolls shot the back of their first album cover in 1973. The Manhattan-based band is credited with spurring punk scenes here and in England. Walk east along St. Marks to No. 19–25, the former site of the Dom Theater and the Electric Circus. Here, in the mid-'60s, Andy Warhol hung out, the Velvet Underground played, and everyone danced until dawn. It closed in '71, one of many happening venues from this era (including Max's Kansas City, just off Union Square, and Fillmore East on 2nd Avenue) that are no more.

Down the block, at No. 96–98 St. Marks is where Led Zeppelin shot the cover for *Physical Graffiti* in 1974. In the early '70s, a new generation of American punk rock bands surfaced in conjunction with a seedy bar called CBGBs. To reach it, backtrack to 4th Avenue and turn left. Fourth becomes the Bowery around 5th Street. In 1973, at 315 Bowery, between 1st and 2nd streets, Hilly Kristal opened his country, bluegrass, and blues venue, hence the CBGB acronym. But Kristal changed his tune, when Television, a pop-ish punk band, persuaded him to host them, and other unsigned rock bands like the Ramones (from nearby Queens), Blondie, the Talking Heads, and Patti Smith for a night of rock. The decision created an era of music that still garners local nostalgia. In 2003, a stretch of 2nd Street at the Bowery, near CBGBs, was renamed Joey Ramone Place to commemorate the singer's death in 2001.

Lafayette St., between E. 4th St. and Astor Pl., East Village ☎ *212/260–2400* ⊕ *www.publictheater.org* Ⓜ *Subway: 6 to Astor Pl.; R, W to 8th St.; B, D, F, Q to Broadway/Lafayette.*

McSorley's Old Ale House. Joseph Mitchell immortalized this spot, which claims to be one of the city's oldest, in the *New Yorker*. McSorley's asserts that it opened in 1854; it didn't admit women until 1970. The mahogany bar, gas lamps, and potbelly stove all hark back to decades past, though it's hard to tell which one. It probably makes no difference: the often crowded saloon attracts many collegiate types enticed by McSorley's own brands of ale, not the history. ⊠ *15 E. 7th St., between 2nd and 3rd Aves., East Village* ☎ *212/473–9148* Ⓜ *Subway: 6 to Astor Pl.*

St. George Ukrainian Catholic Church. Quite the standout on the block with its copper dome and three brightly colored religious murals on its facade, this ostentatious modern church serves as a central meeting place for the local Ukrainian community. Built in 1976, it took the place of the church's more modest Greek Revival–style building nearby. An annual Ukrainian folk festival is held here in the spring. ⊠ *30 E. 7th St., between 2nd and 3rd Aves., East Village* ☎ *212/674–1615* ☉ *Services: Mon.–Sat. 6:15, 7:45, 8:30, Sun. 7, 8:30, 10, and noon* Ⓜ *Subway: 6 to Astor Pl.; R, W to 8th St.*

St. Mark's Church in-the-Bowery. This charming 1799 fieldstone country church stands its ground against the monotonous city block system. The area was once Dutch governor Peter Stuyvesant's *bouwerie*, or farm, and the church occupies the former site of his family chapel. St. Mark's is Manhattan's oldest continually used Christian site, and both Stuyvesant and Commodore Perry are buried here. Over the years St. Mark's has hosted progressive events, mostly in the arts. In the 1920s a pastor injected the Episcopal ritual with Native American chants, Greek folk dancing, and Eastern mantras. William Carlos Williams, Amy Lowell, and Carl Sandburg once read here; and Martha Graham, Ruth St. Denis, Harry Houdini, and Merce Cunningham performed here. Today the dancers of Danspace, poets of the Poetry Project, and theater artists in The Ontological Hysteric-Theater continue the artistic and spiritual tradition. The church offers both English and Spanish services as well. ⊠ *131 E. 10th St., at 2nd Ave., East Village* ☎ *212/674–6377* Ⓜ *Subway: 6 to Astor Pl.; L to 3rd Ave.*

St. Marks Place. The longtime hub of the edgy East Village, St. Marks Place is the name given to East 8th Street between 3rd Avenue and Avenue A. During the 1950s beatniks such as Allen Ginsberg and Jack Kerouac lived and wrote in the area; the 1960s brought Bill Graham's Fillmore East concerts, the Electric Circus, and hallucinogenic drugs. The black-clad, pink-haired, or shaved-head punks followed, and the imaginatively pierced rockers and heavily made-up goths have replaced them. The blocks between 2nd and 3rd avenues have mostly ethnic restaurants, jewelry stalls, and stores selling incense and vinyl clothing. Despite NYU dorms in the vicinity, even the ubiquitous Gap chain couldn't take root on this raggedy and idiosyncratic street.

At 80 St. Marks Place, near 1st Avenue, is the Pearl Theatre Company, which performs classic plays from around the world. The handprints, footprints, and autographs of such past screen luminaries as Joan Crawford, Ruby Keeler, Joan Blondell, and Myrna Loy are embedded in the sidewalk. At 96–98 St. Marks Place (between 1st Ave. and Ave. A) stands the building that was photographed for the cover of Led Zeppelin's *Physical Graffiti* album. The cafés between 2nd Avenue and Avenue A attract customers late into the night. Ⓜ *Subway: 6 to Astor Pl.*

Stuyvesant Street. This diagonal slicing through the block bounded by 2nd and 3rd avenues and East 9th and 10th streets is unique in Manhattan: it's the oldest street laid out precisely along an east–west axis. (This grid never caught on, and instead a street grid following the island's geographic orientation was adopted.) Among the handsome red-brick row houses are the federal-style **Stuyvesant-Fish House** (⊠ *21 Stuyvesant St., East Village* Ⓜ *Subway: 6 to Astor Pl.*), which was built in 1804 as a wedding gift for a great-great-granddaughter of the Dutch governor Peter Stuyvesant, and **Renwick Triangle,** an attractive group of carefully restored unified one- and two-story Anglo-Italianate brick and brownstone residences originally constructed in 1861, which face Stuyvesant and East 10th streets.

CLOSE UP

Keep Your Eyes Peeled

THE EAST VILLAGE'S REPUTATION for quirkiness is evidenced not only among its residents and prominent sites but also in the many incongruous structures that somehow coexist so easily that they can go almost unnoticed. Keep your eyes open (both high and low) as you explore the streets, because you never know what might turn up. Examples include

■ the Hells Angel's Headquarters tucked onto a residential block of 3rd Street between 1st and 2nd avenues

■ the beautiful 19th-century tombstones in the small New York City Marble Cemetery on 2nd Street between 1st and 2nd avenues

■ the shingled Cape Cod–style house perched atop the apartment building at the northwest corner of Houston and 1st Avenue, one of the city's many unique rooftop retreats

■ the Tower of Toys, a 30-foot-tall sculpture of "found" objects—including rocking horses, Barbie dolls, and teddy bears—rising out of a community garden on Avenue B at 6th Street

4

Tompkins Square Park. This leafy spot amid the East Village's crowded tenements is a release valve. The park fills up with locals on mild days year-round, partaking in minipicnics; drum circles; the playground; and, for dog owners, two dog runs. East of the park at 151 Avenue B, near East 9th Street, stands an 1849 four-story white-painted brownstone where renowned jazz musician Charlie Parker lived from 1950 to 1954. The Charlie Parker Jazz Festival packs the park for one day in late August. But it wasn't always so rosy. In 1988 police followed mayor David Dinkins's orders to clear the park of the many homeless who had set up makeshift homes here, and homeless rights and antigentrification activists fought back with sticks and bottles. If you're familiar with the Broadway musical and movie *Rent,* you've seen the general scene. The park was reclaimed and reopened in 1992 with a midnight curfew, still in effect today. ⊠ *Bordered by Aves. A and B and E. 7th and E. 10th Sts., East Village* Ⓜ *Subway: 6 to Astor Pl.; L to 1st Ave.*

East Village & the Lower East Side at a Glance

SIGHTS
Alphabet City
Astor Place Subway Station
Colonnade Row
Cooper Union Foundation Building
Eldridge Street Synagogue
Joseph Papp Public Theater
McSorley's Old Ale House
St. George Ukrainian Catholic Church
St. Mark's Church in-the-Bowery
St. Marks Place
Stuyvesant Street

MUSEUMS & GALLERIES (⇨ Ch. 14)
Gallery Onetwentyeight
Lower East Side Tenement Museum
Merchant's House Museum
Rivington Arms
Ukrainian Museum

PARKS & GARDENS
Tompkins Square Park

WHERE TO EAT (⇨ Ch. 18)
BUDGET DINING
Bond Street
ChikaLicious Dessert Bar
Dok Suni's
Gnocco
Great Jones Cafe
Holy Basil
Il Bagatto
'inoteca
Katz's Delicatessen
La Palapa
Le Gamin
Momofuku Noodle Bar
Moustache
Paladar
Pie by the Pound
Piola
Schiller's Liquor Bar
Serafina Lafayette
Una Pizza Napoletana
Veniero's Pasticceria

MODERATE DINING
Butter
Il Buco
Prune
Tasting Room
wd-50

EXPENSIVE DINING
Jewel Bako

WHERE TO STAY (⇨ Ch. 19)

BUDGET LODGING
Howard Johnson's Express Inn
Second Home on Second Avenue

MODERATE LODGING
Hotel on Rivington

BARS & NIGHTLIFE (⇨ Ch. 16)
Arlene's Grocery, *rock club*
B Bar, *bar*
Beauty Bar, *bar*
Beige, *gay & lesbian*
Bowery Ballroom, *rock club*
BoysRoom, *gay & lesbian*
Cake Shop, *rock club*
CBGB & OMFUG, *rock club*
The Cock, *gay & lesbian*
Continental, *rock club*
Coyote Ugly, *bar*
Decibel, *bar*
Delancey, *rock club*
Girlsroom, *gay & lesbian*
Good World Bar & Grill, *bar*
Joe's Pub, *cabaret*
Living Room, *acoustic & blues*
Local 138, *bar*
Lucky Cheng's, *bar*
Max Fish, *bar*
McSorley's Old Ale House, *bar*
Mercury Lounge, *rock club*
Mo Pitkin's House of Satisfaction, *cabaret*
1984, *gay & lesbian*
Nowhere, *gay & lesbian*
Otto's Shrunken Head, *bar*
The Phoenix, *gay & lesbian*
The Pink Pony, *bar*
Remote, *bar*
Rothko, *rock club*
Rififi, *burlesque*
Sapphire, *dance club*
Sidewalk Café, *acoustic & blues*
Sin-é, *rock club*
The Slide, *gay & lesbian*
Slipper Room, *burlesque*
Starlight, *gay & lesbian*
Subtonic Lounge, *dance club*
Telephone Bar, *bar*
Temple Bar, *bar*
THOR, *bar*
Tonic, *rock club*
Webster Hall, *dance club*

ARTS & ENTERTAINMENT (⇨ Ch. 15)
Amato Opera Theatre, *opera*

Anthology Film Archives, *film*
Bowery Poetry Club, *readings*
Classic Stage Company, *theater*
Danspace Project, *dance*
Dixon Place, *readings*
Gotham Chamber Opera, *opera*
Jean Cocteau Repertory, *theater*
La Mama E.T.C, *theater*
Landmark's Sunshine Cinema, *film*
New York Theater Workshop, *theater*
Nuyorican Poets Café, *readings*
P.S.122, *theater*
The Public Theater, *theater*
Teatro SEA @ Los Kabayitos Puppet & Children's Theater, *theater*
Theater for the New City, *theater*
Village East Cinemas, *film*

SHOPPING (⇨ Ch. 17)
ANTIQUES
Las Venus
Lost City Arts

BOOKS
St. Mark's Bookshop
The Strand

CLOTHING
Bond 07
Foley & Corinna
Frock
Psyche's Tears
Screaming Mimi's
TG-170
Trash and Vaudeville
Urban Outfitters

LEATHER GOODS
Altman Luggage
Fine & Klein

MUSIC
Kim's Video & Music
Other Music
Tower Records

PERFUME/COSMETICS
Bond No. 9
Kiehl's Since 1851

TOYS
Dinosaur Hill

WINE
Astor Wines & Spirits

Greenwich Village
& Chelsea

INCLUDING THE MEATPACKING DISTRICT

WORD OF MOUTH

"This, to me, is the most casual neighborhood in NYC. People here are being themselves and not apologizing to anyone for it."
—Ciaony, about Greenwich Village

"[Chelsea Market] is an exciting, vibrant building, quite busy at lunch hour and a terrific stop on any downtown tour—and right near the far West Village, Hudson River Park, Chelsea Piers and the Meatpacking District."

—mp

Sightseeing
★ ★ ★

Nightlife
★ ★ ★ ★ ★

Dining
★ ★ ★ ★ ★

Lodging
★ ★ ★

Shopping
★ ★ ★ ★

Home of writers, artists, bohemians, and bon vivants, the West Village is a unique section of the city where right angles and office buildings give way to twisting streets and historic homes. In the late 1940s and early 1950s, the abstract expressionist painters Franz Kline, Jackson Pollock, Mark Rothko, and Willem de Kooning congregated here, as did the Beat writers Jack Kerouac, Allen Ginsberg, and Lawrence Ferlinghetti. The 1960s brought folk musicians and poets, notably Bob Dylan. This primarily residential area lacks the blockbuster attractions in other parts of the city, but makes up for it with a warm local feeling and myriad small restaurants, boutiques, and coffee shops. NYU students keep the cafés full and the idealistic vibe of the neighborhood alive. The Meatpacking District, in the far northwest section of the West Village, has cobblestone streets that are gradually giving way from swinging sides of beef to swinging clubs, trendy restaurants, and chic shops.

Chelsea, the stylish neighborhood north of the Meatpacking District, has usurped SoHo as the world's art gallery headquarters and replaced Christopher Street in the West Village as New York's Gay Central. If it's art you're seeking, the high-profile galleries housed in cavernous converted warehouses are easily identified by their ultracool/cold, glass-and-stainless-steel doors. Many former warehouses, unremarkable by day, pulsate after dark and into the dawn as the city's hottest nightclubs. One-of-a-kind boutiques and pet-pampering salons along 7th, 8th, and 9th avenues are sprinkled among unassuming grocery stores and other remnants of Chelsea's immigrant past.

What's Here

Greenwich Village & the Meatpacking District

The heart and spiritual center of Greenwich Village is **Washington Square Park.** At Washington Square Park, the city's central business thoroughfare of 5th Avenue ends, and the student-bohemian feel of the Village begins. Circle the leafy square, but don't expect to find a bench or fountain-side seat that's not occupied by New York University students, professors, pigeon-feeders, or idlers of all ilks. On the park's north side is the grand **Washington Memorial Arch.** On Washington Square North, between University Place and MacDougal Street, stretches **The Row,** two blocks of lovingly preserved Greek Revival and federal-style town houses.

Half a block north, on the east side of 5th Avenue, is **Washington Mews,** a cobblestone private street. A similar Village mews, **MacDougal Alley,** lies between Washington Square North and 8th Street, one block west. West 11th Street between 5th and 6th avenues is one of the best examples of a Village town-house block. One exception to the 19th-century redbrick town houses here is the modern, angled front window of **18 West 11th Street,** usually occupied by a stuffed bear whose outfit changes day to day. At 12th Street you can stop in at the free **Forbes Magazine Galleries** to see the armadas of toy ships and soldiers and exquisite Fabergé eggs that Malcolm Sr. has collected since the 1930s.

The triangle formed by West 10th Street, 6th Avenue, and Greenwich Avenue originally held a market, a jail, and the magnificent towered courthouse that is now the **Jefferson Market Library.** West of 6th Avenue on 10th Street is the wrought-iron gateway to a tiny courtyard called **Patchin Place.** Christopher Street, which veers off from the south end of the library triangle, has long been the symbolic heart of New York's gay and lesbian community. Where Christopher crosses Waverly Place is the 1831 brick **Northern Dispensary building.** At **51–53 Christopher Street,** the historic Stonewall riots marked the beginning of the gay rights movement. Across the street is a green triangle named **Christopher Park,** not to be confused with **Sheridan Square,** another landscaped triangle to the south.

West of 7th Avenue South, the Village turns into a picture-book town of twisting tree-lined streets, quaint houses, and tiny restaurants. Across the busy intersection of 7th Avenue South is the **Village Vanguard,** one of many notable music venues in this neighborhood. Here, Christopher Street continues to the Hudson River, where a landscaped pier with benches marks a stop on the city's riverside path.

Try to allow yourself the luxury of getting a bit lost in the area where Grove and Bedford streets intersect, two blocks southwest. These streets still feel very 19th-century New York. One of the few remaining clapboard structures in Manhattan is **17 Grove Street.** Around the same corner is **Twin Peaks,** an early-19th-century house that resembles a Swiss chalet. Heading west, Grove Street curves in front of the iron gate of **Grove Court,** a group of mid-19th-century brick-front residences. One

GETTING ORIENTED

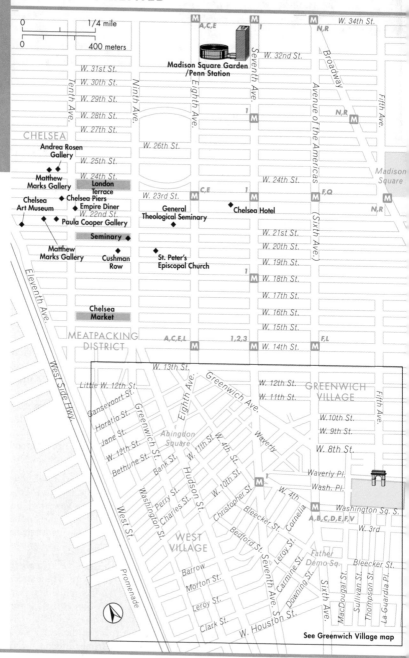

0 _____ 1/4 mile

0 _____ 400 meters

M A,C,E

M

M N,R   W. 34th St.

W. 32nd St.

Seventh Ave.

Broadway

Avenue of the Americas

Fifth Ave.

W. 31st St.

W. 30th St.

W. 29th St.

W. 28th St.

W. 27th St.

Tenth Ave.

Ninth Ave.

Eighth Ave.

Madison Square Garden /Penn Station

M N,R

CHELSEA

Andrea Rosen Gallery

W. 25th St.

Matthew Marks Gallery

W. 24th St.

◆ London Terrace

W. 26th St.

W. 24th St.

M F,Q

Madison Square

Chelsea Art Museum

◆ Chelsea Piers

◆ Empire Diner

◆ Paula Cooper Gallery

C,E

W. 23rd St.   **M**

C,E

General Theological Seminary

W. 22nd St.

◆ Chelsea Hotel

N,R

M

Seminary ◆

W. 21st St.

W. 20th St.

Sixth Ave. (Sixth Ave.)

Matthew Marks Gallery

Cushman Row

St. Peter's Episcopal Church

W. 19th St.

W. 18th St.   **M**

W. 17th St.

Chelsea Market

W. 16th St.

W. 15th St.

MEATPACKING DISTRICT

A,C,E,L

1,2,3

F,L

M   **M**   W. 14th St.   **M**

Eleventh Ave.

West Side Hwy.

W. 13th St.

Little W. 12th St.

Gansevoort St.

Horatio St.

Jane St.

W. 12th St.

Bethune St.

Greenwich St.

Washington St.

Eighth Ave.

Greenwich Ave.

Abingdon Square

Bank St.

W. 11th St.

Perry St.

Charles St.

W. 10th St.

Hudson St.

W. 12th St.

W. 11th St.

W. 4th St.

Waverly

GREENWICH VILLAGE

W. 10th St.

W. 9th St.

W. 8th St.

Fifth Ave.

Christopher St.

Bleecker St.

W. 4th

Waverly Pl.

Wash. Pl.

Washington Sq. S.

M A,B,C,D,E,F,V

W. 3rd

WEST VILLAGE

Bedford St.

Barrow

Morton St.

Leroy St.

Clark St.

West St.

Promenade

Seventh Ave. S.

Leroy St.

Carmine St.

Downing St.

Father Demo Sq.

Sixth Ave.

Bleecker St.

MacDougal St.

Sullivan St.

Thompson St.

La Guardia Pl.

W. Houston St.

See Greenwich Village map

TOP 5

- People-watching in Washington Square Park

- Gallery-hopping in Chelsea

- Getting lost on meandering Barrow and Grove streets

- Sampling the hip shops and hopping nightlife in the Meatpacking District

- Sipping a coffee at an outside café near Bleecker and W. 4th streets

MAKING THE MOST OF YOUR TIME

Weekday afternoons the streets of the West Village are nearly empty. Due to the large number of artists, students, and writers who live here, you'll have just enough company at the cafés and shops to make you feel like an insider instead of a tourist. To truly appreciate Meatpacking, make a 9 PM or later dinner reservation at a hot restaurant a few weeks in advance, then hit the bars to see where the hipsters are this week. If shopping is your pleasure, weekdays are great; come after noon, though, or you'll find most spots shuttered.

Chelsea has a dual life: typical gallery hours are Tuesday-Saturday 10-6, but at night the neighborhood changes into a party town. Swank, hard-to-enter clubs like Bungalow 8 and Bed often don't start cooking until after 10.

GETTING HERE

The West 4th Street subway stop—serviced by the A, C, E, B, D, F, V—puts you in the center of Greenwich Village. Farther west, the 1 train has stops on W. Houston St. and Christopher St./Sheridan Square. The A, C, E, and 1 trains stop at 14th Street for both Meatpacking District and Chelsea. The latter is further served by the A, C, E, 1, F, V lines at the 23rd St. stops and the 1 stop at 28th St.

QUICK BITES

Sandwiches at **Peanut Butter & Co.** (✉240 Sullivan St., at W. 3rd St., Greenwich Village ☎ 212/677–3995) may include a simple slathering of smooth or crunchy on white bread, or more complex concoctions with honey, bananas, and even bacon. Cupcake junkies, and *Sex and the City* devotees, queue up all day for the buttercream-frosted confections at cultishly popular **Magnolia Bakery** (✉ 401 Bleecker St., at 11th St., Greenwich Village ☎ 212/462–2572).

Locals use country-kitsch coffee spot **Jack's Stir Brew** (✉ 138 W. 10th St., between Greenwich Ave. and Waverly St., Greenwich Village ☎ 212/929–0821) as a morning way station, grabbing organic coffee and a fruit-filled muffin from Brooklyn's Blue Sky Bakery on their way to work.

In 1985 **Restaurant Florent** (✉ 69 Gansevoort St., between Washington and Greenwich Sts., Meatpacking District ☎ 212/989–5779), a funky 24-hour neighborhood bistro, was the only eatery here, decidedly built away from the downtown scene. The scene has since come to it, but Florent's vibe—and prices—have remained down to earth.

You can sit for hours without being disturbed at **Le Gamin** (✉ 183 9th Ave., at W. 21st St., Chelsea ☎ 212/243–8864), a rustic French café where soup-bowl-size café au lait, crepes, and salads are de rigueur.

5

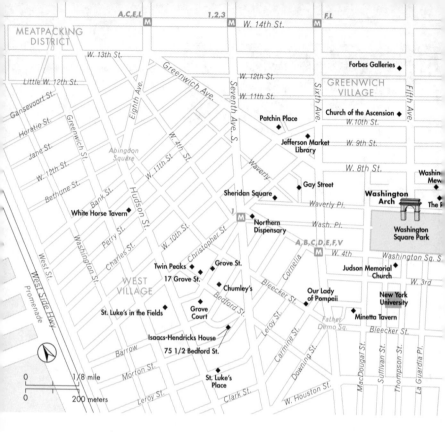

of the most beloved sights in the area is **Chumley's**, a former speakeasy, at 86 Bedford Street. It still has an unmarked door, and book jackets from some of the literary types who frequented here hang on the walls. This landmark eatery is a great place to call it quits and get refueled. But it doesn't serve lunch on weekends.

Bleecker Street, on the other hand, always has something cooking. Because of all the shops and crowds, Bleecker Street between 6th and 7th avenues seems more vital these days than Little Italy does. For authentic Italian ambience, step into one of the fragrant Italian bakeries, such as **Rocco's** (No. 243), or look inside the old-style butcher shops, such as **Ottomanelli & Sons** (No. 285) and Faicco's (No. 260). In a town that's fierce about its pizza, some New Yorkers swear by **John's Pizzeria** (No. 278), the original in a chain of three branches citywide.

On Bleecker Street at Carmine Street is the **Church of Our Lady of Pompeii**, where Mother Cabrini, a naturalized Italian immigrant who became the first American saint, often prayed. Near here, on MacDougal Street, Louisa May Alcott wrote *Little Women* while living at 130–132 MacDougal Street. At 119 MacDougal Street is **Caffe Reggio**, one of the Village's first coffeehouses. Its interior hasn't changed much since it opened in 1927. Partly because of the proximity of NYU, this area still attracts a young crowd to its cafés, bars, jazz clubs, coffeehouses, theaters, and cabarets. The **Meatpacking District** covers a few blocks of the West Village, between the Hudson River and 9th Avenue, from Little West 12th Street north to West 14th Street. This burgeoning area is a meat market in the morning, and a metaphorical one at night, when the city's trendiest frequent the equally trendy restaurants here. The main drag for the rapidly multiplying eateries, galleries, shops, and nightclubs is West 14th Street.

If you're at West 14th and 8th Avenue, walk west and the streets become cobbled; at about 9th Avenue, the shoes traversing them are increasingly well-heeled. Affluent-angled retailers and services line West 14th: hair-cutting extortionist **Sally Herschberger** (whose cuts cost about $800) and the boutiques of fashion designers **Alexander McQueen** and **Stella McCartney.** One block south at 13th Street is **Hogs and Heifers,** a neighborhood "meet market" and drinking hole infamous for its brassiere-covered bar—and the B-movie *Coyote Ugly,* which was based on it. The next corner at Little West 12th Street is the best place to see **The Highline,** a 75-year-old elevated railway track (look right or west, toward the Hudson River). It's now being recycled as a park. Little West 12th Street (the real West 12th Street is four blocks away) where the street merges with Gansevoort Street, was the site of an outdoor food market in 1884. On 9th Avenue is the hip **Hotel Gansevoort,** with a rooftop pool and bar. Take a peek at the sleek Southeast Asian design at Jean-Georges Vongerichten's **Spice Market** (No. 403), on the northeast corner of West 13th Street. but don't expect to score a table in the dining room without a reservation placed weeks in advance. You can always head, instead, to **Pastis,** the French bistro at the end of the block.

Chelsea

North of the Meatpacking District, Chelsea exists at the nexus of the American art scene, and you can get a good feel for the thriving gallery culture by popping into a handful of its more than 190 galleries. The range of contemporary art on display spans almost every imaginable medium and style; if it's going on in the art world, it'll be here. Standouts include the **Robert Miller Gallery** on 26th street, whose proprietor is a titan in the New York art world (he represents the estates of Diane Arbus and Robert Mapplethorpe) as well as the West 24th street galleries of **Andrea Rosen** and **Matthew Marks,** both major players showing the latest in painting, photography, and sculpture. For a taste of the artistic past, there's the **Chelsea Art Museum** on West 22nd street, housed in a former Christmas ornament factory, and home to a fine collection of postwar European art.

The neighborhood's history is on display a few blocks east on 23rd Street at the legendary **Chelsea Hotel,** one of the best-known reminders of the street's heyday as the heart of the entertainment district. Equally distinguished long-term digs can be found on 20th Street in the **Cushman Row** town houses, dating from the 1820s, and at **London Terrace** on 23rd Street, now home to the likes of Isaac Mizrahi and Annie Leibovitz. Regardless of whether they rent or own, nearly all neighborhood residents

Bleecker Street's "Little Italy"

LITTLE ITALY CAN BE BESIEGED by slow-moving crowds, touristy shops, and desperate restaurant owners who call at you like shooting-gallery barkers at Coney Island. These days Bleecker Street between 6th and 7th avenues seems more vital as a true Italian neighborhood. It's nearly Boston's North End.

For authentic Italian ambience, step into one of the fragrant Italian bakeries, such as **A. Zito & Sons** (No. 259), opened in 1924, and **Rocco's** (No. 243). Cannoli, cream puffs, and cookies are packed up in boxes with string for those on the fly, and enjoyed until late in the evenings at the small tables along with an espresso.

Or look inside the old-style butcher shops, such as **Ottomanelli & Sons** (No. 285) and **Faicco's Pork Store** (No. 260), where Italian locals have gotten their pork custom cut since 1900. Now they may also get their nerves wrangled by foodies who come from all corners of the city for the "gourmet" shopping experience they think they've found in these neighborhood ethnic markets.

The sweet (or stinky) smell of success seems nowhere more evident than at **Murray's Cheese** (No. 254), at Cornelia Street. Until recently, the shop opened in 1940 by Murray Greenberg—the only Jewish-owned business on the strip—was not much larger than the cheese case that stocked the stuff. Now it's a fromage fiend's emporium, with everything from imported crackers to bamboo cutting boards.

In a town that's fierce about its pizza, some New Yorkers swear by **John's Pizzeria** (No. 278), the original in a chain of three branches citywide. But be forewarned: they don't deal in individual slices; whole pies only. Got diet-breaking guilt? Head east to Carmine Street and the Church of Our Lady of Pompeii, where Mother Cabrini, a naturalized Italian immigrant who became the first American saint, often prayed.

make frequent pilgrimages south to **Chelsea Market,** a treasure trove of gourmet and specialty stores housed in an industrial building filling the entire block between 9th and 10th avenues on 15th Street.

Along the water, at 23rd Street, is **Chelsea Piers,** a sports and entertainment complex the size of four 80-story buildings lying flat. Sports-starved Manhattanites come here to golf, ice-skate, roller-skate, rock climb, and swim.

Places to Explore

Greenwich Village & the Meatpacking District

You might have to share a bench in tiny **Christopher Park** (✉ Bordered by W. 4th, Grove, and Christopher Sts., Greenwich Village Ⓜ Subway: 1 to Christopher St./Sheridan Sq.) with George Segal's life-size sculptures—a lesbian couple sits on one and gay male partners stand and converse. The statue of Union General Philip Sheridan dates to 1936. It's a convenient place to eat takeout or rest your feet without footing a restaurant bill.

★ **Chumley's.** A speakeasy during the Prohibition era, this still-secret tavern behind an unmarked door on Bedford Street retains its original ambience with oak booths, a fireplace once used by a blacksmith, and a sawdust-strewn floor. For years Chumley's attracted a literary clientele (John Steinbeck, Ernest Hemingway, Edna Ferber, Simone de Beauvoir, and Jack Kerouac), and the book covers of their publications were proudly displayed (and still appear) on the walls. There's another "secret" entrance in Pamela Court, accessed at 58 Barrow Street around the corner. ⊠ *86 Bedford St., near Barrow St., Greenwich Village* ☎ *212/675–4449* Ⓜ *Subway: 1, 9 to Christopher St./Sheridan Sq.*

Gay Street. A curved, one-block lane lined with small row houses circa 1810, Gay Street is named after the *New York Tribune* editor who lived here with his wife and fellow abolitionist, Lucretia Mott. The black neighborhood was a stop on the Underground Railroad and would later become a strip of speakeasies. In the 1930s this darling thoroughfare and nearby Christopher Street became famous nationwide when Ruth McKenney published her somewhat zany autobiographical stories in the *New Yorker,* based on what happened when she and her sister moved to Greenwich Village from Ohio (they appeared in book form as *My Sister Eileen* in 1938). McKenney wrote in the basement of No. 14. Also on Gay Street, Howdy Doody was designed in the basement of No. 12. ⊠ *Between Christopher St. and Waverly Pl., Greenwich Village* Ⓜ *Subway: 1, 9 to Christopher St./Sheridan Sq.*

Isaacs-Hendricks House. Originally built as a federal-style wood-frame residence in 1799, this immaculate structure is the oldest remaining such house in Greenwich Village. Its first owner, Joshua Isaacs, a wholesale merchant, lost the farmhouse to creditors; the building then belonged to copper supplier Harmon Hendricks. The village landmark was remodeled twice; it received its brick face in 1836, and the third floor was added in 1928. ⊠ *77 Bedford St., at Commerce St., Greenwich Village* Ⓜ *Subway: 1 to Christopher St./Sheridan Sq.*

Jefferson Market Library. After Frederick Clarke Withers and Calvert Vaux's magnificent, towered Third Judicial Courthouse was constructed in 1877, critics variously termed its hodgepodge of styles Venetian, Victorian, or Italian. Villagers, noting the alternating wide bands of red brick and narrow strips of granite, dubbed it the "lean bacon style." The veritable Victorian Gothic castle—with its turrets, traceried windows, ironwork and sculpture—was named after the third U.S. president, and the murder trial of architect Stanford White took place here. The building was on the verge of demolition when local activists saved it and turned it into a public library in 1967. Inside are handsome interior doorways and a graceful circular stairway. And if the gate is open, the flower garden behind the library is worth a look. ⊠ *425 6th Ave., at 10th St., Greenwich Village* ☎ *212/243–4334* Ⓜ *Subway: A, C, E, F, V to W. 4th St./Washington Sq.; 1 to Christopher St.*

Judson Memorial Church. Designed by celebrated architect Stanford White, this Greco-Romanesque-style church has long attracted a congregation interested in the arts and community activism. Funded by the Astor family and John D. Rockefeller and constructed in 1892, the yel-

Literary Pub Crawl

WHERE THERE ARE ACADEMICS, writers, and artists, there are pubs and bars nearby in which to swill the pain of procrastination and lament the limits of creativity. A literary lot has long frequented the West Village's "think tanks" and a tour of a few make for a sophisticated pub crusade rather than crawl. Especially since 10-minute walks separate each.

The most famous '50s watering hole is the **White Horse Tavern** (⊠ 567 Hudson St., at 11th St., Greenwich Village ☎ 212/989-3956), where poet Dylan Thomas did not go gentle into that good night as much as he drank himself into the state here. He died at 39 of alcoholism in 1953 after a last drink here.

Walk east one block along 11th Street to Bleecker and take a right. It's a good 10-minute walk southeast on Bleecker, past many mediocre NYU bars, to MacDougal Street, which is one block east of 6th Avenue. Take a left when you reach it. At **Minetta Tavern** (⊠ 113 MacDougal St., between Bleecker and W. 3rd Sts., Greenwich Village ☎ 212/475-3850) Italian fare is now served in the venerable Village watering hole that dates to Prohibition. During those years, the tavern was called the Black

Rabbit, some say for the scandalous 1890s sex shows held here. In 1923, De Witt Wallace printed his first copies of the simply named *Reader's Digest* in the basement. Suffice it to say that Wallace and his wife became benefactors of the Met. More recently poets and lit lions, including Nobel Prize-winning poet Seamus Heaney, have been regulars here.

Take a sobering walk north to Washington Square Park, cross it to Washington Square East, and take a left, walking north on University Place, heading for 11th Street. During the '40s and '50s Abstract Expressionist Jackson Pollock, practiced the *non*dribble method when lifting drink to mouth at the **Cedar Tavern** (⊠ 82 University Pl., between 11th and 12th Sts., Greenwich Village ☎ 212/929-9089). Willem de Kooning and his wife, Elaine, regularly processed their marital troubles from the captain's-chair bar stools during the same time, and rumor has it that Beat writer Jack Kerouac, a regular, lost his drinking privileges here for emptying his bladder in an ashtray. Complete any necessary business of this kind in the traditional WC before waving down a cab for your hotel.

---

low-brick and limestone church was built thanks to Edward Judson, who hoped to reach out to the poor immigrants in adjacent Little Italy. The church has stained-glass windows designed by John La Farge and a 10-story campanile. Inquire at the parish office for weekday access at 239 Thompson Street. ⊠ *55 Washington Sq. S, between Thompson and Sullivan Sts., Greenwich Village* ☎ *212/477-0351* ⊕ *www.judson.org* Ⓜ *Subway: A, C, E, F, V to W. 4th St./Washington Sq.*

Northern Dispensary. Edgar Allan Poe was a frequent patient at the triangular Dispensary, built in 1831 as a private medical clinic for indigent Villagers. The Georgian brick building has *one* side on *two* streets

(Grove and Christopher streets where they meet) and *two* sides facing *one* street—Waverly Place, which splits in two directions. A building as odd as Poe's stories. ✉ *165 Waverly Pl., Greenwich Village* Ⓜ *Subway: 1 to Christopher St./Sheridan Sq.*

Patchin Place. This little cul-de-sac off West 10th Street between Greenwich and 6th avenues has 10 diminutive 1848 row houses. Around the corner on 6th Avenue is a similar dead-end street, **Milligan Place,** consisting of five small homes completed in 1852. The houses in both quiet enclaves were originally built for the waiters (mostly Basques) who worked at 5th Avenue's high-society Brevoort Hotel, long since demolished. Patchin Place later attracted numerous writers, including Theodore Dreiser, e. e. cummings, Jane Bowles, and Djuna Barnes. Milligan Place eventually became the address for several playwrights, including Eugene O'Neill. Ⓜ *Subway: F, V to 14th St.*

The Row. Built from 1833 through 1837, this series of beautifully preserved Greek Revival row houses along Washington Square North, on the two blocks between University Place and MacDougal Street, once belonged to merchants and bankers, then writers and artists such as John Dos Passos and Edward Hopper. Now the buildings serve as NYU offices and faculty housing. ✉ *1–13 and 19–26 Washington Sq. N, between University Pl. and MacDougal St., Greenwich Village.*

The Church of St. Luke's in the Fields. The author of "A Visit from St. Nicholas" (" 'Twas the night before Christmas . . ."), Clement Clarke Moore, was the first warden of the Episcopal parish of St. Luke's. When the chapel was constructed in 1821, this part of the city was still the country—in the fields, so to speak. The chapel was the country branch of downtown's Trinity Church. Today St. Luke's Choir, a professional ensemble, and guest choristers perform regularly. The Barrow Street Garden on the chapel grounds is worth visiting in spring and summer. ✉ *487 Hudson St., at Grove St., Greenwich Village* ☎ *212/924–0562* ⊕ *www.stlukeinthefields.org* ⊘ *Garden open Tues.–Fri. 8–5 (June–Sept. 8–7), weekends 8–4* Ⓜ *Subway: 1 to Christopher St./Sheridan Sq.*

St. Luke's Place. Shaded by graceful gingko trees, this street has 15 classic Italianate brownstone and brick town houses (1851–54). Novelist Theodore Dreiser wrote *An American Tragedy* at No. 16, and poet Marianne Moore resided at No. 14. Mayor Jimmy Walker (first elected in 1926) lived at vine-covered No. 6; the lampposts in front are "mayor's lamps," which were sometimes placed in front of the residences of New York mayors. This block is often used as a film location, too: No. 12 was shown as the Huxtables' home on *The Cosby Show* (although the family lived in Brooklyn), and No. 4 was the setting of the Audrey Hepburn movie *Wait Until Dark*. Before 1890 the playground on the south side of the street was a graveyard where, according to legend, the dauphin of France—the lost son of Louis XVI and Marie Antoinette—is buried. ✉ *Between Hudson St. and 7th Ave. S, Greenwich Village* Ⓜ *Subway: 1 to Houston St.*

75½ Bedford Street. Rising real estate rates inspired the construction of New York City's narrowest house—just 9½ feet wide—in 1873. Built on a lot that was originally a carriage entrance of the Isaacs-Hendricks House next door, this sliver of a building has been home to actor John Barrymore and poet Edna St. Vincent Millay, who wrote the Pulitzer Prize–winning *Ballad of the Harp-Weaver* during her tenure here from 1923 to 1924. ⊠ *75½ Bedford St., between Commerce and Morton Sts., Greenwich Village* Ⓜ *Subway: 1 to Christopher St./Sheridan Sq.*

Twin Peaks. In 1925 financier Otto Kahn gave money to a Village eccentric named Clifford Daily to remodel an 1835 house for artists' use. The building was whimsically altered with stucco, half-timbers, and the addition of a pair of steep roof peaks. The result: an imitation Swiss chalet. ⊠ *102 Bedford St., between Grove and Christopher Sts., Greenwich Village* Ⓜ *Subway: 1 to Christopher St./Sheridan Sq.*

Washington Mews. This mostly cobblestone private street is lined on one side with the former stables of the houses on the Row on Washington Square North. Writer Walter Lippmann and heiress-artist-patron Gertrude Vanderbilt Whitney (founder of the Whitney Museum) once had homes in the mews; today it's mostly owned by NYU. ⊠ *Between 8th St. and Washington Square N., between 5th Ave. and University Pl., Greenwich Village* Ⓜ *Subway: R, W to 8th St.*

★ ⓒ **Washington Square Park.** Earnest-looking NYU students, street musicians, skateboarders, jugglers, chess players, and bench warmers—and those just watching the grand opera of it all—generate a maelstrom of activity in this physical and spiritual heart of the Village. The 9½-acre park had inauspicious beginnings as a cemetery, principally for yellow fever victims—an estimated 10,000–22,000 bodies lie below. In the early 1800s it was a parade ground and the site of public executions; bodies dangled from a conspicuous Hanging Elm that still stands at the northwest corner of the square. The square became the focus of a fashionable residential neighborhood when it was made a public park in 1827. Today, a playground attracts parents with tots in tow, dogs go leash-free inside the popular dog run, and everyone else seems drawn toward the large central fountain where in spring and summer passersby and loungers can cool off in small sprays.

The triumphal **Washington Memorial Arch** stands at the square's north end, marking the start of 5th Avenue, the city's central thoroughfare that's never been marked by understatement. Stanford White designed a wooden version of the arch, which was built in 1889 to commemorate the 100th anniversary of George Washington's presidential inauguration. It was originally placed about half a block north of its present location. The arch was reproduced in Tuckahoe marble in 1892, and the statues—*Washington at War* on the left, *Washington at Peace* on the right—were added in 1916 and 1918, respectively. The civilian version of Washington is the work of Alexander Stirling Calder, father of the renowned artist Alexander Calder. Bodybuilder Charles Atlas modeled for *Peace*. ⊠ *5th Ave. between Waverly Pl. and 4th St., Greenwich Village* Ⓜ *Subway: A, C, E, F, V to W. 4th St.*

Chelsea

Chelsea Hotel. The shabby aura of the hotel is part of its bohemian allure. This 12-story Queen Anne neighborhood landmark (1884) became a hotel in 1905, although it has always catered to long-term tenants with a tradition of broad-mindedness and creativity. Its literary roll call of former live-ins includes Mark Twain, Eugene O'Neill, O. Henry, Thomas Wolfe, Tennessee Williams, Vladimir Nabokov, Mary McCarthy, Brendan Behan, Arthur Miller, Dylan Thomas, William S. Burroughs, and Arthur C. Clarke (who wrote the script for *2001: A Space Odyssey* while living here). In 1966 Andy Warhol filmed a group of fellow artists, including Brigid Polk and Nico, in eight rooms; the footage was included in *The Chelsea Girls* (1967). The hotel was also seen on-screen in *I Shot Andy Warhol* (1996) and in *Sid and Nancy* (1986), a dramatization of the real-life murder of Nancy Spungen, who was stabbed to death here by her boyfriend punk rocker Sid Vicious. Read the commemorative plaques outside, then check out the eclectic collection of art in the lobby, some donated in lieu of rent by residents down on their luck. In the building's basement, accessible from the street, is the plush lounge Serena. ✉ *222 W. 23rd St., between 7th and 8th Aves., Chelsea* ☎ *212/243–3700* ⊕ *www.hotelchelsea.com* Ⓜ *Subway: 1, C, E to 23rd St.*

Chelsea Piers. Beginning in 1910, the Chelsea Piers were the launching point for a new generation of big ocean liners, including the *Lusitania,* the British liner sunk by a German submarine in 1915. Even the *Titanic* planned to dock here at the end of its ill-fated journey. Decades-long neglect ended with the transformation of the four old buildings along the Hudson River into a 1.7-million-square-foot, state-of-the-art sports and recreation facility, providing a huge variety of activities and several restaurants with river views, including the Chelsea Brewing Company, New York State's largest microbrewery. Private trips on the river via speedboat or yacht can be arranged by **Surfside 3 Marina** (☎ 212/336–7873). ✉ *Piers 59–62 on Hudson River from 17th to 23rd Sts.; entrance at 23rd St., Chelsea* ☎ *212/336–6666* ⊕ *www.chelseapiers.com.*

DID YOU KNOW? The *Titanic* was scheduled to arrive at Chelsea Piers on April 16, 1912. Fate intervened and the "unsinkable" ship struck an iceberg on April 14 and sank. Of the 2,200 passengers aboard, 675 were rescued by the Cunard liner *Carpathia,* which arrived at Chelsea Piers eight days later.

Cushman Row. Built in 1840, this string of homes between 9th and 10th avenues represents some of the country's most perfect examples of Greek Revival row houses. Original details include small wreath-encircled attic windows, deeply recessed doorways with brownstone frames, and striking iron balustrades and fences. Note the pineapples, a traditional symbol of welcome, on top of the black iron newels in front of No. 416. ✉ *406–418 W. 20th St., between 9th and 10th Aves., Chelsea* Ⓜ *Subway: C, E to 23rd St.*

Greenwich Village & Chelsea at a Glance

MUSEUMS & GALLERIES
(⇨ Ch. 14)
Alan Klotz Gallery
Andrea Rosen
ATM Gallery
Barbara Gladstone
Casey Kaplan
Cheim & Read
Chelsea Art Museum
Clementine
David Zwirner
Forbes Galleries
Gagosian
Galerie Lelong
Grey Art Gallery
Jack Shainman
Luhring Augustine
Marlborough
Mary Boone
Matthew Marks
Metro Pictures
Pace Wildenstein
Paula Cooper
Postmasters
Robert Miller
Rubin Museum of Art
Sean Kelly
Sonnabend
Tanya Bonakdar
303

WHERE TO EAT (⇨ Ch. 18)

BUDGET DINING
Arturo's
Barbuto
Caffè Dante
Caffè Reggio
Dean & DeLuca
Do Hwa
Florent
Gavroche
Gonzo
Grand Sichuan International
Gray's Papaya
Home
La Bergamote
Le Gamin
Lupa
Macelleria
Magnolia Bakery
Mary's Fish Camp

Mi Cocina
Miracle Grill
Moustache
Paris Commune
Pastis
Patsy's Pizzeria
Pepe Giallo to Go
Petite Abeille
R.U.B. BBQ
Seven
The Spotted Pig
Vento
Voyage

MODERATE DINING
Annisa
Babbo
Blue Hill
Blue Ribbon Bakery
5 Ninth
Gusto
Jarnac
Pearl Oyster Bar
The Red Cat
Sapa
Spice Market
Strip House
Wallsé

EXPENSIVE DINING
Gotham Bar & Grill
The Biltmore Room

SHOPPING (⇨ Ch. 17)

ANTIQUES
Kentshire Galleries
Les Pierre Antiques
Old Japan

BOOKS
Barnes & Noble
Biography Bookshop
Books of Wonder
Oscar Wilde Bookshop
Partners & Crime
Skyline Books
Three Lives & Co

CHOCOLATE
Chocolate Bar
Li-Lac Chocolates

CLOTHING
Alexander McQueen
Balenciaga
Charles Nolan

Comme des Garçons
Cynthia Rowley
DDC Lab
Destination
Fisch for the Hip
Írma
Jeffrey
Loehmann's
New York Vintage
Nicole Farhi
Nom de Guerre
Ralph Lauren
Stella McCartney
Triple 5 Soul

HOME DECOR
Bodum
Design Within Reach
Mxyplyzyk
Olatz
Vitra
William-Wayne & Co

JEWELRY
Ten Thousand Things

LEATHER GOODS
Flight 001
Henry Beguelin
Lulu Guinness

LINGERIE
La Perla
La Petite Coquette

MUSIC
Bleecker Bob's Golden
Oldies Record Shop
Jazz Record Center

PERFUME/COSMETICS
Aedes De Venustas
Ricky's
Sephora

Union Square

INCLUDING GRAMERCY, FLATIRON DISTRICT
& MURRAY HILL

WORD OF MOUTH

"[The Empire State Building] is a landmark not to be missed. Take the last elevator up and hit the deck with someone you love—even if it is foggy or overcast. Print tickets online (for the skyride too) and avoid the line."   —DonielleP

"Union Square is a great gathering spot for all sorts of young people, especially in nice weather. There are always skateboarders, breakdancers, and other street entertainers."

—Jdnyc

www.fodors.com/forums

Sightseeing
★ ★ ★ ★

Nightlife
★

Dining
★ ★ ★ ★

Lodging
★ ★ ★

Shopping
★ ★ ★ ★

Union Square is the beating heart of Manhattan. The square itself hosts everything from concerts to protest rallies to the farmers' market, and its surrounding neighborhoods each borrow its flavor while maintaining their own vibe and identity. The haste and hullabaloo of the city calms considerably as you stroll through the tree-lined neighborhoods of Murray Hill, the Flatiron District, and Gramercy, east of 5th Avenue between 14th and 40th streets. Although its name is fairly unknown, Murray Hill is a charming residential neighborhood—between 34th and 40th streets from 5th Avenue to 3rd Avenue—with some high-profile haunts, including the Morgan Library and King Kong's favorite hangout, the Empire State Building.

A little farther south, the Flatiron District—anchored by Madison Square on the north and Union Square to the south—is one of the city's hottest neighborhoods, bustling with shoppers and lined with trendy stores, restaurants, and hotels. Here stands the photogenic Flatiron Building, Madison Square Park, the Museum of Sex, and an elegant turn-of-the-20th-century skyline.

Gramercy Park, a leafy, dignified, and mostly residential neighborhood, is named for its 1831 gated garden square ringed by historic buildings and pricey hotels. Even though you can't unpack your picnic in this exclusive residents-only park, you can bask in its historic surroundings and literary significance. Gramercy's gems are the Players Club, the National Arts Club, a street named after writer Washington Irving, and the exclusive Gramercy Park.

What's Here

The bustle of **Union Square** reaches its peak on Monday, Wednesday, Friday, and Saturday, when more than 25 farms and food purveyors set up shop at the square's north end to peddle their tasty wares: everything from produce to fresh fish to baked goods. For those who prefer their food prepared, the area also boasts some of the city's best restaurants, including Danny Meyer's **Union Square Café** on 16th Street and the airy and debonair **Gotham Bar and Grill** on 12th Street between University Place and 5th Avenue.

Union Square invites walking, lounging, shopping, and eating in equal measures. The **Virgin Megastore** on the south side is always packed and conveniently open daily until 1 AM, just in case you need to run out for a DVD after midnight. The much-loved **Strand** bookstore is two blocks south on Broadway, and one block to the east, **Irving Plaza** posts a list of upcoming rock shows under its marquee.

During the summer, people stretch out on the shaded lawns to read, eat lunch, or just breathe in the atmosphere. One of Union Square's notable features is The Metronome, the bank of cascading numbers above Circuit City on 14th Street. Half art installation, half timepiece, this is actually a clock that counts both time elapsed and time remaining in the day. At **33 Union Square West**, the building now fronted by Union Square Wines once held Andy Warhol's Factory, birthplace of some of the great works of 20th-century art.

A few blocks north of Union Square up Irving Place, the hustle and flow fades into serenity with the look-but-don't touch primness of **Gramercy Park**. This magnificent park is open only to residents, and nearby buildings house the tony likes of the **Players Club**, at 15 Gramercy Park South, and the **National Arts Club** next door.

Heading north up Broadway from Union Square is an exercise in delightful frustration—it's almost impossible to resist being tugged down a side street, each with its own series of colorful awnings promising cool shops and eateries. Perseverance pays off, though, as Broadway reaches 23rd Street and opens onto the expanse of **Madison Square Park**, with its mighty trees, and even mightier, picturesque skyline. In the northeast corner, the gold-top **New York Life Insurance** building was the tallest in the city when it opened in 1903. The limestone, Beaux-Arts courthouse, one block down at East 25th Street, is the **Appellate Division, New York State Supreme Court**. The lovely **Metropolitan Life Insurance Tower**, between East 23rd and 24th streets, is another classically inspired spire. And turning back to face the southwest corner, one finds the charming and historic **Flatiron Building**, a limestone and terra-cotta vessel sailing uptown. With the surrounding towers lighted to perfection, Madison Square Park positively glows at night.

South on 5th Avenue shopping abounds: **Banana Republic, Kenneth Cole, Lucky Brand** and **Club Monaco** all have locations on 5th between 14th and 23rd streets. North on 5th Avenue at 27th Street, the **Museum of Sex** sits behind an unassuming façade, giving little hint of its salacious interior.

GETTING ORIENTED

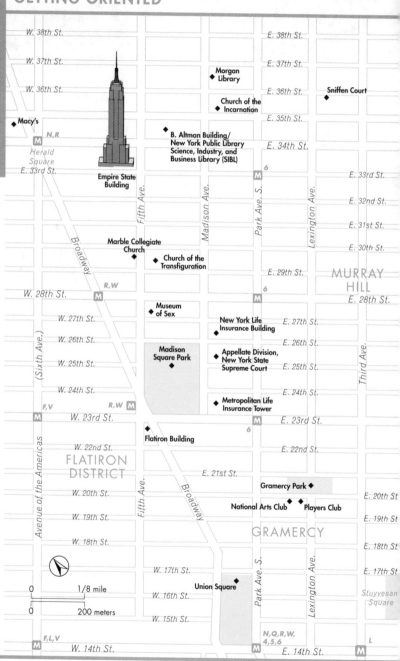

W. 38th St.   E. 38th St.

W. 37th St.   E. 37th St.

Morgan Library

W. 36th St.   E. 36th St.   Sniffen Court

Church of the Incarnation

E. 35th St.

Macy's

N,R

Herald Square

B. Altman Building/ New York Public Library Science, Industry, and Business Library (SIBL)

E. 34th St.

E. 33rd St.

Empire State Building

6

E. 33rd St.

Fifth Ave.

Madison Ave.

Park Ave. S.

Lexington Ave.

E. 32nd St.

E. 31st St.

Marble Collegiate Church

E. 30th St.

Broadway

Church of the Transfiguration

E. 29th St.

MURRAY HILL

R,W

W. 28th St.

6

E. 28th St.

Museum of Sex

W. 27th St.

New York Life Insurance Building

E. 27th St.

(Sixth Ave.)

W. 26th St.

E. 26th St.

Madison Square Park

Appellate Division, New York State Supreme Court

E. 25th St.

Third Ave.

W. 25th St.

W. 24th St.

E. 24th St.

F,V

R,W

Metropolitan Life Insurance Tower

W. 23rd St.

E. 23rd St.

6

Avenue of the Americas

W. 22nd St.

Flatiron Building

E. 22nd St.

FLATIRON DISTRICT

E. 21st St.

Fifth Ave.

Broadway

Gramercy Park

W. 20th St.

E. 20th St

National Arts Club

Players Club

W. 19th St.

E. 19th St

GRAMERCY

W. 18th St.

E. 18th St

W. 17th St.

Park Ave. S.

Lexington Ave.

E. 17th St.

Union Square

Stuyvesan Square

0   1/8 mile

W. 16th St.

0   200 meters

W. 15th St.

F,L,V

N,Q,R,W, 4,5,6

L

W. 14th St.

E. 14th St.

6

TOP 5

■ Sunset from the top of the Empire State Building

■ Dinner and people-watching on Union Square

■ Gazing at the mighty skyline from Madison Square Park

■ Shopping on 5th Avenue

■ Strolling among the rare books at the Morgan Library

MAKING THE MOST OF YOUR TIME

Union Square provides round-the-clock fun. Many establishments in the area are open late, and the square itself sizzles on nights and weekends, when everyone is hanging out on the south steps. During seasonal months, protesters handing out pamphlets share space with young street groups who put on semi-regular dance shows for public consumption. There's not much here in the way of guided tours that need to be attended during business hours, but it's a great place to shop away the day or start the night with dinner and drinks.

Most of the impressive buildings in the skyline around Madison Square and Murray Hill are still office buildings with nothing to see inside. You'll want to visit in the daytime to go into churches or libraries, but these neighborhoods don't have particularly notable nightlife.

GETTING HERE

Both Union Square/14th Street and Herald Square/34th Street are major subway hubs, connected by the 4, 5, 6, N, Q, R, W lines. Any of these trains can bring you right to the center of the action. For Madison Square Park, take the local R or W to 23rd Street. You can reach the Empire State Building via the F or V to 34th Street or the 6 to 33rd Street. The 6 also has stops at 23rd and 28th streets.

QUICK BITES

City Bakery (⌧ 3 W. 18 St., between 5th Ave. and 6th Ave., Flatiron District ☎ 212/366-1414) serves a tempting array of tarts and pastries as well as lunch and dinner menu. On cool days, warm up with a rich marshmallowy hot chocolate. **Rainbow Falafel & Shawarma** (⌧ 26 E. 17th St., between 5th Ave. and Broadway, Union Sq. ☎ 212/691-8641), a hole-in-the-wall off Union Square, has long but fast-moving lunch lines testifying to its reputation for the best falafel in town. Get there early to beat the lunchtime rush and take your baba ghanoush, falafel, and grape leaves with plenty of extra napkins and grab a seat on one of the many benches in Union Square park.

Molly's Shebeen (⌧ 287 3rd Ave., between 22nd and 23rd Sts., Gramercy ☎ 212/889-3361) is a snug Irish pub complete with a friendly Irish staff, log-burning fireplace, and sawdust on the floors. You can enjoy a hearty burger or shepherd's-pie lunch but leave room for dessert—a creamy pint of Guinness.

After visiting, continue north on 5th to receive absolution at the **Marble Collegiate Church** on 29th Street and again at the **Church of the Transfiguration** across the avenue.

At 5th and 33rd, at the edge of Murray Hill looms the most famous building in the city, the state, and perhaps the country: the **Empire State Building.** Canonized in postcards, books, and on film, the building reaches toward the sky with its majestic spire, which is lighted up at night according to an elaborate calendar of dates and corresponding colors. ("Why is it black, red, and yellow?" "For German Reunification Day." "Oh, right.") An excellent view of the ESB can be found on the steps of the nearby **B. Altman Building,** home to the New York Public Library–Science, Industry, and Business Library. From there, it's a quick walk up Madison Avenue to the **Morgan Library,** with its impressive collection of rare books and manuscripts.

West of the Empire State Building at the intersection of 6th Avenue, Broadway, and 34th Street sits a different kind of monument—one dedicated to shopping. **Macy's** has 11 stories and more than a million square feet of floor space, making a good case for its self-proclaimed title as the world's largest department store.

Places to Explore

Appellate Division Courthouse. Sculpted by Frederick Ruckstuhl, figures representing "Wisdom" and "Force" flank the main portal of this imposing Beaux-Arts courthouse, built in 1899 on the eastern edge of Madison Square. Melding the structure's purpose with artistic symbolism, statues of great lawmakers of the past line the roof balustrade, including Moses, Justinian, and Confucius. In total, sculptures by 16 artists adorn the ornate building, a showcase of themes relating to law. This is one of the most important appellate courts in the country: it hears more than 3,000 appeals and 6,000 motions a year, and also admits approximately 3,000 new attorneys to the bar each year. Inside the courtroom is a stunning stained-glass dome set into a gilt-covered ceiling. All sessions are open to the public. ⊠ *27 Madison Ave., entrance on E. 25th St., Flatiron District* ☎ *212/340–0400* ☉ *Weekdays 9–5* Ⓜ *Subway: R, W to 23rd St.*

♻ **B. Altman Building/New York Public Library–Science, Industry, and Business Library (SIBL).** In 1906, department-store magnate Benjamin Altman gambled that his fashionable patrons would follow him here from his popular store on 19th Street in the area now known as the Ladies' Mile Historic District. His new store, one of the first of the grand department stores on 5th Avenue, was an Italian Renaissance–style building that blended with the mansions nearby. In 1996, seven years after the bankruptcy and dismantling of the B. Altman chain, the New York Public Library transferred all scientific, technology, and business materials from its main 42nd Street building to a new state-of-the-art facility here: the **Science, Industry, and Business Library** (SIBL). This sleek and graceful high-tech library heeds Ruskin's words, "Industry without art is brutality," one of many quotations along the undulant upper wall inside the Madison Avenue lobby. Further demonstrating this philosophy is the artwork within Healy Hall, the 33-foot-high atrium that unites the building's two floors, the lending library off the lobby and the research collections below. Downstairs a wall of TVs tuned to business-news stations and electronic ticker tapes beam information and instructions to patrons. On Tuesday and Thursday at 2 you can take a free one-hour tour. ⊠ *188 Madison Ave., between E. 34th and E. 35th Sts., Murray Hill* ☎ *212/592–7000* ⊕ *www.nypl.org* ⊙ *Tues.–Thurs. 10–8, Fri. and Sat. 10–6* Ⓜ *Subway: 6 to 33rd St.*

Church of the Incarnation. Dating from 1864, and subtitled "The Landmark Church of Murray Hill," this brownstone and sandstone Episcopal church was the house of worship for New York's most prominent families in the early 20th century. A fire in 1882 melted all the windows, so they were replaced with English- and American-design stained glass. The north aisle's 23rd Psalm Window is by the Tiffany Glass Works; the south aisle's two Angel windows, dedicated to infants, are by the William Morris Company of London. ⊠ *209 Madison Ave., between E. 35th and E. 36th Sts., Murray Hill* ☎ *212/689–6350* ⊕ *www. churchoftheincarnation.org* ⊙ *Services Wed. 12:15, 6:30; Fri. 12:15; Sun. 8:30 and 11* Ⓜ *Subway: 6 to 33rd St.*

Church of the Transfiguration. Known as the Little Church Around the Corner, this Gothic Revival structure won its memorable nickname in 1870 after a nearby church refused to bury actor George Holland because those in his profession were thought to be "disreputable." His friends were directed to the "little church around the corner," and this Episcopal church has been favored by theater-folk since. The south transept's stained-glass window, by John La Farge, depicts Edwin Booth (brother of Lincoln's assassin) as Hamlet, his most famous role. A lych-gate and quiet garden separates the church from the busy street. Come inside the garden for a lovely view of the Empire State Building to the north. ⊠ *1 E. 29th St., between 5th and Madison Aves., Murray Hill* ☎ *212/684–6770* ⊕ *www.littlechurch.org* ⊙ *Mon.–Sat. 8–6, Sun. 8–3* Ⓜ *Subway: R, W, 6 to 28th St.*

Empire State Building. It's no longer the world's tallest building (it currently ranks seventh), but it's one of the world's most recognizable landmarks, and still worth a visit. Its pencil-slim silhouette is an art deco monument to progress, a symbol for New York City, and a star in some great romantic scenes, on- and off-screen. Its cinematic résumé—the building has appeared in more than 200 movies—means that it remains a fixture of popular imagination and that many visitors come to relive favorite movie scenes. With luck you'll find yourself at the top of the building with the *Sleepless in Seattle* lookalikes or even the building's own *King Kong* impersonators. Today, millions of visitors fill its new 2nd-floor Visitors Center and make the pilgrimage to the top for the astonishing views of the city.

Built in 1931 at the peak of the skyscraper craze, this 103-story limestone giant opened after a mere 13 months of construction. The framework rose at an astonishing rate of 4½ stories per week, making the Empire State Building the fastest-rising skyscraper ever built. Many floors were left completely unfinished so tenants could have them custom-designed. But the

And Then There Was Light

AT NIGHT, THE EMPIRE STATE BUILDING (ESB) ILLUMINATES THE MANHATTAN SKYLINE with a colorful view as awe-inspiring from a distance as the view from the top. The colors are changed regularly to reflect seasons, events, and holidays so New Yorkers always have a reason to look at this icon in a new light, and ne'er a chance to take it for granted.

The building's first light show was in November 1932, when a simple searchlight was used to spread the news that New York–born Franklin Delano Roosevelt had been elected president of the United States. Douglas Leigh, sign designer and mastermind of Times Square's kinetic billboard ads, tried to brighten up prospects at the "Empty State Building" after the Depression by negotiating with the Coca-Cola Company to occupy the top floors. He proposed that Coca-Cola could change the lights of the building to serve as a weather forecast and then publish a small guide on its bottles to decipher the colors. Coca-Cola loved this idea but the deal fell through due to Pearl Harbor when the U.S. government needed office space in the building.

In 1956, the revolving "freedom lights" were installed to welcome people to America; then in 1964 the top 30 floors of the building were illuminated to mark the New York World's Fair. Douglas Leigh revisited the lights of the ESB in 1976 when he was made chairman of City Decor to welcome the Democratic Convention. He introduced the idea of color lighting and so the building's tower was ablaze in red, white, and blue to welcome the convention and to mark the celebration of the American Bicentennial. The color lights were a huge success and they remained red, white, and blue for the rest of the year.

Leigh's next suggestion of tying the lights to different holidays, a variation on his weather theme for Coca-Cola, is the basic scheme still used today. In 1977 the lighting system was updated to comply with energy conservation programs and to allow for a wider range of colors. Leigh further improved this new system in 1984 by designing an automated color-changing system so vertical fluorescents in the mast could be changed with the flick of a switch, the only automated portion of the building's lighting system to date. The lights honor national holidays, the multiethnic population of New York, special local and national events, and charitable causes. The city's greatest nightlight dims respectfully, however, to allow for migrating birds that could otherwise be distracted by the lights.

Memorize these color combinations and corresponding holidays and you'll only have to look to the sky to know what day it is!

Black/green/gold: Jamaican Independence Day

Black/red/yellow: German Reunification Day

Blue: Police Memorial Day, Child Abuse Prevention

Blue/white/blue: Israeli Independence Day, First Night of Hanukkah

Blue/ blue /white: Greek Independence Day, United Nations Day

Dark/no lights: Day without Art/Night without Lights/AIDS Awareness

Green: St. Patrick's Day, March of Dimes, Rain Forest Awareness Day

Green/blue/blue: Earth Day

Green/green/white: Pakistani Independence Day

Green/white/orange: Indian Independence Day

Green/white/red: Mexican Independence Day

Green/yellow/blue: Brazilian Independence

Lavender/lavender/white: Stonewall Anniversary/Gay Pride

Orange/white/blue: NYC marathon

Pink/pink/white: Breast Cancer Awareness

Purple/purple/white: Alzheimer's Awareness

Purple/teal/white: National Osteoporosis Society

Red: Saint Valentine's Day, Fire Department Memorial Day, Big Apple Circus

Red/blue: Equal Parents Day, Children's Rights

Red/black/green: Martin Luther King Jr. Day

Red/red/green: Holiday Season

Red/red/white: Pulaski Day, Red Cross

Red/white/blue: Presidents' Day, Armed Forces Day, Memorial Day, Flag Day, Independence Day, Labor Day, Veterans Day

Red/white/green: Columbus Day

Red/yellow: Autumn

Red/yellow/green: Portugal Day

Yellow: March of Dimes, U.S. Open

Yellow/yellow/white: Spring, Easter week

–Jacinta O'Halloran

6

Great Depression meant that most of the building remained empty, causing critics to deem it the "Empty State Building." The building remained solvent, thanks to the popularity of its 86th-floor observation deck.

However, getting to the observation deck of this behemoth means standing in three lines (security, tickets, and elevators), taking an elevator to the 80th floor, trekking through hallways to the tower shaft, and then taking a second elevator. You can buy tickets in advance on the building's Web site and avoid at least one long line; for an extra $6 you can rent a headset with an audio tour from Tony, a fictional but "authentic" native New Yorker, available in eight languages. The 86th-floor observatory (1,050 feet high) is open to the air (expect strong winds during the winter) and spans the building's circumference. Bring quarters for the high-powered binoculars because the view is one to behold in any weather: on clear days you can see up to 80 mi; on rainy days you can watch the rain travel sideways around the building from the shelter of the enclosed deck; on snowy days you can watch the city's roofs disappear under a blanket of white; and on windy days, bundle up! The Observatory on the 102nd floor has recently reopened. There is an extra $12 charge to visit this floor, and it's well worth the dramatic views. Express tickets can be purchased for front-of-the-line admission for an extra $40.

Time your visit for early or late in the day—morning is the least crowded time—when the sun is low on the horizon and the shadows are deep across the city. But at night the city's lights are dazzling. The French architect Le Corbusier said, "It is a Milky Way come down to earth." Really, both views are a must; one strategy is to go up just before dusk and witness both, as day dims to night. ✉ *350 5th Ave., at E. 34th St., Murray Hill* ☏ *212/736–3100 or 877/692–8439* ⊕ *www.esbnyc.com* ✉ *$16* ⊙ *Daily 8–midnight; last elevator up leaves at 11:15 PM* Ⓜ *Subway: B, D, F, N, Q, R, V, W to 34th St./Herald Sq.*

A major tourist attraction within the Empire State Building, the 2nd-floor **NY SKYRIDE** is a fun-filled presentation of movie, motion, and sights, rolled up into New York's only aerial virtual-tour simulator. Entertaining for visitors of all ages, the ride combines high-definition digital technology and special effects, high-tech platforms, and a two-story high screen as it "flies" above and around New York City. ☏ *212/279–9777 or 888/759–7433* ⊕ *www.skyride.com* ✉ *$23.50; $34 Combo SKYRIDE and Observatory* ⊙ *Daily 8–10.*

DID YOU KNOW?

The first Macy's Thanksgiving Day Parade in 1924 was called "Macy's Christmas Day Parade" although it took place on Thanksgiving. It included camels, goats, elephants, and donkeys. The parade is the world's second-largest consumer of helium after the U.S. government. Each year, balloons are floated through the parade. Due to a helium shortage in 1958, however, the balloons were brought down Broadway on cranes.

Flatiron Building. When completed in 1903, the Fuller Building, as it was originally known, caused a sensation. Architect Daniel Burnham made ingenious use of the triangular wedge of land at 23rd Street, 5th Avenue, and Broadway, employing a revolutionary steel frame, which allowed for its 22-story, 286-foot height. Covered with a limestone and white terra-cotta skin in the Italian Renaissance style, the building was called the Flatiron because of its shape resembling a clothing iron, and became the most popular subject of picture postcards at the turn of the 20th century. When it became apparent that the building generated strong winds, ungallant gawkers would loiter at 23rd Street hoping to catch sight of a young lady's billowing skirts. Local traffic cops had to shoo away the male peepers—coining the phrase "23 skiddoo." Today, the building is occupied by publishing houses and stores. You can visit the lobby to look at photos, but otherwise the building is best enjoyed from Madison Square, across the street. ⊠ *175 5th Ave., bordered by E. 22nd and E. 23rd Sts., 5th Ave., and Broadway, Flatiron District* Ⓜ *Subway: R, W to 23rd St.*

Madison Square Park. The benches of this elegant tree-filled park afford great views of some of the city's oldest and most charming skyscrapers (the Flatiron Building, the Metropolitan Life Insurance Tower, the New York Life Insurance Building, and the Empire State Building) and serves as a perfect vantage point for people-, pigeon-, dog-, or squirrel-watching. Baseball was invented across the Hudson in Hoboken, New Jersey, but the city's first baseball games were played in this 7-acre park circa 1845. On the north end an imposing 1881 statue by Augustus Saint-Gaudens memorializes Civil War naval hero Admiral Farragut. An 1876 statue of Secretary of State William Henry Seward (the Seward of the term "Seward's folly"—as Alaska was originally known) sits in the park's southwest corner, though it's rumored the sculptor placed a reproduction of the statesman's head on a statue of Abraham Lincoln's body. ⊠ *E. 23rd to E. 26th Sts. between 5th and Madison Aves., Flatiron District* Ⓜ *Subway: R, W to 23rd St.*

HERE'S
WHERE

On November 4, 1902, publisher William Randolph Hearst arranged for fireworks at Madison Square to celebrate being elected to Congress. The show, however, was poorly planned and a mortar containing 10,000 shells tipped over and caught fire. The ensuing explosion killed 17 people, injured 100, and blew out doors and windows of the buildings surrounding the square.

Marble Collegiate Church. Built in 1854 for the congregation organized two centuries earlier by Peter Minuit, the canny Dutchman who bought Manhattan for the equivalent of $24, this impressive church takes its name from the Tuckahoe marble that covers the early Romanesque Revival facade. The bell in the tower has tolled the death of every president since Martin Van Buren in 1862. Don't miss the Tiffany-design windows depicting Moses and the burning bush. ⊠ *1 W. 29th St., at 5th Ave., Murray Hill* ☎ *212/686–2770* ⊕ *www.marblechurch.org* ☉ *Weekdays 8:30–8:30, Sat. 9–4, Sun. 8–3* Ⓜ *Subway: 6, R, W to 28th St.*

Metropolitan Life Insurance Company Tower. When it was added in 1909, the 700-foot tower resembling the campanile of St. Mark's in Venice made this 1893 building the world's tallest. The clock's four faces are each three stories high, and their minute hands weigh half a ton each.

Gramercy Park

A WROUGHT-IRON FENCE encloses the tranquil, leafy grounds of Gramercy Park, the only private park in New York City. The beautifully planted 2-acre park, designed by developer Samuel B. Ruggles, dates from 1831, and is flanked by grand examples of early-19th-century architecture and permeated with the character of its many celebrated occupants.

When Ruggles bought the property it was a swamp known as "Krom Moerasje" (little crooked swamp) named by the Dutch settlers. He drained the swamp, and set aside 42 lots for a park to be accessible exclusively to those who bought the surrounding lots in his planned London-style residential square. The park is still owned by the lucky and affluent residents of the surrounding square, although residents of neighboring blocks can now buy visiting privileges.

In 1966 the New York City Landmarks Preservation Commission designated Gramercy Park a historic district. A stroll around Gramercy Park today is a stroll down New York's memory lane. Each building on the square is interesting in its own way. Be sure to stop at the following:

No. 2, the redbrick house at the corner of Gramercy Park West and 20th Street, dates to 1843 and is an example of the earliest houses built

here. The original house would have also included a wrought-iron veranda like that of its 1847 neighbors, **Nos. 3 and 4.** James Harper, founder of Harper Publishing House and former mayor of New York, lived at No. 4 from 1847 to 1869.

No. 15 was once home to Samuel Tilden, governor of New York. It was designed by Calvert Vaux in Gothic Revival brownstone with black granite trim and included a secret passageway to 19th Street so Tilden could escape his political enemies. It is now home to the 100-year-old National Arts Club, founded to support American artists.

Next door at **No. 16** Gramercy Park South lived the actor Edwin Booth, perhaps most famous for being brother to Lincoln's assassin. In 1888 he turned his Gothic-trim home into the Players, a clubhouse for actors and theatrical types, who were not welcome in regular society. A bronze statue of Edwin Booth as Hamlet has pride of place inside the park.

Other notables include the School of Visual Arts at **No. 17,** which occupies the former home of Joseph Pulitzer; the mock-Tudor at **No. 38** was home to John Steinbeck from 1925 to 1926 when he struggled as a reporter for a New York newspaper, and **No. 52** is home to the charming 1920s Gramercy Park Hotel.

The clock chimes on the quarter hour. A skywalk over East 24th Street links the main building to its more austere sibling. The art deco loggias have attracted many film crews—the building has appeared in such films as *After Hours, Radio Days,* and *The Fisher King.* ✉ *1 Madison Ave., between E. 23rd and E. 24th Sts., Flatiron District* Ⓜ *Subway: R, W, 6 to 23rd St.*

New York Life Insurance Company Building. Cass Gilbert, better known for the Woolworth Building, capped this 1928 building with a gilded octagonal spire that is stunning when illuminated. The soaring lobby's coffered ceilings and ornate bronze gates are equally grand. P. T. Barnum's Hippodrome formerly occupied this site from 1837 to 1889, and after that the original Madison Square Garden (designed by Stanford White) from 1890 to 1925. ☒ *51 Madison Ave., between E. 26th and E. 27th Sts., Flatiron District* Ⓜ *Subway: N, R to 28th St.*

Sniffen Court. Just two blocks from the Morgan Library, the 10 brick Romanesque Revival former carriage houses that line this easily overlooked cul-de-sac were built in 1863–64 on a small court perpendicular to E. 36th Street. Peer through the locked gate to see the plaques of Greek horsemen hanging on the rear wall at the end of the flagstone-paved alley. These were created by sculptor and former Sniffen-Court resident Malvina Hoffman. The cover of The Doors album *Strange Days* was shot here. ☒ *150–158 E. 36th St., between Lexington and 3rd Aves., Murray Hill.*

HERE'S WHERE On September 5, 1882, more than 10,000 New York City union workers took an unpaid day off to march from City Hall to Union Square in the city's first Labor Day parade. The day was celebrated with picnics, speeches, and concerts. Twelve years later Congress passed an act making the first Monday in September a legal holiday to celebrate workers.

6

Union Square. A park, farmers' market, meeting place, and site of rallies and demonstrations, this pocket of green space is in the center of a bustling residential and commercial neighborhood. The name "Union" originally signified that two main roads—Broadway and 4th Avenue—crossed here, but it took on a different meaning in the late 19th and early 20th centuries, when the square became a rallying spot for labor protests; many unions, as well as fringe political parties, moved their headquarters nearby. After the terrorist attacks on September 11, 2001, the park became the city's primary gathering point for memorial services. Since then, many anti-Bush groups have led their public campaigns here. Statues in the park include one of George Washington (1856, Henry Kirke Brown) at the north end, Abraham Lincoln (1866, Henry Kirke Brown), and the Marquis de Lafayette (1875, Frederic Auguste Bartholdi, who also sculpted the Statue of Liberty). A statue of Gandhi (1986, Kantilal B. Patel), usually wreathed with flowers, is surrounded by plantings in the southwest corner of the park.

Union Square is at its best on Monday, Wednesday, Friday, and Saturday (8–6), when the largest of the city's 28 **green markets** brings farmers and food purveyors from Long Island and upstate New York. Browse the stands of fruit and vegetables, flowers, plants, fresh-baked pies and breads, cheeses, cider, New York State wines, and fish and meat. Between Thanksgiving and Christmas, red-and-white striped artisan tents (☉ Daily 11–8) set up on the square's southwest end, selling many unique gift items.

So Much Fun It's Scary!

ALL THINGS WEIRD AND
WONDERFUL, ALL CREATURES
GREAT AND SQUALL, ALL THINGS
WITTY AND FANTASTICAL, NEW
YORK CITY HAS THEM ALL—and on
All Hallows' Eve they are freaking
through the streets in New York's
Halloween parade. White-sheeted
ghouls feel duller than dead as
fishnets and leathers, sequins and
feathers pose and prance along 6th
Avenue in this vibrant display of vanity
and insanity.

In 1973, mask maker and puppeteer
Ralph Lee paraded his puppets from
house to house visiting friends and
family along the winding streets of his
Greenwich Village neighborhood. His
merry march quickly outgrew its
original, intimate route and now,
decades later it parades up 6th
Avenue, from Spring Street to 22nd
Street, attracting 50,000 creatively
costumed exhibitionists, artists,
dancers, musicians, hundreds of
enormous puppets, and more than 2
million spectators. Anyone with a

costume can join in, no advance
registration required, although the
enthusiastic interaction between
participants and spectators makes it
as much fun to just watch.

The parade lines up in front of the
HERE Arts Center on 6th Avenue and
Spring Street from 6:30 PM to 8 PM; the
walk itself starts at 7 PM, but it takes
about two hours to leave the staging
area. Get here a few hours early.
Costumes are usually handmade,
clever, and outrageous, and revelers
are happy to strike a pose. The streets
are crowded along the route, with the
most congestion below 14th Street.
You can avoid the crush and take the
subway to 23rd Street and walk south
to find a good vantage point. Of
course the best way to truly
experience the parade is to march—if
you're not feeling the facepaint, you
can volunteer to help carry the
puppets. For information, contact
⊕ www.halloween-nyc.com

– Jacinta O'Halloran

On the north end, the park's 1932 pavilion is flanked by playgrounds
and **Luna Park** (⊠ 1 Union Sq. E ☎ 212/475–8464), an open-air restaurant open from mid-May through October.

New York University dormitories, movie theaters, and cavernous commercial spaces occupy the handsomely restored 19th-century commercial buildings that surround the park. The run of diverse and imaginative
architectural styles on the building at 33 Union Square West (the former name, the **Decker Building,** which is visible above the second floor's
incised decoration) is, indeed, "fabulous"—it was the home of Andy
Warhol's second Factory studio. The redbrick and white-stone **Century
Building** (⊠ 33 E. 17th St., Flatiron District), built in 1881, on the square's
north side, is now a Barnes & Noble bookstore, which has preserved
the building's original cast-iron columns and other architectural details.
The building at 17th Street and Union Square East, now housing the
New York Film Academy and the Union Square Theatre, was the final
home of **Tammany Hall.** This organization, famous in its day as a corrupt and powerful political machine, moved here just at the height of

its power in 1929, but by 1943 it went bankrupt and had to sell the building. A block south on Union Square East is the former U.S. Savings Bank, now the Daryl Roth Theater.

The southern block is dominated by **The Metronome,** a public artwork and abstract timepiece displayed on the exterior wall of the Virgin Records superstore. The 15 digits display time coming and going relative to midnight. Read time going, from left to right and time coming, from right to left. The center three digits count fractions of seconds to reflect the frantic pace and energy of the city. ⊠ *E. 14th to E. 17th Sts. between Broadway and Park Ave. S, Flatiron District* Ⓜ *Subway: N, Q, R, W, 4, 5, 6 to Union Sq./14th St.*

Union Square At a Glance

SIGHTS
Appellate Division Court-
    house
B. Altman Building/New
    York Public Library–
    Science, Industry, and
    Business Library (SIBL)
Church of the Incarnation
Church of the
    Transfiguration
Empire State Building
Flatiron Building
Marble Collegiate Church
Metropolitan Life
    Insurance Company
    Tower
New York Life Insurance
    Company Building
Sniffen Court
MUSEUMS & GALLERIES
    (⇨Ch. 14)
Morgan Library
Museum of Sex
PARKS & GARDENS
Gramercy Park
Madison Square Park
Union Square
WHERE TO EAT (⇨Ch. 18)
BUDGET DINING
Blue Smoke
Cho Dang Gol
City Bakery
Eisenberg's Sandwich
    Shop
Gahm Mi Oak
Hangawi
Kang Suh
Le Pain Quotidien
Mandoo Bar
Republic
Turkish Kitchen
MODERATE DINING
Artisanal
Beppe

BLT Fish
Blue Water Grill
Bolo
Craft
Dévi
Dos Caminos
Eleven Madison Park
I Trulli
Kitchen 22
Les Halles
Olives
Tamarind
Union Square Cafe
EXPENSIVE DINING
Fleur de Sel
Gramercy Tavern
Tabla
Veritas
WHERE TO STAY (⇨Ch. 19)
BUDGET LODGING
Carlton Arms
The Gershwin Hotel
Herald Square Hotel
Red Roof Inn
Thirty Thirty Hotel
Wolcott Hotel
MODERATE LODGING
Carlton on Madison
    Avenue
Hotel Giraffe
The Inn at Irving Place
Jolly Hotel Madison
    Towers
The Kitano
Morgans
Park South Hotel
Roger Williams Hotel
70 Park Avenue
EXPENSIVE LODGING
W New York–The Court
    and W New York–The
    Tuscany
W New York Union
    Square

BARS & NIGHTLIFE
    (⇨Ch. 16)
Cibar, *bar*
Gotham Comedy Club,
    comedy club
Irving Plaza, *rock club*
Jazz Standard, *jazz club*
Luna Park, *bar*
Old Town Bar & Restau-
    rant, *bar*
Pete's Tavern, *bar*
ARTS & ENTERTAINMENT
    (⇨Ch. 15)
Vineyard Theatre,
    theater
SHOPPING (⇨Ch. 17)
BOOKS
The Complete Traveller
    Antiquarian Bookstore
CLOTHING
Paul Smith
Pookie & Sebastian
Space Kiddets
Sude
HOME DECOR
ABC Carpet & Home
JEWELRY
Beads of Paradise
PERFUME/COSMETICS
Jo Malone
SPORTING GOODS
Paragon Sporting
    Goods
TOYS
Compleat Strategist
Kidding Around
WINE
Union Square Wine &
    Spirits

Midtown

INCLUDING TIMES SQUARE &
ROCKEFELLER CENTER

WORD OF MOUTH

"[Grand Central's] main concourse nearly took my breath away. The breadth of the space, the busy New Yorkers rushing by, and— oh my!—that ceiling. And it doesn't end there. You can have a drink at this amazing hideaway called Campbell Apartment, or check out the gourmet food market."   —Lillie

"I love the energy of Times Square. Love the Broadway theatres being just steps away. Even like the kitschy gift shops. It just 'feels' like NYC to me."   —starrsville

Sightseeing
★ ★ ★ ★ ★

Nightlife
★ ★

Dining
★ ★ ★ ★

Lodging
★ ★ ★ ★ ★

Shopping
★ ★ ★ ★ ★

Midtown is the heart of New York City—the center of commerce, media, shopping, transportation, tourism. It's what most people think of when they think of the city. It's a vibrant area known as much for its nose-to-the-grindstone business ethic and its shop-till-you-drop appeal. Per square foot, Midtown has more major landmarks—Grand Central Terminal, Rockefeller Center, Times Square, and the United Nations—than any other part of the city.

Rockefeller Center is in almost every movie filmed here, 5th Avenue is probably the best-known shopping street in the world, Grand Central is not only a commuter hub but an exquisitely beautiful building with its own diversions, and speaking of buildings, architecture buffs won't know where to look first. And the justifiably renowned Museum of Modern Art, along with several other museums, is here. Whirling in a chaos of flashing lights, honking horns, and shoulder-to-shoulder crowds, Times Square is the most frenetic part of New York City. Hordes of people arrive every hour by subway, bus, car, or on foot, drawn by its undeniable gravitational pull. What brings them here? There's not much to do—no great shopping, comparatively few notable restaurants, and, except when they're raising the curtains in the theaters, a dearth of cultural offerings. Simply put, Times Square is a destination in itself.

If you harbor even the vaguest hope that Times Square is still a showcase for sleazy good times, you'll be disappointed. No longer the epicenter of sin in the world's biggest, baddest city, Times Square has been well scrubbed and sanitized and is geared firmly toward family fun. Perky TV show *Good Morning America* calls the Square home, as does Virgin Records, MTV, Disney, and Toys "R" Us. So do take the kids but make sure to keep an eye (and perhaps a hand) on them lest they get swept away by the crowds.

What's Here

Times Square & Midtown West

At the intersection of 7th Avenue and Broadway, the dazzling billboards of **Times Square** will grab your attention. You'll be mesmerized by its usual high-wattage thunder. At the **Times Square Visitors Center**, on Broadway between 46th and 47th streets, you can pick up a plethora of maps, brochures, discount offers, and sightseeing tickets.

Chances are shopping will top your must-do list. The **Virgin Megastore** on Broadway between 45th and 46th streets claims to be the "world's largest entertainment store." At the Times Square **Toys "R" Us**, kids of all ages can ride the giant indoor Ferris wheel with 14 individually themed cabs, visit a 4,000-square-foot, two-story dollhouse filled with Barbie dolls, and marvel at the 5-ton, 20-foot-high animatronic Jurassic Park T. rex dinosaur that will roar if you get too close.

Those who love Toys "R" Us are likely to be enthralled by the high-tech amusement of **Lazer Park.** On the corner of Broadway and 45th street is the **MTV Studios.** Upstairs is the MTV TRL studio. If you're there around 3 PM you'll see the barricades go up to impose some structure on the hordes of excited teenagers who gather here hoping to catch a glimpse of their favorite singer. Across the street **Planet Hollywood** sells their own pricey clothing and accessories.

Duffy Square, a triangle between West 46th and 47th streets, is best known as the home of the TKTS booth. You can score good seats to some of the hottest Broadway shows for half the going rate. Although people think of Broadway as the heart of the theater scene, few theaters actually line the thoroughfare. To see some of Broadway's grand old dames, head west on 45th Street. Here you can see a bevy of Broadway beauties, including the **Booth,** the **Plymouth,** the **Royale,** the **Music Box,** and the **Imperiale.** Farther down the block is the **Hirschfeld,** renamed in honor of the man whose caricatures of theater graced the pages of the *New York Times* for decades. On the southern side of 45th Street you can find the pedestrian-only **Shubert Alley,** distinguished by colorful posters advertising the latest hit plays and musicals. Its name is no mystery, as Schubert Alley takes you to one of Broadway's most lustrous gems, the **Shubert Theater.** Head west along 44th Street to see its neighbors, the **Helen Hayes,** the **Broadhurst,** the **Majestic,** and the **St. James.** Tucked among them, at No. 243, is **Sardi's,** the legendary Broadway watering hole.

Down on 42nd Street is **Madame Tussaud's New York,** where you can see life-size wax figures of famous and infamous folks. If you have the slightest interest in the fine art of photos, you'll want to visit the **International Center of Photography.** Both a museum and one of the largest schools of photography in the world, ICP consistently presents extraordinary exhibitions of photography. Farther west, the *Intrepid* **Sea-Air-Space Museum** is docked in the Hudson River. Formerly the USS *Intrepid,* this 900-foot aircraft carrier is serving out its retirement as the centerpiece of Manhattan's only floating museum.

GETTING ORIENTED

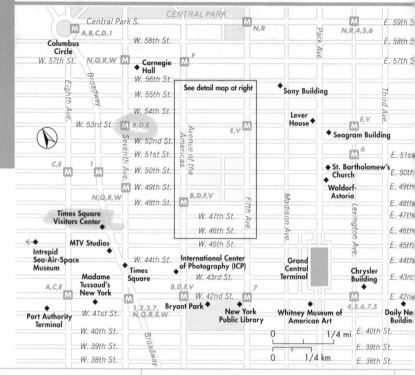

TOP 5	QUICK BITES

■ Strolling through Times Square

■ The skyscrapers of Rockefeller Center

■ The Museum of Modern Art

■ Walking up 5th Avenue

■ The hustle and bustle inside Grand Central

With its myriad food selections, the dining concourse of **Grand Central Terminal** (⊠ E. 42nd St., at Park Ave., Midtown East ☎ 212/935–3960) is a great place to stop for everything from sushi to a piece of Junior's cheesecake.

Café St. Bart's, (⊠ Park Ave. and E. 50th St., Midtown East ☎ 212/888–2664), in the courtyard of St. Bartholomew's Church, is a charming and tranquil indoor/outdoor spot for a relatively inexpensive meal or drink.

If you want to eat in view of the skaters in **Rockefeller Center** (⊠ 30 Rockefeller Plaza, between W. 49th St. and W. 50th St., Midtown West ☎ 212/332–8800) but don't want anything fancy, head downstairs and follow signs to the concourse and skating rink, pick up a slice of Louisiana-inspired pizza at **Two Boots** or a sandwich at **Cucina & Co.,** and snag a table. There are public restrooms nearby.

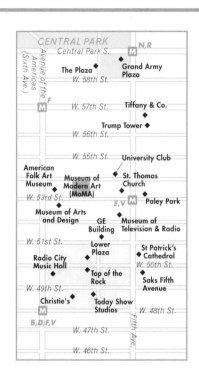

7

GETTING HERE

You can get to Midtown via all subways; many make numerous stops throughout the area. The B, D, F, and V trains serve Rockefeller Center and 42nd Street. The 1, 2, 3, A, C, E, N, R, Q, W serve Times Square and West 42nd Street. The 4, 5, 6 take you to Grand Central.

MAKING THE MOST OF YOUR TIME

Midtown is the busiest area of the city. Packed with so many sights and activities, a visit to Midtown could consume your entire trip. On weekdays, you'll share space with locals, most of whom work in the area, but on the weekends, the area is filled with people from all over the world. The best time to visit is during the week, when there are shorter lines for museums and attractions, and theater and dinner reservations are a little easier to get. Expect to be jostled on the crowded sidewalks if you stand still too long.

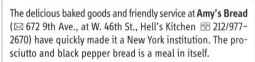

The delicious baked goods and friendly service at **Amy's Bread** (✉ 672 9th Ave., at W. 46th St., Hell's Kitchen ☎ 212/977-2670) have quickly made it a New York institution. The prosciutto and black pepper bread is a meal in itself.

Less than a block from Times Square, **Café Un Deux Trois** (✉ 123 W. 44th St., at 6th Ave., Midtown West ☎ 212/354-6984) serves up a tasty croque monsieur. The Parisian-style bistro is open until midnight, making it a great place to go after a show.

Absolutely the best pizza in the neighborhood, **John's Pizzeria** (✉ 260 W. 44th St., between 7th and 8th Aves., Midtown West ☎ 212/582-8065) is an outpost of the famed John's Pizzeria of Greenwich Village, a New York institution.

In the Edison Hotel, **Edison Cafe** (✉ 228 W. 47th St., between Broadway and 8th Aves., Midtown West ☎ 212/840-5000) is often the choice of neighborhood locals. The price is right—$5–$10 for deli sandwiches and other classic fare.

Some of the most interesting sites in this neighborhood are outside of Times Square proper. **Hell's Kitchen** stretches from West 30th to 59th streets, between the Hudson River and 8th Avenue. On 9th Avenue, you'll find a vast assortment of ethnic cafés, restaurants, and groceries. Argentina, Brazil, Indonesia, and Sri Lanka are just some of the countries represented.

Rockefeller Center & Midtown East

A complex of businesses and attractions and a capital of the communications industry, **Rockefeller Center** has 49 shops, 28 restaurants, 1.4 million square feet of office space, NBC studios, Radio City Music Hall, in winter a skating rink and the world's largest decorated Christmas tree (up the end of November through early January), Christie's auction house, and Top of the Rock in an area that stretches from 47th and 52nd streets between 5th and 7th avenues.

October through April **Lower Plaza** is home to the world's most famous ice-skating rink, which is dominated by the statue of Prometheus. Its backdrop is the 70-story **GE Building**, originally known as the RCA Building (1934). On the right behind the front desk is the former location of a fresco by Diego Rivera, but it was torn down when he wouldn't remove an image of Lenin. On the 65th floor, the elegant **Rainbow Room** has a beautiful view of the city. The observation deck at **Top of the Rock** gives great 360-degree views from both indoor and outdoor areas on the 69th and 70th floors of 30 Rockefeller Plaza. Its timed tickets and central location are big pluses over the Empire State Building's observatory.

The GE Building is home to NBC, but its most famous studio is the **Today Show studio,** which attracts people every morning who hope to get their mugs on national TV. Next door is **Christie's,** where a triple-height entranceway with a mural by Sol LeWitt welcomes you to this famous auction house. One of the most important pieces of art deco architecture, **Radio City Music Hall** has a pink-and-blue neon sign. By West 52nd Street you've left Rockefeller's realm, but yet another communications company made sure its headquarters, the towering black **CBS Building,** stood nearby.

Other attractions in this area include the former speakeasy the **'21' Club,** with its row of jockeys out front; the **Museum of Television & Radio,** as cutting edge as its neighbor is old-fashioned; and on 53rd Street, the **Museum of Arts & Design,** the **American Folk Art Museum,** and a museum whose building is a masterpiece in its own right, the **Museum of Modern Art (MoMA).**

Architecture buffs won't be able to get enough of this part of the city, as it holds examples of every architectural style of the 20th century. The Beaux-Arts **Grand Central Terminal** is one of the city's architectural masterpieces, with a marble floor and staircases, gold chandeliers, and its ceiling now more clearly showcasing an astronomical mural complete with twinkling stars. Inside are destination restaurants like the **Oyster Bar** and **Michael Jordan's The Steakhouse NYC,** bars in the restaurants as well as the little gem the **Campbell Apartment,** a dining concourse, and shops. Nearby is the free **Whitney Museum of American Art at Altria.**

Behind another Beaux-Arts gem, the **New York Public Library (NYPL) Humanities and Social Sciences Library,** is idyllic **Bryant Park.** In the block east of the Whitney there are three architecturally interesting buildings: the Satellite Airlines Terminal, Cipriani, and the Chanin Building. One of the city's tabloids was produced until 1995 in the art deco *Daily News* **Building.** At 42nd and Lexington is the skyscraper many New Yorkers name as their favorite: the art deco **Chrysler Building.**

The modern **Ford Foundation Building** encloses a 160-foot-high, ⅓-acre greenhouse that is open to the public. **Tudor City,** a self-contained complex of a dozen mostly residential buildings with half-timbering and stained glass, encompasses small gardens and playgrounds and a well-regarded Italian restaurant, **L'Impero.** The international-style **United Nations Headquarters** is where the world comes to discuss its problems.

The art deco **Waldorf-Astoria** on Park Avenue is interesting to wander through and **St. Bartholomew's Church** has a pleasant outdoor café in warm weather. Two prime examples of International Style architecture that were pivotal in the history of modern architecture are the **Seagram Building,** the only New York building designed by Ludwig Mies van der Rohe, and **Lever House.** At 560 Madison, you'll recognize the **Sony Building** from its cut-out top and rose-hued granite.

Fifth Avenue & 57th Street

Fifth Avenue's gilt-edged character has been tarnished a bit as mass-market stores such as **H & M** and the **Disney Store** have moved in, but it's still some of the most expensive real estate in the world and you'll still find refined stores such as Bergdorf Goodman and Tiffany & Co.

Across the street from Rockefeller Center's Channel Gardens, **Saks Fifth Avenue** is the flagship of this national chain. An elegant emporium, it helped define the modern department store. Across East 50th Street is the Gothic-style Roman Catholic **St. Patrick's Cathedral. Cartier** displays its wares in a jewel-box turn-of-the-20th-century mansion on the southeast corner of 52nd Street and 5th Avenue. Past **Ferragamo** and **Rolex** and before **Bulgari** and **Dunhill** are two noteworthy churches—**St. Thomas Church** and the 1875 **Fifth Avenue Presbyterian Church**—and the striking **University Club.**

Trump Tower, on the next block between East 56th and 57th streets, is an apartment and office building named for its self-promoting developer, Donald Trump. At 57th Street is **Tiffany & Co.,** which Audrey Hepburn helped make famous in the 1961 movie *Breakfast at Tiffany.* Competitors such as **Fourtonoff, Mikimoto, Bulgari, Piaget,** and **Van Cleef & Arpels** are all lined up on this stretch of 5th Avenue, tempting passersby with their glittering wares. Those with a little time who want to save a hunk of change visit the **Diamond District,** on 47th Street between 5th and 6th Avenues.

East on 57th Street is a stellar lineup of boutiques including **Burberry, Chanel,** and **Yves St. Laurent.** The white-glass building that's home to Christian Dior lends a lighthearted elegance to the block. Tourneau (12 E. 57th St.) is the place to go if you're in the market for a watch. The two **Bergdorf Goodman** stores flank 5th Avenue: women's on the west side of the avenue between 57th and 58th streets, and men's on the east side at 58th Street.

Grand Army Plaza is the open space along 5th Avenue between 58th and 60th streets, across from **The Plaza,** which is due to reopen in 2007 with condos, upscale retailers, and some remaining hotel rooms. On the east side of 5th Avenue at 58th Street is **F.A.O. Schwarz,** a toy emporium for kids of all ages. West on 57th Street you'll pass the **Rizzoli Bookstore,** with a neoclassical-inspired ceiling as elegant as the art books it carries. Across 6th Avenue, you'll know you're in classical-music territory when you peer through the showroom windows at **Steinway & Sons.** Presiding over the southeast corner of 7th Avenue and West 57th Street, **Carnegie Hall** has for decades reigned as a premier international concert hall.

Places to Explore

Beekman Place. This secluded and exclusive two-block-long East Side enclave has an aura of imperturbable calm. Residents of its elegant town houses have included the Rockefellers; Alfred Lunt and Lynn Fontanne; Ethel Barrymore; Irving Berlin; and, of course, Auntie Mame, a character in the well-known Patrick Dennis play (and later movie) of the same name. Steps at East 51st Street lead to an esplanade along the East River. ⊠ *East of 1st Ave. between E. 49th and E. 51st Sts., Midtown East* Ⓜ *Subway: 6 to 51st St./Lexington Ave.; E, V to Lexington–3rd Aves./53rd St.*

☼ **Bryant Park.** Midtown's only major green space has become one of the best-loved and most beautiful small parks in the city. Named for the poet and editor William Cullen Bryant (1794–1878), who sits under a dome at the park's eastern edge, the 8-acre park is filled with London plane trees and formal flower beds, which line the perimeter of its central lawn. In temperate months the park draws thousands of lunching office workers, or even people at work: how-to guides on-site let you know how to log on to the park's wireless network. Four kiosks in the park sell everything from sandwiches to egg creams. In summer, you can check out live jazz and comedy concerts and free outdoor film screenings on Monday at dusk. At the east side of the park, near a squatting bronze cast of Gertrude Stein, is the open-air Bryant Park Café, which is open April 15–October 15, and the stylish Bryant Park Grill, which has a rooftop garden. In February and early September giant white tents spring up here for the New York fashion shows. On the south side of the park is an old-fashioned **carousel** (▨ $1.75) where kids can ride fanciful rabbits and frogs instead of horses. Come late October, the park rolls out the artificial and frozen "**pond**" (☉ Late Oct.–mid-Jan., daily 8 AM–10:30 PM) for ice-skating. Rental for skates and locker will run you $12.50. Surrounding the ice rink are the Christmas market–like stalls of **The Holiday Shops** (☉ Late Nov.–Jan. 1), selling handcrafted and designer goods from around the world. ⊠ *6th Ave. between W. 40th and W. 42nd Sts., Midtown West* ☏ *212/768–4242* ⊕ *www.bryantpark. org* ☉ *Oct.–Apr., daily 7–7; May–Sept., weekdays 7 AM–8 PM, weekends 7 AM–11 PM* Ⓜ *Subway: B, D, F, V to 42nd St.; 7 to 5th Ave.*

★ **Chrysler Building.** An art deco masterpiece designed by William Van Alen and built between 1928 and 1930, the Chrysler Building is one of New York's most iconic and beloved skyscrapers. It's at its best at dusk,

The Great Bright Way

PUT ON YOUR SUNGLASSES —Times Square is dazzling. The city requires signs here to have a minimum "LUTS" rating (Light Unit Times Square) 1½ times brighter than that of the average illuminated billboard. That, combined with the shadows cast by NYC's tall buildings, ensures you'll notice the signs whether you visit at noon or midnight.

It was O. J. Gude, aka "The Botticelli of Broadway," who first coined the phrase "The Great White Way" in reference to the bright lights of Times Square signs. Gude was the first to figure out that Times Square was the perfect spot for big, illuminated signs, or "spectaculars," as they've been called since he started erecting them here at the crossroads of the world in 1917.

Gude put up some dazzling spectaculars during the 1920s—block-long tanks of bubble-blowing fish, 200-foot-high spouting fountains, a 50-foot woman who regularly got caught in gale-force winds. But mid-20th-century crowds were evidently easier to amuse. All it took to draw eyes was a steaming coffee cup (A & P, 1933) or the big poster of the nicotine-loving man who blew 10-foot smoke rings every four seconds (the Camel sign, 1941–1966).

The famous news "Zipper" still circles 1 Times Square as it has since the 1920s, but its been joined by big-screen TVs, animations, fiber optics and light-emitting-diode (LED) technology. Compare the Zipper to the one at 3 Times Square by Reuters, which cost more than $20 million to create and debuted in 2001. A reporter can upload news or photos from anywhere in the world and in less than 90 seconds it can be on display in Times Square. The Reuters sign can also interact with viewers. Recent advertising campaigns have included trivia contests (dial in on your cell phone to answer) and live action games (use your cell phone as a game controller).

The city allows these bodacious billboards only in Times Square, and the space outside the buildings is prime real estate. One Times Square has one tenant, the Warner Bros. store on the first three floors. The other 19 floors are vacant, but the building brings in 26 monthly checks ranging from $40,000 to $250,000, compliments of its illuminated outdoor tenants.

when the stainless-steel spires reflect the sunset, and at night, when its illuminated geometric design looks like the backdrop to a Hollywood musical. The Chrysler Corporation moved out in the mid-1950s, but the building retains its name and many automotive details: gargoyles shaped like car-hood ornaments sprout from the building's upper stories—wings from the 31st floor, eagle heads from the 61st. At 1,048 feet, the building held the world's-tallest title for 40 days before the Empire State Building snatched it away. The Chrysler Building has no observation deck, but the dark lobby with red Moroccan marble walls and yellow Siena marble floors is worth a visit; the ceiling mural salutes transportation and human endeavor. The 32 Otis elevators are each lined with a different inlay of wood, each from a different part of the world.

Rockefeller vs. Rivera

AS ROCKEFELLER CENTER NEARED COMPLETION in 1932, John D. Rockefeller Jr. still needed a mural to grace the lobby of the main building. As was the industrialist's taste, the subject of the 63-foot-by-17-foot mural was to be grandiose: "human intelligence in control of the forces of nature." He hired an artist known for his grand vision, Mexican painter Diego Rivera.

With its depiction of massive machinery moving mankind forward, Rivera's *Man at the Crossroads* seemed exactly what Rockefeller wanted. Everything was going fine until someone noticed that near the center of the mural was a portrait of Soviet Premier Vladimir Lenin surrounded by red-kerchiefed workers. Rockefeller, who was building what was essentially a monument to capitalism, was clearly disappointed. When Rivera was accused of willful propagandizing, the artist famously replied that "All art is propaganda."

Rivera refused to remove the offending portrait (although, as an olive branch, he did offer to add an image of Abraham Lincoln). In early 1934, as Rivera was working on the unfinished work, representatives for Rockefeller informed him that his services were no longer required. Within a half hour tar paper had been hung over the mural. Despite negotiations to move it to the Museum of Modern Art, Rockefeller was determined to get rid of the mural once and for all. Not content to have it painted over, he ordered ax-wielding workers to chip away the entire wall.

Rockefeller ordered the mural replaced by a less offensive one by José María Sert. (This one, interestingly enough, did include Lincoln.) But Rivera had the last word. He re-created the mural in the Palacio de Bellas Artes in Mexico City, adding a portrait of Rockefeller among the champagne-swilling swells ignoring the plight of the workers.

⊠ *405 Lexington Ave., at E. 42nd St., Midtown East* Ⓜ *Subway: 4, 5, 6, 7, S to 42nd St./Grand Central.*

Ⓢ *Daily News* **Building.** This Raymond Hood–designed art deco and modernist tower (1930) has strong vertical lines that make it seem loftier than its 37 stories. The newspaper moved in 1995, but the illuminated, 12-foot-wide globe set into a sunken space beneath a black glass dome in the lobby continues to revolve. The floor is laid out like a gigantic compass, with bronze lines indicating mileage from New York to international destinations. ⊠ *220 E. 42nd St., between 2nd and 3rd Aves., Midtown East* Ⓜ *Subway: 4, 5, 6, 7, S to 42nd St./Grand Central.*

GE Building. This 70-story (850-foot-tall) art deco tower, the tallest building in Rockefeller Center, was known as the RCA Building until 1986, when GE acquired its namesake company. (GE also affixed its logo to the top, which many New Yorkers agree ruins its graceful lines.) Inside the lobby is a monumental mural by José María Sert, *American Progress.* Sert's 1937 mural depicts the muses of poetry, dance, and music along with those of science, technology, and physical effort. A standing

Abraham Lincoln (representing action) and seated Ralph Waldo Emerson (representing thought) are at the center of Sert's mural. Sert's work replaced that of Diego Rivera, which Rockefeller had destroyed because it centered around the likeness of Communist leader Vladimir Lenin. Additional murals by Sert, and by Frank Brangwyn, an English artist, are on the north and south corridors of the lobby.

Today the building also known as 30 Rock is the headquarters of the NBC television network. The two-level, monitor-spiked NBC Experience Store, in the southeast corner of the GE Building, is the departure point for 70-minute tours of the **NBC Studios.** Ticket information for other NBC shows is available here as well. There are also tours of Rockefeller Center, but these don't take you anywhere you can't explore on your own. ✉ *30 Rockefeller Plaza, between 5th and 6th Aves. at 48th St., Midtown West* ☎ *212/664–7174* 💲 *Tour $18* ☞ *Children under 6 not permitted* ☉ *Tours depart from NBC Experience Store at street level of GE Bldg. every 15 mins Mon.–Sat. 8:30–5:30, Sun. 9:30–4:30* Ⓜ *Subway: B, D, F, V to 47th–50th Sts./Rockefeller Center.*

Marble-lined corridors beneath the GE Building house restaurants in all price ranges, from the high-end Sea Grill to sushi and sandwich bars and kid-friendly pizza parlors as well as numerous shops, a post office, and clean public restrooms (a rarity in Midtown). To find your way around the concourse, consult the strategically placed directories or obtain the free "Rockefeller Center Visitor's Guide" at the **information desk** inside the main entrance. ✉ *Bounded by Rockefeller Plaza, 6th Ave., and 49th and 50th Sts., Midtown West* ☎ *212/332–6868* ⊕ *www. rockefellercenter.com* Ⓜ *Subway: B, D, F, V to 47th–50th Sts./Rockefeller Center.*

Fodor'sChoice
★

Grand Central Terminal. Grand Central is not only the world's largest (76 acres) and the nation's busiest (500,000 commuters and subway riders use it daily) railway station, but also one of the world's greatest public spaces, "justly famous," as critic Tony Hiss noted, "as a crossroads, a noble building . . . and an ingenious piece of engineering." A massive four-year renovation completed in October 1998 restored the 1913 landmark to its original splendor—and then some.

The south side of East 42nd Street is the best vantage point from which to admire Grand Central's dramatic Beaux-Arts facade, which is dominated by three 75-foot-high arched windows separated by pairs of fluted columns. At the top are a graceful clock and a crowning sculpture, *Transportation,* which depicts Mercury flanked by Hercules and Minerva. The facade is particularly beautiful at night when bathed in golden light. Doors on East 42nd Street lead past gleaming gold- and nickel-plated chandeliers to the cavernous **main concourse.** This majestic space is 200 feet long, 120 feet wide, and 120 feet—roughly 12 stories—high. Overhead, a celestial map of the zodiac constellations covers the robin's egg–blue ceiling (the major stars actually twinkle with fiber-optic lights). A marble staircase modeled after the Garnier stair at the Paris Opera is on the concourse's east end. Climb it to reach Metrazur restaurant. From this perch you can look across the concourse to the

Art for Art's Sake

THE MOSAICS, MURALS, AND SCULPTURES that grace Rockefeller Center—many of them considered art deco masterpieces—were all part of the plan of John D. Rockefeller Jr. In 1932, as the steel girders on the first of the buildings were heading heavenward, Rockefeller put together a team of advisers to find artists who could make the project "as beautiful as possible." More than 50 artists were commissioned for 200 individual works.

Some artists scoffed at the idea of decorating an office building. Picasso declined to meet with Rockefeller to discuss the project, and Matisse replied that busy business executives would not be in the "quiet and reflective state of mind" necessary to appreciate his art. And some of those who agreed to contribute, including muralists Diego Rivera and José María Sert, were not popular with the public. A group of American artists protested Rockefeller's decision to hire these "alien" artists.

The largest of the original artworks installed at Rockefeller Center, Lee Lawrie's 2-ton sculpture *Atlas*, was controversial because it was said to resemble Italy's fascist dictator, Benito Mussolini. The sculpture, depicting a muscle-bound man holding up the world, drew protests in 1936. Some even derided Paul Manship's golden *Prometheus*, which soars over the ice-skating rink, when it was unveiled the same year. Both are now considered to be among the best public artworks of the 20th century.

Lawrie's sculpture *Wisdom*, perched over the main entrance of 20 Rockefeller Plaza, is another of the gems of Rockefeller Center. Also look for Isamu Noguchi's stainless-steel plaque *News* over the entrance of the Bank of America Building at 50 Rockefeller Plaza and Attilio Piccirilli's 2-ton glass-block panel called *Youth Leading Industry* over the entrance of the International Building. René Chambellan's bronze dolphins in the fountains of the Channel Gardens are also crowd-pleasers.

---

top of the opposite staircase, where diners treat themselves to either Cipriani Dolci or the mahogany-and-leather setting of Michael Jordan's Steak House. Beyond those two restaurants to the left you can find the Campbell Apartment, an extremely comfortable and stylish cocktail and cigar bar in what was once the private office and salon of John W. Campbell, a well-known tycoon from the 1920s through the 1940s.

The Grand Central Market on the east end of the main floor (a street entrance is on Lexington Avenue and East 43rd Street) is a great place to buy fresh fruit, fish, dairy goods, sweets, and breads. Dozens of restaurants (including the historic Oyster Bar, opened the same year as Grand Central Terminal, with vaulted ceilings covered with Guastavino tiles) make the downstairs **Dining Concourse** a destination in its own right.

Despite all its grandeur, Grand Central still functions primarily as a railroad station. Underground, more than 60 ingeniously integrated railroad tracks lead trains upstate and to Connecticut via Metro-North Commuter Rail. The subway connects here as well. The best (and worst) time to visit is at rush hour, when the concourse whirs with the frenzy of commuters dashing every which way. The most popular point for people to meet is at the central information kiosk, topped by a four-faced clock. The **Municipal Art Society** (✉ 457 Madison Ave., Midtown East ☎ 212/935–3960 ⊕ www.mas.org) leads architectural tours of the terminal that begin here on Wednesday at 12:30. A $10 donation is suggested. *Main entrance ✉ E. 42nd St. at Park Ave., Midtown East ☎ 212/935–3960 ⊕ www.grandcentralterminal.com Ⓜ Subway: 4, 5, 6, 7, S to 42nd St./Grand Central.*

Lever House. This gorgeous 1952 skyscraper, built for the Lever Brothers soap company, seems to float above the street and the open plaza. Gordon Bunshaft of Skidmore, Owings & Merrill designed a sheer, slim glass box that rests on the end of a one-story-thick shelf balanced on square chrome columns. Because the International-style tower occupies only half the air space above the lower floors, its side wall reflects a shimmering image of its neighbors. *✉ 390 Park Ave., between E. 53rd and E. 54th Sts., Midtown East Ⓜ Subway: 6 to 51st St./Lexington Ave.; E, V to Lexington–3rd Aves./53rd St.*

A holiday tradition began in 1931 when workers clearing away the rubble for Rockefeller Center erected a 20-foot-tall balsam. It was two years into the Great Depression, and the 4,000 men employed at the site were grateful to finally be away from the unemployment lines. The first official tree-lighting ceremony came in 1933.

Lower Plaza, Rockefeller Center. The gold-leaf statue of the fire-stealing Greek hero **Prometheus,** one of the most famous sights in the complex, floats above the Lower Plaza. A quotation from Aeschylus—PROMETHEUS, TEACHER IN EVERY ART, BROUGHT THE FIRE THAT HATH PROVED TO MORTALS A MEANS TO MIGHTY ENDS—is carved into the red-granite wall behind. The sunken plaza, originally intended to serve as entrance to lower-level retail shops, was a failure until the now-famous ice-skating rink was installed in 1936. Skaters line up October through April, and crowds gather above them on the Esplanade to watch their spins and spills. The rink gives way to an open-air café the rest of the year. Special events and huge pieces of art dominate both plazas during the summer, and in December an enormous twinkling tree towers above. *✉ Between 5th and 6th Aves. and W. 49th and W. 50th Sts., Midtown West ☎ 212/332–7654 for the rink Ⓜ Subway: B, D, F, V to 47th–50th Sts./Rockefeller Center.*

New York Public Library (NYPL) Humanities and Social Sciences Library. This 1911 masterpiece of Beaux-Arts design is one of the great research institutions in the world, with 6 million books, 12 million manuscripts, and 2.8 million pictures. But you don't have to crack a book to make it worth visiting: both inside and out, this awe-inspiring building, a National Historic Landmark, will take your breath away with its opulence. The grand entrance is at 5th Avenue just south of 42nd Street, where a pair of **marble lions** guard a flagstone plaza. Mayor Fiorello La Guardia dubbed them "Patience" and "Fortitude." In good weather you can people-watch from the block-long grand marble staircase or from the chairs and small tables hospitably set out on the plaza.

The library's bronze front doors open into **Astor Hall,** flanked by a sweeping double staircase. Straight ahead is a special exhibit gallery, and to the left down the corridor, a stunning periodicals room with wall paintings of New York publishing houses. Exhibits line the third-floor corridor on the way to the McGraw Rotunda. A large gallery off it features paintings and special exhibits on typography, literature, bookmaking, and maps. Its centerpiece through December 2007 is a Gutenberg Bible (1455). On the same floor, cross through the catalog room to reach the magisterial **Rose Main Reading Room**—297 feet long (almost two full north–south city blocks), 78 feet wide, and just over 51 feet high. Go to the farthest end to best appreciate the original chandeliers, rows of oak tables with bronze reading lamps, and ceiling murals of puffy clouds, inspired by Tiepolo and Tintoretto. In the second-floor corridor overlooking Astor Hall, panels highlight the library's development; it's surprising to see the fortress-like bulk of the site's former reservoir, which was torn down in the 1890s to make way for the library. Free one-hour tours leave Tuesday–Saturday at 11 and 2 from Astor Hall. There are women's rooms on the ground floor and third floor, and a men's room on the third floor. ⊠ *5th Ave. between E. 40th and E. 42nd Sts., Midtown West* ☎ *212/930–0800, 212/869–8089 for exhibit information* ⊕ *www.nypl.org* ☉ *Thurs.–Sat. 10–6, Sun. 1–5, Tues. and Wed. 11–7:30; exhibitions until 6* Ⓜ *Subway: B, D, F, V to 42nd St.*

The Plaza. With Grand Army Plaza, 5th Avenue, *and* Central Park at its doorstep, this world-famous 19-story building claims one of Manhattan's prize real estate corners. A registered historical landmark built in 1907, The Plaza was designed by Henry Hardenbergh, who also built the Dakota apartment building on Central Park West. Here he concocted a birthday-cake effect of highly ornamented white-glazed brick topped with a copper-and-slate mansard roof in French renaissance style. The original hotel was home to Eloise, the fictional star of Kay Thompson's children's books, and has been featured in many movies, including Alfred Hitchcock's *North by Northwest, Plaza Suite,* and *Home Alone 2.* Closed since the end of 2005, The Plaza is scheduled to reopen in fall 2007 after completing an extensive renovation that will result in a multi-use building featuring high-end shops, luxury hotel rooms, and condo hotel units. ⊠ *5th Ave. at W. 59th St., Midtown West* ☎ *212/ 759–3000* Ⓜ *Subway: N, R, W to 5th Ave./59th St.*

★ **St. Bartholomew's Church.** Moviegoers may recognize St. Bart's from *Arthur, The Elf,* and *Maid in Manhattan*; the church has also been featured on TV in *Sex and the City* and *Law & Order.* This handsome 1919 limestone-and-salmon-colored brick church, known to locals as St. Bart's, represents a generation of midtown Park Avenue buildings long since replaced by such modernist landmarks as the Seagram and Lever buildings. The incongruous juxtaposition plays up the church's finest features—a McKim, Mead & White Romanesque triple-arched portal from the congregation's previous (1904) church and the intricately tiled Byzantine dome. St. Bart's sponsors major music events throughout the year, including the summer's Festival of Sacred Music, with full-length masses and other choral works; an annual Christmas concert; and an organ recital series that showcases the church's 12,422-pipe organ, the city's largest. St. Bart's also runs a popular outdoor café. The church has been associated with VIPs in many capacities. ⊠ *109 E. 50th St., at Park Ave., Midtown East* ☎ *212/378–0222, 212/378–0248 for concert information* ⊕ *www.stbarts.org* ⊙ *Daily 8–6* Ⓜ *Subway: 6 to 51st St./Lexington Ave.; E, V to Lexington–3rd Aves./53rd St.*

St. Patrick's Cathedral. This Gothic cathedral is one of the city's largest (seating approximately 2,400) and most striking (note the 330-foot spires) churches. Dedicated to the patron saint of the Irish, the 1859 white marble-and-stone structure by architect James Renwick Jr. was consecrated in 1879. Additions over the years include the archbishop's house and rectory and the intimate Lady Chapel. The original, predominantly Irish, members of the congregation made a statement when they chose the 5th Avenue location for their church: during the week, most of them came to the neighborhood only as employees of the wealthy. But on Sunday, at least, they could claim a prestigious spot for themselves. Among the statues in the alcoves around the nave is a modern depiction of the first American-born saint, Mother Elizabeth Ann Seton. The steps outside the three entrances on 5th Avenue are a convenient, scenic rendezvous spot. Many of the funerals for fallen New York City police and firefighters after 9/11 were held here. ⊠ *5th Ave. between E. 50th and E. 51st Sts., Midtown East* ☎ *212/753–2261 rectory* ⊕ *www. ny-archdiocese.org* ⊙ *Daily 8 AM–8:45 PM* Ⓜ *Subway: E, V to 5th Ave./53rd St.*

Seagram Building. Ludwig Mies van der Rohe, a leading interpreter of International Style architecture, built this simple, boxlike bronze-and-glass tower in 1958. The austere facade belies its wit: I-beams, used to hold buildings up, are here attached to the surface, representing the *idea* of support. The Seagram Building's innovative ground-level plaza, extending out to the sidewalk, has since become a common element in urban skyscraper design. A 52nd Street entrance leads to one of New York's most venerated restaurants, the Four Seasons. Even if you're not dining, peek in to see the Philip Johnson–designed Pool Room (main dining room), a modernist masterpiece. Above the Grill Room's bar hangs a frighteningly sharp sculpture installation. ⊠ *375 Park Ave., between E. 52nd and E. 53rd Sts., Midtown East* ⊡ *Free* ⊙ *Tours Tues. at 3* Ⓜ *Subway: 6 to 51st St./Lexington Ave.; E, V to Lexington–3rd Aves./53rd St.*

⟳ **Sony Building.** Designed by Philip Johnson in 1984, the Sony Building's rose-granite columns and its giant-size Chippendale-style pediment made the skyscraper an instant landmark. The first-floor public arcade is home to electronics stores, a restaurant, a café, and, tables often filled with children and adults playing chess. The four-story **Sony Wonder Technology Lab** (⊠ E. 56th St. entrance between Madison and 5th Aves. ☎ 212/833–8100 ⊕ www.sonywondertechlab.com ⊙ Tues.–Sat. 10–5,

Put It in Your Pocket

WHEN HE WAS RUNNING FOR MAYOR IN 1965, John V. Lindsay came up with an idea that people agreed was a breath of fresh air. With no large tracts of land left in the city, it would have been impossible to build new parks on the scale of Central Park in Manhattan or Prospect Park in Brooklyn. Instead, Lindsay proposed that vacant lots owned by the city be used for "vest-pocket parks." That meant neighborhoods that resembled concrete canyons could have a little bit of green.

After being elected, Lindsay set to work on making these parks a reality. In 1967, the first 10 publicly funded vest-pocket parks were built. Despite the fact that none of them was larger than a quarter of an acre, the puny parks were a huge hit.

At about the same time, privately funded vest-pocket parks began to spring up. This was partly a result of new zoning ordinances that

encouraged buildings to incorporate "public space" into their plans. Other parks were gifts to the city from philanthropists. One of the first privately funded vest-pocket parks was **Paley Park** (⊠ 3 E. 53rd St., between 5th and Madison Aves., Midtown), which opened in 1967. On a sliver of land once occupied by the Stork Club, this swath of green was funded by William Paley, the founder of CBS. More than a dozen honey locust trees and a beautiful water wall keep the park cool even on the hottest days.

Greenacre Park (⊠ 217–221 E. 51st St., between 2nd and 3rd Aves., Midtown) was a gift of John D. Rockefeller's daughter in 1971. She wanted people to experience "some moments of serenity in this busy world." Despite its size, it's a lush landscape. Water cascades over a 25-foot-tall wall at the rear.

Sun. noon–5; last entrance 30 mins before closing) is a carnival of interactive exhibits, including a recording studio, and video-game and TV production studios. Admission is free, but call for a reservation to avoid a line. ⊠ 550 Madison Ave., between E. 55th and E. 56th Sts., Midtown East ☎ Free ☉ Daily 7 AM–11 PM Ⓜ Subway: 6 to 51st St./Lexington Ave.

Top of the Rock. First opened in 1933 and closed since the early 1980s, Rockefeller Center's observation deck reopened at the end of 2005. Arriving just before sunset affords a view of the city that morphs before your eyes into a dazzling array of colors, with a bird's-eye view of the tops of the Empire State Building, the Citicorp Building, and the Chrysler Building, in particular, as well as views northward covering the full expanse of Central Park and southward to the Statue of Liberty. The observation deck, on the 67th–70th floors, includes both indoor and outdoor spaces. Transparent glass-ceilinged elevators bring you into the interior viewing room on the 67th floor. From here, you can take an escalator to the outdoor deck on the 69th floor for views through glass safety panels; the 70th floor is reached by another elevator or by stairs and leads to a 360-degree outdoor panorama of New York City on a deck that is only 20 feet wide and nearly 200 feet long. Reserved-time ticketing eliminates the need to wait in long lines. Indoor multimedia exhibits include films of Rockefeller Center's history as well as a model of the building. Especially interesting is a Plexiglas screen on the floor with footage showing Rock Center construction workers on beams well above the streets; visitors can "walk" across a beam to get a sense of what it might have been like to erect this skyscraper. ⊠ *Entrance on 50th St., between 5th and 6th Aves.* ☎ *877/692–7625 or 212/698–2000* ⊕ *www.topoftherocknyc.com* ✆ *$17* ☉ *Daily 8:30–midnight; last elevator at 11:30 PM.*

FRUGAL FUN

Have kids in tow? The free **Sony Wonder Technology Lab** (⊠ 550 Madison Ave., between E. 55th and E. 56th Sts., Midtown East ☎ 212/833–8100 ⊕ www.sonywondertechlab.com ☉ Tues.–Sat. 10–5, Sun. noon–5; last entrance 30 mins before closing) lets them program robots, edit music videos, or take a peek inside the human body. Call ahead, as it is very popular.

Times Square Visitors Center. When it opened in 1925, the Embassy Theater was an exclusive, high-society movie theater; a few years ago the lobby of this landmark theater was transformed into the city's first comprehensive visitor center. Beyond getting general information about the area, you can buy sightseeing and theater tickets, Metro-Cards, and transit memorabilia; use ATMs; and log on to the Internet for free. There's also a video camera that shoots and e-mails instant photos. Free walking tours of Times Square are given Friday at noon. Perhaps most important, its restrooms are the only facilities in the vicinity open to the nonpaying public. ⊠ *1560 Broadway, between W. 46th and W. 47th Sts., Midtown West* ☎ *212/768–1560* ⊕ *www.timessquarebid.org* ☉ *Daily 8–8* Ⓜ *Subway: 1, 2, 3, 9, N, Q, R, W to 42nd St./Times Sq.*

⑲ Tudor City. Built between 1925 and 1928 to attract middle-income residents, this private Tudor-style "city" on a bluff above East 42nd Street occupies 12 buildings containing 3,000 apartments. Two of the buildings originally had no east-side windows, so the tenants wouldn't be forced to gaze at the slaughterhouses, breweries, and glue factories then crowding the shore of the East River. The terrace at the end of East 43rd Street now affords great views of the United Nations Headquarters and stands at the head of **Sharansky Steps** (named for Natan [Anatoly] Sharansky, the Soviet dissident). The steps run along **Isaiah Wall** (inscribed THEY SHALL BEAT THEIR SWORDS INTO PLOWSHARES); below are **Ralph J. Bunche Park,** named for the African-American former U.N. undersecretary, and **Raoul Wallenberg Walk,** named for the Swedish diplomat and World War II hero who saved many Hungarian Jews from the Nazis. ⊠ *1st and 2nd Aves. from E. 40th to E. 43rd Sts., Midtown East* Ⓜ *Subway: 4, 5, 6, 7 to 42nd St./Grand Central.*

★ United Nations Headquarters. Officially an "international zone," not part of the United States, the U.N. Headquarters is a working symbol of global cooperation. The 18-acre riverside tract, now lushly landscaped, was bought and donated by oil magnate John D. Rockefeller Jr. in 1946. The headquarters were built in 1947–53 by an international team led by Wallace Harrison. The slim, 505-foot-tall green-glass **Secretariat Building;** the much smaller, domed **General Assembly Building;** and the **Dag Hammarskjöld Library** (1963) form the complex, before which fly the flags of member nations in alphabetical order, from Afghanistan to Zimbabwe, when the General Assembly is in session (mid-September to mid-December). Architecturally, the U.N. buildings are evocative of Le Corbusier (the influential French modernist was on the team of architects that designed the complex), and their windswept park and plaza remain visionary: there's a beautiful riverside promenade, a rose garden with 1,400 rosebushes, and sculptures donated by member nations.

A 45-minute-long guided tour (given in 20 languages) is the main attraction; it includes the **General Assembly,** the **Security Council Chamber,** the **Trustee Council Chamber,** and the **Economic and Social Council Chamber,** though some rooms may be closed on any given day. Displays on war, nuclear energy, and refugees are also part of the tour; corridors overflow with imaginatively diverse artwork. Free tickets to assemblies are sometimes available on a first-come, first-served basis before sessions begin; pick them up in the General Assembly lobby. The **Delegates Dining Room** (☎ 212/963–7625) is open for an elegant international buffet lunch weekdays ($25; jackets required for men, no jeans or sneakers; reservations required at least one day in advance). The public concourse, one level down from the visitor entrance, has a coffee shop, gift shops, a bookstore, and a post office where you can mail letters with U.N. stamps. Be sure to bring a photo ID. *Visitor entrance ⊠ 1st Ave. and E. 46th St., Midtown East ☎ 212/963–8687 ⊕ www.un.org ☜ Tour $11.50 ☞ Children under 5 not admitted ⊙ Tours weekdays 9:30–4:45, weekends 10–4:30, no weekend tours Jan. and Feb.; tours in English leave General Assembly lobby every 30 mins; Delegates Dining Room, 11:30–2:30* Ⓜ *Subway: 4, 5, 6, 7 to 42nd St./Grand Central.*

University Club. New York's leading turn-of-the-20th-century architects, McKim, Mead & White, designed this pink Milford granite palace in 1899 for an exclusive midtown club of degree-holding men. (The crests of various prestigious universities hang above its windows.) The club's popularity declined as individual universities built their own clubs and as gentlemen's clubs became less important on the New York social scene. Still, the nine-story Italian High Renaissance Revival building (the facade looks as though it's three stories) is as grand as ever. Architectural critics rate this among Charles McKim's best surviving works. ⊠ *1 W. 54th St., at 5th Ave., Midtown West* Ⓜ *Subway: E, V to 5th Ave./53rd St.*

Midtown At a Glance

WHERE TO EAT (⇨ Ch. 18)
BUDGET DINING
Carnegie Deli
Comfort Diner
Cupcake Café
Grand Sichuan International
Hallo Berlin
Havana Central
Island Burgers and Shakes
Joe's Shanghai
Meskerem
Mint
Scarlatto
Virgil's Real BBQ

MODERATE DINING
Abboccato
Acqua Pazza
Baldoria
Barbetta
Becco
Ben Benson's Steak House
BLT Steak
Brasserie
Brasserie 8 1/2
Bull and Bear
Carmine's
db bistro moderne
District
Esca
Estiatorio Milos
Felidia
Firebird
Four Seasons
Il Gattopardo
Kuruma Zushi
Le Marais
L'Impero
Maloney & Porcelli
Marseille
Metrazur
Michael Jordan's The Steak
  House NYC
Molyvos
Monkey Bar
Nino's Tuscany
Osteria del Circo
Oyster Bar
Palm
The Palm
Pampano
Peacock Alley
Petrossian

Remi
San Domenico
Seppi's
Shun Lee Palace
Solo
Sparks Steak House
Sushi Yasuda
Trattoria Dell'Arte
Triomphe
Uncle Jack's Steakhouse
Victor's Café
Vong

EXPENSIVE DINING
Alain Ducasse
Alto
Aquavit
Churrascaria Plataforma
La Grenouille
Le Bernardin
Le Perigord
March
Oceana
Sugiyama
Town
'21' Club

WHERE TO STAY (⇨ Ch. 19)
BUDGET LODGING
Ameritania Hotel
Belvedere Hotel
The Bentley
Broadway Inn
The Fitzpatrick Manhattan
  Hotel
Hotel Edison
Hotel QT
Pickwick Arms Hotel
Portland Square Hotel
Quality Hotel and Suites
Vanderbilt YMCA
Wellington Hotel

MODERATE LODGING
Affinia Fifty
The Alex
The Algonquin
Beekman Tower
The Benjamin
The Blakely
The Bryant Park
Casablanca
Chambers
City Club Hotel

Crowne Plaza at the United
  Nations
Dream Hotel
The Dylan
Flatotel
Hilton New York
Hilton Times Square
Hotel Elysée
The Hudson
The Iroquois
Le Parker Meridien
Library Hotel
The Mansfield
Marriott Marquis
The Michelangelo
Millennium Hotel New
  York UN Plaza
The Muse
Omni Berkshire Place
The Regency
Renaissance
Rihga Royal
Roger Smith
The Royalton
Sherry-Netherland
The Shoreham
Sofitel New York
The Time Hotel
Waldorf-Astoria
Warwick
The Westin New York at
  Times Square

EXPENSIVE LODGING
The Drake
Essex House, a Westin Hotel
Four Seasons
Mandarin Oriental
New York Palace
The Peninsula
Ritz-Carlton New York,
  Central Park South
The St. Regis
W New York
W Times Square

BARS & NIGHTLIFE
  (⇨ Ch. 16)
Algonquin Hotel, *bar*
Area 10018, *gay & lesbian*
B. B. King Blues Club &
  Grill, *blues club*
Birdland, *jazz club*
Campbell Apartment, *bar*

7

The Upper East Side

WORD OF MOUTH

"NYers would be marooned without this park! I took a walk from my hotel into the park, and I can't believe such a beautiful and peaceful place exists amid all of the chaos. It's perfect for a walk, run, or picnic."

                                                                    –Zooey

"The Mt. Vernon Hotel Museum, one of the oldest buildings in Manhattan, is one of those charming surprise relics hidden away in NYC."
                                                                    –Anonymous

Sightseeing
★ ★ ★ ★

Nightlife
★ ★

Dining
★ ★ ★

Lodging
★ ★

Shopping
★ ★ ★ ★

To many New Yorkers, the Upper East Side connotes old money and high society. Alongside Central Park, between 5th and Lexington avenues, up to about East 96th Street, the trappings of wealth are everywhere apparent: posh buildings, Madison Avenue's flagship boutiques, and doormen in braided livery. But even more impressive, the Upper East Side's museums, including the Metropolitan Museum of Art, the Guggenheim, and the Cooper-Hewitt Museum of Art and Design, stretch along "Museum Mile." The Whitney Museum of American Art on Madison Avenue and the Asia Society Museum on Park Avenue are two world-class museums just off the "Mile."

But like all other New York neighborhoods, this one is diverse, too, and plenty of residents live modestly. The northeast section, which is known as Yorkville, is more affordable and ethnically mixed with a jumble of high and low buildings, old and young people. And east of Lexington Avenue and between the 80s and 90s, young singles reign. On weekend nights, the scene in many bars resembles that of a fraternity and sorority reunion.

What's Here

Amid all the glitzy stores and lavish apartment buildings, the real gems of this neighborhood lie along a stretch known as "Museum Mile" along Fifth Avenue. The **Metropolitan Museum of Art,** one of the world's largest art museums, makes room for itself on Central Park's turf. At the corner of East 85th Street is 1040 5th Avenue, the former home of Jacqueline Kennedy Onassis, from which she could view Central Park and the reservoir that now bears her name. One block north stands the **Neue Galerie New York,** a museum devoted to German and Austrian art in a

1914 Carrère and Hastings mansion. The **Frick Collection** is housed at East 70th Street in an ornate, imposing Beaux-Arts mansion, complete with furnishings. At East 88th Street, Frank Lloyd Wright's striking **Solomon R. Guggenheim Museum** houses an exceptional collection of modern and contemporary art and is the architect's only major New York building. A block north stands the **National Academy of Design**, a prestigious museum and school of fine arts. At East 91st Street you'll find the former residence of industrialist Andrew Carnegie, now the **Cooper-Hewitt National Design Museum–Smithsonian Institution.**
■ TIP➔ Most museums are closed at least one day of the week, usually Monday, and a few have free admission during extended hours on specific days.

After filling up on all this culture, you may want to head for nature: Central Park's Conservatory Garden, a formal, enclosed tract in the rambling park, is the perfect place to sit on a bench and enjoy the scents of whatever's in bloom.

If shopping is your passion, **Bloomingdale's** floor after floor tempts shoppers with gorgeous gets. Another must is **Barneys,** a treasure trove of wares from cutting-edge, hard-to-find designers. Located on Madison Avenue, Barneys is central to the bevy of designer boutiques, art galleries, and specialty stores that extend along the avenue from 59th to 79th streets. But Madison Avenue has more to offer than retail therapy. The distinctive **Whitney Museum of American Art** looms on the right at East 75th Street. Take at least two hours to view the remarkable collection of American arts.

When Upper East Siders are done with their shopping, the bags are usually delivered to homes along Park Avenue. Although apartment buildings now prevail along Park Avenue, a few surviving mansions give you an idea of how the neighborhood once looked. It was grand enough for presidents; Ulysses S. Grant spent his final years right off Park Avenue at 3 E. 66th St. On East 65th Street between Madison and Park avenues at Nos. 47 and 49 are two connected town houses built in 1908 for Sara Delano Roosevelt and her son, Franklin, after his marriage to Eleanor. Park Avenue is more than residences, though. You can check out art from South, Southeast, and East Asia at the **Asia Society and Museum** or stroll by the red Victorian castle-fortress at East 66th Street and Park Avenue that is the **Seventh Regiment Armory.**

If you venture east of Park Avenue, this neighborhood emits a completely different vibe. Many shops and restaurants line 2nd Avenue, three avenues east of Park Avenue, some reflecting the area's Eastern European heritage. At East 81st Street the **Yorkville Packing House** is a Hungarian meat market that serves up fresh-made sausages. At East 86th Street, the German store **Schaller & Weber** entices with bratwurst, imported chocolates, and stollen. Secondhand stores in the area sell all sorts of odds and ends discarded by the well-to-do. On East 86th Street and East End Avenue, the **Henderson Place Historic District** includes 24 small-scale town houses built in the late 1880s. Across the street is **Carl Schurz Park,** overlooking the East River. **Gracie Mansion,** the mayor's house, sits at its north end.

GETTING ORIENTED

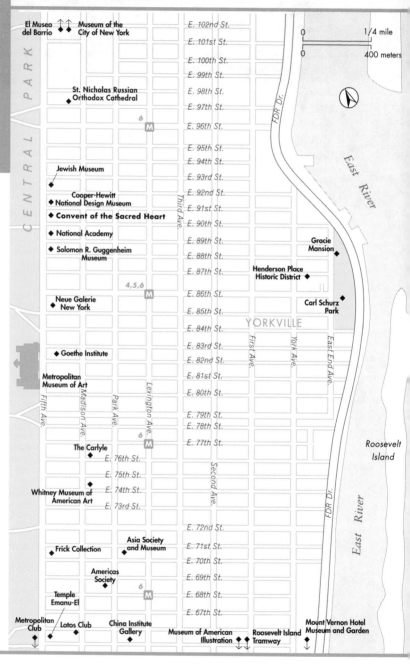

El Museo del Barrio

Museum of the City of New York

St. Nicholas Russian Orthodox Cathedral

Jewish Museum

Cooper-Hewitt National Design Museum

Convent of the Sacred Heart

National Academy

Solomon R. Guggenheim Museum

Neue Galerie New York

Goethe Institute

Metropolitan Museum of Art

The Carlyle

Whitney Museum of American Art

Frick Collection

Asia Society and Museum

Americas Society

Temple Emanu-El

Metropolitan Club

Lotos Club

China Institute Gallery

Museum of American Illustration

Roosevelt Island Tramway

Mount Vernon Hotel Museum and Garden

Gracie Mansion

Henderson Place Historic District

Carl Schurz Park

YORKVILLE

Roosevelt Island

East River

FDR Dr.

CENTRAL PARK

Fifth Ave.

Madison Ave.

Park Ave.

Lexington Ave.

Third Ave.

Second Ave.

First Ave.

York Ave.

East End Ave.

E. 102nd St.
E. 101st St.
E. 100th St.
E. 99th St.
E. 98th St.
E. 97th St.
E. 96th St.
E. 95th St.
E. 94th St.
E. 93rd St.
E. 92nd St.
E. 91st St.
E. 90th St.
E. 89th St.
E. 88th St.
E. 87th St.
E. 86th St.
E. 85th St.
E. 84th St.
E. 83rd St.
E. 82nd St.
E. 81st St.
E. 80th St.
E. 79th St.
E. 78th St.
E. 77th St.
E. 76th St.
E. 75th St.
E. 74th St.
E. 73rd St.
E. 72nd St.
E. 71st St.
E. 70th St.
E. 69th St.
E. 68th St.
E. 67th St.

0   1/4 mile
0   400 meters

TOP 5

- The Metropolitan Museum of Art
- Window shopping on Madison Avenue
- The Solomon R. Guggenheim Museum
- Strolling down 5th Avenue
- A night out at the Carlyle

MAKING THE MOST OF YOUR TIME

It would be impossible to do justice to all these museum collections in one outing; the Metropolitan Museum alone contains too much to see in a week, much less a day. Consider selecting one or two museums or exhibits in which to linger and simply walk past the others, appreciating their exteriors (this in itself constitutes a minicourse in architecture). Save the rest for another day—or for your next trip.

GETTING HERE

Take the Lexington Avenue 4 and 5 express trains to 59th or 86th streets. The 6 local train also stops at 68th, 77th, and 96th streets. If you're coming from Midtown, the F train will let you out at Lexington Avenue at 63rd Street. From the West Side, take one of the crosstown buses, which are the M66, M72, M79, M86, and M96.

QUICK BITES

Classy but unpretentious **Bemelmans Bar** (✉ Carlyle Hotel, 35 E. 76th St., between Madison and Park Aves., Upper East Side ☎ 212/744-1600) is the perfect haunt for a postmuseum or post-shopping drink.

The ultrapopular **DT-UT** (✉ 1626 2nd Ave., at E. 84th St., Upper East Side ☎ 212/327-1327) is one of the few *true* coffee shops in the city, where you can sink into a velvety '70s-era sofa and chain-drink coffee for hours without the waitstaff shooting you dirty looks. Plus it's the place that invented indoor s'mores. In an elegant, high-ceiling space below the Neue Galerie, **Café Sabarsky** (✉ 1048 5th Ave., at E. 86th St., Upper East Side ☎ 212/288-0665) offers Viennese coffee, cakes, strudel, and Sacher torte (Mon. and Wed. 9–6, Thurs.–Sun. 9–9). **Sarabeth's at the Whitney** (✉ Whitney Museum, 945 Madison Ave., at E. 75th St., Upper East Side ☎ 212/570-3670) serves up delicious brunch and tasty sandwiches. But be sure to save room for all the pastries and the life-changing brownies.

A GOOD WALK

One of the most spectacular walks is up or down 5th Avenue, with luxury apartment buildings and museums on one side, Central Park on the other. Duck down the occasional street and check out the town houses, home to many of the wealthiest residents in the city.

8

Places to Explore

Carl Schurz Park. Warm weather is the time to visit this park bordering the East River, as winds off the river can be frigid in winter. Grab a cone at Temptations (York St., between 90th and 91st Sts.) ice-cream shop and head over to take a look at the mayor's residence, **Gracie Mansion,** at the north end of the park. (The last mayor to live here was Rudy Giuliani; Michael Bloomberg apparently prefers his own East 79th Street digs.) Ferryboats depart from the East 90th Street tip of the park to Lower Manhattan and up to Yankee Stadium. A path runs along the churning East River, from where you can see the Triborough and Queensboro bridges; Wards, Randall's, and Roosevelt islands; and, on the other side of the river, Astoria, Queens. The view is so tranquil you'd never guess you're directly above the FDR Drive—-apart from the sound of cars whizzing by below. Along the park walkways are raised flower beds, recreation areas, and a playground. ⊠ *E. 84th to E. 90th St. between East End Ave. and East River, Upper East Side* Ⓜ *Subway: 4, 5, 6 to 86th St.*

Gracie Mansion. Nothing like the many impressive brick-and-stone mansions of the Upper East Side, the federal-style yellow wood frame official residence of the mayor of New York looks like a country manor house, which it was when built in 1799 by wealthy shipping merchant Archibald Gracie. Tours of the interior—which you must schedule in advance—take you through the history of the house and its many objets d'art. The Gracie family entertained many political, civic, and artistic notables here, including Louis-Philippe (later king of France), Alexander Hamilton, James Fenimore Cooper, Washington Irving, and John Jacob Astor. The city purchased Gracie Mansion in 1896, and after a period of use as the Museum of the City of New York, Mayor Fiorello H. La Guardia made it the official mayor's residence in 1942. Since then nine mayors have lived in Gracie Mansion, but don't expect to find New York City's current mayor Michael Bloomberg here, however; he chose to stay in his own 79th Street town house rather than moving to Gracie Mansion when he took office in 2002. ⊠ *Carl Schurz Park, East End Ave. opposite 88th St., Upper East Side* ☎ *212/570–4751* 🖼 *$7* ☉ *Guided tours Wed. 10–2, starting every hr on the hr; all tours by advance reservation only* Ⓜ *Subway: 4, 5, 6 to 86th St.*

Henderson Place Historic District. Tucked away off 86th Street, this cozy half block is a miniature historic district, with 24 connected Queen Anne–style houses in excellent condition. Originally numbering 32 in the enclave, the houses were built in 1881 for "people of moderate means." Richard Norman Shaw designed the stone-and-brick buildings to be comfortable yet romantic dwellings that combined elements of the Elizabethan manor house with classic Flemish details. Note the lovely bay windows, the turrets marking the corner of each block, and the symmetrical roof gables, pediments, parapets, chimneys, and dormer windows. This is one of those "hidden" New York treasures that even most New Yorkers don't know about. ⊠ *Henderson Pl., between 86th and 87th Sts., Upper East Side* Ⓜ *Subway: 4, 5, 6 to 86th St.*

Lotos Club. This private club, which attracts devotees of the arts and literature, got its name in 1870 from the poem "The Lotos-Eaters" by Alfred Lord Tennyson. Mark Twain and Andrew Carnegie were among the founding members. Its current home is a handsomely ornate Beaux-Arts mansion originally built in 1900 by Richard Howland Hunt for a member of the Vanderbilt family. ⊠ *5 E. 66th St., between 5th and Madison Aves., Upper East Side* Ⓜ *Subway: 6 to 68th St./Hunter College.*

HERE'S WHERE

Nathan Hale, of "I have but one life to lose for my country" fame, was likely hanged at a British encampment that was close to the present-day intersection of 66th Street and 3rd Avenue. A plaque on the Banana Republic building on 3rd Avenue (between 65th and 66th Sts.) attests to this.

Metropolitan Club. With a lordly Italian renaissance edifice, this exclusive club was built in 1891–94 by the grandest producers of such structures—McKim, Mead & White. It was established by J. P. Morgan when a friend of his was refused membership in the Union League Club. Because members wanted to have a lounge that overlooked Central Park, the club's entrance was situated on E. 60th Street instead of 5th Ave. Its members today include leaders of foreign countries, presidents of major corporations, and former U.S. President Bill Clinton. ⊠ *1 E. 60th St., near 5th Ave., Upper East Side* Ⓜ *Subway: N, R, W to 59th St./Lexington Ave.*

Mount Vernon Hotel Museum and Garden. Built in 1799, this carriage house is now owned by the colonial Dames of America and is largely restored to look as it did when it served as a bustling day hotel during the 1820s and 1830s. At that time, when the city ended at 14th Street, this area was a country escape for New Yorkers. A docent can give you a 45-minute tour through the eight rooms that display furniture and artifacts of the federal and empire periods. Each room has a hands-on basket with real artifacts that children can handle. The adjoining garden, designed in an 18th-century style, hosts classic music concerts in June and July at 6 PM (extra charge). ⊠ *421 E. 61st St., between York and 1st Aves., Upper East Side* ☎ *212/838–6878* ⊕ *www.mvhm.org* ☑ *$8* ☉ *Sept.–July, Tues.–Sun. 11–4* Ⓜ *Subway: 4, 5, 6, N, R, W to 59th St./Lexington Ave.*

Roosevelt Island Tramway. In 1976 the tramway was born as a means to transport Roosevelt Island residents to and from Manhattan. It's the only commuter cable car in North America. The five-minute trip suspends you 3,000 feet in the air. The views—of Queens, the Bronx, and the Queensboro Bridge—are not spectacular, but it's fun, it's cheap, and there are some interesting bits of history to see on Roosevelt Island (⇨ "Roosevelt Island" CloseUp box). ⊠ *Entrance at 2nd Ave. and either 59th St. or 60th St.* ☎ *212/832–4543* ☑ *$2* ☉ *Sun.–Thurs. 6 AM–2 AM, Fri. and Sat. 6 AM–3:30 AM; leaves every 15 mins.*

Temple Emanu-El. The world's largest Reform Jewish synagogue seats 2,500 worshippers. Built in 1928–29 of limestone and designed in the Romanesque style with Byzantine influences, the building has Moorish and art deco ornamentation, and its sanctuary is covered with mosaics. A free museum displays artifacts detailing the congregation's history and

Roosevelt Island

ROOSEVELT ISLAND is a 2-mi-long East River slice of land, parallel to Manhattan proper from East 48th to East 85th streets. The island became a planned mixed-income residential project in the 1970s and is home to some 9,000 people. It's accessible by the Roosevelt Island Tramway from 2nd Avenue and 59th Street.

In the 1800s and early 1900s, Roosevelt Island was a place for society's rejects: criminals and the mentally and physically ill. A penitentiary was built on the island in 1832 (Mae West and William "Boss" Tweed are among those who served time in Blackwell Penitentiary). The New York Lunatic Asylum followed in 1839. The asylum was made famous in 1888 by journalist Nellie Bly, who posed undercover as a patient to expose the inhumane treatment of the mentally ill. The Smallpox Hospital opened on the island in 1856, followed by several more charity houses and hospitals. It's no wonder, then, that the island was renamed Welfare Island in 1921. Some fragments of the asylums, hospitals, and jails once clustered here remain, but the insane were eventually moved to Ward's Island, the criminals to Riker's Island, and most of the hospitals relocated to Manhattan proper.

Points of interest on the island today are a 19th-century lighthouse, designed by James Renwick Jr. (architect of St. Patrick's Cathedral) and Blackwell House (1794), the fifth-oldest wooden house in Manhattan. Walkways follow the island's edge.

Jewish life. ✉ *1 E. 65th St., at 5th Ave., Upper East Side* ☎ *212/744–1400* ⊕ *www.emanuelnyc.org* ◷ *Sabbath services Fri. 5:15, Sat. 10:30; weekday services Sun.–Thurs. 5:30. Temple open daily 10–5. Museum open Sun.–Thurs. 10–4:30; tours Sun.–Fri., Sat. after services at noon* Ⓜ *Subway: 6 to 68th St./Hunter College.*

Yorkville. Until the 1830s, when the New York & Harlem Railroad and a stagecoach line began racing through, Yorkville was a quiet, remote hamlet with a large German population. Over the years it also welcomed waves of immigrants from Austria, Hungary, and Czechoslovakia, and a few local shops and restaurants keep up this European heritage, though their native-tongue customers have trickled down to a few surviving senior citizens. The quiet blocks of 78th Street between Park and 2nd avenues are home to rows of well-maintained Italianate town houses from the late 1800s. Many shops and restaurants line 2nd Avenue, some reflecting the area's Eastern European heritage. At East 81st Street the Yorkville Packing House (1560 2nd Ave.) is a Hungarian meat market that serves up fresh-made sausages. At East 86th Street, the German store Schaller & Weber (1654 2nd Ave.) entices with bratwurst, imported chocolates, and stollen. Secondhand stores in the area sell all sorts of odds and ends discarded by the well-to-do.

The Upper East Side At a Glance

8

Shanghai Tang
TSE
Valentino
Vera Wang
Vilebrequin
Yves Saint Laurent Rive
  Gauche

DEPARTMENT STORES
Barneys New York

GIFTS
Metropolitan Museum of
  Art Shop
Museum of the City of
  New York

HOME DECOR
Crate & Barrel
Nina Griscom

Scully & Scully
Steuben

JEWELRY
Chanel Fine Jewelry
David Yurman
Fred Leighton

LEATHER GOODS
Anya Hindmarch
Judith Leiber
Longchamp

LINGERIE
Bra Smyth
La Perla

PERFUME/COSMETICS
Floris of London
Fresh
Molton Brown

SHOES
Billy Martin's
Christian Louboutin
Church's English Shoes
J. M. Weston
Jimmy Choo
John Lobb
Robert Clergerie
Santoni
Tod's
Unisa

WINE
Best Cellars
Garnet Wines &
  Liquors
Sherry-Lehmann

Central Park

House Sparrows, Conservatory Gardens

9

WORD OF MOUTH

Don't miss Belvedere Castle on the south end of the Great Lawn. Approach it from the north: enter the park at East 84th Street, for example, passing the Temple of Dendur, then circle around the Great Lawn until you see the castle rising above the Turtle Pond. The view from the castle is excellent, and from there you can easily walk south to the Bow Bridge and Bethesda Fountain. Enjoy our backyard!

–Gekko

OUR BACKYARD

HOW A SWAMP BECAME AN OASIS

1855 New York City acquires 843 acres of undeveloped swamp for the then-obscene sum of $5 million.

1857 Journalist Frederick Law Olmsted becomes superintendent of a park that does not yet exist. He spends days clearing dirt and evicting squatters and evenings working with architect friend Calvert Vaux on what will become the Greensward Plan. The plan is the winning entry in the city's competition to develop a design for the park.

The Panic of 1857 creates widespread unemployment. Thousands of workers begin the task of moving five million cubic yards of dirt and planting more than four million trees, plants, and shrubs. Beleaguered by

bureaucrats, Olmsted and Vaux unsuccessfully submit their resignations several times during the project.

1873 The Greensward Plan is completed. With a few notable departures it has been the blueprint for Central Park ever since.

The goal was simple: Create a place where city dwellers could go to forget the city. And while the town eventually grew far taller than the trees planted to hide it, this goal never falters. A combination escape hatch and exercise yard, Central Park is an urbanized Eden that offers residents and visitors alike a bite of the apple. We can't imagine how insufferably stressed New York City would be without it.

31 > THINGS WE LOVE TO DO IN CENTRAL PARK

1 Take a rowboat out on the Lake

2 Watch the sea lions play at feeding time

3 Walk around the Reservoir

4 Ice-skate at Wollman Rink

5 Watch rollerbladers show off

6 Go bird watching at the Ramble

7 Lie in the grass at Sheep Meadow

8 Rent a bike at the Boathouse

9 Sit on the hill behind the Met Museum

10 See a free concert

11 Catch a softball game

12 Clap for the jugglers

13 Remember John Lennon at Strawberry Fields

14 Run through an icy playground sprinkler

15 Rent a gondola and a gondolier

16 Cross the park on the bridle path

17 Stand under the gnarly 72nd Street pergola

18 Hear the Delacorte Clock's musical chimes

19 Crunch the snow before anyone else

20 Pilot a tiny boat at Conservatory Water

21 Stroll through Shakespeare Garden

22 Fish at Harlem Meer

23 Watch dogs play

24 Smell the Conservatory Garden tulips

25 Shoot photos from Bow Bridge

26 Walk the wide, curvy East Drive steps

27 People-watch at Bethesda Fountain

28 Picnic on the Great Lawn

29 Pet the bronze Balto statue

30 Climb to the top of Belvedere Castle

31 Ride the Carousel, wave at everyone

(top left) Monarch butterfly pollinates at Conservatory Gardens (top center) Hansom driver between fares (top right) Chrysanthemums near Sheep Meadow (center) The skyline with some of the park's 26,000 trees (bottom) Park skaters in the 1860s.

9

PARK BASICS

Several entrances lead into the park. You can enter from the east, west, south, and north by paved pedestrian walkways, just off Fifth Avenue, Central Park North (110th St.), Central Park West, and Central Park South.

Four roads, or transverses, cut through the park from east to west—66th, 79th, 86th, and 96th streets. The East and West drives are both along the north–south axis; Center Drive enters the south edge of the park at Sixth Avenue and connects with East Drive around 80th Street.

Three Visitor Centers—the Dairy (just south of the 66th St. transverse), Belvedere Castle (just north of the 79th Street transverse), and the Charles A. Dana Discovery Center (at the top of the park at Central Park North)—have directions, park maps, event calendars, and volunteers who can guide you.

Central Park's reputation for danger is a remnant of bleaker days. An awareness of one's surroundings and common sense should suffice to protect the wary.

TOURS

The **Central Park Conservancy** gives nine different free walking tours of the park on Wednesday, Saturday, and Sunday. The walks provide a perfect opportunity to explore the Ramble without getting lost, become well versed in the park's history, or get clued into "hidden" aspects you might otherwise have missed. Most tours are 60 to 90 minutes, and custom tours are also available.

WHERE AM I?

Along the main loop and some smaller paths, lampposts are marked with location codes. Posts bear a letter—always "E" (for east) or "W" (for west)—followed by four numbers. The first two numbers tell you the nearest cross street. The second two tell you how far you are from either 5th Avenue or Central Park West (depending on whether it's an "E" or "W" post). So E7803 means you're near 78th Street, three posts in from 5th Avenue. For street numbers above 99, the initial "1" is omitted, for example, E0401 (near 104th Street, one post in from 5th Avenue).

PERFORMERS AND THE PARK: SOULMATES

It was inevitable that Central Park, conceived to give and ask little in return, would attract artists and arts lovers who feel the same way.

Be they superstars like Paul Simon, Diana Ross, or Barbra Streisand or one of the amateur musicians, animal handlers, or jugglers who delight passersby, they all share the urge to entertain and give back to the city, the park, and its visitors.

Information on scheduled events is provided, but if you can't catch one, don't fret: you'll be rewarded by the serendipitous, particularly on summer and autumn days. Just keep your ears peeled for the music, applause and laughter. You won't have to wait long.

The Central Park Conservancy, in cooperation with other arts patrons, drives a series of free events, including the Harlem Meer Performance Festival and the Great Lawn Performances by the Metropolitan Opera and New York Philharmonic. One standout is Summerstage, which yields a cornucopia of worldwide pop.

Perhaps the brass ring of park performances is the more than four-decade-old Shakespeare in the Park, which wows about 80,000 New Yorkers and visitors during any given season. Free tickets (two per person) are given out starting at 1 PM for the performance that evening, but you need to line up by midmorning or earlier depending on the show. The wait is worth it, though, as casts are often studded with the likes of Meryl Streep, Philip Seymour Hoffman, Natalie Portman, Morgan Freeman, Denzel Washington, and Kevin Kline. You can also try for same-day tickets by going to the Public Theater (425 Lafayette St., East Village) at 1 PM.

GOINGS ON

Central Park Film Festival: Five nights at end of summer; Rumsey Playfield, near E. 72nd St. entrance.

Harlem Meer Performance Festival: Late May–early Sept., Sun. 4–6 PM; at Dana Discovery Center, near Lenox Ave. entrance.

New York Grand Opera: Performances Aug.–Sept.; Naumburg Bandshell.

New York Philharmonic: Two performances in July; Great Lawn.

Shakespeare in the Park: Late May–early Sept., Tues.–Sun. evenings.

Storytelling: June–Sept., Sat. 11 AM; Hans Christian Andersen Statue.

SummerStage: Late May–early Sept.; Rumsey Playfield. Big-name, up-and-coming, and international musicians perform here.

Swedish Cottage Marionette Theatre: Since 1947, puppeteers have entertained tiny New Yorkers in this 1876 Swedish schoolhouse. $6 adults/$5 kids. Tue.–Sun, hours vary.

(center) N.Y. Philharmonic associate conductor Xian Zhang (right) Shakespeare's *Much Ado About Nothing*

FROM 59TH TO 72ND ST.

The busy southern section of Central Park is where most visitors get their first impression. Artists line the entrances off Central Park South, and drivers of horse carriages await passengers. But no matter how many people congregate in this area, you can always find a spot to picnic, ponder, or just take in the beauty, especially on a sunny day.

At the southeast corner of the park, you will come upon one of its prettiest areas, the Pond. Swans and ducks cruise on its calm waters, and if you follow the shore line to Gapstow Bridge and look southward, you'll see much of New York City's skyline: to the left (east) are the peak-roofed Sherry-Netherland Hotel, the black-and-white CBS Building, the Chippendale-style top of the Sony Building, and the black-glass Trump Tower. In front of you is the château-style Plaza Hotel.

One of the park's winter gems, Wollman Memorial Rink sits inside the park against a backdrop of Central Park South skyscrapers. You can rent skates there, buy snacks, and have a perfect city-type outing. There's a lively feeling here with lots of great music playing and a terrace so you can watch if you're not into skating.

The Friedsam Memorial Carousel, also known as the Central Park Carousel, was built in 1908. It has 58 oversized hand-carved horses and remains a favorite among young and old. Its original Wurlitzer organ plays calliope waltzes, polkas, and standards. Even if you don't need visitor information, the Dairy is worth a stop for its eclectic Swiss-chalet exterior.

If you saw the film *Madagascar*, you may recognize the Central Park Zoo, officially known as the Central Park Wildlife Center. Here, the polar bears play at the Polar Circle, monkeys frolic in the open-air Temperate Territory, and the Rain Forest showcases flora and fauna that you wouldn't expect to see in Manhattan. An unusual exhibit is the ant colony—even New York City's zoo has a sense of humor. Stick around to see the sea lion feedings (call for times) and to watch the animal statues dance to a variety of nursery rhymes at the Delacorte Musical Clock just outside, on the hour and half-hour from 8 AM to 5 PM.

Wedged between the zoo and the clock is The Arsenal, the second-oldest building in the park. High points here are

park and environmental design exhibits, including Olmsted and Vaux's original plan for Central Park.

North of the clock is Tisch Children's Zoo, where kids can pet and feed sheep, goats, rabbits, cows, and pigs. Enter through the trunk of a make-believe tree and arrive at The Enchanted Forest, filled with huge "acorns," a climbable "spider web," and hoppable "lily pads."

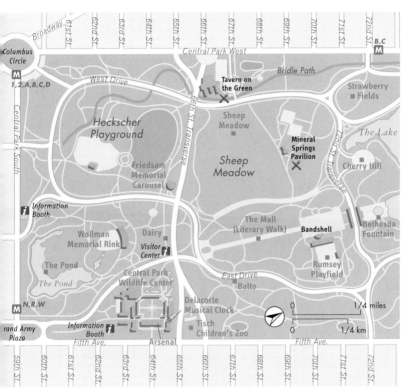

Perhaps more pettable than any of the zoo's occupants is a decidely more inert creature, perched on a rockpile at East Drive and 67th Street: Balto. Shiny in places from constant touching, this bronze statue commemorates a real-life sled dog who led a team of huskies that carried medicine for 60 mi across perilous ice to Nome, Alaska, during a 1925 diphtheria epidemic.

The Mall is at the intersection of Central Drive and East Drive and is arguably the most elegant area of Central Park. In the beginning of the 20th century, it was the place to see and be seen. Today, these formal walkways are still a wonderful place to stroll, meander, or sit and take in the "parade." The Mall's main path, known as Literary Walk, is covered by the majestic canopy of the largest collection of American elms in North America and is lined with statues of authors and artists such as Robert Burns and William Shakespeare.

(from left to right) Riding on the outside track (recommended) of the Carousel; Getting in a workout on a park drive loop; The Mall, where Dustin Hoffman's character famously teaches his son to ride a bike in *Kramer vs. Kramer*.

The large expanse to the west of the Mall is known as Sheep Meadow, the only "beach" that some native New Yorkers have ever known. Join in on a Frisbee or football game, admire the tenacity of kite flyers, or indulge simultaneously in the three simplest meadow pleasures of them all— picnicking, sunbathing, and languorously consuming the newspaper.

There's a reason why the ornate Bethesda Fountain, off the 72nd Street transverse, shows up in so many movies set in New York City: the view from the staircase above is one of the most romantic in the city. The statue in the center of the fountain, The Angel of the Waters, designed by Emma Stebbins, is surrounded by four figures symbolizing Temperance, Purity, Health, and Peace.

There's a good amount of New York–style street entertainment here, too, with break dancers, acrobats, and singers all vying for your spare change. It's also a great place to meet, sit, stretch after a long run, and admire the beautiful lake beyond with its swans and boaters. For a glimpse of the West Side skyline and another view of the lake, walk slightly west to Cherry Hill.

Originally a watering area for horses, this circular plaza has a small wrought-iron-and-gilt fountain. It's particularly beautiful in the spring when the cherry trees are in full pink-and-white bloom.

Across from the Dakota apartment building on Central Park West is **Strawberry Fields,** named for the Beatles' 1967 classic, "Strawberry Fields Forever." This informal memorial to John Lennon is sometimes called the "international garden of peace," and fans make pilgrimages to walk its curving paths, reflect among its shrubs, trees, and flower beds, and lay flowers on the black-and-white "Imagine" mosaic. On December 8, hundreds of Beatles fans mark the anniversary of Lennon's death by gathering at the mosaic.

(top from left to right) Seals cavorting at the zoo; Artist painting the oft-rendered Gapstow bridge, which spans the northeast end of the Pond; Cutting through the park is a classic midday timesaver and post-work respite; Meeting up and chilling out at world-famous Bethesda Fountain
(center left) Nighttime at Wollman Rink serves up twinkling skyscrapers and skaters of all abilities
(center right) The late John Lennon and his widow, Yoko Ono, often visited the site of what would become Strawberry Fields.

FROM 72ND ST. TO THE RESERVOIR

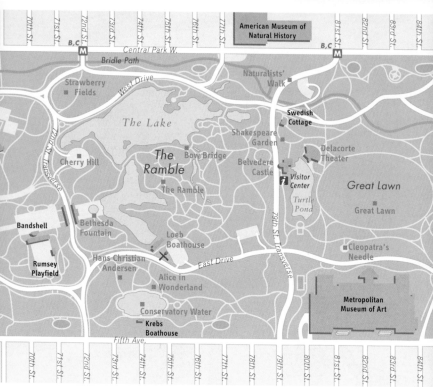

Playgrounds, lawns, jogging and biking paths, and striking buildings populate the midsection of the park. You can soak up the sun, have a picnic, or even play in a pick-up basketball or baseball game by the Great Lawn; get your cultural fix at the Metropolitan Museum of Art; or train for the next New York City Marathon along the Reservoir.

A block from Fifth Avenue, just north of the 72nd Street entrance, is a peaceful section of the park where you'll find the Conservatory Water, named for a conservatory that was never built. Generations of New Yorkers have grown up racing model sailboats here. It's a tradition that happens each Saturday at 10 AM from spring through fall. At the north end is the Alice in Wonderland statue;

on the west side of the pond, a bronze statue of Hans Christian Andersen, the Ugly Duckling at his feet, is the site of Saturday storytelling hours during summer.

At the brick neo-Victorian Loeb Boathouse on the park's 18-acre lake, you can rent a rowboat or a bicycle as well as ride in an authentic Venetian gondola. The attached café is a worthy pit stop.

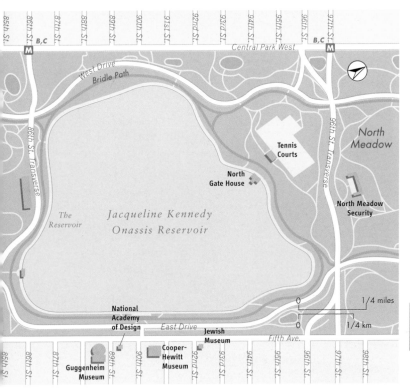

Designed to resemble upstate New York's Adirondack Mountain region, the Ramble covers 38 acres and is laced with twisting, climbing paths. This is prime bird-watching territory, since it's a rest stop along a major migratory route and a shelter for many of the more than 270 species of birds that have been sighted in the park; bring your binoculars. Because the Ramble is so dense and

isolated, however, don't wander here alone, or after dark. Head south through The Ramble and you'll come to the beautiful cast-iron Bow Bridge, spanning part of The Lake between the Ramble and Bethesda Fountain. From the center of the bridge, you can get a sweeping view of the park as well as of the apartment buildings on both the East Side and the West Side.

North of the Ramble atop Vista Rock, Belvedere Castle is the second-highest natural point in the park. If you can't get tickets for Delacorte Theater, you can climb to one of the castle's three terraces

(from left to right) Belvedere means "beautiful view" in Italian, a clue to why we climb to the top of Belvedere Castle; Birders, photographers, and couples of all ages are drawn to Bow Bridge; Red-eared slider turtles frolic in Turtle Pond, at the base of Belvedere Castle.

and look down on the stage. You'll also get a fantastic view of the Great Lawn—it's particularly beautiful during the fall foliage months—and of the park's myriad bird visitors. Since 1919 the castle has served as a U.S. Weather Bureau station, and meteorological instruments are set on top of the tower. If you enter the Castle from the lower level, you can visit the Henry Luce Nature Observatory, which has nature exhibits, children's workshops, and educational programs.

Somewhat hidden behind Belvedere Castle, Shakespeare Garden is an informal jumble of flowers, trees, and pathways, inspired by the flora mentioned in Shakespeare's many plays. The garden is particularly beautiful when the bulbs begin to re-emerge in March and when the antique roses bloom in June.

The Great Lawn hums with action on weekends, on warm days, and on most summer evenings, when its baseball fields and picnic grounds are filled with city folks and visitors alike. Its 14 acres have endured millions of footsteps, thousands of ball games, hundreds of downpours, dozens of

concerts, fireworks displays, and even a papal mass. On a beautiful day, everyone seems to be here.

Chancing upon Cleopatra's Needle always feels a bit serendipitous and delight-fully jarring, even to the most cynical New Yorkers. This weathered hieroglyphic-covered obelisk began life in Heliopolis, Egypt, around 1600 BC, but has nothing to do with Cleopatra—it's just New York's nickname for the work. It was eventually carted off to Alexandria by the Romans in 12 BC, and it landed here on February 22, 1881, when the khedive of Egypt made it a gift to the city.

At the southwest corner of the Great Lawn is the fan-shaped Delacorte Theater, home to the summer Shake-speare in the Park festival.

If you want to take in several sites in a single brisk jaunt, consider walking the Natural-ists' Walk. On this path you

(top, from left to right) A female Canada goose and goslings on Turtle Pond; Cyclists make good use of the bike paths; Bikers as well as joggers boost their egos by outpacing the hansom carriages; Racing boats at Conservatory Water (center) In the 1930s, a flock of mutant sheep was evicted from what would later be known as Sheep Meadow.

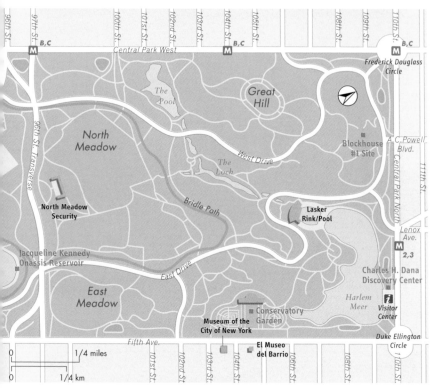

can wind your way toward the Swedish Cottage, the Shakespeare Garden, and Belvedere Castle on a landscaped nature walk with spectacular rock outcrops, a stream that attracts bird life, a woodland area with various native trees, stepping-stone trails, and, thankfully, benches.

North of the Great Lawn and the 86th Street transverse is a popular gathering place for New Yorkers and visitors alike, the Jacqueline Kennedy Onassis Reservoir. Rain or shine, you'll see runners of all ages and paces heading counterclockwise around the 1.58-mi cinder path that encircles the water. The path in turn is surrounded by hundreds of trees that burst into color in the spring and fall. The 106-acre reservoir, built in 1862 as a source of fresh water for Manhattanites, holds more than a billion gallons, but it's no longer used for drinking water; the city's main reservoirs are upstate. From the top of the stairs at 90th Street just off 5th Avenue you have a 360-degree panorama of the city's exciting skyscrapers and often-brilliant sunsets. On the south side, there are benches so you can rest and recharge.

FROM THE RESERVOIR TO 110TH ST.

 More locals than tourists know about the wilder-looking, less-crowded northern part of Central Park, and there are hidden gems lurking here that enable even the most tightly wound among us to decompress, at least for a short while.

Walking along Fifth Avenue to 105th Street, you'll see a magnificent wrought-iron gate—once part of the 5th Avenue mansion of Cornelius Vanderbilt II—that marks the entrance to the Conservatory Garden. As you walk through it, you enter a different world, a quiet place that's positively idyllic for reading and slowing down. The Italian-style Central Garden is a beauty, with an expansive lawn, a strikingly simple fountain, and a wisteria-draped pergola that just oozes romance.

The French-inspired North Garden is a colorful place with plants placed into elaborate patterns. Springtime is magical—thousands of tulips come to life in a circle around the garden's striking Untermeyer Fountain and its three bronze dancers; in the fall, chrysanthemums take their place. The English-style South Garden conjures up images from the classic children's book *The Secret Garden*.

The garden is a beautiful hodgepodge of trees, bushes, and flowers that bloom year-round. A free tour is conducted on Saturday at 11 AM, from April through October.

Yes, there are fish in Central Park. At Harlem Meer, the second-largest body of water in Central Park, you can rent fishing poles (identification required) from mid-April through October and try your hand at catching the large-mouth bass, catfish, golden shiners, and bluegills that are stocked in the water's 11 acres. You can also learn about the upper park's geography, ecology, and history at the Victorian-style Charles A. Dana Discovery Center.

Although only a shell of this stone building remains, Blockhouse #1 serves as a historical marker: the structure was built in 1814 as a cliffside fortification against the British. The area is deserted and dense with trees, so join a guided group if you're exploring there.

(left) A pensive raccoon in the park's northern reaches (center) Indulging in a park favorite, soccer, near East Meadow (right) A 7-foot chain-link fence encircling the Reservoir bit the dust in 2003, giving way to a more viewer-friendly 4-ft. steel enclosure.

CONTACT INFORMATION

Central Park Conservancy
☏ 212/360-2726
⊕ www.centralparknyc.org

Central Park Summerstage
☏ 212/360-2756
⊕ www.summerstage.org

Central Park Wildlife Center (Central Park Zoo)
☏ 212/439-6500
⊕ www.centralparkzoo.org

Central Park Visitor Centers
☏ 212/310-6600 (park events); 212/360-2726 (walking tours)
⊕ www.nycgovparks.org

Charles A. Dana Discovery Center
☏ 212/860-1370

Delacorte Theater
☏ 212/539-8750
⊕ www.publictheater.org

Loeb Boathouse, Boathouse Café
☏ 212/517-2233
⊕ www.thecentral-parkboathouse.com

Swedish Cottage Marionette Theatre
☏ 212/988-9093

Wollman Memorial Rink
☏ 212/439-6900
⊕ www.wollmanskating-rink.com

PALE MALE: IF YOU CAN MAKE IT HERE...

Telescoping the nest from within the park; Pale Male returns home; watching the brood like a hawk; Pale Male's progeny.

Since 1993, the red-tailed hawk Pale Male has sired and raised 23 offspring in a nest on the 12th floor of 927 Fifth Avenue, one of the city's toniest co-ops. Despite his upscale digs, life hasn't always been easy. He's lost mates (current partner Lola is his fourth), eggs, chicks, and even his home. In 2004, the co-op trashed Pale Male and Lola's nest and blocked their return. Under pressure from the news media and protesters (some holding signs that urged passing drivers to "Honk-4-Hawks"), the board relented less than a month later. A platform was installed to hold the nest, and Pale Male and Lola returned immediately and began to rebuild. Today the hawks' numbers are growing—in 2006 Pale Male's son Junior and his mate, Charlotte, hatched two chicks in their nest at the Trump Parc building.

The Upper West Side

INCLUDING MORNINGSIDE HEIGHTS

WORD OF MOUTH

"The exterior of the Seinfeld diner (Monk's) was shot at Tom's restaurant at the corner of 112th Street and Broadway."   —janie

"The Cathedral of St. John the Divine on the Upper West Side has beautiful stained glass and you can tour yourself or go on a guided tour once a day. This could be combined with other interesting things in the neighborhood, like Riverside Church, Grant's Tomb, and the grounds of Columbia University, which has some terrific architecture."   —Caitlin

Sightseeing
★ ★ ★
Nightlife
★ ★
Dining
★ ★ ★ ★
Lodging
★ ★
Shopping
★ ★ ★ ★ ★

Residents of the Upper West Side will proudly tell you that they live in one of the last real neighborhoods in the city. That's arguable (as is most everything in NYC), but people actually do know their neighbors in this primarily residential section of Manhattan, and some small owner-operated businesses still flourish. On weekends, stroller-pushing parents cram the sidewalks and shoppers jam the gourmet food emporiums and interesting stores that line Broadway and Columbus Avenue. Those who aren't shopping are likely to be found in Riverside Park, the neighborhood's communal backyard. Lively avenues, quiet tree-lined side streets and terrific restaurants and museums, all in a relatively compact area, make this the perfect neighborhood to experience life the way the locals do.

Most people think the area north of 106th Street and south of 125th Street on the west side is just part of the Upper West Side. It's actually Morningside Heights, and is largely dominated by Columbia University, along with the cluster of academic and religious institutions—Barnard College, St. Luke's Hospital, and the Cathedral of St. John the Divine, to name a few. Within the gates of the Columbia or Barnard campuses or inside the hushed St. John the Divine or Riverside Church, New York City takes on a different character. This is an *uptown* student neighborhood—less hip than the Village, but friendly, fun, and intellectual.

What's Here

The Upper West Side is a five-block-wide strip between Central Park and the Hudson River, stretching from 59th on its southern border to 110th Street on the northern terminus. Within these boundaries is an entire world; Riverside Drive, a stretch of the most elegant addresses in the city, lively blue-collar Amsterdam Avenue, occasionally affluent West End Avenue, and the two main shopping and walking thoroughfares—Broadway and Columbus.

The West Side story begins at **Columbus Circle,** the bustling intersection of Broadway, 8th Avenue, Central Park West, and Central Park South. The **Time Warner Center** is the centerpiece of the circle. Locals sneer at its mall-like atmosphere but it includes a great collection of shops, a behind-the-scenes tour of *Inside CNN* and **Masa,** a five-star Japanese restaurant, along with more casual dining options. Sample the world's gourmet treats at sprawling shops including **Zabars, Citarella, Fairway,** or the **Garden of Eden** on Broadway, then walk one block east to Amsterdam and purchase "authentic curio" voodoo supplies from one of the tiny botanicas. Keep walking east another block and you're on Columbus Avenue, one of the most eccentric shopping and dining streets in the city. Attend an event at **Lincoln Center** and/or wander over to one of the parks and watch impromptu performance art.

Several world-class museums dot the Upper West Side; the **American Museum of Natural History, the American Folk Art Museum,** and the **New York Historical Society.** You can easily spend an entire day in any of these establishments, but do make sure to spend some time soaking up the everyday life of this culturally diverse neighborhood. In Morningside Heights, on Broadway to 112th Street, stands the **Cathedral Church of St. John the Divine,** the world's largest Gothic cathedral. Walk one block west from Broadway and stroll north on beautiful Riverside Drive to 122nd Street. The white-marble building on the left as you face north/uptown is **Grant's Tomb,** once one of the city's most popular sights. Back on the east side of Riverside Drive, the refined **Riverside Church** seems the antithesis of the rougher hulk of the Cathedral of St. John the Divine—a contrast that sums up this neighborhood nicely: elegant and artsy but not at all precious or overly refined.

10

Places to Explore

Ansonia Hotel. This 1904 Beaux-Arts masterpiece designed by Paul E. M. Duboy commands its corner of Broadway with as much architectural detail as good taste can stand. Inspiration for the former apartment hotel's turrets, mansard roof, and filigreed-iron balconies came from turn-of-the-20th-century Paris. Suites came without kitchens (and with separate quarters for staff that took care of the food). Designed to be fireproof, it has thick, soundproof walls that make it attractive to musicians; famous denizens of the past include Enrico Caruso, Igor Stravinsky, Arturo Toscanini, Florenz Ziegfeld, Theodore Dreiser, and Babe Ruth. Today, the Ansonia is a condominium apartment building.

GETTING ORIENTED

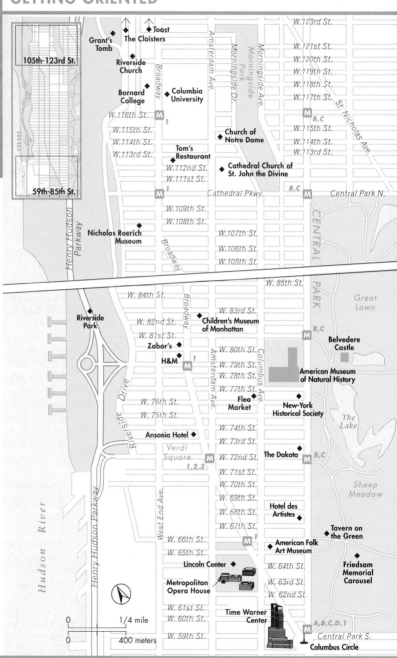

105th–123rd St.

Grant's Tomb
Toast
The Cloisters
Riverside Church
Barnard College
Columbia University
Church of Notre Dame
Tom's Restaurant
Cathedral Church of St. John the Divine
Nicholas Roerich Museum

W.123rd St.
W.121st St.
W.120th St.
W.119th St.
W.118th St.
W.117th St.
B,C
W.115th St.
W.114th St.
W.113th St.

W.116th St.
W.115th St.
W.114th St.
W.113th St.
W.112th St.
W.111th St.
Cathedral Pkwy.
B,C
Central Park N.

W.109th St.
W.108th St.
W.107th St.
W.106th St.
W.105th St.

Amsterdam Ave.
Morningside Dr.
Morningside Park
Morningside Ave.
St. Nicholas Ave.
Broadway

59th–85th St.

Henry Hudson Parkway

CENTRAL PARK

W. 85th St.
Great Lawn

Riverside Park
W. 84th St.
W. 82nd St.
W. 81st St.
Zabar's
H&M
W. 83rd St.
Children's Museum of Manhattan
B,C
Belvedere Castle
W. 80th St.
W. 79th St.
W. 78th St.
W. 77th St.
American Museum of Natural History
Flea Market
New-York Historical Society
The Lake

W. 76th St.
W. 75th St.
Ansonia Hotel
W. 74th St.
W. 73rd St.
The Dakota
B,C
Sheep Meadow

Verdi Square
1,2,3
W. 72nd St.
W. 71st St.
W. 70th St.
W. 69th St.
W. 68th St.
W. 67th St.
Hotel des Artistes
Tavern on the Green
American Folk Art Museum
W. 66th St.
W. 65th St.
Lincoln Center
Metropolitan Opera House
W. 64th St.
W. 63rd St.
W. 62nd St.
Friedsam Memorial Carousel

W. 61st St.
W. 60th St.
W. 59th St.
Time Warner Center
A,B,C,D,1
Central Park S.
Columbus Circle

Broadway
Amsterdam Ave.
Columbus Ave.
West End Ave.
Riverside Drive
Henry Hudson Parkway
Hudson River

0   1/4 mile
0   400 meters

TOP 5

- The dinosaurs on the 4th floor of the American Museum of Natural History
- The Cathedral of St. John the Divine, the largest Gothic cathedral in the world
- Sunset at the Boat Basin Café in Riverside Park
- A performance at Lincoln Center
- Coffee at the Mandarin Hotel, overlooking Central Park

GETTING HERE

The A, B, C, D, and 1 subway lines will take you to Columbus Circle. From there, the B and C lines stop at various points along Central Park (at 72nd, 81st, 86th, 96th, and 110th streets. The 1 train stops at 72nd, 79th, 86th, 96th, 103rd, 110th, 116th, and 125th streets.

A GOOD WALK

This is a great walking neighborhood. West 71st Street or West 74th Street between Broadway and Central Park West are perfect for casual strolling, with shops and restaurants dotting the route. At West 72nd Street, where Broadway cuts across Amsterdam Avenue, is triangular Verdi Square (named for Italian opera composer Giuseppe Verdi); here a marble statue of the composer is flanked by figures from Verdi's operas: *Aida*, *Otello*, and *Falstaff*. The triangle south of West 72nd Street is Sherman Square (named for Union Civil War general William Tecumseh Sherman); the **subway kiosk** is an official city landmark.

QUICK BITES

Absolute Bagel, (✉ 2788 Broadway, at 107th St., Upper West Side) is famed for fresh, warm bagels schmeared (local lingo for "spread") with one of their many flavored cream cheeses (try the sun-dried tomato and basil).

The tree-filled garden at **Café La Fortuna** (✉ 69 W. 71st St., between Columbus Ave. and Central Park W., Upper West Side ☎ 212/724–5846) is a quiet place to sip a cappuccino and snack on a prosciutto-and-mozzarella sandwich.

Overhyped? Definitely. But New York institution and glorified hot-dog stand **Gray's Papaya** (✉ 2090 Broadway, at W. 72nd St., Upper West Side ☎ 212/799–0243) still draws plenty of customers. Two juicy hot dogs with your pick of onions, sauerkraut, or mustard and a tropical fruit drink for less than two bucks is a hard price to beat.

Columbia-area intellectual hangout **Hungarian Pastry Shop** (✉ 1030 Amsterdam Ave., at W. 111th St., Morningside Heights ☎ 212/866–4230) is a cozy—as in small *and* as in comfortable—place for tasty desserts and coffee. The exterior of **Tom's Restaurant** (✉ 2880 Broadway, at 112th St., Morningside Heights ☎ 212/864–6137) made frequent appearances on the TV show *Seinfeld*. Whether you are excited by its claim to fame or not, this diner is still a decently priced place for a quick bite.

10

✉ *2109 Broadway, between 73rd and 74th Sts., Upper West Side* Ⓜ *Subway: 1, 2, 3, 9 to 72nd St.*

Wandering leisurely up Central Park West in the 70s and 80s, and down Upper West Side streets just window shopping, stopping into cafés, or eating ice-cream on a stoop makes you feel like a character in a Woody Allen movie—or at least like a regular old New Yorker.

Fodor'sChoice
★

Cathedral Church of St. John the Divine. Everything about the cathedral is colossal, from its cavernous 601-foot-long nave, which can hold some 5,000 worshippers, to its 162-foot-tall dome crossing, which could comfortably contain the Statue of Liberty (minus its pedestal), and its **Great Rose Window,** the largest stained-glass window in the United States, made from more than 10,000 pieces of colored glass. Even though this divine behemoth is unfinished—the transepts and towers are the most noticeably uncompleted elements—it is already the largest Gothic cathedral in the world. To get the full effect of the building's size, approach it from Broadway on West 112th Street. On the wide steps climbing to the Amsterdam Avenue entrance, five portals arch over the entrance doors. The central **Portal of Paradise** depicts St. John witnessing the Transfiguration of Jesus, and 32 biblical characters, all intricately carved in stone. The 3-ton bronze doors below the portal open only three times a year— on Easter, in October for the Feast of St. Francis, and for the annual "blessing of the bicycles" in the spring. The doors have relief castings of scenes from the Old Testament on the left and from the New Testament on the right.

The cathedral's cornerstone was laid in 1892. The original architects were George Heins and Christopher Grant Lafarge, who had beat out 80 other competitors with a Romanesque-Byzantine design. It took nearly 20 years for just the choir and vaulted dome crossing to be completed. When Heins died, the project came under the direction, in 1911, of Ralph Adams Cram, a Gothic Revival purist who insisted on a French Gothic style for the edifice (his work also shaped Princeton University and West Point). The granite of the original Romanesque-Byzantine design is still visible inside at the crossing, where it has yet to be finished with the Gothic limestone facing. Note that the finished arches are pointed—Gothic—whereas the uncovered two are in the rounded Byzantine style. Although work on the cathedral had continued for nearly 50 years, construction came to a halt during World War II. Work did not resume again until 1979, by which time stonecutting had become something of a lost art in this country; in order to continue building, stonecutters came from Europe to train local craftspeople. This project ended in the early '80s. As it stands, the cathedral is now about two-thirds complete. In January 2005, an ongoing cleaning and restoration project began following a fire on December 18, 2001.

Inside, the **Saint Saviour Chapel** contains a three-panel bronze altar in white-gold leaf with religious scenes by artist Keith Haring (this was his last work before he died in 1990). The more conventional **baptistry** (temporarily closed due to the fire), to the left of the altar, is an exquisite oc-

Holy House Cats

On the first Sunday of October, the Cathedral Church of St. John the Divine is truly a zoo. In honor of St. Francis, the patron saint of animals and nature, the church holds its usual Sunday service with a twist: the service is attended by men, women, children, dogs, cats, rabbits, hamsters, and the occasional horse, sheep, or ant farm. In past years, upwards of 3,500 New Yorkers have shown up to have their pets blessed. A procession is led by such guest animals as elephants, camels, llamas, and golden eagles. Tickets are first-come, first-served. The service starts at 11.

tagonal chapel with a 15-foot-high marble font and a polychrome sculpted frieze commemorating New York's Dutch heritage. The altar area expresses the cathedral's interfaith tradition and international mission—with menorahs, Shinto vases, and, in the **Chapels of the Seven Tongues,** which surround the altar, dedications to various ethnic groups.

A precinct of châteaulike Gothic-style buildings, known as the **Cathedral Close,** is behind the cathedral on the south side. In a corner by the Cathedral School is the **Biblical Garden,** with perennials, herbs, and an arbor. Around the bend from here is a rose garden. Back at Amsterdam Avenue, the **Peace Fountain** depicts the struggle of good and evil. The forces of good, embodied in the figure of the archangel Michael, triumph by decapitating Satan, whose head hangs from one side. The fountain is encircled by small, whimsical animal figures cast in bronze from pieces sculpted by children. ✉ *1047 Amsterdam Ave., at W. 112th St., Morningside Heights* ☎ *212/316–7540, 212/662–2133 box office, 212/932–7347 tours* ⊕ *www.stjohndivine.org* ⌚ *Tours $5* ☉ *Mon.–Sat. 7:30–6, Sun. 7:30–7; tours Tues.–Sat. at 11. A vertical tour with a climb of 124 feet to the top is given on Sat. at noon and 2; reservations required. $15. Sun. services at 8, 9, 9:30, 11, and 6* Ⓜ *Subway: 1, 9 to 110th St./Cathedral Pkwy.*

Church of Notre Dame. A French neoclassical building (1911), this Roman Catholic church has a grand interior, including a replica of the French grotto of Lourdes behind its altar. It once served a predominantly French community of immigrants, but like the neighborhood, today's congregation is more ethnically diverse, with Irish, German, Italian, African-American, Hispanic, and Filipino members. ✉ *405 W. 114th St., between Amsterdam Ave. and Morningside Dr., Morningside Heights* ☎ *212/866–1500* ☉ *Bldg. open 30 mins before and after masses. Mass weekdays at 8 and 12:05, Sat. at 12:05, and Sun. at 8:30, 11:30, and 5:30* Ⓜ *Subway: 1 to 116th St./Columbia University.*

Columbia University. This wealthy, private, coed Ivy League school was New York's first college. Today Columbia's main campus occupies 36 acres, with a formal axial arrangement typical of 19th-century Beaux-Arts architecture. The herringbone-pattern brick paths of College Walk lead into the open main quadrangle, dominated by the **Butler Library** to the south and the **Low Memorial Library** to the north. Butler, built in 1934, holds the bulk of the university's 8 million books. Modeled on the Roman Pantheon, Low is now an administrative center and exhibit hall, but on weekdays you can go inside to see its domed, former Reading Room, marble rotunda, and 16 colossal columns. Low Library also houses the **Visitors Center,** where you can pick up a campus map or go on a campus tour. The steps of Low Library, presided over by Daniel Chester French's statue *Alma Mater,* have been a focal point for campus life, not least during the student protests of 1968.

Before Columbia moved here, this site was occupied by the Bloomingdale Insane Asylum, evidenced today only by Buell Hall (1878), a gabled orange-red brick house east of Low Library. North of Buell Hall is the interdenominational **St. Paul's Chapel,** an exquisite little Byzantine-style dome church with salmon-colored Guastavino tile vaulting inside. ⊠ *Main entrance at 116th St. and Broadway, Morningside Heights* ☎ *212/854–4900* ⊕ *www. columbia.edu* ⊗ *Weekdays 9–5. Tours begin at 11 and 2 weekdays from Room 213, Low Library* Ⓜ *Subway: 1 to 116th St./Columbia University.*

HERE'S WHERE

In 1915, the infamous "Typhoid Mary" Mallon was arrested at her place of employment, the Sloan Women's Hospital near Columbia University, where she was working as a cook after city officials had forbidden her from doing so. In her defense, Mallon didn't believe she carried typhoid fever, since she was never sick from it. And despite her notorious legacy, she passed on only 33 cases of the virus, 3 of which resulted in deaths.

Columbus Circle. Broadway, 8th Avenue, Central Park West, and Central Park South all meet at this busy intersection, which gets its name from the 700-ton granite monument capped by a marble statue of Christopher Columbus in the middle of the park in the center of the traffic circle. Inside the park are wooden benches, a fountain that masks the sounds and sights of passing cars, and rich landscaping. At nighttime, the fountain is especially striking, lighted by almost 300 lights.

The traffic circle sits to the east of the Time Warner Center, which looms over the circle with a concave front that fits into its curve. The 80-story, twin-tower super complex, designed by skyscraper architect David M. Childs, houses an array of shops on the first three floors, among them Sephora, Borders, and Coach. The third and fourth floors have restaurants, including outrageously priced and acclaimed sushi restaurant Masa (a meal for two tops $700), plus Thomas Keller's in-demand Per Se, and Gray Kunz's Café Gray. Above are luxury condos, offices, and the Mandarin Oriental Hotel. The building's paired 750-foot towers rise atop a glass-and-stone base and are shaped like parallelograms, mirroring the angle of Broadway and the lines of the city's side-street grid. Between the columns, allowing views from Central Park West westward is an 85-foot corridor of light. The main entrance, on Columbus Circle itself, is through a 150-foot curvilinear, cable-net glass wall.

Launched in 2004, **Jazz at Lincoln Center** (☎ 212/258–9800 ⊕ www. jalc.org) is the world's first performing-arts center created specifically for jazz. The center includes the large Rose Theater concert hall; the Allen

CLOSE UP

Famous Film Sites

Annie Hall (1977): Alvy waits for Annie in front of the Beekman Theater (2nd Ave. at E. 66th St.). At the end of the movie, Annie and Alvy part ways at 63rd and Columbus.

Breakfast at Tiffany's (1961): Holly Golightly's apartment is at 169 E. 71st Street, between Lexington and 3rd avenues.

Ghostbusters (1984): Dana Barrett's apartment is at 55 Central Park West (between 65th and 66th Sts). Movie magic made it appear taller than its 19 stories. The Columbia University campus appears near the beginning of the movie.

Hannah and Her Sisters (1986): Hannah lives at the Langham (135 Central Park West, between 73rd and 74th Sts.), which was Mia Farrow's own apartment.

Manhattan (1979): The film opens at Elaine's restaurant (2nd Ave. between E. 88th and E. 89th Sts.). Isaac meets his high-school-age girlfriend outside the Dalton School, at 108 East 89th Street.

Rosemary's Baby (1968): Filmed at the Dakota Apartments (Central Park West at 72nd St.).

West Side Story (1961): The tenements where the film was shot were later torn down to build Lincoln Center.

When Harry Met Sally (1989): The titular characters run into each other at the Shakespeare & Company bookstore (Lexington Ave. at 69th St.). Later they walk through the sunny modern art wing at the Metropolitan Museum of Art.

You've Got Mail (1998): Kathleen's bookshop was Maya Schaper Cheese & Antiques (W. 69th St. at Columbus Ave.). Joe stood her up at Café Lalo (W. 83rd St. between Amsterdam and Broadway) and rescued her at the checkout at Zabar's (Broadway at 80th St.). The final scene is at the Riverside Park 91st Street Garden.

Room, with its huge windows and skyline views; the intimate Dizzy's Club Coca-Cola, which overlooks Columbus Circle; and the Nesuhi Ertegun Jazz Hall of Fame, with a 24-foot-long video wall showing historic footage of hall-of-fame inductees. Adding another art installation to Manhattan, the Prow Sculpture at the southeast corner of the building is an environmental sculpture with polycarbonate panels that program a dramatic light show. Changing every 15 minutes, the lights create a meaningful and colorful display, reflecting moods, themes, and holidays. Northeast of Columbus Circle, standing guard over the entrance to Central Park, is the **Maine Monument,** whose gleaming equestrian figures perch atop a formidable limestone pedestal. At the monument's foot are horse-drawn carriages awaiting fares through Central Park, and a newsstand in a Victorian-style pavilion. The **Trump International Hotel and Tower** fills the wedge of land between Central Park West and Broadway; it's also home to the self-named Jean-Georges restaurant, where the celebrity chef works his culinary magic. On the south side, at Two Columbus Circle, is the former Huntington Hartford building, built in 1964 and vacant since 1998, currently undergoing extensive renovations

10

to open in 2007 as the new home of the Museum of Arts & Design. Ⓜ *Subway: A, B, C, D, 1 to 59 St./Columbus Circle.*

The Dakota. Most famous for being the home of John Lennon, the Dakota was designed by Henry Hardenbergh, who also built the Plaza Hotel. It was at the Dakota's gate that, in December 1980, a deranged fan shot and killed Lennon as he came home from a recording session. Other celebrity tenants have included Boris Karloff, Rudolf Nureyev, José Ferrer and Rosemary Clooney, Lauren Bacall, Rex Reed, Leonard Bernstein, Gilda Radner, and Connie Chung. When it was completed in 1884, the Dakota was so far uptown that it was jokingly described as being "out in the Dakotas." Indeed, this buff-color château, with picturesque gables, copper turrets, and a central courtyard, housed some of the West Side's first residents. ⊠ *1 W. 72nd St., at Central Park W, Upper West Side* Ⓜ *Subway: B, C to 72nd St.*

Grant's Tomb. Officially called the General Grant National Memorial, this Classical Revival–style national monument, the final resting place of Civil War general and two-term president Ulysses S. Grant and his wife, Julia Dent Grant, commands a stalwart position overlooking Riverside Park and the Hudson River. Designed by John H. Duncan and opened in 1897, almost 12 years after Grant's death, it was a more popular sight than the Statue of Liberty until the end of World War I. The towering granite tomb, the largest mausoleum in North America, is engraved with the words LET US HAVE PEACE, recalling Grant's speech to the Republican convention upon his presidential nomination. Enclosed in a large rotunda is a crypt housing the Grants' twin Wisconsin granite sarcophagi, visible from above; exhibits around the rotunda display photographs and Grant memorabilia. ⊠ *Riverside Dr. and W. 122nd St., Morningside Heights* ☎ *212/666–1640* ⊕ *www.nps.gov/gegr* 🖼 *Free* ☉ *Daily 9–4; 20-min tours at 10, noon, and 2* Ⓜ *Subway: 1 to 116th St. or 125th St.*

Hotel des Artistes. Built in 1918 with an elaborate, mock-Elizabethan lobby, this "studio building," like several others on West 67th Street, was designed with high ceilings and immense windows, making it ideal "live-work" space for artists. Its tenants have included Isadora Duncan, Rudolph Valentino, Norman Rockwell, Noël Coward, George Balanchine, and contemporary actors Joel Grey and Richard Thomas; another tenant, Howard Chandler Christy, designed the lush, soft-tone murals in the ground-floor restaurant, Café des Artistes. ⊠ *1 W. 67th St., at Central Park W, Upper West Side* Ⓜ *Subway: 1, 9 to 66th St./Lincoln Center.*

Riverside Church. The Riverside Drive–facing facade of this 1930 Gothic-style church, with elaborate stone carvings modeled on the French cathedral of Chartres, is gorgeous. The other reason to visit the church is to take the elevator to the top of the 392-foot tower, with its 72-bell carillon—the heaviest in the world at 200,000 pounds—to get the breathtaking panoramic view of the Hudson River, New Jersey Palisades, and George Washington Bridge from the bell tower. Call ahead to verify whether it is open, as the bell tower has recently been under renovation. ✉ *490 Riverside Dr., between W. 120th and W. 122 Sts., entrance on Claremont Avenue, on opposite side of the building Morningside Heights* ☎ *212/870–6792* 🌐 *www.theriversidechurchny.org* *Free* *Visitor center Tues. 10:30–5, Wed. 10:30–7, Thurs. and Fri. 10:30–5, Sun. 9:45–10:45 and 12:15–3. Service Sun. at 10:45; call for hrs for tower* Ⓜ *Subway: 1 to 116th St./Columbia University.*

DID YOU KNOW?

One of the world's largest Bible collections is on the Upper West Side. The American Bible Society Library (✉ 1865 Broadway, at 61st St. ☎ 212/408–1200) holds nearly 50,000 scriptural items in more than 2,000 languages, including Helen Keller's 10-volume Braille Bible, leaves from a first-edition Gutenberg Bible, and a Torah from China. Tours are by appointment only.

Riverside Park. When you spend your days surrounded by concrete and skyscrapers, it's easy to forget that an expansive waterfront is just blocks away. Riverside Park—bordering the Hudson from 72nd to 159th streets—dishes out a dose of perspective. The park was laid by Central Park's designers Olmsted and Vaux between 1873 and 1888 and is often, somewhat unfairly, outshone by Olmsted's "other" park. But with its waterfront bike- and walking paths and lesser crowds, Riverside Park holds its own.

From the corner of West 72nd Street and Riverside Drive—where a **statue of Eleanor Roosevelt** stands at the park's entrance—head down the ramp (through an underpass beneath the West Side Highway) to the **79th Street Boat Basin,** a rare spot in Manhattan where you can walk right along the river's edge and watch a flotilla of houseboats bobbing in the water. These boats must sail at least once a year to prove their seaworthiness. Behind the boat basin, the **Rotunda** is home in summer to the Boat Basin Cafe, an open-air spot for a burger and river views. From the Rotunda, head up to the **Promenade,** a broad formal walkway extending a few blocks north from West 80th Street, with a stone parapet overlooking the river.

At the end of the Promenade, a community garden explodes with flowers. To the right, cresting a hill along Riverside Drive at West 89th Street, stands the Civil War **Soldiers' and Sailors' Monument** (1902, designed by Paul M. Duboy), an imposing 96-foot-high circle of white-marble columns. From its base is a view of Riverside Park, the Hudson River, and the New Jersey waterfront. ✉ *W. 72nd to W. 159th Sts. between Riverside Dr. and the Hudson River, Upper West Side* Ⓜ *Subway: 1, 2, 3, to 72nd St.*

The Upper West Side At a Glance

SIGHTS
Ansonia Hotel
Cathedral Church of St. John the Divine
Church of Notre Dame
Columbia University
Columbus Circle
The Dakota
Grant's Tomb
Hotel des Artistes
Riverside Church

MUSEUMS & GALLERIES (⇨ Ch. 14)
American Folk Art Museum: Eva and Morris Feld Gallery
Children's Museum of Manhattan
New-York Historical Society
Nicholas Roerich Museum

PARKS & GARDENS
Riverside Park

WHERE TO EAT (⇨ Ch. 18)

BUDGET DINING
Alouette
Artie's Delicatessen
Barney Greengrass
Big Nick's
Cafe Lalo
Café con Leche
Columbus Bakery
Gennaro
Kitchenette
Mughlai
Nice Matin
Nonna
Ollie's
Onera
Patsy's Pizzeria
Saigon Grill
Sarabeth's

MODERATE DINING
Café des Artistes
Café Gray
Café Luxembourg
Carmine's
'Cesca
Compass
Docks Oyster Bar
Ocean Grill
Ouest
Picholine
Shun Lee West
Tavern on the Green

EXPENSIVE DINING
Asiate
Jean Georges
Per Se

WHERE TO STAY (⇨ Ch. 19)

BUDGET LODGING
Excelsior
Hotel Beacon
Malibu Studios Hotel
The Lucerne
YMCA West Side

EXPENSIVE LODGING
Trump International Hotel and Towers

BARS & NIGHTLIFE (⇨ Ch. 16)
Smoke, *jazz club*
Café des Artistes, *bar*
Gabriel's, *bar*
Hi-Life, *bar*
Peter's, *bar*
Shark Bar, *bar*

ARTS & ENTERTAINMENT (⇨ Ch. 15)
ABC Studios, *television*
Big Apple Circus, *circus*
The Cloisters, *music*
Frederick P. Rose Hall, *music*
IMAX Theater, *film*
Lincoln Center for the Performing Arts, *performance venue*
Lincoln Plaza Cinemas, *film*
Loews Lincoln Square Theater, *film*
Makor/Steinhardt Center, *readings*
Merkin Concert Hall, *music*
Metropolitan Opera, *opera*
Miller Theatre, *music*
New York City Opera, *opera*
New York Public Library for the Performing Arts, *library*
Symphony Space, *performance venue*
Walter Reade Theater, *film*
The View, *television*

SHOPPING (⇨ Ch. 17)

BOOKS
Westsider Rare & Used Books

CLOTHING
Allan & Suzi
Intermix
Morris Bros
Pookie & Sebastian
Sude
Z'Baby Company

HOME DECOR
Fishs Eddy

LEATHER GOODS
Coach

MUSIC
Westsider Records

PERFUME/COSMETICS
Kiehl's Since 1851
Lush

WINE
Acker Merrall & Condit

Harlem

WORD OF MOUTH

"We ate dinner at Lenox Lounge in Harlem and it was fantastic! Soul food at its best. I had the rib/seafood combo (ribs, shrimp, mac & cheese, with yams), very very good! . . . The atmosphere here gives you that '70s feel."

—louise1928

Sightseeing
★ ★ ★ ★

Nightlife
★

Dining
★ ★ ★ ★

Lodging
★ ★ ★

Shopping
★ ★ ★ ★

Harlem is known throughout the world as a center of culture, music, and African-American life. Today's Harlem, however, is a very different Harlem from that of 10 years ago, when many considered it too dangerous to visit with little to offer in the way of cultural attractions, business, or residential life. Renovated and new buildings are appearing throughout the area, joining such jewels as the Apollo Theatre, architecturally splendid churches, and cultural magnets like the Studio Museum in Harlem and the Schomburg Center for Research in Black Culture. Black (and, increasingly, white) professionals and young families are restoring many of Harlem's classic brownstone and limestone buildings, bringing new life to the community.

Both residential and commercial rents have doubled as the neighborhood has become more desirable and more affordable relative to other parts of the city. Former President Bill Clinton's selection of 55 West 125th Street as the site of his New York office has also been an inspiration to businesses considering a move to Harlem, with new outposts cropping up by the likes of Starbucks, Old Navy, The Body Shop, MAC Cosmetics, and H & M.

The city's north–south avenues take on different names in Harlem: 6th Avenue is Malcolm X Boulevard (formerly Lenox Avenue), 7th Avenue is Adam Clayton Powell Jr. Boulevard, and 8th Avenue is Frederick Douglass Boulevard; West 125th Street, the major east–west street, is called Martin Luther King Jr. Boulevard.

What's Here

Harlem's commercial centers are on 116th and 125th streets. Traveling west to east along 116th leads from African-American neighborhoods to the area more traditionally known as Spanish Harlem. Even busier, 125th Street is a continuous traffic jam of people and cars that offers a concentrated glimpse into life in the neighborhood.

Harlem has more than 300 churches covering many denominations and with many opening their doors to visitors on the weekends. Among them are the **Abyssinian Baptist Church** on 138th Street; the **Memorial Baptist Church** on 115th Street; and the ornate **First Corinthian Baptist Church,** at the corner of Adam Clayton Powell Jr. Blvd. and 116th Street. In striking contrast, at 116th and Malcolm X Boulevard, the plain but colorful **Masjid Malcolm Shabazz,** with its onion domes and yellow arched windows, is a center of the Muslim community. Also important to the community is the **Malcolm Shabazz Harlem Market,** where you can stock up on jewelry, African masks, and caftans at good prices.

Music buffs will want to stop by the now-defunct **Minton's Playhouse** on 118th Street, the club where bebop was born; or visit the Cotton Club at 125th Street at 12th Avenue, not the original club of legendary jazz fame (which closed in 1935) but a newer, smaller version that continues the tradition of offering jazz and swing concerts along with a terrific weekend gospel brunch. Also on 125th Street, the landmark **Apollo Theatre** now makes an even more striking presence with its new digital marquee and spruced-up facade. In an area literally buzzing with action, the legendary jazz and writer hangout, the **Lenox Lounge** is just south of 125th Street on Lenox Avenue. Harlem's incipient Walk of Fame lies on 135th Street between Adam Clayton Powell Jr. and Frederick Douglass boulevards and includes plaques for notable Harlem musicians like Dizzy Gillespie and Tito Puente.

Parks are an important part of Harlem with open spaces and vistas that are a scarcity in more southern parts of the city. **Marcus Garvey Park,** along Fifth Avenue from 120th Street to 124th Street, has one of Manhattan's original fire watchtowers. Dating from 1855, the Acropolis upon which the tower is set offers a vantage point from which the Empire State Building can be seen. To the south and west of the park and along the side streets are well-preserved late-19th-century brownstones of the Mount Morris Historic District. Recent times have seen an active effort to refurbish these beautiful parkside homes and many command premium prices.

You can find lots of hip-hop clothing shops on 125th Street, along withAfrican hair braiding, and an ever-increasing variety of specialty shops. Familiar chain stores like H & M, Foot Locker, and Old Navy join local favorites like Carol's Daughter and Nubian Heritage Harlem, where body sprays, soaps, and essential oils tantalize with unusual fragrance combinations.

GETTING ORIENTED

Hispanic Society of America

W. 155th St.

Highbridge Park

409 Edgecombe Avenue

W. 153rd St.

◆ **Sugar Hill**

W. 152nd St.

Dance Theatre of Harlem

W. 151st St.

W. 150th St.

Broadway

Amsterdam Ave.

Convent Ave.

Nicholas Ave.

Jackie Robinson Park

Frederick Douglass Blvd. (8th Ave.)

W. 149th St.

W. 148th St.

W. 147th St.

W. 146th St.

W. 145th St.

1,9

A,B,C,D

W. 144th St.

Hamilton Grange National Monument

W. 143rd St.

W. 142nd St.

W. 141st St.

W. 140th St.

City College

W. 138th St.

St. Nicholas Park

◆ **Strivers' Row**

W. 139th St.

Abyssinian Baptist Church

ST. NICHOLAS HISTORIC DISTRICT

W. 137th St.

W. 136th St.

B,C

2,3

E. 135th St.

Adam Clayton Powell Jr. Blvd.

Lenox Ave./Malcolm X Blvd.

W. 135th St.

W. 133rd St.

1,9

Frederick Douglass Blvd.

W. 134th St.

W. 132nd St.

E. 131st St.

W. 130th St.

◆ **Astor Row Houses**

E. 129th St.

◆ **The Cotton Club**

W. 129th St.

W. 128th St.

W. 127th St.

Martin Luther King Jr. Blvd.

Sylvia's Soul Food Restaurant

125th St. Metro North Station

Apollo Theater

A,B,C,D

African Sq.

W. 126th St.

2,3

Studio Museum in Harlem

(8th Ave.)

(7th Ave.)

W. 124th St.

Martin Luther King Jr. Blvd. (125th St.)

Lenox Lounge

W. 123rd St.

W. 122nd St.

W. 121st St.

W. 120th St.

Lenox Ave./Malcolm X Blvd.

Mt. Morris Park West

Marcus Garvey Park

Madison Ave.

E. 119th St.

Barnard College

Morningside Park

Columbia University

1,9

W. 116th St.

Broadway

Amsterdam Ave.

Canaan Baptist Church of Christ

B,C

2,3

◆ **Minton's Play House**

E. 117th St.

Malcolm Shabazz ◆ Harlem Market

St. Nicholas Ave.

First Corinthian Baptist Church

W. 114th St.

W. 113th St.

W. 112nd St.

Masjid Malcolm Shabazz

(Sixth Ave.)

E. 115th St.

W. 111th St.

1,9

B,C

2,3

Central Park North

E. 110th St.

Central Park W.

CENTRAL PARK

Harlem Meer

Riverside Dr.

Henry Hudson Pkwy.

Riverside Park

Harlem River Dr.

145 St. Bridge

Harlem River

Madison Ave. Bridge

Fifth Ave.

Park Ave.

0   1/4 mile

0   400 meters

TOP 5

■ Dinner at Sylvia's Soul Food Restaurant

■ Attending a gospel service

■ Browsing through the Malcolm Shabazz Harlem Market

■ Walking 125th Street

■ A jazz session at Lenox Lounge

GETTING HERE

The 2, 3 subway stops on Lenox Avenue; the 1 goes along Broadway; and the A, B, C, D trains (the A train is of legendary Duke Ellington fame) travel along St. Nicholas and 8th Aves.

QUICK BITES

Sylvia's Soul Food Restaurant (✉ 328 Malcolm X Blvd., between W. 126th and W. 127th Sts. ☎ 212/996-0660), the most famous soul-food spot in Harlem, serves up such Southern specialties as catfish, ribs, eggs, and fried chicken (for breakfast).

For home-style Southern cuisine in a casual, more intimate setting, visit **Amy Ruth's** (✉ 113 W. 116th St., between Lenox Ave. and Adam Clayton Powell Jr. Blvd. ☎ 212/280-8779). Ask for the "Rev. Al Sharpton," a combination of waffles with fried or smothered chicken, one of the more than a dozen choices on their amazing waffle menu.

At **Settepani Bakery** (✉ 197 Malcolm X Blvd./Lenox Ave., at 120th St. ☎ 917/492-4806), an Italian oasis, glass displays are filled with biscotti, pies, and cakes; dining options include Sicilian egg specialties, panini, and pastas.

A GOOD WALK

Walk east on 116th Street from 8th Avenue for a tour of some of Harlem's most interesting religious institutions: ornate **First Corinthian Baptist Church** is first, on your right; across 7th Avenue you come to **Canaan Baptist Church of Christ** and then **Masjid Malcolm Shabazz** mosque. To be in the cultural hub of present-day Harlem walk along 125th Street for an in-your-face flurry of activity that resembles an outdoor strip mall. In front of the towering stores, hawkers sell bootleg CDs and DVDs, books, and homemade essential oils in nondescript bottles.

It is still advisable, however, to use common sense when walking around. Stay close to main commercial areas like 125th Street and Lenox Avenue if you visit at night, and enjoy the side streets and parks during daylight hours.

CLOSE UP

Harlem Gospel Tours

The typical "gospel tour" includes only a 20-minute stop at a church to hear some of the sermon and the gospel music. Then you're off (via bus) to another Harlem sight or to a soul-food brunch. Prices range from $35 to $80. The tours are an expeditious, if not authentic, way to experience a bit of Harlem.

The tours garner mixed reactions from church officials and parishioners. Some see it as an opportunity to broaden horizons and encourage diversity. But others find tours disruptive and complain that tourists take seats away from regular parishioners (churches regularly fill to capacity). If you decide to go on one of these tours, remember that parishioners do not consider the service, or themselves, to be tourist attractions. Also, dress nicely. Harlem churchgoers take the term "Sunday best" to heart and are impressively

decked out. Be as quiet as possible and avoid taking photos or videos.

For a rich gospel-church experience, do your own tour. The following are some of the Uptown churches with gospel choirs:

Abyssinian Baptist Church (⇨ *Harlem*) is one of the few churches that does not allow tour groups. Services are at 9 and 11 AM. **Convent Avenue Baptist Church** (⊠ 429 W. 145th St., between Convent and St. Nicholas Aves. ☎ 212/234–6767 ⊕ www.conventchurch.org) has services at 8 AM, 11 AM, and 6 PM. **First Corinthian Baptist Church** (⇨ *Harlem*) has services at 11 AM.

Greater Refuge Temple (⊠ 2081 7th Ave., at 124th St. ☎ 212/866–1700) has services at 11 AM. **Memorial Baptist Church** (⇨ *Harlem*) has services at 10:45 AM. **Riverside Church** (⇨ *Harlem*) has services at 10:45 AM.

Between Lenox Avenue and Adam Clayton Powell Boulevard on 125th Street, the **Studio Museum in Harlem** showcases contemporary works of Harlem's burgeoning artist community. **El Museo del Barrio** on 5th Avenue and 104th Street is New York's only museum dedicated to Puerto Rican, Caribbean and Latin American art.

Places to Explore

Abyssinian Baptist Church. Charlie Parker's funeral was held here. Adam Clayton Powell Jr., the first black U.S. congressman, and his father, Adam Clayton Powell Sr., have both served as pastors here. Fats Waller's father was also a minister. The Gothic-style building opened its doors in 1923, but the church was founded in 1808 in Lower Manhattan (Worth Street) by a group of parishioners who defected from the segregated First Baptist Church of New York City, making Abyssinian Baptist Church the first African-American Baptist church in New York State. Sermons by pastor Calvin Butts are fiery and the seven choirs are excellent. The Coptic cross on the pulpit was a gift from Haile Selassie, when he was king of Ethiopia. Parishioners take the phrase "Sunday best" to heart, so look the part when you visit. Lineups on holiday Sundays can be intense. Expect to arrive at 6:30 AM on Easter Sunday. ⊠ *132 Odell Clark*

11

Pl. (W. 138th St.), between Adam Clayton Powell Jr. Blvd. (7th Ave.) and Malcolm X Blvd. (Lenox Ave.), Harlem ☎ *212/862–7474* ⊕ *www. abyssinian.org* ☉ *Sun. services at 9 and 11* Ⓜ *Subway: 2, 3 to 135 St.*

Canaan Baptist Church of Christ. The heavenly gospel music that saturates Sunday-morning services makes up for this church's concrete-box-esque exterior. Visitors are allowed to enter on Sunday once the parishioners have been seated. Don your Sunday best to attend an inspirational service to fully experience the passion of the church's choir and sermons. Pastor emeritus Wyatt Tee Walker worked with Dr. Martin Luther King Jr. in the 1960s and is an internationally known human rights activist. Dr. King delivered his famous "A Knock at Midnight" sermon (penned in 1963) here one month before his assassination in 1968. ⊠ *132 W. 116th St., between Malcolm X Blvd. (Lenox Ave./6th Ave.) and Adam Clayton Powell Jr. Blvd. (7th Ave.), Harlem* ☎ *212/866–0301* ☉ *Services Sun. at 10:45* AM Ⓜ *Subway: 2, 3 to 116th St.*

First Corinthian Baptist Church. One of the most ornate structures in Harlem, this church was built in 1913 as the Regent Theatre as the country moved from nickelodeons to elaborate movie palaces. The design is based on the Doges' Palace in Venice, evident in the thin columns and arches of the facade. Architect Thomas W. Lamb went on to design other prominent Manhattan theaters, including the French-inspired Embassy Theater and Cort Theater, and the modernist-baroque Hollywood Theater. The Regent was sold to the church in 1964. ⊠ *1910 Adam Clayton Powell Jr. Blvd. (7th Ave.), Harlem* ☎ *212/864–5796* ☉ *Services Sun. at 10:45* Ⓜ *Subway: 2, 3 to 116th St.*

DID YOU KNOW?

In the decade between 1993 and 2003, Harlem's crime rate dropped 65%, which is more than the crime decrease in famously "safe" neighborhoods Greenwich Village, SoHo, and Gramercy.

Marcus Garvey Park. The bedrock, or Manhattan schist, that anchors New York City's skyscrapers is visible here 70 feet above street level. The 20-acre park's unusual man-made feature is the three-tier, 47-foot cast-iron **watchtower** (Julius Kroel, 1856), the only remaining part of a now defunct citywide network used to spot and report fires in the days before the telephone. Originally Mount Morris Park, the park was renamed in 1973 after Jamaican-born Marcus Garvey (1887–1940), who preached from nearby street corners and founded the United Negro Improvement Association in 1914. Handsome neoclassical row houses of the **Mount Morris Park Historic District** front the west side of the park and line side streets. ⊠ *Interrupts 5th Ave. between W. 120th and W. 124th Sts., Madison Ave. to Mt. Morris Park W, Harlem* ⊕ *www.eastharlem.com/parks_mg.htm* Ⓜ *Subway: 2, 3 to 125th St.*

Masjid Malcolm Shabazz (Mosque). Talk about religious conversions. In the mid-'60s the Lenox Casino was transformed into this house of worship and cultural center. Yellow panels were added above the windows to create arches, and a huge green onion dome sits atop the building. The mosque was named for El-Hajj Malik Shabazz (better known as Malcolm X), who once preached here. Though the mosque was founded on the con-

Harlem's Jazz Age

IT WAS IN HARLEM that Billie Holiday got her first singing job, Duke Ellington made his first recording, and Louis Armstrong was propelled to stardom. Jazz was king during the Harlem Renaissance in the 1920s and '30s, and though Chicago and New Orleans may duke it out for the "birthplace of jazz" title, New York was where jazz musicians came to be heard.

In the 1920s, downtown socialites would flock to Harlem's Cotton Club and Connie's Inn (131st St. and 7th Ave.) to hear "black" music. Both clubs were white-owned and barred blacks from entering, except as performers. (The rules changed years later.) It was at Connie's that New York was introduced to Louis Armstrong. Harlem's most popular nightspot by far, the Cotton Club booked such big names as Fletcher Henderson,

Coleman Hawkins, Duke Ellington, Cab Calloway, and Ethel Waters. After shows ended at the paying clubs, musicians would head to such after-hours places with black patrons as Small's Paradise (229 7th Ave., at 135th St.), Minton's Playhouse, and Basement Brownies, where they'd hammer out new riffs into the wee hours.

Today you can hear great jazz all over the city, but old-time clubs like the Lenox Lounge still hash it out unlike anywhere else. Why? Partly due to history and sense of place, and partly due to—as musicians claim—the more easygoing nature of uptown clubs, which tend to have more flexible sets and open jam sessions. You can't go back in time to Harlem's jazz heyday, but you might catch a modern-day jazz great in the making.

---

cept of pro-black racism that Shabazz urged at one point in his life, the message today is one of inclusion, the philosophy adopted by Shabazz near the end of his life. ✉ *102 W. 116th St. at Malcolm X Blvd. (Lenox Ave./6th Ave.), Harlem* ☎ *212/622–2200* Ⓜ *Subway: 2, 3 to 116th St.*

Strivers' Row. Since 1919, African-American doctors, lawyers, and other professionals have owned these elegant homes designed by such notable architects as Stanford White (his Italian-Renaissance creations stand on the north side of West 139th Street). Musicians W. C. Handy ("The St. Louis Blues") and Eubie Blake ("I'm Just Wild About Harry") were among the residents here. Behind each row are service alleys, a rare luxury in Manhattan. The area, now officially known as the St. Nicholas Historic District, got its nickname because less affluent Harlemites felt that its residents were "striving" to become well-to-do. Note the gatepost between numbers 251 and 253 on W. 138th Street that says, "Private Road. Walk Your Horses." ✉ *W. 138th and W. 139th Sts. between Adam Clayton Powell Jr. and Frederick Douglass Blvds., Harlem* Ⓜ *Subway: B, C to 135th St.*

Sugar Hill. From the 1920s to the 1950s, Sugar Hill, on a hill overlooking Colonial Park (now Jackie Robinson Park), was Harlem's high-society neighborhood. Built from the mid-1880s to the First World War,

A Walk through Hamilton Heights

11

CLOSE UP

THE ENCLAVES OF SUGAR HILL and Hamilton Heights were carved out by Harlem's elite in the late 1800s and early 1900s. From their position on a rocky bluff above lower Harlem, the districts' residents could literally "look down on" their less-fortunate neighbors. The historic district is bordered roughly by Amsterdam Avenue to the east, Edgecombe and St. Nicholas avenues to the west, and 140th and 155th streets to the north and south. Some blocks within these confines are historic in spirit only and appear quite shabby. Other blocks, tree lined and with nicely preserved prewar row houses, are as attractive as those you find in the West Village.

One of the first homes in the area, and a good first stop in Hamilton Heights, is the federal-style mansion built for Alexander Hamilton. The **Hamilton Grange National Memorial** (✉ 147 Convent Ave., between 141st and 142nd Sts. ☎ 212/283-5154 ⊕ www.nps.gov/hagr) is now wedged between a church and an apartment building. Inside, restored rooms give the appearance of the years during Hamilton's residence. Out front stands a statue of Hamilton. Less than a block down pretty Convent Avenue, the Gothic spires of **City College** (✉ Convent Ave. between 138th and 140th Sts.), built in 1905, loom seemingly out of nowhere. The college's campus, stretching from 130th to 141st streets—inspired by Oxford and Cambridge—is worth a meander, especially in spring when trees are flowering. (Bonus points: spot the rebellious sycamore tree that "ate" the KEEP OFF THE GRASS sign.) At 141st Street, go east and then turn left onto **Hamilton Terrace,** a time capsule of elegant stone row houses in mint condition.

Getting There: A, B, C, D to 145th St.

the area encompasses Queen Anne styling, Romanesque Revival, and neo-Renaissance row houses and Beaux-Arts apartment buildings. Some of the most affluent and influential African-Americans lived here—to name a few: activist W.E.B. Du Bois; Supreme Court Justice Thurgood Marshall; NAACP leaders Walter White and Roy Wilkins (all four of whom lived at 409 Edgecombe Ave.); writers Langston Hughes and Zora Neale Hurston; and jazz musicians Duke Ellington, Andy Kirk, Count Basie, and Johnny Hodges, who all lived at 555 Edgecombe Ave., where an open jazz concert happens Sunday afternoons. Despite its wealth of prominent black leaders, Sugar Hill was, and remains, one of the most diverse parts of Harlem. The gradual decline of Sugar Hill, and Harlem, hit bottom in the '70s and '80s when buildings were neglected and criminals roamed the streets. Today, although Sugar Hill hasn't reclaimed its old glory, it is benefiting from Harlem's so-called second renaissance. ✉ *Bounded by 145th and 155th Sts. and Edgecombe and St. Nicholas Aves.*

Harlem At a Glance

SIGHTS
Abyssinian Baptist Church
Canaan Baptist Church of
  Christ
First Corinthian Baptist
  Church
Masjid Malcolm Shabazz
Strivers' Row
Sugar Hill
MUSEUMS & GALLERIES
  (⇨ Ch. 14)

Hispanic Society of
  America
Studio Museum in Harlem
PARKS & GARDENS
Marcus Garvey Park
WHERE TO EAT
  (⇨ Ch. 18)
BUDGET DINING
Bayou
Dinosaur Bar-B-Que

BARS & NIGHTLIFE
  (⇨ Ch. 16)
Lenox Lounge, *jazz club*
ARTS & ENTERTAINMENT
  (⇨ Ch. 15)
Aaron Davis Hall,
  music
It's Showtime at the
  Apollo, *television*

Brooklyn

WORD OF MOUTH

"If you have a long vacation in NYC it's worth the trek out to the [Brooklyn Botanic Gardens]. The Japanese garden is very peaceful, there is a whole indoor area with tropical plants and flowers, and there is also a scent garden. All in all it makes for a lovely morning or afternoon." —Cameron

"There's a great aquarium [at Coney Island]. And the 1940s-style rides and tacky games can be a hoot for the afternoon. And everyone should have a Nathan's famous." —Nytraveler

Sightseeing
★ ★

Nightlife
★ ★ ★

Dining
★ ★

Lodging
★

Shopping
★ ★

Hardly Manhattan's wimpy sidekick, Brooklyn is a metropolis in its own right. It's the most populous of all the boroughs, with nearly 2.5 million residents; if it were independent of New York, it would rank among the five largest cities in the country. Diverse neighborhoods share a down-to-earth character: the steps of brownstone apartments host chats and "stoop sales," family-owned businesses preserve ethnic heritages, and patrons at restaurants and bars are happy to eat and drink rather than "see and be seen." It's largely Brooklyn that has lent New York its streetwise and sincere personality, famously captured in films such as *Do the Right Thing, Moonstruck,* and *Smoke.*

What's Here

Williamsburg

Bedford Avenue and its offshoots are like a catwalk for hipsters who, not living for fashion alone, call in at cafés, galleries, and bars on their way to and from that umbilical cord to Manhattan: the L train. Until the mid-1990s, the industrial area on the East River was better known for its mix of Hasidic Jews, Poles, and Puerto Ricans, but as rents rose in the East Village, artists moved one subway stop into Brooklyn to add some splash to the desolate-looking streetscape. Most of the action can be found between Metropolitan Avenue and North 9th Street along Bedford Avenue, Williamsburg's main drag. The nightlife is great for affordable drinks and eccentric entertainment, especially at **Galapagos,** which hosts everything from burlesque to singing acrobats and film screenings. You don't have to leave Manhattan to taste its brews, but you can only tour the **Brooklyn Brewery** here.

Brooklyn Heights

Residents here have something wealthy Manhattanites never will: a stunning view of the Manhattan skyline from the **Brooklyn Heights Promenade.** First developed in the mid-1800s, much of the Heights was designated New York's first historic district in the 1960s. Some 600 buildings built in the 19th century represent a wide range of American building styles and are in excellent condition. Many of the best line **Columbia Heights,** a residential street that runs parallel to promenade. In the 1940s and '50s, the Heights was a bohemian haven, home to writers that included Carson McCullers, W. H. Auden, Arthur Miller, Truman Capote, Richard Wright, Alfred Kazin, Marianne Moore, and Norman Mailer. Pair a stroll here with a walk to DUMBO and a return trip over the **Brooklyn Bridge,** which has an access stairwell just off Cadman Plaza.

DUMBO

A downhill walk from Brooklyn Heights, the area called DUMBO (*Down Under the Manhattan Bridge Overpass*) hugs the East River and was once known as Fulton Landing, named after the inventor and engineer Robert Fulton, who introduced steamboat ferry service from Brooklyn to Manhattan in 1814. Factories and dry-goods warehouses thrived here until the Manhattan Bridge was built (from 1889 to 1909). Bridge construction eventually made the neighborhood obsolete, but since the 1970s, buildings have been reclaimed by loft residents and businesses. Today the **Fulton Ferry Landing**'s view of Manhattan and the Brooklyn Bridge makes it a favorite site for wedding photos; the New York Water Taxi stops here as well. You can get that same view from the Riverfront Café, which hugs the water next to the landing. Walking up the hill from the landing, save your appetite for pizza at **Grimaldi's Pizzeria,** which serves some of the best pie in the city. North of the Brooklyn Bridge, a deteriorating tobacco redbrick warehouse has been stabilized and incorporated into **Empire-Fulton Ferry State Park.** Those in the know wander the empty, old cobblestone streets for photo ops (try to frame the Empire State Building within the anchorage of the Manhattan Bridge) and to see who has joined the pioneers: galleries, bars and restaurants, home furnishing shops, and even a Starbucks.

Park Slope

The 2005 film *The Squid and the Whale* is set in 1980s Park Slope, and the family-friendly neighborhood is similarly full of academics, writers, and late-blooming couples who have their first child when pushing 40. Follow dog-walkers, joggers, and bicyclists to 526-acre **Prospect Park,** designed by the same landscapers of Central Park and from which the neighborhood streets "slope" down. Leafy side streets are coveted for their stately brownstone apartments with bay windows, and if you can't live in one, you can buy its castoffs at weekend stoop sales. Baby strollers and shoppers fill the cafés and local designer boutiques of 7th and 5th avenues. Adjacent to the park are two of Brooklyn's main attractions: the **Brooklyn Botanic Garden,** a must-see during its springtime Cherry Blossom Festival, and the **Brooklyn Museum,** known for its Egyptian and art collections.

GETTING ORIENTED

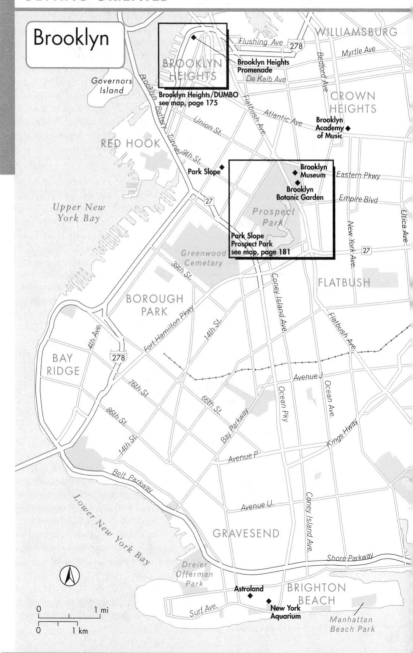

Brooklyn

WILLIAMSBURG

Flushing Ave 278

Myrtle Ave

Bedford Ave

Governors
Island

BROOKLYN
HEIGHTS

Brooklyn Heights
Promenade

De Kalb Ave

CROWN
HEIGHTS

Brooklyn Heights/DUMBO
see map, page 175

Brooklyn Battery Tunnel

Union St.

Atlantic Ave

Flatbush Ave

Brooklyn
Academy
of Music

RED HOOK

9th St.

Park Slope

Brooklyn
Museum

Eastern Pkwy

Brooklyn
Botanic Garden

Empire Blvd

Utica Ave.

Upper New
York Bay

27

Prospect
Park

New York Ave.

27

Park Slope
Prospect Park
see map, page 181

FLATBUSH

Greenwood
Cemetery

39th St.

BOROUGH
PARK

Fort Hamilton Pkwy

14th St.

Coney Island Ave.

Flatbush Ave.

BAY
RIDGE

4th Ave.

278

76th St.

66th St.

Bay Parkway

Avenue J

Ocean Pky

Ocean Ave.

Kings Hwy

86th St.

14th St.

Avenue P

Belt Parkway

Lower New York Bay

Avenue U

Coney Island Ave.

GRAVESEND

Shore Parkway

Dreier
Offerman
Park

Astroland

New York
Aquarium

Surf Ave.

BRIGHTON
BEACH

Manhattan
Beach Park

0   1 mi

0   1 km

12

TOP 5

■ Walking the Brooklyn Heights Promenade

■ Strolling the Brooklyn Botanic Gardens

■ A night out in Williamsburg

■ An afternoon in Coney Island

■ Breakfast, lunch, and a smile at Tom's Restaurant

A GOOD WALK

Start with a walk from Manhattan across the Brooklyn Bridge. (In Manhattan, the Brooklyn Bridge stop on the 6 train puts you at the foot of the pedestrian bridge path.) It takes 40 minutes to an hour to walk across the bridge and into Brooklyn; stay in the pedestrian lane to avoid the crossing bicyclists. To get off the bridge, take the Prospect Street exit (it's in the left lane, and leads down to a set of stairs). Turn left onto Washington Street, and carefully cross Cadman Plaza to Cadman Plaza West. Walk along this road in the direction of Manhattan until you reach the beginning of Middagh Street. Walk a half block up Middagh to Henry Street. Take a left on Henry and walk two blocks to Orange Street. Turn right; midblock, on the right side, between Henry and Hicks streets, is the Plymouth Church of the Pilgrims, a center of abolitionist sentiment in the years before the Civil War. Continue two blocks up Orange Street and turn left onto Willow Street to see the masterful local architecture between Clark and Pierrepont streets. At the corner of Willow and Pierrepont streets, turn right and walk up Pierrepont to its end at one of the most famous vistas in all of New York: the Brooklyn Heights Promenade. After you've soaked in the views, exit at the north side of the promenade and walk along Columbia Heights to Montague Street. Look right to see Nos. 2 and 3 Pierrepont Place, two brick-and-brownstone palaces built in the 1850s. Walk three blocks east on Montague (away from the promenade) to its intersection with Clinton; the Church of St. Ann and the Holy Trinity here is a local landmark. Turn left and walk one block on Clinton to Livingston to visit the impressive architecture and exhibits on display at the Brooklyn Historical Society. Return to Montague and walk one more block along this commercial strip to reach the R train back to Manhattan.

GETTING HERE

To get to **Williamsburg,** take the L train from 14th Street to Bedford Avenue, the first stop in Brooklyn.

You can reach **Brooklyn Heights** by the 2 or 3 to Clark Street, the M or R to Court Street, or the 4 or 5 to Borough Hall. To get to **DUMBO,** take the F train to York Street.

The F train to 7th Avenue will take you to the center of **Park Slope.** You can walk uphill to reach Prospect Park or walk north to sample the shops. The hipper boutiques and eateries are two long blocks west, on 5th Avenue. Closer subway stops to 5th Avenue include the 2 or 3 to Bergen Street or the R to Union Street. To reach the Brooklyn Museum, Brooklyn Botanic Gardens, and Prospect Park take the 2 or 3 train to Eastern Parkway/ Brooklyn Museum.

The last stop on D, F, or Q train is **Coney Island.** Allow a good part of the day for this trip, since it takes at least an hour to get here from Manhattan.

Coney Island

Named Konijn Eiland (Rabbit Island) by the Dutch for its wild rabbit population, the Coney Island peninsula on Brooklyn's southern shore has a boardwalk, a 2½-mi-long beach, a legendary amusement park, a baseball stadium, and the **New York Aquarium.** It's a great place to experience the sounds, smells, and sights of summer: hot dogs and ice cream; suntan lotion; crowds; and old men fishing the sea. And then there are the freakish attractions at **Sideshows by the Seashore** and the **Coney Island Museum,** the heart-stopping plunge of the granddaddy of roller coasters—the Cyclone—within **Astroland,** and the thwack of bats swung by Brooklyn's own minor-league team, the Cyclones, at **Keyspan Park.** The Coney Island boardwalk remains the hub of the action; amble along it to take in the local color. The area's banner day is the raucous Mermaid Parade, held in June.

Places to Explore

Williamsburg

Around 1900, Williamsburg was primarily a German neighborhood, and one with nearly 50 breweries and lots of bars and beer gardens. Those are all gone, but **Brooklyn Brewery** has been trying to bring back those traditions in its own way since it opened a plant here in 1996. Tours, held on Saturday afternoon, end with a tasting of Brooklyn brews, including its signature lager. Friday nights, the brewery hosts a happy hour from 6 to 11 PM. ⊠ *79 N. 11th St.* ☎ *718/486–7422* ⊕ *www. brooklynbrewery.com* ⊠ *Free* ☉ *Tours Sat. on the hr 1–4.*

At the **City Reliquary,** an unusual streetside museum, the windows of a ground-floor storefront have become an exhibit for forgotten pieces of New York history: weird pieces of trash that washed up from a canal, stones from construction sites, a prize from Coney Island, and "devil's nuts," a kind of fruit that grows in the ocean. Press the button to hear a recording explaining what's in front of you. Directions to nearby streets and subway stops are helpfully painted on the Reliquary's walls. ⊠ *307 Grand St., at Havemeyer St.* Ⓜ *Subway: J, M, Z to Marcy Ave.* ☎ *No phone* ⊕ *dhlabsnyc.com* ⊠ *Donations accepted* ☉ *Daily.*

WHERE TO EAT **Mugs Ale House** (⊠ 125 Bedford Ave., at N. 10th St. ☎ 718/486–8232. $6–$13) serves some of the best burgers and fries in the neighborhood—as well as reliable Italian and seafood specials. Try for a seat in the backroom, which has cozy booths and lots of fun beer posters on the walls.

Across the street from the Girdle Building, **Sparky's** (⊠ 135A N. 5th St., between Berry and Bedford Aves. ☎ 718/302–5151. $4) serves steamed, tasty hot dogs in what used to be a warehouse's loading dock. Get some cheese fries with your order.

With its large size, over-the-top, industrial design, **Planet Thailand** (⊠ 133 N. 7th St., between Bedford Ave. and Berry St. ☎ 718/599–5758. $6–$29) serves pad thai, sushi, and other Asian dishes at cheap prices.

Diner (⊠ 85 Broadway, at Berry St. ☎ 718/486–3077. $9–$22) may be inside an old diner car on a windblown crossroads, but the menu includes such sophisticated dishes as mussels, mesclun salad, and hanger steak in addition to great burgers and fries.

Peter Luger Steak House (⊠178 Broadway, at Driggs Ave. ☎718/387–7400. $37) brings meat-loving pilgrims from all over the city—and the world. Other steak houses have better lighting, more elegant dining, bigger wine lists, less brusque service, and comfortable chairs instead of wooden benches, but the steak makes it worth it. You probably won't see a menu, but here's all you need to know: shrimp cocktail, beefsteak tomato and onion salad, home fries, creamed spinach, pecan pie, and porterhouse steak—ordered according to how many are in your party. Be sure to make a reservation, and bring lots of cash—Luger's doesn't take plastic.

SHOPPING One stop on almost everyone's shopping expeditions to Williamsburg should be the **Girdle Building** (⊠ 218 Bedford Ave., at N. 5th St.). No undergarments are made here any more, but the ground floor has become a mall of local shops selling such essentials as books, vintage clothes, cheese, and wine. Taking its cue from its location, the **Girdle Factory** (☎718/486–9599) sells vintage lingerie, much of it in sultry designs from the 1950s and '60s. **Bedford Cheese Shop** (☎ 718/599–7588 ⊕ www. bedfordcheeseshop.com) is full of employees who know their merchandise, which includes imported cheese, olives, and chocolate. **Spoonbill & Sugartown Books** (☎ 718/387–7322 ⊕ www.spoonbillbooks.com) carries a large selection of art and design books and magazines, as well as a fair amount of used general titles.

The handknit sweaters, the messenger bags, the candles, and the perfume at the sunny corner boutique **Spacial Etc.** (⊠199 Bedford Ave. ☎718/ 599–7962 ⊕ www.spacialetc.com) aren't cheap, but they're all wonderfully made and many would be hard to track down elsewhere. **Brooklyn Industries** (⊠ 162 Bedford Ave. ☎ 718/486–6464) carries bags, accessories, knits, T-shirts, and other items for men and women: everything's designed for an urban, casual sensibility. **Beacon's Closet** (⊠ 88 N. 11th St. ☎ 718/486–0816) is a magnet for the young locals in the neighborhood seeking out vintage clothes and accessories. Most items sell for under $20. The store is across the street from Brooklyn Brewery.

THE ARTS Williamsburg's 70-odd galleries are distributed randomly, with no single main drag. Hours vary widely, but almost all are open on weekends. Call ahead. The **Williamsburg Gallery Association** (⊕ www. williamsburggalleryassociation.com) Web site has a handy printable map of its nearly 30 members. Also useful is the *Gallery Guide*, a free publication available at many stores and galleries in the neighborhood.

At the cheerfully nonprofessional-looking **Cinders** (⊠ 103 Havemeyer St., between Hope and Grand Sts. ☎ 718/388–2311 ⊕ www. cindersgallery.com), you can buy zines and clothing as well as crafts and art—paintings, silkscreened cloth, and papier-mâché sculptures.

Galapagos (⊠70 N. 6th St., between Wythe and Kent Aves. ☎718/782– 5188 ⊕ www.galapagosartspace.com) is an all-in-one bar, art gallery, performance space, and movie house. Don't be fooled by this former mayo factory's reflecting pool near the front: it's not that deep.

One of the first art galleries to open in Williamsburg, **Pierogi 2000** (✉ 177 N. 9th St., between Bedford and Driggs Aves. ☎ 718/599–2144) is famous for its "Flat Files," a collection of artists' portfolios that travel to other museums and galleries. **Sideshow Gallery** (✉ 319 Bedford Ave., between S. 2nd and S. 3rd Sts. ☎ 718/486–8180) often has artwork hanging from the floor to the ceiling on its walls.

Inside a beautiful 1867 bank building that's in the midst of being restored, the **Williamsburg Art and Historical Center** (WAH; ✉ 135 Broadway, at Bedford Ave. ☎ 718/486–7372) is a work in progress itself. The annual round of exhibits include the Williamsburg Salon winter show, which highlights local artists.

Brooklyn Heights

Brooklyn Borough Hall. Built in 1848, this Greek Revival landmark is one of Brooklyn's handsomest buildings. The hammered-brass top of the cast-iron cupola was restored by the same French craftsmen who restored the Statue of Liberty. The stately building is adorned with Tuckahoe marble both inside and out; other highlights are the square rotunda and the two-story Beaux-Arts–style courtroom with plaster columns painted to look like wood. Originally Brooklyn's city hall, the building lost this function when Brooklyn became part of New York City in 1898. Today the hall serves as the office of Brooklyn's borough president and the location of the **Brooklyn Tourism & Visitors Center** (☎ 718/802–3846), which has historical exhibits and a gift shop as well as many maps and pamphlets covering the borough's attractions. It's open weekdays 10–6. On Tuesday, Thursday, and Saturday a green market sets up on the flagstone plaza in front. ✉ *209 Joralemon St., between Court and Jay Sts.* ☎ *718/802–3700* ⊕ *www.brooklyntourism.org* ✆ *Free* Ⓜ *Subway: 2, 3, 4, 5 to Borough Hall; R, W to Court St.*

☺ FodorśChoice ★ **Brooklyn Heights Promenade.** Stretching from Cranberry Street on the north to Remsen Street on the south, this ⅓-mi-long esplanade provides enthralling views of Manhattan. Find a bench and take in the view of the skyline, the Statue of Liberty, and the Brooklyn Bridge, the impressive steel suspension bridge designed by John Augustus Roebling and completed in 1883. The small island to your left is Governors Island, a former Coast Guard base that's now partially a national park. Below you are the Brooklyn–Queens Expressway and Brooklyn's industrial waterfront of warehouses, piers, and parking lots. A greenway initiative is moving forward in a bid to replace all but the expressway. At the south end of the promenade, near Montague Street, is a small playground. Ⓜ *Subway: 2, 3 to Clark St.; A, C to High St.*

Brooklyn Historical Society. Housed in a Queen Anne–style National Landmark building from 1881 that's one of the gems of the neighborhood, the Brooklyn Historical Society displays memorabilia, artifacts, art, and other items relating to the borough, from 17th-century Native American tools to contemporary artworks. The core exhibit is a family-focused, interactive one called Brooklyn Works: 400 Years of Mak-

12

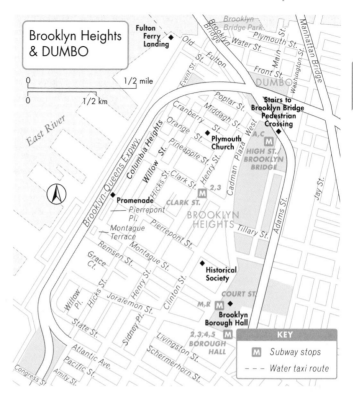

Brooklyn Heights & DUMBO

0 ____ 1/2 mile
0 ____ 1/2 km

East River

Fulton Ferry Landing

Brooklyn Bridge Park

Plymouth St.

Water St.

Manhattan Bridge

Old Fulton St.

Event St.

Front St.

Main St.

Washington St.

DUMBO

Poplar St.

Cranberry St.

Middagh St.

Stairs to Brooklyn Bridge Pedestrian Crossing

Orange St.

Columbia Heights

Pineapple St.

Plymouth Church

A,C

HIGH ST./ BROOKLYN BRIDGE

Willow St.

Henry St.

Clark St.

Hicks St.

Cadman Plaza West

Jay St.

2,3

Promenade

CLARK ST.

BROOKLYN HEIGHTS

Pierrepont Pl.

Pierrepont St.

Montague Terrace

Montague St.

Tillary St.

Adams St.

Remsen St.

Grace Ct.

Willow Pl.

Hicks St.

Henry St.

Joralemon St.

Clinton St.

Historical Society

COURT ST.

M,R

Brooklyn Borough Hall

State St.

Sidney Pl.

2,3,4,5

BOROUGH HALL

Livingston St.

Schermerhorn St.

Atlantic Ave.

Congress St.

Amity St.

Pacific St.

KEY

M Subway stops
- - - Water taxi route

ing a Living in Brooklyn. ✉ *128 Pierrepont St., at Clinton St., Brooklyn Heights* ☎ *718/222–4111* ⊕ *www.brooklynhistory.org* 💲 *$6* ⊙ *Wed.–Sun. noon–5* Ⓜ *Subway: 4, 5, 6 to Borough Hall.*

Columbia Heights. Among the majestic residences on this street, the brownstone grouping of **Nos. 210–220** is sometimes cited as among the most graceful in New York. Norman Mailer lives on this street, and from a rear window in **No. 111,** Washington Roebling, who in 1869 succeeded his father as chief engineer for the Brooklyn Bridge, directed the completion of the bridge after a case of the bends left him an invalid. ✉ *Between Pierrepont and Cranberry Sts.* Ⓜ *Subway: 2, 3 to Clark St.; A, C to High St.*

Plymouth Church of the Pilgrims. Thanks to the stirring oratory of Brooklyn's most eminent theologian and the church's first minister, Henry Ward Beecher (brother of Harriet Beecher Stowe, author of *Uncle Tom's Cabin*), this house of worship was a center of antislavery sentiment in the years before the Civil War. Abraham Lincoln worshipped here twice, and several slave auctions were held in the church both to gain the slaves' freedom and to publicize the inhumanity of slavery. Because it provided refuge to slaves, the church, which was built in 1849, was known as the Grand Central Terminal of the Underground Railroad in its later years.

Added in the early 20th century, the stained-glass windows of the church were designed by Louis Comfort Tiffany. In the gated courtyard beside the church, a statue of Beecher by Gutzon Borglum (known for his work at Mount Rushmore) depicts refugee slaves crouched in hiding behind the base. A fragment of Plymouth Rock is in an adjoining arcade. ⊠ *Orange St. between Henry and Hicks Sts.* ☎ *718/624–4743* ⊕ *www. plymouthchurch.org* ☉ *Service Sun. at 11; tours by appointment* Ⓜ *Subway: 2, 3 to Clark St.; A, C to High St.*

Willow Street. One of the prettiest and most architecturally varied blocks in Brooklyn Heights is Willow Street between Middagh and Pierrepont streets. At **No. 22** stands Henry Ward Beecher's house—a prim Greek Revival brownstone. **Nos. 155–159** are three brick federal row houses that were alleged stops on the Underground Railroad. Look down at a skylight in the pavement by the gate to No. 157. It provided the light for an underground tunnel leading to a post–Civil War stable. Ⓜ *Subway: 2, 3 to Clark St.; A, C to High St.*

WHERE TO EAT   The **Heights Café** (⊠ 84 Montague St., at Hicks St. ☎ 718/625–5555. $9–$20) is a local favorite for American fare. The pan-roasted chicken is especially popular. At **Henry's End** (⊠ 44 Henry St., near Cranberry St. ☎ 718/834–1776. $18–$22) wild game such as elk, buffalo, and quail take center stage; less exotic meats and chicken are also available year-round in the cozy surroundings. **Teresa's** (⊠ 80 Montague St., near Hicks St. ☎ 718/797–3996. $8–$10), like its sister location in the East Village, serves well-prepared Polish and American food. Have a breakfast with the blintzes, pierogi, or kielbasa here, and you won't be ready for lunch for a good long time.

DUMBO

☉ **Brooklyn Bridge Park.** The Brooklyn Bridge Park Coalition combined city and state funds to convert this underused patch of prime real estate, which stretches 1.3 mi from the Manhattan Bridge south along the East River to Atlantic Avenue, into a park. The park closes at 5 PM after Labor Day and stays open later in summer, when the outdoor Brooklyn Bridge Park Summer Film Series is held. ⊠ *Entrance at top of Main St.* ⊕ *www.bbpc. net* Ⓜ *Subway: A, C to High St./Brooklyn Bridge; F to York St.*

☉ **Empire-Fulton Ferry State Park.** Adjacent to Brooklyn Bridge Park, this 9-acre park has picnic tables and benches to accompany great views of the nearby bridges and the Manhattan skyline. If you have kids in tow, the large playground, which includes a replica of a boat to crawl around on, provides a welcome spot for tots. The ruins of the Tobacco Inspection Warehouse (circa 1871), now stabilized and part of the park, are sometimes used for band performances and other events. ⊠ *26 New Dock St.* ☎ *718/858–4708* ⊕ *nysparks.state.ny.us* 🖾 *Free* ☉ *Daily dawn–dusk* Ⓜ *Subway: A, C to High St.; F to York St.*

WHERE TO EAT   A classic New York–style pizza parlor, **Grimaldi's Pizzeria** (⊠ 19 Old Fulton St., between Front and Water Sts. ☎ 718/858–4300. $13–$22), near the Brooklyn Bridge, has red-and-white checkered tablecloths, walls filled with autographed photos, and Frank Sinatra crooning on the juke-box. There's better pizza in town, but the experience here is hard to beat.

With its exposed brick and pool table in a prominent location, **Superfine** (⊠ 126 Front St., between Jay and Pearl Sts. ☎ 718/243–9005. $9–$17) is as much a highly designed hangout as it is a restaurant. Come here for Mediterranean-influence twists on classic American dishes.

THE ARTS Most DUMBO galleries are open afternoons Thursday through Sunday.

The **DUMBO Arts Center** (DAC; ⊠ 30 Washington St., between Water and Plymouth Sts. ☎ 718/694–0831 ⊕ www.dumboartscenter.org) exhibits contemporary art in its 3,000-square-foot gallery. Its Art Under the Bridge festival brings performances, special exhibits, and other events to locations throughout the neighborhood.

The **5 + 5 Gallery** (⊠ 111 Front St., Suite 210 ☎ 718/488–8383) specializes in contemporary prints. The nonprofit **Smack Mellon Studios** (⊠ 92 Plymouth St., at Washington St. ☎ 718/834–8761 ⊕ www.smackmellon.org) specializes in exhibits of local artists, especially those whose art doesn't fit neatly into one category or another.

SHOPPING Even if the surrounding streets are empty, **Jacques Torres Chocolate** (⊠ 66 Water St. ☎ 718/875–9772 ⊕ www.mrchocolate.com), a chocolate factory with a small shop and café operated by the French chocolatier, is almost always packed. It's closed on Sunday. One of the better music stores for dance, house, and electronica, **Halcyon** (⊠ 57 Pearl St. ☎ 718/260–9299 ⊕ www.halcyonline.com) also sells accessories and DJ gear. The DUMBO outpost of **ABC Carpet & Home** (⊠ 20 Jay St. ☎ 718/643–7400) takes up an entire block. Unlike its chaotic headquarters in Manhattan, the sprawling, modern home furnishings shop and showroom is a pleasure to peruse.

Atlantic Avenue

On the busy thoroughfare of Atlantic Avenue, between Court and Clinton streets on the southern border of Brooklyn Heights, are a handful of Middle Eastern restaurants and markets. **Sahadi's** (⊠ 187 Atlantic Ave. ☎ 718/624–4550) sells cheap, good-quality dried fruits, nuts, candies, and olives by the pound as well as many other specialty food items. **Damascus Bakery** (⊠ 195 Atlantic Ave. ☎ 718/625–7070) is a great place to pick up pita bread—and some killer baklava. Next door, **A Cook's Companion** (⊠ 197 Atlantic Ave. ☎ 718/852–6901) carries cookbooks, kitchen gadgets and tools, and lots of paraphernalia for the serious cook.

Farther east on Atlantic, particularly between Hoyt and Bond streets, the leafy street gives way to more than a dozen antique-furniture stores and purveyors of modern housewares. Despite its Dutch-influenced name, **Breukelen** (⊠ 369 Atlantic Ave., near Bond St. ☎ 718/246–0024) is stuck anywhere but in the past. On offer are housewares, lamps, modern furniture, and other items in a design-heavy vein. **In Days of Old** (⊠ 355–57 Atlantic Ave. ☎ 718/858–4233) looks to Victorian and early 1900s for its stock of antiques.

In among the Atlantic Avenue's housewares are many noteworthy boutiques. **Butter** (⊠ 407 Atlantic Ave. ☎ 718/260–9033) was one of the first Brooklyn shops to bring a bit of Manhattan's trend-conscious women's clothes to Atlantic Avenue. At nearby **Jelly** (✉ 389 Atlantic Ave. ☎ 718/858–8214), owned by the sisters who own Butter, it's accessories that take main stage.

To get to the northwest section of this busy stretch, take the subway to the Borough Hall station. To pick up Atlantic Avenue at its southeast edge, take the subway to the Nevins Street station. Both stations are served by a number of subway lines. The blocks between Boerum Place and Smith Street that separate the aforementioned sections is a kind of no-man's-land, looming as it does in the shadow of the Brooklyn House of Detention. Emptied of prisoners in 2004, its fate is currently unknown. A few bail-bond businesses across the street remain for the moment as evidence of its past.

Cobble Hill

On the south side of Atlantic Avenue from Brooklyn Heights, Cobble Hill is a quiet residential area of leafy streets lined with town houses built by 19th-century New York's upper middle class. Court Street is a major drag that runs through the neighborhood. Activity whirls around its cafés, restaurants, bookstores, old-fashioned bakeries, and imported-food shops. Smith Street, which runs parallel to Court Street one block east, is somewhat of a restaurant row, augmented by young designers who have set up shop here. The restaurants are some of Brooklyn's best.

Although many of the streets here contain gorgeous houses, the tiny mews called Verandah Place is especially worth a walk through. South of Congress Street and between Henry Street and Clinton Street, Verandah Place has town houses built in the 1850s; the novelist Thomas Wolfe lived for a time at No. 40 in the 1930s.

WHERE TO EAT   At the creative American restaurant **Saul** (✉ 140 Smith St., between Dean and Bergen Sts., Boerum Hill ☎ 718/935–9844. $17–$20), everything on the seasonal menu is well prepared, from such simple dishes as a grilled hanger steak to more involved items like crispy duck confit. One of the best restaurants on Smith Street, the **Grocery** (✉ 288 Smith St., between Union and Sackett Sts. ☎ 718/596–3335. $20–$25), gets accolades for a New American take on such dishes as slowly rendered duck breast. Be sure to make a reservation; it's very popular. Grocery is open for dinner every day but Sunday.

Brooklyn Academy of Music (BAM)

Young professionals, families, hipsters, and old-timers live side by side in the brownstone-filled neighborhood of Fort Greene, which is anchored by the Brooklyn Academy of Music (BAM). And with the Mark Morris Dance Center (whose troupe performs at BAM) down the street, the area is now becoming interchangeable with its performing-arts scene.

Attracting lots of downtown Manhattanites as well as locals, BAM's program tends to be a bit more experimental than similar institutions across the river in Manhattan. But even if you're not planning on seeing one of its presentations, it's well worth a glimpse at the facade and the interior of BAM's main building. Built in 1908, the cream-color neo-Ital-

Hip-Hop's Birthplace

MAYBE IT'S NOT SO SURPRISING that art forms that depend heavily on competition and audience participation would have developed in New York City, where people spend so much time meeting with friends or just looking for something to do.

Most people date modern graffiti's birth to the late 1960s, when a Greek-American boy began writing his nickname and street number, "Taki 183," with a permanent marker on subway cars. Others, primarily teenagers from the poor areas of Manhattan, the Bronx, Brooklyn, and Queens, began to imitate his "tagging." It wasn't too long afterward that spray paint, with its wealth of colors and looser method of application, became the medium of choice. Spray paint also allowed innovators to start signing their names in the loose "bubble" style that remains prevalent today.

From its start, however, modern graffiti was tied up with petty crime: the ideal "canvas" was the interiors and exteriors of the Metropolitan Transit Authority's trains, and getting to that canvas involved trespassing in the MTA's rail yards, a dangerous place.

Rap music and break dancing arose at the same time. The DJs who supplied music for South Bronx nightclubs and parties were always trying to create better and better mixes of soul and disco music. One innovation, generally credited to DJ Kool Herc, was to use two turntables with the same record on each and switch repeatedly between the two during their breaks—the section of song in which only bass and percussion are playing. By repeating the break indefinitely, he gave MCs a chance to introduce themselves, get the crowd worked up, and lead everyone in a chant. Soon MCs were delivering full-blown rhymes and verses, and rap music was on its way. Break dancing's appearance as a distinct form is due to one man: DJ Afrika Bambaataa. During the late '60s, he began organizing teenagers into a group called the Zulu Kings. A gang alternative, the Zulu Kings would break-dance against other groups and against each other during DJs' breaks, seeing who could move with the most skill and athletic prowess.

By the early 1980s, hip-hop—an umbrella term for rap music, break dancing, and graffiti writing and the culture around them—was almost mainstream. In its embryonic stages, downtown artists such as Jean-Michel Basquiat and Keith Haring blurred the line between legitimate art and graffiti, tagging and making illegal murals at the same time as dealers and art-lovers were snapping up their work. The new wave band Blondie also helped introduce hip-hop to a wide audience with "Rapture," a 1980 hit song that included a rap name-checking hip-hop artist and impresario Fab Five Freddy.

By this time, New York City had declared war on graffiti artists and their vandalism. By using aggressive cleaning methods and by quickly removing cars that had been "bombed" from service, the city succeeded in reducing the amount of graffiti visible on trains, if not perhaps on the streets themselves.

As the graffiti artist Mare 139 put it in the seminal 1984 hip-hop documentary *Style Wars*, "We lost the trains, but we gained the world."

12

ianate building is covered with lots of painted detailing, all of them bright after a 2002 refurbishment.

In addition to the impressive and huge lobby, the BAM building contains an opera house, which seats 2,100, and a movie theater. Nearby is BAM's **Harvey Theater** (⊠ 651 Fulton St.), which is where many of BAM's theatrical works are staged. ⊠ *Peter Jay Sharp Bldg., 30 Lafayette Ave., between Ashland Pl. and St. Felix St.* ☎ *718/636–4100* ⊕ *www. bam.org* Ⓜ *Subway: C to Lafayette Ave.; 2, 3, 4, 5, Q to Atlantic Ave.*

WHERE TO EAT The **BAMcafé**, serving mostly lighter dishes, is open for dinner Thursday through Saturday and also open two hours before performances at the Harvey Theater and Howard Gilman Opera House. Across the street from BAM, **Thomas Beisl** (⊠25 Lafayette Ave., at Ashland Pl. ☎718/ 222–5800. $15–$18) is well acquainted with ensuring its patrons make their show. Viennese specialties here include goulash, sauerbraten, and some wonderfully rich desserts.

Park Slope & Prospect Park

One of Brooklyn's most comfortable places to live, Park Slope contains row after row of immaculate brownstones that date from its turn-of-the-20th-century heyday. At the time, Park Slope had the nation's highest per-capita income. To see some of the neighborhood's most beautiful houses, walk between 7th Avenue and Prospect Park along any of the streets between Sterling Place and 4th Street.

Prospect Park. Brooklyn residents are more than affectionate toward their more naturalistic cousin of Central Park. Prospect Park, designed by Frederick Law Olmsted and Calvert Vaux and completed in the late 1880s, serves as the center of much activity, with attractions not only in the park but next door at Brooklyn Botanic Garden and the Brooklyn Museum. A good way to experience the park is to walk the entirety of its 3⅓-mi circular drive and make detours off it as you wish. Joggers, skaters, and bicyclists have the drive to themselves weekdays 9–5 and 7 PM–10 PM April–October and weekends year-round. On weekends and holidays throughout the year, from noon to 5 PM, the red **"Heart of Brooklyn" trolley** (☎ 718/965–8999 events hotline ⊕ www.prospectpark. org) circles Prospect Park, leaving Wollman Rink on the hour and hitting the zoo, the Botanic Garden, the Band Shell, and most other sights. Best of all, it's free.

The park's north entrance is at **Grand Army Plaza.** In the center of the plaza stands the Soldiers' and Sailors' Memorial Arch, honoring Civil War veterans and patterned after the Arc de Triomphe in Paris. Three heroic sculptural groupings adorn the arch: atop, a four-horse chariot by Frederick MacMonnies, so dynamic it seems about to catapult off the arch; to either side, the victorious Union Army and Navy of the Civil War. The inner arch has bas-reliefs of presidents Abraham Lincoln and Ulysses S. Grant, sculpted by Thomas Eakins and William O'Donovan, respectively. On some warm-weather weekends the top of the arch is

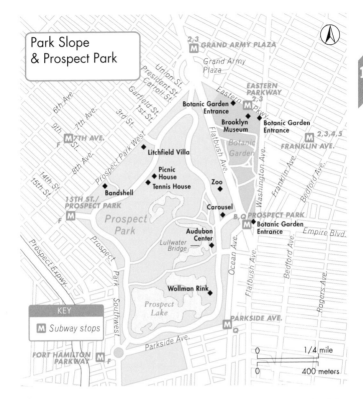

Park Slope & Prospect Park

GRAND ARMY PLAZA 2,3

Grand Army Plaza

Union St.

President St.

Carroll St.

EASTERN PARKWAY 2,3

Garfield St.

1st St.

3rd St.

6th Ave.

7th Ave.

Botanic Garden Entrance

Brooklyn Museum

Botanic Garden Entrance

9th St.

7TH AVE. F

Prospect Park West

8th Ave.

Litchfield Villa

Botanic Garden

FRANKLIN AVE. 2,3,4,5

Flatbush Ave.

Franklin Ave.

Bedford Ave.

14th St.

15th St.

Picnic House

Tennis House

Zoo

Washington Ave.

15TH ST./ PROSPECT PARK

Bandshell

F

Prospect Park

Carousel

PROSPECT PARK

B, Q

Botanic Garden Entrance

Empire Blvd.

Audubon Center

Lullwater Bridge

Ocean Ave.

Flatbush Ave.

Bedford Ave.

Rogers Ave.

Prospect Expwy.

Prospect

Park Southwest

Wollman Rink

Prospect Lake

PARKSIDE AVE.

Q

KEY

Ⓜ Subway stops

Parkside Ave.

FORT HAMILTON PARKWAY Ⓜ F

0 ——— 1/4 mile

0 ——— 400 meters

12

accessible. To the northwest of the arch, Neptune and a passel of debauched Tritons leer over the edges of the **Bailey Fountain,** a popular spot for wedding-party photographs.

Looking like a sleek, modern temple of learning with gold-leaf figures celebrating art and science, the facade of the **Brooklyn Public Library** (☎ 718/230–2100 ⊕ www.brooklynpubliclibrary.org ☉ Tues.–Thurs. 10–9, Fri. and Sat. 10–6, Sun. 1–6) curves to embrace the roundabout between Eastern Parkway and Flatbush Avenue. (The building's meant to resemble an open book, with the entrance the book's spine.) Bright limestone walls, perfect proportions, and ornate decorative details make this a rare 20th-century New York building. The small café inside is the nearest snack and coffee source to Prospect Park.

Ⓒ **Lefferts Historic House** (☎ 718/789–2822 ▨ Free ☉ Thurs.–Sun. noon–5), a gambrel-roof Dutch colonial farmhouse built in 1783 and moved to Prospect Park in 1918, contains a historic house-museum. Rooms are furnished with antiques and reproductions from the 1820s, the period when the house was last redecorated. The museum hosts all kinds of activities for kids; call for information. **Litchfield Villa** (☎ 718/965–8951 ▨ Free ☉ Weekdays noon–5), an Italianate mansion on the western border of Prospect Park, was built in 1857 for a prominent railroad magnate. It has housed the park's headquarters since 1883, but visitors are welcome to step inside and view the domed octagonal rotunda.

☾ Styled after Sansovino's 16th-century Library at St. Mark's in Venice, the **Prospect Park Audubon Center and Visitor Center at the Boathouse**, built in 1904, sits opposite the Lullwater Bridge, creating an idyllic scene on evenings when the lake reflects an exact image of the building. In the Audubon Center, you can learn about nature in the park through interactive exhibits, park tours, and educational programs especially for kids. On a nice day, take a ride on the electric boat or rent a pedal boat and head out onto the Lullwater and Prospect Lake. You can also sign up for a bird-watching tour to see some of the 200 species spotted here. The café is always good for a break, and restrooms are also available here. ☎ *718/287–3400 Audubon Center, 718/282–7789 pedal boats* ⊕ *www.prospectparkaudubon.org* ✉ *Audubon Center free; electric-boat tours $5; pedal boat $15 per hr* ☾ *Audubon Center: Thurs.–Sun. noon–6; call for program and tour times. Electric-boat tours: late Apr.–Labor Day, Thurs.–Sun. noon–4:30; Sept.–mid-Oct., weekends noon–4:30, every 30 mins. Pedal boats: mid-May–June, Thurs.–Sun. noon–5; July–Labor Day, Thurs.–Sun. noon–6; Sept.–mid-Oct., weekends noon–5.*

The **Prospect Park Band Shell** (☎ 718/965–8999 park hotline, 718/855–7882 Celebrate Brooklyn Festival ⊕ www.brooklynx.org/celebrate) is the home of the annual Celebrate Brooklyn Festival, which from mid-June through the last weekend in August sponsors free films and concerts that have included African-Caribbean jazz, Nick Cave, the Brooklyn Philharmonic, and the Mark Morris Dance Company; benefit concerts, which charge admission, also bring big-name acts. The crowd either fills the seats or spreads out blankets on the small hill.

☾ Horses, dragon-pulled chariots, and other colorful animals enliven the restored **Prospect Park Carousel** handcrafted in 1912 by master carver Charles Carmel. ☎ *718/282–7789* ✉ *$1 per ride* ☾ *Apr.–June and Sept.–Oct., Thurs.–Sun. noon–5; July–Labor Day, Thurs.–Sun. noon–6.*

☾ Small and friendly, **Prospect Park Zoo** has 400 inhabitants and 93 species, including a number of unusual and endangered ones. The sea-lion pool is a hit with children, as are the indoor exhibits—"Animal Lifestyles," which explains habitats and adaptations, and "In Living Color," which showcases and explains brightly colored critters. An outdoor discovery trail has a simulated prairie-dog burrow, a duck pond, and kangaroos and wallabies in habitat. ☎ *718/399–7339* ⊕ *www.prospectparkzoo.com* ✉ *$5* ☾ *Apr.–Oct., weekdays 10–5, weekends 10–5:30; Nov.–Mar., daily 10–4:30; last ticket ½ hr prior to closing.*

The most prominent of several neoclassical structures in the park, the **Tennis House** (✉ Free ☾ Tennis House only, weekdays 9–5, weekends 10–5; Tennis House and BCUE gallery, during exhibitions) is a 1910 limestone and yellow-brick building, with triple-bay Palladian arches on both its north and south facade, and a terra-cotta barrel-vaulted arcade on the south side. The building's large tiled central court has amazing acoustics—shout "hello" and listen to your voice bounce back at you. On the lower level, the **Brooklyn Center for the Urban Environment** (BCUE) has rotating exhibitions on urban issues and organizes Brooklyn walking tours. Restrooms are also available here at the back entrance.

☉ A smaller cousin to Wollman Rink in Central Park, **Wollman Memorial Rink** is one of Prospect Park's most popular destinations. Besides skating in winter, pedal-boat rentals are available here from spring through fall. ☎ *718/282–7789* ☒ *$5, with $5 skate rental; pedal boats $15 per hr* ☉ *Rink: Thanksgiving–mid-Mar.; hrs vary, call for specifics. Pedal boats: mid-May–June, Thurs.–Sun. noon–5; July–Labor Day, Thurs.–Sun. noon–6; Sept.–mid-Oct., weekends noon–5.*

On weekends vendors sell snacks and beverages near the 9th Street entrance, and a few are at the Grand Army Plaza entrance. On Saturday year-round, a green market at the plaza sells produce, flowers and plants, cheese, and baked goods to throngs of locals.

★ ☉ **Brooklyn Botanic Garden.** A major attraction at this 52-acre botanic garden, one of the finest in the country, is the beguiling Japanese Hill-and-Pond Garden—complete with a 1-acre pond and blazing red *torii* gate, which signifies that a shrine is nearby. The Japanese cherry arbor nearby turns into a breathtaking cloud of pink every spring, and the Cherry Blossom Festival is the park's most popular event. You can also wander through the Cranford Rose Garden (5,000 bushes, 1,200 varieties); the Fragrance Garden, designed especially for the blind; and the Shakespeare Garden, featuring more than 80 plants immortalized by the Bard.

The Steinhardt Conservatory, a complex of three diverse greenhouses, holds thriving desert, tropical, temperate, and aquatic vegetation, as well as a display charting the evolution of plants over the past 140 million years. The extraordinary C. V. Starr Bonsai Museum in the Conservatory exhibits about 80 miniature Japanese specimens. Near the conservatory are a café and an outstanding gift shop, with bulbs, plants, and gardening books as well as jewelry and children's gardening tools. Free garden tours are given weekends at 1 PM, except for holiday weekends. Entrances to the garden are on Eastern Parkway, next to the subway station; on Washington Avenue, behind the Brooklyn Museum; and on Flatbush Avenue at Empire Boulevard. ☒ *1000 Washington Ave., between Flatbush Ave. and Empire Blvd., Prospect Heights* ☎ *718/623–7200* ⊕ *www.bbg.org* ☒ *$5; free Tues. and Sat. before noon. Weekend combo ticket with Brooklyn Museum of Art $11* ☉ *Apr.–Sept., grounds Tues.–Fri. 8–6, weekends 10–6, conservatory daily 10–5:30; Oct.–Mar., grounds Tues.–Fri. 8–4:30, weekends 10–4:30; conservatory daily 10–4* Ⓜ *Subway: 2, 3 to Eastern Pkwy.; B, Q to Prospect Park.*

★ **Brooklyn Museum.** With more than 1 million pieces in its permanent collection, from Rodin sculptures to Andean textiles and Assyrian wall reliefs, the Brooklyn Museum is the second-largest art museum in New York—only the Met is larger. The massive building was designed by McKim, Mead & White (1893) with allegorical figures in the facade. Look for the freestanding statues of Brooklyn and Manhattan, originally carved by Daniel Chester French for the Manhattan Bridge.

Beyond the changing exhibitions, highlights include Egyptian art (third floor), one of the best collections of its kind in the world, African and pre-Columbian art, and Native American art (first floor). "American Identities" in the Luce Center for American Art (fifth floor) exhibits fine arts and crafts beginning with a focus on Brooklyn, and then continues through Colonial America up to contemporary art. The works by Georgia O'Keeffe, Winslow Homer, John Singer Sargent, George Bellows, Thomas Eakins, and Milton Avery, are stunners. In early 2005, the Luce Center expanded to allow 1,500 more objects to be shown in the compact Visible Storage/Study Center.

Much of the fourth floor will remain closed for 2006 while construction continues for the Elizabeth A. Sackler Center for Feminist Art. Scheduled to open in the spring of 2007, the inaugural exhibit will be Global Feminism. The center is also home to Judy Chicago's installation *The Dinner Party* (1974–79). On the first Saturday of each month, "First Saturdays" is a free evening of art, live music, dancing, film screenings, and readings. ⊠ *200 Eastern Pkwy., at Washington Ave., Prospect Heights* ☎ *718/638–5000* ⊕ *www.brooklynmuseum.org* ⌑ *$8 suggested donation. Weekend combo ticket with Brooklyn Botanic Garden $11* ☉ *Wed.–Fri. 10–5, weekends 11–6; 1st Sat. every month 11–11; call for program schedule* Ⓜ *Subway: 2, 3 to Eastern Pkwy./Brooklyn Museum.*

WHERE TO EAT   At **Blue Ribbon Brooklyn** (⊠ 280 5th Ave., between Garfield and 1st Sts.

★   ☎ 718/840–0404. $13–$30), the Brooklyn branch of a SoHo original, serves updated, carefully prepared versions of bistro dishes, with an especially strong showing in seafood. At comfortably rustic **al di la** (⊠ 248 5th Ave., at Carroll St. ☎ 718/783–4565. $14–$18), the dining room is furnished with a pressed-tin ceiling and communal bare wooden tables. Plenty of care goes into the authentic Italian dishes, but the entrées are on the small side, so go for an appetizer.

For great diner fare and uncommonly friendly service, head to **Tom's Restaurant** (⊠ 782 Washington Ave., at Sterling Pl. ☎ 718/636–9738. $7–$12). The family business (since 1937) is closed Sunday and by 4 PM the rest of the week.

SHOPPING   Seventh Avenue, between Lincoln and 15th streets, is the neighborhood's main shopping street, with long-established restaurants, groceries, bookstores, shops, cafés, bakeries, churches, and real estate agents (one of the favorite neighborhood pastimes is window shopping for homes). More fun, however, are the restaurants, bars, and gift shops along 5th Avenue.

The Clay Pot (⊠ 162 7th Ave., between Garfield and 1st Sts. ☎ 718/788–6564) is known for original wares and ornaments for the home and for one-of-a-kind wedding bands made by local artisans. The **Community Bookstore and Café** (⊠ 143 7th Ave., at Garfield ☎ 718/783–3075) serves pastries, quiche, and additional light offerings in the lovely, little garden out back or indoors among the bookcases. In addition to an astonishing assortment of imported beers (available by the bottle), **Bierkraft**

(⌂ 191 5th Ave., near Union St. ☎ 718/230–7600) also sells cheeses, olives, and some impressively pricey chocolate. **Beacon's Closet** (⌂ 220 5th Ave., between President and Union Sts. ☎ 718/230–1630), like its sister store in Williamsburg, sells vintage clothes, jewelry, and other items at reasonable prices.

12

Coney Island

FodorśChoice
★

Coney Island may have declined from its glory days in the early 1900s, but it's still a great place to experience the sounds, smells, and sights of summer: hot dogs, ice cream, and saltwater taffy; suntan lotion; crowds; and old men fishing the sea. Amid the many attractions here, the Coney Island boardwalk remains the hub of the action; amble along it to take in the local color.

Astroland. The world-famous, wood-and-steel **Cyclone** ($5) is one of the oldest roller coasters still operating (it first rode in 1927); it was moved in 1975 to Astroland, which had first billed itself as a "space-age" theme park. Today a visit is more like stepping into the past than the future, but the rides are still a thrill, as is the Skee-Ball. Farther down the boardwalk, an abandoned Space Needle–like structure, once the Parachute Jump, is testimony to this waning beachside culture. ⌂ *1000 Surf Ave., at W. 10th St., Coney Island* ☎ *718/372–0275* ⊕ *www.astroland. com* ☉ *Palm Sun. (late Mar. or early Apr.)–mid-Oct.; call for seasonal hrs* ▱ *Free; $2–$5 per ride.*

Deno's Wonderwheel Park. You get a new perspective on the island from its 150-foot-tall Wonder Wheel, which was built in 1920 by the Eccentric Ferris Wheel Company. Though it appears tame, it will still quicken your heart rate. Other rides include the Spook-a-rama, the Thunderbolt, bumper cars, and a number of children's rides. ⌂ *1025 Boardwalk, at W. 12th St., Coney Island* ☎ *718/372–2592* ⊕ *www.wonderwheel. com* ☉ *Memorial Day–Labor Day, daily 11–midnight; Apr., May, Sept., Oct., weekends noon–9* ▱ *Free; $5 per ride, 5 rides for $20.*

Keyspan Park. Rekindle your Brooklyn baseball memories (or make some new ones) at a Brooklyn Cyclones game. This single A farm team was bought by the Mets in 1999 and moved from St. Catharine's, Ontario, to Brooklyn, bringing professional baseball to the borough for the first time since 1957. ⌂ *1904 Surf Ave., between 17th and 19th Sts., Coney Island* ☎ *718/449–8497* ⊕ *www.brooklyncyclones.com* ☉ *Games June–Sept.; call for schedule* ▱ *$5–$8* Ⓜ *Subway: D, F, Q to Coney Island Stillwell Ave.*

New York Aquarium. More than 10,000 creatures of the sea make New York City's only aquarium their home. It's an attractive layout in which tropical fish, sea horses, and jellyfish luxuriate in large tanks; otters, walruses, penguins, and seals lounge on a replicated Pacific coast; and a 90,000-gallon tank is home to several different types of sharks. ⌂ *W. 8th St. and Surf Ave., Coney Island* ☎ *718/265–3474* ⊕ *www. nyaquarium.com* ▱ *$12* ☉ *Early Apr.–Memorial Day and Labor Day–Oct., weekdays 10–5, weekends 10–5:30; Memorial Day–Labor*

Day, weekdays 10–6, weekends 10–7; Nov.–early Apr., daily 10–4:30; last ticket sold 45 mins before closing Ⓜ *Subway: D to Coney Island Stillwell Ave. or F, Q, W to 8th St.*

🅒 **Sideshows by the Seashore and the Coney Island Museum.** Step right up for a lively circus sideshow, complete with a fire-eater, sword swallower, snake charmer, and contortionist carrying in what was once billed as the "World's Largest Playground." Upstairs from Sideshows, the museum has historic Coney Island memorabilia and a great deal of tourist information. ✉ *1208 Surf Ave., at W. 12th St., Coney Island* ☎ *718/ 372–5159 for both* ⊕ *www.coneyisland.com* 📧 *Sideshow $5; museum 99¢* ◷ *Sideshows Memorial Day–Labor Day, Wed.–Fri. 2–8, weekends 1–11; Apr., May, and Sept., weekends 1–8. Museum weekends noon–5. Hrs vary, so call ahead.*

WHERE TO EAT   The chewy, deep-fried clams, hot dogs with spicy mustard, and ice-cold lemonade from **Nathan's Famous** (✉ 1310 Surf Ave., at Stillwell Ave. ☎ 718/946–2202) have been nearly inseparable from the Coney Island experience since it opened in 1916. Another branch, on the Boardwalk between Stillwell Avenue and West 12th Street, is open from May through September.

Brooklyn At a Glance

SIGHTS
Astroland
Brooklyn Borough Hall
Brooklyn Brewery
Brooklyn Heights
  Promenade
Brooklyn Public Library
Columbia Heights
Deno's Wonderwheel Park
Keyspan Park
Lefferts Historic House
Litchfield Villa
New York Aquarium
Plymouth Church of the
  Pilgrims
Prospect Park Band Shell
Prospect Park Carousel
Prospect Park Zoo
Sideshows by the Seashore
  and the Coney Island
  Museum
Tennis House
Willow Street
Wollman Memorial Rink
MUSEUMS & GALLERIES
  (⇨ Ch. 14)
Brooklyn Historical Society
Brooklyn Museum
Cinders
City Reliquary
DUMBO Arts Center
5 + 5 Gallery
Galapagos
Pierogi 2000
Sideshow Gallery
Smack Mellon Studios
Williamsburg Art and
  Historical Center
Williamsburg Gallery
  Association
PARKS & GARDENS
Brooklyn Botanic Garden
Brooklyn Bridge Park
Empire-Fulton Ferry State
  Park
Grand Army Plaza

Prospect Park
Prospect Park Audubon
  Center and Visitor Center
  at the Boathouse
WHERE TO EAT (⇨ Ch. 18)
BUDGET DINING
al di la
BAMcafé
Diner
Grimaldi's Pizzeria
Heights Café
Henry's End
Mugs Ale House
Nathan's Famous
Saul
Sparky's
Superfine
Teresa's
Thomas Beisl
Tom's Restaurant
MODERATE DINING
Blue Ribbon Brooklyn
Grocery
Planet Thailand
EXPENSIVE DINING
Peter Luger Steak House
WHERE TO STAY (⇨ Ch. 19)
MODERATE LODGING
New York Marriott
  Brooklyn
BARS & NIGHTLIFE
  (⇨ Ch. 16)
Brooklyn Brewery, *bar*
Brooklyn Social, *bar*
Capone's, *bar*
Cattyshack, *gay & lesbian*
Galapagos Art Space, *bar*
Pete's Candy Store, *bar*
Northsix, *rock club*
River Café, *club*
Southpaw, *rock club*
Superfine, *bar*
ARTS & ENTERTAINMENT
  (⇨ Ch. 15)
BAM Rose Cinemas, *film*

Brooklyn Academy of
  Music (BAM), *arts
  center*
Galapagos Art Space,
  theater
Harvey Theater, *theater*
Puppetworks, *puppet
  shows*
St. Ann's Warehouse,
  theater
SHOPPING (⇨ Ch. 17)
ANTIQUES
Breukelen
In Days of Old
BOOKS
Community Bookstore
  and Café
Spoonbill & Sugartown
  Books
CHOCOLATE
Jacques Torres
  Chocolate
CLOTHING
Beacon's Closet
Brooklyn Industries
Butter
Jelly
Spacial Etc
FOOD
Bedford Cheese Shop
Bierkraft
Sahadi's
Damascus Bakery
HOME DECOR
A Cook's Companion
ABC Carpet & Home
The Clay Pot
LINGERIE
Girdle Factory
MALLS
Girdle Building
MUSIC
Halcyon

12

Queens, the Bronx & Staten Island

WORD OF MOUTH

"A much more authentic 'Little Italy' is Arthur Avenue in the Bronx. Go to the Bronx Zoo or [New York] Botanical Garden and then there for lunch and pastries."

"The Staten Island Ferry is a really pretty ride over and back and I would suggest the best time is just at dusk, so you see the lights of the city coming up on your way back."

—wantsomesun

Sightseeing
★ ★ ★

Nightlife
★ ★ ★

Dining
★ ★ ★ ★ ★

Lodging
★

Shopping
★ ★ ★ ★

Home of LaGuardia and John F. Kennedy International airports, Queens is seen by most visitors only from the window of an airplane and cab. On the ground, however, it's a neighborhood of neighborhoods, each a small world with a distinct culture. All of these communities—especially Astoria and Jackson Heights—are fascinating to explore, particularly if you're interested in some of the city's most interesting cuisine. And with such places as P.S. 1 Contemporary Art Center and the Isamu Noguchi Garden Museum, Queens has become an art-lover's destination.

Although the Bronx has a reputation as a gritty, down-and-out place, the borough is full of vital areas like the Italian neighborhood of Belmont. It has its cultural gems, too—it's the birthplace of hip-hop, and home to the New York Botanical Garden, the Bronx Zoo, and, of course, Yankee Stadium. The Bronx features many interesting sights and scenes, but the borough covers a large area, and its attractions are spread out, making it difficult to take in a variety in one day. Still, whether you're relaxing at a ball game or scoping exotic species at the zoo, there's plenty of fun to be had here.

Staten Island is legally a part of New York City but that's about all the two have in common. The "Forgotten Borough," as some locals refer to it, is significantly more bucolic, politically more conservative, and ethnically less diverse than the rest of the city. Much of the island is now a sprawl of suburban development, but there are also small museums with unexpectedly wonderful offerings, 2,800 acres of walkable woodland, and a historic village that gives a sense of New York's rural past. And for a view of the skyline and the Statue of Liberty, nothing beats the 20- to 30-minute, free ferry trip to Staten Island.

What's Here

Queens

Long Island City and **Astoria,** both just a few minutes from Manhattan, offer great museums and excellent ethnic dining. Astoria earned the nickname Little Athens by the late 1960s, and was the center of Greek immigrant life in New York City until very recently. Today a substantial numbers of Asians, Eastern Europeans, Irish, and Latino immigrants reside in Astoria. Here you can buy kalamata olives and Bulgarian feta cheese from store owners who will tell you where to go for the best spinach pie, or you can sit outside at one of the many pastry shops, drink tall, frothy frappes, and watch the subway's elevated trains roll by. The heart of what remains of the Greek community is on Broadway, between 31st and Steinway streets. You'll know you've arrived when you spot the Greek pastry shops and coffee shops. Farther up, 30th Avenue is another busy thoroughfare with almost every kind of food store imaginable.

Even if you're not interested in lunching on moussaka and baklava, it's worth making a pilgrimage to Astoria to visit the nation's only museum devoted to the art, technology, and history of film, TV, and digital media. The **American Museum of the Moving Image** has slews of hands-on exhibits that allow visitors to edit, direct, and step into favorite movies and television shows. Astoria's nearby neighbor is Long Island City, where you will find a number of Manhattan's most interesting museums, including **Socrates Sculpture Park** and the **P.S. 1 Contemporary Art Center,** where a variety of exhibitions reflect the center's mission to present experimental and formally innovative contemporary art, from the progressive and interactive to the incomprehensible. Nearby **Isamu Noguchi Garden Museum** showcases the work of Japanese-American sculptor Isamu Noguchi in a large, peaceful garden and galleries.

Farther out, **Jackson Heights**'s "Little India" neighborhood, whose center is 74th Street between Roosevelt and 37th avenues, has restaurants, jewelry shops, DVD stores, and other businesses. The site of both the 1939 and 1964 World's Fairs, **Flushing Meadows–Corona Park** puts you within walking distance of some of Queens' major cultural and recreational institutions. Its centerpiece is the Unisphere, in front of the **Queens Museum of Art.** Made entirely of stainless steel, this massive sculpture of Earth is 140 feet high and weighs 380 tons.

Other highlights include the **Queens Zoo; Shea Stadium,** the home of the New York Mets; the **Louis Armstrong House,** the home of the famed jazz legend, which is now a small museum full of mementos and art; the **New York Hall of Science;** and the **Queens Botanical Gardens.**

The Bronx

Perhaps the best-known Bronx attraction is the world-famous **Bronx Zoo,** which opened its gates in 1899 with 843 animals on display. Today, this 265-acre zoo is the world's largest. More than 4,500 animals, representing more than 600 species, mostly live in outdoor settings designed to re-create their habitats. Visitors are often separated from them by no more than a moat.

GETTING ORIENTED

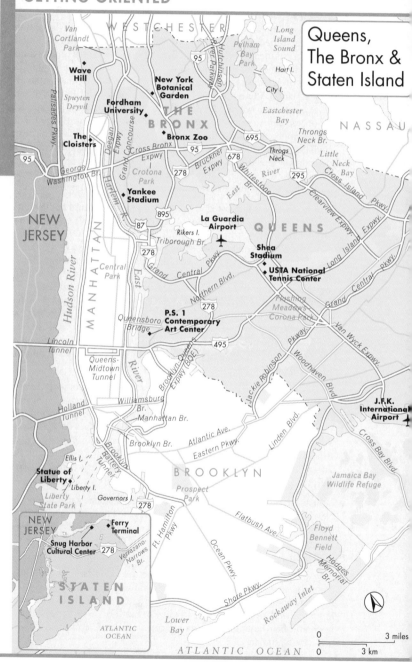

Queens, The Bronx & Staten Island

WESTCHESTER

Van Cortlandt Park

Wave Hill

New York Botanical Garden

Fordham University

THE BRONX

The Cloisters

Bronx Zoo

Cross Bronx Expwy

Crotona Park

Yankee Stadium

Long Island Sound

Pelham Bay Park

Hart I.

City I.

Eastchester Bay

NASSAU

Throngs Neck Br.

Throgs Neck

Whitestone Br.

Little Neck Bay

Cross Island Pkwy.

Clearview Expwy.

Long Island Expwy.

Bruckner Expwy

East River

La Guardia Airport

Rikers I.

Triborough Br.

QUEENS

Shea Stadium

USTA National Tennis Center

Grand Central Pkwy.

Northern Blvd.

Flushing Meadows Corona Park

Van Wyck Expwy.

P.S. 1 Contemporary Art Center

Queensboro Bridge

Central Park

MANHATTAN

East River

Lincoln Tunnel

Queens-Midtown Tunnel

Holland Tunnel

Williamsburg Br.

Manhattan Br.

Brooklyn Br.

Brooklyn Queens Expwy (BQE)

Jackie Robinson Pkwy.

Woodhaven Blvd.

J.F.K. International Airport

Atlantic Ave.

Eastern Pkwy.

Linden Blvd.

Cross Bay Blvd.

Battery Tunnel

Ellis I.

Statue of Liberty

Liberty I.

Governors I.

BROOKLYN

Prospect Park

Jamaica Bay Wildlife Refuge

Floyd Bennett Field

Hodges Memorial Br.

NEW JERSEY

Ferry Terminal

Snug Harbor Cultural Center

Verrazano-Narrows Br.

Ft. Hamilton Pkwy.

Ocean Pkwy.

Flatbush Ave.

Shore Pkwy.

Rockaway Inlet

STATEN ISLAND

ATLANTIC OCEAN

Lower Bay

Liberty State Park

Hudson River

NEW JERSEY

Palisades Pkwy.

Spuyten Deyvil

George Washington Br.

Deegan Expwy

Grand Concourse

Harlem R.

ATLANTIC OCEAN

0   3 miles

0   3 km

TOP 5

- A visit to the P.S.1 Contemporary Art Center

- The Museum of the Moving Image

- An afternoon at the Bronx Zoo

- The Jacques Marchais Museum of Tibetan Art

- Wandering the restored buildings in Historic Richmondtown

MAKING THE MOST OF YOUR TIME

Queens is rich with a diverse selection of museums. A quick afternoon trip to Astoria and Long Island City will enable you to take in the American Museum of Moving Image, Isamu Noguchi Garden, and the P.S. 1 Contemporary Art Center. After that, you could either jump on the 7 train and have dinner in Jackson Heights, or head back into Manhattan.

It takes about an hour to get to the Bronx from Midtown, but you'll certainly be rewarded for your time. Many of the city's most popular attractions are in the Bronx, and though most are within walking distance of each other, you can't possibly see them all in one day. Both the New York Botanical Garden and the Bronx Zoo require at least a half day each to see the highlights. If you want to visit both, start early and plan on a late lunch or early dinner in Belmont. The Zoo and the Garden are less crowded on weekdays.

Staten Island holds unexpected offerings in its small museums and historic villages. As you make your plans, set aside the better part of a day for Historic Richmondtown, and add on a couple of hours for the Tibetan Museum. If you take the bus, ask the driver about the return schedule. Both Historic Richmondtown and the Tibetan Museum are closed Monday and Tuesday and open afternoons only on weekends.

GETTING HERE

Queens is served by many subway lines. To get to Astoria, take the N or W train. For Long Island City, take the E, V, or 7 trains. To get to Jackson Heights, take the 7 subway train to the 74th Street–Broadway stop.

The Bronx is serviced by three different subway lines: 2, 4, 5, 6, B, and D. Since the attractions in the Bronx are spread out across the borough, you'll need to take different lines to get where you want to go, and it's not necessarily convenient to make connections across town. The B, D, and 4 trains all go to Yankee Stadium, and the B and D continue uptown to bring you to Belmont and Arthur Avenue from the west. The 2 and 5 trains take you to the Bronx Zoo and also to Belmont from the east.

The Staten Island Ferry will take you to Staten Island. From the ferry terminal, you can access sights via bus or car service. See individual listings for directions.

Nearby, the **New York Botanical Garden** is considered one of the leading botany centers of the world. Built around the dramatic gorge of the Bronx River, this 250-acre garden is one of the best reasons to make a trip to the Bronx. Die-hard sports nuts and casual fans alike are drawn to **Yankee Stadium,** one of baseball's most revered cathedrals. A stadium tour at noon includes glimpses of the field, dugout, and clubhouse.

For a bit of old-world flavor, check out the "Little Italy of the Bronx": **Belmont** is much more a real, thriving Italian-American community than its Manhattan counterpart, and it's been this way since the late 19th century. The corner of **Arthur Avenue** and 187th Street is the heart of this low-key neighborhood. **Edgar Allan Poe Cottage** is the tiny workman's house in which the poet sought refuge from 1846 to 1849. At the extreme northeast end of the Bronx sits the 230-acre stretch of **City Island.** At its spine is City Island Avenue, which is lined with antiques and gift shops, restaurants, and boat rentals.

Wave Hill—a 28-acre public garden and cultural center with exquisite herb, wildflower, and aquatic gardens—attracts green thumbs from all over the world. Among the 300,000 buried in the ornate and star-studded burial grounds of **Woodland Cemetery** are R. H. Macy, Fiorello La Guardia and four other former mayors of New York, Robert Moses, Herman Melville, Irving Berlin, Miles Davis, and Celia Cruz.

Staten Island

Take the **Staten Island Ferry** from the southern tip of Manhattan. After you disembark, walk into the terminal and grab the S40 bus for a 10-minute (2-mi) ride to the **Snug Harbor Cultural Center.** From Snug Harbor, families with young kids may want to head to the **Staten Island Zoo.**

Photography buffs will want to visit the **Alice Austen House Museum.** Its most famous resident, Alice Austen (1866–1952), was a pioneer of the then-new art of photography. Her work is on display at the museum, which also offers a nice view of the waterfront. For some Italian-American history, head to the **Garibaldi-Meucci Museum.** On the southern end of the island, you can journey back into Staten Island's past at **Historic Richmond Town,** where you can visit many restored buildings, including the **Staten Island Historical Society Museum** and **Stephen's General Store,** which was built in 1837 and looks much as it did in the mid-19th century. High above Richmondtown is the **Jacques Marchais Museum of Tibetan Art** where relaxing gardens await you.

PLACES TO EXPLORE

Queens

Astoria & Long Island City
Museum of the Moving Image. Displays on the evolution of creating moving images begin on the third floor with cool samples of Victorian-era technology (and a modern strobe-light niche; enter the recessed area when the strobe light is off). Interactive, how-to exhibits proceed to modern times, but they don't reach the contemporary era of digital technology.

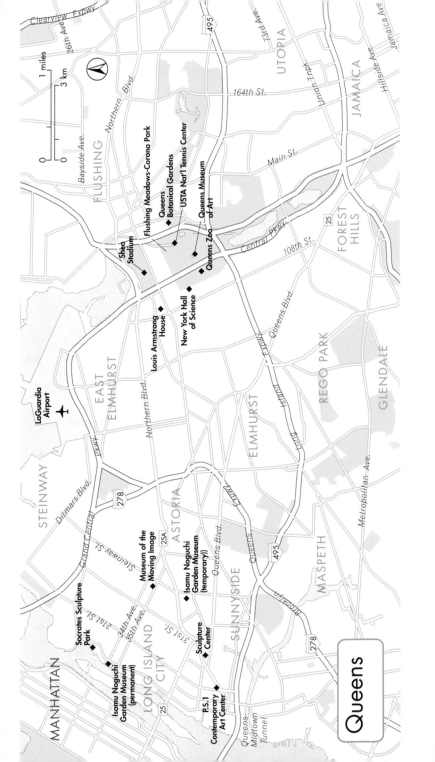

Filmmaking in Astoria

CLOSE UP

IN THE 1920S, when Hollywood was still a dusty small town, such stars as Gloria Swanson, Rudolph Valentino, and Claudette Colbert all came out to the Astoria Studio to act in one of the more than 100 movies produced here. Built in 1919 by the film company that would soon become Paramount, "the Big House" was the largest and most important filmmaking studio in the country. Its location was ideal for the time, when filmmakers needed easy access to Broadway's and vaudeville's stars.

By the '30s, the trickle of studios and stars lured to Hollywood and its near-perfect year-round weather had become a full-blown stream. Astoria was able to hold its own for a while longer, creating such films as the Marx Brothers classics *The Cocoanuts* and *Animal Crackers*. As the decade went on, Paramount continued to moves its operations west, until finally shorts were the only films being made at Paramount's eastern branch.

In 1942 the studio was sold to the U.S. Army, and it became the Signal Corps Photographic Center, producing training films and documentaries that include Frank's Capra's classic seven-film series, *Why We Fight*. The government retained the studio until the early '70s, by which time it had begun to fall into disrepair.

Sold to a foundation and then to the city, in 1982 the studio was transferred to real-estate developer George S. Kaufman and his partners, which included Alan King and the late Johnny Carson. Kaufman-Astoria Studios, with six stages, is a thriving operation once again, used for television series (*Sesame Street, Law and Order*) as well as movies (*The Wiz, Hair, The Manchurian Candidate*).

Funding seems to have dipped after the 1980s, as sound recording displays using artifacts from *The Cosby Show* and *Dangerous Liaisons* seem like ancient history. However, there are flashes of the newish, including costumes from every hot body seen in *Chicago* and daily editing sessions using *Titanic* sequences. The most fun comes from engaging your creativity with stop-action sequences, voice dubbing, and music-score overlay. The second floor, full of memorabilia, begins with a wall of glamorous Hollywood head shots, a minitheater decked out in Egyptian style by artists Red Grooms and Lysiance Long, and loads of spin-off products, from lunch boxes to dolls. It's the latex-and-silicon models used to create possessed children (Regan in *The Exorcist*) or a simple wig (a Mohawk cap worn by Robert De Niro in *Taxi Driver*) that drive home the fact that this museum is perhaps best appreciated by baby boomers and their kids. Those wishing to improve their Ms. Pac-man score should head to the darkened video arcade on the ground floor (games are moving images, too). The museum draws locals with its lectures and film programs, including retrospectives. Next door is the solid block of Kaufman-Astoria Studios, used for filming TV series such as *Law and Order* and *The Sopranos*. ⊠ *35th Ave. at 36th St., Astoria* ☎ *718/784–0077* ⊕ *www.ammi.org* ☒ *$10; free after 4 on Fri.* ⊙ *Wed. and Thurs.*

11–5, Fri. noon–8, weekends 11–6:30; screenings weekends and Fri. 7:30 Ⓜ *Subway: R, V (weekdays only), R, G (weekends only) to Steinway St.; N, W to Broadway.*

Isamu Noguchi Garden Museum. The Japanese-American sculptor Isamu Noguchi (1904–88) bought this former photo-engraving plant, across the street from his studio at the time, as a place to display his work. The large, peaceful garden and the galleries that border it provide ample room to show more than 250 pieces done in stone, metal, clay, and other materials. Temporary exhibits feature his collaborations with others, such as engineer R. Buckminster Fuller and industrial designer Isamu Kenmochi. The museum is not close to subway stops, so check the Web site for complete directions. On Sundays a shuttle bus leaves from in front of Manhattan's Asia Society hourly beginning at 12:30. A round-trip costs $10. ✉ *9–01 33rd Rd., at Vernon Blvd., Long Island City* ☎ *718/204–7088* ⊕ *www.noguchi.org* ✎ *$10; first Fri. of month pay what you wish* ☉ *Wed.–Fri. 10–5, weekends 11–6* Ⓜ *Subway: N, W to Broadway; F to Queensbridge–21st St.*

P.S. 1 Contemporary Art Center. A pioneer in the "alternative-space" movement, P.S. 1 rose from the ruins of an abandoned school in 1976 as a sort of community arts center for the future. Now a partner of the Museum of Modern Art, P.S. 1 still focuses on community involvement, with studio spaces for resident artists and educational programs. In summer, its Saturday afternoon outdoor dance parties with DJs attract a crowd in which everyone looks like an in-the-know art student. P.S. 1's exhibition space is enormous, and every available corner is used—four floors, rooftop spaces, staircases and landings, bathrooms, the boiler room and basement, and outdoor galleries. Exhibitions reflect the center's mission to present experimental and formally innovative contemporary art, from the progressive and interactive to the merely incomprehensible. It's never dull. ✉ *22–25 Jackson Ave., at 46th Ave., Long Island City* ☎ *718/784–2084* ⊕ *www.ps1.org* ✎ *$5 suggested donation* ☉ *Thurs.–Mon. noon–6* Ⓜ *Subway: 7 to 45th Rd.–Courthouse Sq.; V (weekdays only) or E to 23rd St.–Ely Ave.; G to 21st St.–Van Alst.*

Sculpture Center. This large museum not far from P.S. 1 is devoted to contemporary sculpture. A former trolley repair shop that was renovated by artist Maya Lin and architect David Hotson, the Sculpture Center exhibits cutting-edge work in its large indoor and outdoor exhibition spaces. The museum sometimes closes between exhibition periods; call ahead before visiting. ✉ *44–19 Purves St., at Jackson Ave., Long Island City* ☎ *718/361–1750* ⊕ *www.sculpture-center.org* ✎ *$5 suggested donation* ☉ *Thurs.–Mon. 11–6* Ⓜ *Subway: 7 to 45th Rd.–Courthouse Sq.; V (weekdays only), E to 23rd St.–Ely Ave.; G to 21st St.–Van Alst.*

Socrates Sculpture Park. In 1985 local artist Mark di Suvero and other residents rallied to transform what had been an abandoned landfill and illegal dump site into this 4½-acre park devoted to public art. The park was named in honor of the philosopher as well as the local Greek community. Today a superb view of the river and Manhattan frames changing exhibitions of contemporary sculptures and multimedia installations. The park also hosts a variety of free public programs, including art workshops and an annual outdoor film series (July–August, Wednesday evening). ⊠ *Vernon Blvd. at Broadway, Long Island City* ☎ *718/956–1819* ⊕ *www.socratessculpturepark.org* ☒ *Free* ⊙ *Daily 10–sunset* Ⓜ *Subway: N to Broadway, then walk west or take Q104 bus along Broadway to Vernon Blvd.*

WHERE TO EAT   Astoria has emerged as one of the top destinations in Queens for superb ethnic dining. After you're done with the sights, you may want to end your day with dinner at one of Astoria's Greek restaurants (on or near Broadway) or venture to the Middle Eastern restaurants farther out on Steinway Street.

The multilevel **Karyatis** (⊠ 35–03 Broadway, between 35th and 36th Sts., Astoria ☎ 718/204–0666. $15–$24) is among the oldest and most elegant of Queens' neighborhood Greek restaurants. The traditional appetizers, grilled octopus, lamb, grilled fish entrées, and other menu highlights are served by a friendly and professional staff. With live music at night you can make a festive evening of it. **Uncle George's Greek Tavern** (⊠ 33–19 Broadway, at 34th St. ☎ 718/626–0593. $8–$15), which looks much more like a diner than a tavern, serves simple preparations of Greek dishes, especially those involving fish.

Jackson Heights

WHERE TO EAT   Neighborhood folk and Manhattanites alike flock to **Jackson Diner** (⊠ 37–47 74th St., between Roosevelt and 37th Aves. ☎ 718/672–1232. $8–$19) for the cheap, spicy, and authentic fare served in generous portions. Popular choices include chicken tandoori, lentil doughnuts in a tangy broth, and any of the curry dishes, as well as the many vegetarian specialties. Down the block from Jackson Diner, **Delhi Palace** (⊠ 37–33 74th St., between Roosevelt and 37th Aves. ☎ 718/507–0666. $9–$16) serves a similar menu of authentic Indian dishes, but many of them are just a bit better—and spicier. The restaurant's daily buffet (around $8), served daily from 11:30 to 4, stands out from the competition.

SHOPPING   **Sahil Sari Palace** (⊠ 37–39 74th St., between Roosevelt and 37th Aves. ☎ 718/426–9526) is filled with bolts of colorful cloth as well as ready-to-wear saris and other clothing. **Patel Brothers** (⊠ 37–27 74th St., near 37th Ave., Jackson Heights 718/898–3445), like the other members in this large chain of Indian grocery stores, stocks household goods, produce, and lots of other staples. Especially fun to check out are the ice cream, nuts, and other snacks.

Flushing Meadows–Corona Park

The **Queens Museum of Art** shows contemporary works by many interesting local and international artists as well as temporary exhibits on culture, but it's best known for the astonishing Panorama, a nearly 900,000-building model of the five boroughs made for the 1964 World's Fair. The exhibit, brought up to date in 1994, faithfully replicates the city building by building, on a scale of 1 inch per 100 feet. The model's tiny brownstones and skyscrapers are updated periodically to match the

Ethnic Eats on the 7 Train

BEGINNING AT TIMES SQUARE, stopping at Grand Center Terminal, and then moving farther west until it reaches its end on Flushing's Main Street, the 7 train cuts through the middle of Queens and some of its most diverse and interesting neighborhoods. This, of course, is no coincidence—groups and individuals have long chosen neighborhoods along the subway for their relative cheapness and their easy proximity to Manhattan. The 7 train's importance hasn't been overlooked by the nation at large: in 1999 the U.S. government recognized the 7 train's importance to immigrants by designating its 5-mi path in Queens as one of 16 "National Millennium Trails." Just about wherever you may happen to stop on the 7 train's path, you're likely to find something worth seeing. Because the 7 train is elevated throughout its trip through Queens, it's easy to get a handle on your surroundings—and to know where to find the subway once your explorations are through. Restaurants in ethnic neighborhoods are often on a shoestring, with profit margins and cash flow a constant concern. As a result, relatively few such places accept credit cards. Woodside, Queens, which contains the 7 train's 61st Street stop, is a smaller melting pot within the larger one of Queens. To get a little Irish, head first to **Shane's Bakery** (✉ 39–61 61th St. ☎ 718/424–9039), which serves breakfast and lunch and is known for its scones and similar pastries. Nearby is the **Stop Inn Diner** (✉ 60–22 Roosevelt Ave. ☎ 718/779–0290), where you can get British Isle bacon sandwiches, fish and chips, and a proper Irish breakfast. The large pub **Donovan's** (✉ Roosevelt Ave. and

58th St. ☎ 718/429–9339) is reputed to have some of the best burgers in New York City.

Woodside is also home to several different Asian populations. The Thai restaurant **Sripraphai** (✉ 64–13 39th Ave. ☎ 718/899–9599) (pronounced See-PRA-pie) has been getting raves for its brand of uncompromising, often spicy Thai food and has gained a broader and broader contingent of the adventurous. The restaurant is closed on Wednesday.

At Jackson Heights–74th Street, not only can you experience "Little India," but you can also range even farther afield. At the same stop is **Tibetan Yak** (✉ 72–20 Roosevelt Ave. ☎ 718/779–1119). The tea here, made with cow butter rather than that of a yak as it is in Tibet, is definitely an acquired taste, but most of the items on its menu of hearty curries and dumplings and other dishes are easier to like immediately.

The 7 train may save the best for last: Flushing, whose Main Street is at the end of the line, is a neighborhood full of Chinese and South Asian stores, markets, and restaurants. Unlike Manhattan's Chinatown, the streets here are laid out regularly and with wide sidewalks, making it easier to get around. Two notable stops are **Joe's Shanghai** (✉ 136–21 37th Ave. ☎ 718/539–3838), notable for its delicate soup dumplings, and the **Sweet 'n Tart Café** (✉ 136–11 38th Ave. ☎ 718/661–3380), which serves small dishes perfect for a quick snack. Both restaurants have gone on to open branches in Manhattan, but these older versions are both a little more of an adventure.

13

real things (a red, white, and blue ribbon now hangs on the World Trade Center). Another permanent exhibit, the Neustadt Museum Collection, brings together Tiffany lamps and windows, many of which were made in nearby Corona, Queens. In early 2007, Robert Moses, the man who planned—nearly with an iron fist—New York City's parks and roadways between the 1930s and '60s, is the focus of an exhibit. ⊠ *Flushing Meadows–Corona Park* ☎ *718/592–9700* ⊕ *www.queensmuseum. org* ✉ *$5 suggested donation* ⊙ *Sept.–June, Wed.–Fri. 10–5, weekends noon–5; July and Aug., Wed., Thurs., and weekends noon–6, Fri. noon–8* Ⓜ *Subway: 7 to Willets Point/Shea Stadium.*

Animals from the Americas roam in settings loosely approximating their natural habitats at **Queens Zoo.** The residents include spectacled bears, mountain lions, sea lions, prairie dogs, coyotes, bison, elk, thick-billed parrots, and bald eagles. The aviary is inside a geodesic dome made by futurist architect Buckminster Fuller for the 1964 World's Fair. ⊠ *53–51 111th St., at 53rd Ave.* ☎ *718/271–7761* ⊕ *www.wcs.org* ✉ *$5* ⊙ *Early Apr.–late Oct., weekdays 10–5, weekends 10–5:30; late Oct.–early Apr., daily 10–4:30; last ticket sold 30 mins before closing.*

Built in 1964, **Shea Stadium** is named for the lawyer William A. Shea, who was essential in bringing a National League baseball team back to New York. The New York Mets play here from April through September. In addition to its place in sports-making history, Shea Stadium was also the site of a famous Beatles concert in August of 1965. ⊠ *Roosevelt Ave. off Grand Central Pkwy.* ☎ *718/507–8499* ⊕ *www.mets.com* Ⓜ *Subway: 7 to Willets Pt./Shea Stadium.*

The **USTA National Tennis Center,** site of the U.S. Open Tennis Championships, has 42 courts (33 outdoor and 9 indoor, all Deco Turf II) open to the public all year except August and September. Reservations are accepted up to two days in advance, and prices are $20–$50 hourly. ⊠ *Flushing Meadows–Corona Park.* ☎ *718/760–6200* ⊕ *www.usta. com* Ⓜ *Subway: 7 to Willets Pt./Shea Stadium.*

Elsewhere in Queens

Louis Armstrong House. Famed jazz musician Louis Armstrong lived in this three-story redbrick house in a working-class neighborhood of Corona Park with his wife, Lucille, from 1943 until his death in 1971. The 40-minute tour takes you through the large living room, full of mementos and art collected over a lifetime of traveling, the Asian-inspired dining room, and the kitchen, all done up in robin's-egg blue and Lucite. The downstairs bathroom, its walls entirely mirrored and its fixtures plated in gold, is a trip in itself. Amid all this vivid decoration, Louis's den is comparatively drab, with dark wood and a phonograph, ceiling speakers, a bar area, and what were once state-of-the-art reel-to-reel tape recorders. It's here where his spirit shines through most clearly. ⊠ *34–56 107th St., between 37th and 38th Aves., Corona Park* ☎ *718/ 478–8274* ⊕ *www.satchmo.net* ✉ *$8* ⊙ *Tours hourly Tues.–Fri. 10–4, weekends noon–4* Ⓜ *Subway: 7 to 103rd St.–Corona Plaza.*

New York Hall of Science. This top science museum has more than 400 hands-on experiments on subjects ranging from lasers to microbes, plus changing exhibits. In 2004, a 55,000-square-foot addition brought permanent exhibits on sports and the search for life on other planets. Rocket Park includes *Mercury I*, the first U.S. spacecraft used in 1960. You can imagine what John Glenn, the first American astronaut, felt like when climbing in a replica *Friendship Mercury 7* capsule. The Mathematica section is designed by names more often heard in the art world: Charles and Ray Eames. You can get extra tutoring from volunteer "Explainers," who are scientists and teachers in training. Outside, stations on the Science Playground coax youngsters into learning while they're horsing around. ⊠ *111th St. at 46th Ave., Flushing* ☎ *718/699–0005* ⊕ *www.nyscience.org* ✉ *$11; free Fri. 2–5 and Sun. 10–11, Sept.–June* ☉ *Sept.–June, Mon.–Thurs. 9:30–2, Fri. 9:30–5, weekends 10–6; July and Aug., weekdays 9:30–5, weekends 10–6* Ⓜ *Subway: 7 to 111th St.; walk 3 blocks south.*

Queens Botanical Gardens. Built for the 1939 World's Fair, these 39 acres include gardens of roses and herbs, an arboretum, and plantings especially designed to attract bees and birds. Plans slated for completion in 2006 will bring a new environmentally friendly visitor center that will use solar energy and water-filtering plants in its design. ⊠ *43–50 Main St., Flushing* ☎ *718/886–3800* ⊕ *www.queensbotanical.org* ✉ *Free* ☉ *Apr.–Oct., Tues.–Fri. 8–6, weekends 8–7; Nov.–Mar., Tues.–Sun. 8–4:30* Ⓜ *Subway: 7 to Main St.–Flushing.*

The Bronx

The Bronx Zoo. When it opened its gates in 1899, 843 animals were exhibited in small cages and enclosures. Today, this 265-acre zoo is the largest metropolitan zoo in the United States. It has more than 4,500 animals, representing more than 600 species, many of which live in outdoor settings designed to re-create their habitats. You're often separated from them by no more than a moat or wall of glass. One of the zoo's best exhibits is the **Congo Gorilla Forest** (✉ $3) a 6½-acre re-creation of an African rain forest with wooded pathways, lush greenery, and animals including red-river hogs, black-and-white colobus monkeys, and two troops of lowland gorillas. The 3-acre **Tiger Mountain** is a habitat with six Siberian tigers who particularly like being outside in cold weather. They're often napping at midday, but short daily "enrichment sessions" let you see the keepers interacting with them.

From the **Wild Asia Monorail,** open May–October, weather permitting, you can see Asian elephants, Indian rhinoceros, gaur (the world's largest cattle), Mongolian wild horses, and several deer and antelope species. In the summer of 2006, the **African Plains**—home to lions, giraffes, cheetahs, zebras, and other savanna species—made room for a rowdy pack of African wild dogs. The park is open 365 days a year, but planning your trip is important, as it's impossible to see everything here in one day. Try to visit the most popular exhibits, such as Congo Gorilla Forest, early to avoid lines later in the day. In winter the outdoor exhibitions have fewer animals on view, but there's also reduced admission and the Holiday Lights period, when the zoo is decorated and open until 9 PM. ⊠ *Bronx River Pkwy. and Fordham Rd., Fordham* ☎ *718/367–*

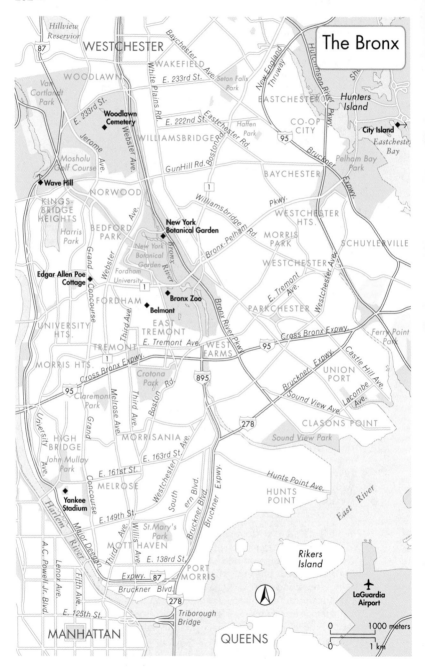

The Bronx

WESTCHESTER

Hillview
Reservoir

WOODLAWN

Van
Cortlandt
Park

Baychester Ave.

WAKEFIELD

E. 233rd St.

Seton Falls
Park

White Plains Rd.

New England
Thruway

EASTCHESTER

Hutchinson River Pkwy.

Hunters
Island

E. 233rd St.

Woodlawn
Cemetery

E. 222nd St.

Eastchester Rd.

Haffen
Park

CO-OP
CITY

95

City Island

Jerome Ave.

Webster Ave.

WILLIAMSBRIDGE

Boston Rd.

Eastchester
Bay

Mosholu
Golf Course

GunHill Rd.

Bruckner Expwy.

Pelham
Bay
Park

BAYCHESTER

Wave Hill

NORWOOD

1

Williamsbridge Rd.

WESTCHESTER
HTS.

KINGS-
BRIDGE
HEIGHTS

BEDFORD
PARK

Pkwy.

SCHUYLERVILLE

Harris
Park

New York
Botanical Garden

Webster Ave.

New York
Botanical
Garden

Bronx-Pelham Rd.

MORRIS
PARK

WESTCHESTER

Edgar Allen Poe
Cottage

Grand Concourse

Fordham
University

1

Bronx River

Bronx Zoo

E. Tremont
Ave.

Westchester Ave.

FORDHAM

Third Ave.

Belmont

PARCHESTER

UNIVERSITY
HTS.

EAST
TREMONT

Bronx River Pkwy.

Ferry Point
Park

TREMONT

E. Tremont Ave.

WEST
FARMS

95

Cross Bronx Expwy.

Castle Hill Ave.

MORRIS HTS.

1

Cross Bronx Expwy.

Crotona
Park

Boston Rd.

895

Bruckner Expwy.

UNION
PORT

Lacombe
Ave.

95

Claremont
Park

Third Ave.

Melrose Ave.

278

Sound View Ave.

CLASONS POINT

University Ave.

HIGH
BRIDGE

Grand

MORRISANIA

Westchester Ave.

Sound View Park

John Mullay
Park

E. 163rd St.

South ern Blvd.

Hunts Point Ave.

East River

E. 161st St.

MELROSE

Bruckner Blvd.

Bruckner Expwy.

HUNTS
POINT

Yankee
Stadium

Concourse

E. 149th St.

Willis Ave.

St. Mary's
Park

Rikers
Island

Harlem River

Major Deegan

Third Ave.

MOTT HAVEN

E. 138th St.

A.C. Powell Jr. Blvd.

Lenox Ave.

Fifth Ave.

Expwy.

87

PORT
MORRIS

LaGuardia
Airport

E. 125th St.

Bruckner Blvd.

278

MANHATTAN

Triborough
Bridge

QUEENS

0   1000 meters

0   1 km

1010 ⊕ www.bronxzoo.com ✉ $11; free Wed., donation suggested; extra charge for some exhibits; parking $7. $8 admission Nov.–Mar. ⊙ Apr.–Oct., weekdays 10–5, weekends 10–5:30; Nov.–Mar., daily 10–4:30; last ticket sold 30 mins before closing Ⓜ Subway: 2, 5 to Pelham Pkwy., then walk 3 blocks west to Bronx Pkwy. entrance; Bx11 express bus to Bronx Pkwy. entrance.

Edgar Allan Poe Cottage. The poet and his sickly wife, Virginia, sought refuge at this tiny workman's cottage from 1846 to 1849. The family was so impoverished that Poe's mother sometimes wandered along the roadside to pick dandelions for dinner. Virginia died of tuberculosis in 1847, and Poe sought solace in the church chimes at nearby St. John's College Church (now Fordham University); word has it that these haunting sounds inspired one of his most famous poems, "The Bells." ✉ *E. Kingsbridge Rd. and Grand Concourse, Kingsbridge Heights* 🕾 *718/ 881–8900 ⊕ www.bronxhistoricalsociety.org ✉ $3 ⊙ Sat. 10–4, Sun. 1–5* Ⓜ *Subway: 4, D to Kingsbridge Rd.*

★ **New York Botanical Garden.** Considered one of the leading botany centers of the world, this 250-acre garden built around the dramatic gorge of the Bronx River is one of the best reasons to make a trip to the Bronx. Outdoor plant collections include the Peggy Rockefeller Rose Garden, with 2,700 bushes of more than 250 varieties; the spectacular Rock Garden, with plants from all seven continents; and the Everett Children's Adventure Garden, a 12-acre, indoor-outdoor museum with a boulder maze, giant animal topiaries, and a plant discovery center. On the grounds by the rushing Bronx River is the Snuff Mill, built in 1840 by two French Huguenot brothers named Lorillard. It powered the grinding of tobacco for snuff and nearby, the Lorillards grew roses to supply fragrance for their blend. A path along the river from the mill leads to the garden's rare 50-acre tract of the native forest that once covered New York City.

Inside the **Enid A. Haupt Conservatory** (✉ $5), a Victorian-style glass house with 17,000 individual panes, are year-round re-creations of misty tropical rain forests and arid African and North American deserts as well as changing exhibitions, such as the annual Holiday Train Show and the Orchid Show. A good way to see the garden is with the **Combination Ticket** (✉ $13, off-peak days), which gives you access to the Conservatory, Rock Garden, Native Plant Garden, Tram Tour, Everett Children's Adventure Garden, and exhibits in the library.

The most direct way to the New York Botanical Garden is via **Metro-North Railroad** (⊕ www.mta.nyc.ny.us/mnr) from Grand Central Terminal, on the Harlem Local Line. The Botanical Garden stop is right across from the entrance. Round-trip tickets are $5 to $12, depending on the time of day. A cheaper alternative is to take the D train or the No. 4 to Bedford Park Boulevard. From the subway station walk east on Bedford Park Boulevard to the entrance. When you decide to leave the grounds, exit via the visitor center and through the main gate. ✉ *200th St. and Kazimiroff Blvd., Bedford Park* 🕾 *718/817–8700 ⊕ www.nybg.org ✉ $6 grounds only; free Sat. 10–noon and Wed.; parking $7 ⊙ Apr.–Oct. and mid-Nov.–first week of Jan., Tues.–Sun. 10–6;*

2nd wk of Jan.–Mar., Tues.–Sun. 10–5 Ⓜ *Subway: D, 4 to Bedford Park Blvd.; Metro-North to Botanical Garden.*

Wave Hill. In the mid- to late 19th century, Manhattan millionaires built summer homes in the suburb of Riverdale, where they had stirring views of the New Jersey Palisades. Wave Hill, a former estate dating back to 1843, is now a 28-acre public garden and cultural center. Today the greenhouse and conservatory, plus 18 acres of exquisite herb, wildflower, and aquatic gardens, attract green thumbs from all over the world. Grand beech and oak trees adorn wide lawns, and elegant pergolas are hidden along curving pathways. Additional draws are gardening and crafts workshops, a summertime dance series, changing art exhibitions, and Sunday concerts, which are held in Armor Hall from fall to spring. Free garden and greenhouse tours take place Sunday at 2:15 year-round. The café, gift shop, greenhouses, and galleries open at 10 AM. ☒ *W. 249th St. and Independence Ave., Riverdale* ☎ *718/549–3200* ⊕ *www.wavehill.org* ▨ *Mar.–Nov. $4, Sat.* AM *and Tues. free; Dec.–Feb. free* ⊙ *Mid-Apr.–mid-Oct., Tues.–Sun. 9–5:30; June–July open Wed. until 9* PM*; mid-Oct.–mid-Apr., Tues.–Sun. 9–4:30. Free garden tours Sun. 2:15* Ⓜ *Subway: 1 to 231st St., then Bx7 or Bx10 bus to 252nd St. and Riverdale Ave.; Metro-North train: Hudson line to Riverdale then 15-min uphill walk.*

★ **Yankee Stadium.** Ever since Babe Ruth hit a home run in the park's inaugural game in 1923, Yankee Stadium has been one of baseball's most revered cathedrals. John Phillip Sousa and the Seventh Regiment Band marked the opening with a fanfare. Many renovations later, the stadium still feels like the place where Lou Gehrig and Micky Mantle performed their heroic deeds. A stadium tour at noon includes glimpses of the field, dugout, and clubhouse. Arrive at least 30 minutes early to buy tickets. If you want to pick up a souvenir, then head to the Yankees gift store, which is open daily. Better yet, come for a game at the "House That Ruth Built": the Yankees play ball from April through September.

Catercorner to Gate 6 of Yankee Stadium and open two hours before and after games, the tiny **Press Café** (☒ 114 E. 157th St., between River and Gerard Aves., Highbridge ☎ 718/401–0545. $5–$8) serves delicious salads and pressed Italian-style sandwiches—all for $8 or less. Look for the striped awning and take a seat at one of the seven bar stools or six tables. On game nights, New York Waterway's ferry *Yankee Clipper* (☎ 800/533–3779 departure information) departs for the stadium from Manhattan's east side. A round-trip ferry ride is $18. ☒ *161st St. and River Ave., Highbridge* ☎ *718/579–4531 tours, 718/293–6000 box office* ⊕ *www.yankees. com* ▨ *Tour $12 Sept.–May, $14 June–Aug.* Ⓜ *Subway: B (weekdays only), D to 167th St., No. 4 to 161st St.–Yankee Stadium.*

Belmont (Arthur Avenue)

Touted as the "Little Italy of the Bronx," Belmont is much more a real, thriving Italian-American community than its Manhattan counterpart, and it's been this way since the late 19th century, when Italian workers were encouraged to move here to help build the Bronx Zoo and other large projects. As the food writer Regina Schrambling puts it, "Arthur Avenue has never catered to fickle tourists, but to passionately loyal shoppers looking for mozzarella so fresh it oozes, for the supplest veal, for fettuccine cut to order, for sausages in a dozen variations."

Don't be surprised to hear people speaking Italian—or Albanian, since the neighborhood has been an enclave for this group since the 1980s. The corner of Arthur Avenue and 187th Street is the heart of this low-key neighborhood—just as Our Lady of Mt. Carmel Roman Catholic Church, at East 187th Street and Belmont Avenue and towering above nearby buildings, is Belmont's spiritual center.

Locals and suburbanites do their shopping on Saturday afternoons, and so should you—you'll find most stores shuttered on Sunday. ⊠ *Bordered by E. Fordham Rd., Southern Blvd., and Crescent and 3rd Aves.* ⊕ *www.arthuravenuebronx.com* Ⓜ *B, D, No. 4 to Fordham Rd., then Bx12 east; No. 2 or 5 to Pelham Pkwy., then Bx12 west; Metro-North to Fordham Rd., then shuttle bus to Belmont.*

13

WHERE TO EAT What might be the best restaurant in Belmont, **Roberto's** (⊠ 603 Crescent Ave., at Hughes Ave. ☎ 718/733–9503. $13–$19), serves classic Southern Italian dishes. At **Dominick's** (⊠ 2335 Arthur Ave., at E. 187th St. ☎ 718/733–2807. $9–$40), no-nonsense waiters preside over communal tables in the sparsely decorated dining room. There are no printed menus, but typical Southern Italian items like veal parmigiana, spaghetti with meat sauce, and shrimp scampi are normally available. Stop for a quick lunch at the **Café al Mercato** (⊠ 2344 Arthur Ave., at E. 187th St. ☎ 718/364–7681. $9–$13), inside the Arthur Avenue Retail Market. Don't pass up the creative pizzas—the tri-color "Italian Flag" is topped with broccoli rabe, artichokes, and sun-dried tomatoes.

SHOPPING The covered **Arthur Avenue Retail Market** (⊠ 2344 Arthur Ave., at E. 187th St. ☎ 718/367–5686 ⊕ www.arthuravenue.com), in a building sheltering more than a dozen different vendors, was opened by Mayor Fiorello LaGuardia in an effort to get the pushcarts off the crowded streets. Inside you'll find piles of fresh arugula and radicchio, barrels full of olives, and lots of gnocchi *freschi* (fresh) and other pastas. Also sold here are cigars and Italian gifts and kitchenware. The market is open Monday through Saturday 7–6.

The brick ovens at **Madonia Bros. Bakery** (⊠ 2348 Arthur Ave., between 187th and Crescent Sts. ☎ 718/295–5573) have been turning out golden-brown loaves since 1918. A ring of salty prosciutto bread makes a great snack. Clams ranging from littlenecks to cherrystones are iced down in wooden bins in front of **Randazzo's Seafood** (⊠ 2327 Arthur Ave., between 187th and Crescent Sts. ☎ 718/367–4139). The front window of **Calandra's Cheese** (⊠ 2314 Arthur Ave., between 187th and Crescent Sts. ☎ 718/365–7572) is stuffed with hunks of cheese the size of truck tires. Mozzarella (with salt or without), mascarpone, and scamorza dangle from the rafters.

At **Egidio's Pastry Shop** (⊠ 622 E. 187th St., between Arthur and Hughes Aves. ☎ 718/295–6077) you can sample delicious desserts, washed down with a strong shot of espresso.

Best Views of Manhattan

CLOSE UP

THE FREE STATEN ISLAND FERRY is justly famous for its views, but taking one of the bridges linking Brooklyn with Manhattan lets you get those scenes from above, and at your own pace. The Brooklyn Bridge, going from City Hall Park to Brooklyn Heights, is beautiful in its own right, and by taking its northern neighbor, the Manhattan Bridge, you can see Brooklyn Bridge with downtown Manhattan's lights as a backdrop.

The Williamsburg Bridge connects the south side of its namesake Brooklyn neighborhood with Delancey Street in Manhattan. As you walk up the bridge toward Brooklyn, you'll be able to get a bird's-eye view of the Lower East Side and Chinatown, with their many tenements, small storefronts, and parks. Both the Williamsburg and Manhattan bridges have a level for the subway as well as for cars and pedestrians: if you're too tired to walk,

you can get the same views from the relative comfort of a subway seat.

Easily reached via the Brooklyn Bridge, the Brooklyn Heights Promenade was built in 1950 to give neighborhood dwellers as well as visitors a great view of Manhattan and nearby sights. If you'd rather get a sea-level view, then walk down into DUMBO, to Fulton Landing and its waterfront parks.

Queens has several great views of its own. Most of its subway trains are elevated for at least part of their distance: as they snake west, the 7, N, R, and W trains all provide good views. Although the waterfront of Long Island City is for the most part taken up by industry and less-than-scenic infrastructure, you can visit Astoria's Socrates Sculpture Park and get a view of midtown Manhattan from there.

Within sight of Our Lady of Mt. Carmel Church, the **Catholic Goods Center** (⊠ 630 E. 187th St., between Belmont and Hughes Aves. ☎ 718/733–0250) sells statues, cards, and books, and many other items of a religious nature. **Borgatti's Ravioli & Egg Noodles** (⊠ 632 E. 187th St., between Belmont and Hughes Aves. ☎ 718/367–3799) is known for its homemade pastas.

Staten Island

Staten Island Ferry. One of Staten Island's biggest attractions for visitors is the phenomenal view of Lower Manhattan and the Statue of Liberty afforded by the free 20- to 30-minute Staten Island Ferry ride across New York Harbor—the only direct route to Manhattan from the island. On weekdays and weekend afternoons you can catch the ferry at least every half hour. On weekend mornings until 11:30 AM, ferries leave the southern tip of Manhattan at Whitehall Terminal every hour on the half hour; from 11:30 AM until 7:30 PM, they run every half hour. ⊹ *Runs between Manhattan's Whitehall Terminal (Whitehall and South Sts.) and Staten Island's St. George Terminal* ⊕ *www.siferry.com* Ⓜ *Whitehall Terminal: 4 or 5 train to Bowling Green, or R or W train to Whitehall St.*

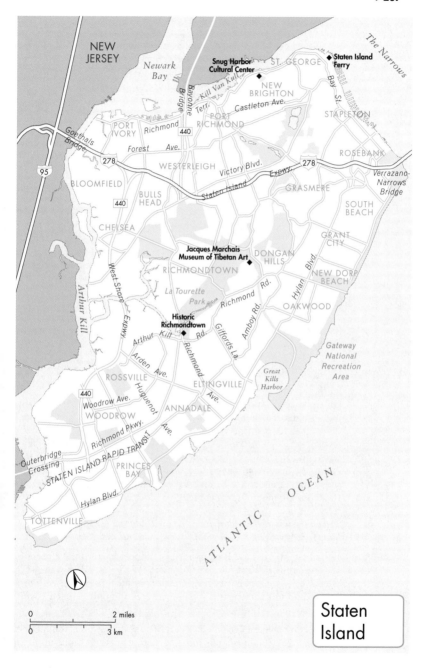

NEW JERSEY

Newark Bay

Snug Harbor Cultural Center

ST. GEORGE

Staten Island Ferry

The Narrows

NEW BRIGHTON

Bayonne Bridge

Kill Van Kull

Castleton Ave.

STAPLETON

Terr.

PORT RICHMOND

PORT IVORY

Richmond 440

Goethals Bridge

Forest Ave.

278

95

WESTERLEIGH

Victory Blvd.

ROSEBANK

278

BLOOMFIELD

Staten Island Expwy.

GRASMERE

Verrazano-Narrows Bridge

BULLS HEAD

440

SOUTH BEACH

CHELSEA

Jacques Marchais Museum of Tibetan Art

DONGAN HILLS

GRANT CITY

Arthur Kill

West Shore Expwy.

RICHMONDTOWN

La Tourette Park

Richmond Rd.

Rd.

Hylan Blvd.

NEW DORP BEACH

OAKWOOD

Historic Richmondtown

Amboy Rd.

Giffords La.

Gateway National Recreation Area

Arthur Kill Rd.

Richmond Rd.

Arden Ave.

ROSSVILLE

Huguenot Ave.

ELTINGVILLE

Great Kills Harbor

440

Woodrow Ave.

ANNADALE

WOODROW

Richmond Pkwy.

Ave.

Outerbridge Crossing

STATEN ISLAND RAPID TRANSIT

PRINCES BAY

Hylan Blvd.

TOTTENVILLE

ATLANTIC OCEAN

0   2 miles
0   3 km

Staten Island

Jacques Marchais Museum of Tibetan Art. One of the largest collections of Tibetan and Himalayan sculpture, scrolls, and paintings outside of Tibet is displayed in this museum resembling a Tibetan monastery. The museum often hosts Buddhist monks from across the world, who demonstrate different parts of their faith—the Dalai Lama visited in 1991. The life of Jacques Marchais, a female art dealer who founded the museum in 1945, will be highlighted in a spring 2007 exhibit. ⊠ *338 Lighthouse Ave., Richmondtown* ☎ *718/987–3500* ⊕ *www.tibetanmuseum.org* ⊡ *$5* ⊙ *Wed.–Sun. 1–5* Ⓜ *S74 bus to Lighthouse Ave. and walk uphill 15 mins.*

Ⓒ **Historic Richmondtown.** These 27 buildings, some constructed as early as 1685, others as late as the 19th century, are part of a 100-acre village that was the site of Staten Island's original county seat. Some of the buildings have been relocated from different spots on the island in order to provide a fuller appreciation of Staten Island's rich history. The Staten Island Historical Society runs the site, and 12 buildings that have been restored are open to the public. Many, such as the Greek Revival courthouse, which serves as the **visitor center** in summer, date from the 19th century; other architectural styles on-site range from Dutch Colonial to Victorian Gothic Revival. The **Staten Island Historical Society Museum,** built in 1848 as the second county clerk's and surrogate's office, now houses furniture, tools, photographs, and other Staten Island artifacts plus changing exhibitions about the island; it serves as the visitor center in winter. **Stephen's General Store,** built in 1837, looks much as it did in the mid-19th century. Adjacent is the late-19th-century **Stephen's House,** which is also filled with artifacts from the period. The **Voorlezer's House,** built in 1695, is one of the oldest buildings on the site; it served as a residence as well as a place of worship and an elementary school.

During special events staff members demonstrate Early American crafts and trades such as printing, tinsmithing, basket making, and fireplace cooking. In summer you might want to make reservations for the traditional dinner (call for details), cooked outdoors and served with utensils of the specific period. Old Home Day in October shows off craftspeople at work; and December brings a monthlong Christmas celebration. A tavern on the historic village grounds hosts a Saturday night concert series showcasing ethnic and folk music; call for details. Take the S74–Richmond Road bus (30 minutes) or a car service (which costs about $12) from the ferry terminal. ⊠ *441 Clarke Ave., Richmondtown* ☎ *718/351–1611* ⊕ *www.historicrichmondtown.org* ⊡ *$5* ⊙ *July and Aug., Wed.–Sat. 10–5, Sun. 1–5; Sept.–June, Wed.–Sun. 1–5* Ⓜ *S74 bus to St. Patrick's Pl.*

WHERE TO EAT For a taste of Historic Richmondtown cuisine, head to the **Parsonage** (⊠ 74 Arthur Kill Rd., Richmondtown ☎ 718/351–7879. $14–$27), which serves twists on American classics (pork chops stuffed with prosciutto and mozzarella, filet mignon covered in apple-smoked bacon) in a restored 19th-century parish house in the complex.

★ **Snug Harbor Cultural Center.** Once part of a sprawling farm, this 83-acre community is Staten Island's most popular attraction. Made up of 26 mostly restored historic buildings, Snug Harbor's center is a row of five columned Greek Revival temples that were built between 1831 and 1880. Its Main Hall—the oldest building on the property and dating from

1833—is home to the **Eleanor Proske Visitors Center** (🎫 $3, including Newhouse Center), which has an exhibit on the history of Snug Harbor and special art exhibits, and the **Newhouse Center for Contemporary Art** (🎫 $3, including Visitors Center), which exhibits contemporary work, normally within a historical context. Thus older works often sit beside multidisciplinary pieces—in costume, video, mixed media, and performance, among others—in the expansive space. Next door to the Main Hall is the **John A. Noble Collection** (🎫 $3) where an old seaman's dormitory has been transformed into classrooms; a library and archive; a printmaking studio; and galleries displaying maritime-inspired photography, lithographs, and artwork.

13

Spread over the cultural center grounds is the **Staten Island Botanical Gardens** (☎ 718/273–8200 ⊕ www.sibg.org 🎫 Free; $5 for Chinese Garden and Secret Garden ⊙ Daily dawn–dusk; Chinese Garden and Secret Garden Apr.–Sept., Tues.–Sun. 10–5; Oct.–Mar., Tues.–Sun. 10–4), which include a perennial garden, orchid collection, Garden of Healing, 9/11 World Trade Center Tribute Building, 20-acre wetland, rose garden, and sensory garden with fragrant, touchable flowers, and tinkling waterfalls intended for people with vision and hearing impairments. An authentic Chinese Scholars' Garden has reflecting ponds, waterfalls, pavilions, and a teahouse. The Carl Grillo Glass House keeps tropical, desert, and temperate plant environments, and the Connie Gretz Secret Garden is wonderfully child friendly in design, with a castle and moat and maze among the flowers. Buy tickets for the Chinese and Secret gardens at the garden's gift shop, on Cottage Row.

☺ The **Staten Island Children's Museum** (☎ 718/273–2060 ⊕ www. statenislandkids.org 🎫 $5 ⊙ During school year, Tues.–Fri. noon–5, weekends 10–5; in summer until 8 on Thurs.) has five galleries with hands-on exhibitions introducing such topics as nature's food chains, storytelling, and insects. Portia's Playhouse, an interactive children's theater, invites youngsters to step up to the stage and try on costumes. Ladder 11 is a thrill for firefighter fans.

To get here from the Staten Island Ferry terminal, take the S40 bus 2 mi to the Snug Harbor Road stop—a trip of about seven minutes. Signal the driver as soon as you glimpse the black iron fence along the edge of the property. You can also grab a car service at the ferry terminal (the ride should cost you about $5). ✉ *1000 Richmond Terr., between Snug Harbor Rd. and Tyson Ave., Livingston* ☎ *718/448–2500* ⊕ *www. snug-harbor.org* 🎫 *$3. Gardens and Galleries Tour $6. Cultural Center grounds free* ⊙ *Tues.–Sun. 10–5. Grounds dawn–dusk; tours Sat. noon–4, Sun. 11–3, meet opposite main hall gift shop.*

WHERE TO EAT **Adobe Blues** (✉ 63 Lafayette St., off Richmond Terr. ☎ 718/720–2583. $11–$19) is a bar and restaurant that serves up more than 160 beers, 40 types of tequila, and Southwestern fare.

Café Botanica (✉ Snug Harbor Cultural Center, Cottage Row ☎ 718/ 720–9737. $8–$9), next to the Staten Island Botanical Garden, serves breakfast and light lunch items daily; its hours are identical to the Chinese Garden nearby.

Queens, the Bronx & Staten Island At a Glance

SIGHTS
Edgar Allan Poe Cottage
Historic Richmondtown
Louis Armstrong House
Shea Stadium
Snug Harbor Cultural
  Center
Staten Island Ferry
USTA National Tennis
  Center
Yankee Stadium

MUSEUMS & GALLERIES
  (⇨ Ch. 14)
American Museum of the
  Moving Image
Eleanor Proske Visitors
  Center
Isamu Noguchi Garden
  Museum
Jacques Marchais Museum
  of Tibetan Art
John A. Noble Collection
New York Hall of Science
Newhouse Center for
  Contemporary Art

P.S.1 Contemporary Art
  Center
Queens Museum of Art
SculptureCenter
Staten Island Children's
  Museum

PARKS & GARDENS
The Bronx Zoo
New York Botanical Garden
Queens Botanical Gardens
Queens Zoo
Socrates Sculpture Park
Staten Island Botanical
  Gardens
Wave Hill

WHERE TO EAT
  (⇨ Ch. 18)

BUDGET DINING
Adobe Blues
Café Botanica
Café al Mercato
Delhi Palace
Jackson Diner
Karyatis

Parsonage
Press Café
Roberto's
Uncle George's Greek
  Tavern

MODERATE DINING
Dominick's

SHOPPING (⇨ Ch. 17)

CLOTHES
Sahil Sari Palace

FOOD
Borgatti's Ravioli & Egg
  Noodles
Calandra's Cheese
Egidio's Pastry Shop
Madonia Bros. Bakery
Patel Brothers
Randazzo's Seafood

GIFTS
Catholic Goods Center

MARKETS
Arthur Avenue Retail
  Market

Museums & Galleries

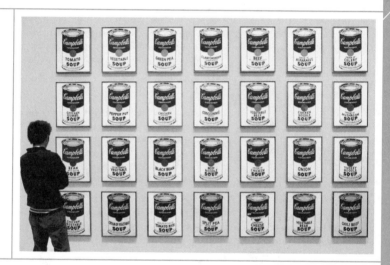

WORD OF MOUTH

"[The Museum of Modern Art] is definitely worth a revisit. The renovation/expansion is so vast, you'll feel like you're visiting a new facility." —HowardR

"The setting alone is superb, the indoor courtyard very quaint, and the [Frick] collection itself very impressive. This is a great way to see wonderful art in a setting that is much more intimate and unique than going through large, standard museums."

—lisa

MUSEUMS & GALLERIES PLANNER

Free Art

Art galleries, including the large numbers that are on the Upper East Side, are always free. Check *New York* magazine, or the *New York Times* Sunday "Arts" section to find out what's showing. Gallery openings often have free food and drink for attendees.

Save Money

Consider purchasing a City-Pass, a group of tickets to six top-notch attractions in New York, including the Guggenheim Museum, the American Museum of Natural History, the Museum of Modern Art, and the *Intrepid* Sea-Air-Space Museum. The $53 pass, which saves you half the cost of each individual ticket, is good for nine days from first use. It also allows you to beat long ticket lines at some attractions. You can buy a CityPass online or at any of the participants' ticket offices.

Beating Museum Burnout

- Don't try to cram several museums into a day. Instead, see one per day and plan something relaxing afterward to rest tired legs, like a long leisurely lunch.

- Hit major museums on weekdays, when crowds lessen.

- Come to terms with the fact that you can't see all of the Met—probably New York's number-one contributor to burnout—in one visit. MoMA and the Museum of Natural History are other museums that can easily overwhelm. The Whitney and the Guggenheim, on the other hand, are small enough that you can do a thorough tour without major burnout.

- Take a look at floor plans on museum Web sites to decide which collections you want to see before you go.

- Spend two to three hours, tops, at each museum.

- If you're with a group, consider splitting up so you can all see what you're most interested in, and plan a meet-up time.

- Break up art viewing with coffee and food breaks. Take advantage of museum cafés.

- If you're with an infant or young child, call to make sure that strollers aren't prohibited on the day you plan to visit, as they are at the Met on Sunday.

Late Hours

Almost all museums have extended hours on Friday nights. See individual listings for times.

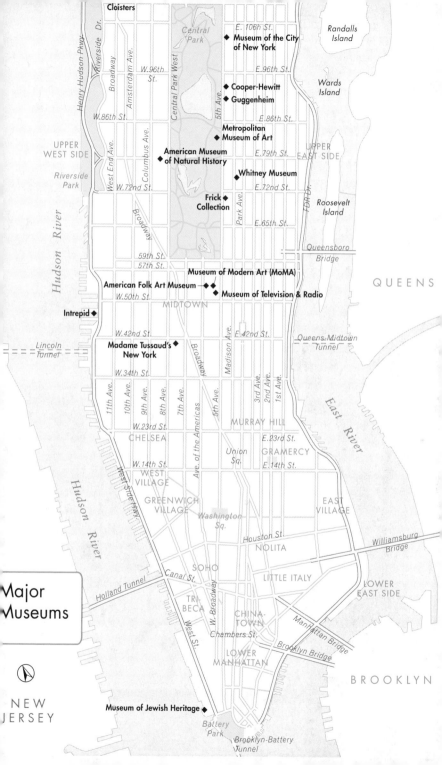

Cloisters

Central Park

E. 106h St.

◆ Museum of the City of New York

Randalls Island

E. 96th St.

Henry Hudson Pkwy.
Riverside Dr.
W. 96th St.
Broadway
Amsterdam Ave.
Central Park West

◆ Cooper-Hewitt
5th Ave.
◆ Guggenheim

Wards Island

W. 86th St.

E. 86th St.

Metropolitan
◆ Museum of Art

UPPER
WEST SIDE

UPPER
EAST SIDE

West End Ave.
Columbus Ave.

American Museum
◆ of Natural History

E. 79th St.

Riverside Park

Whitney Museum ◆

FDR Dr.

W. 72nd St.

E. 72nd St.

Roosevelt Island

Broadway

Frick ◆
Collection

Park Ave.

E. 65th St.

Hudson River

59th St.

Queensboro Bridge

57th St.

Museum of Modern Art (MoMA)

QUEENS

American Folk Art Museum ◆
◆ Museum of Television & Radio

W. 50th St.

MIDTOWN

Intrepid ◆

Lincoln Tunnel

W. 42nd St.

Madison Ave.

E. 42nd St.

Queens-Midtown Tunnel

Madame Tussaud's ◆
New York

W. 34th St.

Broadway

East River

11th Ave.
10th Ave.
9th Ave.
8th Ave.
7th Ave.
Ave. of the Americas
5th Ave.
Madison Ave.
3rd Ave.
2nd Ave.
1st Ave.

W. 23rd St.

MURRAY HILL

CHELSEA

E. 23rd St.

GRAMERCY

Union Sq.

W. 14th St.

E. 14th St.

WEST VILLAGE

GREENWICH VILLAGE

EAST VILLAGE

Washington Sq.

Houston St.

NOLITA

Williamsburg Bridge

West Side Hwy.

SOHO

LITTLE ITALY

LOWER EAST SIDE

Canal St.

Holland Tunnel

TRI-BECA

CHINA-TOWN

Manhattan Bridge

West St.
W. Broadway

Chambers St.

Brooklyn Bridge

LOWER MANHATTAN

Major
Museums

NEW
JERSEY

Museum of Jewish Heritage ◆

Battery Park

Brooklyn-Battery Tunnel

BROOKLYN

INSECTS AND MYRIAPODS   SEGMENTED

Theodore Roosevelt Memorial Hall

AMERICAN MUSEUM
OF NATURAL HISTORY

The largest natural history museum in the world is also one of the most impressive sights in New York. Four city blocks make up its 45 exhibition halls, which hold more than 32 million artifacts and wonders from the land, the sea, and outer space. With all those wonders, you won't be able to see everything on a single visit, but you can easily hit the highlights in half a day.

Before you begin, plan a route before setting out. Be sure to pick up a map when you pay your admission. The museum's four floors (and lower level) are maze-like.

To get the most from the museum's stunning riches, try to allow enough time to slow down and take advantage of the computer stations and the volunteer "Explainers," who are knowledgeable and able to point out their own favorite exhibits.

Getting into the museum can be time consuming. For the shortest lines, use the below-street-level entrance connected to the 81st Street subway station (look for the subway entrance to the left of the museum's steps). This entrance gives you quick access to bathrooms and the food court. The entrance on Central Park West, where the vast steps lead up into the impressive, barrel-ceilinged Theodore Roosevelt Rotunda, is the busiest entrance, and its 2nd-floor location also makes it the least confusing.

The Rose Center for Earth & Space, a must-visit, is attached to the museum. Enter from West 81st Street, where a path slopes down to the entrance, after which elevators and stairs descend to the ticket line on the lower level.

What to see? Check out the museum highlights on the following pages.

> ✉ Central Park W at W. 79th St., Upper West Side
>
> Ⓜ Subway: B, C to 81st St.
>
> ☎ 212/769-5200
>
> 🌐 www.amnh.org
>
> 💵 $14 suggested donation, includes admission to Rose Center for Earth and Space
>
> 🕐 Daily 10–5:45. Rose Center until 8:45 on Fri.

Spectrum of Life Wall

MUSEUM HIGHLIGHTS

Left, Tyrannosaurus rex
Above, Hadrosaurus

Dinosaurs and Mammals

An amazing assembly of dinosaur and mammal fossils covers the entire floor. The organization can be hard to grasp at first, so head to the **Wallace Orientation Center,** where a short film and touch screens explain how each of the Fossil Halls lead into each other. You'll want to spend at least an hour here—the highlights include a *T. rex*, an *Apatosaurus* (the current name for what used to be called a Brontosaurus), and the *Buettneria*, which resembles a modern-day crocodile.

The specimens are not in chronological order; they're put together based on their shared characteristics. Key branching-off points—a watertight egg, a grasping hand—are highlighted in the center of rooms and surrounded by related fossil groups. The large-print explanations here are some of the best and clearest in the museum.

Reptiles and Amphibians

Head for the Reptiles and Amphibians Hall to check out the Komodo dragon lizards and a 23-foot-long python skeleton. The weirdest display is the enlarged model of the Suriname toad *Pipa pipa*, whose young hatch from the female's back. The Primates hall carries brief but interesting comparisons between apes, monkeys, and humans. Also on the third floor is the upper gallery of the famed Akeley Hall of African Mammals.

SPECIAL SHOWS AND NEW EXHIBITS

Special exhibits, the IMAX theater, and the Space Show cost extra. The timed tickets you need to see special shows are sold only at the entrances, so be prepared to choose a time when you go in. Between October and May, you can walk through the warm, plant-filled Butterfly Conservatory, watching blue morphos, monarchs, and other butterflies flit and feed. Ten minutes is probably enough time to enjoy it.

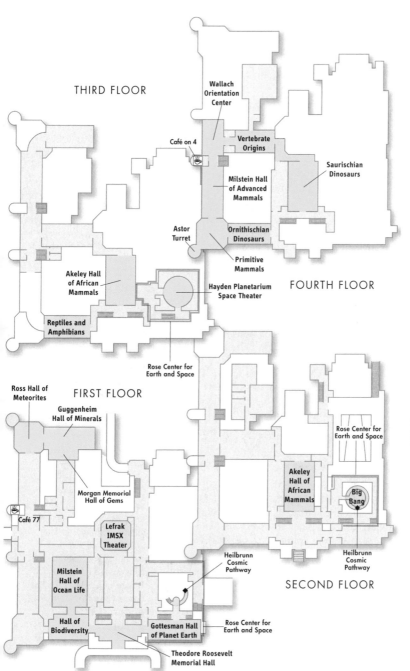

THIRD FLOOR

Wallach
Orientation
Center

Café on 4

Vertebrate
Origins

Saurischian
Dinosaurs

Milstein Hall
of Advanced
Mammals

Astor
Turret

Ornithischian
Dinosaurs

Primitive
Mammals

FOURTH FLOOR

Akeley Hall
of African
Mammals

Hayden Planetarium
Space Theater

Reptiles and
Amphibians

Rose Center for
Earth and Space

Ross Hall of
Meteorites

FIRST FLOOR

Guggenheim
Hall of Minerals

Rose Center for
Earth and Space

Morgan Memorial
Hall of Gems

Akeley
Hall of
African
Mammals

Big
Bang

Café 77

Lefrak
IMSX
Theater

Milstein
Hall of
Ocean Life

Heilbrunn
Cosmic
Pathway

Heilbrunn
Cosmic
Pathway

SECOND FLOOR

Hall of
Biodiversity

Gottesman Hall
of Planet Earth

Rose Center for
Earth and Space

Theodore Roosevelt
Memorial Hall

14

AMERICAN MUSEUM OF NATURAL HISTORY

Akeley Hall of African Mammals

Opened in 1936, this hall is one of the most beloved parts of the museum. Its 28 dramatically lighted dioramas may seem merely kitschy at first glance, but take a little time to let their beauty and technical brilliance shine through.

The hall was the life's work of the explorer Carl Akeley, who came up with the idea for the hall, raised the funds for the expeditions, gathered specimens, and sketched landscape studies for what would become the stunning backgrounds. (The backgrounds themselves were painted by James Perry Wilson, whose works can be found throughout the museum.)

Akeley died a decade before the hall opened on an expedition in what's now Rwanda. His grave site is near the landscape portrayed in the gorilla diorama, completed after his death as a memorial to him and his work. The dioramas make irresistible photo ops. If you want to snap one yourself, it's best to turn off your flash to prevent reflections off the glass.

Rocks and Minerals

Moon rocks introduce the Hall of Meteorites, but the big cheese here is the 34,000-ton Ahnighito meteorite, found in Greenland in 1895. The hall adjoins the **Halls of Minerals and Gems,** which look like a supervillain's lair from a '70s James Bond movie. The specimens' jagged edges and vivid colors are fun to look at, but the captions can be hard to get through. Most people head straight for the small gems room to search for the pale and luminous **Star of India,** the largest sapphire in the world. Many of the gems and stones here are in jewelry settings crafted by Tiffany, Cartier, and other designers.

Hall of Biodiversity

The small **Hall of Biodiversity** includes a shady replica of a Central African Republic rain forest. Within a few yards are 160 species of flora and fauna—and also evidence of the forest's destruction. Nearby, the **Spectrum of Life Wall** showcases 1,500 specimens and models, helping show just how weird life can get. The wall opens into the gaping Milstein Hall of Ocean Life, lighted in such a way to give it an underwater glow and to show off the 94-foot model of a **blue whale** that's suspended from the ceiling.

Blue Whale

ROSE CENTER FOR EARTH & SPACE

The vast expanses of space and time involved in the creation of the universe can be hard to grasp even with the guiding hand of a museum, so visit the center when you're at your sharpest. The stunning glass building's centerpiece is the aluminum-clad Hayden Sphere, 87 feet in diameter. Enclosed within are the planetarium, called the Space Theater, and an audiovisual Big Bang presentation consisting of four minutes of narration by Maya Angelou, indistinct washes of color, and frightening bursts of sound. The rock-filled **Hall of Planet Earth** is particularly timely given the earthquakes and other natural disasters of recent years: one section uses a working earthquake monitor to help explain just what causes such seismic violence.

The Space Theater

At the Space Theater, the stage is the dome above you and the actors, heavenly projections. One of the world's largest virtual reality simulators, the theater uses surround sound and slight vibrations in the seats, to immerse you in scenes of planets, star clusters, and galaxies. The music of U2, Audioslave, and David Byrne among others inspire Sonic Vision, a digitally animated performance given every Friday and Saturday night.

TIME TO EAT?

Inside the Museum: The **main food court** on the lower level serves sandwiches with more than just American cheese for about $7.25; burgers cost about $5.50, and an antipasto and salad bar costs 57 cents an ounce. A real treat are the glazed cookies in the shapes of planets or a whale.

The small **Café on 4,** in a turret next to the fossil halls, sells premade sandwiches and salads, and yogurt and desserts, but nothing warm.

Café 77, on the first floor, is out of the way now, but it will be handier once the human biology and evolution hall reopens next door in the fall of 2006.

Outside the Museum: The nearest restaurants are expensive; to keep to a budget, head to a popular chain: **Pizzeria Uno** (⊠ Columbus Ave. and W. 81st St. ☎ 212/472–5656), where lunch specials run until 3 PM and kids' meals are under $4. The Cajun-Creole **Jacques-Imo's NYC** (⊠ 366 Columbus Ave., at W. 77th St. ☎ 212/799–0150) serves a free meal to kids under 8 for each adult entrée bought. Lunch is served noon–3, Wednesday–Friday only, and on weekends there's brunch. Kids meals cost under $4 and lunch entrees run $8.50–$15.50.

THE METROPOLITAN MUSEUM OF ART

Carvings of ball players adorn the walls of the juego de pelota.

14

THE METROPOLITAN MUSEUM OF ART

If the city held no other museum than the colossal Metropolitan Museum of Art, you could still occupy yourself for days roaming its labyrinthine corridors. Because the Metropolitan Museum has something approaching 3 million works on display over its more than 7 square miles, you're going to have to make choices. Looking at everything here could take a week.

Before you begin exploring the museum, check the museum's floor plan, available at all entrances, for location of the major wings and collections. Ask for a supplemental (and underpublicized) map of the many small galleries in the European painting and sculpture sections at the Great Hall's information desk, where you can also get information on the day's highlights and theme tours and gallery closings.

The posted adult admission, though only a suggestion, is one that's strongly encouraged. Whatever you choose to pay, admission includes all special exhibits and same-day entrance to the Cloisters (see page 231). The Met's audio guide costs an additional $6, and if you intend to stay more than an hour or so, it's worth it. The generally perceptive commentary covers museum highlights and directors' picks, with separate commentary tracks directed at kids.

If you want to avoid the crowds, visit weekday mornings. Also good are Friday and Saturday evenings, when live jazz or classical music plays from the Great Hall balcony. If the Great Hall (the main entrance) is mobbed, avoid the chaos by heading to the street-level entrance to the left of the main stairs, near 81st Street. Ticket lines and coat checks are much less ferocious here.

What to see? Check out the museum highlights on the following pages.

✉ 5th Ave. at 82nd St., Upper East Side

Ⓜ Subway: 4, 5, 6 to 86th St.

☎ 212/535-7710

⊕ www.metmuseum.org

💳 $15 suggested donation

🕙 Tues.-Thurs. and Sun. 9:30-5:30, Fri. and Sat. 9:30-9

Great Hall

MUSEUM HIGHLIGHTS

Egyptian Art

A major star is the **Temple of Dendur** (circa 15 BC), in a huge atrium to itself and with a moatlike pool of water to represent its original location near the Nile. The temple was commissioned by the Roman emperor Augustus to honor the goddess Isis and the sons of a Nubian chieftain. Look for the scratched-in graffiti from 19th-century Western explorers on the inside. Egypt gave the temple as a gift to the U.S. in 1964; it would have been submerged after the construction of the Aswan High Dam.

Temple of Dendur

The Egyptian collections as a whole cover 4,000 years of history, with papyrus pages from the Egyptian Book of the Dead, stone coffins engraved with hieroglyphics, and tombs. The galleries are divided into two routes: the right-hand corridor traces the Ancient Kingdom (2650–2150 BC), and the left covers the period under Roman rule (30 BC–400 AD). In the latter, keep an eye out for the enormous, bulbous **Sarcophagus of Horkhebit**, hand-carved from basalt.

ART TO TAKE HOME

You don't have to pay admission to get to the mammoth gift shop on the first floor. One of the better souvenirs here is also one of the more reasonable: the Met's own **illustrated guide** to 900 of the best items in its collection ($19.95).

American Wing

Charles Engelhard Court contains some of the most beautiful sculptures and architectural decoration in the whole museum—be sure to check out the facade from a former Wall Street bank building that's on display here. Especially outstanding are an enormous **mantelpiece** held up by the figures Amor (love) and Pax (peace). The work was designed by Augustus Saint-Gaudens for Cornelius Vanderbilt II's town house.

The court's northwest corner leads to the glassware of the **Louis Comfort Tiffany Gallery** and the **Frank Lloyd Wright Room,** an Asian-influenced living room from a Minnesota house Wright built and designed in 1914. The room, furnished primarily with original pieces, has been installed so that its windows look out on Central Park.

Englehard Court

John Vanderlyn's *Panoramic View of the Palace and Gardens of Versailles* (1818–19) has a whole gallery to itself. In this rare survivor of this public art form, two long, curved canvases face each other to put you in the center of Versailles. It's like an early example of IMAX.

Tiffany

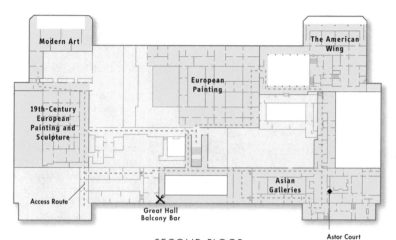

Modern Art

The American Wing

European Painting

19th-Century European Painting and Sculpture

Asian Galleries

Access Route

Great Hall Balcony Bar

Astor Court

SECOND FLOOR

14

THE METROPOLITAN MUSEUM OF ART

MEZZANINES

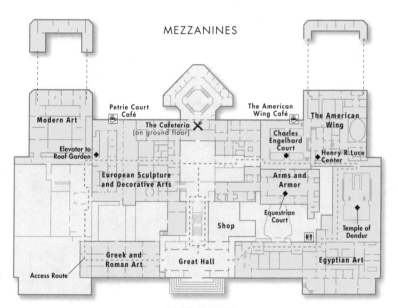

Petrie Court Café

The American Wing Café

Modern Art

The Cafeteria (on ground floor)

The American Wing

Charles Engelhard Court

Elevator to Roof Garden

Henry R. Luce Center

European Sculpture and Decorative Arts

Arms and Armor

Equestrian Court

Shop

Temple of Dendur

Greek and Roman Art

Great Hall

Egyptian Art

Access Route

FIRST FLOOR

5th Avenue

Visitors ponder European paintings on the 2nd floor.

The **Henry R. Luce Center for the Study of American Art**, on a mezzanine between the first and second floors, looks like a storage room, and to some degree it is. Row after row of multilevel glass enclosures hold furniture, decorative objects, and paintings that couldn't otherwise be on display due to space constraints. There are enough works here to make up a small museum of their own—the **Pennsylvania Dutch chests** in row 25 are especially cool.

Also on the mezzanine, near the stairs, is a group of five larger-than-life portraits by **John Singer Sargent.** One of them, *Madame X,* caused a scandal when it was first exhibited in Paris. The woman's pose, with one strap of her gown falling off her shoulder, seemed very suggestive to the onlookers of the time. Sargent later repainted the strap back up in its current, more proper position.

When you see it in person, Emanuel Leutze's *Washington Crossing the Delaware* (1851) is as powerful as it is familiar. For one thing, it's enormous—more than 12 by 21 feet. In the same room, on the opposite wall, is *The Last Moments of John Brown* (1882–84). With more than a little artistic license, the painting depicts the violent abolitionist kissing a black baby on the way to the gallows with a noose around his neck.

TIME TO EAT?
INSIDE THE MUSEUM

The museum's restaurants are almost always full, and going to lunch at 2 PM doesn't mean there won't be a line. The **Petrie Café**, at the back of the 1st-floor European Sculpture Court, has waiter service, but aside from its wall of windows looking onto Central Park, it's very plain. Prices range from $11 for a sandwich to $17 for grilled salmon. Tea, sweets, and savories are served from 2:30 PM to 4:30 PM during the week, until 5 PM on weekends.

The **American Wing Café**, next to the beautiful Charles Engelhard Court, also has good views of the park. Heavier with dessert options, the self-serve restaurant also offers a soup, a few sandwiches ($7.50), and salads ($8), too.

The basement **cafeteria**, which has white tiles and a vaulted ceiling, has stations for pasta, main courses, antipasti, and sandwiches.

Equestrian Court (1930)

Arms and Armor

The **Equestrian Court,** where the knights are mounted on armored models of horses, is one of the most dramatic rooms in the museum. For a bird's-eye view, check it out again from the balconies in the Musical Instruments collection on the second floor.

European Sculpture and Decorative Arts

Among the many sculptures in the sun-filled Petrie Court, **Ugolino and His Sons** still stands out for the despairing poses of its subjects. Ugolino, a nobleman whose family's tragic story is told in Dante's *Inferno,* was punished for treason by being left to starve to death with his grandsons and sons in a locked tower. (It's not clear if putting such a sculpture so near the Petrie Court's café is some curator's idea of a joke or not.) By the way, the redbrick and granite wall on the court's north side is the museum's original entrance.

Modern Art

The museum's most famous Picasso is probably his 1906 portrait **Gertrude Stein** in which the writer's face is stern and masklike. The portrait was bequeathed to the museum by Stein herself.

Of the Georgia O'Keeffes on view, 1931's **Red, White, and Blue** painting of a cow skull is a standout. The color, composition, and natural motif work together to create a work with religious as well as nationalist overtones.

Greek and Roman Art

The urnlike ceramic **kraters** were used by the Greeks for mixing wine and water at parties and other events. Given such a use, it's not surprising that most have scenes that are at least a little racy. Some of the most impressive can be found in the gallery covering 5th and early 4th century BC.

European Paintings

On the second floor, the 13th- to 18th-century paintings are in one block, at the top of the Great Hall's stairs. To get to the 19th-century paintings and sculptures, walk through the the narrow corridor of Drawings, Prints, and Photographs. Both sections can be hard to navigate quickly, so come armed with the supplemental plan available from the Great Hall's information desk.

In 2004, the Met spent about $45 million to buy Duccio di Buoninsegna's **Madonna and Child,** painted circa 1300. The last remaining Duccio in private

14

THE METROPOLITAN MUSEUM OF ART

hands, this painting, the size of a piece of typewriter paper, is unimpressive at first glance. Be sure to get in close to see the detail around the Madonna's halo, as well as the delicate shading in salmon and blue.

The Triumph of Fame, a round, double-sided "commemorative birth tray" by Scheggia, shows a crowd of mounted knights saluting winged Fame, who holds both a cupid and a sword (they symbolize two timeless ways to get famous). The tray heralds the arrival of Lorenzo de' Medici (1449–92), who did indeed become a famed figure of the Italian Renaissance.

Rembrandt's masterful **Aristotle with a Bust of Homer** (1653) emphasizes the philosopher's preference for knowledge over material wealth through its play of light and use of symbols. Around Aristotle is a gold medal of Alexander the Great, one of the philosopher's students.

In the room dedicated to **Monet** you can get to all his greatest hits—poplar trees, haystacks, water lilies, and the Rouen Cathedral. The muted tones of Pissaro follow, and in the next room are the bright and garish colors announcing works by Gauguin, Matisse, and Van Gogh.

Vincent van Gogh, *Wheatfield with Cypresses*

GREAT VIEWS

Looking for one of the best views in town? The Roof Garden (open May–October) exhibits contemporary sculptures, but most people take the elevator here to have a drink or snack while checking out Central Park and the skyline.

Asian Galleries

The peaceful, surreal **Astor Court,** which has its own skylight and pond of real-life koi (goldfish), is a model of a scholar's court garden in Soochow, China.

The Han dynasty (206 BC–220 AD) introduced the practice of sending the dead on to the afterlife with small objects to help them there. Keep an eye out for these **small clay figures,** which include farm animals (enclosed in barnyards) and dancing entertainers.

On display in a glass case in the center of an early-Chinese gallery is a complete set of 14 **bronze altar vessels.** Dating 1100 BC—200 AD, these green and slightly crusty pieces were used for worshipping ancestors. The Met displays some of its finest **Asian stoneware and porcelain** along the balcony overlooking the Great Hall.

The teak dome and balconies from a **Jain meeting hall** in western India were carved in western India around 1600. Just about the entire surface is covered with musicians, animals, gods, and servants.

MUSEUM OF MODERN ART (MOMA)

⊠ 11 W. 53rd St., between 5th and 6th Aves., Midtown East

☎ 212/708-9400

⊕ www.moma.org

🎟 $20

⊗ Sat.-Mon. and Wed.-Thurs. 10:30-5:30, Fri. 10:30-8

Ⓜ Subway: E, V to 5th Ave./53rd St.; B, D, E to 7th Ave.; B, D, F, V to 47th-50th Sts./Rockefeller Center

TIPS:

■ The revitalized museum remains a blockbuster, which means lines are sometimes down the block. If you can manage to come here without bags or backpack, you'll avoid another wait for the checkroom.

■ Consider lining up for the free audio guide, especially if the scribbled and monotone canvases of some modern art confound you.

■ Entrance for children under 16 is free.

★ **Fodors Choice** MoMA is where to come for the masterpieces that even art novices will recognize—Monet's *Water Lilies*, Picasso's *Les Demoiselles d'Avignon*, and Van Gogh's *Starry Night*. The museum's acclaimed $425 million face-lift in 2004 by Yoshio Taniguchi increased exhibition space by nearly 50%, accommodating for the first time large-scale contemporary installations. The museum continues to collect: in 2005 it obtained key works by Henri Matisse, David Hockney, and Alberto Giacometti, as well as numerous contemporary works.

HIGHLIGHTS:

In addition to the impressive collection of artwork, one of the main draws of the museum is the building itself. A maze of glass walkways allows visitors to admire works from surprising new angles.

The 150-foot atrium entrance (accessed from either 53rd or 54th street) features Bronx-born Barnett Newman's *Broken Obelisk* (1962-69) and leads to the movie theater, cafés, and restaurant, The Modern.

Art-lovers have been known to work up an appetite, so with the design came new menus. Both the cafés and The Modern offer excellent food that far exceeds normal museum fare. The Modern offers sections for those with and without reservations to this sophisticated Danny Meyer dining experience.

A favorite area in which to take a break remains the Abby Aldrich Rockefeller Sculpture Garden, designed by Philip Johnson in 1953. A new glass wall lets visitors look directly into the surrounding galleries.

Contemporary art (1970 to the present) from the museum's six curatorial departments share the second floor of a new six-story building, and the skylighted top floor showcases an impressive lineup of changing exhibits.

14

SOLOMON R. GUGGENHEIM MUSEUM

✉ 1071 5th Ave., between
E. 88th and E. 89th Sts.,
Upper East Side

☎ 212/423-3500

🌐 www.guggenheim.org

💲 $18

🕐 Sat.–Wed. 10–5:45, Fri.
10–8

Ⓜ Subway: 4, 5, 6 to 86th
St.

TIPS:

■ Not all of the museum's
works are displayed at one
time, so each trip may provide a pleasing new surprise.

■ The interior nautilus design allows works to be
viewed from several different
angles. Be sure to notice not
only what's in front of you
but also what's across the
spiral from you.

■ Check listings or online
for the latest exhibits. The
museum's director, Thom
Krens, has been known for
his interesting exhibit
choices, including motorcy-
cles and Russia.

★ Fodor's Choice Frank Lloyd Wright's landmark museum building is visited as much for its famous architecture as it is for its superlative art. Opened in 1959, shortly
after Wright died, the Guggenheim is an icon of modernist
architecture. Inside, under a 92-foot-high glass dome, a
¼-mi-long ramp spirals down past changing exhibitions.
The museum has strong holdings in Vasily Kandinsky, Paul
Klee, Marc Chagall, Pablo Picasso, and Robert Mapplethorpe.

HIGHLIGHTS:

The outside of the building is as striking as the inside.
There, Wright's attention to detail is strikingly evident—
in the porthole-like windows on its south side, the circular pattern of the sidewalk, and the hand-plastered concrete.

On permanent display, the museum's Thannhauser Collection is made up primarily of works by French impressionists and neo-impressionists Matisse, Van Gogh,
Toulouse-Lautrec, and Cézanne.

Perhaps more than any other 20th-century painter, Vasily
Kandinsky has been closely linked to the museum's history. Beginning with the acquisition of his masterpiece
Composition 8 (1923) in 1930, the collection has grown
to encompass more than 150 works.

In its Tower galleries, double-high ceilings accommodate
extra-large art pieces, and the Tower's fifth-floor sculpture terrace has a view overlooking Central Park.

WHITNEY MUSEUM OF AMERICAN ART

✉ 945 Madison Ave., at E.
75th St., Upper East Side

☎ 212/570-3676

🌐 www.whitney.org

💲 $12; Fri. 6-9 pay what
you wish

🕒 Sat.-Thurs. 11-6, Fri. 1-9

Ⓜ Subway: 6 to 77th St.

TIPS:

■ After 6 PM on Fridays,
price of admission is pay-
what-you-wish. On some of
those nights, The Sound-
Check series presents up-
and-coming downtown
musicians as well. Be forewarned that this combination
may result in a line wrapped
around the corner.

■ The Whitney also has a
branch across from Grand
Central Terminal in Midtown.

■ Sarabeth's at the Whit-
ney serves a selection of
sandwiches, pastries, and
soups. A popular city restaurant chain famed for its
brunch, Sarabeth's is much
cozier and more interesting
than your standard cafeteria.

14

★ With its bold collection of contemporary art, this museum presents an eclectic mix of over 14,000 works in its
permanent collection. The museum was originally a gallery
in the studio of sculptor and collector Gertrude Vanderbilt Whitney, whose talent and taste were accompanied
by the money of two wealthy families. In 1930 when the
Met turned down an offer to donate her collection of 20th-
century American art, she established an independent
museum. The current minimalist gray-granite building
opened in 1966 and was designed by Marcel Breuer.

HIGHLIGHTS:

Postwar and contemporary attractions from the permanent collection include paintings and sculpture by such
artists as Jackson Pollack, Jim Dine, Jasper Johns, Mark
Rothko, Frank Stella, Chuck Close, Cindy Sherman, and
Roy Lichtenstein.

The fifth floor's eight sleek galleries house "Hopper to
Mid-Century," with works by Reginald Marsh, George
Bellows, Robert Henri, and Marsden Hartley.

Notable pieces include Hopper's *Early Sunday Morning*
(1930), Bellows's *Dempsey and Firpo* (1924), and several
of Georgia O'Keeffe's dazzling flower paintings.

The museum lobby is home to Alexander Calder's beloved
sculpture *Circus* (1926–31) with tiny wire performers
swinging from trapezes and walking on tightropes.

The Whitney Biennial, which showcases the most important developments in American art over the previous two
years, takes place in the spring of even-numbered years.

Updated by
Christina
Knight

The settings of New York's museums are often as impressive as their collections—from the *Intrepid* Sea-Air-Space Museum aboard an aircraft carrier on the Hudson River to the chunks of European monasteries that make up the Cloisters. You can squeeze through the narrow rooms of the Lower East Side Tenement Museum or explore the rich collections of industrial barons and financiers such as J. P. Morgan. For art-lovers of every taste, there's so much to choose from, whether you favor the old masters, abstract expressionism, or quirky conceptual installations.

MAJOR MUSEUMS

American Folk Art Museum. This museum is a work of art itself: an eight-story building designed in 2001 by husband-and-wife team Tod Williams and Billie Tsein. The facade, consisting of 63 hand-cast panels of alloyed bronze, reveals individual textures, sizes, and plays of light. Inside, four gallery floors—dedicated to exhibitions and the collection of arts and decorative objects from the 18th century to the present day—are illuminated by a central skylight. Works include paintings, weather vanes, quilts, pottery, scrimshaw, and folk sculpture. ⊠ *45 W. 53rd St., between 5th and 6th Aves., Midtown West* ☏ *212/265–1040* ⊕ *www. folkartmuseum.org* ☑ *$9; free Fri. 5:30 PM–7:30 PM* ☉ *Tues.–Thurs. and weekends 10:30–5:30, Fri. 10:30–7:30* Ⓜ *Subway: E, V to 5th Ave./53rd St.; B, D, E to 7th Ave.; B, D, F, V to 47th–50th Sts./Rockefeller Center.*

American Museum of Natural History See Page 214

The Cloisters. Atop a wooded hill in Fort Tryon Park, near Manhattan's northernmost tip, the Cloisters houses the medieval collection of the Metropolitan Museum of Art in a monasterylike setting. Colonnaded walks connect authentic French and Spanish monastic cloisters, a French Romanesque chapel, a 12th-century chapter house, and a Romanesque apse. One entire room is devoted to the extraordinarily detailed 15th- and 16th-century Unicorn Tapestries—a must-see. The tomb effigies are another highlight. Three gardens shelter more than 250 species of plants similar to those grown during the Middle Ages, including herbs and medicinals; the Unicorn Garden blooms with flowers and plants depicted in the tapestries. Concerts of medieval music are held here regularly, and an outdoor café decorated with 15th-century carvings serves biscotti and espresso from May through October. ⊠ *Fort Tryon Park, Inwood* ☎ *212/923–3700* ☏ *$15 suggested donation* ⊙ *Mar.–Oct., Tues.–Sun. 9:30–5:15; Nov.–Feb., Tues.–Sun. 9:30–4:45* Ⓜ *Subway: A to 190th St.*

Cooper-Hewitt National Design Museum. More than 2,000 years of international design is on display inside the former 64-room mansion of industrialist Andrew Carnegie. The museum's 250,000 objects include examples of drawings, textiles, furniture, metalwork, ceramics, glass, and woodwork. Changing exhibitions are drawn from the permanent collection, covering everything from cutlery to architecture to animation. The shows are invariably enlightening and often amusing. Between early December 2006 and late July 2007, the National Design Triennial presents the best design projects of the past three years. In summer, some exhibits are displayed in the museum's comfortable garden. A new ground-floor gallery was added in 2005. ⊠ *2 E. 91st St., at 5th Ave., Upper East Side* ☎ *212/849–8400* ⊕ *www.cooperhewitt.org* ☏ *$10* ⊙ *Tues.–Thurs. 10–5, Fri. 10–9, Sat. 10–6, Sun. noon–6* Ⓜ *Subway: 4, 5, 6 to 86th St.*

★ **Frick Collection.** Coke-and-steel baron Henry Clay Frick (1849–1919) amassed this superb art collection far from the soot and smoke of Pittsburgh, where he made his fortune. Édouard Manet's *The Bullfight* (1864) hangs in the East Gallery, which also exhibits the *Chinard* bust (1809; bought in 2004 and the first museum purchase in eight years). Two of the Frick's three Vermeers—*Officer and Laughing Girl* (circa 1658) and *Girl Interrupted at Her Music* (1660–61)—hang by the front staircase. Nearly 50 additional paintings, as well as much sculpture, decorative arts, and furniture, are in the West and East galleries. Three Rembrandts, including *The Polish Rider* (circa 1655) and *Self-Portrait* (1658), as well as a third Vermeer, *Mistress and Maid* (circa 1665–70), hang in the former; paintings by Whistler, Goya, Van Dyck, Lorrain, and David in the latter. An audio guide, available in several languages, is included with admission, as are the year-round temporary exhibits. When you're through, the tranquil indoor garden court with a fountain is a great spot for a rest. ⊠ *1 E. 70th St., at 5th Ave., Upper East Side* ☎ *212/288–0700* ⊕ *www.frick.org* ☏ *$15* ⊙ *Tues.–Sat. 10–6, Sun. 11–5* Ⓜ *Subway: 6 to 68th St./Hunter College.*

☾ **Intrepid Sea-Air-Space Museum.** Formerly the USS *Intrepid*, this 900-foot aircraft carrier is serving out its retirement as the centerpiece of

Manhattan's only floating museum. The carrier's most trying moment of service, the day it was attacked in World War II by kamikaze pilots, is recounted in a multimedia presentation. Aircraft on deck include an A-12 Blackbird spy plane, a Concorde, helicopters, and two dozen other aircraft. Docked alongside, and also part of the museum, is the *Growler*, a strategic-missile submarine. Children can explore the ships' skinny hallways and winding staircases, as well as manipulate countless knobs, buttons, and wheels. For an extra thrill (and an extra $8), they can try the Navy flight simulator and "land" an aircraft on board. The original Iwo Jima sculpture upon which the memorial in Washington, D.C., is based. is one of the museum's most photographed objects. ⊠ *Hudson River, Pier 86, 12th Ave. and W. 46th St., Midtown West* ☎ *212/245-0072 or 877/957-7447* ⊕ *www. intrepidmuseum.org* ✉ *$16.50; free to active and retired U.S. military personnel* ⊗ *Apr.–Sept., weekdays 10–5, weekends 10–6; Oct.–Mar., Tues.–Sun. 10–5; last admission 1 hr before closing* Ⓜ *Subway: A, C, E to 42nd St.; M42 bus to pier.*

Madame Tussaud's New York. Go ahead, whisper in Jennifer Lopez's ear, air-kiss Bette Midler, and stare down Morgan Freeman in the palazzo courtyard–like setting of the "Opening Night Party," complete with party music and the murmur of conversation. The realism of some of these wax figures may creep you out: if a room gets crowded, sometimes you can't tell who's fake anymore. Along with the addition of new figures each year, check out such interactive options as a haunted house based on a horror flick, an *American Idol* karaoke stage in the café, and a photo op where you can transform yourself into a celebrity. Packs of friends and hams will get the most fun out of the place. You're encouraged to pose with the nearly 200 historical, cultural, and popular characters (disposable cameras are on sale), and yes, you can even touch them. ⊠ *234 W. 42nd St., between 7th and 8th Aves., Midtown West* ☎ *212/512–9600* ⊕ *www.madame-tussauds.com* ✉ *$29* ⊗ *Weekdays 10–9, weekends 10 AM–11 PM* Ⓜ *Subway: A, C, E to 42nd St.*

Metropolitan Museum of Art See Page 220

★ ☺ **Museum of the City of New York.** Within a Colonial Revival building designed for the museum in the 1930s, the city's history and quirks are revealed through exhibits that cover anything from political figures to photography. With artifacts and models, permanent exhibits detail firefighting, theater, and New York's role as a port. Period rooms include several that John D. Rockefeller Sr. acquired when he bought a fully furnished New York mansion in the 1880s. The historic toys on view include the beloved Stettheimer Dollhouse, a mansion outfitted down to miniature artworks imitating 20th-century masters. Don't miss

Timescapes, a 22-minute media projection that innovatively illustrates New York's physical expansion and population changes. The museum hosts New York–centric lectures, films, and walking tours. Weekend programs are especially for kids. ⊠ *1220 5th Ave., at E. 103rd St., Upper East Side* ☎ *212/534–1672* ⊕ *www.mcny.org* ✉ *$7 suggested donation* ☉ *Tues.–Sun. 10–5* Ⓜ *Subway: 6 to 103rd St.*

Museum of Jewish Heritage—A Living Memorial to the Holocaust. In a granite 85-foot hexagon at the southern end of Battery Park City, this museum pays tribute to the 6 million Jews who perished in the Holocaust. Kevin Roche and John Dinkeloo, architects, built the museum in the shape of a Star of David, with three floors of exhibits demonstrating the dynamism of 20th-century Jewish culture. You enter through a multiscreen vestibule, perhaps best described as a storytelling gallery, that provides a context for the early-20th-century artifacts on the first floor: an elaborate screen hand-painted for the fall harvest festival of Sukkoth, wedding invitations, and tools used by Jewish tradesmen. Also intriguing is the use of original documentary film footage throughout the museum. The second floor details the rise of Nazism and anti-Semitism, and the ravages of the Holocaust. A gallery covers the doomed voyage of the SS *St. Louis,* a ship of German Jewish refugees that crossed the Atlantic twice in 1939 in search of a safe haven. Signs of hope are on display, as well, including a trumpet that Louis Bannet (the "Dutch Louis Armstrong") played for three years in the Auschwitz-Birkenau inmate orchestra. The third floor covers postwar Jewish life. The east wing contains a theater, memorial garden by artist Andy Goldsworthy, resource center, library, more galleries, classrooms, and a café. ⊠ *36 Battery Pl., Battery Park City, Lower Manhattan* ☎ *646/437–4200* ⊕ *www.mjhnyc.org* ✉ *$10* ☉ *Thurs., Sun.–Tues. 10–5:45, Wed. 10–8, Fri. and eve of Jewish holidays 10–3* Ⓜ *Subway: 4, 5 to Bowling Green.*

Museum of Television & Radio. Three galleries of photographs and artifacts document the history of broadcasting in this 1989 limestone building by Philip Johnson and John Burgee. But the main draw here is the computerized catalog of more than 100,000 television and radio programs. If you want to see a performance of "Turkey Lurkey Time" from the 1969 Tony Awards, for example, type in the name of the song, show, or performer into a computer terminal. You can then proceed to a private screening area to watch your selection. People nearby might be watching classic comedies from the '50s, miniseries from the '70s, or news broadcasts from the '90s. ⊠ *25 W. 52nd St., between 5th and 6th Aves., Midtown West* ☎ *212/621–6800* ⊕ *www.mtr.org* ✉ *$10* ☉ *Tues., Wed., and Fri.–Sun. noon–6, Thurs. noon–8* Ⓜ *Subway: E, V to 5th Ave./53rd St.; B, D, F, V to 47th–50th Sts./Rockefeller Center.*

FodorśChoice ★

NICHE MUSEUMS

🜚 **Alexander Hamilton U.S. Custom House/National Museum of the American Indian.** The Beaux-Arts Alexander Hamilton U.S. Custom House (1907) is one of Lower Manhattan's finest buildings. Massive granite columns rise to a pediment topped by a double row of statues. Daniel Chester French, sculptor of Lincoln in the Lincoln Memorial in Washington, D.C., carved the lower statues, which symbolize continents (left to right: Asia, the Americas, Europe, Africa). The upper row represents the major trading cities of the world. Inside, the side egg-shaped stairwell and rotunda embellished with shipping theme murals (completed in the 1930s) are incredibly impressive. Changing presentations drawn from the National Museum of the American Indian, a branch of the Smithsonian, are exhibited with modern stylishness. You can see everything without being overwhelmed. On view through May 2007 are ceramics from the Americas, both ancient and contemporary. The Diker Pavilion, opening on the ground floor in fall 2006, will provide more exhibit space and a venue for dance, music, and storytelling programs. Videos and films made by indigenous peoples from around the world are shown regularly. ⊠ *1 Bowling Green, between State and Whitehall Sts., Lower Manhattan* ☎ *212/514–3700* ⊕ *www.americanindian.si.edu* 🎫 *Free* ☉ *Mon.–Wed. and Fri.–Sun. 10–5, Thurs. 10–8* Ⓜ *Subway: 4, 5 to Bowling Green.*

American Folk Art Museum: Eva and Morris Feld Gallery. Across from Lincoln Center, this gallery extension of the American Folk Art Museum on West 53rd Street has a small selection of art and decorative objects culled from all over the Americas. You might see painted store signs, outsider art, weather vanes, or carousel mounts. On permanent display is *The National Tribute Quilt,* made up of 3,466 blocks for each person who died on 9/11. The gift shop is worth a browse. ⊠ *2 Lincoln Sq., Columbus Ave. between W. 65th and W. 66th Sts., Upper West Side* ☎ *212/595–9533* 🎫 *$3 suggested admission* ☉ *Tues.–Sat. noon–7:30, Sun. noon–5* Ⓜ *Subway: 1 to 66th St./Lincoln Center.*

Asia Society and Museum. The Asian art collection of Mr. and Mrs. John D. Rockefeller III forms the museum's major holdings, which include South Asian stone and bronze sculptures; art from India, Nepal, Pakistan, and Afghanistan; bronze vessels, ceramics, sculpture, and paintings from China; Korean ceramics; and paintings, wooden sculptures, and ceramics from Japan. Founded in 1956, the society has a regular program of lectures, films, and performances, in addition to changing exhibitions. Trees grow in the glassed-in café, which serves an eclectically Asian menu for lunch and dinner. ⊠ *725 Park Ave., at 70th St., Upper East Side* ☎ *212/288–6400* ⊕ *www.asiasociety.org* 🎫 *$10; free Fri. 6–9* ☉ *July 4–Labor Day, Tues.–Sun. 11–6; Labor Day–July 4, Tues.–Thurs. and weekends 11–6, Fri. 11–9* Ⓜ *Subway: 6 to 68th St./Hunter College.*

Asian American Arts Centre. This space holds impressive contemporary works by Asian-American artists, annual folk-art exhibitions during the Chinese New Year, Asian-American dance performances, and videos of Asian-American art and events. The center also sells unique art objects from all over Asia. The inconspicuous entrance doesn't have a perma-

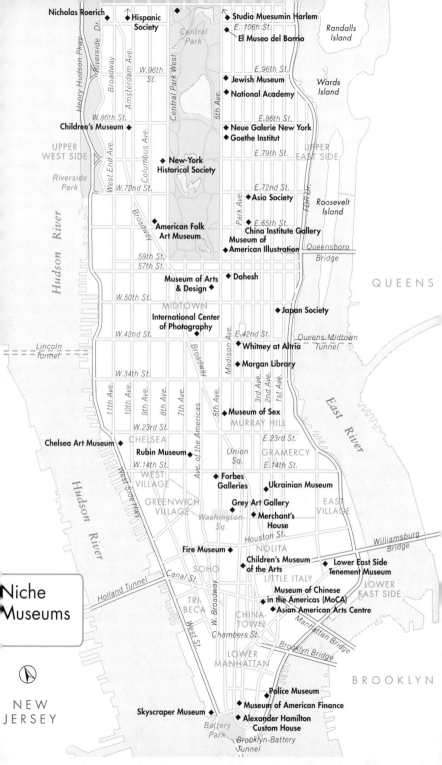

nent sign, but the address is posted on a doorway to the right of the entrance to McDonald's. A steep flight of stairs leads to the third-floor gallery. ⊠ *26 Bowery, between Bayard and Pell Sts., Chinatown* ☎ *212/233–2154* ⊕ *www.artspiral.org* ✉ *Free* ⊙ *Mon.–Wed. and Fri. 12:30–6:30, Thurs. 12:30–7:30* Ⓜ *Subway: 6, J, M, N, Q, R, W, Z to Canal St.*

Chelsea Art Museum. Housed in a former Christmas ornament factory, this contemporary art museum was created to display a collection of postwar European art and to host traveling exhibitions from European museums. Exhibits examine relatively unexplored dimensions of 20th- and 21st-century art, as well as display the work of French abstract painter Jean Miotte. ⊠ *556 W. 22nd St., at 11th Ave., Chelsea* ☎ *212/255–0719* ⊕ *www.chelseaartmuseum.org* ✉ *$6* ⊙ *Tues., Wed., Fri., and Sat. noon–6, Thurs. noon–8* Ⓜ *Subway: C, E to 23rd St.*

☺ **Children's Museum of the Arts.** In this bi-level space a few blocks from Broadway, children ages 1 to 10 can amuse and educate themselves with various activities, including diving into a pool of colorful balls; play-acting in costume; music making with real instruments; and art making, from computer art to old-fashioned painting, sculpting, and collage. ⊠ *182 Lafayette St., between Grand and Broome Sts., SoHo* ☎ *212/941–9198* ⊕ *www.cmany.org* ✉ *$8* ⊙ *Wed. and Fri.–Sun. noon–5, Thurs. noon–6* Ⓜ *Subway: 6 to Spring St.*

Children's Museum of Manhattan. In this five-story exploratorium, children ages 1–10 are invited to paint their own masterpieces, float boats down a "stream," and put on shows at a puppet theater. Art workshops, science programs, and storytelling sessions are held daily. ⊠ *212 W. 83rd St., between Broadway and Amsterdam Aves., Upper West Side* ☎ *212/721–1234* ⊕ *www.cmom.org* ✉ *$8* ⊙ *Wed.–Sun. 10–5* Ⓜ *Subway: 1 to 86th St.*

China Institute Gallery. A pair of stone lions guards the doorway of this pleasant redbrick town house. The institute's gallery is open for two exhibitions each year (September–November and March–June). A two-part exihibit, "Reinventing Books," represents the gallery's foray into the contemporary Chinese art realm through new and innovative creations by contemporary Chinese artists. The first part is in fall 2006, the second in winter 2007–2008. Spring 2007 brings "Tea, Wine & Poetry." The gallery is closed on holidays and between exhibits. ⊠ *125 E. 65th St., between Lexington and Park Aves., Upper East Side* ☎ *212/744–8181* ⊕ *www.chinainstitute.org* ✉ *Gallery $5; free Tues. and Thurs. 6–8* ⊙ *Mon., Wed., Fri., and Sat. 10–5, Tues. and Thurs. 10–8* Ⓜ *Subway: 6 to 68th St./Hunter College.*

Dahesh Museum of Art. On view from the street is the chic, bazaar-like gift store, but downstairs are the elegant galleries filled with Orientalist and classicist works of 19th-century and early-20th-century European academic art. The vivid paintings idealize the human figure and are usually of historical, mythological, or religious subjects. The evolving collection features mostly French and British artists, including works by such painters as Bonheur, Bouguereau, and Gérôme, and sculptor Barye—all of whom have since been upstaged by their contemporaries, the impressionists. The pricey Opaline café on the second floor has a great view over the avenue. ⊠ *580 Madison Ave., between E. 56th and E. 57th Sts., Midtown East* ☎ *212/759–0606* ⊕ *www.daheshmuseum. org* ▣ *$10* ☉ *Tues.–Sun. 11–6* Ⓜ *Subway: E, V to Lexington–3rd Aves./53rd St.; E, V to 5th Ave./53rd St.; 6 to 51st St./Lexington Ave.*

El Museo del Barrio. *El barrio* is Spanish for "the neighborhood" and the nickname for East Harlem, a largely Spanish-speaking, Puerto Rican and Dominican community. The museum, on the edge of this neighborhood, focuses on Latin American and Caribbean art. The 8,000-object permanent collection includes numerous pre-Columbian artifacts, sculpture, photography, film and video, and traditional art from all over Latin America. The collection of 360 *santos*, carved wooden folk-art figures from Puerto Rico, is a popular attraction. ⊠ *1230 5th Ave., between E. 104th and E. 105th Sts., Upper East Side* ☎ *212/831–7272* ⊕ *www. elmuseo.org* ▣ *$6* ☉ *Wed.–Sun. 11–5* Ⓜ *Subway: 6 to 103rd St.*

14

⟳ **Forbes Galleries.** It's free to marvel at the idiosyncratic personal collection of the late publisher Malcolm Forbes, on view in the limestone Forbes Magazine Building. Those who like toys and flea-market finds (see the Trophies room), should definitely take a look. Military music is piped into the displays of warships and ocean liners. The *André* from Paris is gasoline powered; a tiny, dramatic diorama captures the adrenaline of the men on the gun deck of the HMS *Victory* during the Battle of Trafalgar. Of the 10,000 toy soldiers depicted in action, you'll see Aztecs resisting Cortez in 1521, Mussolini marching into Ethiopia in 1935, and a skirmish between "cowboys and Indians." Four galleries have changing exhibits. Recent ones included French military illustrations, letters from First Ladies, and bejeweled objects that belonged to all manner of famous names in history. ⊠ *62 5th Ave., at E. 12th St., Greenwich Village* ☎ *212/206–5548* ⊕ *www.forbesgalleries.com* ▣ *Free* ☉ *Tues.–Sat. 10–4* Ⓜ *Subway: L, N, Q, R, W, 4, 5, 6 to 14th St./Union Sq.*

Goethe Institut. In a 1907 Beaux-Arts town house across from the Met, this German cultural center hosts lectures, films, and concerts; its extensive library includes German newspapers and periodicals. Look for work by young, cutting-edge German photographers and other artists in the gallery space. ⊠ *1014 5th Ave., between E. 82nd and E. 83rd Sts., Upper East Side* ☎ *212/439–8700* ⊕ *www.goethe.de/newyork* ▣ *Exhibitions free* ☉ *Library Tues. and Thurs. noon–7, Wed., Fri., and Sat. noon–5. Gallery weekdays 10–5* Ⓜ *Subway: 4, 5, 6 to 86th St.*

Grey Art Gallery. Within New York University's main building, this gallery presents both traveling shows and its own. During "American Art and Early Film, 1880–1910," films will be projected onto the walls alongside art influenced by the medium (September 13–December 9, 2006). In 2007, fans of the Beat Generation will get to see the works of West Coast artist Wallace Berman and a complete run of the journal *Semina*. The minimalist and conceptual works of Irish artists Brian O'Doherty and Patrick Ireland are on view from April through July 2007. *Silver Center* ⊠ *100 Washington Sq. E, between Waverly Pl. and Washington Pl., Greenwich Village* ☎ *212/998–6780* ▣ *$3 suggested donation* ☉ *Tues., Thurs., and Fri. 11–6, Wed. 11–8, Sat. 11–5* Ⓜ *Subway: R, W to 8th St.*

Hispanic Society of America. This is the best collection of Spanish art outside the Prado in Madrid, with (primarily 15th- and 16th-century) paintings, sculptures, textiles, and decorative arts from Spain, Portugal, Italy, and South America. There are notable pieces by Goya, El Greco, and Velázquez. An entire room is filled with a collection of antique brass knockers. ☒ *Audubon Terrace, Broadway, between W. 155th and W. 156th Sts., entrance up steps to left, Harlem* ☎ *212/926–2234* ⊕ *www. hispanicsociety.org* ☒ *By donation* ☉ *Sept.–July, Tues.–Sat. 10–4:30, Sun. 1–4* Ⓜ *Subway: 1 to 157th St.*

International Center of Photography (ICP). This leading photography venue and school was founded in 1974 by photojournalist Cornell Capa (photographer Robert Capa's brother). From September to late November 2006, the second triennial of photography and video will fill the two floors with works related to global environmental change. The permanent collection consists of 100,000 works and up to three exhibits may be presented at one time. In early 2007, exhibits featuring muses Louise Brooks, Amelia Earhart, and Weimar-era actresses will be on view. ☒ *1133 6th Ave., at W. 43rd St., Midtown West* ☎ *212/857–0000* ⊕ *www.icp.org* ☒ *$10* ☉ *Tues.–Thurs. and weekends 10–6, Fri. 10–8* Ⓜ *Subway: B, D, F, V to 42nd St.*

Japan Society. The stylish and serene lobby of the Japan Society has interior bamboo gardens linked by a second-floor waterfall. Works by well-known Japanese artists are exhibited in the second-floor gallery—past shows have included the first-ever retrospective of Yoko Ono's works and "Hiroshi Sugimoto: History of History." ☒ *333 E. 47th St., between 1st and 2nd Aves., Midtown East* ☎ *212/832–1155* ⊕ *www.japansociety. org* ☒ *$12* ☉ *Building: weekdays 9:30–5:30; gallery: Tues.–Thurs. 11–6, Fri. 11–9, weekends 11–5* Ⓜ *Subway: 6 to 51st St./Lexington Ave.; E, V to Lexington–3rd Aves./53rd St.*

Jewish Museum. Housed within a Gothic-style 1908 mansion, the museum draws on a large collection of art and ceremonial objects to explore Jewish identity and culture. The two-floor permanent exhibition, "Culture and Continuity: The Jewish Journey" displays nearly 800 objects. The wide-ranging collection includes a 3rd-century Roman burial plaque, 20th-century sculpture by Elie Nadelman, and contemporary art. Special exhibits in 2006 and 2007 will include works by painter Alex Katz and sculptor Louise Nevelson, as well as photography and video by international artists living in Israel. ☒ *1109 5th Ave., at E. 92nd St., Upper East Side* ☎ *212/423–3200* ⊕ *www.jewishmuseum.org* ☒ *$10; Thurs. 5–8 pay what you wish* ☉ *Sun.–Wed. 11–5:45, Thurs. 11–8, Fri. 11–3* Ⓜ *Subway: 6 to 96th St.*

Ⓒ **Lower East Side Tenement Museum.** Step back in time and into the partially restored 1863 tenement building at 97 Orchard Street, where you can squeeze through the preserved apartments of immigrants on one of three one-hour tours. This is America's first urban living-history museum dedicated to the life of immigrants—and one of the city's most underrated and overlooked. "Getting By" visits the homes of Natalie Gumpertz, a German-Jewish dressmaker (dating from 1878) and Adolph and Rosaria Baldizzi, Catholic immigrants from Sicily (1935). "Piecing it Together" visits the Levines' garment shop/apartment and the Rogarshevsky family from Eastern Europe (1918). The tour through the Confino family apartment is designed for children, who are greeted by a costumed interpreter playing Victoria Confino. The family of Sephardic Jews came from Kastoria, Turkey, which is now part of Greece (1916). Building tours are limited to 15 people so consider buying tickets in advance. Select tours are followed by free one-hour discussions with snacks provided. Walking tours of the neighborhood are also held regularly. The visitor information center and excellent gift shop displays a video with interviews of Lower East Side residents past and present. An antiques shop at 90 Orchard Street further benefits the museum. ☒ *108 Orchard St., between Delancey and Broome Sts., Lower East Side* ☎ *212/431–0233* ● *www.tenement.org* 🖃 *Tenement and walking tours $15; Confino apartment tour $14* ☉ *Tenement tours leave in 40-minute intervals, Tues.–Fri, 1–4:45, weekends 11–5 (check Web site for full details); Confino apartment tour weekends, hourly noon–3; walking tours Apr.–Dec., weekends 1 and 3. Visitor Center and gift shop Mon. 11–5:30, Tues.–Fri. 11–6, weekends 10:45–6* Ⓜ *Subway: B, D to Grand St.; F to Delancey St.; J, M, Z to Essex St.*

🐾 **Merchant's House Museum.** Built in 1832, this redbrick house, combining federal and Greek Revival styles, provides a glimpse into the family life of that era. Retired merchant Seabury Tredwell and his descendants lived here from 1835 until it became a museum in 1933. The original furnishings and architectural features remain intact; family memorabilia are also on display. Self-guided tour brochures are always available, and guided tours are given on weekends. Kids under 12 get in free. ☒ *29 E. 4th St., between the Bowery and Lafayette St., East Village* ☎ *212/ 777–1089* ● *www.merchantshouse.org* 🖃 *$8* ☉ *Thurs.–Mon. noon–5* Ⓜ *Subway: 6 to Astor Pl. or Bleecker St.; B, D, F, V to Broadway–Lafayette St.; R, W to 8th St.*

Morgan Library. The treasures inside this museum, gathered by John Pierpont Morgan (1837–1913), one of New York's wealthiest financiers, are exceptional: medieval and Renaissance illuminated manuscripts, old-master drawings and prints, rare books, and autographed literary and musical manuscripts. Architect Renzo Piano's redesign of the museum was unveiled in April 2006. The original Renaissance-style building (1906) by Charles McKim of McKim, Mead & White has been preserved, but now there's twice the gallery space, an enlarged auditorium, and two cafés. Crowning achievements produced on paper, from the Middle Ages to the 20th century, are on view here: letters penned by John Keats and Thomas Jefferson; a summary of the theory of relativity in Einstein's own elegant handwriting; three Gutenberg Bibles; drawings by Dürer, Leonardo da Vinci, Rubens, Blake, and Rembrandt; the only known manuscript fragment of Milton's *Paradise Lost;* Thoreau's journals; and original manuscripts and letters by Charlotte Brontë, Jane Austen, Thomas Pynchon, and many others.

The library shop is within an 1852 Italianate brownstone, once the home of Morgan's son, J. P. Morgan Jr. Outside on East 36th Street, the sphinx in the right-hand sculptured panel of the original library's facade was rumored to wear the face of architect Charles McKim. ☒ *225*

Madison Ave., at 36th St., Murray Hill ☎ *212/685–0610* ⊕ *www.*
morganlibrary.org 🖅 *$12* ⊙ *Tues.–Fri. 10:30–5, weekends, 11–6*
Ⓜ *Subway: B, D, F, N, Q, R, W to 34th St./Herald Sq.*

Museum of American Finance. This Smithsonian Institution affiliate has
made it big on Wall Street: in early 2006 it moved from a room in the
Standard Oil Building on Broadway to the grandiose former banking
hall of the Bank of New York. On view are artifacts of the financial market's history, a replica ticker-tape machine that will print out your name,
and well-executed temporary exhibits. ✉ *48 Wall St., at William St.,*
Lower Manhattan ☎ *212/908–4110* ⊕ *www.financialhistory.org* 🖅 *$2*
⊙ *Tues.–Sat. 10–4* Ⓜ *Subway: 2, 3 to Wall St.*

Museum of American Illustration. Founded in 1901, the museum of the
Society of Illustrators presents its annual "Oscars," a juried, international competition, from February to May. The best in children's book
illustrations is featured every November. In between are eclectic exhibitions on everything from cartoons to Norman Rockwell paintings.
✉ *128 E. 63rd St., between Lexington and Park Aves., Upper East Side*
☎ *212/838–2560* ⊕ *www.societyillustrators.org* 🖅 *Free* ⊙ *Tues. 10–8,*
Wed.–Fri. 10–5, Sat. noon–4 Ⓜ *Subway: F to 63rd St.; 4, 5, 6, N, R,*
W to 59th St./Lexington Ave.

Museum of Arts & Design. The irresistible storefront gift shop with colorful jewelry and glass packs in more visitors than the three-level gallery
just beyond it. A convenient match to the American Folk Art museum on
the same street, the museum showcases professional decorative arts in clay,
glass, fabric, wood, metal, paper, and even chocolate. From September
2006 to January 2007 the innovative designs of the international collective Droog will be on display. ✉ *40 W. 53rd St., between 5th and 6th Aves.,*
Midtown West ☎ *212/956–3535* ⊕ *www.americancraftmuseum.org*
🖅 *$9* ⊙ *Fri.–Wed. 10–6, Thurs. 10–8* Ⓜ *Subway: E, V to 5th Ave./53rd*
St.; B, D, E to 7th Ave.; B, D, F, V to 47th–50th Sts./Rockefeller Center.

Museum of Chinese in the Americas (MoCA). The only East Coast museum
dedicated to the history of the Chinese people will move in early 2007
from the second floor of an 1893 schoolhouse at 70 Mulberry Street to
a new 12,000-square-foot space designed by Maya Lin, architect of the
Vietnam Veterans Memorial. The permanent exhibit—"Where Is Home?
Chinese in the Americas"—explores the Chinese-American experience
through displays of artists' creations, personal and domestic artifacts, and
historical documentation. Slippers for binding feet, Chinese musical instruments, a reversible silk gown worn at a Cantonese opera performance, and antique business signs are some of the unique objects on
display. MoCA sponsors workshops, walking tours, lectures, and family events. Its archives (open by appointment only) remain at 70 Mulberry Street and include more than 2,000 volumes. ✉ *141–151 Lafayette*
St. (new address), between Howard and Grand Sts, Chinatown ☎ *212/*
619–4785 ⊕ *www.moca-nyc.org* 🖅 *$3* ⊙ *Tues.–Thurs. and weekends,*
noon–6; Fri. noon–7 Ⓜ *Subway: 6, J, M, N, Q, R, W, Z to Canal St.*

Museum of Sex. Ponder the history and cultural significance of sex while
staring at vintage pornographic photos, Playboy bunny costumes, S&M

paraphernalia, and silent movies. The subject matter is given serious cu-ratorial treatment, though an alternative museum like this has to credit sex product companies for sponsorship rather than foundations, and the gift shop preceding the galleries is full of fun sexual kitsch. On two floors, two special exhibits and the permanent collection may cover Japanese porno-graphic art from the 1700s or the emergence of AIDS. Evenings bring read-ings by cutting-edge authors and performance artists. Check the Web site for a $5 discount on admission. No one under 18 is admitted, unless ac-companied by an adult. ☒ *233 5th Ave., entrance on 27th St., Flatiron District* ☎ *212/689–6337* ⊕ *www.museumofsex.com* ☒ *$14.50* ☺ *Sun.–Fri. 11–6:30, Sat. 11–8* Ⓜ *Subway: N, R to 28th St.*

National Academy. Since its founding in 1825, the Academy has re-quired each member elected to its Museum and School of Fine Arts (the oldest art school in New York) to donate a representative work of art. This criterion produced a strong collection of 19th- and 20th-century American art, as members have included Mary Cassatt, Samuel F. B. Morse, Winslow Homer, Frank Lloyd Wright, Jacob Lawrence, I. M. Pei, Robert Rauschenberg, Maya Lin, Frank Gehry, and Red Grooms. Art and architecture shows highlight both the permanent collection and loan exhibits. The collection's home is a 19th-century mansion do-nated in 1940 by sculptor and academy member Anna Hyatt Hunting-ton. Huntington's bronze, *Diana of the Chase* (1922), is in the academy's foyer. ☒ *1083 5th Ave., between E. 89th and E. 90th Sts., Upper East Side* ☎ *212/369–4880* ⊕ *www.nationalacademy.org* ☒ *$10* ☺ *Wed. and Thurs. noon–5, Fri.–Sun. 11–6* Ⓜ *Subway: 4, 5, 6 to 86th St.*

Neue Galerie New York. Early-20th-century German and Austrian art and design are the focus here, with Gustav Klimt, Vasily Kandinsky, Paul Klee, Egon Schiele, and Josef Hoffman and other designers from the Wiener Werkstatte. Making a guest appearance in 2007 is "Van Gogh and Expressionism" (March 23–July 7, 2007), with pieces from Ams-terdam's Van Gogh Museum. The Neue Galerie was founded by the late art dealer Serge Sabarsky and cosmetics heir and art collector Ronald S. Lauder. The two-floor gallery, a Viennese-style café, and a top-notch design shop are in a 1914 mansion designed by Carrère and Hastings, which was home to Mrs. Cornelius Vanderbilt III, the top social host-ess of the Gilded Age. An audio guide is included with admission.

In an elegant, high-ceiling space below the Neue Galerie, **Café Sabarsky** serves Viennese coffee, cakes, strudel, and Sacher torte (Mon. and Wed. 9–6, Thurs.–Sun. 9–9). If you seek something more than a sugar fix, the savory menu includes trout crepes and Hungarian goulash. ☒ *1048 5th Ave., at E. 86th St., Upper East Side* ☎ *212/628–6200* ⊕ *www. neuegalerie.org* ☒ *$15* ☞ *Children under 12 not admitted; under 16 must be accompanied by an adult* ☺ *Sat.–Mon. and Thurs. 11–6, Fri. 11–9* Ⓜ *Subway: 4, 5, 6 to 86th St.*

New York City Fire Museum. In the former headquarters of Engine 30, a handsome Beaux-Arts building dating from 1904, retired firefighters vol-unteer their time to answer visitors' questions. The collection of fire-fighting tools from the 18th century to the present includes hand-pulled and horse-drawn engines, pumps, and uniforms. A memorial exhibit with photos, paintings, children's artwork, and found objects relating to the September 11 attacks is also on view. On 9/11, the city's fire department lost 343 members at the World Trade Center. The museum is two subway stops (via the E train) north of the Ground Zero site. ⊠ *278 Spring St., near Varick St., SoHo* ☎ *212/691–1303* ⊕ *www. nycfiremuseum.org* 🖃 *$5 suggested donation* ⊙ *Tues.–Sat. 10–5, Sun. 10–4* Ⓜ *Subway: C, E to Spring St.*

⏰ **New York City Police Museum.** Why are police called cops? Why does a police badge have eight points? When was fingerprinting first used to solve a crime? Find the answers at this museum dedicated to New York's finest. The force's history from colonial times through the present is covered through permanent and rotating exhibits, as well as interactive and sometimes chilling displays, including fingerprinting and forensic art stations. A permanent exhibit, "9/11 Remembered," includes a video with interviews with those who were first responders to the attack. The Hall of Heroes honors police officers who have fallen in the line of duty. Special events include a vintage police car show the first weekend in June, and the first Saturday in October, when kids get to meet police officers and demonstrations take place. ⊠ *100 Old Slip, near South St., Lower Manhattan* ☎ *212/480–3100* ⊕ *www.nycpolicemuseum. org* 🖃 *$5 suggested donation* ⊙ *Jan.–Mar., Tues.–Sat. 10–5; Apr.–Dec., Tues.–Sat. 10–5, Sun. 11–5* Ⓜ *Subway: 2, 3 to Wall St.*

New-York Historical Society. The city's oldest museum, founded in 1804, has one of the city's finest research libraries, with a collection of 6 million pieces of art, literature, and memorabilia. Special exhibitions shed light on New York's—and America's—history, everyday life, art, and architecture. Major exhibits in late 2006 through early 2007 include a collection of Hudson River School landscapes and an examination of New York City's role in the slavery debate and the Civil War. The permanent collection is exhibited within glass cases. Exhibits aren't always displayed there to the best effect: the links of a chain that spanned the Hudson River to stop the British is an intriguing artifact, but they're on a darkened bottom shelf beneath an archaelogical-like assortment of World Trade Center artifacts. The items and art are rich and diverse here, but the Museum of the City of New York presents better summaries of New York's history. ⊠ *2 W. 77th St., at Central Park W, Upper West Side* ☎ *212/873–3400* ⊕ *www.nyhistory.org* 🖃 *$10 suggested donation* ⊙ *Tues.–Thurs. and weekends 10–6; Fri. 10–8* Ⓜ *Subway: B, C to 81st St.*

Nicholas Roerich Museum. An 1898 Upper West Side town house contains this small, eccentric museum dedicated to the work of Russian artist Nicholas Roerich, who immigrated to New York in the 1920s and quickly developed an ardent following. Some 200 of his paintings hang here—notably some vast canvases of the Himalayas; other works are in several museums in Russia and India. He also designed sets for ballets, such as Stravinsky's *Rite of Spring,* sketches of which are also on view. Free chamber music concerts are held here most Sunday afternoons at 5, except in summer. ⊠ *319 W. 107th St., between Broadway and Riverside Dr., Morningside Heights* ☎ *212/864–7752* ⊕ *www.roerich.org* 🖃 *By donation* ⊙ *Tues.–Sun. 2–5* Ⓜ *Subway: 1 to 110th St./Cathedral Pkwy.*

Rubin Museum of Art. Opened in 2004, this sleek and serene museum is the first in the Western Hemphispere dedicated to art of the Himalayas. It provides a great deal of the explanation for the colorful works, which are religious and rich with symbols. Six floors hold paintings on cloth, metal sculptures, and textiles dating from the 12th century onward. The works from areas such as Tibet, Nepal, southwest China, and India are all related to either Buddhisim, Hinduism, or the Bon religions. Begin on the second floor, which in a very simple manner, addresses the "why?" "where?" and "how?" surrounding the art. A central circular stairwell leads to each floor, where you can pick up a magnifying glass to better examine the intricate, dense works. The exhibits on the 5th and 6th floors change regularly. A pleasant café and gift shop are on the ground floor. ⊠ *150 W. 17th St., near 7th Ave., Chelsea* ☎ *212/ 620–5000* ⊕ *www.rmanyc.org* ✉ *$10* ⊗ *Mon., Thurs. 11–5; Wed. 11–7; Fri. 11–10; weekends 11–6* Ⓜ *Subway: 1 to 18th St.*

Skyscraper Museum. Opposite the Museum of Jewish Heritage, this small museum will either delight or disappoint skyscraper fans. To evoke space, the stainless steel floor and ceiling are polished to mirror quality, but the open room with column partitions does not include a comprehensive overview of the rise of the skyscraper. Focused exhibits change every few months; on permanent view is the daily photo journal a contractor kept during the Empire State Building's construction. Models of current or future buildings, short videos, and exhibits that reveal the influence of history, real estate, and individuals on architecture are regular features. More of the museum's holdings can be seen and researched online, making the Web site an excellent "branch." "Manhattan Timeformations" uses animation to depict the dynamic relationship between skyscrapers and geology, landfill, settlement patterns, and real estate cycles. ⊠ *39 Battery Pl., Battery Park City, Lower Manhattan* ☎ *212/968–1961* ⊕ *www.skyscraper.org* ✉ *$5* ⊗ *Wed.–Sun. noon–6* Ⓜ *Subway: 4, 5 to Bowling Green.*

Studio Museum in Harlem. Contemporary art by African-American, Caribbean, and African artists is the focus of this small museum with a light-filled sculpture garden. Its changing exhibits have included "Black Artists and Abstraction" and "Africa Comics." Three artists in residence present their works each year. ⊠ *144 W. 125th St., between Lenox Ave. and Adam Clayton Powell Jr. Blvd., Harlem* ☎ *212/864–4500* ⊕ *www. studiomuseuminharlem.org* ✉ *$7 suggested donation* ⊗ *Wed.–Fri. and Sun. noon–6, Sat. 10–6* Ⓜ *Subway: 2, 3 to 125th St.*

Ukrainian Museum. Folk art, fine art, and documentary materials addressing the life of Ukrainians in the Americas make up the permanent collection. Ceramics, jewelry, hundreds of brilliantly colored Easter eggs, and an extensive collection of Ukrainian costumes and textiles are the highlights. The two-floor museum makes its home in the neighborhood where many from Ukraine settled during the years of Soviet domination. ⊠ *222 E. 6th St., between 2nd and 3rd Aves., East Village* ☎ *212/ 228–0110* ⊕ *www.ukrainianmuseum.org* ✉ *$8* ⊗ *Wed.–Sun. 11:30–5* Ⓜ *Subway: 6 to Astor Pl.*

Whitney Museum of American Art at Altria. An enormous atrium with 20th-century sculptures, many of which are simply too big for the Whitney's uptown base, is the centerpiece of the museum's outpost opposite Grand Central Terminal. An adjacent gallery presents four shows a year by living artists. An espresso bar and seating areas make this an agreeable place to rest. ✉ *120 Park Ave., at E. 42nd St., Midtown East* ☎ *917/663–2453* ⊕ *www.whitney.org* ✆ *Free* ☉ *Sculpture court Mon.–Sat. 7:30 AM–9:30 PM, Sun. and holidays 11–7; gallery Mon.–Wed. and Fri. 11–6, Thurs. 11–7:30. Gallery talks Wed. and Fri. at 1* Ⓜ *Subway: 4, 5, 6, 7 to 42nd St./Grand Central.*

ART GALLERIES

Art galleries, including the large numbers that are on the Upper East Side, are always free. Check *New York Magazine,* or the *New York Times* Sunday "Arts" section to find out what's showing. Gallery openings often have free food and drink for attendees.

SoHo

Deitch Projects. This energetic enterprise composed of two gallery spaces shows works from the global art scene, as well as performance groups such as The Citizens Band. Artists on view have included Cecily Brown, Ryan McGinness, and Kihinde Wiley. ✉ *76 Grand St., between Greene and Wooster Sts., SoHo* ☎ *212/343–7300* ⊕ *www.deitch.com* Ⓜ *Subway: C, E to Spring St.* ✉ *18 Wooster St., between Grand and Canal Sts., SoHo* ☎ *212/343–7300* Ⓜ *Subway: C, E to Spring St.*

Drawing Center. At this nonprofit organization, the focus is on contemporary and historical drawings seen nowhere else. Works often push the envelope on what's considered drawing; many projects are commissioned especially by the center. A second gallery is across the street at 40 Wooster Street. ✉ *35 Wooster St., between Broome and Grand Sts., SoHo* ☎ *212/219–2166* ⊕ *www.drawingcenter.org* Ⓜ *Subway: C, E to Spring St.*

Nancy Hoffman. Contemporary painting, sculpture, drawing, prints, and photographic works by an impressive array of international artists are on display here. Gallery artists range from Rupert Deese, known for his conceptual shaped canvases, to Yuko Shiraishi, whose abstract oil paintings explore different tones of a single color. ✉ *429 West Broadway, between Prince and Spring Sts., SoHo* ☎ *212/966–6676* ⊕ *www. nancyhoffmangallery.com* Ⓜ *Subway: R, W to Prince St.*

New York Earth Room. Walter de Maria's 1977 avant-garde work consists of 140 tons of gently sculpted soil (22 inches deep) filling 3,600 square feet of space of a second-floor gallery maintained by the Dia Art Foundation. If you like this work of his, check out de Maria's *Broken Kilometer,* a few blocks away at 393 West Broadway. ✉ *141 Wooster St., between W. Houston and Prince Sts., SoHo* ☎ *212/473–8072* ⊕ *www.earthroom.org* ✆ *Free* Ⓜ *Subway: R, W to Prince St.*

OK Harris Works of Art. This SoHo stalwart hosts a wide range of visual arts: paintings, digitally enhanced photographs, trompe l'oeil reliefs, sculptures. The gallery closes from mid-July to early September. ✉ *383 West Broadway, between Spring and Broome Sts., SoHo* ☎ *212/431–3600* ⊕ *www.okharris.com* Ⓜ *Subway: R, W to Prince St.*

Ronald Feldman Fine Arts. Founded in 1971, this gallery represents over 30 international contemporary artists. It has a large selection of Andy Warhol prints, paintings, and drawings. ✉ *31 Mercer St., between Grand and Canal Sts., SoHo* ☎ *212/226–3232* ⊕ *www.feldmangallery. com* Ⓜ *Subway: R, W to Prince St.*

Lower East Side

Gallery Onetwentyeight. Inside the jewel-box space, artist Kazuko Miyamoto directs crisp and provocative group shows. ✉ *128 Rivington St., between Essex and Norfolk Sts., Lower East Side* ☎ *212/674– 0244* ⊕ *www.galleryonetwentyeight.org* Ⓜ *Subway: F, V to 2nd Ave.*

Rivington Arms. A tiny space with a quirky and casual mind-set, this gallery shows young emerging artists. Look for the photographic-sound works of collective Lansing-Dreiden and portrait paintings by Mathew Cerletty. ✉ *102 Rivington St., between Essex and Ludlow Sts., Lower East Side* ☎ *646/654–3213* ⊕ *www.rivingtonarms.com* Ⓜ *Subway: F, V to 2nd Ave.*

Chelsea

Numbers in the margin correspond to numbers on the Chelsea Galleries map.

❼ Alan Klotz Gallery. Fine 19th- and 20th-century photography is the focus of the exhibitions here. Shows range from the modern photo-realistic natural landscapes of Karen Halverson to the more playful portraits of photojournalist Jonathan Torgovnik. Also here are extensive collections from some of history's most important photographers, including Josef Sudek, Berenice Abbott, and Eugene de Salignac. ✉ *511 W. 25th St., Suite 701, between 10th and 11th Aves., Chelsea* ☎ *212/741–4764* ⊕ *www.klotzgallery.com* Ⓜ *Subway: C, E to 23rd St.*

⓮ Andrea Rosen. The gallery showcases artists on the cutting edge, such as sculptor Andrea Zittel, Felix Gonzalez-Torres, and painter and installation artist Matthew Ritchie. ✉ *525 W. 24th St., between 10th and 11th Aves., Chelsea* ☎ *212/627–6000* ⊕ *www.andrearosengallery.com* Ⓜ *Subway: C, E to 23rd St.*

㉑ ATM Gallery. Eighteen artists, mostly from Japan, are represented at this gallery that began in the East Village in 1999. In 2006–07, look for solo painting shows by Michael Ferris, Alison Fox, and Yoko Kawamoto. ✉ *511 W. 20th St.,, between 10th and 11th Aves, Chelsea* ☎ *212/375– 0349* ⊕ *www.atmgallery.com* Ⓜ *Subway: C, E to 23rd St.*

❽ Barbara Gladstone. The international roster of artists cultivated here include sculptor Anish Kapoor, photographer Sharon Lockhart, and mul-

Chelsea
Galleries

W. 32nd St.
W. 31st St.
W. 30th St.
W. 29th St.
W. 28th St.
W. 27th St.
W. 26th St.
W. 25th St.
W. 24th St.

Tenth Ave.
Eleventh Ave.
Ninth Ave.
Eighth Ave.
Seventh Ave.
Avenue of the Americas

W. 28th St.

W. 24th St.

W. 23rd St.
W. 22nd St.
W. 21st St.
W. 20th St.
W. 19th St.
W. 18th St.
W. 17th St.
W. 16th St.
W. 15th St.
W. 14th St.
W. 13th St.

Chelsea
Piers

Eleventh Ave.

Chelsea
Market

MEATPACKING
DISTRICT

W. 4th St.

KEY

M Subway stops

C,E
1
F,Q
(Sixth Ave.)
A,C,E,L
1,2,3
F,L

0   1/2 mile
0   800 meters

Alan Klotz . . . .**7**   Gagosian . . . .**10**   Pace Wildenstein **6**
Andrea Rosen . . . .**14**   Galerie Lelong . . . .**2**   Paula Cooper **18**
ATM Gallery . . . .**21**   Jack Shainman . . . .**22**   Postmasters **24**
Barbara Gladstone . . . . .**8**   Luhring Augustine . . . .**11**   Robert Miller **4**
Casey Kaplan . . . .**19**   Marlborough . . . .**25**   Sean Kelley **1**
Cheim & Read . . . .**5**   Mary Boone . . . .**12**   Sonnabend **15**
Clementine . . . .**3**   Matthew Marks . . .**13, 17**   Tanya Bonakdar **20**
David Zwirner . . . .**23**   Metro Pictures . . . .**9**   303 . . . .**16**

CLOSE UP

Chelsea Galleries 101

GOOD ART, BAD ART, EDGY ART, DOWNRIGHT DISTURBING ART—it's all here waiting to please and provoke in the contemporary art capital of the world. For the uninitiated, the concentration of more than 250 galleries within a seven-block radius can be overwhelming, and the sometimes cool receptions upon entering, intimidating. Art galleries are not exactly famous for their customer service skills, but they're free, and you don't need a degree in art appreciation to stare at a canvas. Wear your walking shoes, leave your preconceptions of what's art behind, and don't be intimidated—at the very least your gallery experience will provide some interesting dinnertime talk.

There's no required code of conduct, although most galleries are library-quiet. Don't worry, you won't be laughed at if you mistake the fire extinguisher for a cutting-edge statement and you won't be pressured to buy anything; staff will probably be doing their best to ignore you.

Galleries are generally open Tuesday through Saturday from 10 AM to 6 PM. Gallery-hop on a Saturday afternoon—the highest traffic day—if you want company. You can usually find a binder with the artist's résumé, examples of previous work, and exhibit details (usually including prices) at the front desk. If not, ask. You can also ask if there's information you can take with you.

You won't be able to see everything in one afternoon so if you have specific interests, plan ahead. You can find gallery information and current exhibit details at ⊕ www.galleryguide.org (you can pick up a free hard copy at any gallery desk). Sift further through your choices by checking the "Art Guide" in Friday's weekend section of the *New York Times* and the Chelsea Art section of *Time Out New York* magazine. You can also learn more about the galleries and the genres and artists they represent at ⊕ www.artincontext.org.

–Jacinta O'Halloran

14

timedia artists Matthew Barney and Richard Prince. ⊠ *515 W. 24th St., between 10th and 11th Aves., Chelsea* ☎ *212/206–9300* ⊕ *www. gladstonegallery.com* Ⓜ *Subway: C, E to 23rd St.*

⑲ Casey Kaplan. Kaplan has a keen eye for conceptual artists from around the globe. Among them is photographer Anna Gaskell, and Liam Gillik and Simon Starling, who both create architectural sculptures. ⊠ *525 W. 21st St., between 10th and 11th Aves., Chelsea* ☎ *212/645–7335* ⊕ *www.caseykaplangallery.com* Ⓜ *Subway: C, E to 23rd St.*

⑤ Cheim & Read. This prestigious gallery represents artists such as Louise Bourgeois, William Eggleston, Joan Mitchell, Jenny Holzer, Donald Baechler, and Jack Pierson. ⊠ *547 W. 25th St., between 10th and 11th Aves., Chelsea* ☎ *212/242–7727* ⊕ *www.cheimread.com* Ⓜ *Subway: C, E to 23rd St.*

③ Clementine. This gallery is committed to giving artists their first solo shows, so hosts more emerging artists than other Chelsea galleries do. Look for

Mylar collages by Kurt Lightner, graphite on paper by Whitney Biennial alum Robyn O'Neil, and mixed media by Robert Pruitt. ⊠ *623 W. 27th St., between 11th and 12th Aves., Chelsea* ☎ *212/243–5937* ⊕ *www.clementine-gallery.com* Ⓜ *Subway: C, E to 23rd St.*

㉓ **David Zwirner.** Proving his finger is on the pulse of contemporary art, Zwirner shows works in all media by such emerging artists as Luc Tuymans, Stan Douglas, Thomas Ruff, Diana Thater, and Yutaka Sone. ⊠*525 W. 19th St., between 10th and 11th Aves., Chelsea* ☎ *212/727–2070* ⊕ *www.davidzwirner.com* Ⓜ *Subway: C, E to 23rd St.*

❿ **Gagosian.** This enterprising modern gallery has two branches in New York City (the other's on the Upper East Side), one in Beverly Hills, and one in London, all presenting works by heavy hitters, such as sculptor Richard Serra and the late pop-art icon Roy Lichtenstein. ⊠ *555 W. 24th St., at 11th Ave., Chelsea* ☎ *212/741–1111* ⊕ *www.gagosian.com* Ⓜ *Subway: C, E to 23rd St.*

❷ **Galerie Lelong.** This large gallery presents challenging installations and art, as well as many Latin American artists. Look for Alfred Jaar, Andy Goldsworthy, Cildo Meireles, Ana Mendieta, and Petah Coyne. ⊠ *528 W. 26th St., between 10th and 11th Aves., Chelsea* ☎ *212/315–0470* Ⓜ *Subway: C, E to 23rd St.*

㉒ **Jack Shainman.** Both emerging and established artists are shown here, such as Subodh Gupta, a young sculptor from India, and Kerry James Marshall, who deals with African-American issues. You might find works by Phil Frost, whose imagery is derived from graffiti, or Zwelethu Mthethwa, a South African photographer. ⊠ *513 W. 20th St., between 10th and 11th Aves., Chelsea* ☎ *212/645–1701* ⊕ *www.jackshainman. com* Ⓜ *Subway: C, E to 23rd St.*

⓫ **Luhring Augustine.** Since 1985 owners Lawrence Luhring and Roland Augustine have worked with established and emerging artists from Europe, Japan, and America. ⊠ *531 W. 24th St., between 10th and 11th Aves., Chelsea* ☎ *212/206–9100* ⊕ *www.luhringaugustine.com* Ⓜ *Subway: C, E to 23rd St.*

㉕ **Marlborough.** With galleries in London, Monaco, and Madrid, the Marlborough empire also operates two of the largest and most influential galleries in New York City. The Chelsea location (the other's in midtown) shows the latest work of modern artists, with a special interest in sculptural forms, such as the large-scale work of Michele Oka Doner. Red Grooms, Richard Estes, and Fernando Botero are just a few of the 20th-century luminaries represented. ⊠ *211 W. 19th St., between 7th and 8th Aves., Chelsea* ☎ *212/463–8634* ⊕ *www.marlboroughgallery. com* Ⓜ *Subway: C, E to 23rd St.*

⓬ **Mary Boone.** A hot SoHo gallery during the 1980s, this venue now resides both in midtown and in the newer flash point of Chelsea. Boone continues to show established artists such as Barbara Kruger and Eric Fischl, as well as newcomers. ⊠ *541 W. 24th St., between 10th and 11th Aves., Chelsea* ☎ *212/752–2929* ⊕ *www.maryboonegallery.com* Ⓜ *Subway: C, E to 23rd St.*

⑬ ⑰ Matthew Marks. At three Chelsea spaces Marks, one of the most influential art dealers in New York, shows prominent modern artists such as the painters Ellsworth Kelly and Jasper Johns, as well as photographers Andreas Gursky, Inez van Lamsweerde, and Nan Goldin. ✉ *522 W. 22nd St., between 10th and 11th Aves., Chelsea* ☏ *212/243–0200* ⊕ *www.matthewmarks.com* Ⓜ *Subway: C, E to 23rd St.* ✉ *523 W. 24th St., between 10th and 11th Aves., Chelsea* ☏ *212/243–0200* Ⓜ *Subway: C, E to 23rd St.* ✉ *521 W. 21th St., between 10th and 11th Aves., Chelsea* ☏ *212/243–0200* Ⓜ *Subway: C, E to 23rd St.*

⑨ Metro Pictures. The hottest talents in contemporary art shown here include Cindy Sherman, whose provocative photographs have brought her international prominence. ✉ *519 W. 24th St., between 10th and 11th Aves., Chelsea* ☏ *212/206–7100* Ⓜ *Subway: C, E to 23rd St.*

⑥ Pace Wildenstein. The midtown specialist in 20th- and 21st-century art now has two spaces in Chelsea. The West 25th Street location can fit the largest sculpture and installations. Their roster concentrates on upper-echelon artists, sculptors, and photographers, including Elizabeth Murray, Chuck Close, Sol LeWitt, and Robert Rauschenberg. ✉ *534 W. 25th St., between 10th and 11th Aves., Chelsea* ☏ *212/929–7000* ✉ *545 W. 22nd St., between 10th and 11th Aves., Chelsea* ☏ *212/989–4258* ⊕ *www.pacewildenstein.com* Ⓜ *Subway: C, E to 23rd St.*

⑱ Paula Cooper. SoHo pioneer Paula Cooper moved to Chelsea in 1996 and enlisted architect Richard Gluckman to transform a warehouse into a dramatic space with tall ceilings and handsome skylights. Now she has two galleries on the same block that showcase the minimalist sculptures of Carl André, the dot paintings of Yayoi Kusama, and the provocative photos of Andres Serrano, among other works. ✉ *534 W. 21st St., between 10th and 11th Aves., Chelsea* ☏ *212/255–1105* Ⓜ *Subway: C, E to 23rd St.* ✉ *521 W. 21st St., 2nd fl., between 10th and 11th Aves., Chelsea* ☏ *212/255–5247* Ⓜ *Subway: C, E to 23rd St.*

㉔ Postmasters. Postmasters shows new and established conceptual artists, with one room devoted to multimedia shows. Recent exhibits have included Claude Wampler's *Pomerania*—a series of photographs, sculptures, video, and drawings examining the artist's relationship with her pet Pomeranian. ✉ *459 W. 19th St., between 9th and 10th Aves., Chelsea* ☏ *212/727–3323* ⊕ *www.postmastersart.com* Ⓜ *Subway: C, E to 23rd St.*

④ Robert Miller. Miller, a titan of the New York art world, represents some of the biggest names in modern painting and photography, including Tom Wesselma and the estates of Lee Krasner and Alice Neel. ✉ *524 W. 26th St., between 10th and 11th Aves., Chelsea* ☏ *212/366–4774* ⊕ *www.robertmillergallery.com* Ⓜ *Subway: C, E to 23rd St.*

① Sean Kelly. Drop in to this large space for works by top contemporary American and European artists, including Marina Abramovic, Ann Hamilton, Robert Mapplethorpe, Lorna Simpson, and James Casebere. ✉ *528 W. 29th St., between 10th and 11th Aves., Chelsea* ☏ *212/239–1181* ⊕ *www.skny.com* Ⓜ *Subway: 1, 9 to 28th St.*

⑮ Sonnabend. This pioneer of the SoHo art scene continues to show important contemporary artists in its Chelsea space, including Jeff Koons, Ashley Bickerton, and British art duo Gilbert&George. ⊠ *536 W. 22nd St., between 10th and 11th Aves., Chelsea* ☎ *212/627–1018* Ⓜ *Subway: C, E to 23rd St.*

⑳ Tanya Bonakdar. This gallery presents such contemporary artists as Uta Barth, whose blurry photos challenge ideas about perception, and Ernesto Neto, a Brazilian artist who has made stunning room-size installations of large nylon sacks filled with spices. ⊠ *521 W. 21st St., between 10th and 11th Aves., Chelsea* ☎ *212/414–4144* ⊕ *www.tanyabonakdargallery.com* Ⓜ *Subway: C, E to 23rd St.*

⑯ 303. International cutting-edge artists shown here include photographers Doug Aitken and Thomas Demand and installation artist/painter Karen Kilimnik. The gallery is closed in August and weekends between July 5 and Labor Day. ⊠ *525 W. 22nd St., between 10th and 11th Aves., Chelsea* ☎ *212/255–1121* ⊕ *www.303gallery.com* Ⓜ *Subway: C, E to 23rd St.*

Midtown

David Findlay Jr. Fine Art. This gallery concentrates on American 19th- and 20th-century painters from Winslow Homer to Robert Richenburg to op artist Richard Anuszkiewicz. ⊠ *41 E. 57th St., 11th fl., between 5th and Madison Aves., Midtown East* ☎ *212/486–7660* ⊕ *www.findlayart.com* Ⓜ *Subway: F to 57th St.*

Edwynn Houk. The impressive stable of 20th-century photographers here includes Sally Mann, Lynn Davis, and Elliott Erwitt. The gallery also has prints by masters Edward Weston and Alfred Steiglitz. ⊠ *745 5th Ave., between E. 57th and E. 58th Sts., Midtown East* ☎ *212/750–7070* ⊕ *www.houkgallery.com* Ⓜ *Subway: N, R, W to 5th Ave.*

Greenberg Van Doren. This gallery exhibits the works of young artists as well as retrospectives of established masters. You can purchase works here by Georgia O'Keeffe, Ed Ruscha, and Robert Motherwell, among others. ⊠ *730 5th Ave., at E. 57th St., Midtown East* ☎ *212/445–0444* ⊕ *www.agvdgallery.com* Ⓜ *Subway: F to 57th St.*

Marian Goodman. The excellent contemporary art here includes Jeff Wall's staged photographs presented on light boxes, South African artist William Kentridge's video animations, and Gerhard Richter's paintings. ⊠ *24 W. 57th St., between 5th and 6th Aves., Midtown West* ☎ *212/977–7160* ⊕ *www.mariangoodman.com* Ⓜ *Subway: F to 57th St.*

Marlborough. With its latest branch in Chelsea, Marlborough raises its global visibility up yet another notch. The gallery represents modern artists such as Michele Oka Doner, Magdalena Abakanowicz, and Israel Hershberg. Look for sculptures by Tom Otterness—his whimsical bronzes are found in several subway stations. ⊠ *40 W. 57th St., between 5th and 6th Aves., Midtown West* ☎ *212/541–4900* ⊕ *www.marlboroughgallery.com* Ⓜ *Subway: F to 57th St.*

Pace Wildenstein. The giant gallery—now in Chelsea as well—focuses on such modern and contemporary painters as Julian Schnabel, Mark Rothko, and New York School painter Ad Reinhardt. A recent exhibit examined the work of the late Saul Steinberg, whose drawings appeared in the *New Yorker* for decades. ⊠ *32 E. 57th St., between Park and Madison Aves., Midtown East* ☏ *212/421–3292* ⊕ *www.pacewildenstein. com* Ⓜ *Subway: N, R, W to 5th Ave.*

Peter Findlay. Covering 19th- and 20th-century works by European artists, this gallery shows pieces by Mary Cassatt, Paul Klee, and Alberto Giacometti. ⊠ *41 E. 57th St., 8th fl., at Madison Ave., Midtown East* ☏ *212/644–4433* ⊕ *www.findlay.com* Ⓜ *Subway: N, R, W to 5th Ave.*

Spanierman. This venerable gallery deals in 19th- and early-20th-century American painting and sculpture and is the kind museums turn to when seeking out new acquisitions. ⊠ *45 E. 58th St., between Park and Madison Aves., Midtown East* ☏ *212/832–0208* ⊕ *www.spanierman. com* Ⓜ *Subway: N, R, W to 5th Ave.*

Tibor de Nagy. Founded in 1950, this reputable gallery shows work by 20th-century artists such as Biala, Nell Blaine, Jane Freilicher, and Shirley Jaffee. It's closed weekends June through mid-August, and closes up completely from mid-August to Labor Day. ⊠ *724 5th Ave., between W. 56th and W. 57th Sts., Midtown West* ☏ *212/262–5050* ⊕ *www. tibordenagy.com* Ⓜ *Subway: F to 57th St.*

Upper East Side

David Findlay. Descend into a warren of rooms to view contemporary, color-soaked paintings by American and French artists. Represented artists include Pierre Lesieur, Roger Mühl, and (for a brightly hued slice of New York streets) Tom Christopher. ⊠ *984 Madison Ave., between E. 76th and E. 77th Sts., Upper East Side* ☏ *212/249–2909* ⊕ *www. davidfindlaygalleries.com* Ⓜ *Subway: 6 to 77th St.*

Hirschl & Adler. Although this five-floor town house has a selection of European works, it's best known for its American paintings, prints, and decorative arts. The celebrated 19th- and 20th-century artists whose works are featured include Thomas Cole, Frederick Church, Childe Hassam, Camille Pissaro, and William Merritt Chase. ⊠ *21 E. 70th St., between 5th and Madison Aves., Upper East Side* ☏ *212/535–8810* ⊕ *www. hirschlandadler.com* Ⓜ *Subway: 6 to 68th St./Hunter College.*

Jane Kahan. This welcoming gallery represents very lofty works. Besides ceramics by Picasso and modern master tapestries, one of this gallery's specialties, you'll see works by 19th- and 20th-century artists such as Fernand Léger, Joan Miró, and Marc Chagall. ⊠ *922 Madison Ave., 2nd fl., between E. 73rd and E. 74th Sts., Upper East Side* ☏ *212/744– 1490* ⊕ *www.janekahan.com* Ⓜ *Subway: 6 to 77th St.*

Knoedler & Company. Knoedler helped many great American collectors, including industrialist Henry Clay Frick, start their collections. Now it represents 20th-century painters such as Helen Frankenthaler, Sean

Scully, and John Walker. Catherine Murphy and John Duff are some of the contemporary artists featured. ✉ *19 E. 70th St., between 5th and Madison Aves., Upper East Side* ☎ *212/794–0550* ⊕ *www. knoedlergallery.com* Ⓜ *Subway: 6 to 68th St./Hunter College.*

Leo Castelli. Castelli was one of the most influential dealers of the 20th century. An early supporter of pop, minimalist, and conceptual art, he helped foster the careers of many important artists, including one of his first discoveries, Jasper Johns. The gallery moved here from SoHo and continues to show works by Roy Lichtenstein, Ed Ruscha, Jackson Pollock, and others. ✉ *18 E. 77th St., between 5th and Madison Aves., Upper East Side* ☎ *212/249–4470* ⊕ *www.castelligallery.com* Ⓜ *Subway: 6 to 77th St.*

Margo Feiden. Illustrations by the late Al Hirschfeld, whose theatrical caricatures appeared in the *New York Times* for more than 60 years, are the draw here. ✉ *699 Madison Ave., between E. 62nd and E. 63rd Sts., Upper East Side* ☎ *212/677–5330* ⊕ *www.alhirschfeld.com* Ⓜ *Subway: F to 63rd St.; 4, 5, 6, N, R, W to 59th St./Lexington Ave.*

Michael Werner. This German art dealer mounts shows of such early-20th-century masters as Otto Freundlich and Francis Picabia in his East Side town house. The emphasis is on paintings and drawings. ✉ *4 E. 77th St., between 5th and Madison Aves., Upper East Side* ☎ *212/988–1623* Ⓜ *Subway: 6 to 77th St.*

Mitchell-Innes & Nash. This sleek spot specializes in contemporary, impressionist, and modern art; it represents the estates of Willem de Kooning, Tony Smith, and Jack Tworkov. ✉ *1018 Madison Ave., between 78th and 79th Sts., Upper East Side* ☎ *212/744–7400* ⊕ *www.miandn. com* Ⓜ *Subway: 6 to 77th St.*

Wildenstein & Co. This branch of the Wildenstein art empire was the first to take root in New York; its reputation for brilliant holdings was cemented by the acquisition of significant private museum-quality collections. Look for French impressionist exhibitions. ✉ *19 E. 64th St., between 5th and Madison Aves., Upper East Side* ☎ *212/879–0500* ⊕ *www.wildenstein.com* Ⓜ *Subway: 6 to 68th St./Hunter College.*

The Performing Arts

WORD OF MOUTH

"The entire Met experience is worth it. The building, the audience, and the opera itself combine for a fascinating experience and one you can't get anywhere else. It is magical!" —Labfans

"We have enjoyed *Spamalot*, *Sweeney Todd*, *Jersey Boys*, *I Love You, You're Perfect, Now Change* (off B'way), *Wicked*, *Mamma Mia*, and *Hairspray*. The best? *Jersey Boys* (story of Frankie Valli and the Four Seasons) would get my recent choice. Then again, I'm from the '60s!!" —Rogfam

Updated by
Lynne Arany

The Performing Arts Capital of America, New York attracts celebrated artists from around the world. But the city's own artistic resources are what make the performing arts here so special. Thousands of actors, singers, dancers, musicians, and other artists populate the city, infusing New York's cultural scene with unparalleled levels of creative energy. And discerning patrons drive the arts scene as they strive to keep up with the latest—from flocking to a concert hall to hear a world-class soprano deliver a flawless performance to crowding in a cramped basement bookstore to support young writers nervously stumbling over their own prose.

New York has somewhere between 200 and 250 legitimate theaters, and many more ad hoc venues—parks, churches, universities, museums, lofts, galleries, streets, rooftops, and even parking lots. The city also keeps up a revolving door of festivals and special events: summer jazz, one-act-play marathons, international film series, and musical celebrations from the classical to the avant-garde, to name just a few. It's this unrivaled wealth of culture and art that many New Yorkers cite as the reason why they're here.

Getting Tickets

Scoring tickets to shows and concerts is fairly easy—especially if you have some flexibility with dates and times. The only way to ensure you'll get the seats you want, on the day that you want, at the price you want, is to purchase tickets in advance—and that might be months ahead for a hit show. In general, you'll find that tickets are more readily available for evening performances from Tuesday through Thursday and matinees on Wednesday. Tickets for Friday and Saturday evenings and for weekend matinees are tougher to secure.

What do tickets sell for, anyway? For the most part, the top ticket price for Broadway musicals is about $100; the best seats for Broadway plays can run as high as $90. Off-Broadway show tickets average about $50, while off-off-Broadway shows can be as low as $10. Tickets to an opera start at about $25 for nosebleed seats and soar to more than $200 for those in the orchestra. Classical music concerts range from $25 to $90, depending on the venue. Dance performances are usually $15 to $60.

How to Buy Them

For Broadway shows, off-Broadway shows, and other big-hall events, you can order tickets well in advance through **Telecharge** (☎ 212/239–6200 ⊕ www.telecharge.com) and **Ticketmaster** (☎ 212/307–4100 ⊕ www.ticketmaster.com). For off-Broadway shows, also try **SmartTix** (☎ 212/868–4444 ⊕ www.smarttix.com) or **Ticket Central** (✉ 416 W. 42nd St., between 9th and 10th Aves., Midtown West ☎ 212/279–4200 ⊕ www.ticketcentral.org Ⓜ Subway: A, C, E to 42nd St.).

For opera, classical music, and dance performances, call the box office or order tickets from the venue's Web site. Some people prefer to purchase tickets at the box office, where you can see a seating chart and a ticket seller can advise you where to sit. Brokers can get you last-minute seats, but these go for much more than the price listed on the ticket.

THEATER

Broadway—not the Statue of Liberty or even the Empire State Building—is the city's number-one tourist attraction. The renovation and restoration of some of the city's oldest and grandest theaters on and near 42nd Street has drawn everyone's attention to Times Square. But to fully experience theater in New York, you'll also want to consider the many offerings outside of this hearty center. From splashy musical to austere performance piece, from the Battery to the Bronx, New York has shows for every taste and budget—on just about any night (or day) of the week.

Broadway

Broadway is the magical jewel set into the glittering bauble that is Times Square. There's nothing quite like sitting in a plush seat in one of the Great White Way's beautiful theaters, waiting for the lights to dim and the orchestra to play the first notes of the overture. Performances staged here over the decades have ranged from Shakespearean comedies to Victorian melodramas, risqué burlesque to overwrought operettas, and sophisticated dramas to stylish musicals. And no visit to the city is really complete if you haven't seen at least one Broadway show. So don your best clothes, make your curtain call, and let the magic begin!

Among the 40-odd Broadway theaters are some old playhouses as interesting for their history as for their current offerings. The handsomely renovated Selwyn is now known as the **American Airlines Theatre** (✉ 227 W. 42nd St., between 7th and 8th Aves., Midtown West ☎ 212/719–1300 Ⓜ Subway: A, C, E to 42nd St.). After various reincarna-

15

What's Playing

Check out **Broadway.com** (⊕ www. broadway.com) for the skinny on what's playing, who's starring, and what the reviewers said. In *New York* magazine (⊕ www.newyorkmetro. com), check out the section called "The Week" for hot ticket events. *The New Yorker* (⊕ www.newyorker.com) contains succinct reviews of many performances. The *New York Times* (⊕ www.nytimes.com) has listings in its Thursday and Friday papers, as well as online. The *Village Voice*, (⊕ www.villagevoice.com), a weekly tabloid that comes out on Wednesday, has extensive listings as well.

For unbiased briefs on individual performing arts events in all five boroughs—dance, music, theater, and family-friendly fare—contact **NYC/ONSTAGE** (☎ 212/768–1818). The 24-hour service provides reliable information about performances in English and Spanish. You can easily select events by date as well as by type. If you want to purchase tickets, it patches you through to the appropriate company.

tions as a burlesque hall and pornographic movie house, this Venetian-style theater is now home to the Roundabout Theatre Company, which is acclaimed for its revivals of classic musicals and plays, such as a star-studded production of *12 Angry Men*. The lavish **Hilton Theatre** (⊠ 213 W. 43rd St., between 7th and 8th Aves., Midtown West ☎ 212/207–4100 Ⓜ Subway: A, C, E to 42nd St.) is an 1,839-seat house that combines two classic auditoriums, the Lyric and the Apollo. It incorporates architectural elements from both, adding state-of-the-art sound and lighting equipment.

Disney refurbished the art nouveau **New Amsterdam Theater** (⊠ 214 W. 42nd St., between 7th and 8th Aves., Midtown West ☎ 212/282–2907 Ⓜ Subway: A, C, E to 42nd St.), where Eddie Cantor, Will Rogers, Fanny Brice, and the Ziegfeld Follies once drew crowds. *The Lion King* ruled here for the first nine years of its run. The **St. James** (⊠ 246 W. 44th St., between Broadway and 8th Ave., Midtown West ☎ 212/269–6300 Ⓜ Subway: A, C, E to 42nd St.), current home of Mel Brooks's juggernaut *The Producers*, is where Lauren Bacall was an usherette in the '40s and where a little show called *Oklahoma!* changed musicals forever.

Off-Broadway Theaters

The best theater can often be found far from Times Square. Off- and off-off-Broadway houses are where you can find showcases for emerging playwrights, classic plays performed with new twists, and perennial crowd-pleasers like *Blue Man Group* and *Stomp*. The venues themselves are often found in clusters around the city—in Greenwich Village, the East Village, and the Lower East Side, as well as in Brooklyn neighborhoods like DUMBO and Williamsburg.

At the cozy 178-seat theater belonging to the **Classic Stage Company** (⌧ 136 E. 13th St., between 3rd and 4th Aves., East Village ☎ 212/677–4210 ⊕ www.classicstage.org Ⓜ Subway: 4, 5, 6, L, N, Q, R, W to Union Sq.) you can see revivals of older works—such as Chekhov's *Three Sisters*—that still have relevance today. With the help of its resident acting troupe, **Jean Cocteau Repertory** (⌧ Bouwerie Lane Theatre, 330 Bowery, at Bond St., East Village ☎ 212/677–0060, 212/279–4200 tickets ⊕ www.jeancocteaurep.org Ⓜ Subway: B, D, F, V to Broadway–Lafayette St.; 6 to Bleecker St.) revives classics by playwrights such as Genet, Molière, Beckett, and Brecht.

★ **Manhattan Theatre Club (MTC)** (⌧ Biltmore Theatre, 261 W. 47th St., between Broadway and 8th Ave., Midtown West ☎212/239–6200 ⊕www. mtc-nyc.org Ⓜ Subway: R, W to 49th St.) presents challenging new plays and revivals in both the magnificently restored 650-seat Biltmore Theatre and at City Center. Playwrights Terrence McNally, Richard Greenberg, Elaine May, Craig Lucas, Athol Fugard, August Wilson, and A. R. Gurney have all been produced here. Make sure to call ahead, as most of the tickets go to subscribers. The **New York Theater Workshop** (⌧ 79 E. 4th St., between 2nd and 3rd Aves., East Village ☎ 212/460–5475 ⊕ www.nytw.org Ⓜ Subway: F, V to 2nd Ave.; B, D, F, V to Broadway–Lafayette St.; 6 to Bleecker St.) produces new work by playwrights such as Paul Rudnick, Tony Kushner, and Claudia Shear. Jonathan Larson's musical, *Rent,* debuted here in 1996 three months before moving to Broadway.

Playwrights Horizons (⌧ 416 W. 42nd St., between 9th and 10th Aves., Midtown West ☎ 212/564–1235, 212/279–4200 tickets ⊕ www. playwrightshorizons.org Ⓜ Subway: 1, 2, 7, 9, N, Q, R, W to 42nd St./Times Sq.) also produces new work; shows have included Pulitzer Prize winners such as Wendy Wasserstein's *The Heidi Chronicles* and Stephen Sondheim's *Sunday in the Park with George.* **The Public Theater** (⌧ 425 Lafayette St., south of Astor Pl., East Village ☎ 212/260–2400 ⊕ www.publictheater.org Ⓜ Subway: 6 to Astor Pl.; R, W to 8th St.) presents new, innovative theater. Productions of *Bring In 'Da Noise, Bring In 'Da Funk, A Chorus Line,* and *Hair* that began here all went on to successful Broadway runs. In summer you won't want to miss the annual Shakespeare in the Park performances.

Signature Theatre Company (⌧ Peter Norton Space, 555 W. 42nd St., between 10th and 11th Aves., Midtown West ☎ 212/244–7529 ⊕ www. signaturetheatre.org Ⓜ Subway: 1, 2, 7, 9, N, Q, R, W to 42nd St./Times Sq.) devotes each season to works by a single playwright; past luminaries have included Lanford Wilson and Sam Shepard. The **Vineyard Theatre** (⌧ 108 E. 15th St., between Park Ave. S and Irving Pl., Gramercy ☎ 212/353–0303 ⊕ www.vineyardtheatre.org Ⓜ Subway: 4, 5, 6, L, N, R to 14th St./Union Sq.), one of the best-regarded off-Broadway companies, knows how to pick a winner. Its productions of Paula Vogel's *How I Learned to Drive* and Edward Albee's *Three Tall Women* both won Pulitzers; *Avenue Q* began here and went on to become a Tony-winning smash on Broadway.

15

Feeling Spontaneous?

For tickets at 25% to 50% off the usual price, head to **TKTS** (✉ Duffy Sq., W. 47th St. and Broadway ✉ South St. Seaport, at Front and John Sts., Lower Manhattan Ⓜ Subway: 2, 3 to Fulton St.). The kiosks accept cash and traveler's checks—no credit cards. The Times Square location is open Monday–Saturday 3–8 and Sunday 11–7:30, as well as Wednesday and Saturday at 10–2 for matinee shows. South Street Seaport hours are Monday–Saturday 11–6 and Sunday 11–3:30.

Online deals can be found at **TheaterMania** (⊕ www.theatermania. com) and **Playbill** (⊕ www.playbill. com). You can subscribe to weekly e-mail notices or just log in and troll their sites for Broadway and off-Broadway offers. For discounted tickets you'll need to print the page and present it at the box office.

For long-running shows, including popular hits like *Phantom of the*

Opera, numerous vendors offer discount ticket vouchers. Exchange them at the box office for an actual ticket. The **Broadway Ticket Center** (✉ 1560 Broadway, between W. 46th and W. 47th Sts. ☎ No phone), inside the Times Square Visitors Center, is open Monday–Saturday 9–6 and Sunday 10–3. You can find a selection of discount vouchers here; it also serves as a one-stop shopping place for full-price tickets for most shows.

Need to see the hottest show, no matter what it costs? **Continental Guest Services** (☎ 212/944–8910 ⊕ www.intercharge.com) is one of the best-known ticket brokers in Manhattan. Be warned: tickets can be double the usual price. Order "VIP tickets" from **Broadway Inner Circle** (☎ 866/847–8587 ⊕ www. broadwayinnercircle.com).

Brokers can also get you last-minute seats, but these go for much more than the price listed on the ticket.

Elsewhere in the City

The following theaters host works that are often startling in their originality; their shows typically stretch the boundaries of what's usually found on Broadway and off-Broadway.

The **Brooklyn Academy of Music (BAM)** (✉ Peter Jay Sharp Bldg., 30 Lafayette Ave., between Ashland Pl. and St. Felix St., Fort Greene, Brooklyn ☎ 718/636–4100 ⊕ www.bam.org Ⓜ Subway: C to Lafayette Ave.; 2, 3, 4, 5, Q to Atlantic Ave.) built its considerable reputation on its annual Next Wave Festival. BAM stages avant-garde works year-round. **HERE Arts Center** (✉ 145 6th Ave., between Spring and Broome Sts., SoHo ☎ 212/868–4444 tickets ⊕ www.here.org Ⓜ Subway: C, E to Spring St.), home to Eve Ensler's 1997 Obie winner *The Vagina Monologues*, has three theaters, an art gallery, and a café.

The Kitchen (✉ 512 W. 19th St., between 10th and 11th Aves., Chelsea ☎ 212/255–5793 ⊕ www.thekitchen.org Ⓜ Subway: C, E to 23rd St.) is the place for multimedia performance art. Ellen Stewart, also known as La Mama, founded **La Mama E.T.C.** (✉ 74A E. 4th St., between Bowery and 2nd Ave., East Village ☎ 212/475–7710 ⊕ www.lamama.org Ⓜ Subway: F, V to 2nd Ave.; B, D, F, V to Broadway–Lafayette St.; 6 to Bleecker St.) in a tiny basement space in 1961. Her influential "Experimental Theater Club" has grown to include two theaters and a cabaret, and continues to support new works that cross cultures and all

★ performance disciplines. **P.S.122** (✉ 150 1st Ave., at E. 9th St., East Village ☎ 212/477–5288 ⊕ www.ps122.org Ⓜ Subway: 6 to Astor Pl.), housed in a former public school, has served as an incubator for breakout talent like Spalding Gray and Eric Bogosian.

St. Ann's Warehouse (✉ 38 Water St., between Main and Dock Sts., DUMBO Brooklyn ☎ 718/254–8779 ⊕ www.stannswarehouse.org Ⓜ Subway: A, C to High St.; F to York St.) hosts everything from puppet operas to the Wooster Group's latest theatrical productions. A four-theater cultural complex is home to **Theater for the New City** (✉ 155 1st Ave., between E. 9th and E. 10th Sts., East Village ☎ 212/254–1109 ⊕ www.theaterforthenewcity.net Ⓜ Subway: 6 to Astor Pl.). It puts on 30–40 new American plays each year, including works by Moises Kaufman and Mabou Mines.

Theater for Children

Fodor'sChoice The **New Victory Theater** (✉ 209 W. 42nd St., between 7th and 8th
★ Aves., Midtown West ☎ 212/239–6200 ⊕ www.newvictory.org Ⓜ Subway: 1, 2, 7, 9, N, Q, R, W to 42nd St./Times Sq.) presents plays, music, and dance performances, and even minicircuses in a magnificently restored century-old theater. The 500-seat venue attracts top-notch shows enjoyed by children and their parents. The **Paper Bag Players** (✉ Kaye Playhouse, E. 68th St., between Park and Lexington Aves., Upper East Side ☎ 212/772–4448 ⊕ www.paperbagplayers.org Ⓜ Subway: 6 to 68th St./Hunter College), the country's oldest children's theater group, stages original plays for youngsters under 10.

Tada! (✉ 120 W. 28th St., between 6th and 7th Aves., Chelsea ☎ 212/252–1619 ⊕ www.tadatheater.com Ⓜ Subway: 1 to 28th St.) presents vibrant musical theater pieces performed by children for children. **Theatreworks/USA** (✉ Auditorium at Equitable Tower, 787 7th Ave., between W. 51st and W. 52nd Sts., Midtown West ☎ 212/647–1100 Ⓜ Subway: 1 to 79th St.) mounts original productions based on well-known children's books. Popular shows have included *The Adventures of Curious George* and *Junie B. Jones.*

The Circus

New York's wonderful **Big Apple Circus** (✉ Lincoln Center Plaza, Upper West Side ☎ 212/721–6500 or 800/922–3772 ⊕ www.bigapplecircus.org) is a must-see. It entertains kids and their families both in New York and in shows around the country. The world-renowned **Cirque du Soleil** (⊕ www.cirquedusoleil.com) visits New York with some regularity. Cirque offers sophisticated productions—and pricey tickets to go with them—but their acrobatics and atmosphere always amaze.

15

Puppet Shows

Puppet Playhouse (✉ Asphalt Green, 555 E. 90th St., between York and East End Aves., Upper East Side ☎ 212/369–8890 ⊕ www.asphaltgreen. org Ⓜ Subway: 4, 5, 6 to 86th St.) presents original shows every Saturday; hand puppets, marionettes, rod puppets, or shadow puppets could all make an appearance. Finely detailed wooden marionettes and hand puppets are on the bill at **Puppetworks** (✉ 338 6th Ave., at 4th St., Park Slope, Brooklyn ☎ 718/965–3391 ⊕ www.puppetworks.org). Familiar childhood tales like *Little Red Riding Hood* and *Peter and the Wolf* come to life in this 75-seat neighborhood theater.

The **Swedish Cottage Marionette Theater** (✉ Swedish Cottage, W. Park Dr., north of W. 79th St., Central Park ☎ 212/988–9093 ⊕ www. centralparknyc.org Ⓜ Subway: B, C to 79th St.) entertains children year-round. The charming wooden 100-seat state-of-the-art playhouse (originally brought here from Sweden in 1876) presents classics like *Hansel and Gretel, Cinderella,* and *Jack and the Beanstalk*. Latino arts and culture are celebrated with a sly sense of humor at the bilingual **Teatro SEA @ Los Kabayitos Puppet & Children's Theater** (✉ Clemente Soto Vélez Cultural & Educational Center, 107 Suffolk St., between Delancey and Rivington Sts., Lower East Side ☎ 212/260–4080 Ext.14 ⊕ www.seany.org Ⓜ Subway: F to Delancey St.; J, M, Z to Essex St.). All shows in this 50-seat venue are presented in English and Spanish, and you may even see the *Three Little Pigs* dancing to salsa music.

MUSIC

"Gentlemen," conductor Serge Koussevitzky once told the assembled Boston Symphony Orchestra, "maybe it's good enough for Cleveland or Cincinnati, but it's not good enough for New York." In a nutshell he described New York's central position in the musical world. New York possesses the country's oldest symphony orchestra (the New York Philharmonic) as well as three renowned conservatories (the Juilliard School, the Manhattan School of Music, and Mannes College of Music). For more than a century, the best orchestras have made this a principal stop on their tours. The city is also a mecca for an astonishing variety of musicians playing everything from Eastern European klezmer to Senegalese percussion.

Concert Halls

The **Brooklyn Academy of Music (BAM)** (✉ 30 Lafayette Ave., between Ashland Pl. and St. Felix St., Fort Greene, Brooklyn ☎ 718/636–4100 ⊕ www.bam.org Ⓜ Subway: C to Lafayette Ave.; 2, 3, 4, 5, Q to Atlantic Ave.) has two spaces with extraordinary acoustics: the 2,100-seat Howard Gilman Opera House and the smaller Harvey Theater. Both host contemporary and experimental works by renowned artists such as Philip Glass, Laurie Anderson, and Robert Wilson. BAM is also the performing home of the **Brooklyn Philharmonic** (☎ 718/488–5700 ⊕ www.brooklynphilharmonic.org), with a reputation for having the city's most adventurous symphonic programming.

FodorśChoice   **Carnegie Hall** (✉ 881 7th Ave., at W. 57th St., Midtown West ☎ 212/
★   247–7800 ⊕ www.carnegiehall.org Ⓜ Subway: N, Q, R, W to 57th St.;
B, D, E to 7th Ave.) is one of the best venues—anywhere—to hear classical music. The world's top orchestras sound their best because of the
incomparable acoustics of the 2,804-seat **Stern Auditorium.** So do
smaller ensembles and soloists such as soprano Renée Fleming. The subterranean **Zankel Hall,** which also has excellent acoustics, attracts performers such as the Kronos Quartet and Youssou N'Dour. Many young
talents make their New York debuts in the **Weill Recital Hall.**

★   **Lincoln Center for the Performing Arts** (✉ W. 62nd to W. 66th Sts., Broadway to Amsterdam Ave., Upper West Side ☎ 212/546–2656 ⊕ www.
lincolncenter.org Ⓜ Subway: 1 to 66th St./Lincoln Center) is the city's
musical nerve center, especially when it comes to classical music. Intimate Alice Tully Hall hosts the **Chamber Music Society of Lincoln Center** (☎ 212/875–5788 ⊕ www.chambermusicsociety.org,) and is
considered to be as acoustically perfect as a concert hall can get. With
2,738 seats, the formal and U-shaped Avery Fisher Hall presents the
world's great musicians. The concert hall is home to the **New York Philharmonic** (☎ 212/875–5656 ⊕ newyorkphilharmonic.org), one of the
world's finest symphony orchestras. Lorin Maazel conducts performances from late September to early June. In addition, the orchestra occasionally schedules bargain-price weeknight "rush hour" performances
at 6:45 PM and Saturday matinee concerts at 2 PM; orchestra rehearsals
at 9:45 AM are open to the public on selected weekday mornings (usually Wednesday or Thursday) for $15.

15

Other Venues

Aaron Davis Hall (✉ City College, W. 135th St. at Convent Ave.,
Harlem ☎ 212/650–7100 ⊕ www.aarondavishall.org Ⓜ Subway: 1
to 137th St.) is an uptown venue for jazz and world music, hosting
groups like the Abbey Lincoln Quartet. **The Cloisters** (✉ Fort Tryon
Park, Morningside Heights ☎ 212/923–3700 information, 212/650–
2290 tickets ⊕ www.metmuseum.org Ⓜ Subway: A to 190th St.) offers matinee performances of sacred and secular music from the Middle Ages, all of which take place within the authentic ambience of a
12th-century Spanish chapel. **Frederick P. Rose Hall** (✉ Broadway, at
W. 60th St., Upper West Side ☎ 212/258–9800 ⊕ www.jalc.org
Ⓜ Subway: A, B, C, D, 1 to 59th St./Columbus Circle), overlooking
Central Park, is the home of **Jazz at Lincoln Center,** which features
the Lincoln Center Jazz Orchestra under the direction of Wynton
Marsalis. Guest artists range from roots and swing to bop and beyond,
in two swank performance spaces and a club.

The **Knitting Factory** (✉ 74 Leonard St., between Broadway and Church
St., TriBeCa ☎ 212/219–3055 ⊕ www.knittingfactory.com Ⓜ Subway: 1 to Franklin St.) is a funky, three-story complex that hosts an eclectic assortment of downtown musicians. The emphasis is on jazz of all
types. **Merkin Concert Hall** (✉ Kaufman Center, 129 W. 67th St., between
Broadway and Amsterdam Ave., Upper West Side ☎ 212/501–3330

⊕ www.kaufman-center.org/ Ⓜ Subway: 1 to 66th St./Lincoln Center) is a lovely, acoustically advanced 450-seater that presents chamber pieces; it's also a fine spot for jazz, world, and new music. The **Metropolitan Museum of Art** (✉ 1000 5th Ave., at E. 82nd St., Upper East Side ☎ 212/570–3949 ⊕ www.metmuseum.org Ⓜ Subway: 4, 5, 6 to 86th St.) has three stages—the Temple of Dendur; the Grace Rainey Rogers Auditorium; and the Medieval Sculpture Hall—with concerts by leading classical and jazz musicians. Other than Friday and Saturday evenings, when the museum is open late, access is through the street-level entrance at East 83rd Street and 5th Avenue.

The **Miller Theatre** (✉ Columbia University, Broadway at W. 116th St., Morningside Heights ☎ 212/854–1633 ⊕ www.millertheatre.com Ⓜ Subway: 1 to 116th St.) presents a varied program of cutting-edge jazz, classical, and modern music. **Symphony Space** (✉ 2537 Broadway, at W. 95th St., Upper West Side ☎ 212/864–5400 ⊕ www.symphonyspace.org Ⓜ Subway: 1, 2, 3 to 96th St.) presents a fine range of chamber, new music, folk, and pop music in its Peter Jay Sharp Theatre. Well-known soloists and chamber music groups perform in Kaufmann Concert Hall at the **Tisch Center for the Arts** (✉ 92nd St. Y, 1395 Lexington Ave., at E. 92nd St., Upper East Side ☎ 212/996–1100 ⊕ www.92ndsty.org Ⓜ Subway: 6 to 96th St.).

The Town Hall (✉ 123 W. 43rd St., between 6th and 7th Aves., Midtown West ☎ 212/840–2824 ⊕ www.the-townhall-nyc.org Ⓜ Subway: 1, 2, A, C, E, N, R to Times Sq.) hosts programs of jazz and world music. The **Tribeca Performing Arts Center** (✉ 199 Chambers St., at Greenwich St., TriBeCa ☎ 212/220–1460 ⊕ www.tribecapac.org Ⓜ Subway: A, C, E to Chambers St.) celebrates jazz in all its forms; "Highlights in Jazz" and "Lost Jazz Shrines" are two of its special series.

OPERA

The greatest singers in the world all clamor to test their mettle at the Metropolitan Opera, where they can work alongside internationally admired directors and designers. The Met's lavish productions are far from cheap, unless you buy standing-room tickets. The New York City Opera, housed adjacent to the Met in Lincoln Center, is also a fine company, and its ticket prices are lower.

Major Companies

FodorśChoice
★

The titan of American opera companies, the **Metropolitan Opera** (✉ W. 62nd to W. 66th Sts., Broadway to Amsterdam Ave., Upper West Side ☎ 212/362–6000 ⊕ www.metopera.org Ⓜ Subway: 1 to 66th St./Lincoln Center) brings the world's leading singers to its grand stage at Lincoln Center from October to April. Under the direction of James Levine, the company's music director and principal conductor, the orchestra rivals the world's finest symphonies. All performances, including those sung in English, are unobtrusively subtitled on small screens on the back of the seat in front of you. As for standing room, the Met is the rare venue that makes these tickets (195 of them) available in advance. They go on sale at their box office Saturday at 10 AM for the following week, and usually cost $15 to $20.

Although not as famous as its next-door neighbor, the **New York City Opera** (✉ W. 62nd to W. 66th Sts., Broadway to Amsterdam Ave., Upper West Side ☎ 212/870–5570 ⊕ www.nycopera.com Ⓜ Subway: 1 to 66th St./Lincoln Center) draws a crowd to its performances at the New York State Theater. Founded in 1943, the company is known as well for its innovative and diverse repertory. Under the leadership of artistic director Paul Kellogg, City Opera stages rarely seen baroque operas such as *Acis and Galatea* and *Rinaldo,* adventurous new works such as Jack Beeson's *Lizzie Borden,* and beloved classics such as *La Bohème, Carmen,* and the like. Placido Domingo and Beverly Sills began their careers at City Opera; a new generation of great voices is following in their footsteps. City Opera performs September to November and March to April. All performances of foreign-language operas have supertitles—line-by-line English translations—displayed above the stage.

15

Smaller Companies

☺ In New York, small opera companies can be very, very good. The **Amato Opera Theatre** (✉ 319 Bowery, at E. 2nd St., East Village ☎ 212/228–8200 ⊕ www.amato.org Ⓜ Subway: B, D, F, V to Broadway–Lafayette St.; 6 to Bleecker St.; F, V to 2nd Ave.), which claims to be the world's smallest opera house, is a well-established showcase for rising singers and performs classics by Verdi, Mozart, and others. To top it off, it has reasonable prices. "Opera-in-Brief" matinees are tailored to children. The **Gotham Chamber Opera** (✉ Harry de Jur Playhouse, 466 Grand St., at Pitt St., Lower East Side ☎ 212/868–4460 ⊕ www. gothamchamberopera.org Ⓜ Subway: F to Delancey St.; J, M, Z to Essex St.) presents small-scale chamber works. Featuring American premieres of little-known works (such as Handel's *Arianna in Creta*), the 350-seat Georgian Revival theater makes a fine home for pieces from the baroque era to the present. The **New York Gilbert & Sullivan Players** (☎ 212/769–1000 ⊕ www.nygasp.org) present lively productions of operettas such as *The Pirates of Penzance* and *The Mikado* plus rarities like Sullivan's last completed work, *The Rose of Persia.*

DANCE

In a city that seems never to stop moving, dance is a thriving art form. Ballet aficionados are well served in the grand performing arts centers, and those in search of something different will find it in all corners of the city, including more experimental venues downtown.

Ballet

The **American Ballet Theatre (ABT)** (☎ 212/477–3030 ⊕ www.abt.org) is renowned for its brilliant renditions of the great 19th-century classics (*Swan Lake, Giselle, The Sleeping Beauty,* and *La Bayardère*) as well as its more modern repertoire, including works by such 20th-century masters as George Balanchine, Jerome Robbins, and Agnes de Mille.

Since its founding in 1940, the company has nurtured a stellar array of dancers, including Mikhail Baryshnikov, Natalia Makarova, Rudolf Nureyev, Gelsey Kirkland, and Cynthia Gregory. The ballet has two New York seasons—eight weeks beginning in May at its home in the Metropolitan Opera House and two weeks in the fall (usually October) at City Center.

☾ With more than 90 dancers, the **New York City Ballet** (☎ 212/870–5570 ⊕ www.nycballet.com) has an unmatched repertoire of 20th-century works. Its fall season, which runs from mid-November through December, includes the beloved annual production of George Balanchine's *The Nutcracker.* Its spring season runs from April through June; an eight-week Winter Repertory program runs in January and February. The company continues to stress the works themselves rather than individual performers, although that hasn't stopped a number of principal dancers (such as Kyra Nichols, Darci Kistler, Damian Woetzel, and Jock Soto) from earning kudos. The company performs in Lincoln Center's New York State Theater. Family-friendly Saturday matinees are offered throughout the regular season.

Fodor's Choice ★

Modern Dance

The world's most innovative dance companies perform in New York throughout the year, especially in fall and spring, showcasing the thrilling work of such legendary choreographers as Twyla Tharp, Martha Graham, Alvin Ailey, Mark Morris, and Merce Cunningham.

At **City Center** (⊠ 131 W. 55th St., between 6th and 7th Aves., Midtown West ☎ 212/581–1212 ⊕ www.citycenter.org Ⓜ Subway: N, Q, R, W to 57th St./7th Ave.; F to 57th St./6th Ave.), marvelous modern dance troupes such as **Alvin Ailey American Dance Theater** (www.alvinailey. org) and **Paul Taylor Dance Company** (www.ptdc.org) hold sway. **Dance Theater Workshop** (⊠ 219 W. 19th St., between 7th and 8th Aves., Chelsea ☎ 212/924–0077 ⊕ www.dtw.org Ⓜ Subway: 1 to 23rd St.) serves as a laboratory for new choreographers. Performances here are enhanced by a wonderfully renovated space.

★

Danspace Project (⊠ 131 E. 10th St., at 2nd Ave., East Village ☎ 212/674–8194 ⊕ www.danspaceproject.org Ⓜ Subway: 6 to Astor Pl.), founded to foster the work of independent choreographers such as Bill T. Jones, sponsors a series of avant-garde performances that runs from September through June. The **Harkness Dance Project** (⊠ The Duke on 42nd St., 229 W. 42nd St., between 8th and 9th Aves., Midtown West ☎ 212/415–5500 ⊕ www.92ndsty.org Ⓜ Subway: A, C, E to 42nd St.) presents contemporary dance troupes at reasonable prices. In a former art deco movie house in Chelsea, the 500-seat **Joyce Theater** (⊠ 175 8th Ave., at W. 19th St., Chelsea ☎ 212/242–0800 ⊕ www.joyce.org Ⓜ Subway: A, C, E to 14th St.; L to 8th Ave.) has superb sight lines and presents the full spectrum of contemporary dance. The buoyant **David Parsons** (www.parsonsdance.org) is a regular on the lineup. The Joyce is also known for its special family matinees.

★ ☾

Performing Arts Centers

Fodor'sChoice ★ America's oldest performing arts center, the **Brooklyn Academy of Music (BAM)** (✉ Peter Jay Sharp Bldg., 30 Lafayette Ave., between Ashland Pl. and St. Felix St., Fort Greene, Brooklyn ☎ 718/636–4100 ⊕ www.bam.org Ⓜ Subway: C to Lafayette Ave.; 2, 3, 4, 5, Q to Atlantic Ave.), opened in 1859. BAM has a reputation for daring and innovative dance, music, opera, and theater productions, and for its creative film programming. The main performance spaces are the 2,100-seat Howard Gilman Opera House, a white-brick Renaissance Revival palace built in 1908 and now spectacularly restored, and the 874-seat Harvey Theater, an updated 1904 theater a block away at 651 Fulton Street. BAM's annual Next Wave Festival in fall draws a global audience for its cutting-edge productions. Year-round you can catch other live performances (including the Brooklyn Philharmonic) or a movie at BAM Rose Cinemas, or grab a bite—or a meal—at the BAMcafé, which becomes a cabaret venue Thursday through Saturday nights. The **BAMbus** (Whitney Museum of American Art at Altria ✉ 120 Park Ave., at E. 42nd St., Midtown East ☎ 718/636–4100) provides round-trip transportation from Manhattan one hour prior to a performance. Reservations are required.

Carnegie Hall (✉ 881 7th Ave., at W. 57th St., Midtown West ☎ 212/247–7800 ⊕ www.carnegiehall.org Ⓜ Subway: N, Q, R, W to 57th St.; B, D, E to 7th Ave.) is one of the world's most famous concert halls. Virtually every important musician of the 20th century performed in this century-old Italian Renaissance–style building, often at the peak of his or her creative powers. Tchaikovsky conducted the opening-night concert on May 5, 1891, Leonard Bernstein had his famous debut here, and Vladimir Horowitz made his historic return to the concert stage here as well. Performances are given in the grand 2,804-seat Isaac Stern Auditorium, the 268-seat Weill Recital Hall, and the stylish and acoustically superb 644-seat Judy and Arthur Zankel Hall on the lower level. Although the emphasis is on classical music, Carnegie Hall also hosts jazz, pop, cabaret, and folk music concerts.

City Center (✉ 131 W. 55th St., between 6th and 7th Aves., Midtown West ☎ 212/581–1212 ⊕ www.citycenter.org Ⓜ Subway: N, Q, R, W to 57th St./7th Ave.; F to 57th St./6th Ave.) has a neo-Moorish look (no surprise, as it was built in 1923 by the Ancient and Accepted Order of the Mystic Shrine). Saved from demolition in 1943 by Mayor Fiorello La Guardia, its lush 2,750-seat main stage is the primary New York performance space for the Alvin Ailey and Martha Graham dance companies, as well as the New York Gilbert & Sullivan Players. The hugely popular Encores! musicals-in-concert series is staged here, as are annual appearances by other major dance troupes, including the American Ballet Theatre. The smaller City Center Stages I and II host a number of productions and programs of the Manhattan Theatre Club.

15

★ **Lincoln Center for the Performing Arts** (✉ W. 62nd to W. 66th Sts., Broadway to Amsterdam Ave., Upper West Side ☎ 212/546–2656 ⊕ www. lincolncenter.org Ⓜ Subway: 1 to 66th St./Lincoln Center) is a 16-acre complex comprising the Metropolitan Opera House (which also presents American Ballet Theatre), the New York State Theater (home of the New York City Opera and New York City Ballet), Avery Fisher Hall (home of the New York Philharmonic), Alice Tully Hall, the Vivian Beaumont Theater, the Mitzi E. Newhouse Theater, the New York Public Library for the Performing Arts, and the Walter Reade Theater. The predominantly travertine-clad buildings were designed by multiple architects, all of whom applied a relatively classical aesthetic to the angular modern structures. Philharmonic Hall (now Avery Fisher), designed by Max Abramovitz, broke ground first, opening in 1962. The 2,738-seat hall's improved acoustics came with a Philip Johnson and John Burgee renovation in 1976. In 1965 came Eero Saarinen's finely scaled theaters, the 1,047-seat Beaumont (a Broadway house), and the 334-seat Newhouse (an off-Broadway house). The 3,800-seat Met, with its Austrian-crystal chandeliers and Marc Chagall paintings, premiered in 1966. Alice Tully Hall, designed by Pietro Belluschi for a music and film audience of 1,096, followed in 1969.

Seasonal festivals abound and often utilize the huge open plaza surrounding the center's famous fountain and adjacent Damrosch Park. **Midsummer Night Swing** (☎ 212/875–5766) is a monthlong dance party that runs almost every night of the week starting in late June on the central plaza. Dancers swing, hustle, polka, merengue, salsa, tango, and more to the beat of live bands. The **Lincoln Center Festival** (☎ 212/875–5928) runs for three weeks, usually in July. Its programs include classical and contemporary music concerts, dance, film, and theater works. Lincoln Center's longest-running classical series is the August **Mostly Mozart Festival** (☎ 212/875–5399), featuring the music of Mozart and other classical favorites. Lincoln Center itself expanded in 2004 with an outpost dedicated to **Jazz at Lincoln Center,** just a few blocks south of the main campus, in Rafael Viñoly's crisply modern Frederick P. Rose Hall. Stages there feature the 1,100-seat Rose Theater and The Allen Room, an elegant and intimate 310–500 seater.

The **Skirball Center for the Performing Arts at NYU** (✉ 566 LaGuardia Pl., Washington Sq. Park S, Greenwich Village ☎ 212/992–8484 ⊕ www. skirballcenter.nyu.edu Ⓜ Subway: A, B, C, D, E, F, V to W. 4th St./Washington Sq.) is a sleekly designed—Kevin Roche was the architect—877-seat space for music, dance, and theater. Since its 2003 inaugural season its rich spectrum of performances have included Mabou Mines's experimental theater, the Eos Orchestra, and Ballet Hispanico.

Symphony Space (✉ 2537 Broadway, at W. 95th St., Upper West Side ☎ 212/864–5400 ⊕ www.symphonyspace.org Ⓜ Subway: 1, 2, 3 to 96th St.) presents a fabulously diverse program of contemporary dance, musical performances, film, literature events, and theater for adults, with a full complement of similar programming for children and families. Both renovated in 2002, its 760-seat Peter Jay Sharp Theatre adjoins the 176-seat Leonard Nimoy Thalia Theatre.

FILM & TELEVISION

Film

On any given week New York City theaters screen all the major new releases, classics renowned and obscure, foreign films, small independent flicks, hard-to-find documentaries, and cutting-edge video and experimental works. The theaters themselves run the gamut from sleek multiplexes with large screens and rows of stadium seating to shoe-box-size screening rooms with room for barely a hundred people.

Getting Tickets

New York may be the global capital of cineasts, so sold-out shows are common. It's a good idea to purchase tickets in advance. For evening performances, especially for new releases, a good rule of thumb is to get to the box office at least three or four hours ahead of showtime. If you're seeing a blockbuster, you'll need even more lead time. Save arriving around showtime for smaller films, or something's that been out awhile; in those cases you may still have to hunt for the few remaining seats.

Oddly enough, no one phone or online ticket service handles advance ticket purchase for all of the city's screens. For chains, and even many independent houses, you'll need to contact one of the following to purchase tickets ahead with a credit card: **Fandango** (☎ 800/555–8355 ⊕ www.fandango.com) handles Landmark, Loew's, and Regal theaters. Tickets for the remaining chains, including United Artists and Clearview, may be purchased from **AOLMovieFone** (☎ 212/777–3456 ⊕ www.moviefone.com). There's usually a service charge of $1 to $2 for phone or online orders. Note that tickets for some smaller venues—usually independent theaters—may be purchased through that venue's Web site.

Tickets to most theaters in New York are $10 to $10.50. Although there are no bargain matinees in Manhattan, discounts for seniors and children are usually available. For quick access to showtimes and locations, try the ticket services listed above or the *New York Times* (⊕ www.nytimes. com). *Time Out New York* (⊕ www.timeoutny.com) is especially good for its "Alternatives & Revivals" listings.

First-Run Movies

Wherever you are in New York City, you usually don't have to walk far to find a movie theater showing recent releases. And "first-run" in New York is as much about documentaries and foreign films as it is about commercial blockbusters.

Foreign and independent films are screened at the **Angelika Film Center** (✉ 18 W. Houston St., at Mercer St., Greenwich Village ☎ 212/995–2000 ⊕ www.angelikafilmcenter.com Ⓜ Subway: B, D, F, V to Broadway–Lafayette St.; 6 to Bleecker St.). It's incredibly popular, despite its tunnel-like theaters and truncated screens. The upstairs café has food that's a cut above that at your average multiplex. **Cinema Village** (✉ 22 E. 12th St., between University Pl. and 5th Ave., Greenwich Village ☎212/

15

Tribeca Film Festival

FILM FESTIVALS OF INTERNATIONAL REPUTE abound in New York City. But nothing compares with the unusually warm welcome the Tribeca Film Festival received when it was launched in spring 2002.

Born of the aftermath of the World Trade Center disaster, the festival—the brainchild of Jane Rosenthal, Robert De Niro, and Craig Hatkoff—was conceived as a means to not only boost the devastated economy of Lower Manhattan, but to celebrate the city for its preeminence as a filmmaking center. Seeking to capture the excitement and power of film in a fresh way, Rosenthal and De Niro programmed a rich assortment of major studio premieres with independent films, documentaries, restored classics, shorts, and children's films. To keep it lively, the festival also added panel discussions, outdoor screenings, big-name concerts, and a street fair. TriBeCa residents and merchants gave the project wholehearted support, and the first annual Tribeca Film Festival took off.

Since then, the festival has grown into a 10-day event covering two weekends, usually in April or May. It screens about 250 films, from as many as 42 different countries. Prestigious premieres are a hallmark of the festival (*Star Wars: Attack of the Clones* was the starter for 2002; *United 93* launched the 2006 festival). The impressive panels of jurors, chosen from a wealth of arts luminaries, have included the likes of actress Glenn Close and architect Richard Meier. Illuminating panel discussions with actors, directors, producers, cinematographers, and participants from all corners of the film and performing arts world get past the glamour and glitz and focus on the nitty-gritty of filmmaking.

Each year sees a special theme. In 2003 a series on the 10 most influential African-American films of the 20th century celebrated the Black Filmmaker Foundation's 25th anniversary. Outdoor events—like the Family Outdoor Street Fair (with live puppet shows, a "garden of kites," and more), and Tribeca Drive-in Theater (with outdoor screenings of old favorites like *West Side Story*)—contribute to the special neighborhood atmosphere that pervades the festival.

FILM FESTIVAL PLANNER

When: Annually in April/May, for 10 days, covering two weekends.

Where: Screenings and other festival events take place in venues around the city.

Family Features: The Family Festival screens about 15 family films over each of the two weekends of the main festival. Family Outdoor Street Fair takes place on one Saturday.

Tickets, Passes, and Packages: Box office and phone-purchase options are posted on the Web site prior to the festival; you may also register online for e-mail updates. Tickets and discount packages may be purchased online about four to five weeks in advance.

Information: ⊠ *Box Office: 443 Greenwich St., at Vestry St., TriBeCa* ⊕ *www.tribecafilmfestival.org* ☎ *212/321-7400 or 866/941-3378* Ⓜ *Subway: 1 to Franklin St.*

924–3363 Ⓜ Subway: 4, 5, 6, L, N, Q, R, W to 14th St./Union Sq.) has three tiny screening rooms (with surprisingly good sight lines) that show a smart selection of hard-to-find first-run domestic and foreign films. Within a sleekly renovated space that was once a vaudeville theater, **Landmark's Sunshine Cinema** (✉ 143 E. Houston St., between 1st and 2nd Aves., Lower East Side ☎ 212/358–7709 ⊕ www.landmarktheatres.com Ⓜ Subway: F, V to 2nd Ave.) has seven decent-size screens showing mostly independent films.

A comfortable, modern multiplex with good-size screens, **Lincoln Plaza Cinemas** (✉ 1886 Broadway, at 62nd St., Upper West Side ☎ 212/757–2280 Ⓜ Subway: 1 to 66th St./Lincoln Center) is especially big on foreign-language film. Just off Central Park, **The Paris** (✉ 4 W. 58th St., between 5th and 6th Aves., Midtown West ☎ 212/688–3800 Ⓜ Subway: F to 57th St.) is a rare single-screen showcase for new movies, usually those with a limited release.

Movie lovers adore the **Quad Cinema** (✉ 34 W. 13th St., between 5th and 6th Aves., Greenwich Village ☎ 212/255–8800 ⊕ www.quadcinema. com Ⓜ Subway: 4, 5, 6, L, N, Q, R, W to 14th St./Union Sq.), which plays first-run art and foreign films on four very small screens. The **Village East Cinemas** (✉ 181–189 2nd Ave., at E. 12th St., East Village ☎ 212/529–6799 Ⓜ Subway: 6 to Astor Pl.) is housed in a restored Yiddish theater. Catch a film that's screening upstairs and check out the Moorish-style decor.

★ To experience the last of the old-fashioned movie palaces, head to the **Ziegfeld** (✉ 141 W. 54th St., between 6th and 7th Aves., Midtown West ☎ 212/765–7600 Ⓜ Subway: N, Q, R, W to 57th St.). Its crimson decor, good sight lines, and solid sound system make it a special place to view the latest blockbusters; grand-opening galas often take place here as well.

Alternative Spaces, Revival Films & Festivals

New Yorkers have such a ravenous appetite for celluloid that even barely publicized independent projects can expect a full house, as can revivals of obscure movies and foreign film. Besides traditional movie houses, these gems frequently screen at museums, cultural societies, and other performance spaces, such as the **French Institute** (☎ 212/355–6100 ⊕ www.fiaf.org), **Scandinavia House** (☎ 212/879–9779 ⊕ www.scandinaviahouse.org), **Instituto Cervantes** (☎ 212/308–7720 ⊕ www.cervantes.org), and even branches of the **New York Public Library** (⊕ www.nypl.org).

And then there are the festivals. Fans flock to annual events like the **Asian American International Film Festival** (⊕ www.asiancinevision.org) in July; the **Margaret Mead Film & Video Festival** (⊕ www.amnh.org) in November; the **Tribeca Film Festival** (⇨ Tribeca Film Festival); and of course the iconic **New York Film Festival** (see below), which is held—with all the appropriate razzle-dazzle—at Lincoln Center every fall.

Fodor'sChoice
★ In addition to premiering new releases, **Film Forum** (✉ 209 W. Houston St., between 6th Ave. and Varick St., Greenwich Village ☎ 212/727–8110 ⊕ www.filmforum.com Ⓜ Subway: 1 to Houston St.), a nonprofit

theater with three small screening rooms, hosts movies by directors from Hitchcock and Samuel Fuller to Bernardo Bertolucci and Wim Wenders; genre festivals featuring film noir, silents, and even samuri films; and newly restored prints of classic works. The small café serves tasty cakes and fresh-popped popcorn.

The **American Museum of the Moving Image** (✉ 35th Ave. at 36th St., Astoria, Queens ☎ 718/784–0077 ⊕ www.ammi.org Ⓜ Subway: G, R, V to Steinway St.) presents special series, such as a Martin Scorsese marathon. Admission is free to museum patrons; films are shown Friday to Sunday evenings and weekend afternoons. Dedicated to preserving and exhibiting independent and avant-garde film, **Anthology Film Archives** (✉ 32 2nd Ave., at E. 2nd St., East Village ☎ 212/505–5181 ⊕ www.anthologyfilmarchives.org Ⓜ Subway: F to 2nd Ave.) consists of two small screening rooms in a renovated courthouse. This is a good place for hard-to-find films and videos. The Essential Cinema series delves into the works of filmmakers like Stan Brakhage, Robert Bresson, and more. Part of the Brooklyn Academy of Music, the four-screen **BAM Rose Cinemas** (✉ 30 Lafayette Ave., between Ashland Pl. and St. Felix St., Fort Greene, Brooklyn ☎ 718/636–4100 ⊕ www.bam.org Ⓜ Subway: C to Lafayette Ave.; 2, 3, 4, 5, Q to Atlantic Ave.) offers first-run foreign-language and popular independent films, along with BAMcinématek, an eclectic repertory series.

The **Museum of Modern Art (MoMA)** (✉ 11 W. 53rd St., between 5th and 6th Aves., Midtown East ☎ 212/708–9400 ⊕ www.moma.org Ⓜ Subway: E, V to 5th Ave./53rd St.; B, D, E to 7th Ave.; B, D, F, V to 47th–50th Sts./Rockefeller Center) has some of the most engaging international repertory you'll find anywhere; it's shown in the state-of-the-art Roy and Niuta Titus Theaters 1 and 2. Movie tickets are available at the museum for same-day screenings (a limited number are released up to one week in advance for an extra fee); they're free if you have purchased museum admission.

New York's leading annual film event is the **New York Film Festival** (☎ 212/875–5050 ⊕ www.filmlinc.com Ⓜ Subway: 1 to 66th St./Lincoln Center), sponsored by the Film Society of Lincoln Center every September and October. Screenings—which feature many U.S. premieres—are announced more than a month in advance and sell out quickly. Venues are Lincoln Center's Alice Tully Hall (with opening and closing night extravaganzas in Avery Fisher Hall) and Walter Reade Theater. Each March, the Film Society joins forces with MoMA to produce **New Directors–New Films** (☎ 212/875–5050 ⊕ www.filmlinc.com), giving up-and-coming directors their moment to flicker.

★ The comfortable, 268-seat auditorium of the **Walter Reade Theater** (✉ Lincoln Center, 165 W. 65th St., between Broadway and Amsterdam Ave., Upper West Side ☎ 212/875–5600 ⊕ www.filmlinc.com Ⓜ Subway: 1 to 66th St./Lincoln Center) has what may be the best sight lines in town. It presents series devoted to "the best in world cinema" that run the gamut from silents (with occasional live organ accompaniment) and documentaries to retrospectives and recent releases, often on the same theme or from the same country. Purchase tickets at the box office or online up to four weeks in advance.

Film for Children

Several museums sponsor special programs aimed at families and children, including the Museum of Modern Art, the Museum of Television and Radio, and the American Museum of the Moving Image. Children marvel at the nature and science films shown on the huge screen in the **IMAX Theater** (⊠ Central Park W and W. 79th St., Upper West Side ☎ 212/769–5034 ⊕ www.amnh.org Ⓜ Subway: B, C to 79th St.) at the American Museum of Natural History. At the **Loews Lincoln Square Theater** (⊠ 1998 Broadway, at W. 68th St., Upper West Side ☎ 212/336–5020 Ⓜ Subway: 1 to 66th St./Lincoln Center) audience members strap on high-tech headgear for the specially created 3-D films.

Each March, the two-week-long **New York International Children's Film Festival** (☎ 212/349–0330 ⊕ www.gkids.com) screens 60 new films and videos for ages 3–18 at venues around the city. The **SonyWonder Technology Lab** (⊠ 550 Madison Ave., between E. 55th and E. 56th Sts., Midtown East ☎ 212/833–7858 weekdays ⊕ www.sonywondertechlab.com Ⓜ Subway: E, V to 53rd St.), an interactive experience that uses multimedia presentations to demystify technology, shows free films for kids. Selections range from G-rated holiday classics to PG-13 thrillers. Children under 18 must be accompanied by an adult. Call ahead for reserved tickets.

Television

Tickets to tapings of television shows are free, but can be difficult to come by on short notice. For the most popular shows, like *The Daily Show with Jon Stewart*, the request backlog is so deep you might even have to wait a few months before they'll accept any new ones. Most shows accept advance requests by e-mail, phone, or online. Same-day standby tickets are often available but be prepared to wait in line for several hours, sometimes starting at 5 or 6 AM, depending on how hot the show is, or the wattage of the celebrity involved.

The Daily Show with Jon Stewart. With a knowing smirk, the amiable Jon Stewart pokes fun at news headlines on this half-hour cable show. The program tapes from Monday through Thursday, and free tickets can be obtained by calling the studio. Those under 18 may not attend. ⊠ *733 11th Ave., between W. 51st and W. 52nd Sts., Midtown West* ☎ *212/586–2477* ⊕ *www.comedycentral.com* Ⓜ *Subway: C, E to 50th St.*

Emeril Live. The exuberant chef's main show is taped at the Food Network Studios in Chelsea Market. A ticket lottery is held just once a year, and you must check their Web site for the schedule and then apply online. ⊠ *Food Network Studios, 75 9th Ave., at W. 16th St., Chelsea* ⊕ *www.foodnetwork.com* Ⓜ *Subway: A, C, E to 14th St.*

Good Morning America. Diane Sawyer and Charles Gibson co-anchor this early morning news and entertainment stalwart. *GMA* airs live, Monday through Friday from 7 AM to 9 AM, and ticket requests (online only) must be sent four to six months in advance. ⊠ *Times Sq., at W. 44th St. and Broadway, Midtown West* ☎ *212/456–7384* ⊕ *www.*

goodmorningamerica.com Ⓜ *Subway: 1, 2, 3, N, Q, R, W to 42nd St./Times Sq.*

Late Night with Conan O'Brien. This popular late-night variety show attracts consistently interesting guests. Call the **Ticket Information Line** (☎ 212/664–3056) for a maximum of four tickets in advance. Single standby tickets are available on taping days—Tuesday through Friday—at the W. 49th Street side of 30 Rockefeller Plaza; arrive before 9 AM. No one under 16 may attend. ✉ *NBC Studios, 30 Rockefeller Plaza, between W. 49th and W. 50th Sts., Midtown West* Ⓜ *Subway: B, D, F, V to 47th–50th Sts./Rockefeller Center.*

The Late Show with David Letterman. Letterman's famously offbeat humor is as quirky as ever. Call 212/247–6497 at 11 AM on tape days—Monday through Thursday—for standby tickets. For advance tickets (two maximum), you can submit a request online or fill out an application in person at the theater. No one under 18 may attend. ✉ *Ed Sullivan Theater, 1697 Broadway, between W. 53rd and W. 54th Sts., Midtown West* ☎ *212/975–5853* ⊕ *www.lateshowaudience.com* Ⓜ *Subway: 1, C, E to 50th St.*

Live! with Regis and Kelly. The sparks fly on this morning program, which books an eclectic roster of guests. Standby tickets become available weekdays at 7 AM at the **ABC Studios** (✉ W. 66th St., between Columbus Ave. and Central Park W., Upper West Side). Otherwise, write for tickets (four tickets maximum) a full year in advance. Children under 10 may not attend. ⌖ *Live Tickets, Ansonia Station, Box 230777, 10023* ☎ *212/456–3054* Ⓜ *Subway: 1 to 66th St./Lincoln Center.*

Saturday Night Live. Influential from the start, *SNL* continues to captivate audiences. Standby tickets—only one per person—are distributed at 7 AM on the day of the show at the West 50th Street entrance to 30 Rockefeller Plaza. You may ask for a ticket for either the dress rehearsal (8 PM) or the live show (11:30 PM). Requests for advance tickets (two per applicant) must be submitted by e-mail only in August to snltickets@nbc.com; recipients are determined by lottery. No one under 16 may attend. ✉ *NBC Studios, Saturday Night Live, 30 Rockefeller Plaza, between W. 49th and W. 50th Sts., Midtown West* ☎ *212/664–3056* Ⓜ *Subway: B, D, F, V to 47th–50th Sts./Rockefeller Center.*

Today. America's first morning talk/news show airs weekdays from 7 AM to 10 AM in the glass-enclosed, ground-level NBC studio across from its original home at 30 Rockefeller Plaza. You may well be spotted on TV by friends back home while you're standing behind anchors Meredith Vieira and Matt Lauer. ✉ *Rockefeller Plaza at W. 49th St., Midtown West* Ⓜ *Subway: B, D, F, V to 47th–50th Sts./Rockefeller Center.*

The View. The Emmy-winning chitchat and celebrity gossip show has been a hit since it launched in 1997. Join Star Jones Reynolds, Rosie O'Donnell, Joy Behar, Elisabeth Hasselbeck, and, occasionally, Barbara Walters for an often outrageous hour of live television, Monday through Friday from 11 AM to noon. Ticket requests (postcards only) must be sent four to six months in advance; you may also request tickets online. No one under 18 will be admitted. ✉ *Tickets, The View, 320 W. 66th St., at West End Ave., Upper West Side, 10023* ⊕ *www.abc.com* Ⓜ *Subway: 1 to 66th St.*

READINGS & LECTURES

Literary figures great and small share their work at dozens of readings held each week in New York. From formal venues like the New York Public Library, where you might hear well-known panelists comment on local architecture, to the casual Nuyorican Poets Café, where obscure writers show up for an open-mike night, you'll find New Yorkers sharing their thoughts, insight, and their most creative work.

Time Out New York has the most comprehensive listing of reading and lectures; also check out the *New York Press* and the *Village Voice*. Admission to most of these events is usually under $15, although it might go up to $25–$35 for certain luminaries. At small venues they are often free.

Series & Special Events

The **Center for Architecture** (✉ 536 LaGuardia Pl., between W. 3rd and Bleecker Sts., Greenwich Village ☎ 212/683–0023 ⊕ www.aiany.org Ⓜ Subway: A, B, C, D, E, F, V to W. 4th St.), a glass-faced gallery, hosts lively discussions (often accompanied by films or other visuals) on topics like cutting-edge architecture in Mexico City or visionary American architects of the 1930s.

In the historic Villard Houses, the nonprofit **Municipal Art Society** (✉ Urban Center, 457 Madison Ave., at E. 51st St., Midtown East ☎ 212/935–3960 ⊕ www.mas.org Ⓜ Subway: 6 to 51st St.; E, F to 53rd St.; B, D, F, V to 47th–50th Sts./Rockefeller Center) is dedicated to preserving New York's architectural treasures. As well as leading the city's most interesting walking tours, it presents a free lecture series at noon on Thursday. Well-known authors speak on topics ranging from subway ornamentation to houses of worship. The **New York Public Library** (✉ 5th Ave. at 42nd St., Midtown West ☎ 212/869–8089 ⊕ www.nypl. org Ⓜ Subway: B, D, F, V to 42nd St.) presents a rich program of lectures and reading events here, as well as at many of the branches throughout the city.

★ Authors, poets, and playwrights, as well as political pundits, industry leaders, and media bigwigs, take the stage at the **92nd Street Y** (✉ 1395 Lexington Ave., at E. 92nd St., Upper East Side ☎ 212/415–5500 ⊕ www.92ndsty.org Ⓜ Subway: 6 to 96th St.). The **Makor/Steinhardt Center** (✉ 35 W. 67th St., between Central Park W and Columbus Ave., Upper West Side ☎ 212/601–1000 ⊕ www.makor.org Ⓜ Subway: 1 to 66th St./Lincoln Center), part of the 92nd Street Y, is a sleek cultural arts center with excellent literary events geared toward people in their twenties and thirties. **Symphony Space** (✉ 2537 Broadway, at W. 95th St., Upper West Side ☎ 212/864–5400 ⊕ www.symphonyspace. org Ⓜ Subway: 1, 2, 3 to 96th St.) hosts literary events, including the famed "Selected Shorts" series of stories read by prominent actors and broadcast on National Public Radio.

15

Fiction & Poetry Readings

★ "Poetry Czar" Bob Holman's **Bowery Poetry Club** (⊠ 308 Bowery, at Bleecker St., Lower East Side ☎ 212/614–0505 ⊕ www.bowerypoetry. com Ⓜ Subway: B, D, F, V to Broadway–Lafayette St.; 6 to Bleecker St.) serves up coffee and knishes along with its ingenious poetry events. Expect every permutation of the spoken word—and art and music, too. The **Cornelia Street Café** (⊠ 29 Cornelia St., between W. 4th and Bleecker Sts., Greenwich Village ☎ 212/989–9319 ⊕ www.poetz.com Ⓜ Subway: A, B, C, D, E, F, V to W. 4th St./Washington Sq.) is a good bet for original poetry and fiction readings.

Dixon Place (⊠ 258 Bowery, between E. Houston and Prince Sts., Lower East Side ☎ 212/219–0736 ⊕ www.dixonplace.org Ⓜ Subway: F, V to 2nd Ave.), "NYC's laboratory for performance," hosts readings of fiction, science fiction, and poetry, plus the celebrated "Performance Works-in-Progress" series that showcases theater and performance-art pieces. One of the most influential and avant-garde series around town is "Line Reading," which explores how the visual arts and literature interrelate. Readings are held at 6:30 on Tuesday evenings at the **Drawing Center** (⊠ 35 Wooster St., between Grand and Broome Sts., SoHo ☎ 212/219–2166 ⊕ www.drawingcenter.org Ⓜ Subway: R, W to Prince St.), an art space in SoHo.

★ Amid its collection of 45,000 titles, the **Housing Works Used Book Café** (⊠ 126 Crosby St., between E. Houston and Prince Sts., SoHo ☎ 212/ 334–3324 ⊕ www.housingworks.org/usedbookcafe Ⓜ Subway: R, W to Prince St.; B, D, F, V to Broadway–Lafayette St.; 6 to Bleecker St.) sponsors readings—often by breakout local authors or from books on social issues—and a monthly acoustic music series called "Live from Home." Events at this cozy nonprofit store and café benefit homeless people with HIV/AIDS. **The Kitchen** (⊠ 512 W. 19th St., between 10th and 11th Aves., Chelsea ☎ 212/255–5793 ⊕ www.thekitchen.org Ⓜ Subway: C, E to 23rd St.) presents readings from the edges of the world of arts and literature.

The **Lesbian, Gay, Bisexual & Transgender Community Center** (⊠ 208 W. 13th St., between 6th and 7th Aves., West Village ☎ 212/620–7310 ⊕ www.gaycenter.org Ⓜ Subway: F, V to 14th St.) sponsors "In Our Own Write," a series of readings by up-and-coming gay writers, as well as "Second Tuesdays," which features more established writers. The **Nuyorican Poets Café** (⊠ 236 E. 3rd St., between Aves. B and C, East Village ☎ 212/505–8183 ⊕ www.nuyorican.org Ⓜ Subway: F, V to 2nd Ave.) schedules daily readings, open-mike events, and screenplay readings, and hosts the granddaddy of the current spoken word scene, the "Friday Night Poetry Slam."

Nightlife

WORD OF MOUTH

"Listening to jazz at the [Village Vanguard] was like going back in time to the days of John Coltrane." —jeninnyc

"What always impresses me about New York is the endless array of themed bars. Upscale, divey, rock and roll, lounges—the list goes on." —dan1900

"For a cool, upscale/trendy spot, I suggest Brandy Library in Tribeca. If you feel like splurging, ask for a Lagavulin 12." —Gekko

Updated by
Adam Kowit
and Sara
Marcus

Every night of the week you'll find New Yorkers going out on the town. Nobody here waits for the weekend—in fact, many people prefer to party during the week when there's actually room to belly up to the bar. If word gets out that a hot band is playing in a bar on a Tuesday, or if a well-known DJ takes over a dance club on a Thursday, you can be assured these places will be packed like the Saturday nights in most other towns.

The nightlife scene is still largely downtown—in drab-by-day dives in the East Village and Lower East Side, classic jazz joints in the West Village, and the Meatpacking District's and Chelsea's see-and-be-seen clubs—but you don't have to go below 14th Street to have a good time. Midtown, especially around Hell's Kitchen, is developing a reputation, and there are still plenty of preppy hangouts on the Upper East and Upper West sides. And across the East River, Brooklyn's Williamsburg neighborhood has become the place for artists, hipsters, and rock-and-roll fans.

There are enough committed club crawlers to support venues for almost every idiosyncratic taste. But keep in mind that *when* you go is just as important as *where* you go. A spot is only hot when it's hopping—a club that is packed at 11 might empty out by midnight, and a bar that raged last night may be completely empty tonight. These days, night prowlers are more loyal to floating parties, DJs, and club promoters than to any specific addresses.

For the totally hip, **Paper** magazine has a good list of the roving parties and the best of the fashionable crowd's hangouts. You can check their online nightlife guide, PM (NYC), via their Web site, ⊕ www.papermag. com. Another streetwise mag, *The L Magazine* (⊕ www.thelmagazine. com), lists what's happening day by day at many of the city's lounges and clubs, as well as dance and comedy performances. The **Village Voice,** a free weekly newspaper, probably has more club ads than any other rag in the world. Also check out the **New York Press,** which has pages and pages of nightlife listings. The **New York Times** has listings of cabaret shows. You may also get good tips from an in-the-know hotel concierge. Keep in mind that events change almost weekly, and venue life spans are often measured in months, not years. Phone ahead to make sure your target hasn't closed or turned into a trendy polka hall (although that might be fun, too).

Most clubs charge a cover, which can range from $5 to $25 or more, depending on the venue and the night. Be sure to take some cash, because many places don't accept credit cards. (Nothing will enrage the people behind you in line like whipping out the plastic.) Remember to dress properly, something that is easily accomplished by wearing black and leaving your beat-up sneakers at home. Smoking is prohibited in all enclosed public places in New York City, including restaurants and bars. Some bars have gardens or fully enclosed smoking rooms for those who wish to light up, but in most places you'll have to step outside.

CLUBS & ENTERTAINMENT

Classic New York

16

These are the crème de la crème of New York's social venues, distinguished by an unbeatable locale, a unique style, a rich history, or a combination of the three. Reservations are essential, and many places' dress codes require jackets or prohibit jeans, so call ahead to make sure your threads are up to snuff. Admission to the performance venues can be steep—cover charges for big-name acts go as high as $100—but in many cases you can snag a less pricey spot at the bar if you show up several hours before showtime.

Fodor'sChoice ★ **The Carlyle.** The hotel's discreetly sophisticated Café Carlyle hosts such top cabaret performers as Betty Buckley, Elaine Stritch, Barbara Cook, and Ute Lemper. Stop by on a Monday night and take in Woody Allen, who swings on the clarinet with his New Orleans Jazz Band. Bemelmans Bar, with murals by the author of the *Madeline* books, features a rotating cast of pianist-singers. ⊠ *35 E. 76th St., between Madison and Park Aves., Upper East Side* ☎ *212/744–1600* ⊕ *www.thecarlyle.com* Ⓜ *Subway: 6 to 77th St.*

Four Seasons. New York City (and American) history is made here in Philip Johnson's landmarked temple of modern design. Watch for politicos and media moguls in the Grill Room, or enjoy the changing foliage in the romantic pool room. ⊠ *99 E. 52nd St., between Park and Lexington Aves., Midtown East* ☎ *212/754–9494* Ⓜ *Subway: E, V to Lexington Ave./53rd St.; 6 to 51st St.*

Lever House. This spot on the garden level of one of the city's most stylish office buildings was an instant hit, drawing a younger and faster crowd than its closest competition, the Four Seasons. People flock here to see and be seen in a futuristic, honeycombed setting where just about everybody looks like they're somebody. ⊠ *390 Park Ave., at 53rd St. (entrance on 53rd St.), Midtown East* ☎ *212/888–2700* Ⓜ *Subway: E, V to Lexington Ave./53rd St.; 6 to 51st St.*

Oak Room. One of the great classic cabaret venues, the Oak Room is formal (jackets are mandatory; ties are the norm). You might find the hopelessly romantic singer Andrea Marcovicci, among other top-notch performers, crooning here. ⊠ *Algonquin Hotel, 59 W. 44th St., near 6th Ave., Midtown West* ☎ *212/840–6800* Ⓜ *Subway: B, D, F, V to 42nd St.*

Rainbow Room. Several times a month, this romantic institution on the NBC building's 65th floor opens its doors to the public for a dinner dance, where a revolving dance floor and 12-piece orchestra delight swing-dancers and tangoists. Call ahead for the dance schedule, or enjoy dinner and drinks at the Rainbow Grill any night of the week. ⊠ *30 Rockefeller Plaza, between 5th and 6th Aves., Midtown West* ☎ *212/632–5000* ⊕ *www.rainbowroom.com* Ⓜ *Subway: B, D, F, V to 47th–50th Sts./Rockefeller Center.*

Rise. Ensconced on the 14th floor of the Ritz-Carlton New York, this swank lounge has stunning views of the harbor and the Statue of Liberty. In summer you can sit outside and watch the sun set over America. ⊠ *2 West St., at Battery Pl., Lower Manhattan* ☎ *917/790–2626* Ⓜ *Subway: 1 to Rector St.*

River Café. If you're looking for an eminently romantic locale, head out to this restaurant hidden at the foot of the Brooklyn Bridge. The bar has smashing views of the downtown Manhattan skyline across the East River, and after cocktails you can enjoy a very good meal. ⊠ *1 Water St., near Old Fulton St., DUMBO, Brooklyn* ☎ *718/522–5200* Ⓜ *Subway: F to York St.; A, C to High St.*

★ **'21' Club.** A row of lawn jockeys welcomes you to this former speakeasy, celebrated for attracting famous writers and movie stars through most of the past century. Privilege and whimsy are mixed together here: the well tailored order excellent American cuisine in the lively dining room and enjoy drinks next to a roaring fire in the cozy front lounge. ⊠ *21 W. 52nd St., between 5th and 6th Aves., Midtown West* ☎ *212/582–7200* Ⓜ *Subway: B, D, F, V to 47–50th Sts./Rockefeller Center.*

Dance Clubs & DJ Venues

The city's hottest clubs aren't just places to hit the dance floor. Revelers come to socialize with friends, to find romance, to show off their newest clothes, and to be photographed rubbing shoulders with stars. Some clubs are cavernous spaces filled with a churning sea of bodies. Others are like small get-togethers in a basement belonging to a friend of a friend of a friend. Parties—dance and otherwise—with DJs, salsa bands, and themes ranging from '60s bossa-nova nights to soul-and-drag galas have been known to crop up at such places as Irving Plaza and Opaline. A few places host parties only on weekends, so call ahead, or come up with an alternate plan. Also be aware that weeknight parties don't make allowances for early-morning risers: the crowd often doesn't arrive until well after midnight.

Apt. Music is the priority at this polished club, where some of the world's top DJs—those who elevate record spinning to a high art—ply their trade in a tiny, luminous basement room. At the restaurant up-

Room with a View

In New York you can take in the sights without leaving your bar stool. The pot of gold at the **Rainbow Room** (✉ 30 Rockefeller Plaza, between 5th and 6th Aves., Midtown West ☎ 212/632–5000) is the view from the 65th floor of Rockefeller Center. The **River Café** (✉ 1 Water St., near Old Fulton St., DUMBO, Brooklyn ☎ 718/522–5200) under the Brooklyn Bridge, has unobstructed views of the city skyline. The only sight more beautiful than the skyline is its reflection in the East River at the **Water Club** (✉ 500 E. 30th St., at FDR Dr., Midtown East ☎ 212/683–3333).

From the 23rd floor of the Peninsula Hotel, you can nearly touch the sky at the **Pen Top Bar & Lounge** (✉ 700 5th Ave., at W. 55th St., Midtown West ☎ 212/956–2888). Within the Ritz-Carlton New York, **Rise** (✉ 2 West St., at Battery Pl., Lower Manhattan ☎ 917/790–2626) has clear sight lines to the Statue of Liberty.

16

stairs you can order tapas or sip a cocktail while reclining on a double bed. ✉ *419 W. 13th St., between 9th Ave. and Washington St., Meatpacking District* ☎ *212/414–4245* Ⓜ *Subway: A, C, E to 14th St.; L to 8th Ave.*

Avalon. This deconsecrated church, which gained notoriety during the '90s as the Limelight, has been reborn yet again as a staple of the city's club scene. Sunday is gay night. ✉ *47 W. 20th St., at 6th Ave. (enter on W. 20th St.), Chelsea* ☎ *212/807–7780* Ⓜ *Subway: F, V to 23rd St.*

Canal Room. Polished wood floors, elegant potted palms, and stylish Barcelona chairs distinguish this intimate club. Musicians perform here several times a month (the Roots and Tony Bennett were two recent acts), but they also come just to enjoy themselves. The owners' record business connections, a spectacular speaker system, and DJs who keep the crowds moving have drawn the likes of Mariah Carey, Missy Elliott, and Diddy. ✉ *285 West Broadway, at Canal St., TriBeCa* ☎ *212/941–8100* ⊕ *www.canalroom.com* Ⓜ *Subway: A, C, E to Canal St.*

China Club. This symbol of high-living excess occupies an 8,000-square-foot tri-level space in Hell's Kitchen, with the exclusionary velvet ropes still in place. ✉ *268 W. 47th St., between Broadway and 8th Ave., Midtown West* ☎ *212/398–3800* Ⓜ *Subway: R, W to 49th St.*

Cielo. A relatively mature crowd gravitates to this small, super-fashionable Meatpacking District destination to sip cocktails and groove to soulful house music on the sunken dance floor. ✉ *18 Little West 12th St., between 9th Ave. and Washington St., Meatpacking District* ☎ *212/645–5700* Ⓜ *Subway: A, C, E to 14th St.*

Club Shelter. This enormous space is home to some of the best dancing in the city, which is no surprise, as it takes its name and low-key attitude from a long-running after-hours party that was once found at the old TriBeCa club Vinyl. ✉ *20 W. 39th St., between 5th and 6th Aves., Midtown West* ☎ *212/719–4479* Ⓜ *Subway: B, D, F, V to 42nd St.*

★ **Crobar.** Well-heeled professionals and nightlife scenesters alike flock to this high-gloss megaclub. Enter through an art gallery, descend into a packed cocktail lounge, then proceed through a luminous white tunnel with curved walls to the cavernous dance floor. If you prefer, you can find a getaway from the main action in one of the smaller rooms off to the side. ☒ *530 W. 28th St., between 10th and 11th Aves., Chelsea* ☎*212/ 629–9000* Ⓜ *Subway: 1 to 28th St.*

Culture Club. From the Pac-man illustration on the outside awning to the interior murals of Adam Ant and the cast from *The Breakfast Club*, this is the place for those desperately seeking a dose of '80s nostalgia. ☒ *179 Varick St., between Charlton and King Sts., SoHo* ☎ *212/243–1999* Ⓜ *Subway: 1 to Houston St.*

Fodor'sChoice **Exit.** This extravagant multilevel club has everything from a massive dance
★ floor to an outdoor patio. A-list DJs spin for an enthusiastic crowd that often includes a hip-hop star or two. ☒ *610 W. 56th St., between 11th and 12th Aves., Midtown West* ☎ *212/582–8282* Ⓜ *Subway: 1, A, B, C, D to 59th St.*

Luke & Leroy. The real action at this stylish spot is upstairs on the dance floor, where Madonna has spun records and Boy George has partied. A small bar on the first story serves up quality cocktails to a fashionable mixed crowd. ☒ *21 7th Ave. S., at Leroy St., Greenwich Village* ☎ *212/645–0004* Ⓜ *Subway: 1 to Christopher St.*

Roxy. Most nights this huge hall is a standard bridge-and-tunnel magnet, mostly attracting those who live in other New York boroughs and in New Jersey and occasionally drawing a mixed rave crowd. Gay men rule the roost on Saturday, and Wednesday is roller-disco night. Call ahead for special events. ☒ *515 W. 18th St., between 10th and 11th Aves., Chelsea* ☎ *212/645–5157* Ⓜ *Subway: A, C, E to 14th St.*

Sapphire. The party gets started late at this lively Lower East Side hangout, but the well-known DJs keep the diverse crowd going with deep house, hip-hop, soul, funk, and Latin music. Ultrafriendly patrons might drag you onto the floor to strut your stuff. Drinks are half price before 10 PM. ☒ *249 Eldridge St., between E. Houston and Stanton Sts., Lower East Side* ☎ *212/777–5153* Ⓜ *Subway: F, V to 2nd Ave.*

Subtonic Lounge. Experimental DJs present thought-provoking sound collages and electro-acoustic collaborations several nights a week in this basement bar, downstairs from the live music venue Tonic. At this former kosher winery, you can enjoy the music from a comfortable seat inside a massive wine barrel. ☒ *107 Norfolk St., between Delancey and Rivington Sts., Lower East Side* ☎ *212/358–7501* ⊕ *www.tonicnyc.com* Ⓜ *Subway: F, J, M to Delancey St.*

Table 50. Musicheads who like to dance while enjoying obscure house tracks pack into this elegant DJ venue on weekends. The centrally located dance floor and excellent sound system make it a rare beast in this city of byzantine club-licensing regulations: a quality dance club of modest proportions. ☒ *643 Broadway, at Bleecker St., Greenwich Village* ☎ *212/253–2560* Ⓜ *Subway: 6 to Bleecker St.; B, D, F, V to Broadway–Lafayette St.*

Jazz Clubs

With more than a dozen jazz nightclubs, Greenwich Village is still New York's jazz mecca, although many venues are strewn around town.

Cover charges can be steep, and it's common for a venue to present multiple sets each evening.

Arthur's Tavern. Unless there's a festival in town, you won't find many big names jamming here. But you will find nightly performances, without a cover charge, amid the dark-wood ambience of old Greenwich Village. The acts tend to be bluesier and funkier for the late shows. ☒ *57 Grove St., between 7th Ave. S and Bleecker St., Greenwich Village* ☎ *212/675–6879* Ⓜ *Subway: 1 to Christopher St.*

Birdland. This place gets its name from saxophone great Charlie Parker, so expect serious musicians such as John Pizzarelli, Joe Lovano, and Christian McBride. The dining room serves moderately priced American fare with a Cajun accent. If you sit at the bar your cover charge includes a drink. ☒ *315 W. 44th St., between 8th and 9th Aves., Midtown West* ☎ *212/581–3080* ⊕ *www.birdlandjazz.com* Ⓜ *Subway: 1, 2, 3, 7, N, Q, R, W to 42nd St./Times Sq.*

★ **Blue Note.** Considered by many to be the jazz capital of the world, the Blue Note could see on an average month Spyro Gyra, Ron Carter, and Jon Hendricks. Expect a steep cover charge except on Monday, when record labels promote their artists' recent releases for an average ticket price of about $10. ☒ *131 W. 3rd St., near 6th Ave., Greenwich Village* ☎ *212/475–8592* ⊕ *www.bluenote.net/newyork* Ⓜ *Subway: A, B, C, D, E, F, V to W. 4th St.*

Garage Restaurant & Café. There's no cover *and* no minimum at this trilevel Village hot spot, where you can hear live jazz seven nights a week; a fireplace sets the mood upstairs. ☒ *99 7th Ave. S, between Bleecker and Christopher Sts., Greenwich Village* ☎ *212/645–0600* Ⓜ *Subway: 1 to Christopher St./Sheridan Sq.*

Iridium. This cozy, top-notch club is a sure bet for big-name talent like McCoy Tyner, Michael Brecker, and Kenny Baron. The sight lines are good, and the sound system was designed with the help of Les Paul, the inventor of the solid-body electric guitar, who takes the stage on Monday night. The formidable Mingus Big Band, led by the late bassist's widow, owns Tuesday. ☒ *1650 Broadway, at W. 51st St., Midtown West* ☎ *212/582–2121* ⊕ *www.iridiumjazzclub.com* Ⓜ *Subway: 1 to 50th St.; R, W to 49th St.*

Jazz at Lincoln Center. This confusingly titled complex, located several blocks south of Lincoln Center at Columbus Circle, includes two auditoriums, a jazz café, rehearsal studios, classrooms, and a Jazz Hall of Fame. ☒ *Time Warner Center, Broadway at W. 60th St., Midtown West* ☎ *212/258–9800* ⊕ *www.jalc.org* Ⓜ *Subway: A, B, C, D, 1 to 59th St.*

Jazz Standard. This sizable underground room draws the top names in the business. Part of Danny Meyer's Southern-food restaurant Blue Smoke, it's one of the few spots where you can get dry-rubbed ribs to go with your bebop. Bring the kids for the Jazz Standard Youth Orchestra concerts every Sunday afternoon. ☒ *116 E. 27th St., between Park and Lexington Aves., Murray Hill* ☎*212/576–2232* ⊕*www.jazzstandard. net* Ⓜ *Subway: 6 to 28th St.*

Knickerbocker. Piano-and-bass duets are on the menu on Friday and Saturday nights at this old-fashioned steak house, a longtime staple of the

Continued on page 290

NEW YORK NIGHTS by Sarah Gold

New York is the city that never sleeps—and when you come to visit, you might not, either. It doesn't matter if you're a disco dolly, a lounge lizard, a class act, or a rock n' roll headbanger; the nightlife options here will give you your fix. So pop some No-Doz, take a late-afternoon nap, do whatever it is you have to do to get ready. You can catch up on your sleep next time you're in Cleveland.

A NIGHT OF JAZZ
GREENWICH VILLAGE

It's no surprise that the Village, a legendary haunt for Beat poets, avant-garde performance artists, and countercultural politicos, is also a hotbed of jazz. This neighborhood's vibe is all about experimentation and free expression . . . so put on your dark glasses and your artfully distressed leather jacket, grab your Gauloises (for the sidewalk, anyhow), and get ready to improvise.

Making advance reservations may not entirely jibe with jazz's spontaneous sensibility, but it's not a bad idea, especially if you want to get into some of the Village's best-known venues. Booking weeks ahead for a table at the **Blue Note** will only ensure that you have a memorable night;

you'll be able to see jazz greats like Herbie Hancock, McCoy Tyner, Cassandra Wilson, and David Sanborn right up close from one of the cramped 30-or-so tables. This is also a great place to have dinner; the Note serves up some notable barbecue.

Another spot that's worth pre-booking for is the nearby "Carnegie Hall of Cool," the **Village Vanguard**. John Coltrane and Sonny Rollins used to jam here regularly, and modern-day jazz giants like Wynton Marsalis still make appearances. When the headline act's not huge, though, you can sometimes wander in at 8 (when the doors open) and still get a seat.

OUTSIDE THE BOX

Although the Village has the highest concentration of jazz clubs in the city, there are a few fabulous venues that are worth the cab fare uptown. **Smoke**, way up near Columbia University, is a true jazz-lover's haven; Sunday nights, when the scatting and vocal acrobatics of top vocalists fill the tiny space, are not to be missed. A less arduous trip to Midtown will bring you to **Iridium**, where guitar great Les Paul plays on Monday nights. A bit farther south near Times Square is the famous **Birdland**, named for the late great Charlie Parker; the cover charge here includes a drink.

With smaller, less famous Village venues, you can afford to extemporize a bit; these places are almost always packed with nodding jazz fans, but you can show up without a reservation (often without paying a cover charge) and still catch some top-quality music. The **Garage Restaurant & Café** is one such spot; you can have a steak dinner in front of the giant fireplace while listening to great local trios and quartets (or, on Monday, big-band swing). The **Knickerbocker Bar & Grill** is another place where you can satisfy both your gastronomic and musical appetites; on Friday and Saturday nights live ensembles play while diners dig in to seared Pacific salmon and rack of lamb.

Arthur's Tavern is another no-cover venue, with a coolly grotty dark-wood (or, more accurately, dark wood–veneer) ambience; you can chill out in the piano bar or catch a jazz trio from one of the dining room tables. **Sweet Rhythm,** also a great choice, is even greater if you're a starving student; on Monday nights, a jazz ensemble from the nearby New School University's music program takes the stage, and anyone with student ID gets in free. If you're in the mood for an especially creative challenge, you can try visiting **Chumley's** (212/675–4449), the famous onetime speakeasy that's just a few blocks away. The address is 86 Bedford Street, but the fun part is looking for the unmarked entrance, which is actually on Barrow Street. There's no jazz performers here, but you'll likely find yourself wandering, concentrating, and looking for the right place to jump in . . . what could be jazzier than that?

For addresses and phone numbers of these venues, see the main **Nightlife** listings in this chapter.

A NIGHT OF CLUBBING
THE MEATPACKING DISTRICT & CHELSEA

Ever since Studio 54 hung its first mirrored ball and ignited a citywide disco inferno, New York has been a playground for the young late-night club set. The '70s may be over; the multilevel megaclubs of the '80s and pulsing raves of the '90s are now largely in the past. But if DJ-spun grooves and packed dance floors are what you love, there's still plenty of New York spots where you can party like it's 1999 (or 1989, or 1979).

It's best to start your long evening with some sustenance, so your first stop—no earlier than 9 PM—should be one of the Meatpacking District's super-hip eateries. **Spice Market** and **Pastis** serve excellent food (Asian and French bistro, respectively), and will also ease you into the clubland vibe; they both have killer cocktails, a see-and-be-seen crowd, and, more often than not, lines of people waiting to get inside (advance reservations are highly recommended).

Once you've lingered until a more respectable hour (11 PM or so), meander over to one of the neighborhood's more civilized clubs. **APT's** basement room, where funk and soul are in heavy rotation, has just a narrow slice of dance floor between the bar and a seating area; it's a safe place to do some preliminary head-bobbing. **The Double Seven** (418 W.

HOW TO GET IN

Unless you're a model, movie star, or recording artist, there's no surefire way to make sure you'll get past the velvet ropes at top New York clubs. But there are some things you can do to increase your chances.

14th St., 212/981–9099) a few blocks away, plays ambient trip-hop, which is good for subtle booty-shaking as well as for talking over fruity cocktails. Nearby **Cielo,** where deep-house DJs reign, is another relatively chill and intimate place to dance. The smaller size, though, means exclusivity; you'll need to impress the door staff to get in.

When the wee hours arrive, it's time to get serious; New York's biggest and wildest clubs only really come alive around 1 AM Many of these are in Chelsea, the next neighborhood over and just a short cab ride away from the Meatpacking District. **Crobar,** widely considered to be the best club in the city, is a maze of rooms and bars surrounding a huge main dance floor, where pumping techno is spun by the likes of Paul Van Dyk and Danny Tenaglia. **Marquee** (289 10th Ave., 646/473–0202) is similarly fabulous and similarly hard to get into; the DJs aren't as major here but the beautiful-people ratio is high. If you can get in, **Cain** (544 W. 27th St., 212/947–8000), with its safari theme and house beats, is prime celebrity-spotting territory (Lindsey Lohan is a reported regular). And if you're prone to '80s nostalgia, the slightly-farther-east **Happy Valley** (14 E. 27th St., 212/481–2628) is your best bet. Here, the mirrored ceilings, go-go dancers, and outrageous outfits (or lack thereof) bring to mind the good old days of Danceteria and Palladium. Most of these clubs stay open until 5 or 6 AM, which means you'll stagger out into the sunlight just as the rest of the city's waking up.

■ Arranging for bottle service is an expensive proposition, but one of the only ways to reserve a table for you and your friends inside a club. Bottle service means you agree to purchase an entire bottle (or several) of, say, vodka or champagne, which is then used to serve your group. You won't be paying liquor-store prices, though; a bottle of Grey Goose with mixers can easily set you back a couple hundred dollars.

■ Surrounding yourself with good-looking, sexily dressed females is always a good bet when you're trying to catch the doorman's eye (if he's straight, that is). Club owners and managers want to keep their venues packed with eye candy—so if you're a girl, pour yourself into tight jeans, stiletto heels, and some sort of dressy top, and get your friends together. If you're a guy, do your best to cobble together an entourage, and steer clear of sports jerseys, baseball hats, sneakers...in general, wear something that would make your mom feel proud.

■ Showing up early may make you feel like a loser—nothing's more dismal than a cavernous, empty dance floor—but it's easier to get in when the door staff is simply trying to get bodies inside.

■ Cash has been known to part even the most stubborn velvet ropes like the Red Sea. So if you're not famous, good-looking, or rich enough for bottle service, you can always try slipping the doorman a $20 (do it discreetly, and don't consider it a guarantee).

For addresses and phone numbers of these venues, see the main **Nightlife** listings in this chapter.

A NIGHT OF ELEGANCE
MIDTOWN, THE UPPER EAST & UPPER WEST SIDES

I like the city air
I like to drink of it
The more I know New York
The more I think of it

It hardly matters that these Cole Porter lyrics (from "I Happen to Like New York") are decades old. The nighttime Manhattan that Porter knew—of moonlit walks in Central Park, swanky piano bars, chandeliered dining rooms, and dancing cheek to cheek—is still alive and kicking. Some of the city's classiest nightspots have been around since Porter himself was a regular, and some are more newly minted—but all of them share a sense of old-world, uniquely New York style.

Begin your evening by dining among the swirling murals (or just sipping a cocktail in the cozy bar) at **Café des Artistes.** The dining room, with its well-heeled clientele (Katie Couric and Natalie Portman have been spotted here), gleaming crystal, and impeccable waitstaff, is the embodiment of old-school opulence; accordingly, you'll need reservations to beat the upper-crusty regulars to a table. If you prefer a clubbier, less formal but

still elegant meal, try the **'21' Club,** where you can enjoy one of the city's best, and most expensive, hamburgers ($30) in front of a roaring fire. (Ties and jackets are required for men at both of these restaurants at dinnertime.)

For post-dinner drinks, head east to the gorgeously wood-paneled **Campbell Apartment**—a small warren of rooms inside Grand Central that was once the private residence of a New York tycoon. Cocktails with Fitzgerald-esque names will literally help get you in the spirit. Or, head north to the posh Carlyle Hotel, where

CLASSIC CHAMPAGNE COCKTAILS

If sipping bubbly while gazing at the New York skyline sounds like the epitome of class, you're in luck; many of the elegant nightspots listed here serve up signature champagne cocktails. Here are a few you can try:

The Fountain of Youth, at Café des Artistes: Poire Williams-scented champagne with spiced pear

The Flapper's Delight, at the Campbell Apartment: Champagne with papaya juice and amaretto

The Champino, at Bemelmans Bar: A concoction made with champagne, Campari, and sweet vermouth

The Kir Royale, at the Rainbow Room: An oldie but goodie, made with champagne and crème de cassis

you can slip into one of the leather banquettes and listen to live piano music at **Bemelmans Bar.** The Carlyle is also home to the famed **Café Carlyle,** where big-name entertainers like Ute Lemper and Eartha Kitt dazzle in an intimate setting (you'll need to buy tickets well in advance for these shows). Another nearby spot for live music (except in the summeritime, when it's closed) is **Feinstein's** at the Regency Hotel (540 Park Ave., 212/759–4100). Featured performers here have included Nell Carter and Diahann Carroll.

A whirl around the dance floor is just the thing to cap off a night of romantic about-towning, and the obvious place to do it is the **Rainbow Room,** way up on the 65th floor of the NBC building in Rockerfeller Center. You'll need to call ahead before you come (it's open only on certain Friday and Saturday nights), but once you're there, the view of twinkling city lights, the revolving dance floor, and the swinging live big band will transport you back in time. Don't be surprised if you find yourself humming "It's De-Lovely" all the way back to your hotel.

BACK IN THE DAY

Although Café des Artistes and the 21 Club are among the city's classiest restaurants today, both have wildly bohemian pasts. Café des Artistes, so named because its adjoining hotel was home to dozens of painters, sculptors, and performers back in the 1930s, started out as a sort of community kitchen. Because the hotel apartments were so small, residents would routinely buy their own groceries, then have them sent down to the café with instructions for how they should be cooked. Dishes, once they were prepared, were sent back up to the artists' rooms via dumbwaiter. One of the most famous inhabitants of the hotel was illustrator Howard Chandler Christy; rumor has it that he painted the restaurant's sweeping wood-nymph murals to pay off his bar tab.

The '21' Club, founded during Prohibition, began its life as a speakeasy. The club was raided several times, but it never closed, largely because of the ingenious preventive measures set up by its owners, Jack Kreindler and Charlie Berns. One of these was a mechanical system of pulleys that, when activated, immediately swept all the alcohol bottles off the bar shelves and down a chute, away from the prying eyes of police.

16

NEW YORK NIGHTS

For addresses and phone numbers of these venues, see the main Nightlife listings in this chapter.

A NIGHT OF ROCK N' ROLL
THE LOWER EAST SIDE

The Ramones, the New York Dolls, the Velvet Underground, Television, Blondie . . . easily half the bands that are today considered rock and punk legends cut their teeth in the gritty grottoes of the Lower East Side. Now that the neighborhood's undergone a revival—it's now home base for a new generation of jaded, creative twentysomethings—new live-music venues have been popping up around the old dives like weeds in a junkyard. Some of these are full-blown performance spaces, others just bars with a guitarist, an amp, and a drummer crammed into a corner; but the good news is, if you don't like the band playing in one place, you'll have to walk only a block or two to get to the next one. And hey—now that smoking's been banned, you can actually see what's happening on stage.

The venerable **Bowery Ballroom**, a staple of the downtown music scene, is the perfect place to start your a rock n' roll pilgrimage. You'll need advance tickets to see the bands that play here, especially

ultra-hip headliners like The Rapture and the Yeah Yeah Yeahs. But the relatively small size of the auditorium, the great acoustics, and the beer-sloshing enthusiasm of the crowd make it worth the Ticketmaster prices. On your way out, you'll likely pass the entrance to the now-defunct and legendary **CBGB,** a few blocks down Bowery. A battle-scarred, stinking pit even in its heydey, this was nevertheless the place where Patti Smith and David Byrne launched their careers, and where early performers included The Jam, Elvis Costello, and The Damned. So as you walk by, pay some silent respects.

The nearby intersection of Ludlow and Stanton streets is a zenith of sorts; small but rocking clubs seem to radiate in every direction for several blocks. This is the part of the LES that can get as crowded as a suburban mall late at night; between around 11 and 3 or 4 AM., the sidewalks are awash in young hipsters smoking Luckies and parading their thrift-store best. (If you want to blend in here, think scruffy retro-chic; no logos, no Manolos, no bling.) A favorite of this crowd is **Pianos**, once a piano shop (the new owners didn't bother to change the sign) and now an intimate performance space for acoustic and rock bands. **Arlene's Grocery**, just a block away, has been pulling in alternative music acts for more than a decade; The Strokes played here before anyone else had heard of them. If you need to channel your own inner Julian Casablancas, come on Monday night and join in the super-popular Rock n' Roll Karaoke party.

Heading a bit farther east on Stanton will bring you to **Sin-é**, a bare-bones space where packs of bed-headed twentysomethings gather for PBRs and thrashingly loud rock bands. You can also swing by **Tonic**, a former kosher winery that now brings in progressive rock, jazz, and avant-garde acts. Following Ludlow up to Houston, though, will take you right to **Mercury Lounge**, whose back room is famous for hosting big names before they were big. The White Stripes played here in their early days; more recent performers, like Robbers On High Street and Vox Trot are already starting to hit the mainstream.

IF YOUR EARS ARE RINGING...

Hopping from one LES music bar to another is a blast—until the killer headache sets in. If you need a place to chill out between venues and wait for the Tylenol to take effect, try one of these lower-key neighborhood lounges:

▪ Local 138. This unpretentious pub, with neon signs and sports on the television, has a back room with low lighting and couches—perfect for nursing a $3 draft.

▪ The Pink Pony. A book-lined eatery with good café au lait and a sort-of-French menu, the Pony is one of the more relaxing places on the sceney Ludlow strip.

▪ Teany. It's open only until midnight, and there's no alcohol served—just teas and juices, and healthful vegetarian fare. But if you decide early on that going out on a bender was a mistake, you can start doing your penance here.

For addresses and phone numbers of these venues, see the main **Nightlife** listings in this chapter.

16

NEW YORK NIGHTS

city's jazz scene. ✉ *33 University Pl., at E. 9th St., Greenwich Village* ☎ *212/228–8490* Ⓜ *Subway: R, W to 8th St.*

Lenox Lounge. This art deco lounge opened in the 1930s and currently hosts jazz ensembles, blues acts, and jam sessions in the Zebra Room. The restaurant in back serves great food to go with the soulful music. ✉ *288 Malcolm X Blvd., between W. 124th and W. 125th Sts., Harlem* ☎ *212/427–0253* Ⓜ *Subway: 2, 3 to 125th St.*

Smoke. If you can't wait until after dark to get your riffs on, head uptown to this lounge near Columbia University, where the music starts as early as 6:30 PM. Performers include some of the top names in the business, including turban-wearing organist Dr. Lonnie Smith and the drummer Jimmy Cobb (who laid down the beat on Miles Davis's seminal album *Kind of Blue*). ✉ *2751 Broadway, between W. 105th and W. 106th Sts., Upper West Side* ☎ *212/864–6662* ⊕ *www.smokejazz. com* Ⓜ *Subway: 1 to 103rd St.*

Sweet Rhythm. Every Monday at this sleek West Village nightspot, an ensemble from the New School University's famed jazz and contemporary music program takes the stage. On those nights, college students with ID get in for free. ✉ *88 7th Ave. S, between Bleecker and Grove Sts., Greenwich Village* ☎ *212/255–3626* ⊕ *www.sweetrhythmny.com* Ⓜ *Subway: 1 to Christopher St./Sheridan Sq.*

Fodor'sChoice
★
Village Vanguard. This prototypical jazz club, tucked into a cellar in Greenwich Village, has been the haunt of legends like Thelonious Monk. Today you might hear jams from the likes of Wynton Marsalis and Roy Hargrove, among others. ✉ *178 7th Ave. S, between W. 11th and Perry Sts., Greenwich Village* ☎ *212/255–4037* ⊕ *www.villagevanguard. com* Ⓜ *Subway: A, C, E to 14th St.; L to 8th Ave.*

Rock Clubs

If you love rock music, you've come to the right place. New York continues to give birth to compelling rock performers. Catch a rising star at one of the small clubs on the Lower East Side and in Brooklyn or check out the stellar schedules at the city's midsize venues, where more established groups deliver the goods night after night. Buy tickets in advance whenever possible; bands that are obscure to the rest of the country frequently play here to sold-out crowds.

Arlene's Grocery. On Monday night, crowds pack into this converted convenience store for Rock n' Roll Karaoke, where they live out their rockstar dreams by singing favorite punk anthems onstage with a live band. The other six nights of the week are hit-or-miss. ✉ *95 Stanton St., between Ludlow and Orchard Sts., Lower East Side* ☎ *212/995–1652* Ⓜ *Subway: F, V to 2nd Ave.*

Bitter End. This Greenwich Village standby has served up its share of talent; Billy Joel, David Crosby, and Dr. John are among the stars who have played here. These days you're more likely to find lesser-known musicians playing blues, rock, funk, and jazz. ✉ *147 Bleecker St., between Thompson St. and LaGuardia Pl., Greenwich Village* ☎ *212/673–7030* Ⓜ *Subway: A, B, C, D, E, F, V to W. 4th St.*

Fodor's Choice **Bowery Ballroom.** This theater with art deco accents is the city's top mid-
★ size concert venue. Packing in the crowds for a two-night stand is a rite
of passage for musicians on their way to stardom, including Franz Fer-
dinand, Neko Case, and Bright Eyes. You can grab one of the tables on
the balcony or stand on the main floor. There's a comfortable bar in the
basement. ⊠ *6 Delancey St., near the Bowery, Lower East Side* ☎ *212/
533–2111* ⊕ *www.boweryballroom.com* Ⓜ *Subway: F, J, M to Delancey St.*

CBGB & OMFUG. American punk rock and new wave—think the Ramones,
Blondie, the Talking Heads—were born in this long, black tunnel of a
club. The CBGB T-shirts, on sale here, are must-have items, even for
those who have never even heard of these groups. This is truer now than
ever, since the club has announced that it's closing its doors at the end
of October 2006. Until then, you're more likely to hear obscure garage
and hard-core bands than anything cutting edge. Next door, at **CB's 313
Gallery,** a quieter (and older) crowd enjoys mostly acoustic music.
⊠ *315 Bowery, at Bleecker St., East Village* ☎ *212/982–4052* Ⓜ *Subway: B, D, F, V to Broadway–Lafayette St.; 6 to Bleecker St.*

Continental. A favorite haunt of NYU students, this dive is loud, cheap,
and lots of sophomoric fun. Deliberately trashy local bands keep things
from getting too serious. ⊠ *25 3rd Ave., at St. Marks Pl., East Village*
☎ *212/529–6924* Ⓜ *Subway: 6 to Astor Pl.*

Delancey. From the palm-studded rooftop deck (heated in wintertime,
home to barbecues in summertime) down to the basement where noisy
rock and punk bands hold court, this multifaceted bar at the foot of the
Williamsburg Bridge strikes an invigorating balance between classy and
trashy. ⊠ *168 Delancey St., between Clinton and Attorney Sts., Lower
East Side* ☎ *212/254–9920* Ⓜ *Subway: F, J, M, Z to Delancey St.*

Fodor's Choice **Irving Plaza.** This two-story venue has a near-monopoly on the hottest
★ indie-rock bills in town. The good sound system and ample sight lines
don't hurt, either. The space is nothing to look at, just a couple of bars
and a balcony, but people don't come for the atmosphere. ⊠ *17 Irving
Pl., at E. 15th St., Gramercy* ☎ *212/777–6800* ⊕ *www.irvingplaza.com*
Ⓜ *Subway: 4, 5, 6, L, N, Q, R, W to 14th St./Union Sq.*

★ **Knitting Factory.** This art-rock club is one of the city's most enjoyable
performance spaces—the sound system is superb, and the front-room
bar is a convivial retreat when your eardrums need a break. Indie-rock
darlings, Japanese hard-core legends, and avant-garde noise bands are
common sights on the main stage; quieter and more obscure performers prevail in the two smaller rooms on the lower levels. ⊠ *74 Leonard
St., between Broadway and Church St., TriBeCa* ☎ *212/219–3055*
⊕ *www.knittingfactory.com* Ⓜ *Subway: 1 to Franklin St.*

Mercury Lounge. You'll have to squeeze past all the sardine-packed hipsters in the front bar to reach the stage, but it's worth it. This top-quality venue specializes in bands about to hit the big time. The Yeah Yeah
Yeahs played their first show here, opening for the White Stripes. ⊠ *217
E. Houston St., between Ludlow and Essex Sts., Lower East Side* ☎ *212/
260–4700* ⊕ *www.mercuryloungenyc.com* Ⓜ *Subway: F, V to 2nd Ave.*

Northsix. At this spacious Brooklyn club, near the end of Williamsburg's hip North 6th Street, you can take in an indie-rock show while

16

sitting on the gymnasium-style bleachers that dominate the room. ✉ *66 N. 6th St., between Wythe and Kent Aves., Williamsburg, Brooklyn* ☎ *718/599–5103* ⊕ *www.northsix.com* Ⓜ *Subway: L to Bedford Ave.*

Rothko. Come to this club for your fix of underground hip-hop, electronica, dance music, and rock—a typical monthly lineup might include Northern State, DJ Spooky, and Jean Grae. This place hosts what may be the city's only hip-hop karaoke night. ✉ *116 Suffolk St., at Rivington St., Lower East Side* ☎ *No phone* Ⓜ *Subway: F, V to 2nd Ave.*

Sin-é. Back in the early '90s, when this club was in the East Village, it was the center of the city's acoustic rock scene (the late Jeff Buckley was a regular). In its present incarnation, however, it draws quadruple bills of underground rock nearly every night. ✉ *150 Attorney St., at Stanton St., Lower East Side* ☎ *212/388–0077* Ⓜ *Subway: F, J, M, Z to Delancey St.*

Tonic. This former kosher winery presents innovative rock, jazz, and avant-garde music. At Subtonic, the bar in the basement, you can listen to some of the world's most respected DJs without paying a cover. ✉ *107 Norfolk St., between Delancey and Rivington Sts., Lower East Side* ☎ *212/358–7501* ⊕ *www.tonicnyc.com* Ⓜ *Subway: F, J, M to Delancey St.*

World Music Venues

A former mayor once called New York a "gorgeous mosaic" for the rich ethnic mix of its inhabitants. At the clubs listed here, you'll find musical traditions and innovations that mirror the energy of the city's diverse communities as well as those of farther-flung locales.

Connolly's. This tri-level Irish pub with a *Cheers*-like atmosphere often hosts the Irish rock-and-roots hybrid Black 47 on Saturday night. ✉ *121 W. 45th St., between Broadway and 6th Ave., Midtown West* ☎ *212/597–5126* Ⓜ *Subway: B, D, F, V to 42nd St.*

Copacabana. The granddaddy of Manhattan dance clubs (it has been open almost continuously since 1940) hosts music and dancing on three levels. From the disco on the lower level to the salsa and merengue performers in the main ballroom, few other clubs can compare. ✉ *560 W. 34th St., at 11th Ave., Midtown West* ☎ *212/239–2672* Ⓜ *Subway: A, C, E to 34th St.*

★ **S.O.B.'s.** The initials stand for Sounds of Brazil and it's *the* place for reggae, African, and Latin music, in addition to some major hip-hop performances: Common and M.I.A. have both graced the stage recently. Dinner is served as well. ✉ *204 Varick St., at W. Houston St., SoHo* ☎ *212/243–4940* ⊕ *www.sobs.com* Ⓜ *Subway: 1 to Houston St.*

Acoustic & Blues Venues

B. B. King Blues Club & Grill. This lavish Times Square club is vast and shiny and host to a range of musicians from Aretha Franklin to Bo Diddley. Every so often the relentlessly touring owner stops by as well. ✉ *237 W. 42nd St., between 7th and 8th Aves., Midtown West* ☎ *212/997–4144* Ⓜ *Subway: 1, 2, 3, 7, N, Q, R, W to 42nd St./Times Sq.*

FodorsChoice **Living Room.** Singer-songwriters—some solo, some with their bands—are ★ what you'll find at this casually classy club. Enjoy the sweet music while seated at a candlelit table. ☒ *154 Ludlow St., between Stanton and Rivington Sts., Lower East Side* ☎ *212/533–7235* Ⓜ *F, V to 2nd Ave.*

Terra Blues. A second-story haven for blues lovers, this cozy Greenwich Village club is surprisingly short on NYU students and rowdy folk. It must be the candlelit tables. Great national and local acts grace the stage 365 days a year. ☒ *149 Bleecker St., between Thompson St. and La-Guardia Pl., Greenwich Village* ☎ *212/777–7776* Ⓜ *Subway: B, D, F, V to Broadway–Lafayette St.; 6 to Bleecker St.*

Comedy Clubs

Neurotic New York comedy is known the world over, and a few minutes watching these Woody Allen types might just make your own problems seem laughable. Expect to pay about $15 per person on a weekend, sometimes topped off by a drink minimum. Reservations are usually necessary. Only those skilled in the art of repartee should sit in the front; everyone else should hide in a corner or risk being relentlessly heckled.

Caroline's on Broadway. This high-gloss club presents established names as well as comedians on the edge of stardom. Janeane Garofalo, David Allan Grier, Colin Quinn, and Gilbert Gottfried have headlined. ☒ *1626 Broadway, between W. 49th and W. 50th Sts., Midtown West* ☎ *212/757–4100* ⊕ *www.carolines.com* Ⓜ *Subway: 1 to 50th St.*

Fodor'sChoice **Chicago City Limits.** This crew has been doing improvisational comedy for ★ a long time. The shows, heavy on audience participation, seldom fail to whip visitors into a laughing frenzy. ☒ *318 W. 53rd St., between 8th and 9th Aves., Midtown West* ☎ *212/888–5233* Ⓜ *Subway: C, E to 50th St.*

Comedy Cellar. Laughter fills this space beneath the Olive Tree Café. The bill is a good barometer of who's hot. ☒ *117 MacDougal St., between W. 3rd and Bleecker Sts., Greenwich Village* ☎ *212/254–3480* Ⓜ *Subway: A, B, C, D, E, F, V to W. 4th St.*

Comic Strip Live. The atmosphere here is strictly corner bar ("More comfortable than a nice pair of corduroys," says the manager), belying its storied history: for example, Eddie Murphy is said to have discovered Chris Rock here. The stage is brilliantly lighted but minuscule; the bill is unpredictable but worth checking out. ☒ *1568 2nd Ave., between E. 81st and 82nd Sts., Upper East Side* ☎ *212/861–9386* Ⓜ *Subway: 4, 5, 6 to 86th St.*

Dangerfield's. Since 1969 this has been an important showcase for prime comic talent. Prices are reasonable ($12.50 during the week and $15–$20 on the weekends, with no drink minimum). ☒ *1118 1st Ave., between E. 61st and E. 62nd Sts., Upper East Side* ☎ *212/593–1650* Ⓜ *Subway: 4, 5, 6, N, R, W to 59th St.*

Gotham Comedy Club. Housed in a landmark building, this club—complete with a turn-of-the-20th-century chandelier and copper bars—showcases popular headliners such as Dave Chappelle and Jerry Seinfeld. Once a month there's a Latino comedy show. ☒ *208 W. 23rd St., between 5th and 6th Aves., Flatiron District* ☎ *212/367–9000* Ⓜ *Subway: F, V to 23rd St.*

★ **Upright Citizens Brigade Theatre.** Raucous sketch comedy, audience-initiated improv, and stand-up take turns onstage here at the city's go-to place for alternative comedy. There are even classes available; the Up-

16

CLOSE UP

Burlesque Is More

SINCE THE MID-1990S, a not-so-new activity has returned to the New York City nightlife scene–burlesque. The phenomenon is something more (as well as something less) than the elaborate Ziegfeld and Minsky Brother revues of the '20s and '30s and the stripped-down striptease acts of the '50s, which eventually gave way to go-go dancers and strippers of the '60s and '70s and lap dancers of the '80s and '90s. The latter are still around, of course, but the new burlesque stands apart.

Although not exactly family-friendly, many of today's shows are self-consciously feminist, organized and run by women. What's missing, though, are the bright lights and the glamour. There'll probably never be another performer as big as Sally Rand or Gypsy Rose Lee, but the movement's stars carry on in their own underground way. Some of the scene's finest performers include the heavily touring World Famous Pontani Sisters, classy diva Dirty Martini, the coed and glitter-laden Dazzle Dancers (who usually end their shows wearing nothing but glitter and smiles), and Ixion, a troupe that takes its plots straight from Greek mythology, turning epic tales into erotic adventures.

If your trip is timed right, the **New York Burlesque Festival** (⊕ www.thenewyorkburlesquefestival.com) is a must for fans of this adult art form. This three-day event attracts more than 40 performers from all around the world to several snazzy rooms around the Big Apple.

Aficionados recommend heading to the **Cutting Room** (⊠ 19 W. 24th St., between Broadway and 6th Ave., Chelsea ☎ 212/691-1900) on Saturday night. Le Scandal, the troupe behind the fabled Blue Angel Cabaret, runs the show here, offering a bit of belly dancing, sword swallowing, fan dancing, and, of course, lots of skin. High-profile attendees have included Demi Moore, Wesley Snipes, and Drew Barrymore (who joined the show).

The **Slipper Room** (⊠ 167 Orchard St., at Stanton St., Lower East Side ☎ 212/253-7246) is another burlesque headquarters, with shows on Friday and Saturday nights. The Starshine girls bring the pasties to **Rififi** (⊠ 332 E. 11th St., between 1st and 2nd Aves., East Village ☎ 212/677-6309) on Thursday, with the Red Hots taking over on Sunday. On Monday nights the action moves across the East River to Brooklyn's **Galapagos Art Space** (⊠ 70 N. 6th St., between Wythe and Kent Aves. Williamsburg ☎ 718/782-5188).

right Citizens bill their program as the world's largest improv school. ⊠ *307 W. 26th St., between 8th and 9th Aves., Chelsea* ☎ *212/366–9176* Ⓜ *Subway: C, E to 23rd St.*

Cabaret & Performance Spaces

Cabaret takes many forms in New York, from a lone crooner at the piano to a full-fledged song-and-dance revue. Some nightspots have stages; almost all have a cover and a minimum food and/or drink charge. In addition to the Carlyle and the Oak Room (⇨ Classic New York), here are some of the best venues.

Danny's Skylight Room. Housed in Danny's Grand Sea Palace, this fixture on Restaurant Row presents a little bit of everything: jazz performers, crooners, and ivory-ticklers. The porcelain-voiced treasure Blossom Dearie calls this room home Saturday and Sunday evening. ⊠ *346 W. 46th St., between 8th and 9th Aves., Midtown West* ☎ *212/265–8133* Ⓜ *Subway: A, C, E to 50th St.*

Don't Tell Mama. Composer-lyricist hopefuls and established talents show their stuff until 4 AM at this convivial theater-district cabaret. Extroverts will be tempted by the piano bar's open-mike policy. In the club's two rooms you might find singers, comedians, or female impersonators. ⊠ *343 W. 46th St., between 8th and 9th Aves., Midtown West* ☎ *212/ 757–0788* Ⓜ *Subway: 1, 2, 3, 7, N, Q, R, W to 42nd St./Times Sq.*

The Duplex. Since 1951 this music-scene veteran on busy Sheridan Square has hosted young singers on the rise, comedians polishing their acts, and Broadway performers dropping by after a show. No matter who's performing, the largely gay audience hoots and hollers in support. ⊠ *61 Christopher St., at 7th Ave. S, Greenwich Village* ☎ *212/255–5438* Ⓜ *Subway: 1 to Christopher St.*

Feinstein's at the Regency. That the world-touring Michael Feinstein performs here only once a year (usually in winter) and still gets a venue named after him speaks volumes about the charismatic cabaret star. This space presents some of the top names in the business. ⊠ *540 Park Ave., at E. 61st St., Upper East Side* ☎ *212/339–4095* Ⓜ *Subway: 4, 5, 6, N, R, W to 59th St.*

★ **Joe's Pub.** Wood paneling, red-velvet walls, and comfy sofas make a lush setting for top-notch performers and the A-list celebrities who come to see them. There's not a bad seat in the house, but if you want to sit, arrive at least a half hour early for the Italian dinner menu. ⊠ *425 Lafayette St., between E. 4th St. and Astor Pl., East Village* ☎ *212/539– 8770* ⊕ *web.joespub.com* Ⓜ *Subway: 6 to Astor Pl.*

Mo Pitkin's House of Satisfaction. A mix of comedy, music, literary readings, variety shows, and other performances keeps things interesting at this cozy, intelligent downtown venue. The equally eclectic comfort-food menu combines elevated Jewish-deli fare with Latin specialties, reflecting the club's Lower East Side surrounding. ⊠ *34 Ave. A, between E. 2nd and E. 3rd Sts., East Village* ☎ *212/777–5660* Ⓜ *Subway: F, V to 2nd Ave.*

BARS

New York has no shortage of places to wet your whistle. You'll find a glut of mahogany-panel taverns in Greenwich Village; chic lounges in SoHo and TriBeCa; yuppie hangouts on the Upper West and Upper East sides; and hipster bars in the East Village, Lower East Side, and Brooklyn. Most pubs and taverns have a wide draft selection, and bars and lounges often have special drink menus with concoctions no one would ever think up (or perhaps even drink) on their own. A single martini of the increasingly creative variety can send your tab into double digits. If velvet ropes or shoulder-to-shoulder crowds ever rub you the wrong way, feel free to move on and find a more comfortable spot, because there's always another one nearby. Under city liquor laws, bars can stay open until 4 AM.

Lower Manhattan, SoHo & TriBeCa

Bar 89. This bi-level lounge has the most entertaining bathrooms in town: the high-tech doors of unoccupied stalls are transparent, but (ideally) turn opaque when you step inside. Like the neighborhood, the crowd at the perennially popular spot is hip and rich, but the help manages to be remarkably friendly. ⊠ *89 Mercer St., between Spring and Broome Sts., SoHo* ☎ *212/274–0989* Ⓜ *Subway: 6 to Spring St.*

Brandy Library. The only book in this classy, wood-paneled room is the leather-bound menu listing hundreds of brandies and single-malt scotches. Many of the bottles are on gorgeous backlit "bookshelves" (complete with a rolling ladder for reaching those that are high up). Knowledgeable "librarians" help navigate the list, and will even pour a taste or two. ⊠ *25 N. Moore St., between Varick and Hudson Sts., TriBeCa* ☎ *212/ 226–5545* Ⓜ *Subway: 1 to Franklin St.*

Bridge Café. A hop away from South Street Seaport, this busy little restaurant flanking the Brooklyn Bridge is a world apart from that touristy district. The bar, dating from 1794, is one of the oldest in Manhattan. Though the space is small, the selection is huge: choose from over 100 domestic wines and 85 single-malt scotches. ⊠ *279 Water St., at Dover St., Lower Manhattan* ☎ *212/227–3344* Ⓜ *Subway: A, C, 2, 3, 4, 5, 6 to Fulton St./Broadway–Nassau.*

Broome Street Bar. A local hangout since 1972, this casual corner still feels like the old SoHo, before trendy boutiques replaced artists' lofts. There's a fine selection of draft beers and a full menu of hefty burgers and other pub food. ⊠ *363 West Broadway, at Broome St., SoHo* ☎ *212/925–2086* Ⓜ *Subway: C, E to Spring St.*

Double Happiness. On a block where the boundary between Little Italy and Chinatown blurs, an easily missed stairwell descends into a former speakeasy where couples converse in dark nooks beneath a low ceiling. Drinks are as diverse as a green-tea martini and tap beer. The music is often classic rock or old-school hip-hop. ⊠ *173 Mott St., between Broome and Grand Sts., Chinatown* ☎ *212/941–1282* Ⓜ *Subway: B, D to Grand St.; 6 to Spring St.*

Fanelli's. Linger over the *New York Times* at this down-to-earth neighborhood bar and restaurant, which harks back to 1847. ⊠ *94 Prince St., at Mercer St., SoHo* ☎ *212/226–9412* Ⓜ *Subway: R, W to Prince St.*

Lucky Strike. Now that the supermodels party elsewhere, this ultracool bistro is the domain of hipsters who pose at the cozy back tables. DJs play reggae, R&B, and hip-hop on crowded weekend nights. ⊠ *59 Grand St., between West Broadway and Wooster St., SoHo* ☎ *212/941– 0772* Ⓜ *Subway: A, C, E, R, W, 1 to Canal St.*

★ **MercBar.** A chic local crowd and Europeans in the know come to this dark, nondescript bar for the wonderful martinis. Its street number is barely visible—look for the French doors, which stay open in summer. ⊠ *151 Mercer St., between Prince and W. Houston Sts., SoHo* ☎ *212/ 966–2727* Ⓜ *Subway: N, R, W to Prince St.*

Pegu Club. Modeled after an officers' club in what's now Myanmar, the Pegu Club manages to feel expansive and calm even when packed. The well dressed and flirtatious come here partly for the beautiful surroundings, but primarily for the elegant cocktails, which are pricey, carefully prepared, and often ingenious. ☒ *77 W. Houston St., between West Broadway and Wooster St., SoHo* ☎ *212/473–7348* ⊕ *www.peguclub.com* Ⓜ *Subway: B, D, F, V to Broadway–Lafayette St.; 6 to Bleecker St.*

FodorśChoice ★ **Pravda.** Cocktails are the rule at this Eastern European–style bar. Choose from more than 70 brands of vodka, including house infusions, or opt for one of the house martinis. The cellarlike space, with an atmospheric vaulted ceiling, is illuminated with candles. Reserve a table for the Russian-inspired fare, especially on weekends. ☒ *281 Lafayette St., between Prince and E. Houston Sts., SoHo* ☎ *212/226–4944* Ⓜ *Subway: B, D, F, V to Broadway–Lafayette St.; 6 to Bleecker St.*

Raoul's. One of the first trendy spots in SoHo, this arty French restaurant has yet to lose its touch. Expect a chic bar scene filled with model-pretty men and women, and an intriguing fortune-teller upstairs. ☒ *180 Prince St., between Sullivan and Thompson Sts., SoHo* ☎ *212/966–3518* Ⓜ *Subway: C, E to Spring St.*

The Room. The vibe's so relaxed it's like squeezing into someone's living room (be prepared to share couch space) at this minimalist spot, where the great selection of 70 bottled beers draws a friendly mix of locals and international visitors. The alternative rock music is actually played low enough to have a conversation. ☒ *144 Sullivan St., between W. Houston and Prince Sts., SoHo* ☎ *212/477–2102* Ⓜ *Subway: C, E to Spring St.*

Thom Bar. This lounge inside the 60 Thompson boutique hotel is the perfect place to splurge, fireside, on a litchi martini. Pick a weeknight if you want to have a relaxed drink among the other elegant patrons. ☒ *60 Thompson St., between Spring and Broome Sts., SoHo* ☎ *212/219–3200* Ⓜ *Subway: C, E to Spring St.*

Chelsea, the Meatpacking District & Greenwich Village

Bongo. Like its namesake, this bar is small but cool. The decor harkens back to a time when Beat poets recited poetry as a cool cat tapped out a syncopated rhythm on the drum. There are a boomerang-shape coffee table, mod couches, and a crowd that's as stylish as the surroundings. ☒ *299 10th Ave., between W. 27th and W. 28th Sts., Chelsea* ☎ *212/947–3654* Ⓜ *Subway: 1 to 28th St.*

BriteBar. Gallerygoers winding down the day and nightclubbers just revving up both stop by this West Chelsea watering hole for signature drinks made with energy-infused vodka, including the "Fother Mucker" martini. The attitude is casual compared with the more sceney places nearby, and the modern surroundings get a humorous touch from the Lite-Brite toys scattered around for customers to play with. ☒ *297 10th Ave., at W. 27th St., Chelsea* ☎ *212/279–9706* Ⓜ *Subway: 1 to 28th St.*

Café Loup. This restaurant is something of a neighborhood institution, and its cozy, unpretentious bar serves some of the best margaritas in the city. (The secret is fresh fruit juices.) A literary crowd chats as jazz tunes

16

Theme Dreams

Those who relish sitting beneath a hair dryer will feel right at home at **Beauty Bar** (✉ 231 E. 14th St., between 2nd and 3rd Aves., East Village ☎ 212/539–1389). There's even a manicurist on call. Aspiring Peeping Toms dig the surveillance-themed **Remote** (✉ 327 Bowery, between E. 2nd and E. 3rd Sts., East Village ☎ 212/228–0228), where patrons spy on one another with controllable video cameras. Try a more old-fashioned form of communication on the English phone booths while munching fish-and-chips at **Telephone Bar** (✉ 149 2nd Ave., between E. 9th and E. 10th Sts., East Village ☎ 212/529–5000).

play overhead. ✉ *105 W. 13th St., between 6th and 7th Aves., Greenwich Village* ☎ *212/255–4746* Ⓜ *Subway: F, V to 14th St.*

Fodor'sChoice ★ **Chumley's.** There's no sign to help you find this tavern—they took it down during its days as a speakeasy—but when you reach the corner of Bedford and Barrow, you're very close (the main entrance is just north on Bedford; a "secret" entrance leading through a courtyard can be found just east, on Barrow). A fireplace warms the relaxed dining room, where the burgers are hearty and the clientele mostly college age. ✉ *86 Bedford St., at Barrow St., Greenwich Village* ☎ *212/675–4449* Ⓜ *Subway: 1 to Christopher St./Sheridan Sq.*

★ **Cornelia Street Café.** Share a bottle of merlot at a street-side table on a quaint West Village lane. Downstairs you can catch live jazz or a poetry reading, or take in the "Entertaining Science" evenings hosted by the Nobel laureate chemist Roald Hoffmann. ✉ *29 Cornelia St., between W. 4th and Bleecker Sts., Greenwich Village* ☎ *212/989–9319* Ⓜ *Subway: A, B, C, D, E, F, V to W. 4th St./Washington Sq.*

Corner Bistro. Opened in 1961, this neighborhood saloon serves what many think are the best hamburgers in town. The cozy place is so inviting and the professional crowd so friendly, you might think you're in a small town. ✉ *331 W. 4th St., at 8th Ave., Greenwich Village* ☎ *212/242–9502* Ⓜ *Subway: A, C, E to 14th St.; L to 8th Ave.*

★ **Flatiron Lounge.** Soft lighting and smart leather banquettes distinguish this art deco hideout, where guest mixologists, a seasonal drink menu, and owner Julie Reiner's daily "flights" of fanciful mini-martinis elevate bartending to an art form. ✉ *37 W. 19th St., between 5th and 6th Aves., Chelsea* ☎ *212/727–7741* Ⓜ *Subway: F, V to 23rd St.*

Half King. Writer Sebastian Junger (*The Perfect Storm*) is one of the owners of this mellow pub, which draws a friendly crowd of media types and stragglers from nearby Chelsea galleries for its Monday night readings, gallery exhibits, and Irish-American menu. ✉ *505 W. 23rd St., between 10th and 11th Aves., Chelsea* ☎ *212/462–4300* Ⓜ *Subway: C, E to 23rd St.*

Hogs & Heifers. This raucous place is all about the saucy barkeeps berating men over their megaphones and baiting women to get up on the bar and dance (and add their bras to the collection on the wall). Celebrities still drop in from time to time to get their names in the gossip columns.

✉ *859 Washington St., at W. 13th St., Meatpacking District* ☎ *212/ 929–0655* Ⓜ *Subway: A, C, E to 14th St.; L to 8th Ave.*

La Bottega. Vintage Italian posters, international magazines, and a huge Italian oven set the stage at the Maritime Hotel's European-style restaurant and bar. In the winter, bring your drink out to the lobby and nestle in front of the fireplace. ✉ *363 W. 16th St., at 9th Ave., Chelsea* ☎ *212/ 242–4300* Ⓜ *Subway: A, C, E to 14th St.; L to 8th Ave.*

Madame X. The bordello atmosphere here is enhanced by blood-red walls and a sexy crowd. Madame X is across West Houston Street from SoHo, which means it has an attractive clientele, but less attitude. The garden in the back is open year-round, thanks to outdoor heaters. ✉ *94 W. Houston St., between LaGuardia Pl. and Thompson St., Greenwich Village* ☎ *212/539–0808* Ⓜ *Subway: 1 to Houston St.*

★ **Ono.** The O Bar at Ono, Hotel Gansevoort's trendy Japanese restaurant, must be seen to be believed. Designed by Jeffrey Beers International, the bar has elegant touches that include gold-leaf brick walls and a fiber-optic "waterfall" chandelier. Sip on sake in one of the two lounges or the stylish outdoor garden. ✉ *18 9th Ave., at W. 13th St., Meatpacking District* ☎ *212/660–6766* Ⓜ *Subway: A, C, E to 14th St.; L to 8th Ave.*

Serena. This remarkably stylish subterranean lounge, painted an eye-popping shade of pink, draws a chic crowd. The addictive bar snacks are the work of the bar's original owner, caterer Serena Bass. ✉ *Chelsea Hotel, 222 W. 23rd St., between 7th and 8th Aves., Chelsea* ☎ *212/255– 4646* Ⓜ *Subway: C, E to 23rd St.*

Shag. White carpet (shag, of course) lines the walls at this shoe-box-size spot. The vibe is L.A.–pool-party-meets-groovy-bachelor-pad, set to an '80s sound track. ✉ *11 Abingdon Sq., at Bleecker St. and 8th Ave., Greenwich Village* ☎ *212/242–0220* Ⓜ *Subway: A, C, E to 14th St.; L to 8th Ave.*

Fodor'sChoice **Spice Market.** Asian street fare served with a twist accompanies Spice Market's equally exotic cocktails. A multilevel open space with slowly rotating fans, intricately carved woodwork, and sheer flowing curtains lends an aura of calm to this celebrity hangout. ✉ *403 W. 13th St., at 9th Ave., Meatpacking District* ☎ *212/675–2322* Ⓜ *Subway: A, C, E to 14th St.; L to 8th Ave.*

Tortilla Flats. The back room is a tribute to the stars of Las Vegas, from Martin and Lewis to Siegfried and Roy, but the real action is in the main room, where a rambunctious crowd packs the tight quarters for games (bingo on Monday and Tuesday, hula-hooping on Wednesday), tequila, and Mexican food. The Flats is a prime bachelorette-party destination. ✉ *767 Washington St., at W. 12th St., Greenwich Village* ☎ *212/243– 1053* Ⓜ *Subway: A, C, E to 14th St.; L to 8th Ave.*

Vol de Nuit. The Belgian Beer Bar (as everybody calls it) is tucked away from the street. A European-style, enclosed outdoor courtyard and a cozy dark interior draws NYU grad-student types. The selection of beers on tap is superb, as are the fries, which are served Belgian style, in a paper cone with an array of sauces on the side. ✉ *148 W 4th St., between MacDougal St. and 6th Ave., Greenwich Village* ☎ *212/982–3388* Ⓜ *Subway: A, B, C, D, E, F, V to W. 4th St./Washington Sq.*

White Horse Tavern. According to (dubious) New York legend, Dylan Thomas drank himself to death in this historic tavern founded in 1880.

From April to October try to snag a seat at one of the sidewalk tables. ✉ *567 Hudson St., at W. 11th St., Greenwich Village* ☎ *212/989–3956* Ⓜ *Subway: 1 to Christopher St./Sheridan Sq.*

Lower East Side & East Village through East 20s

B Bar. Long lines of people peer through Venetian blinds at the stylish downtown crowd within this long-running but still fairly trendy bar and grill. If the bouncer says there's a private party going on, more likely than not it's his way of turning you away nicely. Dress your best if you want a seat in the covered outdoor space, a far cry from this spot's former gas station days. ✉ *358 Bowery, at E. 4th St., East Village* ☎ *212/475–2220* Ⓜ *Subway: 6 to Astor Pl.*

Beauty Bar. Grab a seat in a barber chair or under a dryer at this made-over hair salon. During happy hour, the manicurist will do your nails for a fee that includes a drink. The DJ spins rock during the week and soul on Saturday nights. ✉ *231 E. 14th St., between 2nd and 3rd Aves., East Village* ☎ *212/539–1389* Ⓜ *Subway: 4, 5, 6, L, N, R to 14th St./Union Sq.*

Cibar. Descend into the warm pink-and-peach basement to find this candlelit martini lounge. Nightly DJs play an eclectic mix of music; the bamboo garden is quieter. ✉ *56 Irving Pl., between E. 17th and E. 18th Sts., Gramercy* ☎ *212/460–5656* Ⓜ *Subway: 4, 5, 6, N, Q, R, W to 14th St./Union Sq.*

Coyote Ugly. At this grimy dive the raucous patrons wail along with the Lynyrd Skynyrd on the jukebox. The pretty countertop-dancing female bartenders are an ironic twist on the bar's name. ✉ *153 1st Ave., between E. 9th and E. 10th Sts., East Village* ☎ *212/477–4431* Ⓜ *Subway: 6 to Astor Pl.*

Decibel. Red paper lanterns dimly illuminate cool couples sipping sake from small wooden boxes at this underground Japanese bar. Polite servers can help navigate the impressive but reasonably priced list, as well as the menu of Japanese bar food. The entrance is easy to miss: look for a small wooden sign at the top of a sidewalk staircase; walk down and ring the buzzer to get in. ✉ *240 E. 9th St., between 2nd and 3rd Aves., East Village* ☎ *212/979–2731* Ⓜ *Subway: 6 to Astor Pl.*

Good World Bar & Grill. On an isolated street in Chinatown is this glass-fronted bar full of artists, writers, and their subjects, as well as cool music, a catwalk-ready staff, and—believe it or not—tasty Swedish specialties like gravlax, herring, and meatballs. ✉ *3 Orchard St., between Canal and Division Sts., Lower East Side* ☎ *212/925–9975* Ⓜ *Subway: F to East Broadway.*

Local 138. If you're looking for a neighborly spot to catch the Yankees, Knicks, or the World Cup, head to this cozy, low-lighted pub. The friendly bartenders and relaxed customers are a nice change of pace from the typical Ludlow Street scene. ✉ *138 Ludlow St., between Stanton and Rivington Sts., Lower East Side* ☎ *212/477–0280* Ⓜ *Subway: F, V to 2nd Ave.*

Lucky Cheng's. Although locals deride its subpar Asian fare, Lucky Cheng's is famous for the drag queens who cavort with the tourists and bachelorettes singing karaoke in the lounge downstairs. ✉ *24 1st Ave.,* *between E. 1st and E. 2nd Sts., East Village* ☎ *212/473–0516* Ⓜ *Subway: F, V to 2nd Ave.*

FodorśChoice ★ **Luna Park.** This open-air café at the pavilion near the northern end of Union Square is a great place for a romantic date on a summer evening. Arrive before the nine-to-five crowd to secure a seat beneath the strings of white lights. ✉ *Union Sq. between Broadway and Park Ave. S, Gramercy* ☎ *212/475–8464* Ⓜ *Subway: 4, 5, 6, N, Q, R, W to 14th St./Union Sq.*

Max Fish. This crowded, kitschy palace on a gentrified Lower East Side strip has one of the most eclectic jukeboxes in town, a pool table and pinball machine in the back, and a crowd of young rocker types that comes for the live music. ✉ *178 Ludlow St., between E. Houston and Stanton Sts., Lower East Side* ☎ *212/529–3959* Ⓜ *Subway: F, V to 2nd Ave.*

McSorley's Old Ale House. One of New York's oldest saloons (it claims to have opened in 1854) and immortalized by *New Yorker* writer Joseph Mitchell, this is a must-see for beer lovers, even if only two kinds of brew are served: McSorley's light and McSorley's dark. Go early to avoid the lines that stretch down the block on Friday and Saturday night. ✉ *15 E. 7th St., between 2nd and 3rd Aves., East Village* ☎ *212/473–9148* Ⓜ *Subway: 6 to Astor Pl.*

Old Town Bar & Restaurant. This proudly unpretentious watering hole is heavy on the mahogany and redolent of old New York—it's been around since 1892. Make sure to try the top-notch tavern food. ✉ *45 E. 18th St., between Broadway and Park Ave. S, Gramercy* ☎ *212/529–6732* Ⓜ *Subway: 4, 5, 6, N, Q, R, W to 14th St./Union Sq.*

Otto's Shrunken Head. A bamboo bar with fish lamps floating overhead sets the mood at this tiki bar with a tattooed, punk crowd. Otto's sells beef jerky to chew on as you play the pinball machine, pose inside the photo booth, or jive to the DJ or band playing anything from '50s to new wave. ✉ *538 E. 14th St., between Aves. A and B, East Village* ☎ *212/228–2240* Ⓜ *Subway: L to 1st Ave.; 4, 5, 6, N, Q, R, W to 14th St./Union Sq.*

Pete's Tavern. This saloon is famous as the place where O. Henry is alleged to have written *The Gift of the Magi* (at the second booth as you come in). These days it's crowded with locals enjoying a beer or a burger. ✉ *129 E. 18th St., at Irving Pl., Gramercy* ☎ *212/473–7676* Ⓜ *Subway: 4, 5, 6, N, Q, R, W to 14th St./Union Sq.*

★ **The Pink Pony.** Maintaining a calm, bohemian feel among the trendier joints of Ludlow Street, this shabby-chic bar-café draws young writers, filmmakers, and designers who come to escape the cacophony from nearby music venues and make conversation over bottles of cheap wine and cup after cup of coffee. ✉ *176 Ludlow St., between E. Houston and Stanton Sts., Lower East Side* ☎ *212/253–1922* Ⓜ *Subway: F, V to 2nd Ave.*

Remote. The tables in the upstairs lounge have video screens on them, and you control the cameras that scan the room. For a technology that's designed to work over long distances, the effect, strangely enough, is to bring people closer together. Maybe there are just more show-offs in New York City than elsewhere. ✉ *327 Bowery, between E. 2nd and E. 3rd*

16

CLOSE UP

Dive In

When dressing up has got you down and casual—really casual—is what you crave, it's time to find one of New York's dive bars. Although there are grittier choices out there, these options ought to satisfy most tastes. At **American Trash** (⊠ 1471 1st Ave., between E. 76th and E. 77th Sts., Upper East Side ☎ 212/988–9008), stuff found in the garbage has been transformed into decor. At **Hogs & Heifers** (⊠ 859 Washington St., at

W. 13th St., Meatpacking District ☎ 212/929–0655) has no pretense of propriety. Women with no intention of dancing for the crowd may find the atmosphere tough to take. In that same vein, but slightly less intense, **Coyote Ugly** (⊠ 153 1st Ave., between E. 9th and E. 10th Sts., East Village ☎ 212/477–4431) puts the hotties behind (and sometimes on top of) the bar.

Sts., East Village ☎ *212/228–0228* Ⓜ *Subway: B, D, F, V to Broadway–Lafayette St.; 6 to Bleecker St.*

Temple Bar. This unmarked haunt is famous for its martinis and romantic atmosphere. Look for the painted iguana skeleton on the facade, and walk past the slim bar to the back where, in near-total darkness, you can lounge on a plush banquette surrounded by velvet drapes. ⊠ *332 Lafayette St., between Bleecker and E. Houston Sts., East Village* ☎ *212/ 925–4242* Ⓜ *Subway: B, D, F, V to Broadway–Lafayette St.; 6 to Bleecker St.*

THOR. The Hotel on Rivington's swanky lounge swarms with beautiful thirtysomethings who stretch their designer jeans to straddle a bar stool and order mixologist Miguel Aranda's excellent cocktails. True, the walls and ceiling look like a Diane von Furstenberg dress exploded onto them, but that's balanced by sapphire lighting and a clean glass wall looking out onto the grafitti-covered tenements outside. ⊠ *107 Rivington St., between Ludlow and Essex Sts., Lower East Side* ☎ *212/475–2600* Ⓜ *Subway: F to Delancey St.*

Midtown & the Theater District

Algonquin Hotel. This venerable bar plays up its history as the home of the Algonquin Roundtable, a literary clique that included sharp-tongued Dorothy Parker. The clubby, oak-panel lobby and comfortable sofas encourage lolling over cocktails and conversation. ⊠ *59 W. 44th St., between 5th and 6th Aves., Midtown West* ☎ *212/840–6800* Ⓜ *Subway: B, D, F, Q to 42nd St.*

Fodor$Choice ★ **Campbell Apartment.** Commuting professionals pack into this Grand Central Terminal bar on their way to catch trains home during the evening rush. One of Manhattan's more beautiful rooms, the restored space dates to the 1920s, when it was the private office of an executive named John W. Campbell. He knew how to live, and you can enjoy his good taste from an overstuffed chair—if you avoid the evening rush. ⊠ *15 Vanderbilt Ave. entrance, Grand Central Station Midtown East* ☎ *212/953–0409* Ⓜ *Subway: 4, 5, 6, 7, S to 42nd St./Grand Central.*

Cellar Bar. This stylish spot inside the Bryant Park Hotel is distinguished by a tiled, arched ceiling. One of the more spectacular spaces in midtown, it attracts an attractive crowd from the fashion industry. A DJ with a taste for classic R&B keeps the crowd on its toes. ⊠ *40 W. 40th St., between 5th and 6th Aves., Midtown West* ☎ *212/642–2260* Ⓜ *Subway: B, D, F, V to 42nd St.*

Divine Bar. Zebra-stripe bar stools downstairs and jewel-tone velvet couches upstairs make this bar unusually chic for midtown. The selection of tapas is complemented by 55 beers from around the world. There are 70 wines by the glass, and the frequently updated wine list includes some hard-to-come-by vintages. ⊠ *244 E. 51st St., between 2nd and 3rd Aves., Midtown East* ☎ *212/319–9463* Ⓜ *Subway: 6 to 51st St.*

ESPN Zone. When there's a play-off game, expect a line at the door of this multistory sports bar. With one 16-foot and two 14-foot video screens, plus scores of high-definition TVs, there isn't a bad seat in the house. Try the sports-theme video games on the top floor, or dig into the kitchen's full menu. ⊠ *1472 Broadway, at 42nd St., Midtown West* ☎ *212/921–3776* Ⓜ *Subway: 1, 2, 3, N, Q, R, W to 42nd St./Times Square.*

Fodor'sChoice
★
Hudson Bar. This swank establishment combines the exclusive feeling of a hot club with the excellent taste of a top hotel. Slip in between the beautiful people mingling under the hand-painted ceiling. The room is illuminated by lights in the glass floor. ⊠ *356 W. 58th St., between 8th and 9th Aves., Midtown West* ☎ *212/554–6303* Ⓜ *Subway: 1, A, B, C, D to 59th St.*

Joe Allen. At this old reliable on Restaurant Row, celebrated in the musical version of *All About Eve,* everybody's en route to or from a show. The posters that adorn the "flop wall" are from Broadway musicals that bombed. ⊠ *326 W. 46th St., between 8th and 9th Aves., Midtown West* ☎ *212/581–6464* Ⓜ *Subway: A, C, E to 42nd St.*

K. There's no mistaking the theme of this stylishly sultry lounge, where the walls are decorated with drawings from the Kama Sutra. More of a boudoir than a bar, the place is done up in crimson velvety splendor, with oversize cushions, cozy banquettes, and plasma screens projecting Bollywood movies. True romance junkies can sip on an Aphrodisiak, a citrus-accented cocktail, or nibble on some Tantric Tikka. ⊠ *30 W. 52nd St., between 5th and 6th Aves., Midtown West* ☎ *212/265–6665* Ⓜ *Subway: E, V to 5th Ave./53rd St.*

Keens Steakhouse. Single-malt scotch aficionados will appreciate the selection of over 200 varieties at this 120-year-old restaurant, just around the corner from Madison Square Garden. Take a look at the ceilings, which are lined with thousands of clay pipes that once belonged to patrons. ⊠ *72 W. 36th St., between 5th and 6th Aves., Midtown West* ☎ *212/947–3636* Ⓜ *Subway: B, D, F, N, Q, R, V, W to 34th St.*

King Cole Bar. A famed Maxfield Parrish mural is a welcome sight at this classic midtown meeting place, where the Bloody Mary was introduced to American drinkers. ⊠ *St. Regis Hotel, 2 E. 55th St., near 5th Ave., Midtown East* ☎ *212/753–4500* Ⓜ *Subway: E, V to 5th Ave./53rd St.*

Monkey Bar. Once a fabled spot where the likes of Tennessee Williams and Tallulah Bankhead gathered, this lounge was restored in the '90s. Despite the simian light fixtures and monkey-themed murals, there's very little barbarism in the mild-mannered banker types who shoot back scotch here. ☒ *60 E. 54th St., between Park and Madison Aves., Midtown East* ☎ *212/838–2600* Ⓜ *Subway: E, V to Lexington Ave./53rd St.; 6 to 51st St.*

Morgans Bar. Willowy supermodels and their kin frequent this dark, perpetually hip lounge in the basement of Ian Schrager's namesake boutique hotel. The after-work crowd of trendy Manhattanites can be overwhelming. Late-night DJs turn up the volume. ☒ *237 Madison Ave., between E. 37th and E. 38th Sts., Midtown East* ☎ *212/726–7600* Ⓜ *Subway: 4, 5, 6, 7, S to 42nd St./Grand Central.*

Morrell Wine Bar and Café. This vibrant bar takes its wine very seriously, with one of the city's best selections of wine by the glass and an epic array of bottles. In summer you can sip at outdoor tables in the heart of Rockefeller Center. ☒ *1 Rockefeller Center, W. 49th St. between 5th and 6th Aves., Midtown West* ☎ *212/262–7700* Ⓜ *Subway: B, D, F, V to 47th–50th Sts./Rockefeller Center.*

Pen-Top Bar & Lounge. Take a break from 5th Avenue shopping at this glass-lined penthouse bar on the 23rd floor. Drinks are pricey but the views are impressive, especially from the rooftop terraces. ☒ *Peninsula Hotel, 700 5th Ave., at W. 55th St., Midtown West* ☎ *212/956–2888* Ⓜ *Subway: E, V to 5th Ave./53rd St.*

P. J. Clarke's. Mirrors and polished wood adorn New York's most famous Irish bar, where scenes from the 1945 movie *Lost Weekend* were shot. The after-work crowd that unwinds here seems to appreciate the old-fashioned flair. ☒ *915 3rd Ave., at E. 55th St., Midtown East* ☎ *212/317–1616* Ⓜ *Subway: 4, 5, 6 to 59th St.*

FodorśChoice ★ **Royalton.** Philippe Starck's minimalist hotel has two places to drink—the large lobby bar furnished with armchairs and chaise longues and the banquette-lined Round Bar. The circular room to your right as you enter, it's the place to sip vodka and champagne. The entrance to the hotel is difficult to find (look for the curved silver railings). ☒ *44 W. 44th St., between 5th and 6th Aves., Midtown West* ☎ *212/869–4400* Ⓜ *Subway: B, D, F, V to 42nd St.*

Sardi's. "The theater is certainly not what it was," said a forlorn feline in the musical *Cats,* and the same could be said for this Broadway institution. Still, theater fans should make time for a drink in one of the red-leather booths, which are surrounded by caricatures of stars past and present. ☒ *234 W. 44th St., between Broadway and 8th Ave., Midtown West* ☎ *212/221–8440* Ⓜ *Subway: A, C, E to 42nd St.*

Top of the Tower. There are lounges at higher altitudes, but this one on the 26th floor feels halfway to heaven. The atmosphere is elegant and subdued. There's live piano music on Thursday, Friday, and Saturday nights. ☒ *Beekman Tower, 3 Mitchell Pl., near 1st Ave. at E. 49th St., Midtown East* ☎ *212/355–7300* Ⓜ *Subway: 6 to 51st St./Lexington Ave.; E, V to Lexington Ave./53rd St.*

Water Club. You're not sailing on the East River, although you might feel as if you are, when you step onto the pleasing outdoor deck at the Water Club. This is a special-occasion place—especially for those who've already been to all the landlocked ones in town. A fireplace warms the downstairs bar, and there's piano music every night except Sunday.

✉ *500 E. 30th St., at FDR Dr., Midtown East* ☎ *212/683–3333* Ⓜ *Subway: 6 to 28th St.*

Upper East Side

American Trash. Bicycle tires, golf clubs, and other castoffs cover the walls and ceiling, ensuring that this bar merits its descriptive name. Eight plasma TVs, three video games, a rock-and-roll jukebox, and a pool table keep the neighborhood crowd busy. Some nights local bands play classic rock. ✉ *1471 1st Ave., between E. 76th and E. 77th Sts., Upper East Side* ☎ *212/988–9008* Ⓜ *Subway: 6 to 77th St.*

Auction House. This bar aims to bring a bit of downtown coolness to the sometimes suburban-feeling Upper East Side. Its tools of the trade include candlelight, high ceilings, a loose dress code (no baseball hats, no sneakers), and a strict music policy: "No Top 40, just good music," proclaims one indie-rock-loving barkeep. Whatever the reason, the neighborhood crowd tends to be better looking and better behaved than those at many other area bars. ✉ *300 E. 89th St., between 1st and 2nd Aves., Upper East Side* ☎ *212/427–4458* Ⓜ *Subway: 4, 5, 6 to 86th St.*

Session 73. Live music sets this sizable restaurant and bar apart from others in the neighborhood. Young locals groove to the nightly mix of funk, jazz, and blues. If the songs don't set your heart racing, there's always the generous assortment of tequilas and beers on tap. ✉ *1359 1st Ave., at E. 73rd St., Upper East Side* ☎ *212/517–4445* Ⓜ *Subway: 6 to 77th St.*

Upper West Side

Café des Artistes. At this restaurant known for its glorious art nouveau murals and old-school, upper-crust clientele, the small, warm bar is one of the city's special hideaways. Here, interesting strangers tell their life stories. The house drink is a pear-flavored champagne. ✉ *1 W. 67th St., between Central Park W and Columbus Ave., Upper West Side* ☎ *212/877–3500* Ⓜ *Subway: 1 to 66th St.*

Gabriel's. It can be hard to find a good grappa in New York, but this highly regarded northern Italian restaurant has a stupendous selection of the strong grape-based elixir, and a 35-foot curved mahogany bar to boot. The atmosphere couldn't be warmer. ✉ *11 W. 60th St., between Broadway and Columbus Ave., Upper West Side* ☎ *212/956–4600* Ⓜ *Subway: A, B, C, D, 1 to 59th St.*

Hi-Life. Padded black walls, large round mirrors, and an L-shape bar give this spot the look of a 1940s movie. Settle into a banquette and watch the budding neighborhood bons vivants in action. ✉ *477 Amsterdam Ave., at W. 83rd St., Upper West Side* ☎ *212/787–7199* Ⓜ *Subway: 1 to 86th St.*

Peter's. A staple of the Upper West Side scene since the early 1980s, this vast, noisy establishment, adorned with copies of the frescoes at Pompeii, hosts a pretheater crowd. Patrons range from their late 20s to their early 40s. ✉ *182 Columbus Ave., between W. 68th and W. 69th Sts., Upper West Side* ☎ *212/877–4747* Ⓜ *Subway: B, C to 72nd St.*

Shark Bar. The classy bar at this soul-food (and soul-music) restaurant fills with eye candy every night. Rapper LL Kool J has been known to stop by, and it's very popular among young black executives, music industry bigwigs, and professional athletes. ⊠ *307 Amsterdam Ave., between W. 74th and W. 75th Sts., Upper West Side* ☎ 212/874–8500 Ⓜ *Subway: 1, 2, 3 to 72nd St.*

Brooklyn

Brooklyn Brewery. At this working brewery, the Friday evening happy hour means $3 beers—try the popular Brooklyn Lager or one of the seasonal brews. Beer buffs can join a guided tour on Saturday afternoon from noon to 5. ⊠ *79 N. 11th St., between Berry St. and Wythe Ave., Williamsburg* ☎ 718/486–7422 Ⓜ *Subway: L to Bedford Ave.; G to Nassau Ave.*

Brooklyn Social. You could walk right past this inconspicuous storefront—no sign, small windows—without even knowing it, but you'll be happier if you walk into the bar, a converted men's social club. Inside, a local crowd carouses amid vintage club memorabilia while a jukebox plays Rubén González piano tunes one minute, Bjork singles the next. Shoot pool, order a killer panini, or just admire the bartender's dapper outfit (and mixing skills). ⊠ *335 Smith St., between President and Carroll Sts., Carroll Gardens* ☎ 718/858–7758 Ⓜ *Subway: F, G to Carroll St.*

Capone's. A free, freshly made, and darn tasty cheese pizza is yours for the scarfing with every drink you buy at this Brooklyn bar. Behind the club's unassuming exterior you'll find the artists and young professionals of Williamsburg (as well as refugees from that other borough across the river) crowd-watching from the slender balcony, chatting in the sunken booths that line the club, enjoying their pizza by the bar, and grooving to rock, funk, soul, and disco. ⊠ *221 N. 9th St., between Driggs Ave. and Roebling St., Williamsburg* ☎ 718/599–4044 Ⓜ *Subway: L to Bedford Ave.*

★ **Galapagos Art Space.** The dark, placid moat in the entryway is your indication that this converted mayonnaise factory is no ordinary bar. A longtime staple of Williamsburg's art and performance scene, Galapagos hosts dance troupes, theater performances, variety shows, and live music that has included folk as well as avant-garde classical. Monday night there's an old-fashioned burlesque show, and on Sunday night the Ocularis series screens experimental and art films and video. ⊠ *70 N. 6th St., between Wythe and Kent Aves., Williamsburg* ☎ 718/782–5188 Ⓜ *Subway: L to Bedford Ave.*

Pete's Candy Store. Williamsburg's beloved outpost has a retro feel, a friendly crowd, and great cocktails. The back room is smaller than a subway car, but it's the nightly stop for some of the city's best free music (Norah Jones once graced this stage). Brainy hipsters start off their Monday nights with spelling bees, Tuesday night locals turn out for bingo, and the trivia contests on Wednesday draws folks from the entire metro area. ⊠ *709 Lorimer St., between Frost and Richardson Sts., Williamsburg* ☎ 718/302–3770 Ⓜ *Subway: L to Lorimer St.*

Superfine. The pool table takes center stage for the young, hip crowd at this sprawling restaurant and bar at the base of the Manhattan Bridge. Rotating artwork, exposed brick walls lined with tall windows, sunken secondhand chairs, and mellow music (including a bluegrass brunch on

Cut the Blarney

With its rich Irish heritage, New York City is far from hurting for authentic Irish pubs. It seems like every corner has its own Blarney Stone. But three establishments in particular merit mention. Offering a binary selection of its own light or dark beer, **McSorley's Old Ale House** (⊠ 15 E. 7th St., between 2nd and 3rd Aves., East Village ☎ 212/473–9148), immortalized in Joseph Mitchell's classic book *Up in the Old Hotel,* is also one of the New York City's oldest standing bars, Irish or otherwise. **P. J. Clarke's** (⊠ 915 3rd Ave., at E. 55th St., Midtown East ☎ 212/317–1616), however, is the city's most famous Irish pub. Scenes from the 1945 film *Lost Weekend* were filmed on the premises. The three-level **Connolly's** (⊠ 121 W. 45th St., between Broadway and 6th Ave., Midtown West ☎ 212/597–5126) often hosts bands from the old country.

Sundays) make for a distinctive scene. ⊠ *126 Front St., between Jay and Pearl Sts., DUMBO* ☎ *718/243–9005* Ⓜ *Subway: F to York St.*

16

GAY & LESBIAN

Any night of the week, gay men and lesbians can find plenty to keep them occupied. For the latest listings of nightlife options, check out gay publications such as *HX* (⊕ www.hx.com), *Next* (⊕ www.nextmagazine. net), *MetroSource,* and the *New York Blade,* as well as *Paper* and *Time Out New York. GO NYC* is good source for lesbian happenings.

Some venues always have a mixed crowd, whereas others are exclusively for gay men or lesbians. Some clubs have one night a week where they roll out the red carpet for one group or the other. We sort it out for you below.

Dance Clubs & Parties

Area 10018. On Friday nights, the five levels of Club Shelter become a gay playground designed to recall the New York club scene's fabulous heyday in the 1970s and early '80s. Drag queens, go-go boys, and club kids cavort among the mixed crowd while the various DJs play house and '80s music, and and bands perform in the basement. ⊠ *Club Shelter, 20 W. 39th St., between 5th and 6th Aves., Midtown West* ☎ *212/719–4479* Ⓜ *Subway: B, D, F, V to 42nd St.*

Avalon. Housed in a converted church (formerly home to the infamous Limelight), the Sunday-night college party here throbs with techno beats, big-name DJs on two dance floors, and lots of sweaty men. ⊠ *660 6th Ave., at W. 20th St., Chelsea* ☎ *212/807–7780* Ⓜ *Subway: F, V to 23rd St.*

Beige. Gay men in fashion and advertising predominate at this long-running Tuesday get-together. An occasional celebrity or two keeps it lively. Dress up, or look as if you don't have to. ⊠ *B Bar, 358 Bowery, at E. 4th St., East Village* ☎ *212/475–2220* Ⓜ *Subway: 6 to Astor Pl.*

Big Apple Ranch. Country-western and other dance styles are in full swing at this venue, with half-hour two-step lessons at 8 PM, line dancing at 8:30 PM, and then a down-home dance party. ⊠ *Dance Manhattan, 39 W. 19th St., 5th fl., between 5th and 6th Aves., Chelsea* ☎ 212/358–5752 Ⓜ *Subway: F, V to 23rd St.*

BoysRoom. Sexy shenanigans abound at this cruisy bar with a small but steamy downstairs dance floor. On Saturday nights, cocky boys compete for the crowd's applause (and cash) in an amateur strip contest. ⊠ *9 Ave. A, between E. 1st and E. 2nd Sts., East Village* ☎ 212/358–1440 Ⓜ *Subway: F, V to 2nd Ave.*

Cattyshack. The Brooklyn girls are purring over this dance club in Brooklyn's Park Slope, which also attracts a sizable crowd from Manhattan. The draw is a sprawling two-level converted warehouse with rotating DJs, backlit bars perfect for prowling, and an outdoor deck with a barbecue pit. ⊠ *249 4th Ave., between President and Carroll Sts., Park Slope, Brooklyn* ☎ 718/230–5740 Ⓜ *Subway: R to Union St.*

1984. Madonna still reigns supreme on Friday night at Pyramid, a two-story bar with an always-packed dance floor where DJs play '80s pop for a hip, young, and enthusiastic mixed crowd. ⊠ *Pyramid, 101 Ave. A, between E. 6th and E. 7th Sts., East Village* ☎ 212/228–4888 Ⓜ *Subway: 6 to Astor Pl.*

SBNY. At this large, perennially crowded Chelsea bar/club, beefy go-go boys vie for attention with equally buff bartenders who are frequently clad in their underwear. The weekday happy hour, with campy music videos on three huge screens, is a hit. Late-night covers can be high. ⊠ *50 W. 17th St., between 5th and 6th Aves., Chelsea* ☎ 212/691–0073 Ⓜ *Subway: 6 to Astor Pl.*

Lounges

Barracuda. The comfy couches in back are one big plus at this hangout where hilarious, unpredictable send-ups of game shows draw a mostly male crowd. ⊠ *275 W. 22nd St., between 7th and 8th Aves., Chelsea* ☎ 212/645–8613 Ⓜ *Subway: C, E to 23rd St.*

Girlsroom. With a funky young clientele, go-go girls, drink specials, and a cozy lounge, this little Lower East Side dance club packs everything you need for a night out, whether you're after mellow conversation or something racier. ⊠ *210 Rivington St., between Pitt and Ridge Sts., Lower East Side* ☎ 212/677–6149 Ⓜ *Subway: F, J, M, Z to to Delancey St.*

Starlight. The East Village goes fashionable at this lounge, which draws hip, stylish boys. The narrow banquette-lined bar in front can become a squeeze; head to the back lounge area, which often hosts cabaret and stand-up comedy. Starlette, on Sunday, is one of the most popular lesbian nights in town. ⊠ *167 Ave. A, between E. 10th and E. 11th Sts., East Village* ☎ 212/475–2172 Ⓜ *Subway: L to 1st Ave.*

★ **Therapy.** With slate floors, wood-panel walls, and a small stone-filled pond, the decor at this spacious lounge in Hell's Kitchen is as upscale as its mostly male clientele, which includes older uptown professionals as well as some twentysomething hipsters. An appetizing menu of small dishes is available. ⊠ *348 W. 52nd. St., between 8th and 9th Aves., Midtown West* ☎ 212/397–1700 Ⓜ *Subway: C, E to 50th St.*

XL. The owners reportedly poured $2.5 million into this stylish multi-level lounge, but all eyes are on the bare-chested bartenders. Check out the fish tanks in the bathroom. ⊠ *357 W. 16th St., between 8th and 9th Aves., Chelsea* ☎ *646/336–5574* Ⓜ *Subway: A, C, E to 14th St.; L to 8th Ave.*

Neighborhood Bars

The Cock. The 2005 relocation may have slightly cleaned up the setting (the couches are no longer Dumpster worthy), but it hasn't besmirched The Cock's delightfully sordid reputation. The air gets thicker and the men-only scene grows cruisier as the night goes on. ⊠ *29 2nd Ave., between E. 1st and E. 2nd Sts., East Village* ☎ *212/777–6254* Ⓜ *Subway: F, V to 2nd Ave.*

The Cubby Hole. Early in the evening the crowd is mixed at this neighborhood institution, where Madonna and Rosie used to hang out. Later on the room belongs to the women. ⊠ *281 W. 12th St., at W. 4th St., Greenwich Village* ☎ *212/243–9041* Ⓜ *Subway: A, C, E to 14th St.; L to 8th Ave.*

Gym Sports Bar. At New York's first gay sports bar, the plentiful flat-screen TVs and lots of cheap Bud draw sports enthusiasts of every stripe, from athlete to armchair. The bar sponsors—and frequently hosts parties for—a number of local gay sports teams. ⊠ *167 8th Ave., at W. 18th St., Chelsea* ☎ *212/337–2439* Ⓜ *Subway: A, C, E, to 14th St.*

Henrietta Hudson. The nightly parties at this laid-back bar attract young professional women, out-of-towners, and longtime regulars. ⊠ *438 Hudson St., at Morton St., Greenwich Village* ☎ *212/924–3347* Ⓜ *Subway: 1 to Christopher St./ Sheridan Sq.*

Nowhere. The quintessential low-key neighborhood bar, but gay. Rarely crowded, it's a comfortable spot to stop for a drink (happy hour runs until 9 PM), and a welcome alternative to the cruisier venues nearby. Monday is ladies' night. ⊠ *322 E. 14th St., between 1st and 2nd Aves., East Village* ☎ *212/477–4744* Ⓜ *Subway: L to 1st Ave.*

The Phoenix. With a pool table, pinball machine, and an outstanding, constantly updated jukebox, this neighborhood bar is packed almost every night of the week with gay men. The $1 beers on Wednesday are always popular. ⊠ *447 E. 13th St., at Ave. A, East Village* ☎ *212/477–9979* Ⓜ *Subway: L to 1st Ave.*

The Slide. In this underground space, a long wooden bar and vaguely Victorian furnishings are a nice contrast to the raunchy go-go boys. ⊠ *356 Bowery, near E. 4th St., East Village* ☎ *212/420–8885* Ⓜ *Subway: F, V to 2nd Ave.*

Stonewall. With its odd assortment of down-to-earth locals and tourists snapping pictures as they chase gay history, the scene here is definitely egalitarian. ⊠ *53 Christopher St., near 7th Ave. S, Greenwich Village* ☎ *212/463–0950* Ⓜ *Subway: 1 to Christopher St./ Sheridan Sq.*

Piano Bars

Brandy's Piano Bar. A singing waitstaff warms up the mixed crowd at this classy lounge, getting everyone in the mood to belt out their favorite tunes. ⊠ *235 E. 84th St., between 2nd and 3rd Aves., Upper East Side* ☎ *212/650–1944* Ⓜ *Subway: 4, 5, 6 to 86th St.*

Marie's Crisis. Everyone seems to know all the words to show tunes you've never even heard of, but after a few drinks you'll be humming along and making lots of new friends. ⊠ *59 Grove St., at 7th Ave., Greenwich Village* ☎ *212/243–9323* Ⓜ *Subway: 1 to Christopher St./ Sheridan Sq.*

The Monster. A longtime meeting place in the West Village, the Monster has a piano bar upstairs and a disco downstairs. It's mostly men, but women won't feel out of place. ⊠ *80 Grove St., between W. 4th St. and 7th Ave. S, Greenwich Village* ☎ *212/924–3558* Ⓜ *Subway: 1 to Christopher St./ Sheridan Sq.*

The Townhouse. Older, well-off men from the Upper East Side as well as their admirers populate the bars of this brownstone, which sometimes has a piano player. ⊠ *236 E. 58th St., between 2nd and 3rd Aves., Midtown East* ☎ *212/754–4649* Ⓜ *Subway: 4, 5, 6, N, R, W to 59th St.*

Shopping

WORD OF MOUTH

"There IS something about the Tiffany's box. Overpriced? Maybe. Iconic? Definitely. . . . Even if it's something small, pulling out that blue box will definitely put a smile on her face."   —starrsville

"For nice one-of-a-kind boutiques, the East Village: 7th, 8th, 9th, and 10th streets between Third Avenue and Avenue A. Many original designer stores as well as charming vintage stores. It's fun to zig and zag east and west on those streets."

—Elizabeth

Updated by
Sandra Ramani

New York shopping is a nonstop eye-opener, from the pristine couture houses flanking Madison Avenue to quirkier shops downtown. No matter which threshold you cross, shopping here is an event. For every bursting department store there's an echoing, minimalist boutique; for every familiar national brand there's a secret local favorite. The foremost American and international companies stake their flagships here; meanwhile, small neighborhood shops guarantee unexpected pleasures. National chains often make their New York branches something special, with unique sales environments and exclusive merchandise.

For most New Yorkers, shopping is a way of life. You don't shop when you need something, you shop all the time, and somehow one shop always leads to another. Manhattan is a place for wandering—new boutiques are constantly springing up, even on streets that were deserted just weeks before. Manhattan's must-hit shopping neighborhoods concentrate their temptations, sometimes with boutiques in nearly every address on a block, so you can easily spend a couple of hours walking and browsing.

Special neighborhood profiles throughout this chapter will point you to the best areas and give you expert navigating tips. The individual reviews in this chapter are organized by type of merchandise, in alphabetical order by category. Many specialty stores have several branches in the city; in these cases, we have listed the locations in the busier shopping neighborhoods. Happy hunting!

ANTIQUES

Antiquing is a fine art in Manhattan. Goods include everything from rarefied museum-quality pieces to wacky and affordable bric-a-brac. Pre-

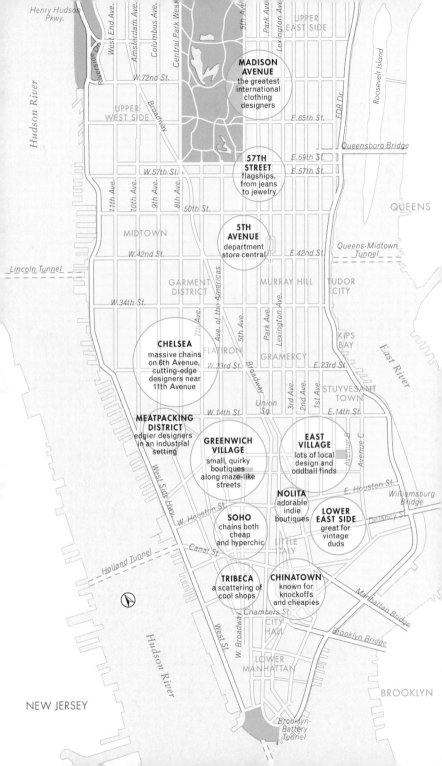

Henry Hudson Pkwy.

West End Ave.

Amsterdam Ave.

Columbus Ave.

Central Park West

5th Ave.

Park Ave.

Lexington Ave.

UPPER EAST SIDE

W.72nd St.

UPPER WEST SIDE

Broadway

Hudson River

MADISON AVENUE
the greatest international clothing designers

E.65th St.

EDR Dr.

Roosevelt Island

Queensboro Bridge

E.59th St.

57TH STREET
flagships, from jeans to jewelry

E.57th St.

QUEENS

W.57th St.

11th Ave.

10th Ave.

9th Ave.

8th Ave.

50th St.

MIDTOWN

5TH AVENUE
department store central

E 42nd St.

Queens-Midtown Tunnel

Lincoln Tunnel

W.42nd St.

GARMENT DISTRICT

MURRAY HILL

TUDOR CITY

W.34th St.

Ave. of the Americas

7th Ave.

5th Ave.

Park Ave.

Lexington Ave.

CHELSEA
massive chains on 6th Avenue, cutting-edge designers near 11th Avenue

FLATIRON

W.23rd St.

GRAMERCY

E.23rd St.

KIPS BAY

East River

Broadway

3rd Ave.

2nd Ave.

1st Ave.

STUYVESANT TOWN

Union Sq.

E.14th St.

MEATPACKING DISTRICT
edgier designers in an industrial setting

W.14th St.

West Side Hwy.

GREENWICH VILLAGE
small, quirky boutiques along maze-like streets

EAST VILLAGE
lots of local design and oddball finds

Avenue B

Avenue C

NOLITA
adorable indie boutiques

E. Houston St.

Williamsburg Bridge

W. Houston St.

SOHO
chains both cheap and hyperchic

LOWER EAST SIDE
great for vintage duds

Delancy St.

Holland Tunnel

Canal St.

LITTLE ITALY

TRIBECA
a scattering of cool shops

CHINATOWN
known for knockoffs and cheapies

Manhattan Bridge

Chambers St.

Hudson River

W. Broadway

W. West

CITY HALL

Brooklyn Bridge

LOWER MANHATTAN

NEW JERSEY

Brooklyn-Battery Tunnel

BROOKLYN

mier shopping areas are on Madison Avenue north of 57th Street, and East 60th Street between 2nd and 3rd avenues, where more than 20 shops, dealing in everything from 18th-century French furniture to art deco lighting fixtures, cluster on one block. Around West 11th and 12th streets between University Place and Broadway, a tantalizing array of settees, bedsteads, and rocking chairs can be seen in the windows of about two dozen dealers, many of whom have TO THE TRADE signs on their doors; a card from your architect or decorator, however, may get you inside. Finally, for 20th-century furniture and fixtures, head south of Houston Street, especially along Lafayette Street. Most dealers are closed Sunday.

American & English

Florian Papp. The shine of gilt—on ormolu clocks, chaise longues, and marble-top tables—lures casual customers in, but this store has an unassailed reputation among knowledgeable collectors. ⊠ *962 Madison Ave., between E. 75th and E. 76th Sts., Upper East Side* ☎ *212/288–6770* Ⓜ *Subway: 6 to 77th St.*

Kentshire Galleries. Pristine furniture is displayed in room settings on eight floors here, with an emphasis on formal English pieces from the 18th and 19th centuries, particularly the Georgian and Regency periods. The collection of period and estate jewelry is a showstopper, from Edwardian pearl earrings to vintage gold watches from Van Cleef & Arpels. ⊠ *37 E. 12th St., between University Pl. and Broadway, Greenwich Village* ☎ *212/673–6644* Ⓜ *Subway: 4, 5, 6, L, N, Q, R, W to 14th St./Union Sq.*

Leigh Keno American Antiques. Twins Leigh and Leslie Keno set an auction record in the American antiques field by paying $2.75 million for a hairy paw–foot Philadelphia wing chair. They have a good eye and an interesting inventory; gaze up at a tall case clock or down at the delicate legs of a tea table. It's best to make an appointment. ⊠ *127 E. 69th St., between Park and Lexington Aves., Upper East Side* ☎ *212/734–2381* Ⓜ *Subway: 6 to 77th St.*

Newel Art Galleries. Near the East Side's interior-design district, this huge collection spans the Renaissance through the 20th century. The nonfurniture finds, from figureheads to bell jars, make for prime conversation pieces. ⊠ *425 E. 53rd St., between 1st Ave. and Sutton Pl., Midtown East* ☎ *212/758–1970* Ⓜ *Subway: 6 to 51st St./Lexington Ave.; E, V to Lexington–3rd Aves./53rd St.*

Asian

Chinese Porcelain Company. Though the name of this prestigious shop indicates one of its specialties, its stock covers more ground, ranging from lacquerware to Khmer sculpture to 18th-century French furniture. ⊠ *475 Park Ave., at E. 58th St., Midtown East* ☎ *212/838–7744* Ⓜ *Subway: N, R, W to 5th Ave.*

Flying Cranes Antiques. Here you can find a well-regarded collection of rare, museum-quality pieces from the Meiji period, the time known as Japan's Golden Age. Items include ceramics, cloisonné, metalwork, carvings, ikebana baskets, and samurai swords and fittings. ⊠ *Manhattan Art and Antiques Center, 1050 2nd Ave., between E. 55th and E. 56th Sts., Midtown East* ☎ *212/223–4600* Ⓜ *Subway: N, R, W, 4, 5, 6 to 59th St./Lexington Ave.*

Jacques Carcangues, Inc. Carrying goods from Japan to India, this SoHo gallery offers an eclectic array of objects, from pillboxes to 18th-century Burmese Buddhas. ✉ *21 Greene St., between Grand and Canal Sts., SoHo* ☎ *212/925–8110* Ⓜ *Subway: 4, 5, 6, R, W to Canal St.*

European

Newel Art Galleries and Florian Papp, covered under American and English antiques, and the Chinese Porcelain Company, listed under Asian antiques, also carry European pieces.

Barry Friedman Ltd. Having championed 20th-century art for decades, Barry Friedman now turns to contemporary decorative objects, such as art glass by Dale Chihuly. Vintage and contemporary photographs are also available. ✉ *32 E. 67th St., between Park and Madison Aves., Upper East Side* ☎ *212/794–8950* Ⓜ *Subway: 6 to 68th St./Hunter College.*

L'Antiquaire & The Connoisseur, Inc. Proprietor Helen Fioratti has written a guide to French antiques, but she's equally knowledgeable about her Italian and Spanish furniture and decorative objects from the 15th through the 18th century, as well as about the medieval arts. ✉ *36 E. 73rd St., between Madison and Park Aves., Upper East Side* ☎ *212/ 517–9176* Ⓜ *Subway: 6 to 77th St.*

Leo Kaplan Ltd. The impeccable items here include art nouveau glass and pottery, porcelain from 18th-century England, antique and modern paperweights, and Russian artwork. ✉ *114 E. 57th St., between Park and Lexington Aves., Upper East Side* ☎ *212/249–6766* Ⓜ *Subway: N, R, W, 4, 5, 6 to 59th St./Lexington Ave.*

Les Pierre Antiques. Pierre Deux popularized French Provincial through reproductions; come here for a strong selection of the real thing. ✉ *369 Bleecker St., at Charles St., Greenwich Village* ☎ *212/243–7740* Ⓜ *Subway: 1 to Christopher St./Sheridan Sq.*

20th-Century Furniture & Memorabilia

Las Venus. Step into this kitsch palace and you may feel as though a time machine has zapped you back to the '50s, '60s, or groovy '70s—depending on which vintage pieces are in stock. Look for bubble lamps, lots of brocade, and Knoll knockoffs; a second location around the corner houses overflow. ✉ *163 Ludlow St., between E. Houston and Stanton Sts., Lower East Side* ☎ *212/982–0608* Ⓜ *Subway: F, V to 2nd Ave.*

Lost City Arts. In addition to mod furniture, like pod and Eames chairs, and industrial memorabilia, such as neon gas-station clocks, Lost City can help you relive the Machine Age with an in-house, retro-modern line of furniture. ✉ *18 Cooper Sq., at E. 5th St., East Village* ☎ *212/ 375–0500* Ⓜ *Subway: 6 to Astor Pl.*

BEAUTY

★ **Aedes De Venustas.** Celebs like Oprah, Madonna, and Jennifer Lopez have called on this West Village boutique for the ultimate in unique, high-end international fragrance and beauty. Swathed in red velvet, the jewel-box-size store stocks a well-edited selection of hard-to-find skin-care lines like Trilogy and Patyka; fragrance from Miller Harris, Lorenzo Villoresi,

Costes, and Nanadebary; and pricey candles from Diptyque and Damien Bash. Their signature gift wrap is as beautiful as what's inside the box. ⊠ *9 Christopher St., between 6th and 7th Aves., Greenwich Village* 🕾 *212/206–8674* Ⓜ *Subway: 1 to Christopher St./Sheridan Sq.*

★ **Bond No. 9.** Created by the same fragrance team as Creed, this line of scents is intended to evoke the New York City experience. Perfumes are named after neighborhoods: Central Park, a men's fragrance, is woodsy and "green"; the feminine Park Avenue is regal and sophisticated, with hints of iris and rose. The downtown shop, with its airy space and wood-panel Tea Library, is a lovely place to linger. ⊠ *9 Bond St., between Lafayette St. and Broadway, East Village* 🕾*212/228–1940* Ⓜ *Subway: 6 to Bleecker St.* ⊠ *897 Madison Ave., between E. 72nd and E. 73rd Sts., Upper East Side* 🕾 *212/794–4480* Ⓜ *Subway: 6 to 68th St./Hunter College* ⊠ *680 Madison Ave., between E. 61st and E. 62nd Sts., Upper East Side* 🕾 *212/ 838–2780* Ⓜ *Subway: N, R, W, 4, 5, 6 to 59th St./Lexington Ave.*

Floris of London. Floral English toiletries adored by British royals stock this re-creation of the cozy London original. If you love lathering, look for the wooden bowls of shaving or bath soap. ⊠ *703 Madison Ave., between E. 62nd and E. 63rd Sts., Upper East Side* 🕾 *212/935–9100* Ⓜ *Subway: 6 to 68th St./Hunter College.*

Jo Malone. Consider this extra incentive to visit the landmark Flatiron Building. Unisex scents such as lime blossom and vetiver can be worn alone or, in the Malone style, layered. Since Malone uses colognes, not perfumes, it's not overpowering. You can also book one of the famed massage-based facials. (The uptown branch offers all the scents, but not the facial.) ⊠ *949 Broadway, at 5th Ave., Flatiron District* 🕾 *212/ 673–2220* Ⓜ *Subway: R, W to 23rd St.* ⊠ *946 Madison Ave., between E. 74th and E. 75th Sts., Upper East Side* 🕾 *212/472–0074* Ⓜ *Subway: 6 to 77th St.*

Fodor'sChoice **Kiehl's Since 1851.** At this favored haunt of top models and stylists, white-★ smocked assistants can help you choose among the lotions and potions, all of which are packaged in deceptively simple-looking bottles and jars. Some of the products, such as the pineapple-papaya facial scrub, Silk Groom hair-styling aid, and the super-rich Creme de Corps, have attained near-cult status among beautyphiles. Kiehl's is also known for being generous with samples, so be sure to ask for your own bag of take-home testers. ⊠ *109 3rd Ave., at E. 13th St., East Village* 🕾 *212/677–3171* Ⓜ *Subway: 4, 5, 6, L, N, Q, R, W to 14th St./Union Sq.* ⊠ *150 Columbus Ave., at W. 67th St., Upper West Side* 🕾 *212/799–3438* Ⓜ *Subway: 1 to 66th St./Lincoln Center.*

★ **L'Artisan Parfumeur.** This tiny, hole-in-the-wall shop may look unassuming—but the line of gorgeous, limited-edition scents sold here is nothing to sneeze at. Some fragrances, like the myrrh-and-vetiver-infused Timbuktu, conjure faraway locales; others, like the rosy, feminine La Chasse aux Papillons ("Chasing the Butterflies") or the manly Mechant Loup ("Big Bad Wolf") evoke nostalgic whimsy. ⊠ *68 Thompson St., between Spring and Broome Sts., SoHo* 🕾 *212/334–1500* Ⓜ *Subway: R, W to Prince St.*

Lush. Some of these products are so fresh you need to keep them in the fridge. Most of the soaps, facial treatments, and lotions have vegetal ingredients and very few preservatives. The Bath Bombs, in such flavors

Holiday Markets

BETWEEN THANKSGIVING AND CHRISTMAS, holiday markets—rows of wooden stalls, many with red-and-white-striped awnings—spring up around town. The gifts and goods vary from year to year, but there are some perennial offerings: colorful handmade knitwear and jewelry; sweet-smelling soaps, candles, and lotions with hand-lettered labels; glittery Christmas ornaments of every stripe; and New York-themed gift items (a group called Gritty City offers T-shirts, coin purses, and undies printed with pictures of taxicabs and manhole covers).

Though the holiday market in **Grand Central Terminal's Vanderbilt Hall** is indoors, most vendors set up outside. There's one every year at **Columbus Circle,** near the southwest entrance to Central Park, and another at **Bryant Park,** behind the New York City Public Library. The largest and most popular, however, is at the south end of **Union Square,** where you can go from the Greenmarket to the stalls like the downtowners who meet in the afternoon or after work to look for unique or last-minute gifts.

as Honey Bee and Ginger Man, dissolve to release essential oils and moisturizers when dropped into a bath. ⊠ *1293 Broadway, at W. 34th St., Midtown West* ☎ *212/564–9120* Ⓜ *Subway: B, D, F, N, Q, R, V, W to 34th St./Herald Sq.* ⊠ *2165 Broadway, at 76th St. Upper West Side* ☎ *212/787–5874* Ⓜ *Subway: 1 to 79th St.*

M.A.C. Fashion hounds pile into these boutiques, both for the basics (foundation and concealer for a huge range of skin tones) and the far-out (eye shadow colors like Electric Eel and Chrome Yellow). Salespeople can offer expert advice—many of them also work as professional makeup artists. ⊠ *113 Spring St., between Mercer and Greene Sts., SoHo* ☎ *212/ 334–4641* Ⓜ *Subway: C, E to Spring St.* ⊠ *1 E. 22nd St., between 5th Ave. and Broadway, Flatiron District* ☎ *212/677–6611* Ⓜ *Subway: F, R, V, W to 23rd St.* ⊠ *202 W. 125th St., at Adam Clayton Powell Jr. Blvd., Harlem* ☎ *212/665–0676* Ⓜ *Subway: A, B, C, D to 125th St.*

Make Up For Ever. The makeup from this Paris-based boutique does not hew to the natural look. The products are pigment-rich and boldly colored; liquid eyeliner could be bright green as well as dark brown, mascara pearly white as well as black. The staff applications help nonprofessionals navigate the spectrum for everyday wear. ⊠ *409 West Broadway, between Prince and Spring Sts., SoHo* ☎ *212/941–9337* Ⓜ *Subway: C, E to Spring St.*

Molton Brown. A staple amenity in British Airways dopp kits, this beloved U.K. brand's only two U.S. emporiums carry the full line of modern bath, body, cosmetics, skin care, and home products, as well as the Luxury collection of travel bags and cashmere accessories. Known for using unusual ingredients from around the world, MB's devoted fans stock up on such items as the Naran Ji Hand Wash, Arctic Birch lotion, and Black Pepper body wash. The Take 5 Bar lets you mix and match travel minis for a reasonable flat fee; free mini-facials and makeup sessions are of-

Continued on page 320

SOHO

Somehow, everything looks a bit more beautiful here. Maybe it's because of the way sunlight filters down the cast-iron facades, glinting off the temptations in shop windows. Maybe it's because the uneven cobblestone streets prompt you to slow down, giving you time to notice details.

Jaded locals call this neighborhood a touristy outdoor mall. True, you'll see plenty of familiar company names, and several common, less-expensive chains, like Banana Republic and Sephora, have made land grabs on Broadway. There's also a certain amount of luxury one-upmanship, as stores like Prada, Chanel, and Louis Vuitton have planted themselves here for downtown cred. But you can still hit a few clothing and housewares boutiques you won't find elsewhere in this country. The hottest shopping area runs west from Broadway over to 6th Avenue, between West Houston and Grand streets. Don't overlook a couple of streets east of Broadway: Crosby and Lafayette each have a handful of intriguing shops. They're also quieter and thus a nice break from the main SoHo scrum. Hard to believe SoHo was an out-of-the-way gallery district not so long ago. . . —by Jennifer Paull

BEST TIME TO GO

Wednesday through Friday afternoons, when all the stores are open and the people-watching is prime, but the streets aren't hideously crowded. On weekends, Broadway and Prince Street can feel like a cattle drive.

BEST SOUVENIR FOR YOUR IN-LAWS

A bottle of New York State wine from **Vintage New York** (after treating yourself to a tasting at the store's wine bar). If they're caffeine fiends, consider the house-blend coffees and teas at **Dean & Deluca,** which you can pair with sophisticated snacks in a D&D tote or metal lunch box.

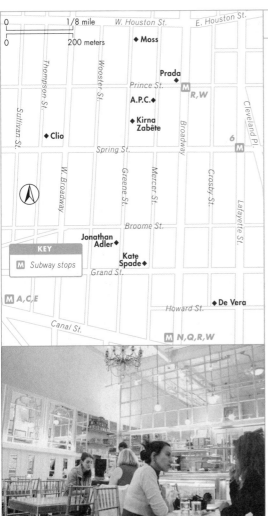

SPOTLIGHT ON SOHO

17

Best For

WHAT TO WEAR

Prada: the high-concept, Rem Koolhaas–designed store steals the spotlight from the clothes.

Kirna Zabête: uncommon, sought-after women's clothing in a cheerful, unpretentious space.

Kate Spade: the motherlode for clever handbags, plus retro-ish shoes and a few baubles.

A.P.C.: deceptively simple casual clothes and excellent narrow, straight-legged jeans.

HOUSEWARES

Moss: exquisite, innovative design for everything from wineglasses to bathtubs.

Clio: low-key vibe but high-scoring selection of unique tableware.

Jonathan Adler: a loving spin on midcentury mod (and kitsch) in ceramics and furniture.

De Vera: eclectic selection of antiques and new objets d'art, from Murano glass to Japanese lacquer.

Refueling

For something on the fly, drop by **Balthazar Bakery** (80 Spring St., between Broadway and Crosby St., 212/965–1785) for a scone, madeleine, or walnut-studded brownie with a potent cup of coffee. If you'd rather have a seat, make your way to the tea room hidden in the back of **Marie Belle** for a cup of their excellent hot chocolate.

fered in private rooms. ⊠ *515 Madison Ave., on E. 53rd St., Midtown East* ☎ *212/755–7194* Ⓜ *Subway: E, V to Lexington Ave./53rd St.* ⊠ *1098 3rd Ave., between E. 64th and E. 65th Sts., Upper East Side* ☎ *212/744–6430* Ⓜ *Subway: 6 to 68th St./Hunter College.*

★ **Santa Maria Novella.** A heavy, iron-barred door leads to a hushed, scented inner sanctum of products from this medieval Florentine pharmacy. Many of the colognes, creams, and soaps are intriguingly archaic, such as the iris toothpaste, the Carta d'Armenia (scented papers that perfume a room when burned), and the Vinegar of the Seven Thieves (a variant on smelling salts). Everything is packaged in bottles and jars with antique apothecary labels. ⊠ *285 Lafayette St., between E. Houston and Prince Sts., SoHo* ☎ *212/925–0001* Ⓜ *Subway: N, R to Prince St.*

SCO. Short for Skin Care Options, this custom-beauty line is all about you. Choose from base products like moisturizers, masks, eye gels, body scrubs, and lip treatments, then add infusions based on your needs. The long list of ingredients includes caffeine to tighten and firm, molasses to even skin tone, and soy to hydrate. Facials, waxing, and body treatments are offered in a back spa area. ⊠ *584 Broadway, between W. Houston and Prince Sts., SoHo* ☎ *212/966–3011* Ⓜ *Subway: Q, R, W to Prince St.*

Shu Uemura. Top-of-the-line Japanese skin-care products, makeup, and tools distinguish this downtown spot; among the best sellers are the Balancing Cleansing Oil, the professional-grade eyelash curler, and lip glosses in such yummy flavors as orange sorbet and lemonade. ⊠ *121 Greene St., between Prince and W. Houston Sts., SoHo* ☎ *212/979–5500* Ⓜ *Subway: R, W to Prince St.*

BOOKS

See National Chains box for Borders and Barnes & Noble locations.

Children's Books

Books of Wonder. The friendly, knowledgeable staff can help select gifts for all reading levels from the extensive, beautiful selection of children's books. Oziana is a specialty. An outpost of the Cupcake Café gives little browsers a second wind. ⊠ *18 W. 18th St., between 5th and 6th Aves., Chelsea* ☎ *212/989–3270* Ⓜ *Subway: F, V to 14th St.*

Foreign Language

Librairie de France/Libreria Hispanica. This store offers one of the country's largest selections of foreign-language books, videos, and periodicals, mostly in French and Spanish. You can also find dozens of dictionaries, phrase books, and other learning materials. ⊠ *610 5th Ave., Rockefeller Center Promenade, Midtown West* ☎ *212/581–8810* Ⓜ *Subway: B, D, F, V to 47th–50th Sts./Rockefeller Center.*

Gay & Lesbian

Oscar Wilde Bookshop. Opened in 1967, this was the first gay and lesbian bookstore in the city and is now the oldest existing one in the country, having weathered a close brush with closure in 2003. It's just steps from the site of the Stonewall riots. The shelves hold everything from cultural studies and biographies to fiction and first editions by the likes of Djuna Barnes and Paul Monette. ✉ *15 Christopher St., between 6th and 7th Aves., Greenwich Village* ☎ *212/255–8097* Ⓜ *Subway: 1 to Christopher St./Sheridan Sq.*

General Interest

Biography Bookshop. Published diaries, letters, biographies, and autobiographies fill this neighborly store. There's also a thoughtful selection of general nonfiction, fiction, guidebooks, and children's books. The sale tables outside have deals on everything from Graham Greene to Chuck Palahniuk. ✉ *400 Bleecker St., at W. 11th St., Greenwich Village* ☎ *212/807–8655* Ⓜ *Subway: 1 to Christopher St./Sheridan Sq.*

The Complete Traveller Antiquarian Bookstore. Founded in the '80s by two former travel writers, this store specializes in rare and antique voyage-related books, and promises the country's largest selection of out-of-print Baedeker travel guides. They stock surprisingly affordable vintage maps, unusual tomes with New York City themes, and a full spectrum of books—from history and geography to poetry and fiction—that emphasize travel. ✉ *199 Madison Ave., at 35th St., Murray Hill* ☎ *212/685–9007* Ⓜ *Subway: 6 to 33rd St.*

★ **Crawford Doyle Booksellers.** You're as likely to see an old edition of Wodehouse as a best seller in the window of this shop. You'll find a quality selection of fiction, nonfiction, and biographies, plus some rare books on the balcony. Salespeople offer their opinions *and* ask for yours. ✉ *1082 Madison Ave., between E. 81st and E. 82nd Sts., Upper East Side* ☎ *212/288–6300* Ⓜ *Subway: 4, 5, 6 to 86th St.*

★ **Gotham Book Mart.** The late Frances Steloff opened Gotham in 1920 with just $200 in her pocket, half of it on loan. But she helped launch James Joyce's *Ulysses,* D. H. Lawrence, and Henry Miller, and is now legendary among collectors and literary types—as is her bookstore. They're one of the few bookstores in town with an extremely large cache of literary journals. There's also a wealth of signed editions of deliciously macabre Edward Gorey books. ✉ *16 E. 46th St., between 5th and Madison Aves., Midtown East* ☎ *212/719–4448* Ⓜ *Subway: B, D, F, V to 47th–50th Sts./Rockefeller Center.*

★ **McNally Robinson.** McNally makes a happy counterpart to the nearby Housing Works bookstore; both places have that welcoming vibe. Check the tables up front for hot-off-the-press novels, nonfiction, and manifestos. Upstairs you'll find fiction arranged by the authors' region of origin, a great way to learn more about, say, Asian or South American writing. (Salman Rushdie gets grouped with the Global Nomads.) The staff are by and large literary themselves, so ask for recommendations, if you're browsing. ✉ *52 Prince St., between Lafayette and Mulberry Sts., SoHo* ☎ *212/274–1160* Ⓜ *Subway: R, W to Prince St.*

Partners & Crime. Imported British paperbacks, helpful staff, a rental library, and whodunits galore—new, out-of-print, and first editions—make this a must-browse for fans. Revered mystery writers give readings here. Check out the Radio Mystery Hour on the first Saturday of every month. ✉ *44 Greenwich Ave., between 6th and 7th Aves., Greenwich Village* ☎ *212/243–0440* Ⓜ *Subway: F, V, 1, 2, 3 to 14th St.*

★ **St. Mark's Bookshop.** Downtown residents, NYU students, and intellectuals in general love this store, and hang out in the aisles, poking through

17

popular and oddball fiction and nonfiction. You'll find a truly eclectic, attitudinal collection of books here, not unlike the salespeople. On the main floor, books on critical theory are right up front, across from new fiction titles—this is perhaps the only place where you can find Jacques Derrida facing off against T. C. Boyle. Cultural and art books are up front as well; literature and literary journals fill the back of the store. ✉ *31 3rd Ave., at 9th St., East Village* ☎ *212/260–7853* Ⓜ *Subway: 6 to Astor Pl.*

Shakespeare & Co. Booksellers. The stock here represents what's happening in just about every field of publishing today: students can grab a last-minute Gertrude Stein for class, then rummage through the homages to cult pop-culture figures. Late hours at the Broadway location (until 11 PM Monday through Saturday; 9 PM on Sunday) are a plus. ✉ *939 Lexington Ave., between E. 68th and E. 69th Sts., Upper East Side* ☎ *212/ 570–0201* Ⓜ *Subway: 6 to 68th St./Hunter College* ✉ *137 E. 23rd St., at Lexington Ave., Gramercy* ☎ *212/505–2021* Ⓜ *Subway: 6 to 23rd St.* ✉ *716 Broadway, at Washington Pl., Greenwich Village* ☎ *212/529– 1330* Ⓜ *Subway: R, W to 8th St.* ✉ *1 Whitehall St., at Beaver St., Lower Manhattan* ☎ *212/742–7025* Ⓜ *Subway: 4, 5 to Bowling Green.*

Fodor'sChoice ★ **The Strand.** The Broadway branch—a downtown hangout—proudly claims to have "18 miles of books." Craning your neck among the tall-as-trees stacks will likely net you something from the mix of new and old. Rare books are next door, at 826 Broadway, on the third floor. The Fulton Street branch is near South Street Seaport; it's decidedly less overwhelming. ✉ *828 Broadway, at E. 12th St., East Village* ☎ *212/473– 1452* Ⓜ *Subway: L, N, Q, R, W, 4, 5, 6 to 14th St./Union Sq.* ✉ *95 Fulton St., between Gold and William Sts., Lower Manhattan* ☎ *212/ 732–6070* Ⓜ *Subway: A, C, J, M, Z, 2, 3, 4, 5 to Fulton St./Broadway-Nassau.*

★ **Three Lives & Co.** Three Lives has one of the city's best book selections. The display tables and counters highlight the latest literary fiction and serious nonfiction, classics, quirky gift books, and gorgeously illustrated tomes. The staff members' literary knowledge is formidable, and they can help you find most any book—even if it's not carried in the store. ✉ *154 W. 10th St., at Waverly Pl., Greenwich Village* ☎ *212/ 741–2069* Ⓜ *Subway: 1 to Christopher St./Sheridan Sq.*

Music

Colony Music. Siphoning energy from Times Square, this place keeps its neon blinking until 1 AM Monday through Saturday, and midnight on Sunday. Inspired by the Broadway musical or concert you've just seen? Snap up the sheet music, CD, or karaoke set here. ✉ *1619 Broadway, at W. 49th St., Midtown West* ☎ *212/265–2050* Ⓜ *Subway: R, W to 49th St.*

Joseph Patelson Music House. A huge collection of scores (some 47,000 pieces of sheet music for piano, organ, strings, woodwind, and brass, and chambers and ensembles) has long made this a hub for music lovers. Fittingly, it's right by Carnegie Hall. ✉ *160 W. 56th St., between 6th and 7th Aves., Midtown West* ☎ *212/582–5840* Ⓜ *Subway: F, N, Q, R, W to 57th St.*

Rare & Used Books

Crawford Doyle Booksellers, Complete Traveller, and the Strand, covered under General Interest, also carry rare and used titles.

Argosy Bookstore. This sedate landmark, established in 1921, keeps a scholarly stock of books and autographs. It's also a great place to look for low-price maps and prints. ✉ *116 E. 59th St., between Park and Lexington Aves., Midtown East* ☎ *212/753–4455* Ⓜ *Subway: N, R, W, 4, 5, 6 to 59th St./Lexington Ave.*

Bauman Rare Books. This successful Philadelphia firm offers New Yorkers the most impossible-to-get titles, first editions, and fine leather sets. ✉ *535 Madison Ave., between E. 54th and E. 55th Sts., Midtown East* ☎ *212/751–0011* Ⓜ *Subway: N, R, W, 4, 5, 6 to 59th St./Lexington Ave.*

★ **Housing Works Used Book Café.** If the jostling sidewalks of SoHo have you on edge, head one block east of Broadway to this sanctuary of a used bookstore. There's lots of room to browse, and plenty of chairs where you can relax and flip through your finds (for hefty art books, you might want to grab a table at the café in back). ✉ *126 Crosby St., between E. Houston and Prince Sts., NoLita* ☎ *212/334–3324* Ⓜ *Subway: R, W to Prince St.*

Skyline Books. Come here for out-of-print and quirky books in all categories, as well as literary first editions. ✉ *13 W. 18th St., between 5th and 6th Aves., Chelsea* ☎ *212/675–4773* Ⓜ *Subway: 4, 5, 6, N, Q, R, W to 14th St./Union Sq.*

Westsider Rare & Used Books. This wonderfully crammed space is a lifesaver on the otherwise sparse Upper West Side. Squeeze in among the stacks of art books and fiction; clamber up the steep stairway and you'll find all sorts of rare books. ✉ *2246 Broadway, between W. 80th and W. 81st Sts., Upper West Side* ☎ *212/362–0706* Ⓜ *Subway: 1 to 79th St.*

Theater

Drama Book Shop. If you're looking for a script, be it a lesser-known Russian translation or a Broadway hit, chances are you can find it here. The range of books spans film, music, dance, TV, and biographies. The shop hosts lots of in-store events, too, such as free writing seminars and talks with well-known playwrights. ✉ *250 W. 40th St., between 7th and 8th Aves., Midtown West* ☎ *212/944–0595* Ⓜ *Subway: A, C, E to 42nd St./Port Authority.*

CAMERAS & ELECTRONICS

Apple Store SoHo. This former post office is now home base for e-mail-generation hipsters. You'll have to elbow through a crowd, but it's the place to check out Mac minis, iPods, and digital moviemaking equipment. Head up the glass staircase for software; the upstairs also houses a demo area and a troubleshooting desk. ✉ *103 Prince St., at Greene St., SoHo* ☎ *212/226–3126* Ⓜ *Subway: R, W to Prince St.*

Fodor'sChoice **B&H Photo Video and Pro Audio.** As baskets of purchases trundle along ★ on tracks overhead, you can plunge into the excellent selection of imaging, audio, video, and lighting equipment. The staff are generous with advice and will happily compare merchandise. Low prices, good customer service, and a liberal returns policy make this a favorite with pros and amateurs alike. Be sure to leave a few extra minutes for the checkout procedure; also, keep in mind that the store is closed Friday evening through Saturday. ⊠ *420 9th Ave., between W. 33rd and W. 34th Sts., Midtown West* ☎ *212/444–5000* Ⓜ *Subway: A, C, E, 1, 2, 3 to 34th St./Penn Station.*

J&R Music World. Just south of City Hall, J&R has emerged, over the years, as the city's most competitively priced one-stop electronics outlet, with an enormous selection of video equipment, computers, stereos, and cameras. The staff is hands-on and superknowledgeable; many of them are A/V wizards who've worked here since the early 1990s. Home-office supplies are at No. 1, computers at No. 15, small appliances at No. 27. ⊠ *23 Park Row, between Beekman and Ann Sts., Lower Manhattan* ☎ *212/ 238–9000* Ⓜ *Subway: 4, 5, 6 to Brooklyn Bridge/City Hall.*

SONY Style. This equipment and music store comes in a glossy package, with imaginative window displays and a downstairs demonstration area for the integrated systems. You'll find all the latest stereo and entertainment systems, video cameras, and portable CD and mp3 players on the shelves. ⊠ *550 Madison Ave., at E. 55th St., Midtown East* ☎ *212/ 833–8800* Ⓜ *Subway: E, V, 6 to 51st./Lexington Ave.*

CHOCOLATE

Chocolate Bar. Sweets from some of New York's finest chocolate chefs fill the cases here. Along with its signature and retro chocolate bars (the latter include such flavors as caramel apple and coconut cream pie) are an array of filled chocolate bonbons. At the café counter you can get a steaming cup of cocoa. The bar is open until 10 PM most nights. ⊠ *48 8th Ave., between Horatio and Jane Sts., Greenwich Village* ☎ *212/366– 1541* Ⓜ *Subway: A, C, E to 14th St.*

Elk Candy Co. This slice of old Yorkville carries European treats such as Mozartkugeln along with specialty chocolates and wonderful marzipan. ⊠ *1628 2nd Ave., between E. 84th and E. 85th Sts., Upper East Side* ☎ *212/650–1177* Ⓜ *Subway: 4, 5, 6 to 86th St.*

★ **Jacques Torres Chocolate Haven.** Visit the café and shop here and you'll literally be surrounded by chocolate. The glass-walled space is in the heart of Torres's chocolate factory, so you can watch the goodies being made while you sip a richly spiced cocoa. Signature taste: the "wicked" chocolate, laced with cinnamon and chili pepper. ⊠ *350 Hudson St., at King St., SoHo* ☎ *212/414–2462* Ⓜ *Subway: 1 to Houston St.*

Kee's Chocolates. Walking into this small store, you might get a whiff of warm chocolate or spy a few smeared spatulas in the back, attesting to the candy's homemade origin. Yet what's in the case looks preternaturally perfect: dark chocolates filled with *yuzu* (a Japanese citrus), covered with freshly crushed pistachios, or flavored with lemon and basil. ⊠ *80 Thompson St., between Broome and Grand Sts., SoHo* ☎ *212/ 334–3284* Ⓜ *Subway: A, C to Spring St.*

★ **La Maison du Chocolat.** Stop in at this chocolatier's small tea salon to dive into a cup of thick, heavenly hot chocolate. The Paris-based outfit sells handmade truffles, chocolates, and pastries that could lull you into a chocolate stupor. ⊠ *1018 Madison Ave., between E. 78th and 79th Sts., Upper East Side* ☎ *212/744–7117* Ⓜ *Subway: 6 to 77th St.* ⊠ *30 Rockefeller Center, between 5th and 6th Aves., Midtown West* ☎ *212/ 265–9404* Ⓜ *Subway: B, D, F, V to 47th–50th St./Rockefeller Center.*

Li-Lac Chocolates. This adorable nook has been feeding the Village's sweet tooth since 1923. You can buy dark-chocolate-dipped marzipan acorns here by the pound, as well as such specialty items as chocolate-molded Statues of Liberty. If you can't get downtown, try a hand-dipped treat at their stand in the Grand Central Market at Grand Central Terminal. ⊠ *40 8th Ave., at Jane St., Greenwich Village* ☎ *212/ 242–7374* Ⓜ *Subway: A, C, E to 14th St.*

Lunettes et Chocolat. Eyeglasses and candy? The better to see your choco-late with. Gaze at the rows of dashing frames by New Yorker favorite Selima and various designer shades for as long as you can withstand the beckoning smell of cocoa. Then melt for the chocolates, with their de-lectable ganache, praline, and cream-based fillings. ⊠ *25 Prince St., be-tween Elizabeth and Mott Sts., NoLita* ☎ *212/925–8800* Ⓜ *Subway: R, W to Prince St.*

★ **MarieBelle.** The handmade chocolates here are nothing less than works of art. Square truffles and bonbons—which come in such flavors as Earl Grey tea, cappuccino, passion fruit, saffron, lemon milk, and lavender— are painted with edible dyes so each resembles a miniature painting, and packaged in decorative leather boxes. Tins of aromatic tea leaves and Aztec hot chocolate are also available. ⊠ *484 Broome St., between West Broadway and Wooster St., SoHo* ☎ *212/925–6999* Ⓜ *Subway: R, W to Prince St.*

Richart Design et Chocolat. This French shop is worth its weight in cacao beans. The sophisticated chocolates are mostly dark, the ganaches and fillings are intense and sometimes unusual, and many are imprinted with intricate and colorful patterns. ⊠ *7 E. 55th St., between 5th and Madi-son Aves., Midtown East* ☎ *212/371–9369* Ⓜ *Subway: N, R, W to 5th Ave./59th St.*

Teuscher Chocolates of Switzerland. Fabulous chocolates (try the cham-pagne truffles) made in Switzerland are flown in weekly for sale in these jewel-box shops, newly decorated each season. ⊠ *620 5th Ave., in Rockefeller Center, Midtown West* ☎ *212/246–4416* Ⓜ *Subway: E, V to 5th Ave./53rd St.* ⊠ *25 E. 61st St., between Madison and Park Aves., Upper East Side* ☎ *212/751–8482* Ⓜ *Subway: N, R, W, 4, 5, 6 to 59th St./Lexington Ave.*

Fodor'sChoice ★ **Vosges Haut Chocolat.** This chandeliered salon takes chocolate couture to a new level. The creations are internationally themed: the Budapest bonbons combine dark chocolate and Hungarian paprika, the Black Pearls contain wasabi, and the Aboriginal collection uses such esoteric ingre-dients as wattleseed and ryeberry. The vibe here is unabashedly arty: films are projected on a section of white wall, T-shirts obsessively repeat the word *chocolate,* and silk-covered handbags are printed with a cocoa-pod design. ⊠ *132 Spring St., between Greene and Wooster Sts., SoHo* ☎ *212/625–2929* Ⓜ *Subway: R, W to Prince St.*

17

Street Vendors

IF YOU'RE LOOKING for original or reproduced artwork, the two areas to visit for street vendors are the stretch of 5th Avenue in front of the Metropolitan Museum of Art (roughly between 81st and 82nd streets) and the SoHo area of West Broadway, between Houston and Broome streets. In both areas, you'll find dozens of artists selling original paintings, drawings, and photographs (some lovely, some lurid), as well as photo reproductions of famous New York scenes (the Chrysler building, South Street Seaport). Prices can start as low as $10.

The east–west streets in SoHo are an excellent place to look for handmade crafts: Spring and Prince streets, especially, are jammed with tables full of beaded jewelry, tooled leather belts, and homemade hats and purses. These streets are also a great place to find deals on art books; several vendors have titles featuring the work of artists from Diego Rivera to Annie Leibovitz, all for about 20% less than you'd pay at a chain. It's

best to know which books you want ahead of time, though; street vendors wrap theirs in clear plastic, and can get testy if you unwrap them but don't wind up buying.

Faux-designer handbags, sunglasses, wallets, and watches are some of the most popular street buys in town–but crackdowns on knockoffs have made them harder to find. The hub used to be Canal Street, roughly between Greene and Lafayette streets, but many vendors there have swept their booths clean of fake Vuitton, Prada, Gucci, and Fendi merchandise. You might have better luck finding a Faux-lex near Herald Square or Madison Square Garden; and good old-fashioned fake handbags are still sold by isolated vendors around such shopping areas as Rockefeller Center and Lexington Avenue near Bloomingdale's. The one thing Canal Street is still good for, though, is cheap luggage: for $30–$40 (be sure to haggle), you can walk away with a giant rolling suitcase to lug home all your loot.

CHILDREN'S CLOTHING

Precious

Bonpoint. The sophistication here lies in the beautiful designs and impeccable workmanship—velvet-tipped coats with matching caps and hand-embroidered jumpers and blouses. ⊠ *1269 Madison Ave., at E. 91st St., Upper East Side* ☎ *212/722–7720* Ⓜ *Subway: 4, 5, 6 to 86th St.* ⊠ *33 E. 68th St., between Park and Madison Aves., Upper East Side* ☎ *212/879–0900* Ⓜ *Subway: 6 to 68th St./Hunter College.*

Calypso Enfant et Bébé. Sailor-stripe tops, polka-dot PJs, lovely party dresses . . . you may find yourself dressing vicariously through your children. ⊠ *426 Broome St., between Lafayette and Crosby Sts., No-Lita* ☎ *212/966–3234* Ⓜ *Subway: 6 to Spring St.*

Flora and Henri. The padded twill coats, slate-blue pleated skirts, and pin-dot cotton dresses here are cute but not overly so. They'll stand up to wear and tear; witness the sturdy Italian-made shoes. ⊠ *943 Madi-*

son Ave., between E. 74th and E. 75th Sts., Upper East Side ☎ 212/ 249–1695 Ⓜ Subway: 6 to E. 77th St.

Infinity. Mothers gossip near the dressing rooms as their daughters try on slinky Les Tout Petits dresses, Miss Sixty Jeans, and cheeky tees with slogans like "chicks ahoy." The aggressively trendy and the rather sweet meet in a welter of preteen accessories. ✉ 1116 Madison Ave., at E. 83rd St., Upper East Side ☎ 212/517–4232 Ⓜ Subway: 4, 5, 6 to 86th St.

Les Petits Chapelais. Designed and made in France, these kids' clothes are adorable but also practical. Corduroy outfits have details like embroidered flowers and contrasting cuffs; soft fleecy jackets are reversible, and sweaters have easy-zip-up fronts and hoodies. ✉ 142 Sullivan St., between Prince and W. Houston Sts., SoHo ☎ 212/505–1927 Ⓜ Subway: C, E to Spring St.

Lilliput. At both locations, which face each other across the street, kids can up their coolness quotient with Paul Smith sweaters, sequined party dresses, and denimwear by Diesel. The difference is that the shop at No. 265 carries it all up to size 8, whereas the original shop goes up to teens. ✉ 240 Lafayette St., between Prince and Spring Sts., SoHo ☎ 212/965–9201 Ⓜ Subway: R, W to Prince St. ✉ 265 Lafayette St., between Prince and Spring Sts., SoHo ☎ 212/965–9567 Ⓜ Subway: 6 to Spring St.

Little Eric. Hip adult shoe styles—Camper knockoffs, brogues—play footsie alongside the familiar loafers and Mary Janes. ✉ 1118 Madison Ave., at E. 83rd St., Upper East Side ☎ 212/717–1513 Ⓜ Subway: 4, 5, 6 to 86th St.

17

Oilily. Stylized flowers, stripes, and animal shapes splash across these brightly colored play and school clothes. ✉ 820 Madison Ave., between E. 68th and E. 69th Sts., Upper East Side ☎ 212/772–8686 Ⓜ Subway: 6 to 68th St./Hunter College.

Z'Baby Company. Outfit the eight-and-unders for dress-up or play, with overalls, tulle-skirted party dresses, even motorcycle jackets. ✉ 100 W. 72nd St., at Columbus Ave., Upper West Side ☎ 212/579–2229 Ⓜ Subway: 1, 2, 3 to 72nd St. ✉ 996 Lexington Ave., at E. 72nd St., Upper East Side ☎ 212/472–2229 Ⓜ Subway: 6 to 68th St.

Play Clothes

Bu and the Duck. Vintage-inspired children's clothing, shoes, and toys distinguish this shop. The Italian-made, two-toned spectator boots might make you wish your own feet were tiny again. ✉ 106 Franklin St., at Church St., TriBeCa ☎ 212/431–9226 Ⓜ Subway: 1 to Franklin St.

Petit Bateau. Fine cotton is spun into comfortable underwear, play clothes, and pajamas; T-shirts come in dozens of colors and to every specification, with V-necks, round necks, snap-fronts, and more. ✉ 1094 Madison Ave., at E. 82nd St., Upper East Side ☎ 212/988–8884 Ⓜ Subway: 4, 5, 6 to 86th St.

Shoofly. Children's shoes and accessories are the name of the game here; you can choose from Mary Janes, wing tips, and Dolce & Gabbana fur-lined booties along with pom-pom hats, brightly patterned socks, and jewelry. ✉ 42 Hudson St., between Thomas and Duane Sts., TriBeCa ☎ 212/406–3270 Ⓜ Subway: 1 to Franklin St.

Continued on page 330

NOLITA

The Nabokovian nickname, shorthand for "North of Little Italy," covers a neighborhood that has taken the commercial baton from SoHo and run with it.

Like SoHo, NoLita has gone from a locals-only, understated area to a crowded weekend magnet, as much about people-watching as it is about shopping. Still, unlike those of its SoHo neighbor, these stores remain largely one-of-a-kind. Running along the parallel north-south spines of Elizabeth, Mott, and Mulberry streets, between East Houston and Kenmare streets, NoLita's boutiques tend to be small and, as real estate dictates, somewhat pricey. –*J.P.*

BEST TIME TO GO

Wednesday through Friday afternoons if you're keen to shop without too many distractions, weekends for more people to scope out. Shops stay open latest (usually until 8 PM) Thursday through Saturday.

BEST SOUVENIR FOR YOUR BABYSITTER

Beautifully packaged, petal-topped candles exclusive to **Red Flower** (13 Prince St., at Elizabeth St., 212/966–5301) in dreamy scents like jasmine and Japanese peony. Or perhaps some calming camomile or lavender bath products from the ancient Italian perfumer-pharmacist **Santa Maria Novella.** Were your children, shall we say, overactive? You may need to include some stomach-soothing lozenges too.

◆ Calypso

◆ Mayle

Jamin Puech ◆
Seize sur Vingt ◆
Calypso Joaillerie ◆   ◆ Me+Ro

Prince St.

Sigerson ◆
Morrison

◆ Hollywould

Resurrection ◆

Spring St.

Kenmare St.

J, M, Z

Calypso
Home

Calypso Enfant ◆

Broome St.

37=1 Atelier ◆   ◆ Calypso
Outlet

Grand St.

KEY
Ⓜ Subway stops

Refueling

Hit the takeout window of **Café Gitane** (242 Mott St., at Prince St., 212/334–9552) for the best espresso; it comes with a little square of dark chocolate for an extra boost. Or, if you don't mind getting your fingers messy, stop by **Café Habana To Go** (17 Prince St., at Elizabeth St., 212/625–2002) for an addictively salty, cheese-topped ear of grilled corn.

Best For

TOO-COOL-FOR-SCHOOL CLOTHES

Mayle: ladylike looks with two dashes of retro flair and a pinch of eccentricity.

Seize sur Vingt: whether customized or off the rack, these button-downs and suits are perfectly cut.

Resurrection: mint-condition vintage Pucci and Courrèges make this a stylist's gold mine.

Calypso: a half-dozen boutiques in NoLita alone for softly exotic clothes and housewares.

FOXY SHOES

Sigerson Morrison: this strappy-sandal success has the biggest footprint in the 'hood.

Hollywould: ballerina flats and mules meet a Palm Beach color palette.

...AND OTHER ACCESSORIES

Jamin Puech: runaway-bohemian-heiress handbags dripping with embroidery and fringe.

3 7 = 1 Atelier: lighter-than-air silk chiffon underpinnings.

Me + Ro: Indian-inspired gold and silver jewelry, from shoulder-duster earrings to tiny lotus-petal pendants.

Space Kiddets. The funky (Elvis-print rompers, onesies made from old concert tees) mixes with the old-school (retro cowboy-print pants, brightly colored clogs) at this casual, trendsetting store. ⊠ *46 E. 21st St., between Broadway and Park Ave., Flatiron District* ☎ *212/420–9878* Ⓜ *Subway: 6 to 23rd St.*

CLOTHING: DISCOUNT

Besides the following spots, don't overlook the discount department stores, especially Century 21.

Duty Free Apparel. Despite the name, it's all bags, all the time—plus a smattering of designer shoes, belts, wallets, and sunglasses—at this bare-bones midtown warehouse. The stock—which is up to 50% off retail—of mainly European names, including Prada, Balenciaga, Bottega Veneta, and Fendi, includes current season merch as well as perennial staples. The goods are guaranteed authentic, but it's best to inspect items before you buy: there's a strict no-returns policy. ⊠ *204 W. 35th St., between 7th and 8th Aves., 2nd fl., Midtown West* ☎ *212/ 967–6548* Ⓜ *Subway: A, C, E, 1, 2, 3 to 34th St./Penn Station.*

Find Outlet. These outlets are like year-round sample sales. Both locations stock up-and-coming and established designer merchandise for 50%–80% off the original price. It's easy to make finds on a regular basis, like Paul & Joe silk chiffon tops or Twinkle sweaters, as the stock is replenished daily. For a wider selection visit the Chelsea shop; it's open only Thursday through Sunday, however. ⊠ *229 Mott St., between Prince and Spring Sts., NoLita* ☎ *212/226–5167* Ⓜ *Subway: 6 to Spring St.* ⊠ *361 W. 17th St., between 8th and 9th Aves., Chelsea* ☎ *212/243–3177* Ⓜ *Subway: A, C, E to 14th St.*

Loehmann's. Label searchers can turn up $40 Polo/Ralph Lauren chinos and Donna Karan and Yves Saint Laurent suits in the men's department here on a regular basis. Head up to the "back room" on the top floor for the best women's designers, but you may need to make a repeat visit or two before emerging victorious. ⊠ *101 7th Ave., at W. 16th St., Chelsea* ☎ *212/352–0856* Ⓜ *Subway: 1, 2, 3 to 14th St.*

CLOTHING: MEN'S & WOMEN'S

Casual & Cool

Agnès b. With this quintessentially French line, women can look like Parisienne schoolgirls—in snap-front tops, slender pants, sweet floral prints—or like a chic *maman* in tailored dark suits and leather jackets. For men, the designer's love for the movies makes it easy to come out looking a little Godard around the edges: turtleneck sweaters, lean black suits, and black leather porkpie hats demand the sangfroid of Belmondo. The Flatiron and Upper East Side stores are women's only. ⊠ *103 Greene St., between Broome and Spring Sts., SoHo* ☎ *212/925–4649* Ⓜ *Subway: 6 to Spring St.* ⊠ *13 E. 16th St., between 5th Ave. and Union Sq. W, Flatiron District* ☎ *212/741–2585* Ⓜ *Subway: F, V to 14th St.* ⊠ *1063*

Madison Ave., between E. 80th and E. 81st Sts., Upper East Side ☎ *212/ 570–9333* Ⓜ *Subway: 6 to 77th St.*

A.P.C. This hip French boutique proves to be deceptively simple. Watch your step on the uneven wooden floorboards while choosing narrow gabardine and corduroy suits or dark denim jeans and jackets, some with a hint of military. ✉ *131 Mercer St., between Prince and Spring Sts., SoHo* ☎ *212/966–9685* Ⓜ *Subway: 6 to Spring St.; R, W to Prince St.*

Christopher Fischer. Featherweight cashmere sweaters, wraps, and throws in Easter-egg colors have made Fischer the darling of Hamptonites. His shop also carries luggage and leather accessories by Henry Beguelin, and such home wares as flokati pillows and wooden bowls from South Africa. ✉ *80 Wooster St., between Spring and Broome Sts., SoHo* ☎ *212/965–9009* Ⓜ *Subway: R, W to Prince St.*

Diesel. The display windows styled like washing machines at the Lexington Avenue superstore will tip you off to Diesel's industrial edge. They give their mainstay, denim, various finishes, from a dusty-looking indigo to superfaded. **Diesel Kids** carries the same hip fashions for kids up to age 16. The **Diesel Denim Gallery** will even launder your purchase for you. ✉ *770 Lexington Ave., at E. 60th St., Upper East Side* ☎ *212/ 308–0055* Ⓜ *Subway: N, R, W, 4, 5, 6 to 59th St./Lexington Ave.* ✉ *1 Union Sq. W, at 14th St., Chelsea* ☎ *646/336–8552* Ⓜ *Subway: L, N, Q, R, W, 4, 5, 6 to 14th St./Union Sq.* ✉ *Diesel Kids, 416 West Broadway, between Prince and Spring Sts., SoHo* ☎ *212/343–3863* Ⓜ *Subway: C, E to Spring St.* ✉ *Diesel Denim Gallery, 68 Greene St., between Spring and Broome Sts., SoHo* ☎ *212/966–5593* Ⓜ *Subway: C, E to Spring St.*

DKNY. Cocktail-party ensembles, chunky-knit sweaters, and knockaround denim vie for notice; the "pure" line is reserved for all-natural fibers. A scattering of vintage pieces, such as leather bomber jackets and 1930s jewelry, ensures that you can have something no one else has. Scout out the nonwearables, too; the candles, toiletries, and home accessories are unfailingly cool. Then you can belly up to the juice bar, log on to an in-store iMac, or listen to a featured CD. ✉ *655 Madison Ave., at E. 60th St., Upper East Side* ☎ *212/223–3569* Ⓜ *Subway: N, R, W, 4, 5, 6 to 59th St./Lexington Ave.* ✉ *420 West Broadway, between Prince and Spring Sts., SoHo* ☎ *646/613–1100* Ⓜ *Subway: C, E to Spring St.*

Foley & Corinna. Images of flowers and butterflies waft along the walls at the women's boutique. The racks divulge both vintage finds, like embroidered leather jackets, and Foley's own line of new clothes. Many looks are lingerie-inspired, with flounces and lace. The men's branch, just around the corner, spins a similar mix of old and artfully rumpled new in tees, button-downs, and denim. ✉ *114 Stanton St., between Ludlow and Essex Sts., Lower East Side* ☎ *212/529–2338* Ⓜ *F to 2nd Ave. or Delancey St.* ✉ *Men's store, 143 Ludlow St., between E. Houston and Stanton Sts., Lower East Side* ☎ *212/529–5043* Ⓜ *F to 2nd Ave. or Delancey St.*

Guess? The denim here seizes on all kinds of trends at once: wide legs and tight low-riders, preshredded hems and pockets, rhinestones, studs, cutoffs, and whatever else holds teenagers' fancy. ✉ *537 Broadway, be-*

tween Prince and Spring Sts., SoHo ☎ *212/226–9545* Ⓜ *Subway: R, W to Prince St.*

H By Hilfiger. With their patriotic red, white, and blue logos, bright colors, and casual, outdoorsy look, these clothes have a recognizably American style. This particular store takes a more upscale tack, with tailored suits for men, smart sweater sets and pencil skirts for women, and broadcloth shirts for both. ✉ *372 West Broadway, at Broome St., SoHo* ☎ *917/237–0774* Ⓜ *Subway: R, W to Prince St.*

Hugo Boss. Hugo Boss is known for its menswear, but women will have no trouble occupying themselves here. Choose a business-meeting wool suit, then cut a dash with something leather or a wild striped shirt. ✉ *717 5th Ave., at E. 56th St., Midtown East* ☎ *212/485–1800* Ⓜ *Subway: F to 57th St.* ✉ *10 Columbus Circle, at W. 59th St., Midtown West* ☎ *212/485–1900* Ⓜ *Subway: 1, A, B, C, D to Columbus Circle.*

Írma. This unprepossessing nook with its squeaky plank floors is actually home to some of the most hard-to-find designers in the city. Besides carrying a good selection of Vivienne Westwood, it stockpiles whisper-light cashmere tees by Fifi, leather trenches by Histoire, and vintage Belstaff motorcycle boots. ✉ *378 Bleecker St., Greenwich Village* ☎ *212/ 206–7475* Ⓜ *Subway: A, C, E, F, V to W. 4th St./Washington Sq.*

Paul Frank. The flat visage of Julius the monkey, the original Paul Frank character, plasters vinyl wallets, flannel PJs, skateboards, and, of course, T-shirts. Also look for tees evoking such formative elements of '80s youth as corn dogs and break dancing. A selection of monkey-free accessories, including perfect weekender bags, are more stylish than sassy. ✉ *195 Mulberry St., at Kenmare St., NoLita* ☎ *212/965–5079* Ⓜ *Subway: 6 to Spring St.*

Phat Farm/Baby Phat. Hip-hop impresario Russell Simmons's logo-heavy parkas, sweatshirts, and oversize polos and jeans have remained consistently popular among New York funk-soul brothers. Wife Kimora Lee's Baby Phat women's-wear line, which is heavy on body-hugging jeans and tops, shares the same space. ✉ *129 Prince St., between West Broadway and Wooster St., SoHo* ☎ *212/533–7428* Ⓜ *Subway: R, W to Prince St.*

R by 45rpm. Japanese interpretations of Western styles, from pea coats to bandannas, are marked by their attention to detail. Look for hand-stressed denim. ✉ *169 Mercer St., between W. Houston and Prince Sts., SoHo* ☎ *917/237–0045* Ⓜ *Subway: R, W to Prince St.*

Reiss. The first American outpost of this U.K.-based chain carries chic, casual-but-tailored clothes with beautiful details. Women's blouses and skirts have delicate pleats and contrast-stitched embroidery; halter dresses have swirly, summery prints. Men's slouchy pants are complemented by shrunken blazers, military-cut shirts, and trim leather jackets. The prices are slightly higher than those at similar chain shops (French Connection, Club Monaco). ✉ *387 West Broadway, between Spring and Broome Sts., SoHo* ☎ *212/925–5707* Ⓜ *Subway: R, W to Prince St.*

Shanghai Tang. Slide into a loose crepe de chine or velvet Tang jacket, silk pajamas, or a form-fitting cheongsam dress; these modern adaptations of Chinese styles come in soft colors or eye-popping lime and fuchsia. ⊠ *714 Madison Ave., between E. 63rd and E. 64th Sts., Upper East Side* ☎ *212/888–0111* Ⓜ *Subway: N, R, W to 5th Ave./59th St.*

High Design

Alessandro Dell'Acqua. Sexiness with a soft touch has become this designer's forte. Chiffon and silk jersey drape and cling in the right places, and the sweaters and polos fit just so. ⊠ *818 Madison Ave., between E. 68th and E. 69th Sts., Upper East Side* ☎ *212/253–6861* Ⓜ *Subway: 6 to E. 68th St.*

Burberry. The signature plaid is hardly square these days, as bikinis, leather pants, and messenger-style bags join the traditional gabardine trench coats. The flagship store on East 57th Street is the mother lode; the SoHo branch has an abbreviated assortment. ⊠ *9 E. 57th St., between 5th and Madison Aves., Midtown West* ☎ *212/407–7100* Ⓜ *Subway: N, R, W to 5th Ave./59th St.* ⊠ *131 Spring St., between Greene and Wooster Sts., SoHo* ☎ *212/925–9300* Ⓜ *Subway: R, W to Prince St.*

Calvin Klein. Though the namesake designer has bowed out, the label keeps channeling his particular style. This stark flagship store emphasizes the luxe end of the clothing line. Men's suits tend to be soft around the edges; women's evening gowns are often a fluid pouring of silk. There are also shoes, accessories, housewares, and makeup. ⊠ *654 Madison Ave., at E. 60th St., Upper East Side* ☎ *212/292–9000* Ⓜ *Subway: N, R, W, 4, 5, 6 to 59th St./Lexington Ave.*

Christian Dior. The New York outpost of one of France's most venerable fashion houses makes its home in the dazzlingly modern LVMH tower. The designs bring elements of everything from raceways to skate punks to haute couture. If you're not in the market for an investment gown, peruse the glam accessories, like the latest stirrup bag. The Dior menswear boutique is next door; the rocking cigarette-thin suits are often pilfered by women. ⊠ *21 E. 57th St., at Madison Ave., Midtown East* ☎ *212/931–2950* Ⓜ *Subway: E, V to 5th Ave./53rd St.* ⊠ *Men's store, 17 E. 57th St., between 5th and Madison Aves., Midtown East* ☎ *212/421–6009* Ⓜ *Subway: E, V to 5th Ave./53rd St.*

Comme des Garçons. The designs in this stark, white, swoopy space consistently push the fashion envelope with brash patterns, unlikely juxtapositions (tulle and neoprene), and cuts that are meant to be thought-provoking, not flattering. Architecture students come just for the interior design. ⊠ *520 W. 22nd St., between 10th and 11th Aves., Chelsea* ☎ *212/604–9200* Ⓜ *Subway: C, E to 23rd St.*

Costume National. Although entering this dramatically murky shop may seem intimidating (the black-wall space evokes a sort of futuristic tomb), the sexy, slim-cut leather coats and sheer black shirts for both men and women are chic and beautifully made. ⊠ *108 Wooster St., between Prince and Spring Sts., SoHo* ☎ *212/431–1530* Ⓜ *Subway: C, E to Spring St.*

D&G. This outpost for the secondary Dolce & Gabbana line sells less pricey, but still over-the-top Italian designs to a young crowd. This isn't the place to shop for basics—the jeans and separates are all trimmed with embroidery, sequins, lace inserts, and neon-colored patent leather accents—but the clothes are nothing if not fun. ⊠ *434 West Broadway, between Prince and Spring Sts., SoHo* ☎ *212/965–8000* Ⓜ *Subway: C, E to Spring St.*

17

National Chains

American Apparel. It's huge with the teenage set for its line of colorful "sweatshop-free" T-shirts and undies. ✉ *121 Spring St., between Mercer and Greene Sts., SoHo* ☎ *212/226-4880* ✉ *183 Houston St., at Orchard St., Lower East Side* ☎ *212/598-4600* ✉ *373 6th Ave., between Waverly Pl. and Washington St., Greenwich Village* ☎ *646/336-6515* ✉ *1090 3rd Ave., at 64th St., Upper East Side* ☎ *212/772-7462.*

Barnes & Noble. Without argument, this is the biggest bookstore presence in the city. ✉ *396 6th Ave., at W. 8th St., Greenwich Village* ☎ *212/674-8780* ✉ *33 E. 17th St., at Union Sq., Flatiron District* ☎ *212/253-0810* ✉ *4 Astor Pl., at Lafayette St., East Village* ☎ *212/420-1322* ✉ *600 5th Ave., at W. 48th St., Midtown West* ☎ *212/765-0592* ✉ *1972 Broadway, at W. 66th St., Upper West Side* ☎ *212/595-6859* ✉ *2289 Broadway, at W. 82nd St., Upper West Side* ☎ *212/362-8835* ✉ *240 E. 86th St., between 2nd and 3rd Aves., Upper East Side* ☎ *212/794-1962.*

Borders. The smart, cheery flagship Columbus Circle branch of this second-biggest bookstore presence in the city is worth a browse. ✉ *461 Park Ave., at E. 57th St., Midtown East* ☎ *212/980-6785* ✉ *576 2nd Ave., at E. 32nd St., Murray Hill* ☎ *212/685-3938* ✉ *100 Broadway, at Wall St., Lower Manhattan* ☎ *212/964-1988* ✉ *10 Columbus Circle, Upper West Side* ☎ *212/823-9775.*

Club Monaco. You'll find manageable prices, neutral palettes, and mild designer knockoffs here. ✉ *121 Prince St., between Wooster and Greene Sts., SoHo* ☎ *212/533-8930* ✉ *2376 Broadway, at W. 87th St., Upper West*

Side ☎ *212/579-2587* ✉ *160 5th Ave., at W. 21st St., Flatiron District* ☎ *212/352-0936* ✉ *6 W. 57th St., between 5th and 6th Aves., Midtown West* ☎ *212/459-9863* ✉ *1111 3rd Ave., at E. 65th St., Upper East Side* ☎ *212/355-2949* ✉ *520 Broadway, between Broome and Spring Sts., SoHo* ☎ *212/941-1511.*

Coach. Classic glove-tanned leather goes into handbags, briefcases, wallets, shoes, and dozens of other accessories. ✉ *2321 Broadway, at W. 84th St., Upper West Side* ☎ *212/799-1624* ✉ *3 W. 57th St., between 5th and 6th Aves., Midtown West* ☎ *212/371-7110* ✉ *595 Madison Ave., at 57th St., Midtown East* ☎ *212/754-0041* ✉ *620 5th Ave., at Rockefeller Center, Midtown West* ☎ *212/245-4148* ✉ *342 Madison Ave., at E. 44th St., Midtown East* ☎ *212/599-4777* ✉ *143 Prince St., at West Broadway, SoHo* ☎ *212/473-6925* ✉ *79 5th Ave., at E. 16th St., Flatiron District* ☎ *212/675-6403* ✉ *10 Columbus Circle, at W. 59th St., Midtown West* ☎ *212/581-4115.*

Fresh. It sounds good enough to eat: a brown-sugar skin-care line, pomegranate hair conditioner, pear-cassis cologne. The 3rd Avenue location offers decadent skin and body treatments—many of which are free with the purchase of product—in a back spa room. ✉ *57 Spring St., between Lafayette and Mulberry Sts., SoHo* ☎ *212/925-0099* ✉ *1367 3rd Ave., at E. 78th St., Upper East Side* ☎ *212/585-3400* ✉ *922 Madison Ave., between 73rd and 74th Sts., Upper East Side* ☎ *212/396-4545* ✉ *388 Bleecker St., between Perry and W. 11th Sts., Greenwich Village* ☎ *917/408-1850.*

H&M. Swarm the racks for up-to-the-minute trends at unbelievably low prices. ✉ *640 5th Ave., at W. 51st St., Midtown West* ☎ *212/489-0390* ✉ *1328 Broadway, at W. 34th St., Midtown West* ☎ *646/473-1165* ✉ *731 Lexington Ave., at E. 59th St., Midtown East* ☎ *212/935-6781* ✉ *558 Broadway, between Prince and Spring Sts., SoHo* ☎ *212/343-2722* ✉ *515 Broadway, between Spring and Broome Sts., SoHo* ☎ *212/965-8975* ✉ *125 W. 125 St., between Lenox Ave. and Adam Clayton Powell Jr. Blvd., Harlem* ☎ *212/665-8300.*

L'Occitane. It's Provençal all the way, with extra-mild orange blossom, rosemary, and lavender soaps, shampoos, and creams. The Prince Street branch also stocks olive oils and other goodies, many of which can be sampled in the in-house café. ✉ *92 Prince St., at Mercer St., SoHo* ☎ *212/219-3310* ✉ *1046 Madison Ave., at E. 80th St., Upper East Side* ☎ *212/639-9185* ✉ *412 Lexington Ave., inside Grand Central Terminal, at E. 43rd St., Midtown East* ☎ *212/557-6754* ✉ *247 Bleecker St., at Leroy St., Greenwich Village* ☎ *212/367-8428* ✉ *10 Columbus Circle, at W. 59th St., Midtown West* ☎ *212/333-4880.*

Sephora. The alphabetical wall houses perfumes and a comprehensive makeup selection ranging from Urban Decay to Nars, to hard-to-find names such as Peter Thomas Roth. Some brands are exclusive to certain branches, so call ahead if you're looking for something specific. ✉ *555 Broadway, between Prince and Spring Sts., SoHo* ☎ *212/625-1309* ✉ *119 5th Ave., at E. 19th St., Flatiron District* ☎ *212/674-3570* ✉ *45 E. 17th St., between Park Ave. S*

and Broadway, Chelsea ☎ *212/995-8833* ✉ *1500 Broadway, at W. 44th St., Midtown West* ☎ *212/944-8168* ✉ *130 W. 34th St., between 7th Ave. and Broadway, Midtown West* ☎ *212/629-9135* ✉ *10 Columbus Circle, at W. 59th St., Midtown West* ☎ *212/823-9383.*

Urban Outfitters. Fashions change a few times a semester in this hipster emporium. ✉ *162 2nd Ave., between E. 10th and E. 11th Sts., East Village* ☎ *212/375-1277* ✉ *374 6th Ave., at Waverly Pl., Greenwich Village* ☎ *212/677-9350* ✉ *582 6th Ave., at W. 14th St., Greenwich Village* ☎ *646/638-1646* ✉ *628 Broadway, between Bleecker and E. Houston Sts., East Village* ☎ *212/475-0009* ✉ *2081 Broadway, at W. 72nd St., Upper West Side* ☎ *212/579-3912.*

Zara. The tags covered with prices in international currencies all boil down to one thing: inexpensive clothes and accessories for the office or a night out. ✉ *689 5th Ave., at E. 54th St., Midtown East* ☎ *212/371-2555* ✉ *750 Lexington Ave., between E. 59th and E. 60th Sts., Midtown East* ☎ *212/754-1120* ✉ *101 5th Ave., between E. 17th and E. 18th Sts., Flatiron District* ☎ *212/741-0555* ✉ *580 Broadway, between Prince and E. Houston Sts., SoHo* ☎ *212/343-1725.*

17

Dolce & Gabbana. It's easy to feel like an Italian movie star amid these extravagant (in every sense) clothes. Pinstripes are a favorite; for women, they could be paired with something sheer, furred, or leopard-print, and for men they elongate the sharp suits. ⊠ *825 Madison Ave., between E. 68th and E. 69th Sts., Upper East Side* ☎ *212/249–4100* Ⓜ *Subway: 6 to 68th St./Hunter College.*

Donna Karan. Collections may swing from raw-edged to refined, but the luxurious materials remain a constant. Cashmere jersey, silk, and deer-skin are drawn into carefully un-precious pieces. A Zen garden is there to relieve sticker shock. ⊠ *819 Madison Ave., between E. 68th and E. 69th Sts., Upper East Side* ☎ *212/861–1001* Ⓜ *Subway: 6 to 68th St./Hunter College.*

Emporio Armani. At this middle child of the Armani trio, the clothes are dressy without quite being formal, and are frequently offered in cream, muted blues, and ever-cool shades of soot. ⊠ *601 Madison Ave., between E. 57th and E. 58th Sts., Midtown East* ☎ *212/317–0800* Ⓜ *Subway: N, R, W, 4, 5, 6 to 59th St./Lexington Ave.* ⊠ *410 West Broadway, at Spring St., SoHo* ☎ *646/613–8099* Ⓜ *Subway: C, E to Spring St.*

Etro. Echoes of 19th-century luxury pervade Etro's clothing. Trademark paisleys sprawl over richly covered suits, dresses, and lustrous pillows. ⊠ *720 Madison Ave., between E. 63rd and E. 64th Sts., Upper East Side* ☎ *212/317–9096* Ⓜ *Subway: 6 to 68th St./Hunter College.*

Gianni Versace. Housed in a five-story flagship store, the sometimes outrageous designs and colors of Versace clothes might not be to every-one's taste (or budget), but they're never boring. ⊠ *647 5th Ave., near E. 51st St., Midtown East* ☎ *212/317–0224* Ⓜ *Subway: E, V to 5th Ave./53rd St.*

Giorgio Armani. Armani managed to beat out Calvin Klein on the exte-rior-minimalism front; inside, the space has a museumlike quality, re-inforced by the refined clothes. Suits for men and women have a telltale perfect drape; a women's suit might be accessorized with a broad, strik-ing, beaded necklace. ⊠ *760 Madison Ave., between E. 65th and E. 66th Sts., Upper East Side* ☎ *212/988–9191* Ⓜ *Subway: 6 to 68th St./Hunter College.*

Gucci. With a female designer in place, the clothing is a tad less aggres-sively sexy than it was in the Tom Ford era. Skintight pants might be paired with a blousey jacket; lace tops leave a little more to the imagi-nation. The accessories, like wraparound shades and studded or snake-skin shoes, continue to spark consumer frenzies. ⊠ *685 5th Ave., between 54th and 55th Sts., Midtown East* ☎ *212/826–2600* Ⓜ *Sub-way: N, R, W to 5th Ave./59th St.* ⊠ *840 Madison Ave., between E. 69th and E. 70th Sts., Upper East Side* ☎ *212/717–2619* Ⓜ *Subway: 6 to 68th St./Hunter College.*

Hermès. Sweep up and down the curving stairway in this contemporary flagship while on the prowl for the classic, distinctively patterned silk scarves and neckties, the coveted Kelly and Birkin handbags, or the beau-tifully simple separates. True to its roots, Hermès still stocks saddles and other equestrian items. ⊠ *691 Madison Ave., at E. 62nd St., Upper East Side* ☎ *212/751–3181* Ⓜ *Subway: N, R, W, 4, 5, 6 to 59th St./Lexing-ton Ave.*

Issey Miyake. Pleats of a Fortuny-like tightness are the Miyake signature—but instead of Fortuny's silks, these clothes are in polyester or ultra-high-tech textiles, often forming sculptural shapes. **Pleats Please** carries a line with simpler silhouettes, from tunics to long dresses. ✉ *992 Madison Ave., between E. 76th and E. 77th Sts., Upper East Side* ☎ *212/439–7822* Ⓜ *Subway: 6 to 77th St.* ✉ *119 Hudson St., at N. Moore St., TriBeCa* ☎ *212/226–0100* Ⓜ *Subway: 1 to Franklin St.* ✉ *Pleats Please, 128 Wooster St., at Prince St., SoHo* ☎ *212/226–3600* Ⓜ *Subway: R, W to Prince St.*

Jeffrey. The Meatpacking District really arrived when this Atlanta-based mini-Barneys opened its doors. You can find an incredible array of designer shoes—Valentino, Lanvin, and red-soled Christian Louboutin are some of the best sellers—plus überlabels like Marni, Gucci, and Collette Dinnigan. ✉ *449 W. 14th St., between 9th and 10th Aves., Meatpacking District* ☎ *212/206–1272* Ⓜ *Subway: A, C, E, L to 14th St./8th Ave.*

Jil Sander. A herringbone coat or a bit of neon trim is about as unruly as this label gets. The designs are unflappable, whether for shirtdresses or boxy jackets, and the colors urban. ✉ *11 E. 57th St., between 5th and Madison Aves., Midtown East* ☎ *212/838–6100* Ⓜ *Subway: F to 57th St.*

Fodor'sChoice ★ **Marc Jacobs.** The ladylike designs filling this shop's SoHo branch are made with luxurious fabrics: silk, cashmere, wool bouclé, and tweeds ranging from the demure to the flamboyant (think teal-color houndstooth). The details, though—oversize buttons, circular patch pockets, and military-style grommet belts—add a sartorial wink. The Bleecker Street spaces carry more casual clothes; look for slouchy pants and cotton sweaters in sherbet colors, or suede sneakers and scalloped-leather pumps in the accessories boutique next door. ✉ *163 Mercer St., between W. Houston and Prince Sts., SoHo* ☎ *212/343–1490* Ⓜ *Subway: R, W to Prince St.* ✉ *Accessories boutique: 385 Bleecker St., at Perry St., Greenwich Village* ☎ *212/924–6126* Ⓜ *Subway: 1 to Christopher St./Sheridan Sq.* ✉ *403–405 Bleecker St., at W. 11th St., Greenwich Village* ☎ *212/924–0026* Ⓜ *Subway: 1 to Christopher St./Sheridan Sq.*

Nicole Farhi. The designer's New York stores represent the convergence of her many design talents and endeavors—men's and women's apparel and home furnishings. The clothing can be engrossing, especially the knits. The housewares mix modern and vintage. ✉ *10 E. 60th St., between 5th and Madison Aves., Upper East Side* ☎ *212/223–8811* Ⓜ *Subway: N, R, W to 5th Ave./59th St.* ✉ *75 9th Ave., between W. 15th and W. 16th Sts., Chelsea* ☎ *646/638–0115* Ⓜ *Subway: A, C, E to 14th St.*

Polo/Ralph Lauren. One of New York's most distinctive shopping experiences, Lauren's flagship store graces the turn-of-the-20th-century Rhinelander mansion. Clothes range from summer-in-the-Hamptons madras to exquisite silk gowns and Purple Label men's suits. **Polo Sport** (✉ 888 Madison Ave., at 72nd St., Upper East Side ☎ 212/434–8000 Ⓜ Subway: 6 to 68th St./Hunter College ✉ 381 West Broadway, between Spring and Broome Sts., SoHo ☎ 212/625–1660 Ⓜ Subway: R, W to Prince St.) carries casual clothes and sports gear, from puffy anoraks to wick-away tanks. The Village branch of **Ralph Lauren**

Continued on page 340

FIFTH AVENUE & 57TH STREET

Fifth Avenue from Rockefeller Center to Central Park South pogos between landmark department stores, glossy international designer boutiques, and casual national chains. What they all have in common: massive flagship spaces.

The intersection of 5th Avenue with 57th Street distills this mix of old and new, exclusive and accessible. From these corners you'll see blue-chip New York classics (jeweler Tiffany & Co., the Bergdorf Goodman department stores), a reinvented luxury giant (the glass box of Louis Vuitton), and show-off digs for informal brands (NikeTown, Abercrombie & Fitch). Capping this shopping stretch at East 58th Street is the colossal, exceptional toy store F.A.O. Schwarz. If you're keen to shop the high end or to see the impressive flagships, it's worth coming to this neighborhood—but if large-scale doesn't do it for you, you're better off heading downtown. –*J.P.*

BEST TIME TO GO

Wednesday through Friday if you're trying to avoid crowds. Weekends before the winter holidays get extremely hectic and can spark "sidewalk rage" in even the most patient shopper—try to come earlier in the week, especially if you want to see the fantastic department store window displays.

BEST SOUVENIR FOR KIDS

An incredibly lifelike stuffed animal from **F.A.O. Schwarz**. They've got exclusive Steiff "purebred" dogs, for instance, that come with authenticity certificates from the American Kennel Club.

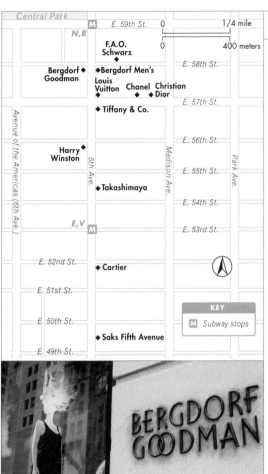

Central Park

M N,R

E. 59th St. 0   1/4 mile

F.A.O.
Schwarz 0   400 meters

Bergdorf ◆   ◆Bergdorf Men's
Goodman   Louis   E. 58th St.
           Vuitton Chanel Christian
              ◆   ◆ ◆ Dior
                              E. 57th St.
           ◆ Tiffany & Co.

                              E. 56th St.

Harry ◆   E. 55th St.
Winston

           ◆Takashimaya   E. 54th St.

                              E. 53rd St.
E,V M

E. 52nd St.
           ◆ Cartier
E. 51st St.

E. 50th St.   KEY

           ◆ Saks Fifth Avenue   M Subway stops
E. 49th St.

Avenue of the Americas (6th Ave.)
5th Ave.
Madison Ave.
Park Ave.

Refueling

Soothe frazzled nerves with a stop at the **Tea Box Café** in the basement of Takashimaya (693 5th Ave., between 54th and 55th Sts., 212/350–0100). The space is quiet and softly lit; in addition to the dozens of teas, you can choose from bento boxes, tea sandwiches, and pastries. Need something more substantial? Nab a table, or a seat with a fold-down tray, at the time-warped **Prime Burger** (5 E. 51st St., between 5th and Madison Aves., 212/759–4729). You'll find all the diner standbys; if you order a burger, you'll have to specify all the toppings you'd like with it.

Best For

DEPARTMENT STORES

Saks Fifth Avenue: fashion and nothing but, with especially strong shoe, makeup, and formalwear departments.

Bergdorf Goodman: these partner stores (one for women, the other for men, guess which has the housewares) are both genteelly tasteful.

Takashimaya: a cool and collected Japanese emporium with a gorgeous florist in the front window.

FLAGSHIP STORES

Louis Vuitton: every permutation of the signature handbags and leather goods, plus the jet-set clothing line upstairs.

Chanel: all the hallmarks, from little black dresses to double-C jewelry, in a building as tailored as the legendary suits.

Christian Dior: madcap designs for women, cigarette-slim looks for men.

SERIOUS JEWELRY

Tiffany & Co.: hum "Moon River," check out the dazzling gems and pearls, then head upstairs for all sorts of silver ornaments.

Cartier: both classic and slinky new designs glitter in a turn-of-the-20th-century mansion.

Harry Winston: the ultimate for diamonds (just ask Marilyn Monroe).

SPOTLIGHT ON FIFTH AVENUE & 57TH STREET

17

(⊠ 380 Bleecker St., at Perry St., Greenwich Village ☎ 212/645–5513 Ⓜ Subway: 1 to Christopher St./Sheridan Sq.), on the other hand, is a small, tightly packed boutique. It stocks items for women (and dogs) only, pulling together sequin-slicked skirts, sturdy cable knits and tweeds, and the odd bit of vintage. ⊠ *867 Madison Ave., at E. 72nd St., Upper East Side* ☎ *212/606–2100* Ⓜ *Subway: 6 to 68th St./Hunter College.*

Fodor'sChoice   **Prada.** The design shop's gossamer silks, slick black suits, and luxe shoes

★   and leather goods are among the all-time great Italian fashion coups. The uptown stores pulse with pale green walls (remember this if you start questioning your skin tone). The 57th Street branch carries just the shoes, bags, and other accessories. The SoHo location, an ultramodern space designed by Rem Koolhaas, incorporates so many technological innovations that it was written up in *Popular Science.* The dressing-room gadgets alone include liquid crystal displays, changeable lighting, and scanners that link you to the store's database. ⊠ *724 5th Ave., between W. 56th and W. 57th Sts., Midtown West* ☎ *212/664–0010* Ⓜ *Subway: Q, W to 5th Ave./60th St.* ⊠ *45 E. 57th St., between Madison and Park Aves., Midtown East* ☎ *212/308–2332* Ⓜ *Subway: E, V to 5th Ave./53rd St.* ⊠ *841 Madison Ave., at E. 70th St., Upper East Side* ☎ *212/327–4200* Ⓜ *Subway: 6 to 68th St./Hunter College* ⊠ *575 Broadway, at Prince St., SoHo* ☎ *212/334–8888* Ⓜ *Subway: R, W to Prince St.*

Roberto Cavalli. Rock-star style (at rock-star prices) delivers denim decked with fur, feathers, prints, and even shredded silk overlays. ⊠ *711 Madison Ave., at E. 63rd St., Upper East Side* ☎ *212/755–7722* Ⓜ *Subway: N, R, W to 5th Ave./59th St.*

TSE. The soft delicacy of the cashmere here doesn't stop at the fabric; TSE's designs are hopelessly refined. ⊠ *827 Madison Ave., at E. 69th St., Upper East Side* ☎ *212/472–7790* Ⓜ *Subway: 6 to 68th St./Hunter College.*

Valentino. The mix here is at once audacious and beautifully cut; the fur or feather trimmings, low necklines, and opulent fabrics are about as close as you can get to celluloid glamour. No one does a better red. ⊠ *747 Madison Ave., at E. 65th St., Upper East Side* ☎ *212/772–6969* Ⓜ *Subway: 6 to 68th St./Hunter College.*

Yohji Yamamoto. Although almost entirely in black and white, these clothes aren't as severe as they seem. Whimsical details, like giant polka dots, shirts with drawstring hems, and slouchy, rolled trouser cuffs, add a dash of levity. ⊠ *103 Grand St., at Mercer St., SoHo* ☎ *212/966–9066* Ⓜ *Subway: J, M, N, Q, R, W, Z, 6 to Canal St.*

Yves Saint Laurent Rive Gauche. Tom Ford's successor, Stephano Pilati, is lightening up the fabled French house; think seduction instead of sexpot, with ruffles, wide belts, and safari-style jackets. ⊠ *855 Madison Ave., between E. 70th and E. 71st Sts., Upper East Side* ☎ *212/988–3821* Ⓜ *Subway: 6 to 68th St./Hunter College* ⊠ *3 E. 57th St., between 5th and Madison Aves., Midtown East* ☎ *212/980–2970* Ⓜ *Subway: N, R, W to 5th Ave./59th St.*

Tailored

Barbour. The company's waxed jackets are built to withstand raw British weather. The tweeds, moleskin pants, lamb's-wool sweaters, and tattersall shirts invariably call up images of country rambles, trusty hunting dog not included. ⊠ *1047 Madison Ave., at E. 80th St., Upper East Side* ☏ *212/570–2600* Ⓜ *Subway: 6 to 77th St.*

Brooks Brothers. The clothes at this classic American haberdasher are, as ever, traditional, comfortable, and fairly priced. At the Madison Avenue store, you can step into a computer scanner to get precisely measured for a custom shirt or suit; appointments are recommended. Summer seersucker, navy blue blazers, and the peerless oxford shirts have been staples for generations. The women's selection has variations thereof. ⊠ *666 5th Ave., at W. 53rd St., Midtown West* ☏ *212/261–9440* Ⓜ *Subway: E, V to 5th Ave./53rd St.* ⊠ *346 Madison Ave., at E. 44th St., Midtown East* ☏ *212/682–8800* Ⓜ *Subway: S, 4, 5, 6, 7 to 42nd St./Grand Central* ⊠ *1 Church St., at Liberty St., Lower Manhattan* ☏ *212/267–2400* Ⓜ *Subway: R, W to Cortlandt St.*

Façonnable. This French company has a lock on the Euro-conservative look. The women's sportswear leans on the men's pillars: tailored shirts in bold stripes or pastels, argyle sweaters, double-breasted coats. The men's Italian-made suits may be expensive, but the craftsmanship and canvas fronting will allow them to withstand years of dry cleaning. ⊠ *636 5th Ave., at W. 51st St., Midtown West* ☏ *212/319–0111* Ⓜ *Subway: E, V to 5th Ave./53rd St.*

Seize sur Vingt. In bringing a contemporary sensibility to custom tailoring, this store realized an ideal fusion. Brighten a men's wool suit or cotton moleskin flat-front pants with a checked or striped shirt; all can be made to order. Women are also the beneficiaries of the store's crisp button-downs and single-pleat trousers. ⊠ *243 Elizabeth St., between Prince and E. Houston Sts., NoLita* ☏ *212/343–0476* Ⓜ *Subway: R, W to Prince St.*

Thomas Pink. Impeccably tailored shirts are the hallmark of this Jermyn Street transplant. The majority of the men's and women's styles—which come in a candy-shop array of stripes, tattersall checks, and ginghams— have spread collars and French cuffs, but there are also more casual button-downs for men and three-quarter-sleeve blouses for women. ⊠ *520 Madison Ave., at E. 53rd St., Midtown East* ☏ *212/838–1928* Ⓜ *Subway: N, R, W to 5th Ave./59th St.* ⊠ *1155 6th Ave., at E. 44th St., Midtown East* ☏ *212/840–9663* Ⓜ *Subway: B, D, F, V to 42nd St.* ⊠ *10 Columbus Circle, at W. 59th St., Midtown West* ☏ *212/823–9650* Ⓜ *Subway: 1, A, B, C, D to Columbus Circle.*

With an Edge

A Bathing Ape. Known simply as BAPE to devotees, this exclusive label has a cult following in its native Tokyo. The shop opened with fanfare in 2005, though at first it's hard to see what the fuss is about. A small selection of camouflage gear and limited-edition T-shirts are placed throughout the minimalist space; the real scene-stealers are the flashy retro-style sneakers in neon colors. ⊠ *91 Greene St., between Prince and Spring Sts., SoHo* ☏ *212/925–0222* Ⓜ *Subway: R, W to Prince St.*

DDC Lab. The superhip offerings at this shop's Meatpacking location include bomber jackets and pleated skirts in paper-thin leather, plus brazenly colored PF Flyers sneakers for men. The overdyed denim comes in hues of supersaturated purple and acid green; you can even buy canisters of special laundry powder to wash it with. ⊠ *427 W. 14th St., at*

17

Washington St., Meatpacking District ☎ *212/414–5801* Ⓜ *Subway: A, C, E to 14th St.*

Nom de Guerre. Brave the narrow staircase at this basement-level hipster hideaway to find racks filled with vintage T-shirts, military-inspired jackets and pants, limited-edition sneakers, and haute-street denim by Rogan and Red Label. There's an Army-Navyish vibe, with camo-green dressing room curtains and a concrete floor, but the staff is militant only about style and fit. ✉ *640 Broadway, at Bleecker St., Greenwich Village* ☎ *212/253–2891* Ⓜ *Subway: F, V to Broadway–Lafayette.*

Patricia Field. If you loved Carrie Bradshaw's wild outfits on *Sex and the City*, this is the place for you. As well as designing costumes for the show, Field has been a longtime purveyor of flamboyant club-kid gear. Her basement-level emporium is chockablock with teeny kilts, lamé, marabou, pleather, and vinyl, as well as wigs in every color and stiletto heels in some very large sizes. ✉ *382 West Broadway, between Spring and Broome Sts., SoHo* ☎ *212/966–4066* Ⓜ *Subway: C, E to Spring St.*

Trash and Vaudeville. Goths, punks, and other nightcrawlers have favored this standby for years. You might hear the Ramones on the sound system while you browse through bondage-inspired pants and skirts covered in straps, buckles, and other hardware. You'll also find striped stovepipe pants, vinyl corsets, and crinolines painted with flames. ✉ *4 St. Marks Pl., between 2nd and 3rd Aves., East Village* ☎ *212/982–3590* Ⓜ *Subway: 6 to Astor Pl.*

Triple 5 Soul. Headquarters for urban, hip-hop gear, this Brooklyn-based label's shop has graffiti murals on the walls and experimental beats playing on the stereo. The label's signature cargo pants, parkas, shoulder bags, and hoodies—many incorporating camo and high-tech fabrics—fill the racks. ✉ *290 Lafayette St., between Prince and Houston Sts., Greenwich Village* ☎ *212/431–2404* Ⓜ *Subway: B, D, F, V to Broadway–Lafayette St.*

CLOTHING: JUST FOR MEN

Duncan Quinn. Shooting for nothing less than sartorial splendor, this designer provides everything from chalk-stripe suits to cuff links in a shop not much bigger than its silk pocket squares. Only a few of each style of shirt are made, so the odds are slim that you will see someone else in your blue, violet, or orange button-down with contrast-color undercuffs. ✉ *8 Spring St., between Elizabeth and Bowery Sts., NoLita* ☎ *212/226–7030* Ⓜ *Subway: 6 to Spring St.*

Dunhill. Corporate brass come here for finely tailored clothing, both ready- and custom-made, and smoking accessories; the walk-in humidor upstairs stores top-quality tobacco and cigars. ✉ *711 5th Ave., between E. 56th and E. 55th Sts., Midtown East* ☎ *212/753–9292* Ⓜ *Subway: F to 57th St.*

John Varvatos. After years with Calvin Klein and Ralph Lauren, Varvatos set off on his own and quickly racked up design awards. There's a casual insouciance in his soft-shouldered, unconstructed suits, cotton crewneck shirts, and jeans in leather, velvet, or denim. ✉ *122 Spring*

St., at Greene St., SoHo ☎ *212/965–0700* Ⓜ *Subway: 6 to Spring St.*

Paul Smith. Dark mahogany Victorian cases complement the dandyish British styles they hold. Embroidered vests, brightly striped socks, scarves, and shirts, and tongue-in-cheek cuff links leaven the classic, dark, double-back-vent suits. Ashtrays, photography books, cordial glasses, and other such oddments beg for a toff's bachelor pad. ✉ *108 5th Ave., at E. 16th St., Flatiron District* ☎ *212/627–9770* Ⓜ *Subway: F, V to 14th St.*

Sean. These snug shops carry low-key, well-priced, and comfortable apparel from France—wool and cotton painter's coats, very-narrow-wale corduroy pants, and a respectable collection of suits and dress shirts. ✉ *132 Thompson St., between W. Houston and Prince Sts., SoHo* ☎ *212/598–5980* Ⓜ *Subway: R, W to Prince St.* ✉ *224 Columbus Ave., between W. 70th and W. 71st Sts., Upper West Side* ☎ *212/769–1489* Ⓜ *Subway: B, C to 72nd St.*

Vilebrequin. Allow St-Tropez to influence your swimsuit; these striped, floral, and solid-color French-made trunks come in sunny hues. Waterproof pocket inserts keep your essentials safe from beachcombers. Many styles come in boys' sizes, too. ✉ *1070 Madison Ave., at E. 81st St., Upper East Side* ☎ *212/650–0353* Ⓜ *Subway: 6 to 77th St.* ✉ *436 West Broadway, between Prince and Spring Sts., SoHo* ☎ *212/431–0673* Ⓜ *Subway: R, W to Prince St.*

CLOTHES: VINTAGE & RESALE

In addition to the selections below, *see* Lyell *in* Women's Clothing, *below.*

Allan & Suzi. The proprietors, whom you'll no doubt find behind the counter, are the godfather and -mother of fashion collecting. Their wacky shop preserves 1980s shoulder pads and 1940s gowns for posterity (or sale). ✉ *416 Amsterdam Ave., between W. 79th and W. 80th Sts., Upper West Side* ☎ *212/724–7445* Ⓜ *Subway: 1, 2, 3 to 72nd St.*

Cheap Jack's. Relocated to midtown in October 2005, Jack's new two-floor, 12,000-square-foot space looks more upscale, but is still jammed with almost everything you could wish for: track suits, bomber jackets, early 1980s madras shirts, old prom dresses, and fur-trimmed wool ladies' suits with the eau-de-mothball stamp of authenticity. Another upgrade from the old location: prices are lower than ever. ✉ *303 5th Ave., at 31st., Midtown West* ☎ *212/777–9564* Ⓜ *Subway: N, Q, R, W, to 34th St. / Herald Sq.*

Fisch for the Hip. These resale racks are evenly split between men's and women's clothes, with a well-edited selection throughout. You may find last season's Catherine Malandrino chiffon dress with its tags intact, or a Zegna jacket for under $300. Look for multiple discounts on such wardrobe warhorses as little black dresses. ✉ *153 W. 18th St., between 6th and 7th Aves., Chelsea* ☎ *212/633–9053* Ⓜ *Subway: F, V, 1, 2, 3 to 14th St.*

Frock. Models and stylists frequent this tiny shop for vintage women's wear from the 1960s, '70s, and '80s. The store carries pieces from such new-wave, mid-'80s designers as Thierry Mugler, Stephen Sprouse, and

Claude Montana, not to mention pumps and lizard clutch purses from Ferragamo, Bruno Magli, and Charles Jourdan. ✉ *148 Orchard St., between Stanton and Rivington Sts., Lower East Side* ☎ 212/594–5380 Ⓜ *Subway: F, J, M, Z to Delancey St./Essex St.*

New York Vintage. No patience to search through the Chelsea flea market? Ransack the racks of women's wear in this narrow space across the way, where the prime picks have been winnowed for you. The 1930s chiffon blouses, '50s circle skirts, and '60s cocktail dresses are well kept; there's a good selection of handbags and pumps, too. ✉ *117 W. 25th St., between 6th and 7th Aves., Chelsea* ☎ 212/647–1107 Ⓜ *Subway: 1 to 28th St.*

Psyche's Tears. Owner Suzanne Pettit, who served as a costumer on such films as *The Hours* and *Sweet and Lowdown,* knows her vintage fashion. Her relaxed East Village boutique offers a diverse selection of women's and men's designer clothing and accessories from a variety of time periods; the common thread is that each item is handpicked for quality and off-the-rack wearability. ✉ *350 E. 9th St., between 1st and 2nd Aves., East Village* ☎ 212/924–3190 Ⓜ *Subway: 6 to Astor Pl.*

★ **Resurrection.** With original Courrèges, Puccis, and foxy boots, this store is a retro-chic gold mine. Prices, however, are decidedly 21st century. ✉ *217 Mott St., between Prince and Spring Sts., NoLita* ☎ 212/625–1374 Ⓜ *Subway: 6 to Spring St.*

Screaming Mimi's. Vintage 1960s and '70s clothes and retro-wear include everything from djellabas to soccer shirts to prom dresses. You can also find a selection of huge tinted sunglasses, in case you feel like channeling Yoko Ono or one of the Olsen twins. ✉ *382 Lafayette St., between 4th and Great Jones Sts., East Village* ☎ 212/677–6464 Ⓜ *Subway: F, V to Broadway–Lafayette St.*

What Comes Around Goes Around. Thanks to the staff's sharp eyes, the denim and leather racks here are reliably choice. You can also find such hip-again items as rabbit-fur jackets, decorative belt buckles, and some terrific vintage rock concert T-shirts. If the idea of forking out $100 for an Alice Cooper number pains you, just remember: unlike the copies everyone else is wearing, you'll be sporting the real deal. ✉ *351 West Broadway, between Grand and Broome Sts., SoHo* ☎ 212/343–9303 Ⓜ *Subway: J, M, N, Q, R, W, Z, 6 to Canal St.*

CLOTHES: WOMEN ONLY

Chic (But Not Cheap)

Anna Sui. The violet-and-black salon, hung with Beardsley prints and alterna-rock posters, is the ideal setting for Sui's bohemian, flapper- and rocker-influenced designs and colorful, quirky beauty products. ✉ *113 Greene St., between Prince and Spring Sts., SoHo* ☎ 212/941–8406 Ⓜ *Subway: R, W to Prince St.*

Anne Fontaine. The white blouses alone might make you swear off plain oxford shirts forever. Rows of snowy tops, most in cotton poplin or organdy, are jazzed up with lacings, embroidery, or ruching. Some shirts are executed in black, and a few warm-weather choices come in watercolory floral prints. ⊠ *93 Greene St., between Prince and Spring Sts., SoHo* ☎ *212/343–3154* Ⓜ *Subway: R, W to Prince St.* ⊠ *687 Madison Ave., between E. 61st and E. 62nd Sts., Upper East Side* ☎ *212/ 688–4362* Ⓜ *Subway: N, R, 4, 5, 6 to 59th St.*

Barbara Bui. Though these designs have a youthful, slightly trendy edge—skinny pants are made for tucking into boots; draped blouses and safari-style jackets hang close to the body—their elegance and soft lines flatter women of all ages. ⊠ *115–117 Wooster St., between Prince and Spring Sts., SoHo* ☎ *212/625–1938* Ⓜ *Subway: R, W to Prince St.*

Bond 07. The clothing by edgy designers might draw you into this store, but the accessories will keep you browsing for an hour: Selima two-tone glasses (with prescription lenses if you need them), inventive handbags, leopard-print cowboy hats, gloves, and even Jean Paul Gaultier striped umbrellas are all here. ⊠ *7 Bond St., between Lafayette St. and Broadway, East Village* ☎ *212/677–8487* Ⓜ *Subway: 6 to Astor Pl.*

Calypso. Spring for something with a tropical vibe, like a sweeping, ruffled skirt in guava-color silk, an embroidered kurta-style top, or a fringed shawl. The jewelry offshoot at 252 Mott Street can doll you up in equally colorful semiprecious stones or shells. Search out a deal at the 405 Broome Street outlet branch or troll the vintage next door at 407; the Home store on Lafayette celebrates furniture and natural textiles from around the world. ⊠ *424 Broome St., at Crosby St., SoHo* ☎ *212/274– 0449* Ⓜ *Subway: 6 to Spring St.* ⊠ *280 Mott St., between E. Houston and Prince Sts., NoLita* ☎ *212/965–0990* Ⓜ *Subway: 6 to Bleecker St.* ⊠ *935 Madison Ave., at E. 74th St., Upper East Side* ☎ *212/535–4100* Ⓜ *Subway: 6 to 77th St.* ⊠ *Bijoux, 252 Mott St., between Prince and E. Houston Sts., NoLita* ☎ *212/334–9730* Ⓜ *Subway: R, W to Prince St.* ⊠ *Outlet, 405 Broome St., between Lafayette and Centre Sts., NoLita* ☎ *212/343–0450* Ⓜ *Subway: 6 to Spring St.* ⊠ *Vintage, 407 Broome St., between Lafayette and Centre Sts., NoLita* ☎ *212/941–9700* Ⓜ *Subway: 6 to Spring St.* ⊠ *Home, 199 Lafayette St., at Broome St., NoLita* ☎ *212/925–6200* Ⓜ *Subway: 6 to Spring St.*

★ **Charles Nolan.** Formerly an exclusive designer for Saks, Nolan opened this shop in winter of 2005. The craftsmanship of his pieces is impeccable: colorful quilted jackets have decorative stitching; body-skimming skirts are beautifully cut; and silken trousers have a creamy drape. There are also a few whimsical styles, such as the black wool coat covered in puli-like cords. ⊠ *30 Gansevoort St., at Hudson St., Meatpacking District* ☎ *212/924–4888* Ⓜ *Subway: A, C, E to 14th St.*

Destination. The model pigs guarding this store fit right in with the Meatpacking District. Inside are clothes and accessories (some for men, too) that marry handmade and sophisticated styles. Heike Javick fitted tweed skirts hang next to Nicholas K striped sweaters, with jeans made from pieced-together denim flowers. Up front, there's a collection of dramatic hats and scarves. ⊠ *32–36 Little West 12th St., between Greenwich and Washington Sts., Meatpacking District* ☎ *212/727–2031* Ⓜ *Subway: 1 to Christopher St./Sheridan Sq.*

Liz Lange Maternity. By using lots of stretch fabrics, even stretch leather, this designer can conjure up maternity versions of the latest trends. ⊠ *958*

CLOSE UP

Deals & Steals

EVEN A TEMPORARY NEW YORKER LOVES A BARGAIN. Scoring a good deal is a rite of passage for everyone, economic bracket be darned. The city offers everything from low-cost departments stores like Century 21 to hawkers of pseudo Rolex watches and Kate Spade bags stationed at street corners and in Canal Street stalls. And then there are the sample sales.

If a seasonal sale makes New Yorkers' eyes gleam, a sample sale throws shoppers into a frenzy. With so many designer flagships and corporate headquarters in town, merchandise fallout periodically leads to tremendous deals. While technically, the phrase "sample sale" refers to stock that's a sample design, show model, leftover, or is already discounted, the term is now also used for sales of current season goods. Location adds a bit of an illicit thrill to the event: Sales are held in hotels, warehouses, offices, or loft spaces, where items both incredible and unfortunate jam a motley assortment of racks, tables, and bins. Generally, there is a makeshift communal dressing room but mirrors are scarce, so veteran sample-sale shoppers come prepared for wriggling in the aisles; some wear skirts, tights, and tank tops for modest quick-changes. Two rules of thumb: grab first and inspect later, and call in advance to find out what methods of payment are accepted. One of the ultimate experiences is the Barneys Warehouse Sale, held in February and August in Chelsea. Other luscious sales range from the Vera Wang bridal-gown sale (early winter) to TSE cashmere (spring and late fall).

How to find out about these events? The level of publicity and regularity of sales vary. The print and online versions of publications like *New York* magazine are always worth checking for sample sale tip-offs, as is a weekly column on Citysearch (newyork. citysearch.com). If you're interested in specific designers, call their shops and inquire—you may get lucky.

Madison Ave., between E. 75th and E. 76th Sts., Upper East Side ☎ *212/879–2191* Ⓜ *Subway: 6 to 77th St.*

Lyell. True vintage meets vintage-inspired. From the enticing few racks, you might slip into a jet-beaded top (old) or a draped silk dress (new) that would do well for dancing to Benny Goodman. Don't miss the vintage shoe selection, ranged in rows on the floor. ✉ *173 Elizabeth St., between Spring and Kenmare Sts., NoLita* ☎ *212/966–8484* Ⓜ *Subway: 6 to Spring St.*

Malia Mills. Fit fanatics have met their match here. Bikini tops and bottoms are sold separately: halters, bandeaus, and triangle tops, plus boy-cut, side-tie, and low-ride bottoms. There are a few one-pieces, too. If you've got a warm-weather honeymoon coming up, you may want the bikini with "Just Married" across your bum. ✉ *199 Mulberry St., between Spring and Kenmare Sts., NoLita* ☎ *212/625–2311* Ⓜ *Subway: 6 to Spring St.* ✉ *1031 Lexington Ave., at E. 74th St., Upper East Side* ☎ *212/517–7485* Ⓜ *Subway: 6 to E. 77th St.*

Marina Rinaldi. These plus-size tailored suits, hip-slung belts, and sweeping coats know just how to flatter. ✉ *800 Madison Ave., between E. 67th and E. 68th Sts., Upper East Side* ☎ *212/734–4333* Ⓜ *Subway: 6 to 68th St./Hunter College.*

Marni. Weaving among the suspended garments in Marni's first U.S. store, you may fall prey to a hemp-cloth duster jacket, brightly striped cotton trousers, or a coyly creased floral blouse. ✉ *161 Mercer St., between W. Houston and Prince Sts., SoHo* ☎ *212/343–3912* Ⓜ *Subway: R, W to Prince St.*

Max Mara. Think subtle colors and plush fabrics—straight skirts in cashmere or heathered wool, tuxedo-style evening jackets, and several choices of wool and cashmere camel overcoats. ✉ *813 Madison Ave., at E. 68th St., Upper East Side* ☎ *212/879–6100* Ⓜ *Subway: 6 to 68th St./Hunter College* ✉ *450 West Broadway, between W. Houston and Prince Sts., SoHo* ☎ *212/674–1817* Ⓜ *Subway: C, E to Spring St.*

Mayle. This boutique basks in the ineffable vapor of cool. Designer Jane Mayle whips up close-fitting knit tops, lanky pants, and retro-inflected dresses that always look effortless, never overdone. ✉ *242 Elizabeth St., between E. Houston and Prince Sts., NoLita* ☎ *212/625–0406* Ⓜ *Subway: 6 to Bleecker St.*

Michael Kors. In his deft reworkings of American classics, Kors gives sportswear the luxury treatment, as with sorbet-color cashmere pullovers. An haute-hippie element is creeping in, too, with keyhole necks, hobo bags, and floppy hats. ✉ *974 Madison Ave., at E. 76th St., Upper East Side* ☎ *212/452–4685* Ⓜ *Subway: 6 to 77th St.*

17

Miu Miu. Prada front woman Miuccia Prada established a secondary line (bearing her childhood nickname, Miu Miu) to showcase her more experimental ideas. Look for Prada-esque styles in more daring colors and cuts, such as orange-and-brown short shorts, Lurex sweaters, brocade coats in pink and scarlet, and aqua wedge shoes. ✉ *100 Prince St., between Mercer and Greene Sts., SoHo* ☎ *212/334–5156* Ⓜ *Subway: R, W to Prince St.* ✉ *831 Madison Ave., at E. 69th St., Upper East Side* ☎ *212/249–9660* Ⓜ *Subway: 6 to 68th St./Hunter College.*

Tory Burch. Bright-orange lacquer zings through this space, which, in a reversal of the usual flow, brings uptown downtown. Orange joins navy, flamingo pink, and mossy green on espadrilles, printed cotton blouses, and zip-backed cashmere turtlenecks. ✉ *257 Elizabeth St., between E. Houston and Prince Sts., NoLita* ☎ *212/334–3000* Ⓜ *Subway: R, W to Prince St.*

Casual & Cool

Intermix. Aimed at those who like to pair denim with silk, chiffon, or just plain revealing tops, this boutique gathers together a solid mid- to high-range lineup, plus a just-enough layout of shoes and accessories. ✉ *210 Columbus Ave., between W. 69th and W. 70th Sts., Upper West Side* ☎ *212/769–9116* Ⓜ *Subway: 1, 2, 3 to 72nd St.* ✉ *1003 Madison Ave., between E. 77th and E. 78th Sts., Upper East Side* ☎ *212/249–7858* Ⓜ *Subway: 6 to 77th St.*

Pookie & Sebastian. Of-the-moment style at a reasonable price is the mission of this Manhattan minichain. In addition to their own label—which quickly replicates the fashion items du jour in a rainbow of

Continued on page 350

MADISON AVENUE

If you're craving a couture fix, cab it straight to Madison Avenue between East 57th and East 79th streets. Here the greatest Italian, French, and American fashion houses form a platinum-card corridor for ladies who lunch. (If you're going to be pointedly overlooked by a salesperson, odds are it will happen here.)

Most occupy large, glass-facade spaces but there are some exceptions, from intimate boutiques in old brownstones to the imposing turn-of-the-20th-century mansion now home to Ralph Lauren. Barneys, a full-fledged if very select department store, fits right in with the avenue's recherché roll call. But Madison isn't just a fashion funnel. A couple of marvelous booksellers and several outstanding antiques dealers and art galleries share this address as well. –*J.P.*

BEST TIME TO GO

Saturday is the busiest day and thus better for people-watching. Perhaps because of the European influence, the pace is calmer here, especially on weekdays. Avoid coming on a Sunday since several stores close, especially in summer when they figure their main clientele is out in the Hamptons.

BEST SOUVENIR FOR AN EX-MANHATTANITE

Take a whiff of the Manhattan-inspired perfumes like Chelsea Flowers and Park Avenue at **Bond No. 9**. Can't decide? Snap up the sampler box with travel-sized spray scents wrapped like bonbons.

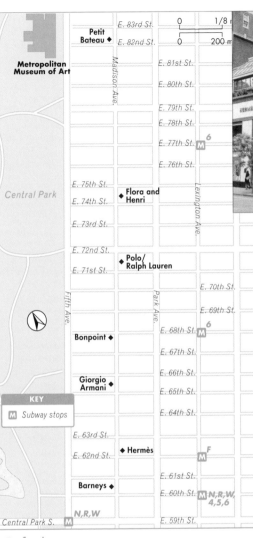

Metropolitan Museum of Art

Petit Bateau ◆

E. 83rd St.
E. 82nd St.
E. 81st St.
E. 80th St.
E. 79th St.
E. 78th St.
E. 77th St. Ⓜ 6
E. 76th St.

Madison Ave.

Central Park

E. 75th St.
E. 74th St.

◆ Flora and Henri

Lexington Ave.

E. 73rd St.
E. 72nd St.
E. 71st St.

◆ Polo/ Ralph Lauren

E. 70th St.
E. 69th St.
E. 68th St. Ⓜ 6
E. 67th St.
E. 66th St.
E. 65th St.
E. 64th St.

Fifth Ave.
Park Ave.

Bonpoint ◆

Giorgio Armani ◆

KEY
Ⓜ Subway stops

E. 63rd St.
E. 62nd St. ◆ Hermès Ⓜ F
E. 61st St.
E. 60th St. Ⓜ N,R,W, 4,5,6

Barneys ◆

N,R,W

Central Park S. Ⓜ

E. 59th St.

0 — 1/8
0 — 200 m

Best For

INTERNATIONAL MEGA-DESIGNERS
Barneys: dozens of the most cutting-edge names, all under one roof.

Polo/Ralph Lauren: haute-WASP style in a Rhinelander mansion.

Hermès: those divine silk scarves and handbags are waiting. . . .

Giorgio Armani: a sleek setting for perfectly cut suits and dramatic evening wear.

FANCY CHILDREN'S CLOTHES
Bonpoint: precious European designs with hand-embroidering, velvet ribbons, you get the picture.

Flora and Henri: sturdy worksmanship and a slightly vintage, but not too cutesy, look.

Petit Bateau: all superfine, hypoallergenic, colorful cotton, all the time.

Refueling

The elegant Italian restaurant **Sant Ambroeus** (1000 Madison Ave., between 77th and 78th Sts., 212/570-2211) has a lovely espresso bar up front where you can stop for an expertly drawn cappuccino, a small sandwich, or an intensely flavored gelato or sorbet.

colors—the four bustling boutiques feature a well-edited collection of trendy separates and flirty dresses; the denim selection offers name brands like Seven and Citizen for Humanity. Hot stock comes and goes quickly, so it's not unusual for fans to pop in at least once a week to see what's new. ⊠ *1488 2nd Ave., between E. 76th and E. 77th Sts., Upper East Side* ☎ *212/861–0550* Ⓜ *Subway: 6 to 77th St.* ⊠ *322 Columbus Ave., at W. 75th St., Upper West Side* ☎ *212/580–5844* Ⓜ *Subway:1, 2, 3 to 72nd St.* ⊠ *541 3rd Ave., at E. 36th St., Murray Hill* ☎ *212/ 951–7110* Ⓜ *Subway: 6 to 33rd St.* ⊠ *Outlet, 249 E. 77th St., between 2nd and 3rd Aves., Upper East Side* ☎ *212/717–1076* Ⓜ *Subway: 6 to 77th St.*

Sude. After the success of her Hell's Kitchen boutique, which helped bring cool to the area before it was so, Sude Dellinger has opened two more mellow city outposts. Though each location caters to a devoted neighborhood following, the stock is the same both uptown and downtown: stylish (and affordable) everyday basics with a smattering of girls-night-out tops and dresses. The roster of mostly American labels includes Free People, Juicy, Splendid, AG Jeans, and Abas leather clutches. ⊠ *829 9th Ave., between W. 54th and W. 55th Sts., Hell's Kitchen* ☎ *212/397– 2347* Ⓜ *Subway: 1, A, B, C, D to 59th St./Columbus Circle* ⊠ *2470 Broadway, between 91st and 92nd Sts., Upper West Side* ☎ *212/721– 5721* Ⓜ *Subway: 1, 2, 3 to 96th St.* ⊠ *240 3rd Ave., at 20th St., Gramercy* ☎ *212/ 420–1422* Ⓜ *Subway: 6 to 23rd St.*

Flirty

BCBG/Max Azria. If flirtation's your sport, you'll find your sportswear here: fluttering skirts, beaded camisoles, chiffon dresses, and leather pants fill the racks. The accessories section has satin evening clutches and strappy sandals. ⊠ *120 Wooster St., between Prince and Spring Sts., SoHo* ☎ *212/625–2723* Ⓜ *Subway: R, W to Prince St.* ⊠ *770 Madison Ave., at E. 66th St., Upper East Side* ☎ *212/717–4225* Ⓜ *Subway: 6 to 68th St./Hunter College.*

Betsey Johnson. The SoHo store departs from the traditional (if such a word can be applied) hot-pink interior; instead its walls are sunny yellow with painted roses, and there's a bordello-red lounge area in back. Besides the quirkily printed dresses, available in all stores, there's a slinky upscale line. This is not the place for natural fibers—it's ruled by rayon, stretch, and the occasional faux fur. ⊠ *138 Wooster St., between Prince and W. Houston Sts., SoHo* ☎ *212/995–5048* Ⓜ *Subway: R, W to Prince St.* ⊠ *251 E. 60th St., between 2nd and 3rd Aves., Upper East Side* ☎ *212/319–7699* Ⓜ *Subway: N, R, W, 4, 5, 6 to 59th St./Lexington Ave.* ⊠ *248 Columbus Ave., between W. 71st and W. 72nd Sts., Upper West Side* ☎ *212/362–3364* Ⓜ *Subway: 1, 2, 3 to 72nd St.* ⊠ *1060 Madison Ave., between E. 80th and E. 81st Sts., Upper East Side* ☎ *212/734–1257* Ⓜ *Subway: 6 to 77th St.*

Catherine Malandrino. Designs here evoke the flapper era: frothy chiffon dresses with embroidered Empire waists, beaded necklines, and tiny matching fur stoles let you pretend you're Daisy Buchanan. ⊠ *468 Broome St., at Greene St., SoHo* ☎ *212/925–6765* Ⓜ *Subway: 6 to Spring St.* ⊠ *652 Hudson St., at W. 13th St., Meatpacking District* ☎ *212/ 929–8710* Ⓜ *Subway: A, C, E to 14th St.*

Cynthia Rowley. As one half of the *Swell* team, you can expect this designer to be a party-outfit pro. She delivers with such flirty picks as bow-top pumps, swingy, swirly halter dresses with heart-shape appliqués, and handbags with small inset mirrors, ideal for checking your lipstick. The *Swell* books are on hand too, natch. ⊠ *376 Bleecker St., between Charles and Perry Sts., Greenwich Village* ☎ *212/242–3803* Ⓜ *Subway: 1 to Christopher St./Sheridan Sq.*

Morgane Le Fay. The clothes here used to have a sort of billowy, Stevie Nicks quality, but though they're still Renaissance-inspired, the designs are more streamlined. Silk organza gowns have Empire waists and crinkly skirts; fitted velvet jackets have covered buttons. ⊠ *746 Madison Ave., between E. 64th and E. 65th Sts., Upper East Side* ☎ *212/ 879–9700* Ⓜ *Subway: 6 to 68th St./Hunter College* ⊠ *67 Wooster St., between Broome and Spring Sts., SoHo* ☎ *212/219–7672* Ⓜ *Subway: C, E to Spring St.*

Nanette Lepore. "Girly" may well be the description that comes to mind as you browse through this cheerful shop; skirts are pleated and adorned with bows, jackets are enhanced by embroidery and floral appliqués; fur shrugs have tiny sleeves. ⊠ *423 Broome St., between Lafayette and Crosby Sts., NoLita* ☎ *212/219–8265* Ⓜ *Subway: 6 to Spring St.*

Rebecca Taylor. Follow the dandelion fluff painted on the walls around racks of lace-overlay dresses and silk-piped trousers. Appliqués and embroideries add fillips of craftiness. ⊠ *260 Mott St., between Prince and W. Houston Sts., NoLita* ☎ *212/966–0406* Ⓜ *Subway: 6 to Spring St.*

Tracy Feith. *Mr.* Feith makes the most of feminine curves by creating vibrant dresses and separates. Necklines on tees scoop wide and low, skirts flirt with flounces and yokes, and the sexy printed silk dresses are light as a feather. ⊠ *209 Mulberry St., between Spring and Kenmare Sts., NoLita* ☎ *212/334–3097* Ⓜ *Subway: 6 to Spring St.*

Vivienne Tam. Tam is known for her playful "China chic" take on familiar Asian images. Cold-weather creations in emerald-and-ruby–color silk are embroidered with dragons and flowers; the warm weather clothes are pale and floaty. ⊠ *99 Greene St., between Prince and Spring Sts., SoHo* ☎ *212/966–2398* Ⓜ *Subway: R, W to Prince St.*

Haute Design

Alexander McQueen. No matter how flouncy McQueen's ensembles become, they retain idiosyncratic, unsettling elements. Delicate, floaty dresses might be crosshatched with bright-red boning; intricate, brocade skirts and jackets could be juxtaposed with stiff leather corsets. ⊠ *417 W. 14th St., between 9th and 10th Aves., Meatpacking District* ☎ *212/ 645–1797* Ⓜ *Subway: A, C, E to 14th St.*

Balenciaga. Nicolas Ghesquière, a recent *amour fou* in the fashion world, took a page from the neighboring galleries for the first U.S. store. His clothing's not always the most wearable, but always stimulating. You might luck onto a reissue from the (Cristobal) Balenciaga archives, made up in modern fabrics. ⊠ *542 W. 22nd St., between 10th and 11th Aves., Chelsea* ☎ *212/206–0872* Ⓜ *Subway: C, E to 23rd St.*

Carolina Herrera. This couture deserves a truly outstanding occasion; the beading and sequin work are stunning. Expect anything from demure, shimmering bands of decoration to knockout swaths of beaded lace.

17

Cool Local Chains

FOLLOWING ARE THE BEST of the local chain stores, the places New Yorkers head to in a fashion pinch.

INA. Although you may spot something vintage, like a 1960s Yves Saint Laurent velvet bolero, most clothing at these small boutiques harks back only a few seasons, and in some cases, the item has never been worn. The Mott Street location racks up menswear; the other three stores carry women's resale. ☒ *101 Thompson St., between Prince and Spring Sts., SoHo* ☎ *212/941-4757* ☒ *21 Prince St., between Elizabeth and Mott Sts., NoLita* ☎ *212/334-9048* ☒ *262 Mott St., between Prince and E. Houston Sts., NoLita* ☎ *212/334-2210* ☒ *208 E. 73rd St., between 2nd and 3rd Aves., Upper East Side* ☎ *212/249-0014.*

Ricky's. Shopping at any one of these wacky stores is a uniquely New York experience. The loud and fun drugstores attract an eclectic, mostly young crowd who come just as often for the crazy-color wigs or fishnet stockings as they do for the body glitter and Neutrogena soap. Every fall the stores turn into Halloween central, with a huge assortment of feather boas, sequined masks, spray-on hair color, and spangled false eyelashes. ☒ *590 Broadway, at Prince St., SoHo* ☎ *212/226-5552* ☒ *7 E. 14th St., Union Sq.* ☎ *212/691-7930* ☒ *466 6th Ave., at W. 12th St., Greenwich Village* ☎ *212/924-3401* ☒ *44 E. 8th St., between Broadway and University Pl., Greenwich Village* ☎ *212/254-5247* ☒ *267 W. 23rd St., between 7th and 8th Aves., Chelsea* ☎ *212/206-*

0234 ☒ *509 5th Ave., at 42nd St., Midtown East* ☎ *212/949-7230.*

Scoop. Chic without trying too hard, these clothes will help you fit in with the too-cool-to-dress-up crowd. They have lots of jeans (limited-edition Levi's, Citizens of Humanity, Chip & Pepper), along with slinky tops for girls and vintage-looking tees and rugby shirts for guys. The SoHo branch is for women only. ☒ *1273-1277 3rd Ave., between E. 73rd and E. 74th Sts., Upper East Side* ☎ *212/535-5577* ☒ *430 W. 14th St., at Washington St., Meatpacking District* ☎ *212/929-1244 men's shop, 212/691-1905 women's* ☒ *532 Broadway, at Spring St., SoHo* ☎ *212/925-2886.*

Searle. Mostly strung along the East Side, these stores have a devoted following for their coats: pea coats, long wool coats, shearlings, leather, and even llama hair. There are plenty of other designer items to layer, from cowl-neck sweaters to fitted tees. ☒ *1051 3rd Ave., at E. 62nd St., Upper East Side* ☎ *212/838-5990* ☒ *635 Madison Ave., between E. 59th and E. 60th Sts., Midtown East* ☎ *212/753-9021* ☒ *805 Madison Ave., between E. 67th and E. 68th Sts., Upper East Side* ☎ *212/628-6665* ☒ *1296 3rd Ave., between E. 74th and E. 75th Sts., Upper East Side* ☎ *212/717-5200* ☒ *1035 Madison Ave., at E. 79th St., Upper East Side* ☎ *212/717-4022* ☒ *1124 Madison Ave., at E. 84th St., Upper East Side* ☎ *212/988-7318* ☒ *156 5th Ave., between W. 20th and W. 21st Sts., Flatiron District* ☎ *212/924-4330.*

⊠ *954 Madison Ave., at E. 75th St., Upper East Side* ☎ *212/249–6552* Ⓜ *Subway: 6 to 77th St.*

Chanel. The midtown flagship has often been compared to a Chanel suit—slim, elegant, and timeless. Inside wait the famed suits themselves, along with other pillars of Chanel style: chic little black dresses and evening gowns, chain-handled bags, and yards of pearls. Downtown's branch concentrates on more contemporary forays, including ski gear, while Madison's boutique is dedicated to shoes, handbags, and other accessories. ⊠ *139 Spring St., at Wooster St., SoHo* ☎ *212/334–0055* Ⓜ *Subway: C, E to Spring St.* ⊠ *15 E. 57th St., between 5th and Madison Aves., Midtown East* ☎ *212/355–5050* Ⓜ *Subway: N, R, W to 5th Ave./59th St.* ⊠ *737 Madison Ave., at E. 64th St., Upper East Side* ☎ *212/535–5505* Ⓜ *Subway: 6 to 68th St./Hunter College.*

Emanuel Ungaro. The vibrant shocking pink of the stairway will keep you alert as you browse through swell ladies-who-lunch daytime suits and grande dame, sometimes bead-encrusted, evening wear. ⊠ *792 Madison Ave., at E. 67th St., Upper East Side* ☎ *212/249–4090* Ⓜ *Subway: 6 to 68th St./Hunter College.*

Herve Leger. Shimmy into something clingy by the man who brought the world the "bandage" dress. Even when you're covered neck to wrists, these looks manage to be come-hither. ⊠ *744 Madison Ave., between E. 64th and E. 65th Sts., Upper East Side* ☎ *212/794–7008* Ⓜ *Subway: 6 to 68th St./Hunter College.*

★ **Kirna Zabête.** A heavy-hitting lineup of prestigious designers—Balenciaga, Viktor & Rolf, Behnaz Sarafour, Matthew Williamson, Sass & Bide—is managed with an exceptionally cheerful flair. Step downstairs for Ella Dish dog hoodies, French Bowl home accessories, and hip infant gear. ⊠ *96 Greene St., between Spring and Prince Sts., SoHo* ☎ *212/941–9656* Ⓜ *Subway: R, W to Prince St.*

O.M.O. Norma Kamali. A fashion fixture from the 1980s has a newly modern, though still '80s-influenced, line. Her luminously white store carries bold black-and-white-patterned bathing suits, slinky separates in velvet and jersey, and poofy "sleeping bag coats." You can also choose from a selection of skin-care products, olive oils, and fragrances. ⊠ *11 W. 56th St., between 5th and 6th Aves., Midtown West* ☎ *212/957–9797* Ⓜ *Subway: E, V to 5th Ave./53rd St.*

Oscar de la Renta. The ladylike yet lighthearted runway designs of this upper-crust favorite got their first U.S. store here. Skirts swing, ruffles billow, embroidery brightens up tweed, and even a tennis dress looks like something you could go dancing in. ⊠ *772 Madison Ave., at E. 66th St., Upper East Side* ☎ *212/288–5810* Ⓜ *Subway: 6 to E. 68th St.*

Philosophy di Alberta Ferretti. The designer's eye for delicate detailing is evident in the perforated hemlines, embroidered stitching, and sprinkling of beads across gauzy fabrics or soft knits. ⊠ *452 West Broadway, between W. Houston and Prince Sts., SoHo* ☎ *212/460–5500* Ⓜ *Subway: F, V to Broadway–Lafayette St.*

Stella McCartney. A devout vegetarian setting up shop in the Meatpacking District may seem odd, but it's further proof that chic trumps many other considerations. You could put together an outfit of head-to-toe satin or chiffon, but it's more in keeping to mix it with shredded denim

17

or a pair of knee-high Ultrasuede cowboy boots (since leather is verboten, shoes and accessories come in satin, canvas, and synthetics). The dressing rooms are so beautiful you might just want to move in. ✉ *429 W. 14th St., at Washington St., Meatpacking District* ☎ *212/255–1556* Ⓜ *Subway: A, C, E to 14th St.*

Vera Wang. The made-to-order bridal and evening wear glows with satin, beading, and embroidery. Periodic pret-a-porter sales offer the dresses for a (relative) song. ✉ *991 Madison Ave., at E. 77th St., Upper East Side* ☎ *212/628–3400* Ⓜ *Subway: 6 to 77th St.*

With an Edge

TG-170. Chiffon Jill Stuart camisoles, pea coats, and a terrific assortment of one-of-a-kind Swiss Freitag messenger bags (made from colorful reused trucking tarps) can be found at this downtown store. ✉ *170 Ludlow St., between E. Houston and Stanton Sts., Lower East Side* ☎ *212/ 995–8660* Ⓜ *Subway: F, J, M, Z to Delancey St./Essex St.*

DEPARTMENT STORES

Most department stores keep regular hours on weekdays and are open late (until 8 or 9) at least one night a week. Many have personal shoppers who can walk you through the store at no charge, as well as concierges who will answer all manner of questions. Some have restaurants or cafés that offer decent meals and pick-me-up snacks.

Fodor'sChoice ★ **Barneys New York.** Barneys continues to provide the fashion-conscious and big-budget shoppers with irresistible, must-have items at its uptown flagship store. The extensive menswear selection has a handful of edgier designers, though made-to-measure is always available. The women's department showcases cachet designers of all stripes, from the subdued lines of Armani and Jil Sander to the irrepressible Alaïa and Zac Posen. The shoe selection trots out Prada boots and strappy Blahniks; the cosmetics department will keep you in Kiehl's, Sue Devitt, and Frederic Malle; jewelry runs from the whimsical (Kazuko) to the classic (Ileana Makri). Expanded versions of the less expensive **Co-op** department occupy the old Barneys' warehouse space on West 18th Street and a niche on Wooster Street. ✉ *660 Madison Ave., between E. 60th and E. 61st Sts., Upper East Side* ☎ *212/826–8900* Ⓜ *Subway: N, R, W, 4, 5, 6 to 59th St./Lexington Ave.* ✉ *Barneys Co-op, 236 W. 18th St., between 7th and 8th Aves., Chelsea* ☎ *212/593–7800* Ⓜ *Subway: A, C, E to 14th St.* ✉ *116 Wooster St., between Prince and Spring Sts., SoHo* ☎ *212/ 965–9964* Ⓜ *Subway: R, W to Prince St.*

Bergdorf Goodman. Good taste reigns in an elegant and understated setting, but remember that elegant doesn't necessarily mean sedate. Bergdorf's carries some brilliant lines, such as John Galliano's sensational couture and Philip Treacy's dramatic hats. In the basement Level of Beauty, find a seat in the manicure/pedicure lounge (no appointments) for a bit of impromptu pampering. The home department has rooms full of magnificent linens, tableware, and gifts. Across the street is another entire store devoted to menswear: made-to-measure shirts, custom suits, designer lines by the likes of Ralph Lauren and Gucci, and scads of accessories, from hip flasks to silk scarves. ⊠ *754 5th Ave., between W. 57th and W. 58th Sts., Midtown West* ⊠ *Men's store, 745 5th Ave., at 58th St., Midtown East* ☎ *212/753–7300* Ⓜ *Subway: N, R, W to 5th Ave./59th St.*

Bloomingdale's. Only a few stores in New York occupy an entire city block; the uptown branch of this New York institution is one of them. The main floor is a crazy, glittery maze of mirrored cosmetic counters and perfume-spraying salespeople. Once you get past this dizzying scene, you can find good buys on designer clothes, bedding, and housewares. The downtown location is smaller, and has a well-edited, higher-end selection of merchandise, so you can focus your search for that Michael Kors handbag or pricey pair of stilettos. ⊠ *1000 3rd Ave., main entrance at E. 59th St. and Lexington Ave., Midtown East* ☎ *212/705–2000* Ⓜ *Subway: N, R, W, 4, 5, 6 to 59th St./Lexington Ave.* ⊠ *504 Broadway, between Spring and Broome Sts., SoHo* ☎ *212/729–5900* Ⓜ *R, W to Prince St.*

Fodor'sChoice
★ **Century 21.** For many New Yorkers, this downtown fixture—right across the street from the former World Trade Center site—remains the mother lode of discount shopping. Four floors are crammed with everything from Gucci sunglasses and half-price cashmere sweaters to Ralph Lauren towels, though you'll have to weed through racks of less-fabulous stuff to find that gem. The best bets in the men's department are shoes and the designer briefs; the full floor of designer women's wear can yield some dazzling finds, such as a Calvin Klein leather trench for less than $600 or a sweeping crinoline skirt from John Paul Gaultier. Since lines for the communal dressing rooms can be prohibitively long, you might want to wear a bodysuit under your clothes for quick, between-the-racks try-ons. ⊠ *22 Cortlandt St., between Broadway and Church St., Lower Manhattan* ☎ *212/227–9092* Ⓜ *Subway: R, W to Cortlandt St.*

Henri Bendel. Behind the graceful Lalique windows you can discover more than the usual fashion suspects. Bendel's dedication to the unusual begins in the ground-floor cosmetics area—filled with lines both big and small, including Trish McEvoy, BeneFit, and Giella Custom Color—and percolates through the floors of women's clothing and accessories. Designers such as Yeohlee, Catherine Malandrino, Rebecca Taylor, and Diane von Furstenberg have room to breathe here; the staircase mezzanine is a minitrove of great handbags and gloves. A first- floor alcove sells Bendel's in-house line, which includes candles in unique scents and the signature brown-and-white dopp kits. ⊠ *712 5th Ave., between W. 55th and W. 56th Sts., Midtown West* ☎ *212/247–1100* Ⓜ *Subway: E, V to 5th Ave./53rd St.*

Lord & Taylor. Comfortably conservative and never overwhelming, Lord & Taylor is a stronghold of classic American designer clothes. Instead of unpronounceable labels, you can find Dana Buchman, Jones New York, and a lot of casual wear. The store tends to attract an older, decidedly untrendy crowd. It also has a large selection of reasonably priced full-length gowns. ⊠ *424 5th Ave., between W. 38th and W. 39th Sts., Midtown West* ☎ *212/391–3344* Ⓜ *Subway: B, D, F, N, Q, R, V, W to 34th St./Herald Sq.*

Macy's. Macy's headquarters store claims to be the largest retail store in America; expect to lose your bearings at least once. Fashion-wise, there's a concentration on the mainstream rather than on the luxe. One strong

17

suit is denim, with everything from Hilfiger and Calvin Klein to Earl Jeans and Paper Denim & Cloth. There's also a reliably good selection of American designs from Ralph Lauren, Tommy Hilfiger, and Nautica. For cooking gear and housewares, the Cellar nearly outdoes Zabar's. ⊠ *Herald Sq., 151 W. 34th St., between 6th and 7th Aves., Midtown West* ☎*212/695–4400* Ⓜ *Subway: B, D, F, N, Q, R, V, W to 34th St./Herald Sq.*

Pearl River Mart. If you want to redecorate your entire apartment with a Chinese theme for less than $1,000, this is the place to do it. Every Asian-style furnishing, houseware, and trinket can be found here, from bamboo rice streamers and ceramic tea sets to paper lanterns and grinning wooden Buddha statues. On the main floor, under a ceiling festooned with dragon kites and rice-paper parasols, you can buy kimono-style robes, pajamas, and embroidered satin slippers for the whole family. There's also a dry-goods section, where you can load up on packages of ginger candy, jasmine tea, and cellophane noodles. ⊠ *477 Broadway, between Broome and Grand Sts., SoHo* ☎ *212/431–4770* Ⓜ *Subway: N, R, Q, W to Canal St.*

Saks Fifth Avenue. A fashion-only department store, Saks sells an astonishing array of apparel. The choice of American and European designers is impressive without being esoteric—the women's selection includes Gucci, Narciso Rodriguez, and Marc Jacobs, plus devastating ball gowns galore. The footwear collections are gratifyingly broad, from Ferragamo to Juicy. In the men's department, sportswear stars such as John Varvatos counterbalance formal wear and current trends. ⊠ *611 5th Ave., between E. 49th and E. 50th Sts., Midtown East* ☎ *212/753–4000* Ⓜ *Subway: E, V to 5th Ave./53rd St.*

Takashimaya New York. This pristine branch of Japan's largest department store carries stylish accessories and fine household items, all of which reflect a combination of Eastern and Western designs. In the Tea Box downstairs, you can have a bento box lunch in the serene, softly lighted tearoom or stock up on green tea. The florist-cum-front-window-display provides a refreshing mini botanical garden. ⊠ *693 5th Ave., between E. 54th and E. 55th Sts., Midtown East* ☎ *212/350–0100* Ⓜ *Subway: E, V to 5th Ave./53rd St.*

HOME DECOR

FodorŝChoice **ABC Carpet & Home.** ABC seems to cover most of the furnishings alpha-
★ bet; over several floors it encompasses everything from rustic furniture to 19th-century repros, refinished Chinese chests, and Vitra chairs, not to mention that loose category, "country French." The ground floor teems with a treasure-attic's worth of accessories. Rugs and carpets are featured across the street at 881 Broadway. ⊠ *888 Broadway, at E. 19th St., Flatiron District* ☎ *212/473–3000* Ⓜ *Subway: L, N, Q, R, W, 4, 5, 6 to 14th St./Union Sq.*

Armani Casa. In keeping with the Armani aesthetic, these minimalist furniture and home wares have a subdued color scheme (cream, black, a crimson accent here and there). You might find lacquered ebony-stain boxes, square-cut porcelain bowls and plates, or silky linens and pillows. ⊠ *97 Greene St., between Prince and Spring Sts., SoHo* ☎ *212/334–1271* Ⓜ *Subway: R, W to Prince St.*

★ **Bellora.** Fine linens for bath and bedroom have been the trademark of this Italian family business since the late 19th century. High-thread-count sheets, duvets, and pillowcases come in soothing color combinations: beachy stripes in pale blue and cream; springtime checks in celadon and rose. There are baffled cotton towels and robes, too, and a line of linen sprays and body lotions to keep everything (including you) smelling lovely. ⊠ *156 Wooster St., at W. Houston St., SoHo* ☎ *212/228–6651* Ⓜ *Subway: R, W to Prince St.; B, D, F, V to Broadway–Lafayette.*

Cath Kidston. Unflaggingly cheery, this British import pushes the retro red, white, and blue for all kinds of houseware essentials and impulses. Pink-and-crimson roses bloom on tote bags, tablecloths, and chintz cushions; polka dots spatter powder-blue and cherry egg cups, bedding, and dog bowls. ⊠ *201 Mulberry St., between Spring and Kenmare Sts., NoLita* ☎ *212/343–0223* Ⓜ *Subway: 6 to Spring St.*

c.i.t.e. Plastic bubble chairs, wavy-looking Holmegaard glassware, bulbous chrome table lamps, and dishes in bright-orange or lime-green enamel are among the fun finds here. ⊠ *120 Wooster St., between Prince and Spring Sts., SoHo* ☎ *212/431–7272* Ⓜ *Subway: R, W to Prince St.*

Clio. Take a shortcut to find the accessories you've seen in the shelter mags. This boutique sets its table with delicate Czech glass vases, bone china with raised dots, and colorful handblown glass bottles. ⊠ *92 Thompson St., between Prince and Spring Sts., SoHo* ☎ *212/966–8991* Ⓜ *Subway: C, E to Spring St.*

★ **De Vera.** The objets d'art and jewelry here all seem to have stories behind them. Many are antique and hint of colonial travels: Indian carvings, Japanese lacquer boxes, 19th-century British garnet earrings. Others exemplify modern forms of traditional workmanship, such as the Murano glass vases or incredibly lifelike glass insects. ⊠ *1 Crosby St., at Howard St., SoHo* ☎ *212/625–0838* Ⓜ *Subway: N, Q, R, W, 6 to Canal St.*

Design Within Reach. "An interesting plainness is the most difficult and precious thing to achieve" reads one of the quotes discreetly placed on the walls here. You can get a lot closer to Mies van der Rohe's ideal with these tasteful mid-20th century pieces, such as Noguchi's paper column lamps and Le Corbusier's steel-frame sofa, plus contemporary furnishings in the same spirit, such as Jesús Gasca's beech "globus" chair. ⊠ *408 W. 14th St., at 9th Ave., Meatpacking District* ☎ *212/242–9449* Ⓜ *Subway: A, C, E to 14th St.* ⊠ *142 Wooster St., between Prince and W. Houston Sts., SoHo* ☎ *212/475–0001* Ⓜ *Subway: F, V to Broadway–Lafayette* ⊠ *27 E. 62nd St., between Park and Madison Aves., Upper East Side* ☎ *212/888–4539* Ⓜ *Subway: N, R, W, 4, 5, 6 to 59th St./Lexington Ave.* ⊠ *341 Columbus Ave., at W. 76th St., Upper West Side* ☎ *212/799–5900* Ⓜ *Subway: 1, 2, 3 to 72nd St.*

Fishs Eddy. The dishes, china, and glassware for resale come from all walks of crockery life, from corporate dining rooms to failed restaurants. New wares often look retro, such as a service with a ticker-tape border. They also stock lots of oddball pieces, such as finger bowls. ⊠ *889 Broadway, at E. 19th St., Flatiron District* ☎ *212/420–9020* Ⓜ *Subway: L, N, Q, R, W, 4, 5, 6 to 14th St./Union Sq.*

17

Continued on page 360

THE MEATPACKING DISTRICT

For nearly a century, this industrial western edge of downtown Manhattan was defined by slaughterhouses and meatpacking plants, blood-splattered cobblestoned streets, and men lugging carcasses into warehouses way before dawn.

But in the late 1990s, the area between West 14th Street, Gansevoort Street, Hudson Street, and 11th Avenue speedily transformed into another kind of meat market. Many of the old warehouses now house ultra-chic shops, nightclubs, and restaurants packed with angular fashionistas. Jeffrey, a pint-sized department store, was an early arrival, followed by edgy but established designers like Stella McCartney and a few lofty furniture stores. Despite the influx of a few chains—albeit stylish ones like Scoop—eclectic boutiques keep popping up. The one thing it's hard to find here is a bargain. –*J.P.*

BEST TIME TO GO

Wednesday through Friday afternoons. Most stores are open daily but a few, like An Earnest Cut & Sew, are closed Monday and Tuesday. A plus if you're here in the late afternoon: a cinematic glow as the light coming off the river burnishes the area's rough edges. On weekends, some stores stay open until 7 or 8 PM, overlapping with the overeager nightlife crowd.

BEST SOUVENIR FOR YOUR GIRLFRIEND (OR BOHO AUNT)

Candy-colored Pyrex rings or quirky dangling earrings from **Auto** (805 Washington St., at Horatio St., 212/229-2292), a boutique focusing on New York–based jewelry designers.

17

Best For

FABULOUS FROCKS

Jeffrey: culls the coolest outfits from high-end labels.

Alexander McQueen: impeccably tailored, take-no-prisoners style.

Catherine Malandrino: romantic chiffon and swingy layers, at more reasonable prices.

DENIM

An Earnest Cut & Sew (821 Washington St., 212/242-3414): customize the cut, buttons, and pockets of your cult jeans.

DDC Lab: high-tech yet earthy, with vegetable indigo dyes, hand-scratching, and sometimes a dash of Lycra.

KILLER ACCESSORIES

Ten Thousand Things: unusual stones in delicate, handwrought settings.

La Perla: the most minxy outpost for this brand's lace lingerie.

Christian Louboutin: vampy heels with telltale crimson soles.

Refueling

Hit the buzzing bistro **Pastis** (9 9th Ave., at Little W. 12th St., 212/929-4844) for a croque monsieur, a bracing coffee, or a cocktail with the namesake hooch. For a quicker stop, follow the smell of cinnamon to the **Little Pie Company** (407 W. 14th St., between 9th Ave. and Washington St., 212/414-2324). Grab a stool along the counter and tuck into a slice of pecan pie, cheesecake, or quiche.

Jonathan Adler. Adler gets mid-20th-century modern and Scandinavian styles to lighten up with his striped, striated, or curvy handmade pottery (ranging from a $30 vase to a chunky $400 lamp) as well as the hand-loomed wool pillow covers, rugs, and throws with blunt graphics (stripes, crosses, circles). ⊠ *47 Greene St., between Broome and Grand Sts., SoHo* ☎ *212/941–8950* Ⓜ *Subway: N, Q, R, W, 6 to Canal St.*

Fodor'sChoice **Moss.** International designers, many of them Italian or Scandinavian, put ★ a fantastic spin on even the most utilitarian objects, which are carefully brought together by Murray Moss at his store–cum–design museum. The latest innovations from Jasper Morrison, Ted Muehling, and Philippe Starck are interspersed with vintage Baccarat crystal and classic chair designs from Frank Gehry. A recent expansion—the Moss Gallery, next to the original space—has allowed the collection to grow even more. ⊠ *146–152 Greene St., between W. Houston and Prince Sts., SoHo* ☎ *212/204–7100* Ⓜ *Subway: R, W to Prince St.*

Mxyplyzyk. Hard to pronounce (*mixy plit sick*) and hard to resist, this is a trove of impulse buys—creative riffs on household standbys such as dishes (covered in psychedelic patterns or made from old vinyl LPs), handbags (made to look like boccie balls), and toothbrush holders (shaped like giant teeth). ⊠ *125 Greenwich Ave., at W. 13th St., Greenwich Village* ☎ *212/989–4300* Ⓜ *Subway: A, C, E, L to 14th St./8th Ave.*

Nina Griscom. Another socialite has joined the commercial fray, allowing those of us without a boldface name to sample the rarified style. The objets d'art, furniture, and jewelry here have an exotic–organic appeal, with natural materials like ivory, sandalwood, and coral turning up as candlesticks, decorative boxes, and chunky cuff bracelets. ⊠ *958 Lexington Ave., at E. 70th St., Upper East Side* ☎ *212/717–7373* Ⓜ *Subway: 6 to E. 68th St.*

★ **Olatz.** The wife and muse of painter Julian, Olatz Schnabel modeled her linen shop on a historic Havana pharmacy after the couple visited Cuba. The black-and white checkerboard floors and mint-green walls breathe a sort of lazy, faded elegance, a spot-on backdrop to her collection of luxurious sheets, blankets, and pajama sets, all of which have sky-high thread counts and are bordered with bold stripes or intricate damask embroidery. ⊠ *43 Clarkson St., between Hudson and Greenwich Sts., Greenwich Village* ☎ *212/255–8627* Ⓜ *Subway: 1 to Houston St.*

Pylones. Even the most utilitarian items get a goofy, colorful makeover from this French company. Toasters and thermoses are coated in stripes or flowers, hairbrushes have pictures of frogs or ladybugs on their backs, and whisks are reimagined as squid. There are plenty of fun gifts for less than $20, such as old-fashioned robot toys and candy-colored boxes. ⊠ *69 Spring St., between Crosby and Lafayette Sts., SoHo* ☎ *212/431–3244* Ⓜ *Subway: 6 to Spring St.*

Steuben. The bowls and vases make for knockout table centerpieces, but if all this shopping gives you sweaty palms, wrap your fingers around a miniature sculpted-animal hand cooler, then head downstairs to view one of the rotating glass exhibitions. ⊠ *667 Madison Ave., between E. 60th and E. 61st Sts., Upper East Side* ☎ *212/752–1441* Ⓜ *Subway: N, R, W to 5th Ave./59th St.*

★ **Terence Conran Shop.** The small glass pavilion beneath the 59th Street Bridge caps this British stylemonger's vast underground showroom of kitchen and garden implements, fabrics, furniture, and glassware. Even the shower curtains are cool. ✉ *407 E. 59th St., at 1st Ave., Midtown East* ☎ *212/755–9079* Ⓜ *Subway: N, R, W to 59th St./Lexington Ave.*

Troy. In this spare space, the clean lines of Lucite, leather, cedar, and resin furniture and home accessories may well wreak havoc with your credit card. In addition to the seriously sleek furnishings, you can also find slightly less-imposing items like stone-shape lamps in Murano glass, teakwood serving trays, and creative ceramic tableware. ✉ *138 Greene St., between Prince and W. Houston Sts., SoHo* ☎ *212/941–4777* Ⓜ *Subway: R, W to Prince St.*

Vitra. A newcomer to the retail market but a seasoned vet in the realm of furniture design, Vitra is the source of many of mid-20th-century modernism's most iconic pieces. The S-curved molded plastic Panton chairs, George Nelson's wall clocks and "marshmallow" sofa, the Eames chairs—they're all here. If you can't swing for the real thing, check out the miniature replicas. ✉ *29 9th Ave., at W. 13th St., Meatpacking District* ☎ *212/929–3626* Ⓜ *Subway: A, C, E to 14th St.*

William-Wayne & Co. Silver julep cups, Viennese playing cards, butler's trays, candelabras made from coral, and other whimsical decorative items all vie for your attention at this shop. ✉ *40 University Pl., at E. 9th St., Greenwich Village* ☎ *212/533–4711* Ⓜ *Subway: 6 to Astor Pl.* ✉ *846 Lexington Ave., at E. 64th St., Upper East Side* ☎ *212/737–8934* Ⓜ *Subway: 6 to 68th St./Hunter College* ✉ *850 Lexington Ave., at E. 64th St., Upper East Side* ☎ *212/288–9243* Ⓜ *Subway: 6 to 68th St./Hunter College.*

JEWELRY

For Everyday

Beads of Paradise. Browse a rich selection of African trade-bead necklaces, earrings, and rare artifacts. You can also create your own designs. ✉ *16 E. 17th St., between 5th Ave. and Broadway, Flatiron District* ☎ *212/620–0642* Ⓜ *Subway: 4, 5, 6, N, Q, R, W to 14th St./Union Sq.*

David Yurman. The signature motifs here—cables, quatrefoil shapes—add up to a classic, go-anywhere look, while the use of semiprecious stones keeps prices within reason. ✉ *729 Madison Ave., at E. 64th St., Upper East Side* ☎ *212/752–4255* Ⓜ *Subway: 6 to 68th St./Hunter Collge.*

Dinosaur Designs. Translucent and colorful, this antipodean work uses an untraditional medium: resin. Some look like semiprecious stone, such as onyx or jade; the rest delve into stronger colors like aqua or crimson. Cruise the stacks of chunky bangles and cuffs or rows of rings; prices start under $50. There's some striking tableware, too. ✉ *250 Mott St., between Prince and E. Houston Sts., NoLita* ☎ *212/680–3523* Ⓜ *Subway: R, W to Prince St.*

Femmegems. If you have finicky taste you can be as choosy as you like here. On one side dangle necklaces and bracelets designed by the staff, on the other hang strands of stones ready for customization. Pick out the beads you like (mostly semiprecious such as topaz, carnelian, and aquamarine), fish out a porcelain or carved-stone pendant, and have a unique bauble assembled in short order. ✉ *280 Mulberry St., between Prince and E. Houston Sts., NoLita* ☎ *212/625–1611* Ⓜ *Subway: R, W to Prince St.*

Fragments. This spot glitters with pieces by nimble new jewelry designers, many of them local. Most use semiprecious stones—you could try on turquoise-bead shoulder-duster earrings, an oversize opal ring, or a tourmaline pendant—but a few bust out the sapphires and rubies. ✉ *116 Prince St., between Greene and Wooster Sts., SoHo* ☎ *212/334– 9588* Ⓜ *Subway: R, W to Prince St.* ✉ *997 Madison Ave., between E. 77th and 78th Sts., Upper East Side* ☎ *212/537–5000* Ⓜ *Subway: 6 to E. 77th St.*

Me + Ro. Eastern styling has gained these designers a cult following. The Indian-inspired, hand-finished gold bangles and earrings covered with tiny dangling rubies or sapphires may look bohemian, but the prices target the trust-fund set. ✉ *241 Elizabeth St., between Prince and E. Houston Sts., NoLita* ☎ *917/237–9215* Ⓜ *Subway: R, W to Prince St.*

Objets du Désir. The wall-hung cases juxtapose terrifically different jewelry styles; one might display dainty clusters of pearls and filigree, while its neighbor could glower with punky stud bracelets and silver skull rings. One great recent find: a cuff etched with a free-form street map of Manhattan. ✉ *241 Mulberry St., between Prince and Spring Sts., No- Lita* ☎ *212/334–9727* Ⓜ *Subway: 6 to Spring St.*

Robert Lee Morris. Gold and silver take on bold, sculptural shapes here: cuff bracelets are chunky but fluidly curved, and necklaces and earrings have dangling hammered disks for a "wind chime" effect. Some pieces incorporate diamonds; others have semiprecious stones like turquoise or citrine. ✉ *400 West Broadway, between Broome and Spring Sts., SoHo* ☎ *212/431–9405* Ⓜ *Subway: C, E to Spring St.*

Stuart Moore. Many of the Teutonic designs are minimalist, almost industrial-seeming: diamonds are set in brushed platinum, and some rings and cuff links have a geometric, architectural aesthetic. Pieces here tend to be modest in scale. ✉ *128 Prince St., at Wooster St., SoHo* ☎ *212/ 941–1023* Ⓜ *Subway: R, W to Prince St.*

Fodor'sChoice ★ **Ten Thousand Things.** Exquisitely delicate, the designs at this boutique incorporate tiny beads of Peruvian opal, chrysophase, ruby, sapphire, and red coral. ✉ *423 W. 14th St., between 9th and 10th Aves., Meatpacking District* ☎ *212/352–1333* Ⓜ *Subway: A, C, E to 14th St.*

Tourneau. Each of these stores stocks a wide range of watches, but the three-level 57th Street TimeMachine, a high-tech merchandising extravaganza, steals the scene. A museum downstairs has timepiece exhibits, both temporary and permanent. The shops carry more than 70 brands, from status symbols such as Patek Philippe, Cartier, and Rolex, to more casual styles by Swatch, Seiko, and Swiss Army. ✉ *500 Madison Ave., between E. 52nd and E. 53rd Sts., Midtown East* ☎ *212/758– 6098* Ⓜ *Subway: 6 to 51st St./Lexington Ave.; E, V to Lexington–3rd Aves./53rd St.* ✉ *12 E. 57th St., between 5th and Madison Aves., Midtown East* ☎ *212/758–7300* Ⓜ *Subway: N, R, W to 5th Ave./59th St.* ✉ *200 W. 34th St., at 7th Ave., Midtown West* ☎ *212/563–6880* Ⓜ *Subway: A, C, E, 1, 2, 3 to 34th St./Penn Station* ✉ *10 Columbus*

Circle, at W. 59th St., Midtown West ☎ *212/823–9425* Ⓜ *Subway: 1, A, B, C, D to Columbus Circle.*

Versani. Silver teams up with all kinds of materials here: leather, denim, and snakeskin, as well as semiprecious stones. There's a good selection of silver rings and pendants under $50. ✉ *152 Mercer St., between Prince and W. Houston Sts., SoHo* ☎ *212/941–9919* Ⓜ *Subway: R, W to Prince St.* ✉ *227 Mulberry St., between Prince and Spring Sts., NoLita* ☎ *212/431–4944* Ⓜ *Subway: 6 to Spring St.*

Money's No Object

A La Vieille Russie. Stop here to behold bibelots by Fabergé and others, enameled or encrusted with jewels. ✉ *781 5th Ave., at E. 59th St., Midtown East* ☎ *212/752–1727* Ⓜ *Subway: N, R, W to 5th Ave./59th St.*

Asprey. Having split from Garrard, Asprey has spread its net to cater to all kinds of luxury tastes, from leather goods and rare books to polo equipment and cashmere sweaters. Its claim to fame, though, is jewelry; its own eponymous diamond cut has A-shaped facets. ✉ *723 5th Ave., at E. 56th St., Midtown East* ☎ *212/688–1811* Ⓜ *Subway: F to 5th Ave.*

Bulgari. This Italian company is certainly not shy about its name, which encircles gems, watch faces, even lighters. There are beautiful, weighty rings, pieces mixing gold with stainless steel or porcelain, and the latest Astrale line, which incorporates delicate motifs, like concentric circles of small diamonds, into drop earrings and necklaces. ✉ *730 5th Ave., at W. 57th St., Midtown West* ☎ *212/315–9000* Ⓜ *Subway: N, R, W to 5th Ave.* ✉ *783 Madison Ave., between E. 66th and E. 67th Sts., Upper East Side* ☎ *212/717–2300* Ⓜ *Subway: 6 to 68th St./Hunter College.*

Chanel Fine Jewelry. Besides the showstopper pieces based on Chanel's own jewels, there are stars and comets sparkling with diamonds and gold worked into a quilted design. ✉ *733 Madison Ave., at E. 64th St., Upper East Side* ☎ *212/535–5828* Ⓜ *Subway: 6 to 68th St./Hunter College.*

H. Stern. Sleek designs pose in an equally modern 5th Avenue setting; smooth cabochon-cut stones, most from South America, glow in pale wooden display cases. The designers make notable use of semiprecious stones such as citrine, tourmaline, and topaz. ✉ *645 5th Ave., between E. 51st and E. 52nd Sts., Midtown East* ☎ *212/688–0300* Ⓜ *Subway: E, V to 5th Ave./53rd St.* ✉ *301 Park Ave., between E. 49th and E. 50th Sts., in Waldorf-Astoria, Midtown East* ☎ *212/753–5595* Ⓜ *Subway: 6 to 51st St.*

Fred Leighton. If you're in the market for vintage diamonds, this is the place, whether your taste is for tiaras, art deco settings, or sparklers once worn by a Vanderbilt. ✉ *773 Madison Ave., at E. 66th St., Upper East Side* ☎ *212/288–1872* Ⓜ *Subway: 6 to 68th St./Hunter College.*

Jacob & Co. The designs at the new home of Diamond District legend "Jacob the Jeweler" are anything but subtle; in Jacob's parlance, bigger is better. Diamond-encrusted watches (favored by such celebs as Paris Hilton, P. Diddy, and Busta Rhymes) are nearly saucer-size, and carats for rings go up into the double digits. If you're not blinded by the glare, head to the back of the shop for a giggle at some of the novelty items: giant pendants shaped like guitars, dice, and Jesus. ✉ *48 E. 57th St., between 5th and Madison Aves., Midtown West* ☎ *212/719–5887* Ⓜ *Subway: N, R, W, 4, 5, 6 to 59th St./Lexington Ave.*

The Diamond District

STEPPING ONTO 47TH STREET between 5th and 6th avenues is like entering an alternate universe. On this single city block, where crowds surge and more than 2,500 independent businesses operate, everything and everyone you see is here for the same reason: to buy, sell, deliver, design, or repair jewelry, most specifically, diamonds.

While some of the merchants here have the usual kinds of storefront jewelry shops, most of the buying and selling is done in the 25 different jewelry "exchanges" scattered along the block. These are cavernous emporiums, where scores of different jewelers man their counters under a single roof. (Many of these, you'll notice, are Hasidic Jews wearing their traditional uniform of black coats and wide-brimmed black hats. Jews have a long history as jewelers, mainly because in many parts of Europe, they weren't allowed to own land, and had to invest in a more portable source of wealth.)

These merchants sell loose diamonds and gemstones, as well as ones already set in rings, bracelets, and necklaces; you can choose a particular stone and have it custom-set in a design you like. Each proprietor will

have different stones and settings to offer, so you should definitely shop around before making a purchase. You should also comparison-shop to make sure you're getting a good price. Although the stiff competition here helps to keep prices reasonable, the best way to be sure a price is fair is to check out stones or jewelry of similar quality in a few different places.

Though most diamond-district merchants are reputable, there are some swindlers out there (as there are everywhere). So it's a good idea to take some self-protective measures when buying here. First, make sure to educate yourself about the gemstones you're looking to purchase before you even approach the merchants, and once you're there, ask them lots of questions. Second, be sure to inquire about refund and exchange policies before you buy; in many of the businesses, these aren't posted. Last, and most important, be sure you get a sales slip from the merchant, with all the information about the stones or jewelry (such as grade, cut, and clarity) written on the slip. In most cases, this will be the only proof you'll have of the claims the merchant has made to you.

Mikimoto. The Japanese originator of the cultured pearl, Mikimoto presents a glowing display of high-luster pearls. Besides the creamy strands from their own pearl farms, check out the dazzlingly colored South Sea pearls, dramatic black-lip and silver-lip varieties, and rare conch pearls. ⊠ *730 5th Ave., between W. 56th and W. 57th Sts., Midtown West* ☎ *212/ 457–4600* Ⓜ *Subway: F to 57th St.*

New York Classics

Cartier. Pierre Cartier allegedly won the 5th Avenue mansion location by trading two strands of perfectly matched natural pearls with Mrs. Morton Plant. The jewelry is still incredibly persuasive, from such established favorites as the interlocking rings to the more recent additions such as the handcufflike Menotte bracelets. ✉ *653 5th Ave., at E. 52nd St., Midtown East* ☎ *212/753–0111* Ⓜ *Subway: E, V to 5th Ave./53rd St.* ✉ *828 Madison Ave., at E. 69th St., Upper East Side* ☎ *212/472–6400* Ⓜ *Subway: 6 to 68th St./Hunter College.*

Harry Winston. Ice-clear diamonds of impeccable quality sparkle in Harry Winston's inner sanctum. They're set in everything from emerald-cut solitaire rings to wreath necklaces resembling strings of flowers. No wonder the jeweler was immortalized in the song "Diamonds Are a Girl's Best Friend." ✉ *718 5th Ave., at W. 56th St., Midtown West* ☎ *212/245–2000* Ⓜ *Subway: F to 57th St.*

Fodor'sChoice   **Tiffany & Co.** The display windows can be soigné, funny, or just plain
★   breathtaking. Alongside the $80,000 platinum-and-diamond bracelets, a lot here is affordable on a whim—and everything comes wrapped in that unmistakable Tiffany blue. ✉ *727 5th Ave., at E. 57th St., Midtown East* ☎ *212/755–8000* Ⓜ *Subway: N, R, W to 5th Ave./59th St.*

LINGERIE

Agent Provocateur. The bustiest mannequins in Manhattan vamp in the front window of this British underpinnings phenom. Showpieces include boned corsets, lace sets with contrast-color trim, bottoms tied with satin ribbons, and a few fetish-type leather ensembles. A great selection of stockings is complemented by the garter belts to secure them. ✉ *133 Mercer St., between Prince and Spring Sts., SoHo* ☎ *212/965–0229* Ⓜ *Subway: R, W to Prince St.*

Bra Smyth. Chic and sweetly sexy French and Canadian underthings in soft cottons and silks line the shelves of this East Side staple. In addition to the selection of bridal-ready white bustiers and custom-fit swimsuits (made, cleverly, in bra-cup sizes), the store is best known for its knowledgeable staff, many of whom can offer tips on proper fit and size you up on sight. Cup sizes run from AA to H. ✉ *905 Madison Ave., at 73rd St., Upper East Side* ☎ *212/772–9400* Ⓜ *Subway: 6 to 68th St./Hunter College.*

La Perla. From the Leavers lace, soutache, and embroidery to unadorned tulle, these underthings are so gorgeous they've inspired a trilogy of books. Look for the sets of sheer underwear embroidered with the days of the week in Italian—a grown-up alternative to Bloomie's classic bloomers. ✉ *803 Madison Ave., between E. 67th and E. 68th Sts., 3rd fl., Upper East Side* ☎ *212/459–2775* Ⓜ *Subway: 6 to 68th St./Hunter College* ✉ *93 Greene St., between Prince and Spring Sts., SoHo* ☎ *212/219–0999* Ⓜ *Subway: R, W to Prince St.* ✉ *425 W. 14th St., between 9th and 10th Aves., Meatpacking District* ☎ *212/242–6662* Ⓜ *Subway: A, C, E to 14th St.*

La Petite Coquette. Among the signed photos on the walls is one of ultimate authority—from Frederique, longtime Victoria's Secret model. The store's own line of silk slips, camisoles, and other underpinnings comes in a range of colors, and as befits the name, they have special petite cuts. ✉ *51 University Pl., between E. 9th and E. 10th Sts., Greenwich Village* ☎ *212/473–2478* Ⓜ *Subway: R, W to 8th St.*

Le Corset. This lovely boutique naturally stocks its namesake, plus lacy underwear and negligees from such designers as Chloe and Collette Dinnigan, and even powder-pink vintage slips and girdles. ⊠ *80 Thompson St., between Spring and Broome Sts., SoHo* ☎ *212/334–4936* Ⓜ *Subway: C, E to Spring St.*

Mixona. The minx-at-heart will have a field day among the lace-encrusted Huit and the gauzy bras of Passion Bait. Some lines trace back to such major design houses as Blumarine, Galliano, and D & G. There are usually good finds on the sales racks in back. ⊠ *262 Mott St., between Prince and E. Houston Sts., NoLita* ☎ *646/613–0100* Ⓜ *Subway: R, W to Prince St.*

37 = 1 Atelier. The ethereal silk chiffon pieces here bring delicacy to a new level. Many are made to match various skin tones, and the use of ribbon and fine seams, rather than elastics, means that you might forget you're wearing anything at all. ⊠ *37 Crosby St., between Broome and Grand Sts., NoLita* ☎ *212/226–0067* Ⓜ *Subway: 4, 5, 6 to Canal St.*

LUGGAGE, LEATHER GOODS & HANDBAGS

Altman Luggage. Great bargains—a Samsonite Pullman for a little more than $100—are the thing at this discount store, which also stocks tough Timberland and Swiss Army backpacks. ⊠ *135 Orchard St., between Delancey and Rivington Sts., Lower East Side* ☎ *212/254–7275* Ⓜ *Subway: F, J, M, Z to Delancey St./Essex St.*

Anya Hindmarch. Although some of these divine British handbags in calf, satin, or velvet are ready for a very proper occasion, others cut loose with funny silk-screened photos or sequined designs of candy or painkillers. ⊠ *29 E. 60th St., between Madison and Park Aves., Upper East Side* ☎ *212/750–3974* Ⓜ *Subway: N, R, W to 5th Ave./59th St.* ⊠ *115 Greene St., between Prince and Spring Sts., SoHo* ☎ *212/343–8147* Ⓜ *Subway: R, W to Prince St.*

Bottega Veneta. The signature crosshatch weave graces leather handbags, slouchy satchels, and shoes; the especially satisfying brown shades extend from fawn to deep chocolate. ⊠ *699 5th Ave., between E. 54th and E. 55th Sts., Midtown East* ☎ *212/371–5511* Ⓜ *Subway: N, R, W, 4, 5, 6 to 59th St./Lexington Ave.*

Crouch & Fitzgerald. Since 1839 this store has offered an unimpeachable selection of hard- and soft-sided luggage, as well as a huge number of attaché cases. ⊠ *400 Madison Ave., at E. 48th St., Midtown East* ☎ *212/755–5888* Ⓜ *Subway: B, D, F, V to 47th–50th St./Rockefeller Center.*

Fendi. Once known for its furs, Fendi is now synonymous with decadent handbags. The purses are beaded, embroidered, and fantastically embellished within an inch of their lives, resulting in prices that skyrocket over $1,000. Fancy leathers, furs, and other accessories are also available. ⊠ *677 5th Ave., between E. 53rd and E. 54th Sts., Midtown East* ☎ *212/759–4646* Ⓜ *Subway: E, F to 5th Ave./53rd St.*

Fine & Klein. Among the Orchard Street veterans, this is a reliable stop for handbags, although it's not quite the bargain it used to be, as many bags now cost upwards of $200. Some purses bear a marked resemblance to those of well-known designers. ✉ *119 Orchard St., between Ludlow and Delancey Sts., Lower East Side* ☎ *212/674–6720* Ⓜ *Subway: F, J, M, Z to Delancey St./Essex St.*

Flight 001. Frequent flyers can one-stop-shop at this travel-theme store. Carry-on bags, passport holders, and personal-size down pillows share shelf space with mini–alarm clocks, satin sleep masks, and mellow music CDs for soothing frazzled nerves. ✉ *96 Greenwich Ave., between W. 12th and Jane Sts., Greenwich Village* ☎ *212/691–1001* Ⓜ *Subway: A, C, E to 14th St.*

Furla. Shoulder bags, oblong clutches, and roomy totes can be quite proper or attention-getting, from a cocoa-brown, croc-embossed zipper-top to a patent leather, cherry-red purse. ✉ *598 Madison Ave., at E. 57th St., Midtown East* ☎ *212/980–3208* Ⓜ *Subway: N, R, 4, 5, 6 to 59th St.* ✉ *727 Madison Ave., between E. 63rd and E. 64th Sts., Upper East Side* ☎ *212/755–8986* Ⓜ *Subway: N, R, W, 4, 5, 6 to 59th St./Lexington Ave.*

Henry Beguelin. The aroma of leather pervades this boutique on the ground floor of the Hotel Gansevoort, and it's no wonder: everything here, even the floor, is made from it. Many of the pieces have an ethnic-bohemian look, with fringe and beading on jackets and swingy skirts. ✉ *18 9th Ave., at W. 13th St., Meatpacking District* ☎ *212/647–8415* Ⓜ *Subway: A, C, E to 14th St.*

High Way. Some of these breezy, colorful handbags come trimmed with grosgrain ribbon or with a coin-purse-like snapping closure. Others open like mini garment bags to disclose a wealth of inner pockets. ✉ *238 Mott St., between Prince and Spring Sts., NoLita* ☎ *212/966–4388* Ⓜ *Subway: 6 to Bleecker St.*

Jamin Puech. Wanderlust is evident in many of these bags; the colors, embroideries, fringes, and fabrics may suggest Morocco and Polynesia, and the bags can cost as much as an off-season plane ticket to the Continent. ✉ *247 Elizabeth St., between E. Houston and Prince Sts., NoLita* ☎ *212/431–5200* Ⓜ *Subway: R, W to Prince St.*

Judith Leiber. A door handle twinkling with Swarowski crystals signals the entrance to the Kingdom of Sparkle. Instantly recognizable handbags are completely frosted in crystals, from simple, colorful rectangles to minaudières shaped like animals or flowers. Crystals also spangle the heels of satin pumps and the bows of oversized (to cut the glare?) sunglasses. ✉ *680 Madison Ave., at E. 61st St., Upper East Side* ☎ *212/223–2999* Ⓜ *Subway: 4, 5, 6 to E. 59th St.*

Fodor'sChoice **Kate Spade.** These eminently desirable (and oft-copied) handbags in ★ lush-color leather, tweed, and canvas have a classic but kicky retro style. Totes and shoulder bags are lined in fun fabrics; wicker baskets for summer are jazzed up with bright leather accents or shaped like birdhouses. The expanded Broome Street shop also carries shoes, hats, scarves, linens, and sunglasses. Around the corner at **Jack Spade** (✉ *56 Greene St., between Broome and Spring Sts., SoHo* ☎ *212/625–1820* Ⓜ *Subway: C, E to Prince St.*), Kate's husband peddles his own line of bags, dopp kits, and other men's accessories in a nostalgic setting. The original storefront on Thompson Street now carries baby accessories. ✉ *454 Broome St., between Mercer and Greene Sts., SoHo* ☎ *212/274–*

17

Continued on page 370

LOWER EAST SIDE

Once home to multitudes of Jewish immigrants from Russia and Eastern Europe, the Lower East Side has traditionally been New Yorkers' bargain beat. The center of it all is Orchard Street, where vendors still holler, "Lady, have I got a deal for you!"

Here tiny, no-nonsense clothing stores and scrappy stalls hang on to the past, while funky local designers gradually claim more turf. A few cool vintage clothing and furniture spots bridge the two camps. Ludlow Street, one block east of Orchard, has become the main drag for twentysomethings with attitude, its boutiques wedged in between bars and low-key restaurants. Anything too polished is looked on with suspicion—and that goes for you, too. For the full scope of this area, prowl from Allen to Essex streets, south of East Houston Street down to Broome Street. A tip: wear closed shoes to stay clear of broken glass and other crud on the sidewalks. –J.P.

BEST TIME TO GO

For the full-blown LES experience come on a Sunday afternoon, when Orchard Street between East Houston and Delancey streets becomes a vehicle-free pedestrian zone. On Saturday, the old-school stores close for the Jewish Sabbath.

BEST SOUVENIR FOR YOUR FAVE KITCHEN AIDE

Raid the **Lower East Side Tenement Museum gift shop** (108 Orchard St., between Delancey and Broome Sts., 212/431-0233) for a cheery reproduction 1950 Empire State souvenir kitchen towel and some retro fridge magnets with skyscrapers trumpeting "New York the Wonder City." Bonus point: wrapping paper with a 1930s NYC map design. Top things off with a portable delicatessen treat.

SPOTLIGHT ON LOWER EAST SIDE

17

Map showing subway stops and store locations: Russ & Daughters, TG-170, Las Venus, Foley & Corinna, Frock, Edith Machinist, Guss' Pickles, along E. 1st St., E. Houston St., Stanton St., Rivington St., Delancey St., and Forsyth St., Allen St., Orchard St., Ludlow St., Essex St., Norfolk St., Eldridge St., Chrystie St.

KEY

M Subway stops

Best For

VINTAGE

Frock: big names from the 1970s and '80s, whopping shoulder pads, and often hefty price tags.

Las Venus: Danish modern furniture, princess phones, boomerang ashtrays in punchy colors.

Edith Machinist: the largest stash of women's boots and bags (and well priced, too).

CLOTHES WITH BITE

TG-170: rock-chick wardrobe staples like superdark, tight jeans and tough Freitag bags.

Foley & Corinna: mixes vintage-y new clothes with the truly vintage, for both men and women.

OLD-WORLD FOOD

Russ & Daughters: smoked salmon, pickled herring, and babka, oh my.

Guss' Pickles (85 Orchard St., no phone): move beyond the half-sours to the zingy full-sour and spicy pickle spears.

Refueling

Get your calcium with a stop at **il laboratorio del gelato** (95 Orchard St., between Delancey and Broome Sts., 212/343–9922) for creamy scoops in unusual flavors like nutmeg, ricotta, or ginger. Cake with your gelato? Zip to **Sugar Sweet Sunshine** (126 Rivington St., between Essex and Norfolk Sts., 212/995–1960), a homey little bakery where you can nibble on a cupcake with chocolate-almond frosting or a slice of red velvet cake. For something healthier, get a table at the **teany café** (90 Rivington St., between Orchard and Ludlow Sts., 212/475–9190), a vegetarian spot with light meals, sweets, and over 90 teas to try.

1991 Ⓜ *Subway: C, E to Spring St.* ✉ *59 Thompson St., between Spring and Broome Sts., SoHo* ☎ *212/965–8654* Ⓜ *Subway: C, E to Spring St.*

Longchamp. Its nylon bags have become an Upper East Side staple and can be spotted everywhere in the Hamptons. The store carries the entire line of luggage, wallets, and totes in a rainbow of colors. ✉ *713 Madison Ave., between E. 63rd and E. 64th Sts., Upper East Side* ☎ *212/223–1500* Ⓜ *Subway: N, R, W, 4, 5, 6 to 59th St./Lexington Ave.*

Fodor'sChoice **Louis Vuitton.** In the mammoth 57th Street store, vintage examples of Vuitton's famous monogrammed trunks float above the fray on the ground
★ floor, where shoppers angle for the latest accessories. Joining the initials are the Damier check pattern and colorful striated leathers, plus devastatingly chic clothes and shoes designed by Marc Jacobs. ✉ *1 E. 57th St., at 5th Ave., Midtown East* ☎ *212/758–8877* Ⓜ *Subway: E, V to 5th Ave./53rd St.* ✉ *116 Greene St., between Prince and Spring Sts., SoHo* ☎ *212/274–9090* Ⓜ *Subway: R, W to Prince St.*

Lulu Guinness. Hit this lavender-upholstered salon for such whimsically retro accessories as handbags adorned with appliqué, beads, and bows; polka-dot scarves; and umbrellas patterned with poodles. ✉ *394 Bleecker St., between W. 11th and Perry Sts., Greenwich Village* ☎ *212/367–2120* Ⓜ *Subway: 1 to Christopher St.*

Manhattan Portage. You know you want one, so visit the source of the messenger-bag fad. Although they're a dime a dozen around these parts, these sturdy nylon and canvas numbers cost real money—$20–$100— and will impress the folks back home. ✉ *301 W. Broadway, between Canal and Grand Sts., SoHo* ☎ *212/226–4557* Ⓜ *Subway: A, C, E to Canal St.*

★ **Sigerson Morrison Handbags.** Ready to seduce your shoulder as well as your feet, Sigerson Morrison devises bags in calfskin, pigskin, suede, and the occasional fabric, often equipped with zippered exterior pockets for cell phones and other things you need close at hand. ✉ *242 Mott St., between Prince and E. Houston Sts., NoLita* ☎ *212/941–5404* Ⓜ *Subway: R, W to Prince St.*

T. Anthony. The trademark coated-canvas luggage with leather trim can be classic (black or beige) or eye-catching (red or purply blue). Those who like to carry it all with them can outfit themselves with hatboxes and shirt cases, plus totes, trunks, and hard- and soft-sided suitcases. ✉ *445 Park Ave., at E. 56th St., Midtown East* ☎ *212/750–9797* Ⓜ *Subway: E, V to 5th Ave./53rd St.*

MUSIC & VIDEO

The city's best record stores provide browsers with a window to New York's groovier subcultures. The East Village is especially good for dance tracks and used music.

Bleecker Bob's Golden Oldies Record Shop. One of the oldest independent record stores in town, this pleasingly shabby-looking shop with its old-fashioned neon sign sells punk, jazz, metal, and reggae, plus good old rock on vinyl, until the wee hours. ✉ *118 W. 3rd St., at MacDou-*

gal St., Greenwich Village ☎ *212/475–9677* Ⓜ *Subway: A, C, E, F, V to W. 4th St./Washington Sq.*

Jazz Record Center. Long-lost Ellingtons and other rare pressings come to light here; the jazz-record specialist also stocks collectibles, DVDs, videos, posters, and LPs. ✉ *236 W. 26th St., between 7th and 8th Aves., 8th fl., Chelsea* ☎ *212/675–4480* Ⓜ *Subway: 1 to 28th St.*

J&R Music World. Not only will you find a huge selection of pop music and videos, as well as Latin, jazz, and classical, you'll also get good prices on major releases. You can even buy music by telephone. ✉ *23 Park Row, between Beekman and Ann Sts., Lower Manhattan* ☎ *212/238–9000* Ⓜ *Subway: 4, 5, 6 to Brooklyn Bridge/City Hall.*

Kim's Video & Music. Scruffy and eclectic, Kim's crystallizes the downtown music scene. Its top-20 list is a long, long way from the Top 40; instead, there's a mix of electronica, jazz, lounge, and experimental. ✉ *6 St. Marks Pl., between 2nd and 3rd Aves., East Village* ☎ *212/598–9985* Ⓜ *Subway: 6 to Astor Pl.* ✉ *2906 Broadway, between W. 113th and W. 114th Sts., Morningside Heights* ☎ *212/864–5321* Ⓜ *Subway: 1 to 116th St.*

Fodor's Choice ★ **Other Music.** Across the way from Tower Records, both spatially and spiritually, this store carries hard-to-find genres on CD and vinyl, from Japanese electronica and Krautrock to acid folk and Americana. There's also a great selection of used CDs, including seminal punk classics from the Clash and the Stooges. ✉ *15 E. 4th St., between Lafayette St. and Broadway, East Village* ☎ *212/477–8150* Ⓜ *Subway: 6 to Astor Pl.*

17

Tower Records. Uptown, patrons discuss jazz; downtown, many customers are multipierced and rainbow-haired. ✉ *692 Broadway, at E. 4th St., East Village* ☎ *212/505–1500* Ⓜ *Subway: B, D, F, V to Broadway–Lafayette* ✉ *1961 Broadway, at W. 66th St., Upper West Side* ☎ *212/799–2500* Ⓜ *Subway: 1 to 66th St.* ✉ *725 5th Ave., basement level of Trump Tower, between E. 56th and E. 57th Sts., Midtown East* ☎ *212/838–8110* Ⓜ *Subway: N, R, W to 5th Ave.* ✉ *20 E. 4th St., at Lafayette St., East Village* ☎ *212/505–1166* Ⓜ *Subway: B, D, F, V to Broadway–Lafayette.*

Virgin Megastore. In megastores in both Times Square and Union Square, you'll find rows upon rows of CDs, videos, books, and DVDs. Both have room for live band appearances. ✉ *1540 Broadway, between W. 45th and W. 46th Sts., Midtown West* ☎ *212/921–1020* Ⓜ *Subway: 1, 2, 3, N, Q, R, W to 42nd St./Times Sq.* ✉ *52 E. 14th St., at Broadway, East Village* ☎ *212/598–4666* Ⓜ *Subway: 4, 5, 6, N, Q, R, W to 14th St./Union Sq.*

MUSEUM STORES

Metropolitan Museum of Art Shop. Of the three locations, the store in the museum has a phenomenal book selection, as well as posters, art videos, and computer programs. Reproductions of jewelry, statuettes, and other *objets* fill the gleaming cases in every branch. ✉ *5th Ave. at E. 82nd St., Upper East Side* ☎ *212/879–5500* Ⓜ *Subway: 4, 5, 6 to 86th St.* ✉ *12–14 Fulton St., between Front and South Sts., Lower Manhattan* ☎ *212/248–0954* Ⓜ *Subway: 4, 5, A, C to Fulton St./Broadway–Nas-*

sau ⊠ *15 W. 49th St., between 5th and 6th Aves., Rockefeller Center, Midtown West* ☎ *212/332–1360* Ⓜ *Subway: B, D, F, V to 47th–50th Sts./Rockefeller Center.*

Museum of Arts and Design. The tie-ins to ongoing exhibits can yield beautiful handmade glassware, unusual jewelry, or enticing textiles. ⊠ *40 W. 53rd St., between 5th and 6th Aves., Midtown West* ☎ *212/956– 3535* Ⓜ *Subway: E, V to 5th Ave./53rd St.*

Museum of Modern Art Design and Book Store. The redesigned MoMA expanded its in-house shop with a huge selection of art posters and more than 2,000 titles on painting, sculpture, film, and photography. Across the street is the **MoMA Design Store** (⊠ 44 W. 53rd St., between 5th and 6th Aves., Midtown West ☎ 212/767–1050 Ⓜ Subway: E, V to 5th Ave./53rd St.), where you can find Frank Lloyd Wright furniture reproductions, vases designed by Alvar Aalto, and lots of clever trinkets. The SoHo branch combines most of the virtues of the first two, although its book selection is smaller. It also has the city's only cache of Muji, a line of addictively inexpensive and minimalist daily necessities like notebooks and aluminum card carriers. ⊠ *11 W. 53rd Sts., between 5th and 6th Aves., Midtown West* ☎*212/708–9700* Ⓜ*Subway: E, V to 5th Ave./53rd St.* ⊠ *81 Spring St., between Broadway and Crosby St., SoHo* ☎ *646/ 613–1367* Ⓜ *Subway: 6 to Spring St.*

Museum of the City of New York. Satisfy your curiosity about New York City's past, present, or future with the terrific selection of books, cards, toys, and photography posters. If you've something classic in mind, look for the Tin Pan Alley tunes and stickball sets. ⊠ *1220 5th Ave., at E. 103rd St., Upper East Side* ☎ *212/534–1672* Ⓜ *Subway: 6 to 103rd St.*

PAPER, GREETING CARDS & STATIONERY

Industries Stationery. The date books, calendars, and paper goods here are all clean-lined and bold. Journals might have wooden or bright yellow leather covers, and note cards are patterned in Marimekko-ish designs. ⊠ *91 Crosby St., between Prince and Spring Sts., SoHo* ☎ *212/ 334–4447* Ⓜ *Subway: N, R to Prince St.*

Fodor'sChoice ★ **Kate's Paperie.** Avid correspondents and gift givers adore Kate's, which rustles with fabulous wrapping papers, ribbons, blank books, writing implements of all kinds, and more. ⊠ *561 Broadway, between Prince and Spring Sts., SoHo* ☎ *212/941–9816* Ⓜ *Subway: R, W to Prince St.* ⊠ *8 W. 13th St., between 5th and 6th Aves., Greenwich Village* ☎ *212/ 633–0570* Ⓜ *Subway: F, V to 14th St.* ⊠ *1282 3rd Ave., between E. 73rd and E. 74th Sts., Upper East Side* ☎ *212/396–3670* Ⓜ *Subway: 6 to 77th St.* ⊠ *140 W. 57th St., between 6th and 7th Aves., Midtown West* ☎ *212/459–0700* Ⓜ *Subway: F to 57th St.*

Smythson of Bond Street. Keep notes on your purchases, deepest thoughts, or conquests in softbound leather diaries with appropriate gilded titles, such as Passions & Pleasures, and Juicy Gossip. They also carry an array of elegant formal stationery, address books, and buttery leather travel accessories. ⊠ *4 W. 57th St., between 5th and 6th Aves., Midtown West* ☎ *212/265–4573* Ⓜ *Subway: F to 57th St.*

Untitled. One wall displays art books, the other flutters with all kinds of greeting cards. There's also a long row of motley postcards alphabetized by topic, such as Degas pastels and fruit-crate labels. ✉ *159 Prince St., between Thompson St. and West Broadway, SoHo* ☎ *212/982–2088* Ⓜ *Subway: C, E to Spring St.*

PERFORMING ARTS MEMORABILIA

Drama Book Shop. The comprehensive stock here includes scripts, scores, and librettos. ✉ *250 W. 40th St., between 7th and 8th Aves., Midtown West* ☎ *212/944–0595* Ⓜ *Subway: A, C, E to 42nd St./Port Authority.*

Movie Star News. As you flip through images from blockbusters, cult faves, and memorable bombs, it's hard to doubt their claim that they have the world's largest variety of movie photos and posters. Behind the counter are signed photos of many of the stars seen on the posters. A poster of a New York film such as *Manhattan, The Royal Tenenbaums,* or *Taxi Driver* makes for a good souvenir for under $20. ✉ *134 W. 18th St., between 6th and 7th Aves., Chelsea* ☎ *212/620–8160* Ⓜ *Subway: 1, 2, 3 to 14th St.*

One Shubert Alley. Souvenir posters, tees, and other knickknacks memorializing past and present Broadway hits reign at this theater district shop. ✉ *1 Shubert Alley, between W. 44th and W. 45th Sts., Midtown West* ☎ *212/944–4133* Ⓜ *Subway: N, Q, R, S, W, 1, 2, 3 to 42nd St./Times Sq.*

Triton Gallery. Theatrical posters large and small are available, and the selection is democratic, with everything from Marlene Deitrich's *Blue Angel* to recent Broadway shows represented. ✉ *323 W. 45th St., between 8th and 9th Aves., Midtown West* ☎ *212/765–2472* Ⓜ *Subway: A, E to 42nd St./Port Authority.*

SHOES

For dressy, expensive footwear, Madison Avenue is always a good bet, but West 8th Street between 5th and 6th avenues is what most New Yorkers mean when they refer to Shoe Street; it's crammed with small storefronts that hawk funky styles, from steel-toe boots to outrageous platforms.

Men's & Women's Shoes

Bally. A few curveballs, like olive green or slate blue wing tips, liven up the mainly conservative selection. Carry-ons and clothing, such as deerskin or lamb jackets, join the shoe leather. ✉ *628 Madison Ave., at E. 59th St., Midtown East* ☎ *212/751–9082* Ⓜ *Subway: N, R, W, 4, 5, 6 to 59th St./Lexington Ave.*

Camper. These Euro-fave walking shoes, with their sturdy leather uppers and nubby rubber soles, have also proved popular on the cobblestone streets of SoHo. Comfort is a priority; all the slip-ons and lace-ups here have generously rounded toes and a springy feel. ✉ *125 Prince St., at Wooster St., SoHo* ☎ *212/358–1841* Ⓜ *Subway: R, W to Prince St.*

Cole-Haan. No longer wedded to staid moccasin styles, Cole-Haan has of late broken into stylish territory. Shoes for both sexes now come in exotic skins like python and crocodile; for warm weather, check out the orange suede thongs for men and metallic stiletto sandals for women. The handbag line is much more playful, too. ✉ *620 5th Ave., at Rockefeller Center, Midtown West* ☎ *212/765–9747* Ⓜ *Subway: E, V to 5th Ave./53rd St.* ✉ *667 Madison Ave., at E. 61st St., Upper East Side* ☎ *212/ 421–8440* Ⓜ *Subway: N, R, W, 4, 5, 6 to 59th St./Lexington Ave.* ✉ *10 Columbus Circle, at W. 59th St., Midtown West* ☎ *212/823–9420* Ⓜ *Subway: 1, A, B, C, D to Columbus Circle.*

J. M. Weston. Specially treated calfskin for the soles and handcrafted construction have made these a French favorite; they could also double the price of your outfit. High heels, a more recent addition to the selection, started gradually with stacked-heel pumps. ✉ *812 Madison Ave., at E. 68th St., Upper East Side* ☎ *212/535–2100* Ⓜ *Subway: 6 to 68th St./Hunter College.*

John Fluevog Shoes. The inventor of the Angelic sole (protects against water, acid . . . "and Satan"), Fluevog designs chunky, funky shoes and boots. ✉ *250 Mulberry St., at Prince St., NoLita* ☎ *212/431–4484* Ⓜ *Subway: R, W to Prince St.*

Fodor'sChoice ★ **Otto Tootsi Plohound.** Downtown New Yorkers swear by this large selection of supercool shoes. Many, including the store's own line, are Italian-made. Styles range from Tyrolean fur boots to vampy Dries Van Noten pumps to Paul Smith rain booties with swirly-print soles. ✉ *413 West Broadway, between Prince and Spring Sts., SoHo* ☎ *212/925–8931* Ⓜ *Subway: C, E to Spring St.* ✉ *273 Lafayette St., between Prince and E. Houston Sts., East Village* ☎ *212/431–7299* Ⓜ *Subway: R, W to Prince St.* ✉ *137 5th Ave., between E. 20th and E. 21st Sts., Flatiron District* ☎ *212/460–8650* Ⓜ *Subway: F, V to 23rd St.* ✉ *38 E. 57th St., between Park and Madison Aves., Midtown East* ☎ *212/231–3199* Ⓜ *Subway: N, R, W, 4, 5, 6 to 59th St./Lexington Ave.*

Salvatore Ferragamo. Elegance typifies these designs, from black-tie patent to weekender ankle boots. The company reworks some of their women's styles from previous decades, like the girlish Audrey (as in Hepburn) flat, available in the original black, or seasonal takes like bone or leopard. ✉ *655 5th Ave., at E. 52nd St.* ☎ *212/759–3822* Ⓜ *Subway: E, V to 53rd St.*

Fodor'sChoice ★ **Sigerson Morrison.** The details—just-right T-straps, small buckles, interesting two-tones—make the women's shoes irresistible. Prices rise above $300, so the sales are big events. ✉ *28 Prince St., between Mott and Elizabeth Sts., NoLita* ☎ *212/219–3893* Ⓜ *Subway: F, V to Broadway–Lafayette St.*

Stuart Weitzman. The broad range of styles, from wing tips to strappy sandals, is enhanced by an even wider range of sizes and widths. ✉ *625 Madison Ave., between E. 58th and E. 59th Sts., Midtown East* ☎ *212/ 750–2555* Ⓜ *Subway: N, R, W, 4, 5, 6 to 59th St./Lexington Ave.* ✉ *10 Columbus Circle, at W. 59th St., Midtown West* ☎ *212/823–9560* Ⓜ *Subway: 1, A, B, C, D to Columbus Circle.*

Men's Shoes

Billy Martin's. Quality hand-tooled and custom-made boots for the Urban Cowboy are carried here. To complete the look, you can add a suede shirt or a turquoise-and-silver belt. ✉ *220 E. 60th St., between 2nd and*

3rd Aves., Upper East Side ☎ *212/861–3100* Ⓜ *Subway: N, R, 4, 5, 6 to 59th St.*

Church's English Shoes. The high quality of these shoes is indisputable; you could choose something highly polished for an embassy dinner, a loafer or a crepe-sole suede ankle boot for a weekend, or even a black-and-white spectator style worthy of Fred Astaire. ⊠ *689 Madison Ave., at E. 62nd St., Upper East Side* ☎ *212/758–5200* Ⓜ *Subway: N, R, 4, 5, 6 to 59th St.*

John Lobb. These British shoes often use waxed leather, the better to contend with London levels of dampness. Ankle boots with padded collars or zips join the traditional oxfords and derbys; some shoes have elegantly tapered toes. ⊠ *680 Madison Ave., between E. 61st and E. 62nd Sts., Upper East Side* ☎ *212/888–9797* Ⓜ *Subway: N, R, 4, 5, 6 to 59th St.*

Santoni. Those who equate Italian with slightly flashy haven't seen these discreet, meticulously finished, handmade shoes. ⊠ *864 Madison Ave., between E. 70th and E. 71st Sts., Upper East Side* ☎ *212/794–3820* Ⓜ *Subway: 6 to 68th St./Hunter College.*

Women's Shoes

Christian Louboutin. Bright-red soles are the signature of Louboutin's delicately sexy couture slippers and stilettos, and his latest, larger downtown store has carpeting to match. The pointy-toe creations come trimmed with brocade, tassels, buttons, or satin ribbons. ⊠ *941 Madison Ave., between E. 74th and E. 75th Sts., Upper East Side* ☎ *212/396–1884* Ⓜ *Subway: 6 to 77th St.* ⊠ *59 Horatio St., between Hudson and Greenwich Sts., Meatpacking District* ☎ *212/255–1910* Ⓜ *Subway: A, C, E to 14th St.*

Hollywould. Colorful ballet flats with long grosgrain ties close ranks along the floorboards, and cinematic high heels patrol the shelves above. Padded soles make even the most soaring pumps surprisingly wearable. ⊠ *198 Elizabeth St., between Prince and Spring Sts., NoLita* ☎ *212/219–1905* Ⓜ *Subway: 6 to Spring St.*

Jimmy Choo. Pointy toes, low vamps, narrow heels, ankle-wrapping straps—these British-made shoes are undeniably vampy, and sometimes more comfortable than they look. ⊠ *716 Madison Ave., between E. 63rd and E. 64th Sts., Upper East Side* ☎ *212/759–7078* Ⓜ *Subway: 6 to 68th St./Hunter College* ⊠ *645 5th Ave., at E. 51st St., Midtown East* ☎ *212/593–0800* Ⓜ *Subway: B, D, F, V to 47th–50th Sts./Rockefeller Center.*

Manolo Blahnik. These are, notoriously, some of the most expensive shoes money can buy. They're also devastatingly sexy, with pointed toes, low-cut vamps, and spindly heels. Mercifully, the summer stock includes flat (but still exquisite) sandals; look for gladiator styles with ankle laces, or thongs embellished with sparkly beads. Pray for a sale. ⊠ *31 W. 54th St., between 5th and 6th Aves., Midtown West* ☎ *212/582–3007* Ⓜ *Subway: E, V to 5th Ave./53rd St.*

Robert Clergerie. Not without its sense of fun, this place is often best in summer, when the sandal selection includes curvaceous soles and beaded starfish shapes. ⊠ *681 Madison Ave., between E. 61st and E. 62nd Sts., Upper East Side* ☎ *212/207–8600* Ⓜ *Subway: N, R, W, 4, 5, 6 to 59th St./Lexington Ave.*

17

Tod's. Diego Della Valle's coveted driving moccasins, casual loafers, and boots in colorful leather, suede, and ponyskin are right at home on Madison Avenue. An increasing selection of high heels is bent on driving sales, rather than cars. ⊠ *650 Madison Ave., near E. 60th St., Upper East Side* ☎ *212/644–5945* Ⓜ *Subway: N, R, W to 5th Ave./59th St.*

Unisa. Try on a gentle riff on a current trend, from bow-top slides to driving mocs; most pairs are under $150, sometimes well under. ⊠ *701 Madison Ave., between E. 62nd and E. 63rd Sts., Upper East Side* ☎ *212/753–7474* Ⓜ *Subway: N, R, W to 5th Ave./59th St.*

SOUVENIRS OF NEW YORK CITY

Major tourist attractions keep their gift shops well stocked, and dozens of souvenir shops dot the Times Square area. If you're looking for grungier souvenirs of downtown (T-shirts with salty messages, tattoos), troll St. Marks Place between 2nd and 3rd avenues in the East Village.

City Store. Discover all kinds of books and pamphlets that explain New York City's government, from pocket maps, NYPD T-shirts, and cocktail napkins printed with subway routes to manhole-cover coasters and a New York City–scented candle (don't worry, it smells like apple pie, not exhaust). The store is closed weekends. ⊠ *1 Centre St., at Chambers St., Lower Manhattan* ☎ *212/669–8246* Ⓜ *Subway: 4, 5, 6 to City Hall/Brooklyn Bridge.*

New York City Transit Museum Gift Shop. In the symbolic heart of New York City's transit system, all the store's merchandise is somehow linked to the MTA, from straphanger ties to skateboards decorated with subway-line logos. ⊠ *Grand Central Terminal, Vanderbilt Pl. and E. 42nd St., Midtown East* ☎ *212/878–0106* Ⓜ *Subway: 4, 5, 6, 7 to 42nd St./Grand Central Terminal.*

SPORTING GOODS

The NBA Store. Push through the bronze-armed door and you'll find yourself in a basketball temple. Every imaginable item having to do with pro b-ball is here, from jerseys, hats, and bags emblazoned with team logos to balls signed by Yao Ming and Larry Bird. Players grin in the digital-photo station, but they also make live appearances on the store's half-court. ⊠ *666 5th Ave., at W. 52nd St., Midtown West* ☎ *212/515–6221* Ⓜ *Subway: E, V to 5th Ave./53rd St.*

NikeTown. A fusion of fashion and sports arena, Nike's "motivational retail environment" is its largest sports-gear emporium. Inspirational quotes in the floor, computer-driven foot sizers, and a heart-pumping movie shown on an enormous screen in the entry atrium make it hard to leave without something in the latest wick-away fabric or footwear design. ⊠ *6 E. 57th St., between 5th and Madison Aves., Midtown East* ☎ *212/891–6453* Ⓜ *Subway: E, V to 5th Ave./53rd St.*

Paragon Sporting Goods. Tennis rackets, snowshoes, kayaks, swim goggles, scuba gear, croquet mallets: Paragon stocks virtually everything any athlete needs, no matter what the sport. It keeps up with the trends (heart-rate monitors) and doesn't neglect the old-fashioned (Woolrich shirts). ⊠ *867 Broadway, at E. 18th St., Flatiron District* ☎ *212/255–8036* Ⓜ *Subway: L, N, Q, R, W, 4, 5, 6 to 14th St./Union Sq.*

TOYS & GAMES

Most of these stores are geared to children, but a few shops that cater to grown-up toy-lovers are mixed in. During February's Toy Week, when out-of-town buyers come to place orders for the next Christmas season, the windows of the Toy Center at 23rd Street and 5th Avenue display the latest thing. In addition to the stores listed below, *see* Pylones *in* Home Decor.

American Girl Place. No toy pink convertibles here; instead, the namesake dolls are historically themed, from Felicity of colonial Virginia to Kit of Depression-era Cincinnati. Each character has her own affiliated books, furniture, clothes, and accessories. There's a doll hairdressing station, a café, and even a theater showing a musical based on the dolls' stories. ⊠ *609 5th Ave., at E. 49th St., Midtown East* ☎ *212/371–2220* Ⓜ *Subway: B, D, F, V to 47th–50th Sts./Rockefeller Center.*

Compleat Strategist. This store puts on a great spread—from board games and classic soldier sets to fantasy games. ⊠ *11 E. 33rd St., between 5th and Madison Aves., Murray Hill* ☎ *212/685–3880* Ⓜ *Subway: 6 to 33rd St.*

Dinosaur Hill. These toys leave the run-of-the-mill far behind, with mini bongo drums, craft kits, jack-in-the-boxes, and a throng of marionettes and hand puppets, from mermaids to farmers to demons. ⊠ *306 E. 9th St., between 1st and 2nd Aves., East Village* ☎ *212/473–5850* Ⓜ *Subway: R, W to 8th St.; 6 to Astor Pl.*

FodorśChoice
★ **F.A.O. Schwarz.** Back in business and better than ever, this children's paradise more than lives up to the hype. The ground floor is a zoo of extraordinary stuffed animals, from cuddly $20 teddies to towering, life-size elephants and giraffes (with larger-than-life prices to match). F.A.O. Schweets stocks M&Ms in every color of the rainbow; upstairs, you can dance on the giant musical floor keyboard, browse through Barbies wearing Armani and Juicy Couture, and design your own customized Hot Wheels car. ⊠ *767 5th Ave., at E. 58th St., Midtown East* ☎ *212/644–9400* Ⓜ *Subway: 4, 5, 6 to E. 59th St.*

Geppetto's Toy Box. Many toys here are handmade, from extravagantly costumed dolls and furry animal hand puppets to tried-and-true favorites such as Lego, building blocks, and rubber duckies. ⊠ *10 Christopher St., at Greenwich Ave., Greenwich Village* ☎ *212/620–7511* Ⓜ *Subway: 1 to Christopher St./Sheridan Sq.*

Kid Robot. Even if you've never heard of Urban Vinyl Toys, which, in quainter times, were simply referred to as "action figures," you can get a kick out of this shop, where adult and kid collectors flock to stock up on the latest toys from Asian designers. ⊠ *126 Prince St., between Greene and Wooster Sts., SoHo* ☎ *212/966–6688* Ⓜ *Subway: N, R to Prince St.*

Kidding Around. This unpretentious shop is piled high with old-fashioned wooden toys, Playmobil and Brio sets, and a fun selection of hand puppets. The costume racks are rich with dress-up potential. ✉ *60 W. 15th St., between 5th and 6th Aves., Flatiron District* ☎ *212/645–6337* Ⓜ *Subway: L, N, Q, R, W, 4, 5, 6 to 14th St./Union Sq.*

Toys "R" Us. The Times Square branch of this megastore is so big that a three-story Ferris wheel revolves inside. With all the movie tie-in merchandise, video games, pogo sticks, stuffed animals, and what seems to be the entire Mattel oeuvre, these stores have a lock on sheer volume. ✉ *1514 Broadway, at W. 44th St., Midtown West* ☎ *800/869–7787* Ⓜ *Subway: 1, N, Q, R, W to 42nd St./Times Sq.*

World of Disney New York. Expect to be flooded with merchandise relating to Disney films and characters—pajamas, toys, figurines, you name it. There's also the largest collection of Disney animation art in the country. ✉ *711 5th Ave., between E. 55th and E. 56th Sts., Midtown East* ☎ *212/702–0702* Ⓜ *Subway: F to 57th St.*

WINE

Acker Merrall & Condit. Known for its selection of red burgundies, this store has knowledgeable, helpful personnel. ✉ *160 W. 72nd St., between Amsterdam and Columbus Aves., Upper West Side* ☎ *212/787–1700* Ⓜ *Subway: 1, 2, 3 to 72nd St.*

Astor Wines & Spirits. This is a key spot for everything from well-priced champagne to Poire Williams to Riesling, in a beautiful new location featuring temperature-controlled storage and a wine library. ✉ *399 Lafayette St., at E. 4th St., East Village* ☎ *212/674–7500* Ⓜ *Subway: 6 to Astor Pl.*

Best Cellars. In a novel move, the stock here is organized by the wine's characteristics (sweet, fruity) rather than by region. Even better, the prices are amazingly low—between $10 and $14 a bottle. ✉ *1291 Lexington Ave., between E. 86th and E. 87th Sts., Upper East Side* ☎ *212/426–4200* Ⓜ *Subway: 4, 5, 6 to 86th St.*

Morrell & Company. Peter Morrell is a well-regarded and very colorful figure in the wine business, and his store reflects his expertise. Free wine tastings are held several times a month (for serious oenophiles, ask about the rare vintage auctions). Next door is his café, where dozens of fine wines are available by the glass. ✉ *1 Rockefeller Plaza, at W. 49th St., Midtown West* ☎ *212/981–1106* Ⓜ *Subway: B, D, F, V to 47th–50th Sts./Rockefeller Center.*

Union Square Wine & Spirits. The store stocks a great selection and has a regular schedule of wine seminars and special tasting events. ✉ *33 Union Sq. W, at W. 16th St., Flatiron District* ☎ *212/675–8100* Ⓜ *Subway: L, N, Q, R, W, 4, 5, 6 to 14th St./Union Sq.*

★ **Vintage New York.** The vintages here, from cabernet sauvignon all the way to gewürztraminer, hail exclusively from New York State. Try your top choices at the tasting bar in the back; every wine sold is available by the glass. Unusually, the business is open seven days a week. ✉ *482 Broome St., at Wooster St., SoHo* ☎ *212/226–9463* Ⓜ *Subway: J, M, N, Q, R, W, Z, 6 to Canal St.* ✉ *2492 Broadway, between W. 92nd and W. 93rd Sts., Upper West Side* ☎ *212/721–9999* Ⓜ *Subway: 1, 2, 3 to 96th St.*

Where to Eat

WORD OF MOUTH

"The tasting menu [at Gramercy Tavern] was superb. Each dish was exquisitely presented and was absolutely delicious. We were treated like royalty. The wine menu is excellent, as well. We can't wait to go back." —Leila

"[Joe's Shanghai] is one of my favorite Chinese restaurants. Their steamed crab dumplings are the best! If you go, go during non-rush hour to avoid having to share a table with strangers!" —Wendy

www.fodors.com/forums

Updated by
Adam Kowit
and Tom Steele

Besides satisfying a taste for the finer things in life, restaurants serve Gothamites and visitors in other crucial ways. They're a vital catalyst for exploring the city (the hunt on Museum Mile for a bite before museum-hopping), a communication device ("Let me tell you about this great little Mexican place way uptown"), and a standby of cocktail-party one-upmanship ("What? You haven't been to Per Se yet?!"). Perhaps most important, restaurants serve as extensions of New Yorkers' usually minute kitchens and nonexistent dining rooms.

Restaurants have consistently demonstrated a savvy sensitivity to the financial times, and a wide array of midprice restaurants somehow manages to serve high-end food. Quite a few have devised bargain prix-fixe three-course dinners. All in all, though, prices have remained steady.

Still, New York is about extremes, and the metropolis remains a mecca of the moneyed. So the upswing in thrift-minded diners hasn't stopped new celebrity-chef-driven (and wildly expensive) restaurants such as Thomas Keller's Per Se from opening. Nor has the statewide smoking ban in all indoor public spaces caused more than a mild ripple in restaurant patronage. If anything, more people are dining out as a result of the ban.

So whether you decide to go for a delectable downtown banh mi Vietnamese hero with its surprising counterpoint of flavors and textures, or a prime porterhouse for two with creamed spinach and pommes Lyonnaise at a fancy uptown steak house, note that some of the dishes recommended in the following reviews may not be on the menu you receive when you sit down to eat. Many menus around town are market-driven and seasonal. Use our recommendations as guidelines and you won't be disappointed.

LOWER MANHATTAN

Although the Financial District's post–September 11th physical recovery was remarkably speedy, psychologically the turnaround took a while—New Yorkers were understandably slow to return to the neighborhood to make merry. Now back up to speed, the restaurants in this most historic of the city's enclaves are largely busy lunch spots, expense-account dining rooms, and after-work watering holes, with the streets quiet by 9.

American

$$–$$$ ✕ **Delmonico's.** As the oldest continually operating restaurant in New York City, opened in 1837, Delmonico's is steeped in cultural, political, and culinary history. Lobster Newburg and baked Alaska were invented here—and are still served. Inside the stately mahogany-panel dining room, tuck into the classic Delmonico's steak, a 20-ounce boneless rib eye smothered with frizzled onions, dry-aged and spoon tender, and don't forget to order creamed spinach on the side. ⊠ *56 Beaver St., at William St., Lower Manhattan* 🕾 *212/509–1144* ⌔ *Reservations essential* ▱ *AE, D, DC, MC, V* ☉ *Closed weekends* Ⓜ *Subway: 2, 3 to Wall St.; R, W to Whitehall St./South Ferry; 4, 5 to Bowling Green.*

Cafés

¢–$ ✕ **Financier.** On Manhattan's oldest paved street, a cobblestone alley that dates from the 1600s, sits this small patisserie with great homemade food, especially soup. Celery root with walnut pesto is always offered along with a daily special, and there are paninis, salads, and quiche, too. Afterward, settle in with a financier (an almond tea cake), a madeleine, or one of the more elegant French pastries and a cup of Illy coffee. If the weather's nice, you can sit outside. ⊠ *62 Stone St., at Pell St., Lower Manhattan* 🕾 *212/344–5600* ⌔ *Reservations not accepted* ▱ *AE, DC, MC, V* ☉ *Closed Sun. No dinner Sat.* Ⓜ *Subway: 2, 3, 4, 5 to Wall St.*

Contemporary

$$$$ ✕ **Bayard's.** Chef Eberhard Müller's austere, classic cooking fits well in this historic, nautical-theme setting. Some of the produce comes direct from his Long Island farm, and is incorporated into seasonal dishes such as roasted monkfish in a savory bacon broth and vegetable risotto with fennel fondue. The restaurant, housed in a stately 1851 Italianate mansion, remains a private club at lunch. At dinner the energy of the subtly lit room exudes a quiet dignity. If you can't get a reservation for a fine meal anywhere on a Saturday night, you can probably get in here. ⊠ *1 Hanover Sq., between Pearl and Stone Sts., Lower Manhattan* 🕾 *212/514–9454* ⌔ *Reservations essential* ▱ *AE, D, DC, MC, V* ☉ *Closed Sun. No lunch* Ⓜ *Subway: 2, 3 to Wall St.*

Pan-Asian

$$–$$$ ✕ **Roy's New York.** Roy's New York guarantees you're getting primo Pacific Ocean fish. The restaurant, part of Hawaii-born pioneering chef Roy Yamaguchi's growing empire of Pacific Rim eateries, ships in Sandwich Island delicacies such as *opakapaka* (snapper) and mahimahi a few times a week. For starters, the blackened tuna in spicy soy-mustard but-

18

PLANNER

How to Use This Chapter

This chapter divides the restaurants in Manhattan by neighborhood. Within each neighborhood the restaurants are grouped first by type of cuisine and then by price range. For restaurants in the Outer Boroughs, *see* the Brooklyn and Queens, the Bronx, and Staten Island chapters.

Reservations

At the hottest restaurants reservations need to be made weeks or months in advance. Tables are especially hard to come by if you want to dine between 7 and 9, or on Friday or Saturday night. If you change your mind or your plans, cancel your reservation—it's only courteous, plus some of the busiest places have started to charge up to $25 a head for a no-show (they take a credit card number when you reserve). Many restaurants will ask you to call the day before or the morning of your scheduled meal to reconfirm: remember to do so or you could lose out.

What to Wear

While casual attire is acceptable most of the time, your concept of the term may change while in New York. Think "casual chic." Only a very few of the most formal places still require ties, and only a few dozen require jackets. As a rule, dress at restaurants in Midtown and around Wall Street is more conservative than in other, more residential neighborhoods, especially at lunch. Shorts are appropriate only in the most casual spots. Don't be embarrassed to call and ask.

Tipping & Taxes

In most restaurants, tip the waiter at least 15%–20%. (To figure the amount quickly, just double the tax noted on the check—it's 8.625% of your bill—and, if you like, add a little more.) Bills for parties of six or more sometimes include the tip already. Tip at least $1 per drink at the bar, and $1 for each coat checked. Never tip the maître d' unless you're out to impress your guests or expect to pay another visit soon.

Hours

New Yorkers seem ready to eat at any hour. Many restaurants stay open between lunch and dinner, some offer late-night seating, and still others serve around-the-clock. Restaurants that serve breakfast often do so until noon. Restaurants in the East Village, the Lower East Side, SoHo, TriBeCa, and Greenwich Village are likely to remain open late, while Midtown spots and those in the theater and financial districts generally close earlier. Unless otherwise noted, the restaurants listed in this guide are open daily for lunch and dinner.

Children

Though it is unusual to see children in the dining rooms of Manhattan's most elite restaurants, dining with your young-sters in New York does not have to mean culinary exile. Many of the restaurants reviewed in this chapter are excel-lent choices for families, and are marked with a ☺ symbol.

Wine

Although some of the city's top restaurants still include his-toric French vintages, most sommeliers are now focusing on small-production, lesser-known wineries. Some are even keeping their wine lists purposefully small, so that they can change them frequently to match the season and the menu. Half bottles are becoming more prevalent, and good wines by the glass are everywhere. Don't hesitate to ask for recommendations. Many restaurants with no som-melier on staff designate special people to lend a hand.

Smoking

Smoking is prohibited in all enclosed public spaces in New York City, in-cluding restaurants and bars.

What It Costs

18

Entrée prices in general have fallen by a few dollars, and the $60-plus prix-fixe menu has given way to the standard à la carte. Of course, the top-tier restaurants remain impervious to market changes. Beware of the $10 bottle of water poured eagerly for unsuspecting diners.

If you are watching your budget, be sure to ask the price of daily specials recited by the waiter or captain. The charge for specials at some restaurants is noticeably out of line with the other prices on the menu. And of course, always review your bill.

If you eat early or late you may be able to take advantage of a prix-fixe deal not offered at peak hours and get more attentive service in the bargain. Most upscale restaurants offer fantas-tic lunch deals with special menus at cut-rate prices designed to give a true taste of the place.

Credit cards are widely accepted, but many restaurants (particularly smaller ones down-town) accept only cash. If you plan to use a credit card it is a good idea to double-check its acceptability when making reservations or before sitting down to eat.

	$$$$	$$$	$$	$	¢
At Dinner	over $35	$28–$35	$19–$27	$10–$18	under $10

Prices are per person for a main course at dinner. Some restaurants are marked with a price range ($$–$$$, for example). This indicates one of two things: either the average cost straddles two categories, or if you order strate-gically, you can get out for less than most diners spend.

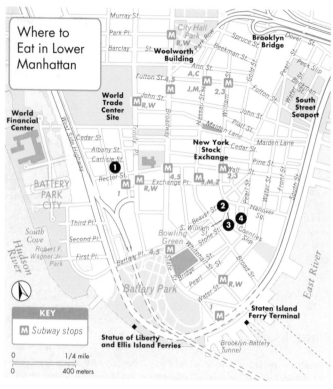

ter works well with entrées such as misoyaki butterfish. Roy's stands in high culinary contrast to its largely meat-and-potatoes Wall Street neighbors. ⊠ *Marriott Financial Center Hotel, 130 Washington St., between Albany and Carlisle Sts., Lower Manhattan* ☎ *212/266–6262* ⊟ *AE, D, DC, MC, V* ☉ *No lunch Sat.* Ⓜ *Subway: 1 to Rector St.*

LITTLE ITALY & CHINATOWN

As Chinatown encroaches from the south, Little Italy keeps getting littler, but from a culinary standpoint nobody's grieving the loss of tourist-trap Italian restaurants. Great Italian food, made with fresh seasonal ingredients, now crops up all over Manhattan. Chinatown is known for cheap, authentic food, but don't let the similar bare-bones look of the many restaurants fool you: a tremendous variety of food can be found here, ranging from modest storefront noodle shops to Hong Kong–style dim sum palaces, and a multitude of regional cuisines, from spicy Szechuan to rich and hearty Shanghainese. Below are some of the best. For dessert, duck into one of the many Chinese bakeries to sample their sweet-salty pastries and delicate, creamy cakes, or try one of the original flavors of ice cream (like litchi or pumpkin pie) at the Chinatown Ice Cream Factory (65 Bayard St., between Elizabeth and Mott Sts.).

Cafés

⟡ ¢ ✕ **Saint's Alp Teahouse.** Join the hip Asian youth crowding the small tables at Saint's Alp Teahouse, part of a Hong Kong–based international chain. They're here for bubble tea—frothy, pastel-color, flavored black or green tea speckled with beads of tapioca or sago (they look like tadpoles). Passion-fruit green tea with chewy tapioca is refreshing. You can also order snacks such as spring rolls, dumplings, or sweets. ⊠ *51 Mott St., between Canal and Pell Sts., Chinatown* ☎ *212/393–9009* ⟿ *Reservations not accepted* ▭ *No credit cards* Ⓜ *Subway: 6, J, M, N, Q, R, W, Z to Canal St.*

Chinese

⟡ ¢–$$$ ✕ **Ping's Seafood.** Although the original location in Queens still has the most elaborate menu with the most extensive selection of live seafood, the Manhattan location is more accessible both geographically and gastronomically. Helpful menus have pictures of most of the specialties. Among them are Dungeness crab in black bean sauce, crisp fried tofu, silken braised *e-fu* noodles, and crisp Peking duck. Pricier than some other Chinatown haunts, Ping's is also a notch above in setting and service. ⊠ *22 Mott St., between Bayard and Pell Sts., Chinatown* ☎ *212/602–9988* ⟿ *Reservations essential* ▭ *AE, MC, V* Ⓜ *Subway: 6, J, M, N, Q, R, W, Z to Canal St.*

¢–$$ ✕ **Jazzi Wok.** One of the new generation of Chinese restaurants, Jazzi Wok looks more like a high-tech Shiseido cosmetics shop than the Hong Kong–style eatery that it is. At night, the place bustles with young, hip neighborhood locals eating Cantonese comfort food like *congee* (rice porridge) topped with assorted meats and vegetables and Sterno-heated miniwoks filled with sizzling stewlike dishes. Jazzi Wok, a marriage of NoLita cool and Chinatown taste, is an intriguing pit stop while touring the neighborhood. ⊠ *176 Mott St., at Broome St., Little Italy* ☎ *212/965–8386* ▭ *AE, MC, V* Ⓜ *Subway: 6 to Spring St.*

⟡ ¢–$$ ✕ **Joe's Shanghai.** Joe opened his first Shanghai restaurant in Queens, but buoyed by the accolades accorded his steamed soup dumplings—magically filled with a rich, fragrant broth and a pork or pork-and-crab-meat mixture—he saw fit to open in Manhattan's Chinatown, and then Midtown. There's always a wait, but the line moves fast. Try the crisp turnip shortcakes to start, ropey homemade Shanghai noodles and traditional lion's head—rich pork meatballs braised in brown sauce—to follow. Other, more familiar Chinese dishes are also excellent. ⊠ *9 Pell St., between the Bowery and Mott St., Chinatown* ☎ *212/233–8888* ▭ *No credit cards* Ⓜ *Subway: 6, J, M, N, Q, R, W, Z to Canal St.*

⟡ ¢–$ ✕ **Great New York Noodletown.** Although the soups and noodles are unbeatable at this no-frills restaurant, what you should order are the window decorations—the hanging lacquered ducks, roasted pork, and crunchy pig. All three are superb, especially if you ask for the pungent garlic-and-ginger sauce on the side. Seasonal specialties such as duck with flowering chives and salt-baked soft-shell crabs are excellent. So is the congee, available with any number of garnishes. Solo diners may end up at a communal table. ⊠ *28 Bowery, at Bayard St., Chinatown* ☎ *212/349–0923* ▭ *No credit cards* Ⓜ *Subway: 6, J, M, Z to Canal St.; B, D to Grand St.*

18

Where to Eat in Little Italy, Chinatown, TriBeCa, SoHo & NoLita

KEY

M *Subway stops*

☼ ¢–$ ✕ **Jing Fong.** Come to this authentic dim sum palace for a taste of Hong Kong. On weekend mornings people pour onto the escalator to Jing Fong's third-floor dining room. Chinese women push carts to offer *hargow* (steamed shrimp dumplings), *shu mai* (steamed pork dumplings), *chow fun* (wide rice noodles with dried shrimp or beef), and much more. For the adventurous: chicken feet, tripe, and snails. Arrive early for the largest and freshest selection. ⊠ *20 Elizabeth St., between Bayard and Canal Sts., Chinatown* ☎ *212/964–5256* ⊟ *AE, MC, V* Ⓜ *Subway: 6, J, M, N, Q, R, W, Z to Canal St.*

★ ¢–$ ✕ **Sweet 'n' Tart Restaurant & Café.** You'll be handed four different menus at this multilevel restaurant. One lists dim sum prepared to order; another offers special dishes organized according to principles of Chinese medicine; a third lists more familiar-sounding dishes, such as hot-and-sour soup; and the final one lists beverages, curative "teas" (more like soups or fruit shakes, really). The original café, with a more limited menu, is up the street at 76 Mott Street, and some think it has better food. ⊠ *20 Mott St., between Chatham Sq. and Pell St., Chinatown* ☎ *212/964–0380* ⊟ *AE* Ⓜ *Subway: 6, J, M, N, R, Q, W, Z to Canal St.*

☼ ¢–$ ✕ **XO Kitchen.** Chinese students throng this eclectic, Hong Kong–style eatery. The walls resemble bulletin boards—they're tacked haphazardly with dozens of sheets announcing a mind-boggling variety of foods, from dim sum to Thai (there is also a menu). Even with the variety, the food is some of Chinatown's best. Try the delicate shrimp wonton soup, or the refreshingly light Hong Kong–style lo mein, where you pour a rich broth over thin wheat noodles topped with meat. ⊠ *148 Hester St., between Elizabeth St. and Bowery, Chinatown* ☎ *212/965–8645* ⊟ *AE, MC, V* Ⓜ *Subway: B, D to Grand St.; 6, J, M, Z to Canal St.*

Italian

☼ ¢–$ ✕ **Bread.** At this stylish little *paninoteca*, owner Luigi Comandatore, a Mercer Kitchen alum, takes advantage of his location, buying top-notch ingredients from neighborhood purveyors such as Di Palo's Fine Foods and Balthazar Bakery to make perfect panini. Italian expats, windows open to the street in summer, and lots of red vino give Bread star-lingering quality. ⊠ *20 Spring St., between Elizabeth and Mott Sts., Little Italy* ☎ *212/334–1015* ⊟ *AE, D, MC, V* Ⓜ *Subway: 6 to Spring St.*

Malaysian

¢–$ ✕ **Sanur.** Malaysian restaurants are popping up like bamboo shoots in Chinatown, and this dingy subterranean spot is one of the best. Locals crowd the dining room from morning (it opens at 8 AM) to night for the fragrantly spiced food. Indonesian-style chicken, crunchy in a sweet soy sauce; long-simmered beef *rendang*; and whole crabs in a big bowl of spicy curry sauce and vermicelli get hearty nods of approval from anyone who's been to Jakarta or Kuala Lumpur. ⊠ *18 Doyers St., at Pell St., Chinatown* ☎ *212/267–0088* ⊟ *No credit cards* ◔ *Closed Mon.* Ⓜ *Subway: 6, J, M, N, Q, R, W, Z to Canal St.*

Pizza

★ ☼ $–$$ ✕ **Lombardi's.** Brick walls, red-and-white check tablecloths, and the aroma of thin-crust pies emerging from the coal oven set the mood for some of the best pizza in Manhattan. Lombardi's has served pizza since

1905 (though not in the same location), and business has not died down a bit. The mozzarella is always fresh, resulting in an almost greaseless slice, and the toppings, such as homemade meatballs, pancetta, or imported anchovies, are also top quality. ⊠ *32 Spring St., between Mott and Mulberry Sts., Little Italy* ☎*212/941–7994* ⊟*No credit cards* Ⓜ*Subway: 6 to Spring St.; B, D, F, V to Broadway–Lafayette St.*

Vietnamese

¢–$ ✕**Nha Trang.** You can get a good meal at this inexpensive Vietnamese restaurant if you know how to order. Start with a steaming bowl of spicy sweet-and-sour seafood soup (the small feeds three to four) and shrimp grilled on sugarcane. Follow that up with paper-thin pork chops grilled until crisp and crunchy deep-fried squid on shredded lettuce with a tangy dipping sauce. If the line is long, which it usually is, even with a second location around the corner, you may be asked to sit at a table with strangers. ⊠ *87 Baxter St., between Bayard and Canal Sts., Chinatown* ☎ *212/233–5948* ⊟ *No credit cards* Ⓜ *Subway: 6, J, M, N, Q, R, W, Z to Canal St.* ⊠ *148 Centre St., at Walker and White Sts., Chinatown* ☎ *212/941– 9292* ⊟ *No credit cards* Ⓜ *Subway: 6, J, M, N, Q, R, W, Z to Canal St.*

TRIBECA

This once industrial neighborhood attracts affluent residents seeking large lofts. The ground floors of these glamorized former warehouses and factories provide dramatic settings for some of the best restaurants in the city. Residents like Robert De Niro and Harvey Keitel can pop down to their favorite haunts. TriBeCa retains a ghostly, deserted feel at night—part of its charm—but the quiet will be shattered when you walk into one of the many fashionable dining rooms.

American

★ $$–$$$ ✕ **The Harrison.** Partners Danny Abrams and Jimmy Bradley's formula for the perfect neighborhood eatery, which they mastered at the Red Cat in Chelsea, works like a charm in TriBeCa. The warm, woody room serves as a relaxed backdrop for chef Brian Bistrong's seasonal American food, like biscuits and gravy with clams and chorizo, and meaty Long Island duck breast with roast figs. Desserts, like a not-too-sweet chocolate cake with *café con leche* ice cream, are at once simple and sophisticated. ⊠ *355 Greenwich St., at Harrison St., TriBeCa* ☎ *212/274–9310* ✍ *Reservations essential* ⊟ *AE, D, DC, MC, V* ◷ *No lunch* Ⓜ *Subway: 1 to Franklin St.*

American–Casual

☺ ¢–$$ ✕ **Bubby's.** Crowds clamoring for coffee and freshly squeezed juice line up for brunch at this TriBeCa mainstay. The dining room is homey and comfortable with big windows; in summer, neighbors sit at tables outside with their dogs. For brunch you can order almost anything, including homemade granola, sour cream pancakes with bananas and berries, and huevos rancheros with guacamole and grits. Eclectic comfort food—macaroni and cheese, Southern fried chicken, barbecue, and Mexican dishes—make up the lunch and dinner menus. ⊠ *120 Hudson St., at N. Moore St., TriBeCa* ☎ *212/219–0666* ⊟ *D, DC, MC, V* Ⓜ *Subway: 1 to Franklin St.*

18

$ ✕ **Kitchenette.** This small, comfy restaurant lives up to its name with tables so close together you're likely to make new friends (especially if you share your wine—it's BYOB). The dining room feels like a neighbor's breakfast nook, and the food tastes like your mom made it—provided she's a great cook. There are no frills, just solid cooking, friendly service, and a long line at peak times. For brunch don't miss the blackberry-cherry pancakes or the pear streusel French toast. ✉ *80 West Broadway, at Warren St., TriBeCa* ☎ *212/267–6740* 🖃 *AE, D, MC, V* Ⓜ *Subway: 1, 2, 3, A, C to Chambers St.*

Belgian

$–$$ ✕ **Petite Abeille.** This consistently good but modest chain of Belgian bistros tempts with salads, frites, sandwiches, omelets, and other light fare early in the day. Come evening, sausages, *stoemp* (mashed potatoes and vegetables), steak, and stew satisfy. Waffles are always available: both *de Bruxelles* (made fresh and topped with ice cream, whipped cream, and fresh fruit) and the true Belgian waffle, *de Liège* (imported and reheated until the subtle caramelized sugar coating crunches and melts in your mouth). ✉ *134 West Broadway, between Duane and Thomas Sts., TriBeCa* ☎ *212/791–1360* 🖃 *AE, MC, V* Ⓜ *Subway: 1, 2, 3, A, C to Chambers St.*

Contemporary

$$–$$$ ✕ **Tribeca Grill.** Anchored by the bar, this cavernous brick-wall restaurant displays art by the late Robert De Niro Sr., whose movie-actor son is one of restaurateur Drew Nieporent's partners. Chef Stephen Lewandowski oversees the kitchen, but his contemporary American food doesn't seem quite as important to the nightly crowd as does the prospect of sighting somebody famous—a regular occurrence. Still, you can eat well with braised short ribs or the herb-roasted, free-range chicken. ✉ *375 Greenwich St., at Franklin St., TriBeCa* ☎ *212/941–3900* ♨ *Reservations essential* 🖃 *AE, D, DC, MC, V* ☽ *No lunch Sat.* Ⓜ *Subway: 1 to Franklin St.*

French

$$$$ ✕ **Chanterelle.** Soft peach walls, luxuriously spaced tables, and towering floral arrangements set the stage for what is the most understated of New York's top French restaurants. Chef David Waltuck's simple, elegant creations include delicious signature grilled seafood sausage that will always be available, but the bulk of the prix-fixe menu is dictated by the season. Roger Dagorn, the restaurant's exceptional sommelier, can help find value in the discriminating, well-chosen wine list. ✉ *2 Harrison St., at Hudson St., TriBeCa* ☎ *212/966–6960* ♨ *Reservations essential* 🖃 *AE, D, DC, MC, V* ☽ *Closed Sun. No lunch Mon.* Ⓜ *Subway: 1 to Franklin St.*

FodorśChoice
★

$$$–$$$$ ✕ **Bouley.** David Bouley has replaced Bouley Bakery with what can only be described as a throwback to his original formal French restaurant on Duane Street. He's reinstalled the 18th-century wooden door from the old location and even arranged apples in the vestibule to perfume the air the way he did before. His contemporary French fare remains precise and pristine (he has the magic touch with foie gras; a seared slab with molten prunes and Armagnac sauce tastes impossibly light), with

Continued on page 395

CHOW DOWN NYC

The late, great actor and writer Spalding Gray put it best when he said that New York City is "a place that tolerates differences and can incorporate them and embrace them. . . . So it's the melting pot that is a purée rather than individual vegetables. I think of New York as a purée and the rest of the United States as vegetable soup."

It's no wonder why he and so many others use food imagery to convey the boundless diversity of New York City. The variety of cuisines all over the city makes the perfect metaphor. Within walking distance of most downtown neighborhoods are restaurants, cafés, street vendors of all manner of ethnic foods (or hot dogs or pretzels or sugar-roasted peanuts), and food shops of every imaginable persuasion—thousands of unusual and off-the-beaten-track places that (for the most part) don't dumb-down their cuisines for the rest of us Americans.

New Yorkers have famously strong opinions about everything you can name, but when it comes to food, they have been known to come to blows over who makes and serves the best pizza, the tastiest bagels, or the juiciest burgers. Despite the implicit danger, then, what follows is the best of the best.

TASTE 1 | BAKERY BLISS

Bagels and Bialys

There are few things better in this life than a fresh, still-warm bagel slathered with a schmear of cream cheese, especially if that fresh, still-warm bagel slathered with a schmear of cream cheese is from **Ess-a-Bagel.** True New Yorkers know this, and they willingly line up for up to 45 minutes in prime time (mornings, especially Sundays) for the privilege. The best branch is on 1st Avenue near 21st Street. And New York wouldn't be New York without bialys, those flour-dusted, low, chewy rolls with a small heap of onion compote in the middle. No one comes close to **Kossar's Bialys,** a kosher landmark down on Grand Street, where less has changed than practically anywhere else in Manhattan.

Ess-a-Bagel, 359 1st Ave., at 21st Street, Gramercy Park, 212/260–2252. **Kossar's Bialys,** 367 Grand St., between Essex and Norfolk Sts., Lower East Side, 212/473–4810.

Croissants

Maury Rubin's passion-fruit tart at **City Bakery** cannot fail to enthrall, but almost everything there is worth braving the often-long lines, including unutterably rich croissants made the true French way, with butter—and lots of it!—as the only shortening. Get there by about 10 AM, and the croissants will usually still be warm. In season, City Bakery also features New York's best hot chocolate, and the space features one of the only salad bars that can actually make you salivate.

City Bakery, 3 W. 18th St., near 5th Ave., Chelsea, 212/366–1414.

Doughnuts

After trying **Doughnut Plant**'s large but surprisingly light products—with flavors like Valrhona chocolate, rosewater (made with fresh rose petals), pumpkin, and powdered

THE ORIGINS OF THE BAGEL

New York's bagels are supposed to be the best in the world, allegedly because the mineral content of our water gives the bagel a tang and texture unequaled elsewhere. Bagels are made by tossing rings of risen dough into ferociously boiling water for just a few seconds; then the bagel is drained and baked in a very hot oven until it's shiny and golden. The bagel (which means "bracelet" in German) was the staple bread for Eastern European Jews, but the first bagels are believed to have been made in southern Germany. It was in the Polish shtetls (small Jewish villages) that the bagel really took shape. Their shape symbolizes the eternal cycle of life—they were traditionally believed to ward off evil spirits, and therefore were, and are, routinely served at important events, from circumcisions to funerals.

maple sugar—you'll turn up your nose at Krispy Kremes, even the ones that are still warm. The Plant uses an heirloom family recipe from the founder's grandfather Herman Israel who once owned the most popular bakery in Greensboro, North Carolina. The varieties rotate seasonally, and new ones are regularly rolled out.

Doughnut Plant, 379 Grand St., between Essex and Norfolk Sts., Little Italy, 212/505–3700.

TASTE 2 | ETHNIC EATS

Arepas

It used to be necessary to make a trip to deepest Queens to find great arepas, irresistibly buttery Venezuelan corn cakes that are usually filled with a white cheese such as *paisa* or *guayanés*. At **Caracas Arepa Bar,** in the East Village, the arepas are filled with practically anything you can think of, from grilled eggplant and sun-dried tomatoes to (our favorite) chorizo, *paisa* cheese, and grilled red and jalapeño peppers.

Caracas Arepa Bar, 91 E. 7th St., between 1st Ave. and Avenue A, East Village, 212/228-5062.

Cubanos

One of the best Cuban sandwiches in town can be found at the cozy **Cafecito.** With pride of place among the dozen sumptuous sandwiches on the menu, the Cuban here starts with authentic bread, pressed in a grill press with a rich filling of moist shredded pork, fresh ham, Swiss cheese, mayonnaise, mustard, and piquant sliced dill pickles. By the second bite, it's likely you'll be swooning.

Cafecito, 185 Avenue C, between 11th and 12th Sts., East Village, 212/253-9966.

Dumplings

Relentless in his commitment to freshness, **Dumpling Man's** Lucas Lin creates dumplings with decidedly lively fillings: ground pork with chives, ginger, and scallion juice; ground chicken with Asian radish, scallions, and sesame oil; soft and firm tofu with wheat protein, shiitake mushrooms, and minced bok choy; and shrimp, whitefish, corn, garlic, and white pepper. The tender doughs are flavored and colored with carrot or spinach or beet juice, and the dumplings are served steamed or "seared" (fried). The dumplings are 65 to 85 cents apiece, or six for $3.49–$4.99. You can get cheaper dumplings in this town, God knows, but not fresher.

Dumpling Man, 100 St. Marks Pl., between 1st Ave. and Avenue A, East Village, 212/505-2121.

Falafel

Chickpea serves a very refreshing take on Middle Eastern (specifically, Israeli) street food. First of all, the pita bread is baked on the premises so constantly that the bread enveloping your falafel will usually still be quite soft and warm. Also on the menu are shawarma (grilled marinated turkey or chicken, rather than the more customary lamb, thinly sliced from a turning spit) and a nice hefty combination they call "shawafel." (The sandwiches are $2.95–$4.95.) You can also create your own salad, with a mixed green base for $3.25, and all manner of fresh add-ons, from chickpeas to toasted almonds to plump, ripe avocado. The setting is sleek and streamlined, with comfortable high stools at the counter, and even a Moroccan lounge in back.

Chickpea, 23 3rd Ave., between St. Marks Place and 9th St., East Village, 212/254-9500.

TASTE 3 | GOTHAM GRUB

Burgers

There are a lot of great burgers served in New York, but it is generally agreed that one of the best is at Danny Meyer's hugely popular **Shake Shack**. The diminutive, unusually juicy burger is a blend of freshly ground chuck and brisket, formed into a stubby 4-ounce patty and grilled to order, then tucked into an extremely soft bun. The burger is so juicy and the bread so tender that burger and bun quickly become one in their little waxed paper bag, which keeps the sandwich from dripping all over you. They also serve some of the best hot dogs going, including "Chicago-style" (all-beef frank on a poppy-seed bun topped with lettuce, tomato, sport peppers, green peppers, pickles, onion, neon relish, cucumber, celery salt, and mustard). Shake Shack opens in early April and runs bravely through late December. As a backup, you can find the burger that many a chef declares the best and juiciest in town at **Corner Bistro**, with all the trimmings.

Shake Shack, Madison Square Park at 23rd Street and Madison, Gramercy Park, 212/889-6600. www.shakeshacknyc.com

Corner Bistro, 331 W. 4th St., at Jane Street, West Village, 212/242-9502.

Hero Sandwiches

Sometimes only a hero sandwich will do, although they may be a submarine,

hoagie, or grinder to you. When that particular craving hits, only the **Italian Food Center** will do. Huddling stalwartly in what little is left of Little Italy, this shop give a starring role to the New Yorker, in which freshly sliced prosciutto, Genoa salami, provolone, and marinated mushrooms are wed in a sliced house-baked hero roll for $6.29/pound (about one sandwich). Better? Where?

Italian Food Center, 186 Grand St., at Mulberry St., Little Italy, 212/925-2954.

Pizza

Some people behave as if there's no such thing as a bad pizza, and in fact, quite a lot of great pizza is served up in Manhattan. The current contender for best is the flashy and debonair **Piola**, where a dizzying array of over 60 "international" varieties of thin-crusted pies are baked, from the Copenhagen (mozzarella and Brie cheeses, smoked salmon, and parsley) to the Brooklyn (tomato sauce, mozzarella and Gorgonzola cheeses, broccoli, and chicken). If you can't make up your mind, there's always the less-is-more Margherita (tomato sauce, mozzarella, and basil). The chefs were all trained in Rome, and it shows.

Piola, 48 E. 12th St., between Broadway and University Place, East Village, 212/777-7781.

occasional Asian accents of ginger and soy. Whatever you think about Bouley's media persona, there's no question the man can cook. ✉ *120 West Broadway, between Duane and Reade Sts., TriBeCa* ☎ *212/964– 2525* ⌕ *Reservations essential* ▭ *AE, DC, MC, V* Ⓜ *Subway: 1, 2, 3, A, C to Chambers St.*

$$–$$$$ ✕ **Montrachet.** Chris Gesualdi's seasonal three- and seven-course menus are still among the best in the city for fine French cuisine. The ever-changing menu might have the succulent frogs' legs with red wine, fricassee of escargots and morel mushrooms, or a truffle-crusted salmon. The distinguished wine list emphasizes smaller regional vineyards. The rooms are warm and intimate, but designed with plenty of space between parties for privacy. ✉ *239 West Broadway, between Walker and White Sts., TriBeCa* ☎ *212/219–2777* ⌕ *Reservations essential* ▭ *AE, D, DC, MC, V* ☉ *Closed Sun. No lunch Mon.–Thurs. and Sat.* Ⓜ *Subway: 1 to Franklin St.; A, C to Canal St.*

♺ **$–$$$** ✕ **Odeon.** New Yorkers change hangouts faster than they can press speed-dial on their cell phones, but this spot has managed to maintain its quality and flair for 25 years and counting. The neo–art deco room is still packed nightly with revelers. Now, children are also welcome. The pleasant service, relatively low prices, and well-chosen wine list are always in style. The bistro-menu highlights include *frisée aux lardons,* grilled skirt steak, and mussels with frites. ✉ *145 West Broadway, between Duane and Thomas Sts., TriBeCa* ☎ *212/233–0507* ▭ *AE, D, DC, MC, V* Ⓜ *Subway: 1, 2, 3, A, C to Chambers St.*

Japanese

$–$$$ ✕ **Nobu.** New York's most famous Japanese restaurant is getting competition. But while there are some better options if all you want is sushi (for some of the best, readers suggest Sushi Yasuda), this is still the destination for the innovative Japanese cuisine Nobu Matsuhisa made famous, like paper-thin hamachi spiced up with jalapeño, or sea bass with black truffle slivers. Put yourself in the hands of the chef by ordering the tasting menu, the *omakase*—specify how much you want to spend (the minimum is $80 per person) and the kitchen does the rest. Can't get reservations? Try your luck at the first-come, first-served sushi bar inside or at **Next Door Nobu,** with a similar menu plus a raw bar. ✉ *105 Hudson St., at Franklin St., TriBeCa* ☎ *212/219–0500, 212/219–8095 for same-day reservations* ⌕ *Reservations essential* ▭ *AE, D, DC, MC, V* ☉ *No lunch weekends* Ⓜ *Subway: 1 to Franklin St.* ✎ *Next Door Nobu* ✉ *105 Hudson St., at Franklin St., TriBeCa* ☎ *212/334– 4445* ▭ *AE, D, DC, MC, V* ☉ *No lunch* Ⓜ *Subway: 1 to Franklin St.*

Seafood

$–$$$ ✕ **Fresh.** Fish doesn't get any meatier than it does at Fresh, where you can get oven-roasted monkfish steak and charred "Kobe" tuna (sublimely fatty seared belly flesh). Chef Daniel Angerer continues to reinvent the seafood menu in surprising ways. Halibut cheeks are as tender as the foie gras with which they're paired, and English batter-fried haddock may be the best in the city. Fresh's offerings really are the catches of the day—one of the restaurant's co-owners is also the proprietor of Early Morning Seafood. ✉ *105 Reade St., between Church St. and West*

18

Broadway, TriBeCa ☎ *212/406–1900* ▤ *AE, MC, V* ✆ *Closed Sun.;*
No lunch Sat. Ⓜ *Subway: 1, 2, 3, A, C to Chambers St.*

Steak

$$–$$$$ ✕ **Dylan Prime.** With a softer and more sophisticated environment than
that in any of the legendary midtown steak houses, Dylan's proffers good,
dry-aged steaks (from the petite filet mignon to the 32-ounce porter-
house), along with rustic dishes like seared halibut with jumbo lump
crab, and dressed-up sides like butternut squash risotto. The fashion-
able bar and lounge is a scene unto itself; it serves lighter food and killer
cocktail inventions like the TriBeCa Town Car, a sidecar made with apri-
cot brandy. ✉ *62 Laight St., at Greenwich St., TriBeCa* ☎ *212/334–
4783* ▤ *AE, DC, MC, V* ✆ *No lunch weekends* Ⓜ *Subway: 1, A, C,
E to Canal St.*

SOHO & NOLITA

Old-timers bemoan the fact that SoHo has evolved from red-hot art dis-
trict to a mall—Chanel, Prada, and Banana Republic have replaced Mary
Boone and Gagosian (two seminal galleries that fled to Chelsea). But any
way you shop it, the neighborhood still means good eating, whether you
feel like a bracing three-tiered iced seafood platter at Balthazar, Jean-Georges
Vongerichten cuisine, or hot chocolate at MarieBelle's. NoLita (North of
Little Italy), the trendy next-door neighborhood of independent bou-
tiques and restaurants, is reminiscent of a bygone SoHo, with fresh new
eateries popping up every month. Expect beautiful crowds dressed in black
and service that is refreshingly unpretentious given the clientele.

American

$–$$ ✕ **Rialto.** The shabby-chic dining room with pressed-tin walls, plain
wooden chairs, and burgundy banquettes provides a backdrop for sea-
sonal food that is interesting without being fussy, well suited to the noisy
space where people-watching can often distract you from your plate.
But those who like to eat will have no trouble focusing on such dishes
as five-pepper steak au poivre in cognac-cream sauce or an excellent hamburger. The back garden is a great spot for alfresco summer dining; in
winter it's canopied and heated. ✉ *265 Elizabeth St., between E. Houston and Prince Sts., NoLita* ☎ *212/334–7900* ▤ *AE, MC, V* Ⓜ *Subway: 6 to Spring St.*

Cafés

★ ☾ **¢–$** ✕ **Le Pain Quotidien.** The concept here and at all Le Pain Quotidien
branches is to provide good, mostly organic food shared around a communal table. Many other tables for two or more make for more private
dining, but it's interesting to listen to how many languages are being spoken at the big one. Excellent bread, fresh soup and sandwiches, the best
croissants, hot chocolate, and caffe latte in big cups keep neighbors coming back again and again. The granola parfait tastes as good as it looks.
✉ *100 Grand St., at Mercer St., SoHo* ☎ *212/625–9009* ⚹ *Reservations
not accepted* ▤ *AE, DC, MC, V* Ⓜ *Subway: N, Q, R, W to Canal St.*

★ ☾ **¢** ✕ **MarieBelle.** Practically invisible from the front of the chocolate emporium, the back entry to the Cacao Bar opens into a sweet, high-ceil-

ing, 12-table hot chocolate shop. Most people order the Aztec, English-style (that's 63% chocolate mixed with hot water—no cocoa powder here!). The first sip is startlingly rich but not too dense. American-style, made with milk, is sweeter. Preface it with a salad or sandwich from the dainty lunch menu, or request one of the expensive but ravishing flavored chocolates sold out front, like passion fruit, or *dulce de leche.* ✉ *484 Broome St., between West Broadway and Wooster St., SoHo* ☎ *212/ 925–6999* ⌛ *Reservations not accepted* ▭ *AE, D, MC, V* Ⓜ *Subway: A, C, E to Canal St.*

Contemporary

$$–$$$ ✕ **The Mercer Kitchen.** New York celebrity-chef Jean-Georges Vongerichten runs this downtown outpost in the basement of the hip Mercer Hotel. The sleek, modern, industrial space sizzles with the energy of the downtown elite, though these days the restaurant draws its share of average Joes checking out the beautiful people. The seasonal menu's organized by preparation area—raw bar, salad bar, pizza oven, rotisserie, pastry oven, and tea bar—with an eclectic mix of possibilities. ✉ *Mercer Hotel, 99 Prince St., at Mercer St., SoHo* ☎ *212/966–5454* ⌛ *Reservations essential* ▭ *AE, D, DC, MC, V* Ⓜ *Subway: R, W to Prince St.*

★ **$$–$$$** ✕ **Savoy.** Chef-owner Peter Hoffman's two-story restaurant has the coziness of a country inn, with blazing fireplaces upstairs and downstairs, soft wood accents, and windows looking onto the cobblestone street. Hoffman is one of the city's (and country's) strongest proponents of using local, seasonal ingredients, which shows in disarmingly simple dishes like a thick-cut pork chop with roasted Seckel pears, and salt-baked duck. The winter prix-fixe menu includes a dish grilled in the dining-room hearth. The wine list emphasizes small producers. ✉ *70 Prince St., at Crosby St., SoHo* ☎ *212/219–8570* ▭ *AE, MC, V* ⊗ *No lunch Sun.* Ⓜ *Subway: R, W to Prince St.; 6 to Spring St.; F, V to Broadway–Lafayette St.*

Eclectic

¢–$$$ ✕ **Blue Ribbon.** After more than a decade, Blue Ribbon remains *the* late-night foodie hangout. Join the genial hubbub for some midnight specialness, namely the beef marrow with oxtail marmalade and the renowned raw-bar platters. Trust funders, literary types, designers—a good-looking gang fills this dark box of a room until 4 AM. The menu appears standard but it's not. Instead of the usual fried calamari, exceptionally tender squid is lightly sautéed with garlic. ✉ *97 Sullivan St., between Prince and Spring Sts., SoHo* ☎ *212/274–0404* ⌛ *Reservations not accepted* ▭ *AE, DC, MC, V* ⊗ *No lunch* Ⓜ *Subway: C, E to Spring St.; R, W to Prince St.*

¢–$ ✕ **Rice.** All meals are built on a bowl of rice at this dark and narrow storefront. Choose from an array of rices, such as basmati, brown, Thai black, or Bhutanese red, and create a meal by adding a savory topping such as jerk chicken wings, Thai coconut curry, or Indian chicken curry. The fresh, well-seasoned, budget-price menu affords a satisfying mix of multicultural cuisine and comfort food. ✉ *227 Mott St., between Prince and Spring Sts., SoHo* ☎ *212/226–5775* ⌛ *Reservations not accepted* ▭ *No credit cards* Ⓜ *Subway: 6 to Spring St.*

18

Ethiopian

★ **$–$$** ✕ **Ghenet.** A rotating exhibit of local, African-inspired art hangs on the walls of this welcoming spot where the food is authentic and delicious. Order one of the combination platters mounded on a platter lined with spongy *injera* flat bread, which is your edible utensil. In addition to the tasty poultry and meat options is a good selection of vegetarian dishes such as rich collard greens with Ethiopian spices, fiery potatoes and cabbage, and carrots in an onion sauce. ✉ *284 Mulberry St., between E. Houston and Prince Sts., NoLita* ☎ *212/343–1888* ▭ *AE, MC, V* ⊙ *Closed Mon. No dinner Sun.* Ⓜ *Subway: R, W to Prince St.; 6 to Spring St.; B, D, F, V to Broadway–Lafayette.*

French

$–$$$$ ✕ **Balthazar.** Even with long waits, noise, and crowds, most agree it's worth making reservations to experience this painstakingly accurate reproduction of a Parisian brasserie. Like the decor, entrées re-create French classics: onion soup, steak frites, steak tartare—it's all good, and the raw bar is shellfish heaven. Brunch is equally chaotic (but turns out flawless eggs Benedict); for a quieter, more civilized affair, go before 10 AM for a Continental breakfast of café au lait and croissants and pains au chocolat from the restaurant's own bakery. ✉ *80 Spring St., between Broadway and Crosby St., SoHo* ☎ *212/965–1785* ⚐ *Reservations essential* ▭ *AE, MC, V* Ⓜ *Subway: 6 to Spring St.; N, R to Prince St.; B, D, F, V to Broadway–Lafayette.*

¢–$ ✕ **Snack.** Misleadingly named Snack serves big Greek flavors in SoHo. Local residents and shop owners come to the sliver of a storefront for toothsome sandwiches, vegetarian souvlaki, and heartier dishes like *keftedes* (veal meatballs with almonds, pine nuts, and prunes in a red wine reduction). Don't expect a greasy gyro shack—Snack is a pretty space. You'll wish there were more than just a handful of chairs. ✉ *105 Thompson St., between Prince and Spring Sts., SoHo* ☎ *212/925–1040* ⚐ *Reservations not accepted* ▭ *AE, MC, V* Ⓜ *Subway: C, E to Spring St.*

Italian

$$–$$$ ✕ **Peasant.** The crowd at this rustic-yet-hip restaurant is stylishly urban. Inspired by the proverbial "peasant" cuisine where meals were prepared in the kitchen hearth, Frank DeCarlo cooks all of his wonderful food in a bank of wood- or charcoal-burning ovens, from which the heady aroma of garlic perfumes the room. Don't fill up on the crusty bread and fresh ricotta. Sizzling sardines (crisp on the outside, moist inside) arrive at the table in the terra-cotta pots in which they were baked. Rotisserie lamb is redolent of fresh herbs. ✉ *194 Elizabeth St., between Spring and Prince Sts., NoLita* ☎ *212/965–9511* ⚐ *Reservations essential* ▭ *AE, MC, V* ⊙ *Closed Mon. No lunch* Ⓜ *Subway: 6 to Spring St.; R, W to Prince St.*

¢–$ ✕ **Pepe Rosso to Go.** The chalkboard at this mostly take-out joint announces pastas (freshly made and generously portioned), antipasti, salads, entrées, and panini. Gnocchi are as fluffy as can be, and pesto is fragrant with basil. It's worth waiting for the few seats: dinner with wine (only $4.50 a glass) can cost under $17, making this and the other "Pepe" restaurants some of the best values for good Italian in the city. ✉ *149*

Sullivan St., between W. Houston and Prince Sts., SoHo ☎ *212/677–4555* ⌖ *Reservations not accepted* ⊟ *No credit cards* Ⓜ *Subway: 1 to Houston St.; C, E to Spring St.*

Japanese

$–$$$ ✕ **Blue Ribbon Sushi.** Sushi, like pizza, attracts opinionated fanatics. Stick to the excellent raw fish and specials here if you're a purist. Others might want to try one of the more experimental rolls: the Blue Ribbon—lobster, shiso, and black caviar—is popular. The dark, intimate nooks, stylized design, and servers with downtown attitude attract a stylish crowd that doesn't mind waiting for a table or for the sake served in traditional wooden boxes. ⊠ *119 Sullivan St., between Prince and Spring Sts., SoHo* ☎ *212/343–0404* ⌖ *Reservations not accepted* ⊟ *AE, DC, MC, V* Ⓜ *Subway: C, E to Spring St.; R, W to Prince St.*

¢–$$ ✕ **Honmura An.** At Honmura An, you can watch the art of making buckwheat soba noodles at the back of the teak-lined dining room. Like the best restaurants in Tokyo, where the original Honmura An still operates, this one focuses on doing one thing well. The true test of quality is the cold soba, served on square trays with a dipping sauce and a ladle full of cooking water you are expected to slurp as you eat. But everything on the menu—including seasonal sashimi and crisp tempura—is exquisite. ⊠ *170 Mercer St., between W. Houston and Prince Sts., SoHo* ☎ *212/334–5253* ⊟ *AE, DC, MC, V* ☺ *Closed Mon. No lunch Tues. and Sun.* Ⓜ *Subway: R, W to Prince St.; 6 to Spring St.; B, D, F, V to Broadway–Lafayette St.*

Korean

$–$$ ✕ **Woo Lae Oak.** Not so much an authentic Korean eatery, Woo Lae Oak uses traditional Korean flavors to create an elevated cuisine. The food is spicy and flavorful: kimchi burns the lips and prepares the palate for such dishes as *kesalmari* (Dungeness crab wrapped in spinach crepes), and *o ree mari* (duck slices wrapped in miso blini sweetened with date sauce). But fans of tabletop grilling will still be able to get their tender sliced beef *bul go gi.* Since this is SoHo, the tables are dark marble slabs and the lighting is low. ⊠ *148 Mercer St., between Prince and W. Houston Sts., SoHo* ☎ *212/925–8200* ⌖ *Reservations essential* ⊟ *AE, DC, MC, V* Ⓜ *Subway: R, W to Prince St.; 6 to Spring St.; B, D, F, V to Broadway–Lafayette St.*

Latin

¢–$ ✕ **Café Habana.** The simple Cuban-Latin menu at this small neighborhood hangout reflects the friendly, casual atmosphere: Cubano sandwiches, rice and beans, and *camarones al ajillo* (shrimp in garlic sauce), all at budget prices. Just try to get a seat, though: on any given night the sidewalk outside the cheery space with blue booths and pale green Formica tables is littered with belly-baring people waiting to get in. Some fans prefer **Café Habana to Go** around the corner, where the *tortas* and grilled corn are cheap and tasty. ⊠ *17 Prince St., at Elizabeth St., NoLita* ☎ *212/625–2001* ⌖ *Reservations not accepted* ⊟ *AE, MC, V* ⊠ *229 Elizabeth St., between E. Houston and Prince Sts., NoLita* ☎ *212/625–2002* ⊟ *AE, MC, V* Ⓜ *Subway: 6 to Spring St.*

18

Celebrity Chefs

NEW YORKERS LOVE TO EAT, and they are an incredibly demanding bunch. For a restaurant to truly flourish, especially over time, it must overcome the two-edged sword of trendiness and rise on its own merits of consistency, originality, and integrity. The multistar chefs behind these restaurants are celebrities not so much because they have a TV show or a handful of cookbooks to their name but because they can successfully translate their passions into an experience that becomes, for some, transcendent. These are masters of their craft who have apprenticed, practiced, and earned their achievements with distinction. Here's a partial list of some of the city's brightest culinary stars:

Mario Batali and Joseph Bastianich happily expand their mostly Italian empire year after year (**Babbo, Esca, Lupa, Otto, 'inoteca, 'ino, Bistro du Vent**). **David Bouley,** one of the early

new French masters, oversees **Bouley, Upstairs at Bouley Bakery & Market,** and Austrian **Danube. Daniel Boulud** shows off his skills at **Daniel, Café Boulud, and db Bistro Moderne. Alain Ducasse** delivers one of the best French meals in the city at **Alain Ducasse.** Some foodies consider **Thomas Keller's** tasting menu at **Per Se** to be the city's best. Much-copied **Nobu Matsuhisa** pioneered a new style of sushi—it's still going strong at **Nobu** and **Nobu Next Door.** Jean-**Georges Vongerichten** almost seems to synthesize new flavors at his restaurants (**Jean Georges, Jo Jo, Vong, 66, Spice Market**). Other masters are **Lidia Bastianich, Tom Colicchio, Wylie Dufresne, Bobby Flay, Kurt Gutenbrunner, Gray Kunz, Zarela Martinez, Tadashi Ono, Alfred Portale, Eric Ripert, Michael Romano, Masayoshi Takayama,** and **David Waltuck,** to name a few.

Mexican

☾ ¢–$ ✕ **Dos Caminos SoHo.** Its enviable location on the corner of West Houston Street and West Broadway makes for primo people-watching (request a street-side patio table), yet this trendy Mexican spot remains remarkably attitude-free. Start with guacamole, served in a traditional granite mortar called a *molcajete*, and peruse the selection of 150 tequilas. Fancier entrées tend toward style over substance, but tacos (like slow-roasted pork with green salsa), sopes, and enchiladas are all solid. ✉ *475 West Broadway, at W. Houston St., SoHo* ☎ *212/277–4300* ▭ *AE, DC, MC, V* Ⓜ *Subway: R, W to Prince St.; C, E to Spring St.*

Seafood

$–$$ ✕ **Aquagrill.** Aquagrill's friendly staff and extensive all-things-marine menu place it among the best. Chef-owner Jeremy Marshall mans the stove, while his wife, Jennifer, works the host stand. Specialties include roasted Dungeness crab cake napoleon and falafel-crusted salmon served on hummus with tomato and cucumber, not to mention the grilled fresh fish and a rotating selection of East and West Coast oysters. The chocolate tasting plate includes exceptional handmade chocolates. ✉ *210 Spring*

St., at 6th Ave., SoHo ☎ *212/274–0505* ⟨⟩ *Reservations essential* ⊟ *AE, MC, V* ⊘ *Closed Mon.* Ⓜ *Subway: C, E to Spring St.*

GREENWICH VILLAGE & THE MEATPACKING DISTRICT

One of the most complicated Manhattan neighborhoods to navigate, Greenwich Village has enchanted many a tourist (and frustrated many a cab driver). Cornelia Street is a mini Restaurant Row, and tiny alcoves around the neighborhood have been transformed into serious eateries. To the far west, the Meatpacking District—where you can still see people carting around sides of beef—has blossomed into one of the most chic restaurant destinations in town. Celebrities and models and their friends and followers fill the new restaurants, organized with a true Parisian feeling and appearance. This effect was more or less created by trailblazing restaurateur Keith McNally, whose impeccable eye and sensibility drew him to the area to create his Pastis, Balthazar's little brother, which looks more like the Left Bank than a lot of the Left Bank itself these days. Pastis set the visual tone for the nouvelle Meatpacking District in more ways than one.

American

$–$$ ⤬ **Home.** Owners David Page and his wife, Barbara Shinn, have re-created that mythic heartland home in this sliver of a storefront restaurant, where the walls are clapboard and the floorboards wide. Page's Midwestern background sets the menu's tone: perennial favorites include cornmeal-fried oysters, moist roast chicken, and fennel-seed-crusted pork rib chop with sweet potatoes and apples. And what's a home-cooked meal without some creamy chocolate pudding? Brunch is especially nice in the garden on weekends. ⊠ *20 Cornelia St., between Bleecker and W. 4th Sts., Greenwich Village* ☎ *212/243–9579* ⊟ *AE, MC, V* Ⓜ *Subway: A, B, C, D, E, F, V to W. 4th St.*

Austrian

$$–$$$$ ⤬ **Wallsé.** Kurt Gutenbrunner's modern Austrian menu at this neighborhood restaurant with a quasi–Wiener Werkstatt look is soulful and satisfying, with a strong emphasis on Austrian tradition and an urban New York attitude. It's hard to argue with such dishes as Wiener schnitzel with potato-cucumber salad and lingonberries or slow-cooked lobster with spaetzle, corn, and Concord grape sauce. And the desserts do Vienna proud: a special Sacher torte is gilded with chocolate sorbet. ⊠ *344 W. 11th St., at Washington St., Greenwich Village* ☎ *212/352–2300* ⟨⟩ *Reservations essential* ⊟ *AE, DC, MC, V* Ⓜ *Subway: A, C, E, L to 14th St./Union Sq.*

Belgian

$–$$ ⤬ **Petite Abeille.** This consistently good but modest chain of Belgian bistros tempts with salads, mussels four ways with frites, sandwiches, omelets, and other light fare early in the day. Come evening, sausages, *stoemp* (mashed potatoes and veggies), steak, and stew satisfy. Waffles are always available: both *de Bruxelles* (made fresh and topped with ice

18

cream, whipped cream, and fresh fruit) and the true Belgian waffle, *de Liège* (imported and reheated until the subtle caramelized sugar coating crunches and melts in your mouth). ⊠ *466 Hudson St., at Barrow St., Greenwich Village* ☎ *212/741–6479* ▭ *AE, MC, V* Ⓜ *Subway: 1 to Christopher St./Sheridan Sq.*

Cafés

¢ ✕ **Caffè Dante.** A longtime Village haunt, this convivial coffee bar on a quiet side street has superlative espresso and knockout gelato. The regulars have been coming for years, long before Starbucks made its mark on the city. Sitting at one of the outdoor tables is a bit like going back in time, a reminder of when the Village was the bohemian center of Manhattan. ⊠ *79–81 MacDougal St., between W. Houston and Bleecker Sts., Greenwich Village* ☎ *212/982–5275* ⌲ *Reservations not accepted* ▭ *No credit cards* Ⓜ *Subway: 1 to Houston St.; A, B, C, D, E, F, V to W. 4th St.*

¢ ✕ **Caffè Reggio.** In the neighborhood's oldest Italian coffeehouse (established 1927), a huge, antique espresso machine (from 1902) gleams among the tiny, packed tables. How often can you eat pasta or sip a latte under an original painting from the school of Caravaggio and pay $5.50 for the plate of pasta? ⊠ *119 MacDougal St., between W. 3rd and Bleecker Sts., Greenwich Village* ☎ *212/475–9557* ⌲ *Reservations not accepted* ▭ *No credit cards* Ⓜ *Subway: A, B, C, D, E, F, V to W. 4th St.*

★ ♻ ¢ ✕ **Magnolia Bakery.** Sky-high home-style cakes, fabulous cupcakes, puddings, and pies keep this adorable take-out bakery packed into the wee hours. They will even serve you a glass of milk to wash it all down. ⊠ *401 Bleecker St., at W. 11th St., Greenwich Village* ☎ *212/462–2572* ▭ *AE, D, DC, MC, V* Ⓜ *Subway: A, C, E to 14th St.; L to 8th Ave.*

Contemporary

$$$–$$$$ ✕ **Gotham Bar & Grill.** A culinary landmark, Gotham Bar & Grill is every
Fodor'sChoice   bit as thrilling as it was when it opened in 1984. Celebrated chef Alfred
★   Portale, who made the blueprint for "architectural food" (towers of stacked ingredients), builds on a foundation of simple, clean flavors. People come to gorge on transcendent dishes: no rack of lamb is more tender, no scallop sweeter. A stellar 20,000-bottle cellar provides the perfect accompaniments—at a price. There's also a perfectly splendid three-course $25 prix-fixe lunch from noon to 2:30 weekdays. ⊠ *12 E. 12th St., between 5th Ave. and University Pl., Greenwich Village* ☎ *212/620–4020* ▭ *AE, D, DC, MC, V* ☉ *No lunch weekends* Ⓜ *Subway: L, N, Q, R, W, 4, 5, 6 to 14th St./Union Sq.*

$$–$$$ ✕ **Annisa.** Dining at Annisa is an experience in sweetness and light: chef Anita Lo's ethereal, creative cooking is served in a spare bone-colored room. Modern French technique mixes with Asian influences to create seared foie gras with soup dumplings and jicama, and pan-roasted chicken stuffed with pig's feet and truffles. This is one of the few A-list restaurants in Manhattan that is owned and operated by two women. Thus, the wine list, created by Roger Dagorn of Chanterelle, features the work of women winemakers and winery owners. From the innovative hors d'oeuvres to the delicate petit fours, Annisa raises the bar on neighborhood dining. ⊠ *13 Barrow St., between 7th Ave. and W. 4th*

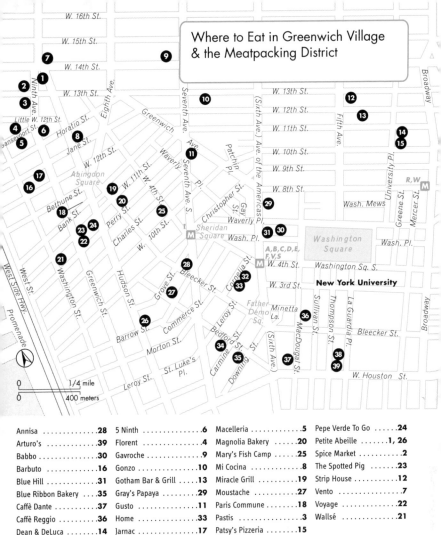

Where to Eat in Greenwich Village & the Meatpacking District

St., Greenwich Village ☎ *212/741–6699* ⊟ *AE, D, DC, MC, V* ☉ *No lunch* Ⓜ *Subway: 1 to Christopher St./Sheridan Sq.*

$$–$$$ ✕ **Blue Hill.** This tasteful, sophisticated chocolate-brown den of a restaurant—formerly a speakeasy—on a quiet, quaint side street maintains a reputation for excellence and consistency other restaurants can only hope for. Part of the "slow food," sustainable agriculture movement, Blue Hill mostly uses ingredients grown or raised around New York, including on a farm at their second restaurant in Pocantico Hills in nearby Westchester. The chefs produce precisely cooked and elegantly constructed food such as Chatham cod with squash and marcona almonds in a shellfish and almond broth. ⊠ *75 Washington Pl., between Washington Sq. W and 6th Ave., Greenwich Village* ☎ *212/539–1776* ⌂ *Reservations essential* ⊟ *AE, DC, MC, V* ☉ *No lunch* Ⓜ *Subway: A, B, C, D, E, F, V to W. 4th St.*

$–$$ ✕ **The Spotted Pig.** Part cozy English pub, part laid-back neighborhood hangout, part gatronome's lure, The Spotted Pig showcases the impeccable food of Londoner April Bloomfield (Mario Batali and partners consulted). Pair the tang of roasted radishes with meltingly delicious prosciutto, or sautéed quail with cippolini onions and marinated figs for studies in contrasts. Shoestring potatoes accompany their namesake Old Speckled Hen cream ale. ⊠ *314 W. 11th St, at Greenwich St., Greenwich Village* ☎ *212/620–0393* ⌂ *Reservations not accepted* ⊟ *AE, D, DC, MC, V* ☉ *Closed Mon.* Ⓜ *Subway: A, C, E to 14th St.; L to 8th Ave.*

Eclectic

★ $$$ ✕ **5 Ninth.** Nestled in a resonant 200-year-old town house, take in the view out the restaurant's front that's so Left Bank you'll repeatedly pinch yourself. Chef Zak Pelaccio's fascinating fusions never fail to enthrall. If mackerel is on the menu, seize it—Pelaccio understands mackerel as few chefs do. Steamed whole *loup de mer* (branzino) is fall-apart tender, seasoned with stinging Thai lime paste and plated with Shanghai bok choy and young ginger. Finish with luscious banana pudding and float out into the Parisian night. Now open for lunch weekdays and brunch weekends. ⊠ *5 9th Ave., at Gansevoort St., Meatpacking District* ☎ *212/929–9460* ⌂ *Reservations essential* ⊟ *AE, MC, V* Ⓜ *Subway: A, C, E to 14th St.; L to 8th Ave.*

$–$$$ ✕ **Blue Ribbon Bakery.** When the owners renovated this space, they uncovered a 100-year-old wood-burning oven. They relined it with volcanic brick, and let it dictate the destiny of their restaurant. The bakery-restaurant has an eclectic menu featuring substantial sandwiches on homemade bread (from the oven, of course), small plates, a legendary bread pudding, and entrées that span the globe. The basement dining room (which has more atmosphere) is dark and intimate; upstairs is a Parisian-style café. ⊠ *35 Downing St., at Bedford St., Greenwich Village* ☎ *212/337–0404* ⊟ *AE, DC, MC, V* Ⓜ *Subway: 1 to Houston St.*

$–$$$ ✕ **Spice Market.** Spice Market is sensual and dazzling. Amid terra-cotta backgrounds, heavy embroidered curtains, and real artifacts from Burma,

Rajasthan (India), and Malaysia, the New York elite gather to eat family-style. Chef Jean-Georges Vongerichten's playful takes on Southeast Asian street food will keep you asking the waiters for more information: What exactly was in that? Sometimes the playfulness works, and sometimes it just doesn't, but don't miss the butter garlic lobster or the hot and cold squid salad with spicy slaw and cooling papaya. ✉ *403 W. 13th St., at 9th Ave., Greenwich Village* ☎ *212/675–2322* ✍ *Reservations essential* ▭ *AE, D, DC, MC, V* Ⓜ *Subway: A, C, E to 14th St.; L to 8th Ave.*

$–$$ ✕ **Voyage.** From the front lounge with the digital fireplace to the swank rear dining room (the padded walls catalyze great tête-à-têtes), Voyage makes you feel like one of the beautiful people without all the fuss. Unusual combinations abound. For example, rich Atlantic salmon is roasted and plated with mashed basil, artichokes, and shiitake mushrooms. ✉ *117 Perry St., at Greenwich St., Greenwich Village* ☎ *212/255–9191* ▭ *AE, DC, MC, V* ⏲ *No lunch Sun.–Fri.* Ⓜ *Subway: 1 to Christopher St./Sheridan Sq.*

Fast Food

¢ ✕ **Gray's Papaya.** It's a stand-up, take-out dive. And, yes, limos do sometimes stop here for the incredibly cheap but good hot dogs. More often than not, though, it's neighbors or commuters who know how good the slim, traditional, juicy all-beef dogs are. Fresh-squeezed orange juice, a strangely tasty creamy banana drink, and the much-touted, healthful papaya juice are available along with more standard drinks—and all 24/7. ✉ *402 6th Ave., at W. 8th St., Greenwich Village* ☎ *212/260–3532* ✍ *Reservations not accepted* ▭ *No credit cards* Ⓜ *Subway: A, C, E, F, S, V to W. 4th St.*

18

French

★ $$ ✕ **Jarnac.** At this corner spot with wraparound windows, in a lovely part of Greenwich Village, Maryann Terillo, Jarnac's multifaceted bistro chef, oversees a market-driven menu that usually includes luscious duck and pork rillettes, rib-eye steak Diane, and braised pork cheeks. Terillo's cassoulet of beans with pork, duck confit, and pork sausage is perfection: supple, smooth, and rich without being too oily or—a more frequent problem—too salty. Desserts are all sublime, and the wine list is carefully selected. ✉ *328 W. 12th St., at Greenwich St., Greenwich Village* ☎ *212/924–3413* ▭ *AE, DC, MC, V* Ⓜ *Subway: A, C, E to 14th St.; L to 8th Ave.*

$–$$ ✕ **Florent.** When it's 4 AM and a slice of pizza just won't cut it, head to Florent, the true pioneer of dining in the Meatpacking District. Open 24 hours, this brushed-steel-and-Formica diner is always a blast—expect loud music, drag queens, and members of every walk of city life. The simple French menu features decent versions of everything you crave—onion soup, mussels steamed in white wine, pâté as well as some inventive dishes like grilled chicken with merguez sausage couscous—and from midnight on, you can also order from a full breakfast menu. ✉ *69 Gansevoort St., between Greenwich and Washington Sts., Greenwich Village* ☎ *212/989–5779* ▭ *No credit cards* Ⓜ *Subway: A, C, E to 14th St.; L to 8th Ave.*

Fast, Cheap & Tasty

PEANUTS AND PRETZELS are reliably good, but let's face it, sometimes you want more. Good thing Manhattan's street-food vendors have taken it up a notch. Beyond the usuals, there are a handful of "destination" food carts that deliver restaurant-quality food at a fraction of the cost and hassle.

Gyro Truck, on the corner of Wall and Pearl streets, doles out killer chicken and cheesesteak sandwiches. Nearby is a **Sausage Truck** with Italian sausage sandwiches and grilled cheesesteaks (Whitehall and Pearl Sts.). **Dosa Man** fills rice and dal "shells" with heavenly spiced veggies at the southern end of Washington Square Park (4th and Sullivan Sts.). At **Daisy Mae's BBQ** chili carts (E. 50th St. near 6th Ave.; Broadway and W. 39th St.; 40 Wall St.), be sure to order the chunky Texas chili.

People rave about the goat stew and jerk chicken at **Yvonne's Mobile Jamaican Restaurant** (E. 71st St. and York Ave.). On weekdays, **Hallo Berlin** restaurants stock "the 'wurst' pushcart in New York" with bratwurst, Hungarian kielbasa, and other treats, in addition to red cabbage and potato pancakes (5th Ave. and E. 54th St.). Street-side falafel varies considerably in quality; look no further than **Moshe's Falafel,** which sells some of the crunchiest fried chickpea balls in town (6th Ave. and W. 46th St.; lunch only). At dinnertime, the well-reputed **Taco Truck** parks near the corner of West 96th Street and Broadway. If you want caffeine, the bright-orange **Mudtruck** sells upscale coffee drinks for less than most cafés (at Astor Pl. on 4th Ave.).

So what are you waiting for?

$-$$ ✕ **Gavroche.** Inside this cozy lantern-lit bistro, authentic Provençale cuisine is created from the skilled hands of the French-trained Mexican Esteban Ortegan. Chances are excellent that you'll be greeted by enchanting owner Camilla Cassin, who lovingly oversees her domain. A voluptuous garden in back invites alfresco diners, with a gurgling stone fountain at the center and ivy climbing the brick walls. The menu features *les planches*—boards piled with charcuterie, cheese, or smoked fish—the best way to start. Roasted fillet of salmon is lightly smoked to order and served with braised lentils and a lemony vinaigrette. Duck breast is roasted just to medium-rare, sliced, and served with duck leg confit and braised cabbage. The profiteroles are the perfect ending. ⊠ *212 W. 14th St., between 7th and 8th Aves., Greenwich Village* ☎ *212/647–8533* ▭ *AE, DC, MC, V* Ⓜ *Subway: 1, 2, 3 to 14th St.*

$-$$ ✕ **Paris Commune.** Wraparound floor-to-ceiling windows, dark cherry banquettes, and papered-and-clothed tables characterize this old favorite's new space, along with a certain self-assurance. Begin with an extraordinarily tender crab cake, carefully seasoned and given a certain edge by an apple-horseradish rémoulade. Grilled ostrich steak isn't something you run across too often; it's surprisingly rich in flavor for such a lean meat. Herbed polenta and a dried-fruit compote make the perfect partners for the ostrich. Finish with a wedge of flourless chocolate cake topped with bourbon-infused crème anglaise and mixed-berry coulis. ⊠ *99 Bank St., at Greenwich St., Greenwich Village* ☎ *212/929–0509* ▤ *AE, MC, V* Ⓜ *Subway: 1 to Chrisopher St./Sheridan Sq.*

$–$$ ✕ **Pastis.** A trendy spin-off of Balthazar in SoHo, Pastis looks like it was shipped in, tile by nicotine-stained tile, from the Left Bank. At night, throngs of whippet-thin cell-phone-slinging boys and girls gather at the bar up front to sip martinis and be seen. French bistro and Provençale fare are front and center, including toothsome steak frites with béarnaise, mussels steamed in Pernod, frisée salad with duck confit, and tasty apple tartlet with phyllo crust. ⊠ *9 9th Ave., at Little W. 12th St., Meatpacking District* ☎ *212/929–4844* ⌁ *Reservations essential* ▤ *AE, DC, MC, V* Ⓜ *Subway: A, C, E to 14th St.; L to 8th Ave.*

Italian

★ $–$$$$ ✕ **Gusto.** From the stunning black-and-white decor to the marvelous cooking of chef Jody Williams, Gusto is all about taste, for which it was named. A gorgeous 27-foot bar runs along the north side of the main dining room, when an opulent Viennese chandelier offsets the semi-starkness of the room's furnishings. The menu is pan-Italian, covering cuisines from Sicily to Venice. From the latter comes a tangled mound of freshly fried whole baby anchovies and squid rings—glorious tempura northern Italian–style. Grilled squab halves are dramatically stacked on a large plate festooned with roasted grapes and salty speck shards. Pear slices with gooseberries and fontina cheese are lightly splashed with grappa. ⊠ *60 Greenwich Ave., at Perry St., Greenwich Village* ☎ *212/924–8000* ▤ *AE, MC, V* Ⓜ *Subway: 1 to Christopher St./Sheridan Sq.*

$–$$$ ✕ **Babbo.** After one bite of the ethereal homemade pasta or the tender suckling pig, you'll understand why it's so hard to get reservations at Mario Batali's flagship restaurant. A full, complex, yet ultimately satisfying menu includes such high points as spicy lamb sausage and fresh mint "love letters," and rich beef-cheek ravioli. There's something for everyone from simple dishes like succulent whole fish baked in salt to custardy brain ravioli for the adventuresome eater. Service is friendly and helpful. ⊠ *110 Waverly Pl., between MacDougal St. and 6th Ave., Greenwich Village* ☎ *212/777–0303* ⌁ *Reservations essential* ▤ *AE, DC, MC, V* ☻ *No lunch* Ⓜ *Subway: A, B, C, D, E, F, V to W. 4th St.*

Fodor's Choice ★

★ $–$$ ✕ **Barbuto.** In this structural, airy space, you'll be facing either the kitchen or the quiet street on the edge of the Meatpacking District. The Italian bistro food depends deeply on fresh seasonal ingredients, so the menu changes almost completely every day—but no entrée is over $20. Legendary chef Jonathan Waxman, who was the first to bring California cuisine to the East Coast back in the 1980s, shows quite a deft hand in the kitchen. On one visit, homemade, firm duck sausage contrasted nicely with creamy, lumpy polenta. On another, peppery, al dente pasta with ragu of boar was light and perfectly seasoned. ⊠ *775 Washington St., between Jane and W. 12th Sts., Greenwich Village* ☎ *212/924–9700* ▤ *AE, D, MC, V* ☻ *No lunch Sat.* Ⓜ *Subway: A, C, E, L to 14th St.; 1 to Christopher St./Sheridan Sq.*

★ $–$$ ✕ **Gonzo.** Once you're seated in the cathedral-ceilinged dining room, you'll swear you're in Florence. The restaurant is usually packed and can be

18

noisy, but that's part of the scene. Chef Vincent Scotto once cooked at the legendary Al Forno in Providence, where grilled cracker-thin pizza rules, and he was the first to bring the technique to Manhattan. The half-dozen varieties of toppings vary from night to night—broccoli with red onion, ricotta, bel paese, and Romano cheeses one night; wild mushrooms, caramelized onions, taleggio and bel paese cheeses the next. The fried olives stuffed with mortadella and Romano cheese are not to be missed. ⊠ *140 W. 13th St., between 6th and 7th Aves., Greenwich Village* ☎ *212/645–4606* ⚑ *Reservations essential* ▭ *AE, MC, V* Ⓜ *Subway: 1, 2, 3 to 14th St.*

★ **$-$$** ✕ **Lupa.** Even the most hard-to-please connoisseurs have a soft spot for Lupa, Mario Batali and Joseph Bastianich's "downscale" Roman trattoria (they also run higher-end hits Babbo and Esca). Rough-hewn wood, great Italian wines, and simple preparations with top-quality ingredients define the restaurant. People come repeatedly for dishes such as bucatini with sweet-sausage ragù, house-made salamis and hams, and fried baby artichokes. The front room of the restaurant is seated on a first-come, first-served basis; reservations are taken for the back. ⊠ *170 Thompson St., between Bleecker and W. Houston Sts., Greenwich Village* ☎ *212/982–5089* ▭ *AE, DC, MC, V* Ⓜ *Subway: A, B, C, D, E, F, V to W. 4th St.*

$-$$ ✕ **Vento.** If these walls could talk! The site of one of the city's most notorious sex clubs—gay *and* straight—Vento is as light and breezy as it was dark and sleazy. Chef Michael White has devised the perfect menu, going from lightly charred octopus and perfectly moist meatballs in a ruddy gravy, to mushroom pizzas with white truffle oil, to grassy sea bream, braised and dappled with mint-coriander pesto. Nice chewy zeppole come in a paper cone, like frites. ⊠ *675 Hudson St., at W. 14th St., Meatpacking District* ☎ *212/699–2400* ▭ *AE, MC, V* Ⓜ *Subway: A, C, E to 14th St.; L to 8th Ave.*

$ ✕ **Macelleria.** Italian for "butcher shop"—the perfect name for an Italian Meatpacking District restaurant—Macelleria's minimalist decor manages to feel simultaneously homey and chic. Start with a meaty *salumi misti*, a platter of prosciutto, salami, olives, and pecorino. Piping hot clams casino are state-of-the-art, with a winey tart lemon gravy. Dry-aged porterhouse for two ($69) sets a standard few could match, yielding such a surprising array of juicy flavors. ⊠ *48 Gansevoort St., between Greenwich and Washington Sts., Meatpacking District* ☎ *212/741–2555* ▭ *AE, MC, V* Ⓜ *Subway: A, C, E to 14th St.; L to 8th Ave.*

¢-$ ✕ **Pepe Verde to Go.** A long list of specials changes daily here, but the menu always includes generously portioned pastas (prepared fresh in the open kitchen), antipasti, salads, entrées, and sandwiches. The gnocchi nearly float above your plate and the pesto sauce is fragrant with basil and garlic. Inexpensive wine is available by the glass or the bottle. Dinner can cost less than $17 at any one of the four "Pepe" restaurants—among the best Italian values in the city. ⊠ *559 Hudson St., between Perry and W. 11th Sts., Greenwich Village* ☎ *212/255–2221* ▭ *No credit cards* Ⓜ *Subway: 1 to Christopher St./Sheridan Sq.*

Korean

$–$$ ✕ **Do Hwa.** If anyone in New York is responsible for making Korean food cool, it is the mother-daughter team behind this perennially popular restaurant and its East Village sister, Dok Suni's. Jenny Kwak and her mother, Myung Ja, serve home cooking in the form of *kalbi jim* (braised short ribs), *bibimbop* (a spicy, mix-it-yourself vegetable and rice dish), and other favorites that may not be as pungent as they are in Little Korea but are satisfying nevertheless. ⊠ *55 Carmine St., between Bedford St. and 7th Ave., Greenwich Village* ☎ *212/414–1224* ⊟ *AE, D, MC, V* Ⓜ *Subway: 1 to Houston St.*

Mexican

★ **$–$$** ✕ **Mi Cocina.** Chef-owner Jose Hurtado-Prud'homme was taught to cook by his grandmothers in Mexico. The dishes served in this charming, inviting restaurant are as personal as they are authentic. Enchiladas in mole sauce with poblanos have deep layers of aromas—along with flavors—that enthrall. The sauce for the dish alone takes an entire day to make. Finish with lemony crepes filled with caramelized goat cheese, raisins, and walnuts—a perfect marriage of divergent flavors and textures. ⊠ *57 Jane St., at Hudson St., Greenwich Village* ☎ *212/627–8273* ⊟ *AE, DC, MC, V* Ⓜ *Subway: A, C, E to 14th St.*

Middle Eastern

¢–$ ✕ **Moustache.** There's nearly always a crowd waiting outside for one of the copper-top tables at this appealing Middle Eastern neighborhood restaurant. The focal point is the pita—the perfect vehicle for the tasty salads, lemony chickpea and spinach, and hearty lentil and bulghur among them. Also delicious is *lahambajin*, spicy ground lamb on a crispy flat crust. For entrées, try the leg of lamb or merguez sausage sandwiches. Although the service can be slow, it's always friendly. ⊠ *90 Bedford St., between Barrow and Grove Sts., Greenwich Village* ☎ *212/229–2220* ✍ *Reservations not accepted* ⊟ *No credit cards* Ⓜ *Subway: 1 to Christopher St./Sheridan Sq.*

Pizza

☾ **$–$$** ✕ **Arturo's.** Few guidebooks list this brick-walled Village landmark, but the jam-packed room and the smell of well-done pies augur a good meal to come. The pizza is terrific, smoky from its searing roast in a coal-fired oven. Monday to Thursday, you can call ahead to reserve a table; weekends, be prepared to wait and salivate. ⊠ *106 W. Houston St., near Thompson St., Greenwich Village* ☎ *212/677–3820* ⊟ *AE, MC, V* Ⓜ *Subway: 1 to Houston St.; F, V to Broadway–Lafayette St.*

☾ **$** ✕ **Patsy's Pizzeria.** The original Patsy's opened back in 1933 in East Harlem, when the neighborhood was largely Italian. The pizzeria still serves some of the best slices in New York. The secret is in the thin, crisp, coal-oven-baked crust, with thick sauce and fresh toppings. ⊠ *67 University Pl., between E. 10th and E. 11th Sts., Greenwich Village* ☎ *212/ 533–3500* ✍ *Reservations not accepted* ⊟ *No credit cards* Ⓜ *Subway: L, N, Q, R, W, 4, 5, 6 to 14th St.*

Seafood

★ **$–$$$** ✕ **Pearl Oyster Bar.** With only 50 seats, chances are there's likely to be a wait for Pearl's fresh seafood: chilled oysters to start, followed by bouillabaisse, a whole fish, or perhaps the famous lobster roll. Locals know to come by for a lazy lunch at the bar, when you can down some Bluepoints and beer in peace. ⊠ *18 Cornelia St., between Bleecker and W. 4th Sts., Greenwich Village* ☎ *212/691–8211* ⌕ *Reservations not accepted* ▭ *MC, V* ⊘ *Closed Sun. No lunch Sat.* Ⓜ *Subway: A, B, C, D, E, F, V to W. 4th St.*

$–$$ ✕ **Mary's Fish Camp.** The neighborhood's second New England fish house (the result of a split between Pearl Oyster Bar's partners) proves you can't have too much of a good thing. Casual Mary's Fish Camp usually has a wait for fried oysters, chowder, moist grilled catches of the day, and, of course, the sweet lobster roll with impeccable frites. A neighborhood favorite is the lobster roll, which usually runs out early. ⊠ *64 Charles St., at W. 4th St., Greenwich Village* ☎ *646/486–2185* ⌕ *Reservations not accepted* ▭ *AE, MC, V* ⊘ *Closed Sun.* Ⓜ *Subway: 1 to Christopher St./Sheridan Sq.*

Southwestern

☾ **¢–$$** ✕ **Miracle Grill.** The margaritas are fabulous here, and the food reasonably priced and tasty: after all, Bobby Flay got his start—and left his culinary imprint—at the original flagship, now closed, in the East Village. Appetizers such as cornmeal-crusted catfish soft tacos are crowd-pleasers. Entrée portions are huge, and Miracle Macaroni and Cheese comes with or without a grilled split chorizo sausage. ⊠ *415 Bleecker St., between Bank and W. 11th Sts., Greenwich Village* ☎ *212/924–1900* ⌕ *Reservations not accepted* ▭ *AE, MC, V* Ⓜ *Subway: A, C, E, L to 14th St.*

Steak

★ **$$–$$$$** ✕ **Strip House.** With vintage nude photographs and cerise leather banquettes that line the red velvet walls, Strip House is decked out like a very high-end brothel. Viennese-born chef Rene Lenger picks up where founding chef David Walzog left off, producing strip steak with an incomparable depth of luscious and beefy flavor. A potato finished in goose fat becomes an exercise in irresistible textures, and truffled creamed spinach is even more resonant. The 8-inch wedge of cheesecake is enough for eight football players. ⊠ *13 E. 12th St., between 5th Ave. and University Pl., Greenwich Village* ☎ *212/328–0000* ▭ *AE, D, DC, MC, V* ⊘ *No lunch* Ⓜ *Subway: L, N, Q, R, W, 4, 5, 6 to 14th St./Union Sq.*

EAST VILLAGE & LOWER EAST SIDE

Once Manhattan's bohemian and immigrant enclave, the East Village has become yet another high-rent neighborhood. The Lower East Side is undergoing similar changes; however, it's slightly edgier and grittier than the East Village—for now, anyway. The influx of deeper pockets is radically changing the restaurant scene, too, in both places. Amid the cheap diners, sushi houses, and tiny Thai restaurants is an army of mid-priced Italian spots and a growing number of high-end reservations-only eateries. But there's still something for everyone.

American

$$–$$$ ✕ **Butter.** A hip spot for celebrity-spotting, Butter features a particularly beautiful decor with sexy lighting. Chef Alexandra Guarnaschelli (daughter of the renowned cookbook editor) brings out the best in such seasonal fare as cavatappi pasta in a yellow tomato sauce with Colorado lamb sausage, and tender grilled halibut with a satiny gold squash emulsion. Desserts include raspberry beignets with vanilla dipping sauce and chocolate tastings. Specialty cocktails include the Butter Martini: Ketel One Citron, butterscotch schnapps, pineapple juice, and Triple Sec. ✉ *415 Lafayette St., between Astor Pl. and E. 4th St., East Village* ☎ *212/ 253–2828* ⊟ *AE, DC, MC, V* Ⓜ *Subway: 6 to Astor Pl.*

$–$$$ ✕ **Prune.** There's just something very right-on about the food at Prune, a cozy treasure of a restaurant serving eclectic, well-executed American food. The choices change with the season, but you might find roasted suckling pig with pickled tomatoes, sweetbreads topped with smoky bacon, or a pasta "kerchief" with poached egg and brown butter. There's usually a wait and the quarters are very cramped, so don't expect to linger at your table. ✉ *54 E. 1st St., between 1st and 2nd Aves., East Village* ☎ *212/677–6221* ⌂ *Reservations essential* ⊟ *AE, MC, V* ⊙ *No lunch weekdays* Ⓜ *Subway: F, V to 2nd Ave.*

Cafés

¢–$ ✕ **Le Gamin.** It's easy to confuse New York for Paris at this hip little haven, where the menu includes all the French café standards: croque monsieur, quiche Lorraine, salade niçoise, crepes (both sweet and savory), and big bowls of café au lait. All the desserts—crème brûlée and tarte tatin, among them—are homemade. Service can be desultory, but the upside is that you're free to lounge for hours. ✉ *536 E. 5th St., between Aves. A and B, East Village* ☎ *212/254–8409* ⊟ *AE* Ⓜ *Subway: F, V to 2nd Ave.*

↻ ¢ ✕ **Veniero's Pasticceria.** More than a century old, this bustling bakery-café sells every kind of Italian *dolci* (sweet), from cherry-topped cookies to creamy cannoli and flaky *sfogliatelle* that are especially delicious when they're still warm. A liquor license means you can top off an evening with a nightcap of Kahlua-spiked cappuccino or a dessert wine. ✉ *342 E. 11th St., near 1st Ave., East Village* ☎ *212/674–7264* ⌂ *Reservations not accepted* ⊟ *AE, D, DC, MC, V* Ⓜ *Subway: 6 to Astor Pl.; L to 1st Ave.*

Cajun–Creole

¢–$ ✕ **Great Jones Cafe.** When you pass through the bright-orange door into this small, crowded Cajun joint, known for its jukebox, you'll feel like you're in a honky-tonk. The daily changing menu, posted on the brightly colored walls, always features cornmeal-fried or blackened catfish, gumbo, jambalaya, po'boy sandwiches, and rice. Brunch is also festive, and if the strong coffee isn't enough to wake you up, a Bloody Mary might. ✉ *54 Great Jones St., between the Bowery and Lafayette St., East Village* ☎ *212/674–9304* ⊟ *MC, V* Ⓜ *Subway: R, W to 8th St.; 6, B, D, F, V to Bleecker St.*

18

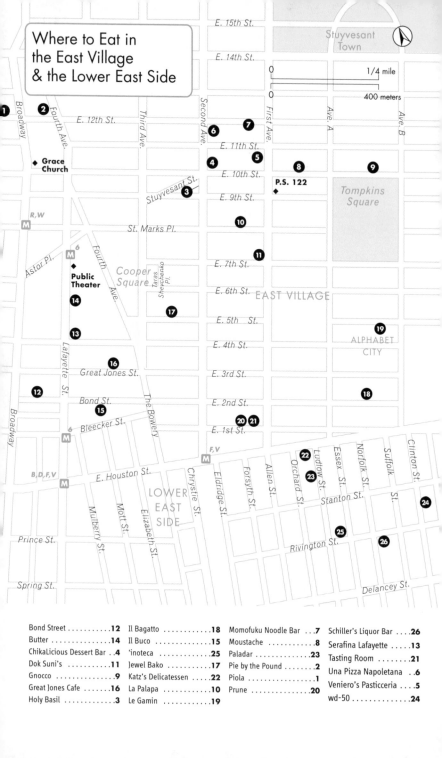

Where to Eat in the East Village & the Lower East Side

Contemporary

$$–$$$ ✕ **wd–50.** The chef's been called a mad genius. Chef Wylie Dufresne
Fodor'sChoice mixes colors, flavors, and textures with a master hand. His staff encour-
★ ages people to feel at ease trying things like pickled tongue with fried mayonnaise on an onion streusel, or foie gras with a grapefruit, basil, and crouton
dice and a leaf of caramelized nori (seaweed). ✉ *50 Clinton St., between
Rivington and Stanton Sts., Lower East Side* ☎ *212/477–2900* ▭ *AE,
D, DC, MC, V* Ⓜ *Subway: F to Delancey St.; J, M, Z to Essex St.*

¢–$$$ ✕ **Tasting Room.** Ignoring any sense of proportion, this 11-table spot fits
more than 300 different bottles on its American-only wine list. The dozen
wines offered by the glass and the menu change nightly. Owners Colin
and Renée Alevras challenge you to make your own tasting menu with
small ("tastes") and large ("shares") portions. Two examples: poached
brook trout with apples and burdock, and roasted Vermont lamb shoul-
der with black beans, turnips, and rocambole garlic. ✉ *72 E. 1st St.,
near 1st Ave., East Village* ☎ *212/358–7831* ▭ *AE, DC, MC, V*
☽ *Closed Sun. and Mon. No lunch* Ⓜ *Subway: F, V to 2nd Ave.*

Delicatessens

¢–$$ ✕ **Katz's Delicatessen.** Everything and nothing has changed at Katz's since
it first opened in 1888, when the neighborhood was dominated by Jew-
ish immigrants. The rows of Formica tables, the long self-service counter,
and such signs as "send a salami to your boy in the army" are all completely authentic. What's different are the area's demographics, but all
types still flock here for succulent hand-carved corned beef and pastrami
sandwiches, soul-warming soups, juicy hot dogs, and crisp half-sour pickles. ✉ *205 E. Houston St., at Ludlow St., Lower East Side* ☎ *212/254–
2246* ▭ *AE, MC, V* Ⓜ *Subway: F, V to 2nd Ave.*

Dessert

$–$$ ✕ **ChikaLicious Dessert Bar.** It's easy to walk past this small shop with
big flavors. Sign on for the three-course prix-fixe dessert, and two
women will dole out incomprehensible combinations and irresistibly rich
offerings. This is the land of kiwi-marinated-in-lavender soup with yogurt sorbet or warm chocolate tart with pink-peppercorn ice cream and
red wine sauce. To top things off, they've hired a sommelier to pair wines
with each course. ✉ *203 E. 10th St., between 1st and 2nd Aves., East
Village* ☎ *212/995–9511* ⌖ *Reservations not accepted* ▭ *MC, V*
☽ *Closed Mon. and Tues.* Ⓜ *Subway: 6 to Astor Pl.; L to 3rd Ave.*

Eclectic

� $–$$ ✕ **Schiller's Liquor Bar.** Day and night, it's the kind of hip Lower East
Side hangout where you'd be equally comfortable as a celebrity or a parent with a baby stroller. The folks at Schiller's have worked hard to make
it feel as if it's decades old. Vintage mirrored panels with flecked and
peeling silver, forever-in-style subway tiles, a high tin ceiling, and a
checkered floor lend an almost Parisian feel. Huevos rancheros, Cuban
sandwiches, and steak frites reveal a steady hand in the kitchen. Dollar
doughnuts, toasted baguettes with sweet or savory fillings, and a more
standard bar menu fill out the list. ✉ *131 Rivington St., at Norfolk St.,
Lower East Side* ☎ *212/260–4555* ▭ *AE, MC, V* Ⓜ *Subway: F, J, M,
Z to Delancey St.*

18

Brunch It

SOME MAKE IT A SOCIAL OCCASION, others have a one-on-one date with the Sunday paper. Either way, brunch is an event, a tradition in New York City. Many of the best places, however, don't take reservations. So, line up with the natives and take in the sights as you wait.

If you're on the Upper West Side, try the famous, caught-in-time **Barney Greengrass,** *the* place to go for bagels and nova (541 Amsterdam Ave., between W. 86th and W. 87th Sts.). Bistro **Nice Matin**'s (201 W. 79th St., at Amsterdam Ave.) tables outside are a delight; inside, it's very light and airy. On the Upper East Side, **Sarabeth's** offers more casual yet still sophisticated food, including moist pumpkin muffins and great fresh fruit plates (1295 Madison Ave., between 92nd and 93rd Sts.; 423 Amsterdam Ave., near 80th St.). **Jo Jo** (160 E. 64th St., between Lexington and 3rd Aves.) serves transcendent brunch fare in a sumptuous town-house setting. The hip and elegant **Aquavit** (65 E. 55th St., between Madison and Park Aves.) sets out a Swedish smorgasbord every Sunday—it's also great for people-watching. For the ultimate sumptuous (and pricey) hotel buffet—the one that has a bit of everything, including shrimp and a dozen desserts—head to the Essex House's **Café Botanica** (160 Central Park S., between 6th and 7th Aves.).

Go to **Home** (20 Cornelia St., between Bleecker and W. 4th Sts.) for American basics plus a heated garden out back. For French fundamentals—croissants, eggs, and croque monsieur—try **Le Quinze** (132 W. Houston St., between MacDougal and Sullivan Sts.); sit up front for a sunny table.

If you're craving challah French toast or anything made with poached eggs, head for **Blue Ribbon Bakery** (35 Downing St., at Bedford St.). **Aquagrill** is elegant without being fussy; order from the classic brunch selections or exotic seafood entrées (210 Spring St., at 6th Ave.). **Jerry's** (101 Prince St., between Greene and Mercer Sts.) is a barely dressed-up diner with roots that go back to SoHo's art gallery days. Kids knock knees with models and Apple store aficionados, who come for salads and sandwiches in addition to brunch classics.

In Tribeca, **Bubby's** (120 Hudson St., at N. Moore St.) presents a slightly Southern take on American standards; its fresh-squeezed citrus juices and buttermilk pancakes draw crowds of all ages. Warm, welcoming, elegant, quiet, and spacious **Capsouto Frères** (451 Washington St., at Watts St.) caters to those who want room to breathe when they eat or who want to talk and—maybe—try the savory soufflés. Quirky and small, the Lower East Side's **Prune** (54 E. 1st St., between 1st and 2nd Aves.) draws brunchers with its legendary Bloody Marys (several creative versions to choose from) and surprising food combinations. Get there early to avoid a crowd. **Miss Mamie's Spoonbread Too** (366 W. 110th St., between Columbus and Manhattan Aves.) is well known for its friendly staff as well as its fried chicken, grits, and corn bread. Former President Clinton dined there, and local politicians are sometimes seen elbow-to-elbow with the students who gather there.

Italian

$–$$$ ✕ **Il Buco.** The unabashed clutter of vintage kitchen gadgets and tableware harkens back to Il Buco's past as an antiques store. The tables, three of which are communal, are each unique—the effect is a festive, almost romantic country-house atmosphere. Chef Ed Witt uses meats and produce from local farms for the daily entrées and Mediterranean tapas-like appetizers. Book the inspirational wine cellar (with more than 300 varieties) for dinner. ⊠ *47 Bond St., between the Bowery and Lafayette St., East Village* ☎ *212/533–1932* ▭ *AE, MC, V* ⊙ *No lunch Sun. and Mon.* Ⓜ *Subway: 6 to Bleecker St.; F, V to Broadway–Lafayette St.*

¢–$$ ✕ **Gnocco.** Owners Pierluigi Palazzo and Rossella Tedesco named the place not after gnocchi but after a regional specialty—deep-fried dough, sort of like wontons, served with salami and prosciutto. Head to the roomy rear canopied garden for savory salads, house-made pastas (tagliatelle with sausage ragù is a winner), pizza, and hearty entrées like pork tenderloin in a balsamic emulsion with flakes of grana padano cheese. Homesick expats come here for a dose of comfort. ⊠ *337 E. 10th St., between Aves. A and B, East Village* ☎ *212/677–1913* ▭ *No credit cards* Ⓜ *Subway: L to 1st Ave.*

¢–$ ✕ **Il Bagatto.** You have to be a magician (*il bagatto* in Italian) to get a table before 11:30 PM at this hip, inexpensive restaurant, but as the reservationist says in her Italian-accented drawl, "You go home, take a shower, relax, everyone else will be tired and drunk, you will come to dinner refreshed and happy." How true. The rich Italian food (try the homemade tagliolini with seafood in a light tomato sauce) and fun, rustic decor make it feel like a party. ⊠ *192 E. 2nd St., between Aves. A and B, East Village* ☎ *212/228–0977* ⌖ *Reservations essential* ▭ *AE* ⊙ *Closed Mon. and Aug. No lunch* Ⓜ *Subway: F, V to 2nd Ave.*

¢–$ ✕ **'inoteca.** The Italian on the menu may be a little daunting, but the food is not. A wine and sandwich bar, 'inoteca strives for authenticity. Come for the grilled-cheese-like pressed panini and the truffle-egg toast with asparagus and runny egg bruschette. Fresh, unusual salads and antipasti supplement the dozen or so entrées. Or select from their list of tempting, mostly Italian cheeses. At night, there's a din. Daytime's much quieter. ⊠ *98 Rivington St., at Ludlow St., Lower East Side* ☎ *212/614–0473* ⌖ *Reservations not accepted* ▭ *AE, MC, V* Ⓜ *Subway: F, J, M, Z to Delancey.*

¢–$ ✕ **Piola.** Festive rainbow lighting fills the spacious dining room of Piola, which has 14 restaurants around the world. But it couldn't feel less like a chain as it bursts with character and Italian-Brazilian bonhomie. The entire kitchen staff was trained in Rome, and the menu lists 60 thin-crust pizzas, from a simple tomato-mozzarella-Parmesan-arugula to the Brooklyn, which features broccoli, chicken, and Gorgonzola cheese. There are some fine pastas and salads as well, and delicious profiteroles for dessert. It's the perfect place to slake those late-night hunger pangs: Piola is open every night until 1 AM. ⊠ *48 E. 12th St., between Broadway and University Pl., East Village* ☎ *212/777–7781* ▭ *AE, DC, MC, V* Ⓜ *Subway: 4, 5, 6, N, Q, R, W to Union Sq./14th St.*

18

Japanese

$$$–$$$$ ✕ **Jewel Bako.** In a minefield of cheap, often inferior sushi houses gleams tiny Jewel Bako. In one of the best sushi restaurants in the East Village, the futuristic bamboo tunnel of a dining room is gorgeous, but try to nab a place at the sushi bar and put yourself in the hands of Masato Shimizu (his *omakase*, or chef's menu, starts at $85). He will serve you only what's best. ✉ *239 E. 5th St., near 2nd Ave., East Village* ☎ *212/ 979–1012* ⏴ *Reservations essential* ▱ *AE, DC, MC, V* ⊘ *Closed Sun. No lunch* Ⓜ *Subway: 6 to Astor Pl.*

$–$$ ✕ **Bond Street.** The minimalist setting of sleek black tables and taupe screens doesn't seem as chic as it once did, nor does the crowd. But the cooking of the resourceful Linda Rodriguez and the creative sushi of Hiroshi Nakahara have not lost their luster. Try the lobster tempura with yuzu and tomato dressing or rib-eye steak with caramelized shallot teriyaki. As for the sushi bar, you can find a selection of 10 kinds of hamachi and four types of yellowtail. ✉ *6 Bond St., between Broadway and Lafayette St., East Village* ☎ *212/777–2500* ⏴ *Reservations essential* ▱ *AE, MC, V* ⊘ *No lunch* Ⓜ *Subway: 6 to Bleecker St.; F, V to Broadway–Lafayette St.*

¢–$ ✕ **Momofuku Noodle Bar.** It's not authentic, but it sure is good. The chef (a Craft alum) created his own special ramen mixture, with a hint of sake in it to create an haute broth. He uses only the best ingredients throughout the menu—Berkshire pork, free-range chicken, and organic produce (when he can). His modern take on pork buns with cucumber and scallions is not to be missed. A sake card explains what the differences are among the drinks. ✉ *163 1st Ave., between E. 10th and E. 11 Sts., East Village* ☎ *212/475–7899* ⏴ *Reservations not accepted* ▱ *No credit cards* Ⓜ *Subway: L to 1st Ave.*

Korean

$ ✕ **Dok Suni's.** Here, and at the restaurant's more upscale Greenwich Village sister, Do Hwa, Korean home cooking marries hip downtown clientele. The combination works to make Korean food more accessible, and a little less pungent, for those on the prowl for good ethnic food. The *bulgogi* (rib eye), *bibimbop*, and pancakes are favorites. ✉ *119 1st Ave., between E. 7th St. and St. Marks Pl., East Village* ☎ *212/477– 9506* ▱ *No credit cards* ⊘ *No lunch* Ⓜ *Subway: 6 to Astor Pl.; F, V to 2nd Ave.*

Latin

¢–$ ✕ **Paladar.** Kitsch 'n' cool Paladar is a party cabana where the drinks are fruity and the pan-Latin dishes are snappy updates of old favorites. Empanadas are filled to bursting with chicken picadillo, and a plantain "canoe" is split down the middle and stuffed with a *bacalao* mash. The bold flavors (and meek prices) are courtesy of chef-heartthrob Aaron Sanchez, the son of restaurateur Zarela Martinez. On weekends, be prepared to perch at the bar and endure your wait with a passion-fruit *agua fresca* or two. ✉ *161 Ludlow St., between E. Houston and Stanton Sts., Lower East Side* ☎ *212/473–3535* ▱ *No credit cards* ⊘ *No lunch weekdays* Ⓜ *Subway: F, V to 2nd Ave.*

Mexican

★ ☺ **$–$$** ✕ **La Palapa.** Aztec-style pottery inset into the wall, embossed-tin mirrors, and a terra-cotta tile floor provide a cozy setting in which to explore traditional ingredients like *epazote* (an herb), *guajillo* (a chili), and *chayote* (a crunchy vegetable). Revelatory sauces combine ingredients such as chilis, tamarind, and chocolate to create multidimensional flavor. Baked cod fillet with guajillo, garlic, and achiote barbecue sauce has layers of flavor; chili barbecue lamb shank and enormous chiles rellenos are among several dishes that may well ruin you for other Mexican restaurants. ✉ *77 St. Marks Pl., between 1st and 2nd Aves., East Village* ☎ *212/777–2537* ▭ *AE, DC, MC, V* Ⓜ *Subway: 6 to Astor Pl.*

Middle Eastern

¢–$ ✕**Moustache.** The focal point here is the pita, steam-filled pillows of dough rolled before your eyes and baked in a searingly hot oven. They are the perfect vehicle for the tasty salads—lemony chickpea and spinach, and hearty lentil and bulghur among them. For entrées, try the leg of lamb or merguez sausage sandwiches. Although the service can be slow, it's always friendly. ✉ *265 E. 10th St., between Ave. A and 1st Ave., East Village* ☎*212/228–2022* ⌣ *Reservations not accepted* ▭ *No credit cards* Ⓜ *Subway: 6 to Astor Pl.; L to 1st Ave.*

Pizza

☺ **$–$$** ✕ **Serafina Lafayette.** Mediterranean-hue friezes and an inviting upstairs terrace grace this roomy restaurant. The real draw here is some of Manhattan's most authentic Neopolitan pizza. Beyond the pies are antipasti, salads, pastas including a number of ravioli dishes, and second courses such as veal scaloppine and sea scallops wrapped in zucchini, seared, and sauced with a brandy curry cream. ✉ *393 Lafayette St., at E. 4th St., East Village* ☎ *212/995–9595* ▭ *AE, DC, MC, V* Ⓜ *Subway: 6 to Bleecker St.; F, V to Broadway–Lafayette St.*

☺ ¢–$$ ✕ **Pie by the Pound.** At this sparkling, cheery spot, oblong designer pizzas are sold by the pound. Ask the server to cut you as small or as large a wedge as you want. The pies are resourcefully topped, with everything from fried eggs to lemon. Even the plain cheese pie is superb. Don't overlook the irresistible dessert pies as well, such as the nice and sloppy Nutella-ricotta-banana pie. No wonder this place is so popular. ✉ *124 4th Ave., between E. 12th and E. 13th Sts., East Village* ☎ *212/475–4977* ▭ *AE, D, MC, V* Ⓜ *Subway: 4, 5, 6 L, N, Q, R, W to Union Sq./14th St.*

$ ✕ **Una Pizza Napoletana.** Owner Anthony Mangieri raises pizza to an art, simply. Only San Marzano or cherry tomatoes touch his crust. The cheese: fresh buffalo mozzarella. His pizzas need only two minutes in the wood-burning oven. You'll find no slices here; the crisp 12-inch pies are relatively costly but well worth it. An important point: the restaurant is open only Thursday through Sunday, from 5 PM until they run out of dough, so it's best to get there early. ✉ *349 E. 12th St., at 2nd Ave., East Village* ☎ *212/477–9950* ⌣ *Reservations not accepted* ▭ *No credit cards* ⌴ *BYOB* ☉ *Closed Mon.–Wed.* Ⓜ *Subway: 4, 5, 6 L, N, Q, R, W to Union Sq./14th St.*

18

Thai

¢–$ ✕**Holy Basil.** It's not often you get to enjoy good Thai food within a clubby setting of dark-wood floors, brick-face walls, huge gilt-framed mirrors, and old-fashioned paintings. The vibrant food—enlivened by chilies, opal basil, and Kaffir lime—comes carefully composed in layer-cake form. Taste buds awaken to *Talay Thai* (sautéed seafood with lemongrass, holy basil leaves, galangal, Kaffir lime leaves, ground chili pepper, and mushrooms in a white wine sauce). A large and informative wine list is an added bonus. ⊠ *149 2nd Ave., between E. 9th and E. 10th Sts., East Village* ☏ *212/460–5557* ▭ *AE, DC, MC, V* ⊘ *No lunch* Ⓜ *Subway: 6 to Astor Pl.*

MURRAY HILL, FLATIRON DISTRICT & GRAMERCY

Quiet, residential Murray Hill, home to some of the city's most charming boutique hotels, has now become the neighborhood of choice for some of the city's most notable restaurants. Lexington Avenue between 26th and 28th streets is known as Curry Hill for its wall-to-wall subcontinental restaurants and take-out joints. Little Korea is near Herald Square in the West 30s. South of Murray Hill, genteel Gramercy is dotted with fashionable eateries in the neighborhood's stately buildings, especially on lower Madison Avenue. Part of the Flatiron District, Park Avenue South and the streets leading off it may be the city's hottest restaurant district, packed with crowd-pleasers like Dos Caminos and top-tier foodie havens such as Gramercy Tavern, Craft, BLT Prime, and Bolo.

American

$$$$
Fodor'sChoice
★
✕**Gramercy Tavern.** Danny Meyer's intensely popular restaurant tops many New Yorkers' "favorite restaurant" list. In front, the first-come, first-served tavern presents a somewhat lighter menu than the main dining room. The more formal dining room has a prix-fixe American menu overseen by founding chef and co-owner Tom Colicchio. For $76, choose from seasonal dishes such as roasted monkfish with pancetta, red cabbage, Jerusalem artichokes, and truffle vinaigrette, or braised lamb shoulder with escarole in a minestrone with tiny goat-cheese ravioli. Meyer's restaurants (which include, in order of appearance, Union Square Cafe, Tabla, Eleven Madison Park, Blue Smoke, and The Modern, at MoMA) are renowned for their knowledgeable, accommodating service, and Gramercy Tavern sets the gold standard. ⊠ *42 E. 20th St., between Broadway and Park Ave. S, Flatiron District* ☏ *212/477–0777* ⊜ *Reservations essential* ▭ *AE, DC, MC, V* Ⓜ *Subway: 6, R, W to 23rd St.*

$$–$$$
Fodor'sChoice
★
✕**Craft.** Crafting your ideal meal here is like choosing from a gourmand's well-stocked kitchen—one supervised by the endlessly gifted Tom Colicchio, also chef at Gramercy Tavern. The bounty of simple yet intriguing starters and sides on the menu makes it easy to forget there are also main courses to partner them. Seared scallops, braised veal, seasonal vegetables—just about everything is exceptionally prepared with little fuss. The serene dining room features burnished dark wood, custom tables,

Ethnic Eats

YOU CAN TOUR THE WORLD eating in New York City. Cuisines of all kinds flourish throughout Manhattan, so it becomes even more special that areas like Chinatown and Little Italy (to a lesser extent) remain, adapting to gentrification instead of being overcome by it. As emigrants set down new roots, they bring with them restaurants and traditions that enrich their new neighborhoods.

The Ukrainian church on East 7th Street (between 2nd and 3rd Aves.) is the epicenter of Eastern European cooking in Manhattan. Nearby, between East 5th Street and East 11th Street along 2nd and 3rd Avenues, a growing crop of Japanese restaurants serves the NYU community. Curry Hill (also known as Little India), the area surrounding the corner of East 27th Street and Lexington Avenue, is rich with South Asian spice shops and restaurants. Offices and warehouses hide some of the restaurants near Koreatown, as some call it (5th and 6th Aves. on W. 32nd St.). On the Upper West Side, a healthy crop of Senegalese and Malian cafés cater to French-speaking African nationals and their American counterparts.

Chinatown no longer dishes out only Cantonese, Szechuan, Hong Kong, and Hunan food. Fujianese, Shanghai, Taiwanese, Uighur, and more northern cuisines find representation as the food demands become more complex. Malaysian and Vietnamese eateries are taking root, too. **Dumpling House** (118A Eldridge St., between Broome and Grand Sts.), gives the famous Joe's Shanghai a run for its money. The tasty potstickers here run $1–$2 each, so you can afford to supplement them with classic almond cookies from nearby **Fay Da Bakery** (83–85 Mott St., near Canal St.).

Although the best Italian fare does not come from Mulberry Street anymore, a few survivors serve good solid food. Even if you come from uptown, you're a tourist here; but it's worth it for a cannoli at **Ferrara Bakery and Cafe** (195 Grand St., between Mulberry and Mott Sts.).

As you sit at the 12-person counter, take a peek behind the white half curtain to watch the Ukrainian ladies preparing goulash, stuffed cabbage, pierogi, blintzes, and more. At **The Stage**'s (128 2nd Ave., between 7th and 8th Sts.) Thursday night homage to corned beef, watch the meat being sliced right in front of you.

The classic Indian food coming out of **Curry Leaf** (99 Lexington Ave., at 27th St.) highlights fresh ingredients like the ones that are sold at the owner's grocery down the street at 123 Lexington Avenue. For a visual and aromatic treat, poke around one of the many small stores that sell beautiful spices, fragrant teas, and unusual grains. Try the fresh halvah, too.

Malians, Guineans, and people from the Ivory Coast—along with their American counterparts—frequent the cafés along West 116th Street to get a dose of French news and a taste of home. **La Marmite** (2264 Frederick Douglass Blvd., at W. 121st St.) is a few blocks uptown, but it's worth the trek for the *debe*, lamb chops, and *cheb*, the Senegalese version of paella.

18

a curved leather wall, and a succession of dangling radiant bulbs. ☒ 43 E. 19th St., between Broadway and Park Ave. S, Flatiron District ☎ 212/780–0880 ☖ Reservations essential ☴ AE, D, DC, MC, V ☉ No lunch Ⓜ Subway: R, W, 6 to 23rd St.

★ $$–$$$ ✕**Union Square Cafe.** When he opened Union Square Cafe in 1985, Danny Meyer changed the American restaurant landscape. The combination of upscale food and unpretentious but focused service sparked a revolution. Today chef Michael Romano still draws devotees with his crowd-pleasing menu. Mahogany moldings outline white walls hung with splashy modern paintings; in addition to the three dining areas, there's a long bar ideal for solo diners. The cuisine is American with a thick Italian accent: for example, the signature tuna burger can land on the same table as homemade gnocchi. ☒ 21 E. 16th St., between 5th Ave. and Union Sq. W, Flatiron District ☎ 212/243–4020 ☖ Reservations essential ☴ AE, D, DC, MC, V Ⓜ Subway: L, N, Q, R, W, 4, 5, 6 to 14th St./Union Sq.

$$ ✕ **Kitchen 22.** Chef and restaurant mogul Charlie Palmer (Aureole, Métrazur) made a clever move when he replaced his restaurant Alva with streamlined Kitchen 22. Where a single entrée once cost about $25, now a three-course prix-fixe costs the same amount. A young, professional crowd willingly waits 45 minutes on weeknights (reservations aren't accepted) for the creative dishes. Choose from five starters and five entrées—say, chicken-liver mousse with pickled red onions and rye toast, followed by herb-baked pollack with warm tomato and shrimp napped with a basil vinaigrette. Homey desserts include the likes of red velvet cake with cream cheese icing and flourless chocolate cake. The appealing '50s airport-lounge look of teal booths and white plastic chairs is so chic, you'll feel like you should be paying more. ☒ 36 E. 22nd St., between Broadway and Park Ave. S, Flatiron District ☎ 212/228–4399 ☖ Reservations not accepted ☴ AE, DC, MC, V ☉ Closed Sun. No lunch Ⓜ Subway: R, W, 6 to 23rd St.

American–Casual

¢ ✕**Eisenberg's Sandwich Shop.** Since the 1930s this narrow coffee shop with its timeworn counter and cramped tables has been providing the city with some of the best tuna, chicken, and egg-salad sandwiches. The staff still use the cryptic language of soda jerks, in which "whisky down" means rye toast and "Adam and Eve on a raft" means two eggs on toast. Considering the feeling of mayhem in the place, it's always a pleasant surprise when you actually get your sandwich, quickly and precisely as ordered. ☒ 174 5th Ave., between E. 22nd and E. 23rd Sts., Flatiron District ☎ 212/675–5096 ☴ AE ☉ Closed Sun. Ⓜ Subway: R, W, 6 to 23rd St.

Barbecue

$–$$ ✕ **Blue Smoke.** Ever the restaurant pioneer, Danny Meyer led the way for barbecue in Manhattan, and not without considerably difficult months of meeting the city's strict smoke regulations. To keep everyone happy, the menu offers the best regional barbecue from all over the country, all at friendly prices. Feast on deviled eggs, oysters, and three styles of ribs—St. Louis, Memphis, and Kansas City styles. If mac and cheese is a weakness, many insist there's none better than here. And downstairs is the commodious Jazz Standard, one of the best jazz clubs in New York. ⊠ *116 E. 27th St., between Lexington and Park Aves., Gramercy* ☎ *212/447–7733* ⊟ *AE, DC, MC, V* Ⓜ *Subway: 6 to 28th St.*

Cafés

★ ☕ ¢–$ ✗ **City Bakery.** This self-service bakery-restaurant has the urban aesthetic to match its name. Chef-owner Maury Rubin's baked goods—giant cookies, flaky croissants, elegant tarts—are unstintingly rich. A major draw is the pricey salad bar, worth every penny—a large selection of impeccably fresh food, including whole sides of baked salmon, roasted vegetables, and several Asian-flavored dishes. Much of the produce comes from the nearby farmers' market. In winter, the bakery hosts a hot-chocolate festival; in summer it's lemonade time. Weekend brunch includes some table-side service. ⊠ *3 W. 18th St., between 5th and 6th Aves., Flatiron District* ☎ *212/366–1414* ⊟ *AE, MC, V* ⊘ *No dinner* Ⓜ *Subway: L, N, Q, R, W, 4, 5, 6 to 14th St./Union Sq.; F, V to 14th St.*

¢–$ ✗ **Le Pain Quotidien.** This international Belgian chain brings its homeland ingredients with it, treating New Yorkers to crusty breads and delicious jams. Specialty sandwiches include beef carpaccio with basil and Parmesan, and a tempting platter of Tuscan meats and cheeses. Best of all is the Belgian chocolate sweetening the café mochas and hot chocolate. For a more substantial meal, take a seat at the long wooden communal table and sample hearty sandwiches like roast beef with caper mayonnaise or roasted turkey with herb dressing. ⊠ *38 E. 19th St., between Broadway and Park Ave. S, Flatiron District* ☎ *212/673–7900* ⊟ *No credit cards* Ⓜ *Subway: R, W, 6 to 23rd St.*

Contemporary

★ $$$$ ✗ **Veritas.** What do you do when you own more wine than you can drink? Veritas's wine-collecting owners decided to open a restaurant. Chef Scott Bryan's prix-fixe contemporary menu runs from such rich, earthy dishes as short ribs braised in Barolo wine with parsnip puree, porcini mushoorms, and glazed carrots to seared diver scallops with hen-of-the-woods mushrooms, leeks, peas, and herb emulsion. A glass of Tokaj and a hazelnut mousse positively sing together. The dining room is distinguished by clean, natural lines, with one wall of Italian tile and another flaunting a collection of handblown vases. ⊠ *43 E. 20th St., between Broadway and Park Ave. S, Flatiron District* ☎ *212/353–3700* ◈ *Reservations essential* ⊟ *AE, DC, MC, V* ⊘ *No lunch* Ⓜ *Subway: R, W, 6 to 23rd St.*

★ $$–$$$$ ✗ **Eleven Madison Park.** Like Tabla, this Danny Meyer restaurant occupies the lobby of the landmark Metropolitan Life Building and has views of Madison Square Park. The design incorporates the original art deco fixtures, but the place feels like a modern train station—in a good way. Chef Kerry Heffernan's seasonal menu always includes a delicious braised beef dish (the braised and grilled short ribs are superb), plus skate, squab, and lobster, each prepared in his simple, elegant French manner. The bar is particularly exquisite. ⊠ *11 Madison Ave., at E. 24th St., Flatiron District* ☎ *212/889–0905* ◈ *Reservations essential* ⊟ *AE, D, DC, MC, V* ⊘ *No lunch Sun.* Ⓜ *Subway: R, W, 6 to 23rd St.*

18

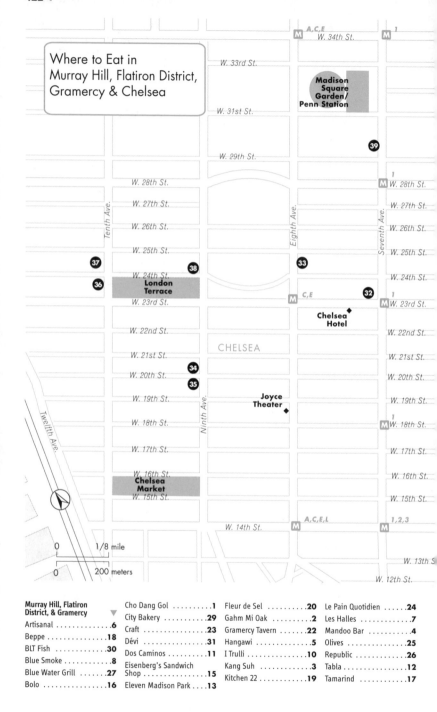

Where to Eat in
Murray Hill, Flatiron District,
Gramercy & Chelsea

W. 34th St.

W. 33rd St.

Madison
Square
Garden/
Penn Station

W. 31st St.

39

W. 29th St.

W. 28th St.   W. 28th St.

W. 27th St.   W. 27th St.

W. 26th St.   W. 26th St.

W. 25th St.   W. 25th St.

37   W. 24th St.   **38**   **33**   W. 24th St.

36   London   **32**
              Terrace
              W. 23rd St.   C,E   W. 23rd St.

                                              Chelsea
                                              Hotel
              W. 22nd St.   W. 22nd St.

              W. 21st St.   CHELSEA   W. 21st St.

              W. 20th St.   **34**   W. 20th St.

              W. 19th St.   **35**   Joyce   W. 19th St.
                                             Theater
              W. 18th St.   W. 18th St.

              W. 17th St.   W. 17th St.

              W. 16th St.   W. 16th St.
              Chelsea
              Market
              W. 15th St.   W. 15th St.

                              W. 14th St.   A,C,E,L   1,2,3

                                                            W. 13th St.

0   1/8 mile

0   200 meters

                                                            W. 12th St.

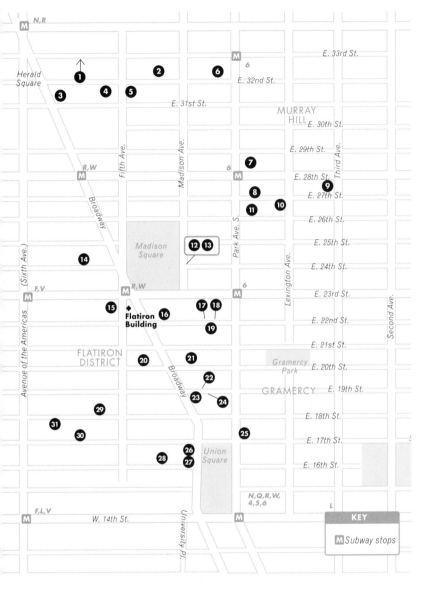

Eclectic

★ $$$$ ✕**Tabla.** In concert with restaurant guru Danny Meyer, chef Floyd Car-doz creates exciting cuisine based on the tastes and traditions of his na-tive India, filtered through his formal European training. Indian ingredients, condiments, and garnishes, such as *kasundi* (tomato sauce), *rawa* (a blend of spices), and *kokum* (dried black plum) garnish famil-iar fish and meats like skate, lobster, oxtail, and chicken. At the more casual Bread Bar downstairs, you can get in and out faster and for less money while watching fresh naan emerge from the searing tandoori ovens. ⌧ *11 Madison Ave., at E. 25th St., Flatiron District* ☎ *212/889–0667* ⌕ *Reservations essential* ▤ *AE, D, DC, MC, V* ☉ *No lunch weekends* Ⓜ *Subway: R, W, 6 to 23rd St.*

French

$$$$ ✕**Fleur de Sel.** Chef-owner Cyril Renaud, who's danced behind the stoves at such highfalutin restaurants as La Caravelle and Bouley, has settled down nicely in a lovely restaurant of his own. His watercolors adorn the walls and the creative menus. The prix-fixe menu is limited and varies often, but is perfectly tuned to the season and the scale of the dining room. Venison loin is simply roasted, napped with a beet-licorice sauce, and served with a sweet potato gratin, and halibut is seared and served with horseradish cream, shallot confit, and blood orange jus. Desserts follow suit: a Bartlett pear tartar comes with a sable Breton cookie and hazelnut ice cream. ⌧ *5 E. 20th St., between 5th Ave. and Broadway, Flatiron District* ☎ *212/460–9100* ⌕ *Reservations essen-tial* ▤ *AE, MC, V* Ⓜ *Subway: R, W, 6 to 23rd St.*

★ ☾ $–$$$ ✕**Les Halles.** Chef Anthony Bourdain is famous not only for his cook-ing, but for his Food Network programs and best-selling books *Kitchen Confidential, A Cook's Tour,* and the splendid Les Halles cookbook. But his original restaurant, which recently doubled in size, remains strik-ingly unpretentious, like a true French bistro–cum–butcher shop. A good bet is steak frites—the fries alone are widely regarded as the best in New York. Other prime choices include crispy duck-leg confit and frisée salad, and firm blood sausage with caramelized apples. ⌧ *411 Park Ave. S, between E. 28th and E. 29th Sts., Murray Hill* ☎ *212/ 679–4111* ⌕ *Reservations essential* ▤ *AE, DC, MC, V* Ⓜ *Subway: 6 to 33rd St.*

★ $$ ✕**Artisanal.** This brasserie is a beloved shrine to cheese, the favorite food of chef-owner Terrence Brennan (Picholine) and past-master cheese man Max McCalman, who has written two superb books on the sub-ject. The cheese is pampered and watchfully aged right in the dining room in a temperature-controlled "cave," and it's all over the menu: fondues, *gougères,* onion soup gratinée, and/or selections from the ever-chang-ing cheese list will leave you simpering and happy. The raw bar is ex-emplary, and the brasserie fare is thrilling, as is the ample by-the-glass wine list. ⌧ *2 Park Ave., at E. 32nd St., Murray Hill* ☎ *212/725–8585* ▤ *AE, MC, V* Ⓜ *Subway: 6 to 33rd St.*

Indian

★ $–$$$ ✕**Dévi.** Boasting an ecstatically colored interior, with nearly every sur-face padded and silked, Dévi is almost as beautiful as the amply spiced dishes that co-executive chefs Suvir Saran and Hemant Mathur devise. Set things right with a Maharani—Belvedere vodka with saffron infusion and a splash of orange—then tear into simply humongous shrimp, sizzling out of the tandoori oven. Manchurian cauliflower is happily marinated in spicy ketchup, and lamb chops have never been slathered in more flavors. ⊠ *8 E. 18th St., between Broadway and 5th Ave., Flatiron District* ☎ *212/691–1300* ▤ *AE, MC, V* Ⓜ *Subway: 4, 5, 6, N, Q, R to Union Sq. 14th St.*

★ **$–$$$** ✕ **Tamarind.** Many consider Tamarind Manhattan's best Indian restaurant. Forsaking the usual brass, beads, sitar, and darkness, you'll find a lustrous skylighted dining room awash in soothing neutral colors and tantalizing fragrances. The kitchen also departs from tradition, offering multi-regional dishes, some familiar (tandoori chicken, a searing lamb vindaloo), some unique (succulent venison chops in spiced cranberry sauce, she-crab soup with saffron, nutmeg, and ginger juice). The more intriguing a dish sounds, the better it turns out to be. Next door is a quaint teahouse/café/take-out shop. ⊠ *41–43 E. 22nd St., between Broadway and Park Ave. S, Flatiron District* ☎ *212/674–7400* ⌂ *Reservations essential* ▤ *AE, DC, MC, V* Ⓜ *Subway: N, R, 6 to 23rd St.*

Italian

$$–$$$$ ✕ **I Trulli.** Rough-hewn gold walls, a fireplace, a garden for summer dining, and a whitewashed open grill with the traditional beehive shape of early Pugliese houses distinguish this Italian winner from its competitors. The appetizers are certainly enticing—rabbit pâté with pecorino and prosciutto brioche, or grilled baby octopus with fennel-orange supreme salad—and nearly all the pasta is handmade. Main courses include a luscious rack of lamb with fava bean puree and dandelions. ⊠ *122 E. 27th St., between Lexington Ave. and Park Ave. S, Murray Hill* ☎ *212/481–7372* ⌂ *Reservations essential* ▤ *AE, DC, MC, V* ⊘ *Closed Sun. No lunch Sat.* Ⓜ *Subway: 6 to 28th St.*

$–$$$ ✕ **Beppe.** There are a lot of restaurants claiming to be Tuscan in New York, but chef Cesare Casella's labor of love is one of the few that can wear the mantle. The chef presents a playful menu of Tuscan specialties, such as *farro* cooked risotto-style, and clever concoctions, like semiboneless quail stuffed with pancetta and sage, roasted and served over Sardinian *fregola* and roasted red peppers. The seasonally changing pastas may be the best part of the satisfying menu. The bright dining room simulates a cheery trattoria. ⊠ *45 E. 22nd St., between Broadway and Park Ave. S, Flatiron District* ☎ *212/982–8422* ▤ *AE, DC, MC, V* ⊘ *Closed Sun. No lunch Sat.* Ⓜ *Subway: R, W, 6 to 23rd St.*

Korean

¢–$$ ✕ **Cho Dang Gol.** Situated a few blocks away from the main drag of Little Korea, this restaurant specializes in tofu (*doo-boo* in Korean), and myriad varieties are made on the premises and incorporated into a vast array of traditional Korean dishes of varying heat and spice. Anyone who thinks of tofu as a bland, jiggling substance should try doo-boo *dong-ka-rang-deng,* puffy rounds of tofu filled with shredded vegetables, egg, and ground pork. The staff members don't speak enough English to be of much help. ⊠ *55 W. 35th St., between 5th and 6th Aves.,*

18

Murray Hill ☎ 212/695–8222 ▭ *AE, DC, MC, V* Ⓜ *Subway: B, D, F, N, Q, R, S, W to 34th St.*

¢–$$ ✕ **Kang Suh.** "Seoul" food at its best is served at this lively, second-floor restaurant. Cook thin slices of ginger-marinated beef (*bul go gui*) or other meats over red-hot coals; top them with hot chilies, bean paste, and pickled cabbage; and wrap them all up with lettuce for a satisfying meal. A crisp oyster-and-scallion pancake, sautéed yam noodles, and other traditional dishes are all expertly prepared. The waitstaff speaks little English, but the menu has lots of pictures, so you can just point and smile. ⊠ *32 W. 32nd St., between 5th and 6th Aves., Murray Hill* ☎ 212/947–8482 ▭ *AE, MC, V* Ⓜ *Subway: B, D, F, N, Q, R, S, W to 34th St.*

¢–$ ✕ **Gahm Mi Oak.** The deconstructed industrial design, inexpensive menu, and late-night hours attract a young and stylish crowd here. Every item on the very limited menu has a photo to help you order. But all you need to remember to order are oxtail-and-bone-marrow soup—a subtle, satisfying milky-white bowl of soup with rice noodles and beef that you season at your table with Korean sea salt and chopped scallions—and mung bean pancakes, made fresh with scallions, and fried until crisp and chewy. ⊠ *43 W. 32nd St., between 5th and 6th Aves., Murray Hill* ☎ 212/695–4113 ᐦ *Reservations not accepted* ▭ *No credit cards* Ⓜ *Subway: B, D, F, N, Q, R, V, W to 34th St.*

¢–$ ✕ **Mandoo Bar.** At this appealing little dumpling shop on Little Korea's main drag, you can watch the ladies making the little oval treats in the window on your way to one of the blond-wood cafeterialike tables in the back. There are plenty of dumplings, or *mandoo,* to choose from, such as broiled shrimp and sea cucumber, Korean kimchi, beef, pork, or leek. Rounding out the menu are noodle and rice dishes and a couple of specialties like *tangsuyook*—fried pork with sweet-and-sour sauce. ⊠ *2 W. 32nd St., between 5th Ave. and Broadway, Murray Hill* ☎ 212/ 279–3075 ▭ *AE, MC, V* Ⓜ *Subway: 6 to 33rd St.*

Mediterranean

★ $$–$$$ ✕ **Olives.** The New York branch of Boston-based Todd English's growing international Olives empire resides in the capacious lobby of the hip W Hotel on Union Square. His executive chef, Mike Crain, sustains English's penchant for complexity of flavors and ingredients with a level hand. Handmade veal agnolotti is enrobed with prosciutto and Parmesan cheese, and finished with truffle butter. A seared yellowfin tuna loin rests on curried polenta, and is dappled with gingered spinach and crispy calamari. Finish with a vanilla soufflé and you'll float out of the bustling lobby with a big grin. ⊠ *201 Park Ave. S, at E. 17th St., Flatiron District* ☎ 212/353–8345 ᐦ *Reservations essential* ▭ *AE, D, DC, MC, V* Ⓜ *Subway: L, N, Q, R, W, 4, 5, 6 to 14th St./Union Sq.*

Mexican

$–$$$ ✕ **Dos Caminos.** Stephen Hanson, the visionary restaurateur behind a dozen New York restaurants, including Blue Water Grill, has created quite a sophisticated hit. The array of 150 tequilas will put you in the right frame of mind for anything chef Scott Linquist creates. Kobe beef tacos are given searing heat by cascabel chilies, and slow-roasted pork ribs in achiote barbecue sauce achieve quite a depth of flavor. Be forewarned: it can

Special Spots

ALMOST EVERY NEIGHBORHOOD
lays claim to at least one restaurant
with a great hidden space, be it a
back garden or patio (there are over
200 in the city), a table by the water,
or a bird's-eye view of Manhattan.

Asiate's views of Central Park can
make you feel as if you've stepped
back in time to the days when
Frederick Law Olmsted first planned
his 843-acre escape. The deck outside
of the food court on the third floor of
Pier 17 (at South Street Seaport) has
not-to-be-missed views of the East
River. You can spend hours watching
ships go by and people-watching—for
free! On the other side of town, bike-
ride or walk to the ultracasual **Boat
Basin Café**, for Hudson River vistas
and sunsets. It's open from April to
October, and is located by the bike
path at West 79th Street. **The Central
Park Boathouse Restaurant** in
Central Park overlooks the gondola
lake, where you can watch rowboaters
and occasionally see cormorants
fishing. On a warm spring day,
though, you might have to fight for a

table. Head to the **Metropolitan
Museum of Art** for drinks in their
rooftop garden from May to October.
In the Meatpacking District, the
ultrahip Hotel Gansevoort's rooftop
restaurant, **Plunge**, touts views and
gardens, 15 floors up.

In the East Village, **Miracle Grill's**
claim to fame is its fragrant peach
tree, which serves as perfect backdrop
for masterful margaritas and great
Southwestern-influenced food; kids
and romantics welcome. Big, modern,
and Italian, **Barolo**'s SoHo garden is
packed in the warm weather with the
beautiful SoHo elite; come to relax,
not to fuss over the food. Old-world
charm flows from the fountain in the
middle of **Barbetta**'s handsome
garden in a 1906 town house in the
theater district. The kitchen keeps
turning out good, solid northern
Italian specialties. A lush, year-round
alternative is rustic, romantic **I
Coppi**'s covered garden on the Lower
East Side. A Tuscan-style charmer, it
serves up good antipasti, pizzas,
pasta, and fish.

18

get pretty noisy here. ⊠ *373 Park Ave. S, between E. 26th and E. 27th
Sts., Flatiron District* ☎ *212/294–1000* ⟜ *Reservations essential* ⊟ *AE,
DC, MC, V* Ⓜ *Subway: 6 to 28th St.*

Pan-Asian

¢ ✕ **Republic.** Epicureans on a budget flock to this Asian noodle emporium that looks like a cross between a downtown art gallery and a Japanese school cafeteria. The young waitstaff dressed in black T-shirts and
jeans hold remote-control ordering devices to accelerate the already speedy
service. Sit at the long, bluestone bar or at the picnic-style tables and
order appetizers such as smoky grilled eggplant and luscious fried wontons. Entrées are based on noodles or rice. Spicy coconut chicken soup
and Vietnamese-style barbecued pork are particularly delicious. ⊠ *37
Union Sq. W, between E. 16th and E. 17th Sts., Flatiron District* ☎ *212/
627–7172* ⊟ *AE, DC, MC, V* Ⓜ *Subway: L, N, Q, R, W, 4, 5, 6 to
14th St./Union Sq.*

Seafood

$$–$$$$ ╳ **BLT Fish.** Two stories above the less formal Fish Shack, BLT Fish is an elegantly appointed dining room set under a spectacular skylight. "BLT" stands for Bistro Laurent Tourondel, and he proves once again, as at BLT Steak uptown, that he embroiders his dishes more successfully than nearly anyone. Buffalo Rock Shrimp are tempura-battered shrimp fried and sauced in the manner of Buffalo wings with shockingly delicious results. Tourondel's signature roasted Alaskan black cod involves simply marinating a fillet overnight in honey, soy sauce, grapeseed oil, and white wine vinegar, then roasting it in a very hot oven for seven minutes. The piping-hot result is among the best seafood dishes in town. ⊠ *21 W. 17th St., between 5th and 6th Aves., Flatiron District* ☎ *212/ 691–8888* ⚷ *Reservations essential* ⊟ *AE, DC, MC, V* Ⓜ *Subway: 4, 5, 6, N, Q, R, W to Union Sq./14th St.*

$–$$$ ╳ **Blue Water Grill.** A copper-and-tile raw bar anchors one end of this warm, sweeping room of indigo, sienna, and yellow. Strong on fresh seafood served neat (chilled whole lobster, shrimp in the rough), the constantly changing menu also has international flair—sushi and sashimi, porcini-crusted halibut with pumpkin risotto, lobster and scallop open-faced ravioli—and simple preparations that issue forth from a wood-burning oven. Lobster mashed potatoes are a must. ⊠ *31 Union Sq. W, at E. 16th St., Flatiron District* ☎ *212/675–9500* ⚷ *Reservations essential* ⊟ *AE, DC, MC, V* Ⓜ *Subway: L, N, Q, R, W, 4, 5, 6 to 14th St./Union Sq.*

Spanish

★ ╳ **Bolo.** Although Bolo was already the most vivid and convincing
☕ $$–$$$ Spanish restaurant in New York, celebrity-chef Bobby Flay decided to add tapas to Bolo's menu, making the place even better. Choose—if you can—from over a dozen possibilities, but don't miss the sautéed squid and bacon with garlic oil or white anchovies with tangerine. Another must-try is the roasted rabbit haunch wrapped in serrano ham with yellow-pepper risotto. In fact, everything on the menu is marvelous. ⊠ *23 E. 22nd St., between Broadway and Park Ave. S, Flatiron District* ☎ *212/228–2200* ⚷ *Reservations essential* ⊟ *AE, MC, V* Ⓜ *Subway: 6 to 23rd St.*

Turkish

$–$$ ╳ **Turkish Kitchen.** This striking multilevel room with crimson walls, chairs with red skirted slipcovers, and colorful kilims is Manhattan's busiest and best Turkish restaurant. For appetizers, choose from the likes of velvety char-grilled eggplant or tender octopus salad, creamy hummus, or poached beef dumplings. The luscious stuffed cabbage is downright irresistible. The restaurant also hosts one of the most alluring Sunday brunch buffets in town, featuring 90 items, Turkish and American—all house-made, including a dozen breads. ⊠ *386 3rd Ave., between E. 27th and E. 28th Sts., Murray Hill* ☎ *212/679–1810* ⊟ *AE, D, DC, MC, V* ⊙ *No lunch Sat.* Ⓜ *Subway: 6 to 28th St.*

Vegetarian

$–$$ ╳ **Hangawi.** Hangawi, serving "vegetarian mountain Korean cooking," holds a special place in the city's collection of vegetarian restaurants. For the full experience choose the "emperor's menu," a parade of more than 10 courses with a prix fixe of $35, designed as a complete introduction to this unusual cuisine. Offerings include delicate soups, such as miso broth or pumpkin porridge with marinated wild mountain herbs; and a main-course spread of more than 15 bowls of assorted earthy and/or spicy kimchi. Exotic teas, including one made from a puree of dates, are good accompaniments to the meal. ⊠ *12 E. 32nd St., between 5th and Madison Aves., Murray Hill* ☎ *212/213–0077* ⚲ *Reservations essential* ▭ *AE, DC, MC, V* Ⓜ *Subway: B, D, F, N, Q, R, V, W to 34th St.*

CHELSEA

Soon after the art galleries and gay men surged into the area, Chelsea underwent a residential building boom, bringing a new wave of luxury-condo dwellers to this relentlessly trendy neighborhood. But there has been no congruent influx of great restaurants. Chelsea may not be a white-hot dining destination like, say, its Flatiron neighbor to the east, but you can eat very well if you know where to go.

American

★ **$$$$** ✕ **The Biltmore Room.** In the most soigné Beaux Arts dining room in town, set about with antique marble preserved from the old Biltmore Hotel, feast on brilliant chef Gary Robins's highly imaginative and deeply delicious fare, like marjoram-scented grilled quail with morel risotto, grilled merguez sausage, or coriander-anise-crusted wild king salmon with red lentils, steamed spinach, spicy carrot butter, and watermelon pickle. The room is a bit crowded, the seats are a bit low for the tables, but the gorgeous and quicksilver staff makes everything come together beautifully. ⊠ *289 8th Ave., between W. 24th and W. 25th Sts., Chelsea* ☎ *212/807–0111* ▭ *AE, DC, MC, V* ⊘ *No lunch* Ⓜ *Subway: C, E to 23rd St.*

$$ ✕ **The Red Cat.** Chef-owner Jimmy Bradley oversees this comfortable neighborhood restaurant. Try the seasonal appetizers like sautéed zucchini with almonds and pecorino, or pancetta-wrapped rabbit loin with favas, cipollini onions, cherries, and violet mustard. Sumptuous entrées include grilled brook trout with spaetzle and mushrooms, and shell steak and Yukon gold potatoes with cabernet sauce. The service is friendly and welcoming, and the wine list is reasonably priced. ⊠ *227 10th Ave., between W. 23rd and W. 24th Sts., Chelsea* ☎ *212/242–1122* ▭ *AE, DC, MC, V* ⊘ *No lunch* Ⓜ *Subway: C, E to 23rd St.*

$–$$ ✕ **Seven.** In the culinary wasteland around Macy's and Penn Station, there actually are a few serious restaurants. The contemporary American menu runs the gamut from overstuffed sandwiches (at lunch), to seasonal soups, to homemade pastas, to creative entrées such as roasted skate with lobster coral, capers, and brown butter. The decor, like the menu, plays it safe but sophisticated. In another neighborhood this restaurant might not warrant attention, but as an oasis in a desert of fast-food outlets it deserves special mention. ⊠ *350 7th Ave., between W. 29th and W. 30th Sts., Chelsea* ☎ *212/967–1919* ▭ *AE, MC, V* Ⓜ *Subway: 1 to 28th St.*

18

Barbecue

$-$$ ✕ **R.U.B. BBQ.** Among the American barbecue capitals, Kansas City's smoked fare stands out as perhaps the most versatile, characterized by dry rubs with sauces strictly on the side. Executive chef Paul Kirk is from Kansas City, and is a legend on the growing New York City barbecue competition circuit. This is not a restaurant for the timid of appetite. Platters are so bountiful that even the side dishes come in overwhelming quantities. The shameless menu promises everything from beef, pork, ham, pastrami, and turkey to chicken, sausage, and of course ribs. Burnt ends—delicious charred-crisp, rich edges of beef brisket—are legendary, and they sell out every night. In fact, many items on the menu sell out by 8 PM, so it's wise to get here fairly early. ⊠ *208 W. 23rd St., between 7th and 8th Aves., Chelsea* ☎ *212/524–4300* ⌲ *Reservations essential* ⊟ *AE, DC, MC, V* Ⓜ *Subway: 1, C, E to 23rd St.*

Cafés

¢–1$ ✕ **Le Gamin.** It's easy to confuse New York for Paris at this hip little haven (one of four in town), where the menu includes all the French-café standards: croque monsieur, quiche Lorraine, salade niçoise, crepes (both sweet and savory), and big bowls of café au lait. Service can be desultory, but the upside is that you're free to lounge for hours. ⊠ *183 9th Ave., at W. 21st St., Chelsea* ☎ *212/243–8864* ⊟ *AE, MC, V* Ⓜ *Subway: C, E to 23rd St.*

♻ **¢** ✕ **La Bergamote.** Exemplary French pastries are served in this simple café. Try the buttery pain au chocolat and chewy meringues with a steaming bowl of café au lait. ⊠ *169 9th Ave., at W. 20th St., Chelsea* ☎ *212/627–9010* ⊟ *No credit cards* Ⓜ *Subway: A, C, E, L to 14th St.*

Chinese

¢–$ ✕ **Grand Sichuan International.** This regional Chinese restaurant serves a vast menu of specialties, many of which you won't find anywhere else. The emphasis is on fiery Sichuan (Szechuan) cooking, but Cantonese, Hunan, Shanghai, and even American Chinese food are represented (a handy treatise and guide to Chinese food comes with the menu). Spicy *dan dan* noodles, shredded potatoes in vinegar sauce, crab soup dumplings, minced pork with cellophane noodles or fermented green beans, and sautéed loofah (a sponge gourd) are among the hauntingly delicious dishes. ⊠ *229 9th Ave., at W. 24th St., Chelsea* ☎ *212/620–5200* ⊟ *AE, MC, V* Ⓜ *Subway: C, E to 23rd St.*

Eclectic

★ **$$–$$$** ✕ **Sapa.** Proving yet again that she is among the most nuanced and imaginative chefs in the world, Patricia Yeo triumphs in a spectacular, shimmering new space. Dishes are creative concoctions, mostly Asian with a French accent. Don't miss the roasted loin chops and sweet-and-sour fried wontons, and fat, medium-rare slices of king salmon tightly wrapped in rice paper and served with toasted sesame–dappled eggplant and a searing tamarind-chili sauce. Onion rings are tempura battered and sweet. Finish with baby banana bread pudding with caramelized ginger chips and white-chocolate ice cream. ⊠ *43 W. 24th St., between 5th and 6th Aves., Chelsea* ☎ *212/929–1800* ⌲ *Reservations essential* ⊟ *AE, MC, V* Ⓜ *Subway: C, E to 23rd St.*

Italian

¢–$ ✕ **Pepe Giallo to Go.** The crown of a chain of four tiny Italian eateries, this Chelsea branch is the most spacious and charming of the lot. A long list of specials changes daily, but the menu always includes generously portioned pastas (prepared fresh in the open kitchen), antipasti, salads, entrées, and sandwiches. The gnocchi are as light as little clouds, and the veal scallops are tender. Inexpensive wine is served. Considering dinner can cost less than $17, these restaurants are among the best Italian values in the city. ⊠ *253 10th Ave., at W. 25th St., Chelsea* ☎ *212/242–6055* ▤ *AE, MC, V* Ⓜ *Subway: C, E to 23rd St.*

MIDTOWN WEST

Big hotels, big businesses, and blockbuster Broadway shows dominate the western half of Midtown, and that means plenty of big hungry crowds around the clock. Capitalizing neatly on that fact is an ever-burgeoning plethora of restaurants ranging from inexpensive ethnic eateries and theme restaurants to fine French dining rooms. Be sure to make an informed choice, or you could easily find yourself in a tourist trap. Now that Times Square and the theater district resemble theme parks and Hell's Kitchen has been gentrified (you'll hear it called Clinton), the seedy edge of the area is all but gone. In fact, Times Square is beginning to look more and more like Shinjuku in Tokyo.

American

$$$$ ✕ **'21' Club.** It's undeniably exciting to hobnob with celebrities and tycoons at this four-story town-house landmark, a former speakeasy that first opened on December 31, 1929. Chef Stephen Trojahn tries to satisfy everyone by retaining signature dishes like the famous '21' burger, game potpie, and other New American food, while also offering more eclectic fare, such as pomegranate-scented halibut with baby eggplant. Such fare comes at quite a high price. Service is seamless throughout. It's worth noting that this is one of only two restaurants in Manhattan that still requires a jacket *and* tie. ⊠ *21 W. 52nd St., between 5th and 6th Aves., Midtown West* ☎ *212/582–7200* 🎩 *Jacket and tie* ▤ *AE, D, DC, MC, V* ☾ *Closed Sun. No lunch Sat.* Ⓜ *Subway: E, V to 53rd St./5th Ave.; B, D, F, V to 47th–50th Sts./Rockefeller Ctr.*

$$ ✕ **District.** The plush design of this contemporary American restaurant in the Muse Hotel incorporates clever stage references meant to evoke the (theater) district for which it is named. Chef Robert Curran creates quite grown-up food, like cavatelli and veal ragù with sage sauce, or brick-pressed half boneless chicken with chorizo-cheddar grits and braised Swiss chard. A pretheater three-course $48 prix fixe is available. ⊠ *130 W. 46th St., between 5th and 6th Aves., Midtown West* ☎ *212/485–2999* ⌕ *Reservations essential* ▤ *AE, D, DC, MC, V* Ⓜ *Subway: R, W to 49th St.*

American–Casual

🐾 ¢ ✕ **Island Burgers and Shakes.** Belly-busting burgers rule at this bright and cheery café with multicolor round tables and funky chairs. Every sandwich can be ordered with grilled chicken instead of the usual beef patty, but true believers stick to the real thing and choose from a staggering

18

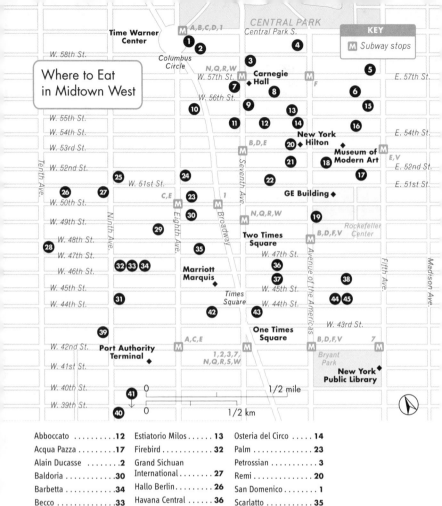

Where to Eat in Midtown West

KEY

Ⓜ Subway stops

Time Warner Center

Columbus Circle

W. 58th St.

CENTRAL PARK

Central Park S.

Carnegie Hall

New York Hilton

Museum of Modern Art

GE Building

Rockefeller Center

Two Times Square

Marriott Marquis

Times Square

One Times Square

Port Authority Terminal

Bryant Park

New York Public Library

variety of toppings. If you're in the mood for even more calories, the tempting selection of shakes is extremely difficult to resist. The only drawback is that there are no french fries—you'll have to settle for "dirty potato chips." ☒ *766 9th Ave., between W. 51st and W. 52nd Sts., Midtown West* ☎ *212/307–7934* ▭ *No credit cards* Ⓜ *Subway: C, E to 50th St.*

Barbecue

☾ **$–$$** ✕ **Virgil's Real BBQ.** Neon, wood, and Formica set the scene at this massive roadhouse in the theater district. Start with stuffed jalapeños or—especially—unbelievably succulent barbecued chicken wings. Then, what the hell: go for the "pig out"—a rack of pork ribs, Texas hot links, pulled pork, rack of lamb, chicken, and, of course, more. It's that kind of place. There are also five domestic microbrews on tap and a good list of top beers from around the world. The place is absolutely mobbed pretheater, so if that's when you're going, arrive by 6 PM. ☒ *152 W. 44th St., between 6th Ave. and Broadway, Midtown West* ☎ *212/921–9494* ⌕ *Reservations essential* ▭ *AE, MC, V* Ⓜ *Subway: N, Q, R, S, W, 1, 2, 3, 7 to 42nd St./Times Sq.*

Brazilian

★ **$$$$** ✕ **Churrascaria Plataforma.** This sprawling, boisterous shrine to meat, with its all-you-can-eat prix-fixe menu, is best experienced with a group of ravenous friends, preferably teenaged football players. A *caipirinha* (sugarcane liquor and lime) will kick you off nicely, then hit the vast salad bar groaning with vegetables, meats, cheeses, and hot tureens of *feijoada* (beans, pork, greens, and manioc). But restrain yourself—there's an ongoing parade of all manner of grilled meats and poultry, brought to the table on long skewers until you beg for mercy. ☒ *316 W. 49th St., between 8th and 9th Aves., Midtown West* ☎ *212/245–0505* ⌕ *Reservations essential* ▭ *AE, DC, MC, V* Ⓜ *Subway: C, E to 50th St.*

Cafés

¢ ✕ **Cupcake Café.** Intensely buttery, magnificently decorated cakes and cupcakes, as well as doughnuts, pies, coffee cake, and hearty soup, are worth the trek to this funky spot on the western flank of the Port Authority Bus Terminal (a somewhat sketchy area). ☒ *522 9th Ave., at W. 39th St., Midtown West* ☎ *212/465–1530* ▭ *No credit cards* Ⓜ *Subway: A, C, E to 42nd St.*

Chinese

$–$$ ✕ **Joe's Shanghai.** Joe opened his first Shanghai restaurant in Queens, but, buoyed by the accolades accorded his steamed soup dumplings—magically filled with a rich, fragrant broth and a pork or pork-and-crabmeat mixture—he saw fit to open in Manhattan's Chinatown, and then here in Midtown. Menu highlights include turnip shortcakes and dried bean curd salad to start, and succulent braised pork shoulder, ropey homemade Shanghai noodles, and traditional lion's head—rich pork meatballs braised in brown sauce—to follow. ☒ *24 W. 56th St., between 5th and 6th Aves., Midtown West* ☎ *212/333–3868* ▭ *AE, DC, MC, V* Ⓜ *Subway: F to 57th St.*

¢–**$$** ✕ **Grand Sichuan International.** This regional Chinese restaurant serves a vast menu of specialties you probably won't find anywhere else. The

18

emphasis is on fiery Sichuan (Szechuan) cooking, but Cantonese, Hunan, Shanghai, and even American Chinese food are represented (a handy treatise and guide on Chinese food comes with the menu). Spicy dan dan noodles, shredded potatoes in vinegar sauce, crab soup dumplings, minced pork with cellophane noodles or fermented green beans, and sautéed loofah are among the hauntingly delicious dishes. ⊠ *745 9th Ave., between W. 50th and W. 51st Sts., Midtown West* ☎ *212/582–2288* ▤ *AE, MC, V* Ⓜ *Subway: C, E to 50th St.*

Contemporary

★ **$$$$** ✕ **Town.** It's difficult to decide which is more soigné in this bi-level restaurant: the design, the food, or the crowd. Ubiquitous architect David Rockwell has created a contemporary restaurant with a truly international feel. Geoffrey Zakarian's cooking is every bit as sophisticated as the environment. The prix-fixe menu lists such dishes as a lovely escargot risotto, wild striped bass roasted with foie gras butter, and tender duck steak with buckwheat pilaf. All are intricate exercises in culinary craft. ⊠ *15 W. 56th St., between 5th and 6th Aves., Midtown West* ☎ *212/582–4445* ⌓ *Reservations essential* ▤ *AE, D, DC, MC, V* Ⓜ *Subway: F to 57th St.*

Continental

$$–$$$$ ✕ **Petrossian.** Set like a magnificent jewel in the glorious historic Alwyn
Fodor'sChoice Court Building, Petrossian closely resembles a haute Parisian restaurant.
★ In addition to the highly luxurious caviars and silky smoked salmon, masterful chef Michael Lipp will pan-roast a wild sturgeon, or roast caviar-crusted sea scallops and plate them with seared foie gras. For dessert, go for roasted pineapple and coconut cake. The café next door serves an enticing selection of creative treats—plus caviar, of course. ⊠ *182 W. 58th St., at 7th Ave., Midtown West* ☎ *212/245–2214* ⌓ *Reservations essential* ▤ *AE, DC, MC, V* Ⓜ *Subway: F, N, R, Q, W to 57th St.*

Cuban

$–$$$ ✕ **Victor's Café.** The heady aroma of authentic Cuban cooking greets you as you enter this Technicolor restaurant, a neighborhood fixture since 1963. The high-back booths and rattan chairs evoke golden-age movies set in Old Havana. Better than average, the food is a contemporary transcription of Cuban, Puerto Rican, and Latin dishes, such as hearty adobo, paella, adobo-rubbed prime steak, and suckling pig marinated and roasted on a plantain leaf. The staff couldn't be friendlier. ⊠ *236 W. 52nd St., between Broadway and 8th Ave., Midtown West* ☎ *212/ 586–7714* ▤ *AE, DC, MC, V* Ⓜ *Subway: C, E to 50th St.*

¢–$$ ✕ **Havana Central.** There are 1950s "Cuban" touches throughout this two-story restaurant, from the enormous ceiling fans to glimmering palm trees. The bar keeps busy turning out the best mojitos in town—rummy, not too sweet, with limes and mint muddled just enough to sharpen the edges. Chef Stanley Licairic prodigiously produces truly authentic Cuban home cooking, often in massive portions. Empanadas are well-stuffed pockets of dough the size of your fist, brimming with tangy beef picadillo, chicken sofrito, shrimp, or broccoli and cheese. Don't miss the churros—sugared flutes of dough that are flash-fried to order and served piping hot with ramekins of *dulce de leche* and thick chocolate sauce. ⊠ *151*

W. 46th St., between 6th and 7th Aves., Midtown West ☎ *212/398–7440* ⊟ *AE, DC, MC, V* Ⓜ *Subway: R, W to 49th St.*

Delicatessens

☺ **$–$$** ✕ **Carnegie Deli.** Although not what it once was, this no-nonsense deli is still a favorite with out-of-towners. The portions are so huge you feel like a child in some surreal culinary fairy tale. The matzo balls could eat Chicago, the knishes hang off the edge of the plates, and some combination sandwiches are so tall they have to be held together with bamboo skewers. Don't miss the cheesecake, to some palates the best in the city. ⊠ *854 7th Ave., at W. 55th St., Midtown West* ☎ *212/757–2245* ⊟ *No credit cards* Ⓜ *Subway: B, C, D, E to 7th Ave.; N, R, Q, W to 57th St.*

Ethiopian

¢–$ ✕ **Meskerem.** The tasty Ethiopian delicacies offered in this Hell's Kitchen storefront include *kitfo* (spiced ground steak), which you can order raw, rare, or well done, and *yebeg alecha,* tender pieces of lamb marinated in Ethiopian butter flavored with curry, rosemary, and an herb called *kosart,* and then sautéed with fresh ginger and a bit more curry. The vegetarian combination, served on injera (a yeasty flat bread used as a utensil to sop up the food) is a seriously good deal. ⊠ *468 W. 47th St., near 10th Ave., Midtown West* ☎ *212/664–0520* ⊟ *AE, DC, MC, V* Ⓜ *Subway: C, E to 50th St.*

French

$$$$ ✕ **Alain Ducasse.** Created by France's most copiously decorated chef, this FodorsChoice special-occasion shrine to French cuisine is an exercise in unbridled lux-
★ ury. If you manage to reserve a table in the hushed 65-seat dining room, it's yours for the entire evening, and you'll need the time to navigate your way through some of the most luscious food in town. Let sommelier André Compeyre partner your dishes with exquisite wines. Be fully aware that such exquisiteness comes at a hefty price. Two people could very easily drop $1,000 or more. But you'll never forget the meal. ⊠ *Essex House, 155 W. 58th St., between 6th and 7th Aves., Midtown West* ☎ *212/265–7300* ⩘ *Reservations essential* ⌂ *Jacket and tie* ⊟ *AE, D, DC, MC, V* ⊗ *Closed Sun. No lunch* Ⓜ *Subway: B, C, D, E to 7th Ave.; N, Q, R, W to 57th St.*

$$$$ ✕ **Le Bernardin.** Owner Maguy LeCoze presides over the plush, teak-panel FodorsChoice dining room at this trendsetting French seafood restaurant, and endlessly
★ handsome chef-partner Eric Ripert works magic with anything that swims—preferring at times not to cook it at all. Deceptively simple dishes such as poached lobster in rich coconut-ginger soup or crispy spiced black bass in a Peking duck bouillon are typical of his style. There's no beating Le Bernardin for thrilling French cuisine, seafood or otherwise, coupled with some of the finest desserts in town. ⊠ *155 W. 51st St., between 6th and 7th Aves., Midtown West* ☎ *212/489–1515* ⩘ *Reservations essential* ⌂ *Jacket required* ⊟ *AE, DC, MC, V* ⊗ *Closed Sun. No lunch Sat.* Ⓜ *Subway: R, W to 49th St.; B, D, F, V to 47th–50th Sts./Rockefeller Ctr.*

$$–$$$ ✕ **Brasserie 8 1/2.** Brasserie's quieter younger sister is a subterranean restaurant with some visual and culinary charms all its own. The dramatic staircase releases you into a spacious cocktail lounge with black leather sofas

18

and a plush dining room beyond. The menu is flush with the creative cooking of Julian Alonzo. Nothing Felliniesque, just solid contemporary French cooking: Chatham cod with cassloulet, rabbit cooked three ways, truffle-crusted loin of lamb. The frites alone are worth a trip to Midtown. ⊠ *9 W. 57th St., between 5th and 6th Aves., Midtown West* ☏ *212/829–0812* ⊟ *AE, D, MC, V* Ⓜ *Subway: R, W to 5th Ave.*

★ **$$–$$$** ✕ **db bistro moderne.** Daniel Boulud's "casual bistro" (it's neither, actually) consists of two elegantly appointed rooms. The menu is organized by the French names of seasonal ingredients—lobster (*homard*), tuna (*thon*), and mushroom (*champignon*), *par exemple*. Within each category, appetizers and main courses are listed. There was quite a fuss made over the $29 hamburger, available at lunch and dinner. But considering it is gloriously stuffed with braised short ribs, foie gras, and black truffles, it's almost a bargain. ⊠ *55 W. 44th St., between 5th and 6th Aves., Midtown West* ☏ *212/391–5353* ⌕ *Reservations essential* ⊟ *AE, MC, V* ⊘ *No lunch Sun.* Ⓜ *Subway: B, D, F, V to 42nd St.*

★ **$$–$$$** ✕ **Triomphe.** You have to be pretty self-confident to name your restaurant Triomphe, but indeed the team behind this jewel box in the Iroquois Hotel has triumphed. The intimate dining room is pleasing but unfussy, and chef Steve Zobel's focused menu is bold and ambitious yet understated. Appetizers include such lusciousness as pan-seared sea scallops with porcini mushroom foie gras butter, and entrées are the likes of lamb rack with foie gras–stuffed prunes (known as French kisses). ⊠ *49 W. 44th St., between 5th and 6th Aves., Midtown West* ☏ *212/453–4233* ⌕ *Reservations essential* ⊟ *AE, D, MC, V* ⊘ *Closed Sun. No lunch Sat.* Ⓜ *Subway: B, D, F, V to 47th–50th Sts./Rockefeller Ctr.*

$–$$$ ✕ **Marseille.** A fetching brasserie outfitted with dark-cherry leather banquettes beautifully showcases the soulful Mediterranean–North African cooking of Andy D'Amico. Begin with mezes (think tapas), like juicy merguez sausages or marinated sardines with an orange-saffron glaze. Grilled octopus is deeply flavored, and bouillabaisse is classically prepared, with four North Atlantic fillets and a nice garlicky rouille on the side. Service is skillful. The place is often mobbed before and after theater, usually restful from 8 to 10:30, but always intensely delicious. ⊠ *630 9th Ave., at W. 44th St., Midtown West* ☏ *212/333–3410* ⌕ *Reservations essential* ⊟ *AE, D, MC, V* Ⓜ *Subway: A, C, E to 42nd St.*

$–$$$ ✕ **Seppi's.** With a prime location just steps from Carnegie Hall and City Center, reasonable prices, and a 2 AM closing time, this luscious French bistro attracts a devoted clientele, including more than a few celebrities. Tender tarte flambée (Alsatian pizza) is carved into manageable finger-length rectangles, escargots are given their classic—and rapidly vanishing—presentation, and steak au poivre is as good as it gets, with deeply beefy gravy. All this and much more—including 15 desserts—are served until closing. ⊠ *123 W. 56th St., between 6th and 7th Aves., Midtown West* ☏ *212/453–4233* ⌕ *Reservations essential* ⊟ *AE, D, MC, V* ⊘ *No lunch Sat.* Ⓜ *Subway: B, D, E to 7th Ave., F, N, Q, R, W to 57th St.*

German

¢–$ ✕ **Hallo Berlin.** When nothing but bratwurst will do, lunge for this Hell's Kitchen café. There are more than 10 varieties of wursts, accompanied

Food Festivals

NEW YORK LOVES ITS STREET FAIRS—there are more than 150 in Manhattan alone. These giant block parties are host to crafts vendors, local shops' sale tables, and fast food from all over the city. Typically, you can sample Greek gyros, Belgian fries in a cone, Israeli couscous, Egyptian falafel, Thai spring rolls—and the list keeps going with Chinese, Mexican, and French.

Whole sections of streets, sometimes 10 to 20 blocks long, are blocked off, so pedestrians can walk freely. But even with the additional space it's a mad crush of bodies, strollers, and bikes. If you're lucky, it's a pleasant stroll down the middle of the street, but more often it's quite a squeeze. A less-crowded alternative is **Pickle Day,** when the Lower East Side's pickle geniuses strut their stuff, selling everything from pickled mangos to kimchi to New York's finest kosher dills.

Many ethnic organizations sponsor festivals throughout the year—countries from Brazil (early Sept.) to Romania (early May) are represented. Chinatown's **Lunar New Year Festival** has lion dances, regulated firecracker displays, and moon cakes (mid-Feb.). The **National Tartan Day Parade,** which gathers together Scotsmen from all over North America, features bagpipe and drum marching bands and a whisky tasting (early Apr.). Taste fresh shad and watch how it's planked (a special way of cooking it) while listening to Native American drumming at the **Shad Festival** along the Hudson (May). Billed as New York's biggest and oldest street fest, Little Italy's **Feast of San Gennaro** has parades, a cannoli-eating contest, and a candlelight procession with a statue of the saint (mid- to late Sept.).

18

by traditional German side dishes such as sauerkraut, spaetzle, or particularly addictive panfried potatoes. The atmosphere is low-budget Berlin beer garden, and the low, low prices match the lack of pretension. There are other authentic dishes on the menu, but none can compete with a sausage paired with a cold pint of German beer. ⊠ *402 W. 51st St., between 9th and 10th Aves., Midtown West* ☎ *212/541–6248* ⊟ *No credit cards* ⊗ *No lunch Sun.* Ⓜ *Subway: C, E to 50th St.*

Greek

★ **$$$–$$$$** ✕ **Estiatorio Milos.** This dramatic, dazzling restaurant flaunts whitewashed walls, table umbrellas, and sultry European diners. Classic spreads—*tzatziki* (yogurt-cucumber), *tarama* (smoked carp roe–olive oil–lemon), and *scordalia* (almonds-garlic)—make a delicious appetizer. If you're feeling flush, select from the glimmering display of fresh Mediterranean seafood flown in every day. Your choice will be weighed (fair warning: you pay by the pound), grilled whole, and filleted tableside. For dessert, don't pass up thick Greek-style goat's-milk yogurt with thyme honey. ⊠ *125 W. 55th St., between 6th and 7th Aves., Midtown West* ☎ *212/245–7400* ✐ *Reservations essential* ⊟ *AE, D, MC, V* Ⓜ *Subway: F, N, Q, R, W to 57th St.*

★ **$$–$$$$** ✕ **Molyvos.** Fresh ingredients, lusty flavors, fine olive oil, and fragrant herbs emerge from Jim Botsacos's marvelous kitchen at this upscale taverna. Start with a bang: *saganaki* (fried *kefalotiri* cheese), or a lump meat crab cake aching with flavor. Seasonal entrées include traditional Greek dishes, such as a perfected moussaka, lamb *yuvetsi* (marinated lamb shanks braised in a clay pot), and cabbage *dolmades* (cabbage stuffed with ground lamb in a lemon-dill sauce). The baklava will make you completely rethink that poor abused dessert. ⊠ *871 7th Ave., between W. 55th and W. 56th Sts., Midtown West* ☎ *212/582–7500* ⌣ *Reservations essential* ▤ *AE, D, DC, MC, V* Ⓜ *Subway: F, N, Q, R, W to 57th St.*

Italian

$$–$$$$ ✕ **Osteria del Circo.** Opened by the sons of celebrity-restaurateur Sirio Maccioni, this less-formal restaurant celebrates the Tuscan cooking of their Mamma Egi. The contemporary menu offers a wide selection and includes some traditional Tuscan specialties, such as Egi's ricotta-and-spinach-filled ravioli, tossed in butter and sage and gratinéed with imported Parmesan, and a stew of prawns, cuttlefish, octopus, monkfish, clams, and mussels. Don't miss the fanciful Circo desserts, especially the filled *bomboloncini* doughnuts. ⊠ *120 W. 55th St., between 6th and 7th Aves., Midtown West* ☎ *212/265–3636* ⌣ *Reservations essential* ▤ *AE, DC, MC, V* ☉ *No lunch Sun.* Ⓜ *Subway: F, N, Q, R, W to 57th St.*

$–$$$$ ✕ **Baldoria.** It's not possible to get into Frank Pellegrino's restaurant Rao's, an institution in Harlem, so try Frank Jr.'s theater district edition. The bi-level restaurant is almost 10 times the size of Rao's, but the atmosphere is still homey and personal. The raw bar is one of the best-stocked in town. Seared octopus is plated with broccoli rabe, cippolini onions, and balsamic reduction. Fluffy gnocchi are napped with a ground veal, pork, and beef tomato sauce. And the lemon chicken in a red vinegar, oregano, and garlic sauce is even tastier than Dad's uptown. ⊠ *249 W. 49th St., between Broadway and 8th Ave., Midtown West* ☎ *212/582–0460* ⌣ *Reservations essential* ▤ *AE, D, MC, V* ☉ *No lunch weekends* Ⓜ *Subway: C, E to 50th St.*

$–$$$$ ✕ **Trattoria Dell'Arte.** This popular trattoria near Carnegie Hall is known for the oversize renderings of body parts (like the giant nose in the front window) displayed alongside portraits of Italian artists in its three dining rooms. The food commands attention, too, from the mouthwatering antipasti on the bar to the tasty pasta, pizza, hot focaccia sandwiches, and gargantuan grilled double veal chop served with shoestring potatoes. Check out the wonderful cannoli, great wine list, and flavored grappas. ⊠ *900 7th Ave., between W. 56th and W. 57th Sts., Midtown West* ☎ *212/245–9800* ⌣ *Reservations essential* ▤ *AE, DC, MC, V* Ⓜ *Subway: F, N, Q, R, W to 57th St.*

$$–$$$ ✕ **Abboccato.** Making a delightful attempt to convey the wide regional Italian palate in its near entirety, Abboccato is the third marvelous restaurant to be opened by the Livanos family (after Oceana and Molyvos). There are some highly unusual—in this country—dishes, like Umbrian quail, boned and stuffed with mortadella, formed into a ball, breaded, and fried. The richest possible carbonara sauce features creamy duck eggs and duck prosciutto. You'd have to look a long time in Italy to find this dish, but vanilla-scented veal cheeks that melt in your mouth are plated with chocolate and spice-stewed wild boar and luscious po-lenta. ⊠ *136 W. 55th St., between 6th and 7th Aves., Midtown West* ☎ *212/265–4000* ⌯ *Reservations essential* ▭ *AE, DC, MC, V* Ⓜ *Subway: N, R to 57th St.*

$$–$$$ ✕ **Barbetta.** Operated by the same family since it opened in 1906, Bar-betta offers a uniquely authentic Piedmontese experience in a throwback of a dining room that evokes the tired, old-world charm of Turin. The vast menu highlights dishes from the restaurant's past, as well as tradi-tional Piedmontese cooking. Pasta, like the eggy tajarin, and risotto stand out. A beautiful garden affords a lovely summertime setting. Inciden-tally, Barbetta claims to be the first restaurant in New York to serve white truffles, in 1962. ⊠ *321 W. 46th St., between 8th and 9th Aves., Mid-town West* ☎ *212/246–9171* ▭ *AE, D, DC, MC, V* ⊘ *Closed Sun. and Mon.* Ⓜ *Subway: A, C, E to 42nd St.*

$$–$$$ ✕ **Becco.** An ingenious concept makes Becco a prime Restaurant Row choice for time-constrained theatergoers. There are two pricing scenarios: one includes an all-you-can-eat selection of antipasti and three pastas served hot out of pans that waiters circulate around the dining room; the other adds a generous entrée. The selection changes daily but often includes gnoc-chi, fresh ravioli, and something in a cream sauce. The entrées include braised veal shank, rack of lamb, and various fish. ⊠ *355 W. 46th St., between 8th and 9th Aves., Midtown West* ☎ *212/397–7597* ⌯ *Reservations es-sential* ▭ *AE, DC, MC, V* Ⓜ *Subway: A, C, E to 42nd St.*

★ **$$–$$$** ✕ **San Domenico.** A dedicated ambassador of authentic Italian cuisine, dapper owner Tony May presides over his lush dining room, where gauzy drapes swathe the wraparound windows that gaze onto Central Park. Don't miss chef Odette Fada's signature truffle-butter-dribbled ravioli pocketing a quivering egg yolk filling. Reconstituted salt cod is whipped into submission with house olive oil, and served with polenta crostini. Goat—in line to be the hot "new" ingredient on next year's toniest menus—is done three delicious ways: pureed, fried, and braised on the bone. ⊠ *240 Central Park S, between Broadway and 7th Ave., Mid-town West* ☎ *212/265–5959* ⌯ *Reservations essential* ⌂ *Jacket required* ▭ *AE, DC, MC, V* ⊘ *No lunch weekends* Ⓜ *Subway: A, B, C, D, 1, 2 to 59th St./Columbus Circle.*

$–$$$ ✕ **Acqua Pazza.** Endlessly chic and sexy, Acqua Pazza attracts all sorts of clever people. The kitchen has widened its focus from a nearly all-seafood menu to include meat and poultry, as well as some highly imaginative pastas, like espresso-flavor tagliolini with rock shrimp and porcini mush-rooms. For a Milanese presentation, a large veal rib chop is flattened, breaded, and plated with fluttery arugula, tomatoes, and buffalo moz-zarella—quite a delicious bargain at $24. The wine list is especially user-friendly. ⊠ *36 W. 52nd St., between 5th and 6th Aves., Midtown West* ☎ *212/582–6900* ⌯ *Reservations essential* ▭ *AE, D, DC, MC, V* Ⓜ *Subway: B, D, F, V to 47th–50th Sts./Rockefeller Center.*

Ⓒ **$–$$$** ✕ **Il Gattopardo.** As sleek and poised as the leopard it is named for, this southern Italian newcomer attracts plenty of soigné regulars. Rare and juicy beef-veal meatballs swathed and braised in savoy cabbage leaves are a marvelous signature dish and a must. Tender house-made pastas are imaginatively sauced. Thick veal scallops are bundled

18

around eggplant and smoked mozzarella cheese for great depth of flavor. Finish with *pastiera*, traditional Neapolitan cheesecake—Christmas in your mouth! ☒ *33 W. 54th St., between 5th and 6th Aves., Midtown West* ☎ *212/246–0412* ▭ *AE, DC, MC, V* Ⓜ *Subway: B, N, Q, R to 57th St.*

★ **$–$$$** ✕ **Nino's Tuscany.** Debonair restaurateur Nino Selimaj's fifth restaurant is his best and most beautiful. Designer Nick Grande has imbued the capacious and elegant restaurant with just the right romantic glow, and Michael Litzig's beautiful murals of Tuscan landscapes give the space an idyllic splendor that will make you sigh. The wine list is intelligently assembled, and service is seamless, expert, and rapt. Chef Sal Maurocco's soups and sauces are especially wonderful, and dense lamb meatballs are perked up by their light lemony broth reduction. The only thing keeping fluffy potato gnocchi from dancing on the ceiling is their deeply delicious Gorgonzola cream sauce. Don't leave without trying a flask of zabaglione, prepared table-side. ☒ *117 W. 58th St., between 6th and 7th Aves., Midtown West* ☎ *212/757–8630* ▭ *AE, DC, MC, V* Ⓜ *Subway: B, N, Q, R to 57th St.*

$–$$$ ✕ **Remi.** A Venetian sensibility pervades this stylish restaurant, with its skylit atrium, blue-and-white stripe banquettes, glass chandeliers, and a soaring room-length mural of the city of canals. And its Venetian cuisine is equally stylish: fresh sardines make a lovely beginning, with their contrasting toasted pine nut–and–golden raisin sauce, and you can't go wrong with the luscious pastas, expertly prepared rack of lamb, or any of the wonderful desserts. ☒ *145 W. 53rd St., between 6th and 7th Aves., Midtown West* ☎ *212/581–4242* ⌢ *Reservations essential* ▭ *AE, DC, MC, V* ⊘ *No lunch weekends* Ⓜ *Subway: E, V to 5th Ave./53rd St.*

Ⓒ **$$** ✕ **Carmine's.** Savvy New Yorkers line up early for the affordable family-style meals (read: massive portions to share) at this large, busy eatery. There are no reservations taken for parties of fewer than six people after 7 PM, but those who wait are rewarded with mountains of such popular, toothsome items as fried calamari, linguine with white clam sauce, chicken parmigiana, and veal saltimbocca. You'll inevitably order too much, but most of the food tastes just as wonderful the next day. ☒ *200 W. 44th St., between Broadway and 8th Ave., Midtown West* ☎ *212/ 221–3800* ▭ *AE, D, DC, MC, V* Ⓜ *Subway: N, Q, R, S, W, 1, 2, 3, 7 to 42nd St./Times Sq.*

$–$$ ✕ **Scarlatto.** In the theater district, amidst the tourist traps, chain restaurants, and purveyors of just plain mediocre fare, often at ghastly prices, have arrived some truly choice alternatives. The latest to join this group is Scarlatto. Pale sage leather-upholstered chairs and candles are everywhere in the track-lighted space. Venetian Roberto Passon gently fries baby calamari and plates them with roasted eggplant puree and dots of a balsamic reduction. Fusilli commingle deliciously with chopped chicken livers in a gentle white wine sauce. Wild boar is braised slowly in burgundy with juniper, carrots, and zucchini, and plated alongside some particularly well-seasoned polenta. A banana tart makes a great finish, and it's none too sweet. ☒ *250 W. 47th St., between Broadway and 8th Ave., Midtown West* ☎ *212/730–4535* ⌢ *Reservations not accepted* ▭ *D, DC, MC, V* Ⓜ *Subway: R, W to 49th St.*

Japanese

$$$$ ✕ **Sugiyama.** Acquaint yourself with the Japanese style of eating known as *kaiseki*, a meal of small portions presented in a ritualized order, at this charming prix-fixe-only restaurant. First timers should order the omakase (chef's tasting) to appreciate the true breadth of the genre. It may start with a wild mountain plum floating in a glassy cube of gelatin, and proceed to a gurgling pot of blowfish or to sweet lobster to be cooked on a hot stone. The experience is exhilarating. ⊠ *251 W. 55th St., between Broadway and 8th Ave., Midtown West* ☎ *212/956–0670* ▭ *AE, D, MC, V* ⊘ *Closed Sun. and Mon. No lunch* Ⓜ *Subway: A, B, C, D, 1, 2 to 59th St.–Columbus Circle.*

Kosher

$–$$$ ✕ **Le Marais.** The appetizing display of meats and terrines at the entrance, the bare-wood floors, tables covered with butcher paper, the French wall posters, and maroon banquettes will remind you of a Parisian bistro. Yet the clientele (mostly male) is strictly kosher (as is the food), and they don't speak French. Start with pan-seared sweetbreads with wild mushrooms, and follow with perfect steak au poivre (dairy-free, of course). The accompanying fries are perfect. ⊠ *150 W. 46th St., between 6th and 7th Aves., Midtown West* ☎ *212/869–0900* ▭ *AE, MC, V* ⊘ *Closed Sat. No dinner Fri.* Ⓜ *Subway: R, W to 49th St.*

Russian

$$$–$$$$ ✕ **Firebird.** Eight dining rooms full of objets d'art and period antiques lie within these two brownstones resembling a pre-Revolutionary St. Petersburg mansion. Staples of the regional cuisine range from caviar and *zakuska* (assorted Russian hors d'oeuvres) to porcini-crusted monkfish, hot-smoked salmon with saffron orzo and herb salad, and beet borscht with duck, beef, smoked pork, and mushroom pirogi. Great desserts (an assortment of Russian cookies steals the show) and an extraordinary vodka selection are giddy indulgences. ⊠ *365 W. 46th St., between 8th and 9th Aves., Midtown West* ☎ *212/586–0244* ⌕ *Reservations essential* ▭ *AE, DC, MC, V* ⊘ *Closed Mon. No lunch Sun.* Ⓜ *Subway: A, C, E to 42nd St.*

Seafood

$$–$$$ ✕ **Esca.** Mario Batali's Esca, Italian for "bait," lures diners in with delectable raw preparations called *cruda*—such as tilefish with orange and Sardinian oil or pink snapper with a sprinkle of crunchy red clay salt—and hooks them with such entrées as whole, salt-crusted *branzino* (sea bass), or *bucatini* pasta with spicy baby octopus. The menu changes daily. Some find the food here too salty, some don't, but if you're a low-sodium kind of diner, you should probably cast your net elsewhere. Batali's partner, Joe Bastianich, is in charge of the wine cellar, so expect an adventurous list of esoteric Italian bottles. ⊠ *402 W. 43rd St., at 9th Ave., Midtown West* ☎ *212/564–7272* ⌕ *Reservations essential* ▭ *AE, DC, MC, V* ⊘ *No lunch Sun.* Ⓜ *Subway: A, C, E to 42nd St.*

Steak

★ **$$$–$$$$** ✕ **Uncle Jack's Steakhouse.** Surpassing even its celebrated flagship restaurant in Bayside, Queens, Uncle Jack's soars directly into the pantheon

18

of the best steak houses in Manhattan. As in most great steak houses, you can feel the testosterone throbbing all through the place. The space is vast and gorgeously appointed, and service is swift and focused. USDA Prime steaks are dry-aged for 21 days. Australian lobster tails are so enormous they have to be served carved, yet the flesh is meltingly tender. ⊠ *440 9th Ave., between W. 34th and W. 35th Sts., Midtown West* ☎ *212/244–0005* ⚜ *Reservations essential* ▤ *AE, DC, MC, V* ✸ *Closed Sun. No lunch weekends* Ⓜ *Subway: A, C, E to 34th St.*

★ **$$–$$$$** ✕ **Ben Benson's Steak House.** Among the most venerable steak houses around, Ben Benson's feels like a clubby hunting lodge. The gracefully choreographed, intensely focused staff will bring you only the finest dry-aged USDA-graded prime meats and only the freshest seafood, all classically prepared, teeming with familiar and beloved flavors. All the trimmings are ravishing, too: perfect creamed spinach, sizzling onion rings, and decadent hash browns are essential. Power lunches were practically invented here; just being in the place makes you feel important. ⊠ *123 W. 52nd St., between 6th and 7th Aves., Midtown West* ☎ *212/581–8888* ⚜ *Reservations essential* ▤ *AE, DC, MC, V* ✸ *No lunch weekends* Ⓜ *Subway: B, D, F, V to 47th–50th Sts./Rockefeller Center.*

$–$$$$ ✕ **Palm.** They may have added tablecloths, but it would take more than that to hide the brusque, no-nonsense nature of this West Side branch of the legendary steak house. The steak is always impeccable, and the lobsters are so big—4 pounds and up—there may not be room at the table for such classic side dishes as rich creamed spinach. The "half and half" side combination of cottage-fried potatoes and fried onions is particularly addictive. ⊠ *250 W. 50th St., between Broadway and 8th Ave., Midtown West* ☎ *212/333–7256* ⚜ *Reservations essential* ▤ *AE, DC, MC, V* ✸ *No lunch weekends* Ⓜ *Subway: F, N, Q, R, W to 57th St.*

MIDTOWN EAST

Power brokers like to seal their deals over lunch on the East Side, so that means more than a few suits and ties at the restaurants during the day. At night the streets are relatively deserted, but the restaurants are filled with people celebrating success over some of the finest, most expensive, and most formal food in town.

American

★ **$$$–$$$$** ✕ **Four Seasons.** The landmark Seagram Building houses one of America's most famous restaurants, truly an only-in-New York experience. The stark Grill Room, birthplace of the power lunch, has one of the best bars in New York. Illuminated trees and a gurgling Carrara marble pool characterize the more romantic Pool Room. The menu changes seasonally; there's a $55 prix-fixe pretheater dinner—quite a good bargain. You can't go wrong with Dover sole, sumptuous crab cake, or crispy duck, which features a table-side final preparation with considerable flourish. ⊠ *99 E. 52nd St., between Park and Lexington Aves., Midtown East* ☎ *212/754–9494* ⚜ *Reservations essential* ⋒ *Jacket required*

= *AE, DC, MC, V* ⊗ *Closed Sun. No lunch Sat.* Ⓜ *Subway: E, F, 6 to 51st St.*

$–$$$$ ✕ **Monkey Bar.** Tucked deep inside the swank Elysée Hotel, behind the adjoining Monkey Bar itself, is this highly cinematic art deco restaurant. Starters include the colossal lump crab cake with red Russian kale and a vegetable tartar sauce. For the main course, try something from the grill—a rib chop or toothsome lamb chops or achingly fresh seafood. ⊠ *60 E. 54th St., between Madison and Park Aves., Midtown East* ☎ *212/838–1600* = *AE, DC, MC, V* Ⓜ *Subway: N, R, W, 4, 5, 6 to Lexington Ave./59th St.*

$$–$$$ ✕ **Metrazur.** A beautiful new "wine wall" highlights the reimagined Metrazur, in the Grand Central Station concourse, where chef Michael Lockard has gussied up the menu considerably. The platter of shellfish comes with a quarter of a lobster, littleneck clams, Peconic Bay oysters, and jumbo shrimp. "Ten-hour cross-cut of veal" turns out to be extravagant osso bucco, with the shank simmered into spoon-tender submission. Bittersweet chocolate mousse is plated on chocolate shingles and dotted with dried cherries reconstituted in cognac. ⊠ *Grand Central Station, E. 42nd St., at Park Ave. Midtown East* ☎ *212/687–4600* = *AE, DC, MC, V* Ⓜ *Subway: 4, 5, 6 to 42nd St./Grand Central.*

American-Casual

🐣 **¢–$** ✕ **Comfort Diner.** If you're in search of a quick, casual, and satisfying meal, true to its name, Comfort Diner is more than happy to oblige, with a menu of such deeply American fare as buffalo wings, Caesar salad, grilled chicken club sandwich, macaroni and cheese, meat loaf, and burgers. The pies and cakes are baked fresh daily. The chrome and terrazzo may look a bit faded, but at least the price is right. Prepare to wait in line for the popular weekend brunch. ⊠ *214 E. 45th St., between 2nd and 3rd Aves., Midtown East* ☎ *212/867–4555* ⌲ *Reservations not accepted* = *D, DC, MC, V* Ⓜ *Subway: S, 4, 5, 6, 7 to 42nd St./Grand Central.*

Chinese

$$–$$$ ✕ **Shun Lee Palace.** If you want inexpensive Cantonese food without pretensions, head to Chinatown; but if you prefer to be pampered and don't mind spending a lot of money, this is the place. The cuisine is absolutely classic Chinese. Beijing panfried dumplings make a good starter, and rack of lamb Szechuan style is a popular entrée. Beijing duck is sure to please. ⊠ *155 E. 55th St., between Lexington and 3rd Aves., Midtown East* ☎ *212/371–8844* ⌲ *Reservations essential* = *AE, DC, MC, V* Ⓜ *Subway: N, R, W, 4, 5, 6 to 59th St./Lexington Ave.*

Contemporary

$$$$ ✕ **March.** This romantic restaurant is tucked into an enchanting town house. Co-owner Joseph Scalice supervises the polished service and the intriguing wine list that complement the cuisine of his partner, chef Wayne Nish, master of classical French technique with a strong Asian influence. The prix-fixe menu is organized into tasting categories. Select any number of courses, then choose from a list of seasonal dishes, such as five-spice salmon with wild mushrooms, and luxury plates, like duck foie gras with Indian spices and port wine, apple, and sultana raisin

18

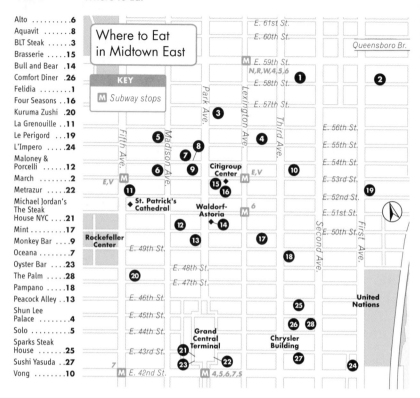

Where to Eat
in Midtown East

KEY

Ⓜ Subway stops

puree. Finish with banana marquise with chocolate-and-banana mousse, spice cake, and ice cream. ✉ *405 E. 58th St., between 1st Ave. and Sutton Pl., Midtown East* ☎ *212/754–6272* ⌕ *Reservations essential* ▭ *AE, DC, MC, V* Ⓜ *Subway: N, R, W, 4, 5, 6 to 59th St./Lexington Ave.*

$$–$$$$ ✕ **Maloney & Porcelli.** Known for generous portions of whimsical American food, this comfortable restaurant (named for the owner's lawyers) is ideal when you're dining with a hungry crowd of people (especially men) who can't decide where to eat. Lunge for a huge, juicy, crackling pork shank served on a bed of poppy-seed sauerkraut with a Mason jar of tangy, homemade "Firecracker" jalapeño-spiced apple sauce. "Drunken doughnuts," served warm with three small pots of liqueur-flavor jam, are one of the fun desserts. ✉ *37 E. 50th St., between Madison and Park Aves., Midtown East* ☎ *212/750–2233* ⌕ *Reservations essential* ▭ *AE, DC, MC, V* Ⓜ *Subway: 6 to 51st St.–Lexington Ave.*

$$–$$$$ ✕ **Peacock Alley.** When the illustrious Peacock Alley was shuttered shortly after 9/11, many a jaw dropped. But in part because you must come all the way inside the Waldorf-Astoria to find the restaurant—there is no separate entrance—the place never attracted the audience it so richly deserved. After a face-lift, however, the restaurant has returned, better than ever. Alsatian chef Cedric Tovar has created some especially enthralling dishes, such as slow-poached organic egg in a black truffle–and–mushroom sauce scattered with crisp bits of pancetta, and a plump and perfectly roasted guinea hen thigh sliced and plated in a pool of luscious ginger consommé. Pastry chef Nancy Olson's apple tart is as good as any in town. ⊠ *301 Park Ave., between E. 49th and E. 50th Sts., Midtown East* ☎ *212/872–4896* ⌖ *Reservations essential* ▭ *AE, DC, MC, V* Ⓜ *Subway: 6 to 51st St./Lexington Ave.*

French

★ **$$$$** ✕ **La Grenouille.** This is such a quintessential Manhattan French restaurant that it almost feels like a retro theme restaurant. At more than 40 years old, it's also one of the very few remaining classic French restaurants in town. The menu presents an $87 menu of three courses (with tempting supplements that fatten your bill). Choices include lobster-tarragon ravioli to start, followed by grilled Dover sole with mustard sauce, or sautéed frogs' legs Provençale. Finish with the lightest soufflé ever born. This isn't just about having memorable food—it's about having an unforgettable experience. ⊠ *3 E. 52nd St., between 5th and Madison Aves., Midtown East* ☎ *212/752–1495* ⌖ *Reservations essential* ▭ *AE, DC, MC, V* ⊘ *Closed Sun.* Ⓜ *Subway: E, V to 5th Ave./53rd St.*

$$$$ ✕ **Le Perigord.** Owner Georges Briguet has presided over his beautiful kingdom of high-end French cuisine for more than three decades, and he's the very definition of bonhomie; chef Joel Benjamin has pedigree and considerable flair. Start with succulent smoked salmon with a corn muffin, sour cream, and salmon roe. One of the restaurant's signature dishes, turbot with a comté cheese crust in champagne sauce, is alone worth a visit—or two. Don't forget to order a soufflé at the beginning of your meal. ⊠ *405 E. 52nd St., between FDR Dr. and 1st Ave., Midtown East* ☎ *212/755–6244* ⌖ *Reservations essential* 🍴 *Jacket required* ▭ *AE, DC, MC, V* ⊘ *No lunch weekends* Ⓜ *Subway: 6 to 51st St.*

FodorśChoice
★

$–$$$ ✕ **Brasserie.** This midtown ultramodern brasserie has an unmistakably downtown vibe. Architects Diller & Scofidio have created quite an otherworldly environment. The contemporary brasserie fare—served from morning to late night—is perfectly scrumptious. Order from the ample raw bar, dive into frisée aux lardons or blue crab bisque, and move on to bouillabaisse with lobster, scallops, clams, shrimp, and sea bass. Save room for dessert—it's special here. ⊠ *100 E. 53rd St., between Lexington and Park Aves., Midtown East* ☎ *212/751–4840* ⌖ *Reservations essential* ▭ *AE, D, DC, MC, V* Ⓜ *Subway: 6 to 51st St.*

Italian

★ **$$$$** ✕ **Alto.** Chef Scott Conant, known for his innovative Italian cuisine at the marvelous L'Impero, takes his originality to the outer extremes at this newcomer. Pale turquoise backlights the 1,000-square-foot wine cellar that brackets the smartly appointed main dining room. Rich, silky polenta makes a fine opening, scattered with chanterelle mushrooms, white asparagus, truffles, and snails. Yukon gold potato gnocchi disintegrate on the tongue. Conant dismantles a guinea hen, poaching the breast and roasting the legs, and plates the bird with a foie gras emulsion, bacon, and haricots verts. Finely textured vanilla soufflé comes together almost like cake with white-ivory foam and a creamy sauce. ⊠ *520 Madison Ave., entrance on E. 53rd St., Midtown East* ☎ *212/308–1099* ⚐ *Reservations essential* ▤ *AE, DC, MC, V* Ⓜ *Subway: E, V to 5th Ave./53rd St.*

★ **$$$** ✕ **Felidia.** Manhattanites frequent this *ristorante* as much for the winning enthusiasm of owner/cookbook author/Public Television chef Lidia Bastianich as for the food. The menu emphasizes authentic regional Italian cuisines, with a bow to dishes from Bastianich's homeland, Istria, on the Adriatic. Sit in an attractive front room with a wooden bar, a rustic room beyond, or in the elegant second-floor dining room. Order risotto, fresh homemade pasta, or roasted whole fish, and choose from a wine list representing Italy's finest vineyards. ⊠ *243 E. 58th St., between 2nd and 3rd Aves., Midtown East* ☎ *212/758–1479* ⚐ *Reservations essential* ▤ *AE, DC, MC, V* ☉ *Closed Sun. No lunch Sat.* Ⓜ *Subway: N, R, W, 4, 5, 6 to 59th St./Lexington Ave.*

★ **$–$$$** ✕ **L'Impero.** Rather than flaunt its proximity to the United Nations by offering a view, L'Impero instead provides a comfortable escape. Scott Conant's Italian cooking is respectful of the cuisine's fine traditions, yet quite resourceful. Not to be missed: unforgettable braised rabbit risotto flickered generously with black truffles (the only entrée on the menu over $30). Another signature is moist roasted baby goat wound with artichoke and mounded on a potato *groestle* (pancake). Finish with a lovely cheese course and warm pumpkin bread pudding-polenta. ⊠ *45 Tudor City Pl., between E. 42nd and E. 43rd Sts., Midtown East* ☎ *212/599–5045* ▤ *AE, DC, MC, V* ☉ *Closed Sun. No lunch Sat.* Ⓜ *Subway: S, 4, 5, 6, 7 to 42nd St./Grand Central.*

Indian

★ **$–$$** ✕ **Mint.** With a delightful dining room splashed with bright, cheery colors and flattering lighting, and chef Wilson Tushar Gomes's brightly seasoned dishes, this newcomer has quickly joined the ranks of the best Indian restaurants in town. The large menu includes rarely encountered specialties from Goa and Sikkim. Freshly grilled moist ground lamb kebabs deliver a nice slow burn to the palate. Chili heat punctuates other spices in the lamb vindaloo, resulting in a well-rounded array of savory flavors. Finish with a fine carrot pudding with saffron and coconut flakes. ⊠ *150 E. 50th St., between Lexington and 3rd Aves., Midtown East* ☎ *212/644–8888* ▤ *AE, DC, MC, V* Ⓜ *Subway: 6, E, V to 51st St./Lexington Ave.*

Japanese

★ **$$–$$$$** ✕ **Kuruma Zushi.** Only a small sign in Japanese indicates the location of this extraordinary restaurant that serves only sushi and sashimi. Bypass the tables, sit at the sushi bar, and put yourself in the hands of Toshihiro Uezu, the owner and chef. Among the selections are hard-to-find fish that Uezu imports directly from Japan. The most quietly attentive, pampering service staff in the city completes the wildly expensive experience. ⊠ *7 E. 47th St., 2nd fl., between 5th and Madison Aves., Mid-*

town East ☎ *212/317–2802* ⌖ *Reservations essential* ▤ *AE, MC, V* ☾ *Closed Sun.* Ⓜ *Subway: 4, 5, 6, 7 to 42nd St./Grand Central.*

$–$$$ ✕ **Sushi Yasuda.** The sleek bamboo-lined space in which chef Maomichi Yasuda works his aquatic sorcery is as elegant as his food. Whether he's using fish flown in daily from Japan or the creamiest sea urchin, Yasuda makes sushi so fresh and delicate it melts in your mouth. A number of special appetizers change daily (crispy fried eel backbone is a surprising treat), and a fine selection of sake and beer complements the lovely food. ✉ *204 E. 43rd St., between 2nd and 3rd Aves., Midtown East* ☎ *212/972–1001* ▤ *AE, D, MC, V* ☾ *Closed Sun. No lunch Sat. Closed for dinner 2nd and 4th Sat. of each month* Ⓜ *Subway: 4, 5, 6, 7 to 42nd St./Grand Central.*

Kosher

$$$–$$$$ ✕ **Solo.** Rather than considering kosher dietary laws restrictive, chef Hok Chin sees them as creative challenges for his "Mediterranean" cuisine. Dark bluefin tuna carpaccio is pressed to ⅛-inch thickness to cover an entire plate, cowboy steak au poivre is an enormous rib steak preening on a bed of spicy cayenne-dusted steak fries, and piping-hot vanilla soufflé is poured with caramel sauce and sided by nondairy vanilla ice cream. In the swanky dining room, Plexiglas is everywhere, and the entire front of the restaurant is a clear wall lighted with rows and rows of vibrant neon that continually change colors. ✉ *Sony Plaza Atrium, 550 Madison Ave., between E. 55th and E. 56th Sts., Midtown East* ☎ *212/833–7800* ⌖ *Reservations not accepted* ▤ *D, DC, MC, V* Ⓜ *Subway: E, V to 5th Ave./53rd St.; 6 to 51st St.*

Mexican

★ $$–$$$ ✕ **Pampano.** Richard Sandoval, who gave New Yorkers the great Maya uptown, here turns his attention to Mexican seafood. Start with a tart, meaningful margarita, or choose from about 50 tequilas available by the snifter. An addictive smoked swordfish is served with freshly fried tortilla chips, but careful: you could well spoil your appetite. Continue with a sampling of three highly complex ceviches, then go for pompano sautéed with chorizo, cactus leaves, tomato, and black bean puree, and napped with a roasted garlic-chili guajillo sauce. ✉ *209 E. 49th St., at 3rd Ave., Midtown East* ☎ *212/751–4545* ⌖ *Reservations essential* ▤ *AE, DC, MC, V* ☾ *No lunch weekends* Ⓜ *Subway: 6 to 51st St./Lexington Ave.*

Pan-Asian

★ $–$$$$ ✕ **Vong.** Jean-Georges Vongerichten's intensely delicious French–Thai menu changes seasonally, but reliable standbys include chicken and coconut soup with galangal (a gingerlike root) and shiitake mushrooms (one of the best soups in town); braised rabbit and carrot curry; and grilled beef and noodles in a tangy ginger broth. A good strategy for two or more: order set assortments of five appetizers ($21 per person) and five terrific desserts ($14), including a spiced peach tarte tatin. ✉ *200 E. 54th St., at 3rd Ave., Midtown East* ☎ *212/486–9592* ⌖ *Reservations essential* ▤ *AE, DC, MC, V* ☾ *No lunch weekends* Ⓜ *Subway: 6 to 51st St./Lexington Ave.; E, V to Lexington–3rd Aves./53rd St.*

18

Scandinavian

★ **$$$$** ✕ **Aquavit.** The dearly beloved restaurant relocated a block northeast to an even more Scandinavian space, leaving the famous waterfall behind. There's a café, lounge, bar, and 80-seat dining room, all decorated with more precise brushstrokes. Emboldened by the move, celebrity-chef Marcus Samuelsson is doing his best cooking ever. Don't miss the ingenious herring preparations—four of them, served in glass bowls with Carlsberg beer and aquavit. Duck breast never had it so good, lemon cured and partnered by potato-braised duck-leg hash, walnut vinaigrette, and a duck egg. ⊠ *65 E. 55th St., between Madison and Park Aves., Midtown East* ☎ *212/307–7311* ⟶ *Reservations essential* ⊟ *AE, DC, MC, V* ⊙ *No lunch Sat., except in café* Ⓜ *Subway: E, V to 5th Ave./53rd St.*

Seafood

★ **$$$$** ✕ **Oceana.** With all the dignity and hushed importance of a stateroom in a luxury ocean liner, Oceana is as nautical as it gets on land. Deeply gifted chef Cornelius Gallagher's ever-changing menus are not without distinctive whimsy. Thus, striped bass is pan-roasted and plated with creamy endive and speck ham with a lingonberry-chicken jus, and Maine skate is stuffed with pastrami and served with cabbage, walnuts, and huckleberries. ⊠ *55 E. 54th St., between Madison and Park Aves., Midtown East* ☎ *212/759–5941* ⊟ *AE, D, DC, MC, V* Ⓜ *Subway: E, V to 53rd St./5th Ave.*

$$–$$$ ✕ **Oyster Bar.** Nestled deep in the belly of Grand Central Station, the Oyster Bar has been a worthy seafood destination for over nine decades. Sit at the counter and slurp an assortment of bracingly fresh oysters, or a steaming bowl of clam chowder, and wash it down with an ice-cold brew. Or experience the forgotten pleasure of fresh, unadorned seafood such as lobster with drawn butter or matjes herring in season. Avoid anything that sounds newfangled. ⊠ *Grand Central Station, dining concourse, E. 42nd St. and Vanderbilt Ave., Midtown East* ☎ *212/490–6650* ⟶ *Reservations essential* ⊟ *AE, D, MC, V* ⊙ *Closed Sun.* Ⓜ *Subway: S, 4, 5, 6, 7 to 42nd St./Grand Central.*

Steak

$$–$$$$ ✕ **BLT Steak.** Chef Laurent Tourondel sets a new steak house standard
Fodor's Choice in this classy space decked out in beige and suede and resined black ta-
★ bles. The no-muss, no-fuss menu is nonetheless large, and so are the portions of supple crab cakes and luscious ruby tuna tartare. As soon as you're settled, puffy Parmesan popovers arrive still steaming. A veal chop is crusted with rosemary and Parmesan, which imbue the veal with more flavor than veal ever has. The quintessential BLT includes Kobe beef, foie gras, bacon, and tomato in a split ciabatta. Sides and desserts are all superior. ⊠ *106 E. 57th St., between Lexington and Park Aves., Midtown East* ☎ *212/752–7470* ⟶ *Reservations essential* ⊟ *AE, DC, MC, V* Ⓜ *Subway: 4, 5, 6, N, R to 59th St.*

$$–$$$$ ✕ **Bull and Bear.** Among the most masculine spaces in Manhattan, the sheer power in the air here is palpable. This is the only kitchen on the eastern seaboard that has access to Certified Angus Beef Prime, less than 1% of all U.S. beef. Go with a 24-ounce porterhouse, and you'll have two days of absolute succulence. All the sides are terrific, especially hash browns sizzling away in a 6-inch cast-iron skillet. ✉ *Waldorf Astoria, 570 Lexington Ave., at E. 49th St., Midtown East* ☎ *212/872–4900* ⚏ *Reservations essential* ▭ *AE, DC, MC, V* Ⓜ *Subway: 6 to 51st St.*

$$–$$$$ ✕ **Sparks Steak House.** Magnums of wines that cost more than most people earn in a week festoon the large dining rooms of this classic New York steak house. Although seafood is given fair play on the menu, Sparks is about dry-aged steak. The lamb chops and veal chops are also noteworthy. Classic sides of hash browns, creamed (or not) spinach, mushrooms, onions, and broccoli are all you need to complete the experience. ✉ *210 E. 46th St., between 2nd and 3rd Aves., Midtown East* ☎ *212/687–4855* ⚏ *Reservations essential* ▭ *AE, D, DC, MC, V* ⊘ *Closed Sun. No lunch Sat.* Ⓜ *Subway: S, 4, 5, 6, 7 to 42nd St.–Grand Central.*

★ $–$$$$ ✕ **Michael Jordan's The Steak House NYC.** Don't be dissuaded by the fact that this place is technically part of a chain: there's nowhere like it. This handsomely appointed space overlooks one of the most famous interiors in America. Start with inch-square logs of toasted bread brushed with garlic butter resting on a creamy pool of hot Gorgonzola fondue. Follow with pristine oysters, then lunge for a prime dry-aged rib eye or a 2½-pound lobster, grilled, steamed, sautéed, or broiled. Finish with luscious 5-inch 1,000-layer chocolate cake. ✉ *Grand Central Terminal, West Balcony, 23 Vanderbilt Ave., between E. 43rd and E. 44th Sts., Midtown East* ☎ *212/655–2300* ⚏ *Reservations essential* ▭ *AE, DC, MC, V* Ⓜ *Subway: 4, 5, 6, 7 to 42nd St./Grand Central.*

$–$$$$ ✕ **The Palm.** They may have added tablecloths, but it would take more than that to hide the brusque, no-nonsense nature of this legendary steak house. The steak is always impeccable, and lobsters are so big there may not be room at the table for such classic side dishes as rich creamed spinach. Overflow from the restaurant caused the owners to open Palm Too, a slightly less raffish version of the original, across the street, and another edition across town. ✉ *837 2nd Ave., between E. 44th and E. 45th Sts., Midtown East* ☎ *212/687–2953* ⚏ *Reservations essential* ▭ *AE, DC, MC, V* ⊘ *Closed Sun. No lunch Sat.* ✉ *Palm Too, 840 2nd Ave., between E. 44th and E. 45th Sts., Midtown East* ☎ *212/697–5198* Ⓜ *Subway: S, 4, 5, 6, 7 to 42nd St./Grand Central.*

UPPER EAST SIDE

Long viewed as an enclave of the privileged, the Upper East Side has plenty of elegant restaurants to serve ladies who lunch, denizens of Museum Mile, and bankers who look forward to a late-night meal and single malt at the end of the day. However, the eastern and northern reaches of the area have some quite affordable spots, too. Whether you want to celebrate a special occasion or have simply worked up an appetite after a long museum visit, you're sure to find something appropriate for almost any budget.

American

$–$$$ ✕ **Lenox Room.** This small neighborhood restaurant keeps a clubby low profile; nevertheless, insiders know it's a serious place to dine. Although the menu changes seasonally, such items as shrimp cocktail, oysters, Earl Grey–poached salmon, and crisp duck breast with a cider glaze are mainstays, as are "Tiers of Taste"—think American tapas. Thanks to congenial and charming host Tony Fortuna, everything runs smoothly. The crimson dining room is always comfortable, and the lively lounge is often crowded with well-heeled locals. ⊠ *1278 3rd Ave., between E. 73rd and E. 74th Sts., Upper East Side* ☏ *212/772–0404* ▭ *AE, D, MC, V* Ⓜ *Subway: 6 to 77th St.*

Contemporary

★ **$$$$** ✕ **Aureole.** Celebrity-chef Charlie Palmer's protégé Dante Boccuzzi is in charge of the kitchen at Palmer's top-rated restaurant. Several distinct flavors work their way into single dishes such as thyme-scented rabbit with foie gras jus, caramelized pear, and acorn squash chutney. Desserts, too, are breathtaking. The town-house setting on two floors has striking floral displays. For a romantic evening, reserve a table on the ground floor. ⊠ *34 E. 61st St., between Madison and Park Aves., Upper East Side* ☏ *212/319–1660* ⚠ *Reservations essential* ▭ *AE, DC, MC, V* ⊙ *Closed Sun. No lunch Sat.* Ⓜ *Subway: N, R, W to 5th Ave.*

★ **$$$–$$$$** ✕ **Mark's Restaurant.** Dignified yet relaxed, staid yet festive, Mark's excels in every way. Jean-Pierre Bagnato's showy menu is cleverly divided into four sectors with two appetizers and two entrées in each: Asian, "Equinox," Modern Classics, and Mediterranean take you from lobster medallions in a mild red curry–coconut broth to poussin with truffled mashed potatoes. Finish with pink grapefruit in a strawberry consommé with an almond chantilly and candied pistachios. To enhance your meal, choose a bottle from the abundant and rewarding wine cellar. Service is particularly focused and prompt. ⊠ *25 E. 77th St., at Madison Ave., Upper East Side* ☏ *212/879–1864* ⚠ *Reservations essential* ▭ *AE, DC, MC, V* Ⓜ *Subway: 6 to 77th St.*

$$–$$$ ✕ **Etats-Unis.** The open kitchen and shelves lined with cookbooks should tell you that the food is the primary focus at this small restaurant. The menu changes daily, but dishes lean toward the traditional, with some modern combinations to liven things up. Good examples are roasted boneless chicken stuffed with mascarpone and rosemary on truffled polenta, or charcoal-grilled rack of lamb with olive tapenade and fresh mint. The same dinner menu is available across the street at The Bar@Etats-Unis. ⊠ *242 E. 81st St., between 2nd and 3rd Aves., Upper East Side* ☏ *212/517–8826* ▭ *AE, DC, MC, V* ✉ *Bar@Etats-Unis, 247 E. 81st St., Upper East Side* ☏ *212/396–9928* ▭ *AE, DC, MC, V* Ⓜ *Subway: 6 to 77th St.*

French

$$$$ ✕ **Daniel.** Celebrity-chef Daniel Boulud has created one of the most memorable dining experiences in Manhattan today. The prix-fixe–only menu is predominantly French, with such modern classics as pan-roasted Dover sole with Japanese mushrooms, braised Swiss chard, and a marcona almond emulsion. Equally impressive is the professional service and primarily French wine list. Don't forget the decadent desserts and overflowing cheese trolley. For a more casual evening, you can reserve a table in the lounge area, where entrées range from $36 to $50. ⊠ *60 E. 65th*

FodorśChoice
★

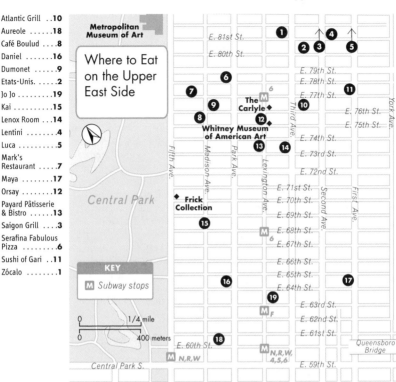

Metropolitan Museum of Art

Where to Eat on the Upper East Side

The Carlyle ◆

Whitney Museum of American Art

◆ **Frick Collection**

Central Park

KEY

Ⓜ *Subway stops*

0 ——— 1/4 mile

0 ——— 400 meters

E. 60th St.

Central Park S.

St., between Madison and Park Aves., Upper East Side ☎ *212/288–0033*
⌕ Reservations essential ⌂ Jacket required ═ AE, DC, MC, V ⊘ Closed
Sun. No lunch Ⓜ Subway: 6 to 68th St./Hunter College.

★ **$$$-$$$$** ✕ **Café Boulud.** Both the food and service are top-notch at Daniel
Boulud's conservative (but not overly stuffy) bistro in the Surrey Hotel.
The menu is divided into four short parts: under *La Tradition* you'll find
such classic French dishes as dry-aged *cote de boeuf* with baby spinach,
carrots, and rustic garlic potatoes; *Le Potager* tempts with handmade
ricotta tortellini; *La Saison* follows the rhythms of the season and re-
ally shines in early autumn; and *Le Voyage,* where the kitchen reinter-
prets the myriad cuisines of the world. ⊠ *20 E. 76th St., between 5th*
and Madison Aves., Upper East Side ☎ *212/772–2600 ⌕ Reserva-*
tions essential ═ AE, DC, MC, V ⊘ No lunch weekends Ⓜ Subway:
6 to 77th St.

$$-$$$$ ✕ **Orsay.** It's hard to believe that this elegant, sedate brasserie was once
the socialite hangout Mortimers—gone are the party favors, the mini-
hamburgers, and the snooty staff. Instead, it's a serious French restaurant featuring a menu that includes a list of whimsical tartares and an
array of house-smoked items. Traditional brasserie fare such as steak
frites as well as more creative options like a choice of five tartares or
pheasant with a barley-and-chorizo risotto are skillfully executed. A rea-

18

sonably priced wine list and professional service complete the dining experience. ⊠ *1057 Lexington Ave., at E. 75th St., Upper East Side* ☎ *212/517–6400* ⌖ *Reservations essential* ▤ *AE, D, MC, V* Ⓜ *Subway: 6 to 77th St.*

★ **$–$$$$** ✕ **Jo Jo.** After a million-dollar face-lift, this gorgeous town-house restaurant feels much roomier even when it's packed, as it usually is. It's the flagship restaurant in the glittering empire of chef Jean Georges Vongerichten (Jean Georges, Vong, The Mercer Kitchen, Spice Market). The food combines classic cooking techniques with infused oils and reductions. Seared foie gras is partnered with a lacy quince puree and plated with a corn pancake, and duck is rubbed with "medieval spices" and roasted with root vegetables. ⊠ *160 E. 64th St., between Lexington and 3rd Aves., Upper East Side* ☎ *212/223–5656* ⌖ *Reservations essential* ▤ *AE, MC, V* Ⓜ *Subway: 6 to 68th St./Hunter College.*

$$–$$$ ✕ **Payard Pâtisserie & Bistro.** Pastry chef François Payard is the force behind this combination bistro and pastry shop, festooned by bosomy, exuberant lanterns. Snazzy people come here in droves, and you'll quickly discover why. The wine list is particularly fine and focused. Start with an insanely rich and delicious cheese soufflé with Parmesan-cream sauce. Follow with stacked fat fillets of red snapper with a curry cauliflower puree, apples, yellow foot and chanterelle mushrooms, all dribbled with a golden raisin–cider–brown butter sauce. Payard's tarts, soufflés, and other French pastries are simply unforgettable. ⊠ *1032 Lexington Ave., between E. 73rd and E. 74th Sts., Upper East Side* ☎ *212/717–5252* ⌖ *Reservations essential* ▤ *AE, MC, V* ☉ *Closed Sun.* Ⓜ *Subway: 6 to 77th St.*

Italian

$–$$$ ✕ **Lentini.** The dining room, from its inlaid marble floors to the honeyed lighting from overhead frosted flute sconces and chandeliers, is clean and warm. Giuseppe Lentini's passionate cooking favors the dishes of Sardinia, Sicily, Piedmont, and especially Puglia, where he is from. Fresh sardines are butterflied, gently fried, and minced with raisins and pine nuts and usually a hint of fennel, then tossed vigorously with spaghetti and buttered dry bread crumbs. Veal Milanese usually involves a rib chop breaded and fried and plated under a heap of lemony arugula, but Giuseppe replaces the arugula with thinly sliced marinated artichoke hearts. This is one of the most comfortable and authentic regional Italian restaurants on the Upper East Side. ⊠ *1562 2nd Ave., at E. 81st St., Upper East Side* ☎ *212/628–3131* ▤ *AE, DC, MC, V* Ⓜ *Subway: 4, 5, 6 to 86th St.*

¢–$$ ✕ **Luca.** This casual spot happens to serve some of the best Northern Italian food on the Upper East Side, including fresh pastas like pappardelle with duck ragù and ravioli filled with spinach and ricotta and sauced with classic butter and sage. Main courses—including potato-crusted salmon with caper sauce on sautéed vegetables and chicken breast rollatini stuffed with goat cheese and pesto—leave regulars satisfied. Chefowner Luca Marcato wanders the clean, sparse restaurant when he's not performing Italian sorcery in the kitchen. ⊠ *1712 1st Ave., between E. 88th and E. 89th Sts., Upper East Side* ☎ *212/987–9260* ▤ *MC, V* ☉ *No lunch* Ⓜ *Subway: 4, 5, 6 to 86th St.*

Japanese

$$$–$$$$ ✕ **Kai.** One flight up from a glamorous stretch of Madison Avenue you'll find serenity and sheer culinary bliss in this jewel box. Three prix-fixe menus consisting of five to 10 small courses of chef Hitoshi Kagawa's premium Japanese fare—like lily-bulb soup with eel dumpling and pristine sashimi—are paired with exceptional teas and/or sakes. Many of the teas are available for sale in the elegant shop downstairs. All this indulgence comes at a price, but you'll leave feeling restored. ⊠ *822 Madison Ave., between E. 68th and E. 69th Sts., Upper East Side* ☎ *212/988–7277* ⊟ *AE, D, MC, V* ⊘ *Closed Sun. and Mon.* Ⓜ *Subway: 6 to 68th St./Hunter College.*

$–$$$$ ✕ **Sushi of Gari.** Options at this popular sushi restaurant range from the ordinary (Alaska maki, California roll) to such exotic items as salmon with guacamole, broiled whole squid with teriyaki sauce, and meltingly delicious lightly fried cream cheese dumplings. Japanese noodles (udon or soba) and meat dishes such as teriyaki and negimaki (scallions rolled in thinly sliced beef) are all well prepared. Reservations are strongly recommended. ⊠ *402 E. 78th St., at 1st Ave., Upper East Side* ☎ *212/517–5340* ⊟ *AE, D, MC, V* ⊘ *Closed Mon. No lunch* Ⓜ *Subway: 6 to 77th St.*

Mexican

★ $–$$ ✕ **Maya.** The upscale hacienda appearance of this justifiably popular restaurant showcases some of the best Mexican food in the city. Begin with a delicious fresh mango margarita, then tuck into intensely delicious roasted corn soup, poblano pepper stuffed with seafood and Gouda cheese, and smoky butterflied beef tenderloin marinated in lime and plated with a mole cheese enchilada or ancho chili–crusted striped bass with roasted tomato–chile de arbol sauce. Finish with crepes dribbled with goat's milk dulce de leche and you'll leave wearing a great big grin. ⊠ *1191 1st Ave., between E. 64th and E. 65th Sts., Upper East Side* ☎ *212/585–1818* ⌕ *Reservations essential* ⊟ *AE, DC, MC, V* ⊘ *No lunch* Ⓜ *Subway: 6 to 68th St./Hunter College.*

$–$$ ✕ **Zócalo.** Explore the unusual menu while enjoying a first-class margarita and chunky guacamole or stinging ceviche. Among the frolicsome and inventive entrées are crispy whole (boneless) red snapper and slow-cooked pork ribs with chipotle barbecue sauce and grilled corn and cactus slaw. There are also such classics as quesadillas and enchiladas. Burnt-orange and blue walls add zest to the attractive main dining room, although it can get a bit crowded. ⊠ *174 E. 82nd St., between Lexington and 3rd Aves., Upper East Side* ☎ *212/717–7772* ⌕ *Reservations essential* ⊟ *AE, DC, MC, V* ⊘ *No lunch* Ⓜ *Subway: 4, 5, 6 to 86th St.*

Pizza

☺ ¢–$$ ✕ **Serafina Fabulous Pizza.** Mediterranean-hue friezes, a most inviting upstairs terrace, and a steady stream of models and celebrities grace this very Italian café. Scene aside, the real draw here is some of Manhattan's most authentic Neopolitan pizza—they even filter the water for the pizza dough to make it closely resemble the water in Naples. Beyond the pies are antipasti, salads, pastas including a number of ravioli dishes, and

18

second courses like veal scaloppine with lemon and capers. ⊠ *1022 Madison Ave., at E. 79th St., Upper East Side* ☎ *212/734–2676* ⊟ *AE, DC, MC, V* Ⓜ *Subway: 6 to 77th St.* ⊠ *29 E. 61st St., between Madison and Park Aves., Upper East Side* ☎ *212/702–9898* ⊟ *AE, MC, V* Ⓜ *Subway: N, R, W, 4, 5, 6 to 59th St.–Lexington Ave.*

Seafood

$–$$ ✕ **Atlantic Grill.** It may be one of Manhattan's most popular dining rooms, but oddly, few people outside of New York have heard of this seafood restaurant. The combination of friendly service, fair prices, and reliably fresh fish means the large dining room is usually filled to capacity. Traditional appetizers are joined by sushi and sashimi starters. Straight-ahead entrées like roasted organic Scottish salmon and crab cakes usually make better choices than rococo concoctions like barbecue-glazed mahimahi. ⊠ *1341 3rd Ave., between E. 76th and E. 77th Sts., Upper East Side* ☎ *212/988–9200* ⚖ *Reservations essential* ⊟ *AE, MC, V* Ⓜ *Subway: 6 to 77th St.*

Vietnamese

¢–$ ✕ **Saigon Grill.** Serving some of the best Vietnamese food in Manhattan, this is also quite affordable. The appetizers are so delicious you might never make it to the entrées—standout starters include the shrimp summer roll, chicken satay, and barbecued spareribs with plum sauce. Main courses like basil prawns and grilled marinated pork chops with lemongrass are also worth a try. The sparse dining room is nothing special to look at, but the waiters are both speedy and polite. ⊠ *1700 2nd Ave., at E. 88th St., Upper East Side* ☎ *212/996–4600* ⚖ *Reservations not accepted* ⊟ *AE, D, DC, MC, V* Ⓜ *Subway: 4, 5, 6 to 86th St.*

UPPER WEST SIDE & HARLEM

Considering the fact that Lincoln Center's theaters can seat more than 18,000 audience members at one time, you would certainly expect the Upper West Side to be jammed with competitive, wonderful restaurants catering to all tastes and budgets. The main avenues are indeed lined with restaurants, but many of them are mediocre; they survive by catering to a local population that has neither the time nor the inclination to cook at home. Progress is being made, with the opening of the Time Warner Center in 2004, which houses a handful of New York's most high-end restaurants, and with the steady gentrification uptown into Harlem, where there are plenty of great cheap offerings beyond a slice of pizza.

American–Casual

$–$$ ✕ **Sarabeth's.** Lining up for brunch here is as much an Upper West Side tradition as taking a sunny Sunday afternoon stroll in nearby Riverside Park. Locals love the bric-a-brac–filled restaurant for unbeatable morning-time dishes like lemon ricotta pancakes, as well as for the comforting dinners. The afternoon tea includes buttery scones with Sarabeth's signature jams, savory nibbles, and outstanding baked goods. ⊠ *423*

Amsterdam Ave., between W. 80th and W. 81st Sts., Upper West Side ☎ *212/496–6280* ▤ *AE, DC, MC, V* Ⓜ *Subway: 1 to 79th St.*

¢–$ ✕ **Big Nick's.** This cramped neighborhood diner is decorated with photographs of the celebrities who've visited, but the primary draw is the burgers, which are huge and juicy. The tomelike menu lists every conceivable burger topping, from avocado and bacon to Greek tsatsiki sauce. The classic Bistro Burger has mushrooms, cheddar, and fried onions on toasted challah bread. Nick's is open later than most burger joints—until 5 AM. ✉ *2175 Broadway, between W. 76th and W. 77th Sts., Upper West Side* ☎ *212/362–9238* ▤ *AE, MC, V* Ⓜ *Subway: 1, 2, 3 to 72nd St.*

¢–$ ✕ **Kitchenette.** Many a hungry Columbia student arriving intent on a meal has gotten waylaid by the gooey cakes, cookies, and other goodies displayed at the bakery counter of this country kitchen, amid decorative old signs and cookware. Those who hold out are rewarded with good, solid cooking, like turkey meat loaf or rich baked cheese macaroni at dinner, or gingerbread French toast and thick-cut bacon at brunch. ✉ *1272 Amsterdam Ave., between W. 122nd and W. 123rd Sts., Morningside Heights* ☎ *212/531–7600* ▤ *AE, D, MC, V* Ⓜ *Subway: 1 to 125th St.*

Barbecue

¢–$$ ✕ **Dinosaur Bar-B-Que.** New York's reputation for inferior barbecue instantly improved when John Stage opened the third outpost of his Syracuse-based joint in 2004, installing it in a riverside meatpacking warehouse in Harlem. Here, the city's friendliest waitstaff serves piled-high plates of pulled pork, ribs, chicken, brisket, and knockout wings; a thoughtfully stocked bar corrals the Columbia students. ✉ *646 W. 131st St., at 12th Ave., Harlem* ☎ *212/694–1777* ◬ *Reservations not accepted* ▤ *AE, D, DC, MC, V* ⊘ *Closed Mon.* Ⓜ *Subway: 1 to 125th St.*

Cafés

¢–$ ✕ **Café Lalo.** The plentiful pastries, floor-to-ceiling French windows, and vintage posters attract enough people to make seating a squeeze, but the Parisian setting and decadent cakes, pies, tarts, and cheesecakes keep the chairs filled into the wee hours (it's one of the few nearby places open late—until 4 AM on weekends). Somehow a camera crew fit in here to film Tom Hanks and Meg Ryan parleying in *You've Got Mail.* ✉ *201 W. 83rd St., between Broadway and Amsterdam Ave., Upper West Side* ☎ *212/496–6031* ◬ *Reservations not accepted* ▤ *No credit cards* Ⓜ *Subway: 1 to 86th St.*

¢ ✕ **Columbus Bakery.** Aside from the addictive cookies, muffins, and other baked goods, Columbus Bakery carries fresh, homemade sandwiches, soups, salads, and frittatas. It's great for breakfast or a pit stop after exploring Central Park or the nearby Museum of Natural History. If you can snag a table outdoors, the seating area is lovely for sipping a cappuccino (or a glass of wine) and watching the neighborhood's endless parade of oversize baby strollers and pedigree dogs. ✉ *474 Columbus Ave., between W. 82nd and W. 83rd Sts., Upper West Side* ☎ *212/724–6880* ◬ *Reservations not accepted* ▤ *AE, MC, V* Ⓜ *Subway: B, C to 81st St.*

18

Artie's
Delicatessen ..**15**

Alouette **3**

Asiate **36**

Barney
Greengrass ...**11**

Bayou **5**

Big Nick's **23**

Café Con
Leche **6, 18**

Café des
Artistes **30**

Café Gray **35**

Cafe Lalo **14**

Café
Luxembourg ...**28**

Carmine's **9**

'Cesca **24**

Columbus
Bakery **17**

Compass **27**

Dinosaur
Bar-B-Que **1**

Docks
Oyster Bar **10**

Gennaro **7**

Jean
Georges **34**

Kitchenette **4**

Mughlai **25**

Nice Matin **20**

Nonna **16**

Ocean Grill **22**

Ollie's .**2, 12, 29**

Onera **21**

Ouest **13**

Patsy's
Pizzeria **26**

Per Se **37**

Picholine **33**

Saigon Grill **8**

Sarabeth's **19**

Shun Lee
West **32**

Tavern on the
Green **31**

KEY

Ⓜ *Subway stops*

American
Museum
of Natural
History

The Dakota ◆

Lincoln
Center

0 — 1/4 mile

0 — 400 meters

Where to Eat on
the Upper West Side
& in Harlem

Columbus
Circle

Central
Park S.

Chinese

$–$$$ ✕ **Shun Lee West.** For Chinese food without pretensions, head to Chinatown; but if you'd rather be pampered and are willing to pay for it, this is the place. The dramatically lighted dining room, accented by images of white dragons and monkeys, serves classic dishes like crispy prawns with XO sauce and rack of lamb Szechuan-style. Less expensive Shun Lee Café next door has pretty good dim sum. ⌂ *43 W. 65th St., between Columbus Ave. and Central Park W, Upper West Side* ☎ *212/595–8895* ⌂ *Reservations essential* ═ *AE, D, DC, MC, V* Ⓜ *Subway: 1 to 66th St./Lincoln Center.*

¢–$ ✕ **Ollie's.** This no-frills Chinese chain is a blessing for locals and Lincoln Center patrons in search of a quick budget meal. The best dishes are the noodle soups (with dumplings, vegetables, and meat), ribs, and the dim sum prepared by speedy chefs. The portions are generous, but don't expect any culinary revelations. ⌂ *1991 Broadway, at W. 67th St., Upper West Side* ☎ *212/595–8181* ⌂ *Reservations not accepted* ═ *AE, MC, V* Ⓜ *Subway: 1 to 66th St./Lincoln Center* ⌂ *2315 Broadway, at W. 86th St., Upper West Side* ☎ *212/362–3111* Ⓜ *Subway: 1 to 86th St.* ⌂ *2957 Broadway, at W. 116th St., Morningside Heights* ☎ *212/932–3300* Ⓜ *Subway: 1 to 116th St.*

Contemporary

$$$$ ✕ **Asiate.** The view alone is reason enough to visit Asiate's pristine dining room, perched on the 35th floor of the Time Warner Center in the Mandarin Oriental Hotel. Artfully positioned tables draw the eye to the great floor-to-ceiling window, which looks onto the expanse of Central Park and midtown; at night, the crystalline lighting reflects in the glass to haunting effect. Efficient service and mostly successful French-Asian dishes (like black cod with foie gras–miso sauce) do not break the spell. ⌂ *Time Warner Center, 80 Columbus Circle, 35th fl., at W. 60th St., Upper West Side* ☎ *212/805–8881* ⌂ *Reservations essential* ═ *AE, D, DC, MC, V* Ⓜ *Subway: A, B, C, D, 1, 2 to 59th St.–Columbus Circle.*

$$$$ ✕ **Per Se.** Thomas Keller, who gave the world butter-poached lobster and the Napa Valley's French Laundry restaurant, has given New York Per Se, which serves his witty, magical creations to 16 lucky tables. Come with an open mind and open wallet, and discover his inventive combinations of flavors reduced to their essences. Waiters can (and may) recite the provenance of the tiniest turnip. For reservations, call exactly two months in advance; hit redial, repeat. ⌂ *Time Warner Center, 10 Columbus Circle, 4th fl., Upper West Side* ☎ *212/823–9335* ⌂ *Reservations essential* 🍴 *Jacket required* ◷ *No lunch Mon.–Thurs.* ═ *AE, MC, V* Ⓜ *Subway: A, B, C, D, 1, 2 to 59th St.–Columbus Circle.*

FodorśChoice ★

★ **$$–$$$$** ✕ **Café Gray.** Four-star chef Gray Kunz, creator of the culinary temple Lespinasse (now closed), has shifted his talents to preparing a more reasonably priced menu of top-notch Asian-accented French dishes, like braised short ribs with grits and mustard sauce. You can watch them being made in the open kitchen which runs the length of the dining room, or head to the lively bar area, which serves the full menu plus other tidbits also worth trying. ⌂ *Time Warner Center, 10 Columbus Circle, 3rd*

18

fl., Upper West Side ☎ *212/823–6338* ⌖ *Reservations essential* ▭ *AE, DC, MC, V* Ⓜ *Subway: A, B, C, D, 1, 2 to 59th St.–Columbus Circle.*

$$–$$$$ ✕ **Compass.** Mixing downtown decor with an uptown lack of attitude makes Compass both stylish and friendly—a rare combination in New York. Chef John Fraser's seasonally informed menu likewise puts great concepts together: contemporary dishes like roast monkfish with Indian spices, and a selection of meats seared in a 1,600° broiler. The *Wine Spectator*-award-winning wine list and $32 three-course prix-fixe menu (served until 6:30 Friday and Saturday) are more reasons to go. ⌧ *208 W. 70th St., between Amsterdam and West End Aves., Upper West Side* ☎ *212/875–8600* ▭ *AE, DC, MC, V* ☉ *No lunch Mon.–Sat.* Ⓜ *Subway: 1, 2 to 72nd St.*

$$–$$$$ ✕ **Ouest.** Celebrity-chef Tom Valenti's contemporary American restaurant, which paved the way for fine cooking on the Upper West Side when it opened in 2001, still reigns supreme with intense flavors that rock, whether you order stick-to-the-ribs fare like braised lamb shanks or grilled meats, or go lighter with roasted sturgeon, chanterelles, and truffled rice. If that's not enough, the $27 multicourse Sunday brunch is a caloric orgy that will make you an instant convert. ⌧ *2315 Broadway, between W. 83rd and W. 84th Sts., Upper West Side* ☎ *212/580–8700* ⌖ *Reservations essential* ▭ *AE, D, DC, MC, V* ☉ *No lunch Mon.–Sat.* Ⓜ *Subway: 1, 2 to 86th St.*

$$–$$$$ ✕ **Tavern on the Green.** As you might expect given the kitchen's near-impossible task of accommodating over 1,000 guests at once, the food and service vary wildly, depending on the craziness. Nonetheless, people throng (by foot, by taxi, even by horse and carriage) to this fantastical maze of dining rooms in Central Park. In good weather (May through October), try for a spot in the lovely garden area under a canopy of lighted trees. Simple dishes like prime rib are best bets—or skip the grub and grab a drink at the charming upstairs bar. ⌧ *In Central Park at W. 67th St., Upper West Side* ☎ *212/873–3200* ⌖ *Reservations essential* ▭ *AE, D, DC, MC, V* Ⓜ *Subway: 1, 2 to 66th St.–Lincoln Center.*

Continental

$$–$$$$ ✕ **Café des Artistes.** Howard Chandler Christy's murals of naked nymphs at play grace the walls of this thoroughly romantic restaurant, which opened in 1917 (to add to the romance). Although the haute French cuisine may no longer be among New York's best, the menu always has some stunners, like pan-roasted squab with chanterelles and garlic flan over a potato cake. Desserts like hot fudge napoleon or a perfect apple strudel are champions. The prix-fixe dinner is $45. ⌧ *1 W. 67th St., at Central Park W, Upper West Side* ☎ *212/877–3500* ⌖ *Reservations essential* ▭ *AE, DC, MC, V* Ⓜ *Subway: 1, 2 to 66th St.–Lincoln Center.*

Creole

$–$$ ✕ **Bayou.** Harlem is still known for its casual soul-food spots, but trendy restaurants like Bayou are beginning to move in, too. The modern Creole menu includes classics like crawfish étouffée, as well as more inventive choices like a grilled pork chop with green peppercorn demi-glace. Bayou's dining room has a pressed-tin ceiling and brass lamps, an accommodating waitstaff, and even a small wine list. ☒ *308 Lenox Ave., between W. 125th and W. 126th Sts., Harlem* ☎ *212/426–3800* ▭ *AE, DC, MC, V* ⊗ *No lunch Sat.* Ⓜ *Subway: 2, 3 to 125th St.*

Delicatessen

¢–$$ ✕ **Barney Greengrass.** At this old–New York Jewish landmark, brusque waiters send out stellar smoked salmon, sturgeon, and whitefish to a happy crowd packed to the gills at small Formica tables. Split a fish platter with bagels, cream cheese, and other fixings, or get your fish with scrambled eggs. If you're still hungry, go for a plate of scrumptious cheese blintzes or the to-die-for chopped liver. Beware: the weekend brunch wait can exceed an hour. ☒ *541 Amsterdam Ave., between W. 86th and W. 87th Sts., Upper West Side* ☎ *212/724–4707* ⌔ *Reservations not accepted* ▭ *No credit cards* ⊗ *Closed Mon. No dinner* Ⓜ *Subway: 1, 2 to 86th St.*

¢–$ ✕ **Artie's Delicatessen.** From the look of it, you'd think you were in an old-time Jewish deli, but Artie's opened in 1999. The pastrami is moist, and appropriately fatty, and the pickles, coleslaw, and homemade hot dogs are all worth trying. The shocker: the staff is actually friendly and accommodating, unlike most joints of this kind. ☒ *2290 Broadway, between W. 82nd and W. 83rd Sts., Upper West Side* ☎ *212/579– 5959* ⌔ *Reservations not accepted* ▭ *AE, D, MC, V* Ⓜ *Subway: 1, 2 to 86th St.*

French

$$$$ ✕ **Jean Georges.** This culinary temple focuses wholly on *chef celebre* Jean-
Fodor'sChoice   Georges Vongerichten's spectacular creations. Some approach the lim-
★   its of the taste universe, like trout sashimi with trout eggs, lemon foam, dill, and horseradish. Others are models of simplicity, like young garlic soup with frogs' legs. Exceedingly personalized service and a well-selected wine list contribute to an unforgettable meal. (For Jean Georges on a budget, try the $20 lunch at **Nougatine** in the front area.) ☒ *1 Central Park W, at W. 59th St., Upper West Side* ☎ *212/299–3900* ⌔ *Reservations essential* ⌂ *Jacket required* ▭ *AE, DC, MC, V* ⊗ *Closed Sun.* Ⓜ *Subway: A, B, C, D, 1, 2 to 59th St.–Columbus Circle.*

★ $$$–$$$$ ✕ **Picholine.** With an elegant, mellow dining room painted in soft colors and accented by gorgeous dried flowers, Picholine is made for special occasions. Whatever you order, allow fromager Max McCalman to discuss his celebrated cart of cheeses, which ripen to glorious maturity in a "cave" in the back. Terrance Brennan's Mediterranean-accented French cuisine is considered among the best in Manhattan: top dishes include Maine lobster with caramelized endive and vanilla brown butter, and daily Scottish game. ☒ *35 W. 64th St., between Broadway and Central Park W, Upper West Side* ☎ *212/724–8585* ⌔ *Reservations essential* ▭ *AE, DC, MC, V* ⊗ *No lunch Sun. and Mon.* Ⓜ *Subway: 1, 2 to 66th St.–Lincoln Center.*

$–$$$ ✕ **Café Luxembourg.** The old soul of the Lincoln Center neighborhood seems to inhabit the tiled and mirrored walls of this lively, friendly bistro, where West End Avenue regulars are greeted with kisses, and musicians and audience members pack the room after a concert. The menu (served until 11:45) includes classic bistro dishes like steak au poivre

18

Up All Night

CAN'T DECIDE between a burger, blintzes, or bibimbop at 2 AM? Here are some favorite late-night spots:

For gracious dining, opt for **Mas** (39 Downing St., between Bedford and Varick Sts.), **Blue Ribbon Bakery,** and the **Tasting Room.** The many bistros and upscale diners open late make choosing hard: classic French **Balthazar**; 24-hour almost-divey French **Florent**; industrial-chic, eclectic **Dinerbar** (1569 Lexington Ave., between E. 100th and E. 101st Sts.); and modern **Diner 24** (102 8th Ave., at W. 15th St.) are among the best. If you just want to see and be seen, follow the models to **Schiller's Liquor Bar, Pop** (127 4th Ave., between W. 12th and W. 13th Sts.), and sushi hot spot **Cube 63** (63 Clinton St., between Rivington and Stanton Sts.).

More worldly choices include **La Marmite** (2264 Frederick Douglass Blvd., at W. 121st St.), Little Senegal's all-night café; Korean table grilling at **Kum Gang San** (49 W. 32nd St., at Broadway); Ukrainian pierogis and blintzes to all-American grilled cheese at **Veselka**; the no-atmosphere, taxi-drivers' pit stop, Turkish **Bereket** (187 E. Houston St., at Orchard St.); Chinese noodles at **Great New York Noodletown;** and **Sushi Seki** (1143 1st Ave., at E. 62nd St.), which offers adventurous variations on a sushi theme.

Burger or hot dog more your style? Try the minis at **Pop Burger** (58–60 9th Ave., between W. 14th and W. 15th Sts.), classic dive burgers at **Corner Bistro** (331 W. 4th St., at Jane St.), all-beef dogs at **Gray's Papaya,** or cool veggie or meat dogs at **Crif-Dogs** (113 St. Marks Pl., between 1st Ave. and Ave. A).

and hamburgers alongside more contemporary spins like rack of lamb with tomato-orange relish. ⊠ *200 W. 70th St., between Amsterdam and West End Aves., Upper West Side* ☎ *212/873–7411* ⌲ *Reservations essential* ☰ *AE, DC, MC, V* Ⓜ *Subway: 1, 2, 3 to 72nd St.*

$–$$ ✕ **Alouette.** Yes, there really is a good French restaurant north of 96th Street. And although Alouette may not be able to compete with most bistros in other parts of Manhattan, people in the immediate area are more than happy to take what they can get. Signature dishes include escargots with garlic, and sirloin steak au poivre with frites. Although the prices are high for the locale, the quality is certainly there. And the casual bistro setting is comfortable and unstuffy. ⊠ *2588 Broadway, between W. 97th and W. 98th Sts., Upper West Side* ☎ *212/222–6808* ⌲ *Reservations essential* ☰ *AE, DC, MC, V* ☉ *No lunch* Ⓜ *Subway: 1, 2, 3 to 96th St.*

$–$$ ✕ **Nice Matin.** The French Riviera meets New York at this bustling brasserie where bright colors and lighted carousel-like columns add a festive air and tables spill onto the sidewalk. The menu mixes authentic Niçoise dishes—like bouillabaisse, and chickpea-flour french fries called *panisses*—with more Americanized standards like steak frites. The requisite salade niçoise goes the extra kilometer by using olive oil–poached tuna instead of canned. ⊠ *201 W. 79th St., at Amsterdam Ave., Upper*

West Side ☎ *212/873–6423* ⌔ *Reservations essential* ▭ *AE, D, MC, V* Ⓜ *Subway: 1 to 79th St.*

Greek

★ **$–$$** ✕ **Onera.** This intimate town-house restaurant (a foyer-size bar leads to a clean white- and navy-walled dining room) feels like a tastefully appointed home. Chef Michael Psilakis's Greek-inspired but inventive menu goes far beyond grilled fish and lamb chops, with dishes like diver scallops with fried capers and brown butter, and sheep's milk dumplings with quail ragout. The Greek-focused wine list is unique and lovely; ask the sommelier for a suggestion, or order by the glass. ✉ *222 W. 79th St., between Broadway and Amsterdam Ave., Upper West Side* ☎ *212/ 873–0200* ▭ *AE, MC, V* Ⓜ *Subway: 1 to 79th St.*

Indian

¢**–$$** ✕ **Mughlai.** Standing well above the neighborhood's just-average offerings, Mughlai serves excellent Indian food in a pleasant glass-enclosed setting. The slightly higher-than-average prices reflect noticeably fresher ingredients, and less greasy, more expertly prepared dishes than you'll find elsewhere. Order one of the well-prepared classics, like chicken tikka masala; or grab a round of samosas and wait a little longer for succulent meats and vegetables to come out of the tandoori oven. ✉ *320 Columbus Ave., at W. 75th St., Upper West Side* ☎ *212/724–6363* ▭ *AE, DC, MC, V* ☺ *No lunch weekdays* Ⓜ *Subway: B, C to 72nd St.*

Italian

$–$$$$ ✕ **Carmine's.** This family-friendly restaurant serves truly huge portions of garlicky Italian-American food, like linguine with clam sauce, chicken parmigiana, and lobster fra diavolo. The dining room has dark woodwork and black-and-white tiles; outdoor seating is available in the front. Although it's impossible not to order too much, everything tastes just as satisfying the next day. ✉ *2450 Broadway, between W. 90th and W. 91st Sts., Upper West Side* ☎ *212/362–2200* ▭ *AE, DC, MC, V* Ⓜ *Subway: 1, 2, 3 to 96th St.*

$–$$$ ✕ **'Cesca.** Chef Tom Valenti's foray into Southern Italian cuisine provides intense, comforting-yet-sophisticated flavors in a rambling but stylish space. The shrimp raviolini has urban sophistication, but true Italophiles might opt for a heady bowl of tripe with red wine and pancetta. Desserts are excellent, but for a really authentic finish, try one of the amari, Italian bitters: this place easily has the best selection of them in New York, if not the country. ✉ *164 W. 75th St., at Amsterdam Ave., Upper West Side* ☎ *212/787–6300* ▭ *AE, D, DC, MC, V* ☺ *No lunch* Ⓜ *Subway: 1, 2, 3 to 72nd St.*

¢**–$$** ✕ **Nonna.** Grandma would have to cook for weeks to prepare all the rustic Italian dishes served at this farmhouse-inspired, family trattoria. You could make a meal just from the vast antipasti menu, which ranges from simple marinated mushrooms to baked clams and arancini (fried risotto balls). The menu rolls on with spaghetti carbonara and chicken under a brick. When everyone's full, sit back with a classic negroni and digest! ✉ *520 Columbus Ave., at W. 85th St., Upper West Side* ☎ *212/ 579–3194* ▭ *AE, MC, V* Ⓜ *Subway: 1 to 86th St.*

18

¢–$ ✕**Gennaro.** A small space and excellent food equal long waits at this neighborhood restaurant, but an expansion has helped ease the crush. The pleasant dining room has brick walls and tables covered with white tablecloths. Start with the huge antipasto platter filled with hot and cold vegetables, prosciutto, fresh mozzarella, and shrimp, and then move on to the pastas or entrées like lemony roasted Cornish hen or red wine–braised lamb shank. ⊠ *665 Amsterdam Ave., between W. 92nd and W. 93rd Sts., Upper West Side* ☎ *212/665–5348* ⚠ *Reservations not accepted* ▭ *No credit cards* ☉ *No lunch* Ⓜ *Subway: 1, 2, 3 to 96th St.*

Pizza

¢–$ ✕**Patsy's Pizzeria.** Not quite on par with the original Patsy's (which opened in 1933 in then-Italian East Harlem and continues to serve great pies from its coal oven), this outpost nevertheless serves some of the best pizza on the Upper West Side. The crust is thin, the sauce is thick, the cheese is bubbling, and the toppings are fresh. ⊠ *61 W. 74th St., between Columbus Ave. and Central Park W, Upper West Side* ☎ *212/579–3000* ▭ *No credit cards* Ⓜ *Subway: B, C to 72nd St.*

Seafood

$$–$$$ ✕**Ocean Grill.** Known for its expansive raw bar, this stylish seafood spot is consistently packed with couples who look grateful that the babysitter didn't cancel. The drinks are generous, the prices are reasonable, and the fish is impeccably fresh. Best bets beyond the great raw bar are the selection of sushi rolls and simple grilled entrées, such as tuna, salmon, and swordfish, although there are also more elaborate creations. ⊠ *384 Columbus Ave., between W. 78th and W. 79th Sts., Upper West Side* ☎ *212/579–2300* ▭ *AE, D, DC, MC, V* Ⓜ *Subway: B, C to 81st St.; 1 to 79th St.*

$–$$$ ✕**Docks Oyster Bar.** As the name implies, this casual spot serves oysters galore (both raw and fried) as well as raw clams, shrimp cocktail, steamed lobster, and other fruits of the sea. Shellfish is the way to go here, although there's a large selection of grilled fish. And save room for key lime pie. ⊠ *2427 Broadway, between W. 89th and W. 90th Sts., Upper West Side* ☎ *212/724–5588* ▭ *AE, D, DC, MC, V* Ⓜ *Subway: B, C to 86th St.*

Vietnamese

¢–$ ✕**Saigon Grill.** Some of New York's best is served at lightening speed at this affordable no-atmosphere restaurant, which packs in families and students alike thrilled to have found Chinatown-quality food uptown. The appetizers are so delicious you might never make it to the entrées—standout starters include the shrimp summer roll, chicken satay, and barbecued spareribs with plum sauce. Main courses include basil shrimp and grilled marinated pork chops. ⊠ *620 Amsterdam, at W. 90th St., Upper West Side* ☎ *212/875–9072* ⚠ *Reservations not accepted* ▭ *AE, D, DC, MC, V* Ⓜ *Subway: 1 to 86th St.*

Where to Stay

WORD OF MOUTH

"[Four Seasons] is the best of the best. Rooms are huge and many offer outstanding views of the New York skyline as well as furnished balconies. All have walk-in closets and gigantic bathrooms."

—jfd

"The [Inn on 23rd] was the perfect base for it all. We stayed in the Cabin Room, spacious, spotless, I want that couch! The neighborhood and the location are perfect."

—Nancy

Updated by
Melissa
Klurman

Staying at a hotel in New York is symbolic of what it's like to live in New York. It's a competitive market and price is dictated by high demand. Rooms, like apartments, are on the whole smaller than you would have ever thought possible, noise is sometimes a nuisance, and what New Yorkers call "quality-of-life issues"—pollution, crowding—are often a problem. Why put up with it? Easy. There's no equivalent experience to being in the city that never sleeps. To truly get the center-of-the-universe energy and excitement that New York is famous for, you have to live here, even if it's only for one night.

To get the most out of your hotel experience, it pays to research and ask questions. If size is important to you, ask the reservationist how many square feet a room has, not just if it's big. A hotel room in New York is considered quite large if it's 500 square feet. Very large rooms, such as those at the Four Seasons, are 600 square feet. To stay anywhere larger you'll have to get a multiroom suite. Small rooms are a tight 150 to 200 square feet. Very small rooms are under 100 square feet; you'll find these at inns and lodges and they're sold as a single for only one person. There are studio apartments in the city that are 250 square feet and include a kitchen; 1,000 square feet is considered a huge abode in this very compact and crowded urban playland.

Now you need to consider price. For top-tier hotels in prime locations, such as the Ritz-Carlton Central Park or Mandarin-Oriental, in high season from September to December, prices start at $750. That's without a park view. Special events, such as the New York City Marathon in November, leave prime hotel areas without a single room, as hard as it to believe when you see prices hovering around $1,000. The least expensive time to book a hotel room in New York is January and February. If you're flexible, ask reservations if there's a cheaper time to stay during your preferred traveling month; that way you can avoid crowded weeks, such as Fashion Week and the marathon.

What can you expect for your very inflated dime? At almost all the top- and middle-ranking hotels you'll be pampered with 300-plus thread count sheets and goose-down duvets; you may also find plush robes, terry slippers, and designer toiletries. High-tech electronics such as plasma-screen TVs and wireless phones are often available; and more noticeably, service includes evening turndown, fine dining, room service, and a concierge who's at your beck and call.

Remember the Realtor's adage "location, location, location," and bear in mind that you'll pay prime prices for your prime piece of real estate. Many visitors to New York cram themselves into hotels in the hectic Midtown area, but it's worth noting that Manhattan is so small and dense that other neighborhoods are often just as convenient for travelers. Several less-touristed areas, such as Gramercy, Murray Hill, and the Upper East Side, offer a far more accurate sense of the pace and feel of New York life. If space is important to you, consider a suite at a smaller hotel such as the Kitano. You'll receive great service since you're staying in a suite, and get an extra room or two for the same price as a regular room at a more expensive property.

Deals do exist if you know where to look. Weekdays in the Financial District are full price, but weekends, when most businesspeople have vacated, is a great time to get a discounted spot at the Millennium Hilton or Ritz-Carlton Battery Park. Many chains have started to call New York home and offer well-priced options; in addition to old favorites such as Sheraton, Hilton, and Hyatt, there are Best Westerns, and Days, Hampton, and Comfort inns. However, don't expect the same low rates you'll find in nonurban areas; on a busy November evening the Hampton Inn in Chelsea was charging as much as $350.

Finally, remember to enjoy your little piece of New York. Live like a local, stroll the neighborhood, visit the corner deli, and you'll remember fondly the time you were able to call New York home.

Lower Manhattan

★ $$$$ 🖭 **Ritz-Carlton New York, Battery Park.** Sweeping views over the Statue of Liberty, Ellis Island, and Lower Manhattan are some of the highlights of a stay at this elegant tower on the tip of Manhattan. The hotel is an oasis of fine living; the luxurious, large rooms and suites with plush fabrics and furnishings seem more like expensive living rooms than hotel rooms. The superlative staff includes a bath butler who can fill your deep soaking tub with anything from rose petals to rubber duckies. Take advantage of the quiet weekends to sample the Kobe beef at 2 West restaurant or imbibe at the View bar with its spectacular sight lines of Lady Liberty. ⊠ *2 West St., at Battery Pl., Battery Park 10004* ☎ *212/ 344–0800 or 800/241–3333* 🖷 *212/344–3801* ⊕ *www.ritzcarlton. com* 🛏 *254 rooms, 44 suites* ⚒ *Restaurant, minibars, cable TV with video games, in-room DVD, in-room data ports, 2 bars, piano, laun-*

PLANNER

How to Use This Chapter

This chapter divides the hotels in New York City by neighborhood then by price. Within each neighborhood, properties are assigned price categories based on the range from their least expensive standard double room at high season (excluding holidays) to the most expensive. We always list the facilities that are available–but we don't specify whether they cost extra: when pricing accommodations, always ask what's included and what costs extra.

Reservations

Hotel reservations are an absolute necessity when planning your trip to New York–hotels fill up quickly, so book your room as far in advance as possible. Fierce competition means properties undergo frequent improvements, especially during July and August, so when booking inquire about any ongoing renovations lest you get a room within earshot of noisy construction. In this ever-changing city, travelers can find themselves temporarily, and most inconveniently, without commonplace amenities such as room service or spa access if their hotel is upgrading.

Services

Unless otherwise noted in the individual descriptions, all the hotels listed have private baths, central heating, air-conditioning, and private phones. Almost all hotels have data ports and phones with voice mail, as well as valet service. Many now have wireless Internet (Wi-Fi) available, although it's not always free. Most large hotels have video or high-speed checkout capability, and many can arrange babysitting. Pools are a rarity, but most properties have gyms or health clubs, and sometimes full-scale spas; hotels without facilities usually have arrangements for guests at nearby gyms, sometimes for a fee.

Bringing a car to Manhattan can significantly add to your lodging expenses. Many properties in all price ranges do have parking facilities, but they are often at independent garages that charge as much as $20 or more per day, and valet parking can cost up to $60 a day. The city's exorbitant 18¾% parking tax makes leaving your lemon out of the Big Apple a smart idea.

What It Costs

With square footage coming at a hefty premium in this town, some accommodations provide more space for more money, while others can only entreat you with more amenities. If it's a bargain you long for, that's one amenity few New York hotels provide. But don't be put off by printed rates—the priciest hotels often have deals that cut room rates nearly in half. Be sure to ask about promotional rates and to check the hotel's Web site and Fodors.com.

FOR 2 PEOPLE				
$$$$	**$$$**	**$$**	**$**	**¢**
over $475	$350–$475	$225–$350	$110–$225	under $110

Prices are for a standard double room, excluding 13.625% city and state taxes.

dry service, concierge, meeting rooms, parking (fee), no-smoking rooms, ▭ *AE, D, DC, MC, V* Ⓜ *Subway: 1, R, W to Rector St.*

$$$ 🏨 **Millennium Hilton.** This sleek black skyscraper directly across the street from the World Trade Center site was badly damaged by the disaster but was renovated and reopened in less than two years. The business-class modern, beige-and-wood rooms have a streamlined look, with contoured built-in desks and night tables as well as enormous plasma TVs; almost all have expansive views reaching to both the Hudson and the East rivers. The health club has an Olympic-size pool with windows that look out on St. Paul's Church. ✉ *55 Church St., between Dey and Fulton Sts., Lower Manhattan 10007* ☎ *212/693–2001 or 800/ 445–8667* 🖷 *212/571–2317* ⊕ *www.hilton.com* ⤶ *463 rooms, 102 suites* ⬧ *2 restaurants, room service, in-room safes, minibars, cable TV with movies, in-room data ports, Wi-Fi, indoor pool, gym, massage, 3 bars, piano, babysitting, dry cleaning, laundry service, concierge, business services, meeting rooms, parking (fee)* ▭ *AE, D, DC, MC, V* Ⓜ *Subway: R, W to Cortlandt St.*

$$ 🏨 **Embassy Suites Hotel New York.** Directly across from the World Trade Center site is Manhattan's first Embassy Suites Hotel. As the name suggests, every one of the modern rooms here is at least a one-bedroom suite, with a living area that includes a pull-out sofa, dining table, microwave oven, and refrigerator. Not only is this hotel practical and reasonably priced, but it's also unusually attractive with original contemporary artwork in the atrium and lobby. Take advantage of the complimentary evening cocktail reception and breakfast bonanza. ✉ *102 North End Ave., at Murray St., Lower Manhattan 10281* ☎ *212/945–0100 or 800/362–2779* 🖷 *212/945–3012* ⊕ *www.embassysuites.com* ⤶ *463 suites* ⬧ *Restaurant, room service, in-room fax, in-room safes, refrigerators, in-room data ports, bar, concierge, business services, meeting rooms, parking (fee)* ▭ *AE, D, DC, MC, V* ⍾❘ *BP* Ⓜ *Subway: R, W to Cortlandt St.*

★ **$–$$** 🏨 **Holiday Inn Wall Street.** You know the future has arrived when a Holiday Inn provides T-1 Internet access in every room, express check-in lobby computers that dispense key cards, and both Web TV and Nintendo on 27-inch TVs. Half the rooms have desktop PCs, and on the "smart floor" wireless laptops and printers are at the ready. The comfortable rooms are surprisingly spacious—many have 14-foot ceilings. Thoughtful touches include ergonomically designed workspaces, full-length mirrors that open to reveal ironing boards, and oversize showerheads that simulate falling rain. ✉ *15 Gold St., at Platt St., Lower Manhattan 10038* ☎ *212/232–7700 or 800/465–4329* 🖷 *212/425– 0330* ⊕ *www.holidayinnwsd.com* ⤶ *136 rooms, 1 suite* ⬧ *Restaurant, room service, in-room safes, minibars, cable TV with movies and video games, in-room broadband, gym, bar, dry cleaning, laundry service, business services, meeting rooms, parking (fee), some pets allowed (fee), no-smoking floors* ▭ *AE, D, DC, MC, V* Ⓜ *Subway: A, E, J, M, 2, 3, 4, 5 to Fulton St./Broadway Nassau.*

$ 🏨 **Best Western Seaport Inn.** This thoroughly pleasant, restored 19th-century building is one block from the waterfront, close to South Street Seaport. Its cozy, librarylike lobby has the feel of a Colonial sea captain's

19

house, though the reasonably priced rooms are clearly those of a chain hotel. For around $25–$35 extra, you can have a room with a whirlpool tub and/or an outdoor terrace with a view of the Brooklyn Bridge. ✉ *33 Peck Slip, between Front and Water Sts., Lower Manhattan 10038* ☎ *212/766–6600 or 800/468–3569* 🖷 *212/766–6615* ⊕ *www. bestwestern.com* ⇨ *72 rooms* ⚴ *In-room safes, refrigerators, cable TV with video games, in-room VCRs, in-room data ports, gym, dry cleaning, laundry service, parking (fee), no-smoking floors* ⊟ *AE, D, DC, MC, V* Ⓜ *Subway: A, E, 2, 3, 4, 5 to Fulton St./Broadway Nassau.*

Chinatown, SoHo & TriBeCa

★ **$$–$$$$** ⬚ **60 Thompson.** A superb and original design by Thomas O'Brien, along with a popular lounge and restaurant, instantly anchored this stunning hotel into the downtown scene. The generous use of dark woods and full-wall leather headboards gives the retro-classic rooms a welcoming warmth; a decadent touch are the FatWitch brownies at turndown. Marble-swathed bathrooms have oversize showers, mosaic tile floors, and Philosophy bath products. Chic Thai restaurant Kittichai on the ground floor has patio dining and a gold-suffused bar; rooftop lounge A60 is a warm-weather haven for hipsters. ✉ *60 Thompson St., between Broome and Spring Sts., SoHo 10012* ☎ *877/431–0400* 🖷 *212/431–0200* ⊕ *www.60thompson.com* ⇨ *82 rooms, 8 suites* ⚴ *Restaurant, room service, in-room fax, in-room safes, minibars, cable TV with movies, in-room DVD, in-room broadband, 2 bars, concierge, meeting rooms, parking (fee), no-smoking rooms* ⊟ *AE, D, DC, MC, V* Ⓜ *Subway: C, E to Spring St.*

$$$ ⬚ **Mercer Hotel.** Owner Andre Balazs, known for his Château Marmont Fodor'sChoice in Hollywood, has a knack for channeling a neighborhood sensibility. Here, ★ it's SoHo loft all the way. In the hushed lobby, the reception desk is unmarked. Guest rooms are generously sized with long entryways, high ceilings, and walk-in closets. Dark African woods and custom-designed furniture upholstered in muted solids lend serenity. The bathrooms steal the show with their decadent two-person marble tubs—some surrounded by mirrors—but beware: not all rooms come with a tub. Downstairs is the happening Mercer Kitchen, where the cool still congregate. The lowest-priced rooms here are a slightly snug 250 square feet. For grander spaces, expect much higher prices. ✉ *147 Mercer St., at Prince St., SoHo 10012* 🖷 *212/966–6060 or 888/918–6060* 🖷 *212/965–3838* ⊕ *www.mercerhotel. com* ⇨ *67 rooms, 8 suites* ⚴ *Restaurant, room service, in-room safes, minibars, cable TV with movies and video games, in-room DVD, Wi-Fi, 2 bars, concierge, business services, some pets allowed, no-smoking rooms* ⊟ *AE, D, DC, MC, V* Ⓜ *Subway: R, W to Prince St.*

$$ ⬚ **SoHo Grand.** This hardy pioneer of SoHo's hotel boom still holds its own against newer arrivals. Public spaces as well as guest rooms use an industrial chic design to mimic the original architecture of the neighborhood. Comfortable contemporary rooms are mainly focused on the view out the 8-foot windows; bathrooms are stark but have deep soaking tubs. The high-ceiling lounge is outfitted in pony and mohair, but better yet is the large outdoor yard area where you can have a drink or

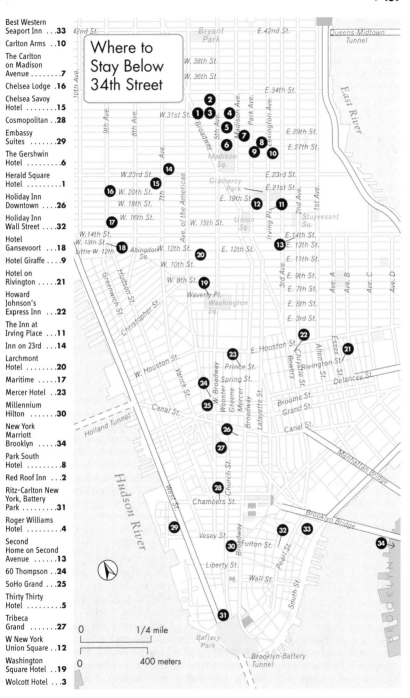

meal and then spread out on the grassy lawn—the only one of its kind at a city hotel. ⊠ *310 West Broadway, at Grand St., SoHo 10013* ☎ *212/965–3000 or 800/965–3000* 🖷 *212/965–3244* ⊕ *www. sohogrand.com* ⟿ *365 rooms, 2 suites* ⚖ *Restaurant, room service, in-room safes, minibars, cable TV with movies, in-room VCRs, in-room data ports, Wi-Fi, gym, hair salon, massage, 2 bars, babysitting, dry cleaning, laundry service, concierge, business services, meeting rooms, parking (fee), some pets allowed, no-smoking rooms* ▭ *AE, D, DC, MC, V* Ⓜ *Subway: 6, J, M, N, Q, R, W to Canal St.*

$$ 🏨 **Tribeca Grand.** Enter this industrial-looking giant via a curving, 30-foot cleft-stone ramp and you'll find yourself looking up into an eight-story atrium onto which all rooms open. Movie- and music-industry types hang out at the Church Lounge—a bar, café, and dining room—well into the night, sometimes to the dismay of quiet-minded guests. Twin glass elevators housed in a steel cage whisk you to hallways overlooking the atrium. Modern-design rooms have low platform beds, large work spaces, and podlike bathrooms with aluminum consoles reminiscent of those in airplanes. Like its sister, the SoHo Grand, the Tribeca Grand welcomes pets. ⊠ *2 Ave. of the Americas, between Walker and White Sts., TriBeCa 10013* ☎ *212/519–6600 or 800/965–3000* 🖷 *212/519–6700* ⊕ *www.tribecagrand.com* ⟿ *197 rooms, 6 suites* ⚖ *Restaurant, café, room service, in-room fax, in-room safes, minibars, cable TV with movies and video games, in-room VCRs, in-room data ports, Wi-Fi, gym, bar, dry cleaning, laundry service, concierge, business services, meeting rooms, parking (fee), some pets allowed, no-smoking rooms* ▭ *AE, D, DC, MC, V* Ⓜ *Subway: A, C, E to Canal St.*

$ 🏨 **Cosmopolitan.** For those on a budget, this spot is one of the better buys, especially if you want a room with a private bath. The decor is modern and clean, and the location is ideal for exploring Chinatown, Little Italy, Wall Street, SoHo, and the South Street Seaport. The building dates to 1850, and Abraham Lincoln slept here. A repeat clientele comes for the "miniloft" rooms. ⊠ *95 West Broadway, at Chambers St., TriBeCa 10007* ☎ *212/566–1900 or 888/895–9400* 🖷 *212/566–6909* ⊕ *www.cosmohotel.com* ⟿ *105 rooms* ⚖ *In-room data ports, gym, babysitting, dry cleaning, laundry service, concierge, parking (fee)* ▭ *AE, DC, MC, V* Ⓜ *Subway: 1, 2, 3, A, C to Chambers St.*

$ 🏨 **Holiday Inn Downtown.** Historical features such as oversize arched windows, high ceilings, and a classic exterior remain in this former factory building, but the lobby is a cross-cultural affair mixing marble and Asian accents. Excellent dim sum at Pacifica Restaurant attracts plenty of Asian business travelers. Many Europeans and young budget travelers are also drawn by the reasonable rates and proximity to Little Italy, TriBeCa, and SoHo. The rooms are standard issue, but clean and well maintained, and they do have nice touches such as in-room coffeemakers and CD players. The staff is well trained and works hard to please. Nearby is bustling Canal Street. ⊠ *138 Lafayette St., near Canal St., Chinatown 10013* ☎ *212/966–8898 or 800/465–4329* 🖷 *212/966–3933* ⊕ *www.holidayinn-nyc.com* ⟿ *215 rooms, 12 suites* ⚖ *Restaurant, room service, refrigerators, cable TV with movies, in-room data ports, bar, dry cleaning, laundry service, concierge, parking (fee), no-*

smoking floors ⊟ *AE, D, DC, MC, V* Ⓜ *Subway: 6, M, N, Q, R, W to Canal St.*

Greenwich Village

$$$ ▦ **Hotel Gansevoort.** Modern and hip, the hotel is a shining beacon in the trendy Meatpacking District. Most notable is the extensive rooftop deck comprising a heated 45-foot pool, myriad terraces, a restaurant where complimentary breakfast is served, and happening bar–lounge that fills with late-night scene-seekers. Sleek, sexy rooms have sweeping views of the city or the Hudson River; slate-and-marble bathrooms have unique showers that double as steam rooms. Original New York–centric artwork, including Warhols and local gallery pieces, hangs in rooms and hallways. Downstairs, Japanese restaurant Ono has a vibrant Asian interior and an extensive outdoor bar and lounge space. ✉ *18 9th Ave., at 13th St., Greenwich Village 10014* ☎ *212/206–6700 or 877/426–7386* 🖷 *212/255–5858* ⊕ *www.hotelgansevoort.com* 🛏 *166 rooms, 21 suites* ♢ *2 restaurants, room service, in-room safes, cable TV with movies, in-room data ports, Wi-Fi, pool, gym, spa, bar, dry cleaning, laundry service, concierge, business services, meeting rooms, parking (fee), some pets allowed* ⊟ *AE, MC, V* ⦿| *CP* Ⓜ *Subway: A, C, E, L to 14th St.*

$ ▦ **Washington Square Hotel.** This low-key hotel with a distinguished history and a Continental feel is catercorner to Washington Square Park's magnificent arch. Most striking is the intimate bar, entered through an ornate wrought-iron-and-gleaming-brass gate from Paris, and decorated with mosaic floors and elegant mirrors. Request one of the lovely, crimson-fuchsia colored renovated rooms. Its proximity to New York University keeps it busy with visiting parents. ✉ *103 Waverly Pl., at MacDougal St., Greenwich Village 10011* ☎ *212/777–9515 or 800/222–0418* 🖷 *212/979–8373* ⊕ *www.washingtonsquarehotel.com* 🛏 *160 rooms* ♢ *Restaurant, in-room safes, cable TV, in-room data ports, Wi-Fi, gym, massage, bar, meeting rooms* ⊟ *AE, MC, V* ⦿| *CP* Ⓜ *Subway: A, B, C, D, E, F, V to W. 4th St./Washington Sq.*

¢–$ ▦ **Larchmont Hotel.** You might miss the entrance to this Beaux-Arts
Fodor'sChoice town house, whose geranium boxes and lanterns blend right in with the
★ old New York feel of West 11th Street. If you don't mind shared bathrooms and no room service, the residential-style accommodations are all anyone could ask for the price. The small rooms have a tasteful safari theme; your own private sink and stocked bookshelf will make you feel right at home. Guests have use of a communal kitchen, and a Continental breakfast is included. ✉ *27 W. 11th St., between 5th and 6th Aves., Greenwich Village 10011* ☎ *212/989–9333* 🖷 *212/989–9496* ⊕ *www.larchmonthotel.com* 🛏 *60 rooms, none with bath* ♢ *Café, fans, business services, no-smoking rooms* ⊟ *AE, D, DC, MC, V* ⦿| *CP* Ⓜ *Subway: A, B, C, D, E, F, V to W. 4th St./Washington Sq.*

The East Village & the Lower East Side

★ **$$–$$$** ▦ **Hotel on Rivington.** The hip Lower East Side finally gets a hotel cool enough to call its own. What's pleasantly surprising here, considering

19

Kids in Tow

MANY NEW YORK HOTELS go out of their way to accommodate families with special amenities and family-size rooms. However, a hotel claiming it's child friendly doesn't always translate to true kid-welcoming style. Ask if cribs come with linens, whether there are high chairs and children's menus in the dining room, and if there are in-house babysitters. Some hotels will even clear out the minibar, baby-proof a room, or provide baby-proofing materials if you alert them in advance. Here are some of the top picks for traveling with kids.

SUITE LIFE. Space is at a premium in New York hotels, and if you have more than two people in a standard room, you'll really start to feel the squeeze. The answer? A suite, where you can spread out in style. The **Embassy Suites Hotel New York** (⇨ Lower Manhattan), a tried-and-true family option, is even more kid friendly in New York since it's in the same building as a multiplex movie theater and several reasonably priced dining options. With newly renovated, super-spacious suites, **Affinia Fifty** (⇨ Midtown East) is the family hotel of choice on the residential East Side.

LUXE LIFE. Just because you have children in tow doesn't mean your dream of a pampering vacation needs to go down the drain. Several top New York hotels go out of their way to accommodate families. The **Ritz-Carlton**'s two hotels (⇨ Lower Manhattan *and* Midtown West) offer special healthful children's menus, rubber-duck-filled baths, and toy menus from FAO Schwarz. The Battery Park location has children's etiquette classes the first Saturday of the month; the Central Park branch holds special teddy bear teas. At **The Pierre** (⇨ Upper East Side), your little one can luxuriate in a child's bathrobe while perusing the menu of children's favorites that includes everything from Froot Loops to Kraft Macaroni and Cheese, not to mention the complimentary cookies and milk served in bed. The hotel can also find a babysitter with as little as five hours' notice.

NEW YORK SPECIAL. Hotel QT (⇨ Midtown West) might make the perfect respite if you have teens in tow. There's a funky lobby pool; a lobby kiosk that stocks sweets with which to fill the in-room refrigerators; and rooms with ingenious bunk beds that levitate out of the walls and have their own plasma TVs—all in the heart of Times Square. At the hip **Hotel on Rivington** (⇨ East Village & the Lower East Side), a special family suite has two full bedrooms, one with two sets of bunk beds and a big bin of toys, two full baths, and a Japanese tub that could easily fit four preschoolers. Bonus points: the hotel is across from Economy Candy.

Family-friendly **Le Parker Meridien** (⇨ Midtown West) has a large pool, a restaurant that serves decadent breakfast foods such as chocolate French toast until 3 PM, and another dining spot that serves nothing but burgers and shakes. Kid heaven. Upon check-in at the **Omni Berkshire Place** (⇨ Midtown East), kids get a goodie bag and a loaner backpack. Both contain toys galore from cards and puzzles to coloring books and bedtime reading. On the room's Web TV, kids can log on to ⊕ www.omnikidsrule.com to participate in polls and contests.

its off-the-beaten-path location, is just how refined, comfortable, and cutting-edge the rooms are. If you like baths, request a room with a super-deep, two-person Japanese soaking tub. Steam showers have glass walls that look onto the street (privacy curtains are available on request—make sure to ask for them when you check in if you're at all modest) and bathrooms have heated floors. High-tech wake-up calls remotely open the blinds on the floor-to-ceiling windows. Most rooms have balconies. The public areas have an Alice-through-the-looking-glass feeling, with amorphous entryways and velvet settees. High-end, small-plate, well-reviewed THOR restaurant is worth visiting even if you're not staying here. ⊠ *107 Rivington St., between Ludlow and Essex Sts., Lower East Side 10002* ☎ *212/475–2600 or 800/915–1537* 🖷 *212/475–5959* ⊕ *www. hotelonrivington.com* ⇨ *110 rooms* ⚏ *Restaurant, room service, in-room safes, minibars, cable TV with movies, in-room data ports, Wi-Fi, Japanese baths, bar, lounge, dry cleaning, laundry service, concierge, meeting rooms, parking (fee), some pets allowed* ⊟ *AE, D, DC, MC, V* Ⓜ *Subway: F, J, M, Z to Delancey/Essex Sts.*

$ 🏠 **Howard Johnson's Express Inn.** This hotel at the nexus of East Village and Lower East Side nightlife is perfect if you want to check out the downtown scene. A corner location increases your chances of having a view when you eventually rise to meet the day, and next door is a century-old knish bakery. The tastefully done rooms each have enough space for a desk; a few have hot tubs or microwaves and mini-refrigerators. With amenities such as in-room hair dryers, irons, coffeemakers, and voice mail, plus free local calls, you're getting more than your money's worth in New York's hotel market. ⊠ *135 E. Houston St., at Forsyth St., Lower East Side 10002* ☎ *212/358–8844 or 800/446–4656* 🖷 *212/ 473–3500* ⊕ *www.hojo.com* ⇨ *46 rooms* ⚏ *Some microwaves, cable TV, in-room data ports, laundry service, no-smoking floors* ⊟ *AE, D, DC, MC, V* ⍢⏐ *CP* Ⓜ *Subway: F, V to 2nd Ave.*

FodorśChoice ★

¢–$ 🏠 **Second Home on Second Avenue.** The rooms at this budget hotel are themed: modern, Caribbean, Peruvian, skylight, and tribal. Local calls are free; a skylight illuminates common areas; and the staff is friendly. Not all rooms, however, have private baths, and the single rooms are only for those who don't mind extremely small quarters (think large walk-in closet). This is a popular place, so book well in advance. ⊠ *221 2nd Ave., between 13 and 14th Sts., East Village 10002* ☎ *212/677–3161* ⊕ *secondhomesecondavenue.com* ⇨ *7 rooms, 2 with bath* ⚏ *Cable TV* ⊟ *AE, D, DC, MC, V* Ⓜ *Subway: 4, 5, 6, L, N, Q, R, W to 14th St./Union Sq.; L to 3rd Ave.*

Flatiron District & Gramercy

$$$$ 🏠 **W New York Union Square.** Starwood's W Hotel brand has owned Union Square since it bought the landmark Guardian Life building at the park's northeast corner. Both the interior and exterior of the 1911 Beaux Arts-style building retain many original granite and limestone details. Modernism permeates each room, from shiny sharkskin bed coverings to overstuffed velvet armchairs. Generally, the service staff look as though they just stepped out of a photo shoot, and at times it feels like that's where they'd rather be. Celebrity chef Todd English's first New York restau-

19

rant, Olives, and the comfortable lobby bar draw huge crowds. ⊠ *201 Park Ave. S, at E. 17th St., Flatiron District 10003* ☎ *212/253–9119 or 877/946–8357* 🖷 *212/779–0148* ⊕ *www.whotels.com* ⥂ *253 rooms, 17 suites* △ *Restaurant, café, room service, in-room fax, in-room safes, minibars, cable TV with movies, in-room DVD/VCR, Wi-Fi, Web TV, gym, health club, spa, 2 bars, babysitting, dry cleaning, laundry service, concierge, business services, meeting rooms, parking (fee), some pets allowed, no-smoking rooms, no-smoking floors* ☰ *AE, D, DC, MC, V* Ⓜ *Subway: 4, 5, 6, L, N, Q, R, W to 14th St./Union Sq.*

$$–$$$$

Fodor'sChoice

★

🏨 **The Inn at Irving Place.** The city's most romantic small inn occupies two grand 1830s town houses just steps from Gramercy Park. Its cozy tea salon (complete with a working fireplace), antiques-filled living room, and original curving banister evoke a more genteel era. Rooms have ornamental fireplaces, four-poster beds with embroidered linens, wood shutters, and glossy cherrywood floors. The room named after Madame Olenska (the lovelorn Edith Wharton character) has a bay window with sitting nook. In the morning, steaming pots of tea and coffee are served in the tea salon, along with a free Continental breakfast including homemade pastries and breads. ⊠ *56 Irving Pl., between E. 17th and E. 18th Sts., Gramercy 10003* ☎ *212/533–4600 or 800/685–1447* 🖷 *212/533–4611* ⊕ *www.innatirving.com* ⥂ *5 rooms, 6 suites* △ *Restaurant, room service, minibars, refrigerators, cable TV with movies, in-room VCRs, in-room data ports, massage, bar, dry cleaning, laundry service, business services, parking (fee); no kids under 8* ☰ *AE, D, DC, MC, V* ⑩ *CP* Ⓜ *Subway: 4, 5, 6, L, N, Q, R, W to 14th St./Union Sq.*

Murray Hill

$$$$

🏨 **W New York–The Court and W New York–The Tuscany.** Big black "W"s transform guest-room headboards into billboards at these self-consciously stylish sister properties. The design-for-design's-sake lobbies might strike some as cold, but an exceedingly attentive staff goes a long way toward warming things up. Spacious rooms have vaguely Oriental black-and-blond wood furnishings and ottomans with chenille throws. If you're accustomed to W hotels being the coolest kids in the 'hood, you may be disappointed at these properties. Both are older hotels that were given W makeovers; head to Times Square or Union Square for truly modern Ws. Both properties, however, uphold the W chain's hip nightlife standards with Tuscany's Cherry, a rock-and-roll vision in red, and the Court's popular Wet Bar. *Court* ⊠ *130 E. 39th St., between Lexington and Park Aves., Murray Hill 10016* ☎ *212/685–1100 or 877/946–8357* 🖷 *212/889–0287* ⊕ *www.whotels.com* ⥂ *Court: 150 rooms, 39 suites; Tuscany: 122 rooms, 12 suites* △ *Restaurant, café, room service, in-room safes, minibars, cable TV with movies, in-room VCRs, in-room data ports, Wi-Fi, exercise equipment, gym, spa, 2 bars, babysitting, dry cleaning, laundry service, concierge, business services, meeting rooms, parking (fee), no-smoking rooms, no-smoking floors* ☰ *AE, D, DC, MC, V* ⊠ *Tuscany* ⊠ *120 E. 39th St., near Lexington Ave., Murray Hill 10016* ☎ *212/779–7822, 800/223–6725 for reservations* 🖷 *212/696–2095* Ⓜ *Subway: 4, 5, 6, 7, S to 42nd St./Grand Central.*

$$–$$$$ 🖼 **Carlton on Madison Avenue.** A five-year, $60 million renovation has turned a nearly invisible old dowager into a modern scene-stealer. A two-story lobby designed by David Rockwell is infused with a golden glow and highlighted by a shimmering wall of water. Happily, many of the original 1904 Beaux-Arts details are still intact, such as the Tiffany-style stained-glass dome (created by workers from the venerable factory but not by Louis Comfort himself) and the elegant mosaic tile floors in upscale Country restaurant adjacent to the lobby. Spacious rooms, some with views of the Empire State Building, have mahogany accents, fabric-framed beds, and marble bathrooms. The residential tone of the neighborhood is often reflected in the reasonable Web-only rates. ☒ *88 Madison Ave., between 28th and 29th Sts., Murray Hill 10016* 🖀 *212/ 532–4100 or 800/601–8500* 🖷 *212/889–8683* ⊕ *www.carltonhotelny. com* ↪ *294 rooms, 22 suites* ↻ *Restaurant, room service, in-room safes, minibars, cable TV with movies, in-room data ports, Wi-Fi, bar, dry cleaning, laundry service, concierge, business services, meeting rooms, parking (fee), no-smoking floors* ▭ *AE, D, MC, V* Ⓜ *Subway: 6 to 33rd St.*

$$$ 🖼 **70 Park Avenue.** Kimpton hotels have something of a cult following with design enthusiasts, and whether you're one of the devout or not, you should be pleased with New York's first offering from this contemporary hotel group. The lobby, with its limestone fireplace and thick-pillowed couches, replicates a well-appointed living room, and is the location for complimentary evening cocktails. The rest of the hotel channels a prosperous Park Avenue abode; neutral-palette rooms have Ultrasuede chairs and couches, plasma TVs, and woven silk blankets. Silverleaf Tavern serves a modern-American menu, and the bar is comfortable even if you're alone. ☒ *70 Park Ave., at 38th St., Murray Hill 10016* 🖀 *212/973–2400 or 800/707–2752* 🖷 *212/ 973–2401* ⊕ *www.70parkavenuehotel.com* ↪ *201 rooms, 4 suites* ↻ *Restaurant, room service, in-room safes, in-room DVD, in-room data ports, Wi-Fi, bar, laundry service, concierge, meeting rooms, some pets allowed, no-smoking rooms* ▭ *AE, D, DC, MC, V* Ⓜ *Subway: 6 to 33rd St.*

$$–$$$ 🖼 **Hotel Giraffe.** Inspired by the colors and sleek lines of European moderne, this retro-glam property aspires to the sophisticated style of the 1920s and '30s. Guest rooms with 10-foot ceilings are adorned with antique-rose velveteen armchairs, sorbet-hue sheer curtains, and pearlized platinum wall covers. Deluxe rooms have French doors opening onto private balconies from which you can survey Park Avenue. For the ultimate in entertaining (or an exorbitant romantic getaway), reserve the spectacular penthouse suite with baby grand piano and rooftop garden. The civilized service here includes complimentary breakfast, coffee beverages, and weekday evening champagne reception. ☒ *365 Park Ave. S, at E. 26th St., Murray Hill 10016* 🖀 *212/685–7700 or 877/296–0009* 🖷 *212/ 685–7771* ⊕ *www.hotelgiraffe.com* ↪ *52 rooms, 21 suites* ↻ *Restaurant, room service, in-room safes, minibars, cable TV, in-room VCRs, in-room data ports, Wi-Fi, 2 bars, piano, dry cleaning, laundry service, concierge, business services, parking (fee), no-smoking rooms, no-smoking floors* ▭ *AE, DC, MC, V* ⧮ *CP* Ⓜ *Subway: 6 to 28th St.*

19

\$\$ 🏨 **Jolly Hotel Madison Towers.** The Italian Jolly Hotels chain brings a European air to this friendly hotel on a residential Murray Hill corner, combining an Italian aesthetic with an art deco design. The tasteful, traditional rooms have elegant cherry furniture and travertine marble bathrooms. Deluxe rooms on the top floors have a sleek, contemporary design, grand bathrooms with separate soaking tubs, and views of the Empire State Building. Cinque Terre serves Northern Italian cuisine, and the cozy Whaler Bar has a fireplace and a wood-beam ceiling. A separate concession on the premises offers shiatsu massage and a Japanese sauna. Note that the name appears as "Madison Towers" on the flags marking the entrance. ⊠ *22 E. 38th St., between Madison and Park Aves., Murray Hill 10016* ☎ *212/802–0600 or 800/225–4340* 🖷 *212/447–0747* ⊕ *www.jollymadison.com* ⤶ *238 rooms, 6 suites* ⚐ *Restaurant, in-room safes, minibars, cable TV with movies and video games, in-room data ports, Wi-Fi, massage, sauna, steam room, bar, dry cleaning, laundry service, concierge, business services, meeting rooms, parking (fee), some pets allowed, no-smoking floors* ▭ *AE, DC, MC, V* Ⓜ *Subway: 6 to 33rd St.*

★ **\$\$** 🏨 **The Kitano.** A virtual Zen relaxation garden of a hotel, this Japanese-owned property, a few blocks from Grand Central, is an oasis of tranquility. The Asian-influenced airy marble lobby has an austere grandeur that flows through the rest of the property. Handsome cherry and mahogany furnishings, tea makers, and watercolor still lifes decorate the large rooms, which would benefit from a little sprucing up; soundproof windows, however, make them among Manhattan's quietest. The authentic sushi and Japanese food at Nadaman restaurant is a favorite of Mayor Bloomberg; the second-floor lounge hosts a jazz band several nights a week. Vacationers can take advantage of discounted weekend rates as well as the large multiroom suites that sell here for the same price as a regular room at trendier hotels. ⊠ *66 Park Ave., at E. 38th St., Murray Hill 10016* ☎ *212/885–7000 or 800/548–2666* 🖷 *212/885–7100* ⊕ *www.kitano.com* ⤶ *149 rooms, 18 suites* ⚐ *2 restaurants, room service, in-room fax, in-room safes, minibars, cable TV with movies, in-room broadband, Web TV, bar, babysitting, dry cleaning, laundry service, concierge, business services, meeting rooms, parking (fee), no-smoking floors* ▭ *AE, D, DC, MC, V* Ⓜ *Subway: 6 to 33rd St.*

★ **\$\$** 🏨 **Morgans.** Überhotelier Ian Schrager launched New York's boutique hotel craze way back in 1984 when he opened this hip hotel, but Morgans is still up-to-the-minute. Comfortable rooms have a minimalist, high-tech look, with low-lying, futonlike beds, long window seats, and original Mapplethorpe photographs; the tiny but functional bathrooms have steel surgical sinks and poured-granite floors. An incredibly friendly and hospitable staff is one of the reasons that the hotel is filled with return guests. The chic Asia de Cuba created the Latin-fusion craze and is still standing-room only. The cavelike, candlelit Morgans Bar downstairs also lives up to all its hype. ⊠ *237 Madison Ave., between E. 37th and E. 38th Sts., Murray Hill 10016* ☎ *212/686–0300 or 800/334–3408* 🖷 *212/779–8352* ⊕ *www.morganshotel.com* ⤶ *87 rooms, 26 suites* ⚐ *Restaurant, room service, in-room safes, minibars, refrigerators, cable TV with movies, in-room VCRs, Wi-Fi, 2 bars, babysitting, dry*

Romantic Retreats

EVEN IF YOU LIVE IN NEW YORK, treat yourself to a stay in one of these romantic hotels where you can order everything from breakfast in bed to a rose-petal-filled bath.

At the **Ritz-Carlton New York, Battery Park** (⇨ Lower Manhattan), your wish is their command. Take advantage of lower-than-normal weekend rates to book a Liberty Suite, with sweeping views of the Statue of Liberty. A quick call to the concierge before you arrive can take care of everything from having champagne and strawberries waiting on your arrival to a silver-framed picture of your sweetie by the bedside. A bath butler can then fill your marble tub with a potion of bath oils and flower petals. If you're here in February, don't miss a trip to the penthouse

Chocolate Bar with its aphrodisiacal chocolate and champagne buffet.

The Inn at Irving Place (⇨ Flatiron District & Gramercy) does romance the old-fashioned way, with four-poster beds, fireplaces, fur throws, and lots of privacy in an elegant 1800s brownstone. The complimentary breakfast is served on fine bone china either in the cozy sitting room or in bed.

All of the rooms at the **Library Hotel** (⇨ Midtown East) have a certain inviting charm that makes them a good choice for a romantic weekend away, but if you're looking for a little mood reading, ask for the Erotic Literature room or the Love room, curated by Dr. Ruth.

---

cleaning, laundry service, concierge, business services, meeting rooms, parking (fee), some pets allowed, no-smoking rooms, no-smoking floors ▤ AE, D, DC, MC, V Ⓜ Subway: 4, 5, 6, 7, S to 42nd St./Grand Central.

19

$$ ▥ **Park South Hotel.** In this beautifully transformed 1906 office building, restful rooms are smartly contemporary although they've retained some period detailing. Beware rooms with half-size closets and those that overlook noisy 27th street; try instead for views of the Chrysler Building. The New York flavor permeates from a mezzanine library focusing on local history to the ubiquitous black-and-white photos of city scenes from the 1880s through 1950s. The Black Duck bar and restaurant warms patrons with its wood-burning fireplace. Despite the reasonable rates, you have a host of high-end niceties such as complimentary Continental breakfast, free Internet, and nightly turndown service. ✉ 122 E. 28th St., between Lexington and Park Aves., Murray Hill 10016 ☎ 212/448–0888 or 800/315–4642 🖷 212/448–0811 ⊕ www. parksouthhotel.com ⇋ 139 rooms, 2 suites ⊛ Restaurant, in-room fax, cable TV, in-room DVD, in-room broadband, gym, bar, dry cleaning, laundry service, concierge, business services ▤ AE, D, DC, MC, V № CP Ⓜ Subway: 6 to 28th St.

★ $$ ▥ **Roger Williams Hotel.** A masterpiece of industrial chic, the cavernous Rafael Viñoly-designed lobby—clad with sleek maple walls accented with fluted zinc pillars—was dubbed "a shrine to modernism" by *New York* magazine. Rooms have a clean, California-beach feel—the parent hotel is in Santa Monica—with blond-birch furnishings, chartreuse enamel bathroom accents, and brightly colored quilts and pillows. A small splurge will buy you an upgrade to a room with a full-size terrace; you'll make up the fee with the bargain $12 buffet breakfast, which is filled with New York specialties. ☒ *131 Madison Ave., at E. 31st St., Murray Hill 10016* ☎ *212/448–7000 or 877/847–4444* 🖷 *212/448–7007* ⊕ *www.rogerwilliamshotel.com* ↪ *185 rooms, 2 suites* ⚒ *Restaurant, room service, cable TV, in-room VCRs, Wi-Fi, exercise equipment, gym, bar, piano, concierge, business services, parking (fee), no-smoking rooms, no-smoking floors* ▱ *AE, D, MC, V* ⚏ *CP* Ⓜ *Subway: 6 to 33rd St.*

★ **$** 🖳 **The Gershwin Hotel.** Young, foreign travelers flock to this budget hotel–cum–hostel, housed in a converted 13-story Greek Revival building adjacent to the Museum of Sex. A giant Plexiglas and metal sculpture of glowing pods by Stefan Lindfors creeps down the facade and winds its way into the lobby. With Andy Warhol as muse, there's pop art on every floor. Rooms are painted in bright colors and are basically distinguished by being simple and cheap. For bargain seekers, the dormitory offers a basic bunk for just $40. On any given night there's something going on—film series, stand-up comedy, performance art—at this slightly cheesy center for avant-garde activities. ☒ *7 E. 27th St., between 5th and Madison Aves., Murray Hill 10016* ☎ *212/545–8000* 🖷 *212/684–5546* ⊕ *www.gershwinhotel.com* ↪ *120 rooms, 64 beds in dorm rooms, 12 suites* ⚒ *Restaurant, café, cable TV, Wi-Fi, bar, no-smoking floors; no TV in some rooms* ▱ *AE, MC, V* Ⓜ *Subway: 6, R, W to 28th St.*

$ 🖳 **Herald Square Hotel.** Sculpted cherubs on the facade and vintage magazine covers adorning the common areas hint at this building's previous incarnation as *Life* magazine's 1886 headquarters. Rooms are basic and clean; all have TVs and phones with voice mail. There's no concierge and no room service, but the staff is friendly and nearby restaurants will deliver. A no-frills option, to be sure, but it's a great bargain for the convenient neighborhood. ☒ *19 W. 31st St., between 5th Ave. and Broadway, Murray Hill 10001* ☎ *212/279–4017 or 800/727–1888* 🖷 *212/643–9208* ⊕ *www.heraldsquarehotel.com* ↪ *120 rooms* ⚒ *In-room safes, cable TV, Wi-Fi, airport shuttle, some pets allowed* ▱ *AE, D, MC, V* Ⓜ *Subway: B, D, F, N, Q, R, V, W to 34th St./Herald Sq.*

$ 🖳 **Thirty Thirty Hotel.** The former Martha Washington women's residence is still haunted by many of its female senior-citizen tenants, who remain in the building despite the fact that a busy hotel has been built around them. This is an efficient and pleasant place, with a friendly staff. The rooms are clean, modern, simple, and sparsely decorated in dusty shades of beige, purple, and green. For a few dollars more you can upgrade to a room with a kitchenette. ☒ *30 E. 30th St., between Park Ave. S and Madison, Murray Hill 10016* ☎ *212/689–1900 or 800/497–6028* ⊕ *www.thirtythirty-nyc.com* ↪ *243 rooms* ⚒ *Room service, some kitchenettes, cable TV with movies, in-room broadband, dry cleaning, laundry service* ▱ *AE, D, DC, MC, V* Ⓜ *Subway: 6, R, W to 28th St.*

$ 🖳 **Wolcott Hotel.** Edith Wharton stayed at this unassuming hotel back when it was a Beaux-Arts glamour palace. Now students, international travelers, and conventioneers grab the unimpressive rooms' impressively low rates. Tilt your head back when you enter the lobby and the chandeliers, marble columns, and ornate moldings will give you an idea of the grandeur that was once here. Now, however, rooms are tiny and the furnishings old, and the elevator is old and slow. The location, however, is still one of the best in New York. ⊠ *3 W. 31st St., between 5th Ave. and Broadway, Murray Hill 10001* ☎ *212/268–2900 or 212/563–0096* ⊕ *www.wolcott.com* ⯈ *180 rooms* ⟁ *In-room safes, cable TV with movies and video games, gym, laundry facilities, laundry service, concierge, business services* ☰ *AE, MC, V* Ⓜ *Subway: B, D, F, N, Q, R, V, W to 34th St./Herald Sq.*

¢–$ 🖼 **Red Roof Inn.** Two blocks from the Empire State Building, Penn Station, Madison Square Garden, and Macy's, this chain hotel has pleasant, spacious rooms and a mezzanine bar overlooking the smart lobby. Weekday newspapers are free, as is the Continental breakfast. ⊠ *6 W. 32nd St., between 5th Ave. and Broadway, Murray Hill 10001* ☎ *212/643–7100 or 800/567–7720* 🖶 *212/643–7101* ⊕ *www.applecorehotels. com* ⯈ *171 rooms* ⟁ *Some microwaves, some refrigerators, cable TV with movies and video games, Wi-Fi, health club, bar, dry cleaning, laundry service, concierge, business services, meeting rooms, parking (fee), no-smoking rooms* ☰ *AE, D, DC, MC, V* ⎢◎⎥ *CP* Ⓜ *Subway: B, D, F, N, Q, R, V, W to 34th St./Herald Sq.*

¢ 🖼 **Carlton Arms.** So creepy, it's cool—every wall and ceiling in this bohemian dive is covered with a mural. Each room has a theme, such as the Versailles Room with its outré symphony of trompe l'oeil trellises and classical urns and the "child's dream" room with its puzzle-covered floor and a bed the shape of a car with monsters underneath. But these are tame compared to the room devoted to sadomasochism. Children are allowed, but you may consider leaving them with relatives. All rooms have double-glaze windows; many are almost free of furniture, and some of baths, and none have TVs or phones. ⊠ *160 E. 25th St., at 3rd Ave., Murray Hill 10010* ☎ *212/684–8337, 212/679–0680 for reservations* ⊕ *www.carltonarms.com* ⯈ *54 rooms, 20 with bath* ⟁ *Some pets allowed; no room phones, no room TVs* ☰ *MC, V* Ⓜ *Subway: R, W to 28th St.*

19

Chelsea

$$ 🖼 **Maritime Hotel.** The soaring white-ceramic tower that is the Maritime earns the title of the first luxury hotel in the heart of the Chelsea gallery scene. And with the Meatpacking District two blocks away, you are near some of the city's chicest boutiques and hippest nightclubs. Rooms here resemble modern ship's cabins, with burnished teak paneling, sea-blue drapes and bed accents, and large porthole windows that face the Hudson River skyline. Matsuri, the cavernous Japanese restaurant below the hotel, is an experience in itself. ⊠ *363 W. 16th St., at 9th Ave., Chelsea 10011* ☎ *212/242–4300* 🖶 *212/242–1188* ⊕ *www.themaritimehotel. com* ⯈ *120 rooms, 4 suites* ⟁ *2 restaurants, room service, in-room safes, minibars, cable TV, in-room DVD, Wi-Fi, bar, dry cleaning, concierge, business services, no-smoking rooms* ☰ *AE, MC, V* Ⓜ *Subway: A, C, E to 14th St.*

$ ▣ **Chelsea Savoy Hotel.** Affordable rates and a friendly though often harried young staff make this a sensible choice. Jade-green carpets, butterscotch wood furniture, and perhaps a framed Van Gogh print enliven the small, basic rooms. The Bull Run Grill is next to the bland lobby. ⊠ *204 W. 23rd St., at 7th Ave., Chelsea 10011* ☎ *212/929–9353 or 866/929–9353* 🖷 *212/741–6309* ⊕ *www.chelseasavoynyc.com* ⟿ *90 rooms* ♿ *Restaurant, café, room service, in-room safes, refrigerators, cable TV, in-room data ports, bar, no-smoking rooms* ▤ *AE, MC, V* Ⓜ *Subway: F, V to 23rd St.*

★ **$** ▣ **Inn on 23rd.** Innkeepers Annette and Barry Fisherman were inspired to restore this 19th-century commercial building in the heart of Chelsea, making each of the guest rooms spacious and unique. One exotic and elegant room is outfitted in bamboo, another in the art moderne style of the 1940s. Although it's small and homey, the inn provides private baths and satellite TV in all rooms, an elevator, and breakfast. ⊠ *131 W. 23rd St., between 6th and 7th Aves., Chelsea 10011* ☎ *212/463–0330* 🖷 *212/463–0302* ⊕ *www.innon23rd.com* ⟿ *13 rooms, 1 suite* ♿ *In-room data ports, Wi-Fi; no smoking* ▤ *AE, MC, V* ⧄�Ⓞⵏ *CP* Ⓜ *Subway: F, V to 23rd St.*

¢–**$** ▣ **Chelsea Lodge.** On a quiet neighborhood street near the galleries of Chelsea and the nightlife of the Meatpacking District, this country-inn-style brownstone is a great budget option if you don't need a lot of services or amenities. The majority of the petite rooms share a toilet, but have a sink and shower in the room. There are small bedrooms with reach-in closets, no phones, and small TVs. However, meticulous attention to cleanliness, lovely period detailing such as decorative wainscoting, and truly helpful staff make a visit here worthwhile. A few doors past the main building are "suites," really small apartments with kitchens and kitchenettes. At $199, these are a great option if you're planning an extended stay or want to take advantage of the gourmet wares at nearby Chelsea Market. ⊠ *318 W. 20th St., between 8th and 9th Aves., Chelsea 10011* ☎ *212/243–4499* 🖷 *212/243–7852* ⊕ *www.chelsealodge. com* ⟿ *22 rooms, 20 with shared bath, 4 suites* ♿ *Some kitchenettes* ▤ *AE, D, MC, V* Ⓜ *Subway: C, E to 23rd St.; 1 to 18th St.*

Midtown West

$$$$ ▣ **Essex House, a Westin Hotel.** The lobby of this stately Central Park South property is an art deco masterpiece, with inlaid marble floors and bas-relief elevator doors. Reproductions of Chippendale or Louis XV antiques decorate guest rooms, all of which have marble bathrooms and luxuriously comfortable beds. The top 20 floors of the hotel, called the St. Regis Club, provide even more lavish rooms, all with park views, as well as butler service. For all-out decadence, book a table at Alain Ducasse's restaurant, where caviar and truffles are de rigueur and prix-fixe dinners starting at $150 buy you your table for the entire evening. ⊠ *160 Central Park S, between 6th and 7th Aves., Midtown West 10019* ☎ *212/247–0300 or 800/937–8461* 🖷 *212/315–1839* ⊕ *www. westin.com/essexhouse* ⟿ *526 rooms, 79 suites* ♿ *2 restaurants, room service, in-room fax, in-room safes, minibars, cable TV, in-room VCRs, in-room data ports, gym, spa, bar, babysitting, dry cleaning, laundry serv-*

ice, concierge, business services, meeting rooms, parking (fee), no-smoking rooms ☐ *AE, D, DC, MC, V* Ⓜ *Subway: F, N, R, Q, W to 57th St.*

★ $$$$ 🏨 **Mandarin Oriental.** No standard hotel rooms in Manhattan are larger or more luxe than those at the Mandarin. Black-enamel furniture is embellished with Asian-inspired silver drawer pulls; silk-encased throw pillows nearly cover the plush beds; marble-ensconced bathrooms are larger than some New York apartments. Since the hotel begins on the 35th floor, views of the city, especially Central Park, are paramount; even the swimming pool has floor-to-ceiling windows and park vistas. Contemporary art, notably two glass sculptures by Dale Chihuly, graces the cavernous public spaces; the hotel also contains an elaborate spa, glass-enclosed lounge, and the high-end Asiate restaurant. You'll pay for all this pleasure—rates start at $725 per night. ☒ *80 Columbus Circle, at 60th St., Midtown West 10019* ☎ *212/805–8800* 🖨 *212/805–8888* ⊕ *www.mandarinoriental.com* ⇦ *203 rooms, 48 suites* ☖ *Restaurant, room service, minibars, cable TV, in-room DVD, in-room data ports, pool, gym, spa, bar, dry cleaning, laundry service, concierge, business services* ☐ *AE, D, DC, MC, V* Ⓜ *Subway: A, B, C, D, 1 to 59th St./Columbus Circle.*

$$$$ 🏨 **Ritz-Carlton New York, Central Park South.** A luxurious retreat with stellar views of Central Park, the former St. Moritz hotel is easily one of the top properties in the city. No request is too difficult for the superlative Ritz staff, one reason the hotel's a favorite of celebrities and royalty. Quietly elegant rooms and suites are sumptuous without feeling stiff or stuffy, with high thread-count sheets and rich, plush fabrics throughout. Exceptional French cuisine is served at jewel-box Atelier restaurant, and La Prairie salon is a pampering treat. ☒ *50 Central Park S, at 6th Ave., Midtown West 10019* ☎ *212/308–9100 or 800/241–3333* 🖨 *212/207–8831* ⊕ *www.ritzcarlton.com* ⇦ *261 rooms, 48 suites* ☖ *Restaurant, room service, in-room safes, minibars, cable TV with movies, in-room DVD, in-room data ports, gym, spa, bar, lobby lounge, babysitting, dry cleaning, laundry service, concierge, meeting rooms, some pets allowed, no-smoking floors* ☐ *AE, D, DC, MC, V* Ⓜ *Subway: F, V to 57th St.*

FodorsChoice ★

★ $$$$ 🏨 **W Times Square.** Times Square finally goes hip on a grand scale with the opening of this super-sleek 57-floor monolith, the flagship of the white-hot W line. After passing through an entrance of cascading, glass-enclosed water, you alight to the seventh-floor lobby where Kenneth Cole–clad "welcome ambassadors" await. The Jetsons experience continues in the space-age, white-on-white lobby and the futuristic rooms with multiple shades of gray. The bi-level Blue Fin restaurant with its sushi bar and floor-to-ceiling windows caps the architectural wonderment. ☒ *1567 Broadway, at W. 47th St., Midtown West 10036* ☎ *212/930–7400 or 877/946–8357* 🖨 *212/930–7500* ⊕ *www.whotels.com* ⇦ *413 rooms, 89 suites* ☖ *Restaurant, café, room service, in-room safes, minibars, cable TV with movies, in-room DVD, in-room data ports, Wi-Fi, exercise equipment, gym, massage, 4 bars, shop, dry cleaning, laundry service, concierge, business services, parking (fee), some pets allowed (fee), no-smoking rooms, no-smoking floors* ☐*AE, D, DC, MC, V* Ⓜ*Subway: 1, 2, 3, 7, S, N, Q, R, W to 42nd St./Times Sq.*

19

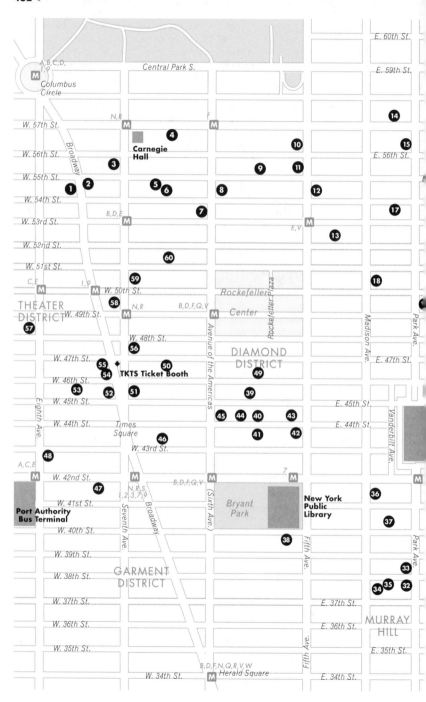

E. 60th St.

E. 59th St.

Central Park S.

M A,B,C,D,
1,9
Columbus
Circle

M N,R
W. 57th St.

Carnegie
Hall

W. 56th St.

W. 55th St.

W. 54th St.

M B,D,E
W. 53rd St.

W. 52nd St.

W. 51st St.

C,E M
W. 50th St.

W. 49th St.

THEATER
DISTRICT

W. 48th St.

W. 47th St.

TKTS Ticket Booth

W. 46th St.

W. 45th St.

W. 44th St.

Times
Square

W. 43rd St.

A,C,E
M
W. 42nd St.

W. 41st St.

Port Authority
Bus Terminal

W. 40th St.

W. 39th St.

GARMENT
DISTRICT

W. 38th St.

W. 37th St.

W. 36th St.

W. 35th St.

W. 34th St.

E. 56th St.

Rockefeller
Center

Rockefeller Plaza

DIAMOND
DISTRICT

E. 47th St.

E. 45th St.

E. 44th St.

Bryant
Park

New York
Public
Library

E. 37th St.

E. 36th St.

E. 35th St.

E. 34th St.

MURRAY
HILL

Herald Square

Madison Ave.

Park Ave.

Vanderbilt Ave.

Fifth Ave.

Eighth Ave.

Seventh Ave.

Broadway

Avenue of the Americas

(Sixth Ave.)

Where to Stay Between 34th & 57th Streets

$$$–$$$$ ▣ **The Bryant Park.** Carved out of the bones of the former American Radiator Building that towers over the New York Public Library and Bryant Park, this brilliant blend of '20s Gothic Revival exterior and sleekly modern rooms delivers the pizzazz worthy of the city's moniker, Gotham. Rooms are furnished at the apex of minimalist chic with sumptuous travertine bathrooms, hardwood floors with Tibetan rugs, and killer views. Since it's at the apex of Fashion Week activities, expect a designer-filled crowd and a runway feel in the stark red lobby. Both the restaurant, Koi, and bars here are popular with the after-work crowd. ⊠ *40 W. 40th St., between 5th and 6th Aves., Midtown West 10018* ☎ *212/869–0100 or 877/640–9300* 🖷 *212/869–4446* ⊕ *www.bryantparkhotel. com* ⇨ *107 rooms, 22 suites* △ *Restaurant, room service, in-room safes, minibars, cable TV with movies, in-room broadband, Web TV, gym, health club, spa, 2 bars, dry cleaning, laundry service, concierge, business services, meeting rooms, parking (fee), some pets allowed (fee), no-smoking floors* ▭ *AE, DC, MC, V* Ⓜ *Subway: B, D, F, V to 42nd St.; 7 to 5th Ave.*

$$$–$$$$ ▣ **Le Parker Meridien.** This chic midtown hotel provides two things that don't always come together in New York: sleek styling and top-of-the-line service. The lobby's striking atrium combines cherry paneling, hand-painted columns, and contemporary art. Crisp, modern rooms include low platform beds, rotating ceiling-to-floor entertainment units, Aeron chairs, CD players, and Central Park or skyline views. A 15,000-square-foot health club has a glass-enclosed rooftop pool and spa services. Norma's serves the morning meal from 6:30 AM to 3 PM; the discreetly hidden Burger Joint is a neighborhood favorite. ⊠ *118 W. 57th St., between 6th and 7th Aves., Midtown West 10019* ☎ *212/245–5000 or 800/543–4300* 🖷 *212/307–1776* ⊕ *www.parkermeridien.com* ⇨ *701 rooms, 249 suites* △ *2 restaurants, room service, in-room safes, minibars, microwaves, cable TV, in-room DVD/VCR, in-room broadband, indoor pool, health club, spa, basketball, racquetball, bar, babysitting, dry cleaning, laundry service, concierge, business services, meeting rooms, parking (fee), some pets allowed, no-smoking rooms, no-smoking floors* ▭ *AE, D, DC, MC, V* Ⓜ *Subway: B, D, E, N, Q, R, W to 57th St.*

$$$–$$$$ ▣ **Rihga Royal.** This discreet establishment—the only luxury all-suites hotel in Manhattan—has a loyal following among celebrities and business travelers. Each of its contemporary-style suites—many of them quite spacious—has a living room, bedroom, and large marble bath with glass-enclosed shower and separate tub. Some suites have French doors and bay windows, and the pricier Pinnacle Suites include personalized business cards, cellular phones, printer-copiers, and even complimentary town-car service from and to airports. Big plans are currently under way now that the hotel is part of the Luxury Resorts group and no longer connected to the Rihga hotel chain. Expect a name change to The London, renovated rooms with grand Waterworks bathrooms, and a Gordon Ramsay—helmed restaurant, the first on this side of the pond for the British superchef. ⊠ *151 W. 54th St., between 6th and 7th Aves., Midtown West 10019* ☎ *212/307–5000 or 800/937–5454* 🖷 *212/765–6530* ⊕ *www.rihgaroyalny.com* ⇨ *507 suites* △ *Restaurant, room* *service, in-room fax, in-room safes, in-room hot tubs, kitchenettes, minibars, refrigerators, cable TV with movies and video games, in-room VCRs, in-room data ports, gym, health club, massage, bar, babysitting, dry cleaning, laundry service, concierge, business services, meeting rooms, parking (fee), no-smoking floors* ⊟ *AE, D, DC, MC, V* Ⓜ *Subway: B, D, E to 7th Ave.; N, Q, R, W to 57th St.*

$$$ ⊞ **Chambers.** Midtown is the new downtown in David Rockwell's gorgeous showcase, where more than 500 works of art hang and each guestroom floor has a mural installation. Loftlike rooms with hand-troweled concrete walls are decorated warmly, and the bathroom floors of poured concrete shimmer with glass mosaic tiles. After entering through the magnificent carved teak doors and passing through the intimate yet grand lobby with soaring ceilings, double-sided fireplace, and Hugo Boss–uniformed staff, head downstairs to the restaurant Town, which also provides room service, for one of the most sublime culinary experiences around. ⊠ *15 W. 56th St., off 5th Ave., Midtown West 10019* ☎ *212/974–5656 or 866/204–5656* 🖷 *212/974–5657* ⊕ *www.chambershotel. com* ⤶ *72 rooms, 5 suites* ⚹ *Restaurant, in-room safes, minibars, cable TV with movies, in-room DVD, in-room data ports, massage, bar, lounge, babysitting, dry cleaning, laundry service, concierge, parking (fee), some pets allowed, no-smoking floors* ⊟ *AE, D, DC, MC, V* Ⓜ *Subway: F, V to 57th St.*

★ **$$$** ⊞ **The Iroquois.** Built during the Depression, this once-prosaic hotel is now among the neighborhood's better properties, and significantly more modern than its traditional exterior. Service is smiling and top-notch, and rooms are a quiet retreat from the frenetic neighborhood. Children can enjoy in-room Nintendo systems and pint-size Frette bathrobes. The large, restful cream-and-white standard rooms have ultracomfortable beds, and the marble-and-brass bathrooms contain phones and pedestal sinks. Off the tiny lobby are a homey reading area with a laptop, a bar, and the intimate and refined Triomphe restaurant. ⊠ *49 W. 44th St., between 5th and 6th Aves., Midtown West 10036* ☎ *212/840–3080 or 800/332–7220* 🖷 *212/398–1754* ⊕ *www. iroquoisny.com* ⤶ *105 rooms, 9 suites* ⚹ *Restaurant, room service, in-room safes, minibars, cable TV with movies and video games, Wi-Fi, gym, health club, massage, sauna, bar, dry cleaning, laundry service, concierge, business services, meeting rooms, parking (fee), no-smoking floors* ⊟ *AE, D, DC, MC, V* Ⓜ *Subway: B, D, F, V to 42nd St.; 7 to 5th Ave.*

$$$ ⊞ **The Mansfield.** Built in 1901 as lodging for distinguished bachelors, this small, clubby hotel has an Edwardian sensibility from the working fireplace in the lounge to the lobby's coffered ceiling and marble and cast-iron staircase. Rooms, with their black-marble bathrooms, dark-wood venetian blinds, and sleigh beds never disappoint. Suites are especially grand. A machine dispenses complimentary 24-hour coffee and tea, and the hotel's swank M Bar serves cocktails, caviar, and desserts until midnight. For a romantic, if refined, getaway, ensconce yourself in the duplex penthouse suite. ⊠ *12 W. 44th St., between 5th and 6th Aves., Midtown West 10036* ☎ *212/944–6050 or 800/255–5167* 🖷 *212/764–4477* ⊕ *www.mansfieldhotel.com* ⤶ *124 rooms, 25 suites* ⚹ *Room*

19

service, in-room safes, some microwaves, refrigerators, cable TV, in-room VCRs, Wi-Fi, bar, cinema, concert hall, library, dry cleaning, laundry service, concierge, business services, meeting rooms, parking (fee), some pets allowed, no-smoking rooms, no-smoking floors ▭ *AE, D, DC, MC, V* Ⓜ *Subway: B, D, F, V to 42nd St.*

★ **$$$** 🏨 **The Muse.** In the heart of the theater district, the Muse has a display of artwork that includes photos of such "muses" as Katharine Hepburn and Nureyev. Fans of the hotel rave about the oversize rooms and bathrooms, super-comfortable beds, and thoughtful touches such as luxe bathroom goodies and complimentary business cards. Note that although the prime theater district location may be a draw for some, the noise that may accompany it is also part of the atmosphere. The hotel's stagelike restaurant, District, serves globally influenced American cuisine. ✉ *130 W. 46th St., between 6th and 7th Aves., Midtown West 10036* ☎ *212/485–2400 or 877/692–6873* 🖷 *212/485–2900* ⊕ *www.themusehotel.com* 🛏 *200 rooms, 19 suites* ♨ *Restaurant, room service, in-room safes, minibars, cable TV with movies, in-room data ports, gym, massage, bar, dry cleaning, laundry service, concierge, business services, meeting rooms, parking (fee), some pets allowed, no-smoking floors* ▭ *AE, D, DC, MC, V* Ⓜ *Subway: B, D, F, V to 47th–50th Sts./ Rockefeller Center.*

$$$ 🏨 **The Royalton.** During the '90s, the lobby restaurant "44" started the craze of local A-listers meeting and greeting in hotel boîtes. Although many of the movers and shakers have moved on, the minimalist Philippe Starck space with its sumptuous sofas and secluded Vodka Bar still gives off a cool vibe. Before you can get to your room, you'll have to transverse this hipster lounge, and then feel your way down the dimly lit hallways. Guest rooms have low-lying, custom-made beds, tasteful lighting, and fresh flowers. Some of the rooms have working fireplaces, and all have CD players. Slate bathrooms with stainless-steel-and-glass fixtures may also include round, two-person tubs. ✉ *44 W. 44th St., between 5th and 6th Aves., Midtown West 10036* ☎ *212/869–4400 or 800/635– 9013* 🖷 *212/575–0012* ⊕ *www.royaltonhotel.com* 🛏 *141 rooms, 27 suites* ♨ *Restaurant, room service, in-room safes, minibars, refrigerators, cable TV, in-room VCRs, in-room data ports, Wi-Fi, exercise equipment, gym, massage, bar, babysitting, dry cleaning, laundry service, concierge, business services, meeting rooms, parking (fee), some pets allowed, no-smoking rooms* ▭ *AE, DC, MC, V* Ⓜ *Subway: B, D, F, V to 42nd St.*

$$$ 🏨 **Sofitel New York.** The European hotel group's property is a dramatic, contemporary 30-story curved tower overlooking 5th Avenue. The place feels professional, with a spacious, quiet lobby, an elegant French brasserie (Gaby, named for a Parisian model who made a name for herself in the Big Apple in the 1920s), and courteous staff who are always on hand. Upstairs, the rooms are what you expect to find in a big corporate hotel—lots of earth tones and mahogany—but what they lack in aesthetics they more than make up for in simple comforts; the best rooms have balconies and views of the Chrysler Building. ✉ *45 W. 44th St., between 5th and 6th Aves., Midtown West 10036* ☎ *212/354– 8844* 🖷 *212/782–3002* ⊕ *www.sofitel.com* 🛏 *398 rooms, 52 suites*

◕ *Restaurant, room service, minibars, cable TV with movies, in-room data ports, gym, massage, bar, dry cleaning, laundry service, concierge, business services, meeting rooms, parking (fee), no-smoking floors*  *AE, D, DC, MC, V* Ⓜ *Subway: B, D, F, V to 42nd St.*

★ **$$$**  **Warwick.** Astonishingly, this palatial hotel was built by William Randolph Hearst in 1927 as a private hotel for his friends and family. The Midtown favorite is well placed for the theater district. The marble-floor lobby buzzes with activity; the Randolph restaurant is on one side and Murals on 54, a Continental restaurant, is on the other. Handsome, Regency-style rooms have soft pastel color schemes, mahogany armoires, and marble bathrooms, and some have fax machines. The Cary Grant suite was the actor's New York residence for 12 years, and encapsulates a more refined moment in New York glamour. ✉ *65 W. 54th St., at 6th Ave., Midtown West 10019* ☎ *212/247–2700 or 800/223–4099*  *212/713–1751* 🌐 *www.warwickhotels.com* ⇝ *359 rooms, 67 suites* ◕ *2 restaurants, room service, in-room safes, minibars, cable TV with movies and video games, in-room data ports, Wi-Fi, exercise equipment, gym, bar, babysitting, dry cleaning, laundry service, concierge, business services, meeting rooms, parking (fee), no-smoking rooms*  *AE, DC, MC, V* Ⓜ *Subway: E, V to 5th Ave.; N, Q, R, W to 57th St.*

$$–$$$  **The Algonquin.** Even Matilda the resident cat, who holds court in the parlorlike lobby, seems to know that the draw here is the ghost of its literary past. Hordes of literary enthusiasts fill the lobby; signed works of former Round Table raconteurs can be checked out of the library, and their witticisms grace guest room doors. *New Yorker* cartoon–strewn wallpaper covers hallways. Small and boxy, the rooms, though spotless, have a less-than-cheerful feel, but the hotel has been upgraded to meet a higher technological standard. The renowned Oak Room is one of the city's premier cabaret performance venues, and the publike Blue Bar makes visitors from around the world feel at home. ✉ *59 W. 44th St., between 5th and 6th Aves., Midtown West 10036* ☎ *212/840–6800 or 800/555–8000*  *212/944–1419* 🌐 *www.algonquinhotel.com* ⇝ *150 rooms, 24 suites* ◕ *2 restaurants, room service, in-room safes, cable TV with movies, Wi-Fi, gym, bar, cabaret, library, dry cleaning, laundry service, concierge, business services, meeting rooms, parking (fee), no-smoking floors*  *AE, D, DC, MC, V* Ⓜ *Subway: B, D, F, V to 42nd St.*

$$–$$$  **City Club Hotel.** Like Cary Grant's ocean-liner suites, City Club rooms are brisk, bright, and masculine, with Jonathan Adler ceramics, baseball photos from the '50s, Hermes bathroom products, and "City Club" banner wool blankets. The bathroom marble is chocolate color, and the wallpaper flecked with mica. Privacy, not publicity, is the emphasis at this luxe property owned by young man-about-town Jeff Klein and designed by celebrity decorator Jeffrey Bilhuber. The lobby is tiny, and guests who wish to drink are sent across the street to the Royalton. Top chef Daniel Boulud opened his db Bistro Moderne downstairs. ✉ *55 W. 44th St., between 5th and 6th Aves., Midtown West 10036* ☎ *212/921–5500*  *212/944–5544* 🌐 *www.cityclubhotel.com* ⇝ *62 rooms, 3 suites* ◕ *Restaurant, minibars, cable TV with movies, in-room DVD, in-room data ports, parking (fee), no-smoking rooms*  *AE, D, DC, MC, V* Ⓜ *Subway: B, D, F, V to 42nd St.; 7 to 5th Ave.*

19

$$–$$$ ⊞ **Hilton New York.** New York City's largest hotel and the epicenter of the city's hotel-based conventions, the Hilton has a Vegas-size range of business facilities, eating establishments, and shops, all designed for convenience. Considering the size of this property, guest rooms are well maintained, and all have coffeemakers, hair dryers, and ironing boards. A variety of local ethnic cuisines is available at the New York Marketplace, a mall-style food court in the hotel lobby. ⊠ *1335 6th Ave., between W. 53rd and W. 54th Sts., Midtown West 10019* ☎ *212/586–7000 or 800/445–8667* 🖶 *212/315–1374* ⊕ *www.newyorktowers.hilton.com* ⇋ *2,079 rooms, 2 penthouses, 5 suites* ♢ *2 restaurants, café, room service, in-room safes, minibars, cable TV, in-room data ports, gym, health club, hair salon, massage, 2 bars, sports bar, shops, babysitting, dry cleaning, laundry service, concierge, concierge floors, convention center, parking (fee)* ▭ *AE, D, DC, MC, V* Ⓜ *Subway: B, D, F, V to 47th–50th Sts./Rockefeller Center.*

$$–$$$ ⊞ **Marriott Marquis.** This brash behemoth in the heart of the theater district is a place New Yorkers love to hate. With its own little city of restaurants, a sushi bar, shops, meeting rooms, and ballrooms—there's even a Broadway theater—it virtually defines "over-the-top." As at other Marriotts, all of the nearly 2,000 rooms here look alike and are pleasant and functional. Some have more dramatic urban views than others. The View, the revolving restaurant and bar on the 49th floor, provides one of the most spectacular panoramas in New York, but it's only open in the evening. Make a reservation to get in. ⊠ *1535 Broadway, at W. 45th St., Midtown West 10036* ☎ *212/398–1900 or 800/843–4898* 🖶 *212/704–8930 or 212/704–8931* ⊕ *www.marriott.com* ⇋ *1,889 rooms, 58 suites* ♢ *3 restaurants, café, coffee shop, room service, in-room safes, minibars, cable TV, in-room data ports, exercise equipment, health club, hair salon, massage, 3 bars, theater, babysitting, dry cleaning, laundry service, concierge, business services, convention center, parking (fee), some pets allowed, no-smoking rooms* ▭ *AE, D, DC, MC, V* Ⓜ *Subway: 1, 2, 3, 7, S, N, Q, R, W to 42nd St./Times Sq.*

★ **$$–$$$** ⊞ **The Michelangelo.** Italophiles will feel that they've been transported to the good life in the boot at this deluxe hotel, whose long, wide lobby lounge is clad with multihue marble and Veronese-style oil paintings. Upstairs, the decor of the relatively spacious rooms (averaging 475 square feet) varies. You can choose contemporary, neoclassic, art deco, or French country—all have marble foyers and marble bathrooms equipped with bidets and oversize 55-gallon tubs. The larger rooms have sitting areas and king beds. Complimentary cappuccino, pastries, and other Italian treats are served each morning in the baroque lobby lounge. ⊠ *152 W. 51st St., at 7th Ave., Midtown West 10019* ☎ *212/765–1900 or 800/237–0990* 🖶 *212/581–7618* ⊕ *www.michelangelohotel.com* ⇋ *123 rooms, 55 suites* ♢ *Restaurant, room service, in-room fax, in-room safes, minibars, cable TV with movies, in-room DVD, in-room data ports, exercise equipment, gym, bar, babysitting, dry cleaning, laundry service, concierge, business services, meeting rooms, parking (fee), no-smoking floors* ▭ *AE, D, DC, MC, V* ⦿ℂ *CP* Ⓜ *Subway: B, D, E to 7th Ave.; 1 to 50th St.; B, D, F, V to 47th–50th Sts./Rockefeller Center.*

$$–$$$ ⊞ **The Shoreham.** This is a miniature, low-attitude version of the ultra-cool Royalton—and it's comfortable to boot. Almost everything is metal or of metal color, from perforated steel headboards (lighted from behind) to steel sinks in the shiny, tiny bathrooms to the silver-gray carpets. Pleasant touches include CD players and cedar-lined closets. There's complimentary Continental breakfast as well as free cappuccino and other hot drinks in the lobby, and the Shoreham Restaurant & Bar serves an eclectic, light menu of sandwiches and salads. ✉ *33 W. 55th St., between 5th and 6th Aves., Midtown West 10019* ☎ *212/247–6700 or 877/847–4444* 🖨 *212/765–9741* ⊕ *www.shorehamhotel.com* ✒ *174 rooms, 37 suites* ⟁ *Restaurant, room service, Wi-Fi, in-room safes, cable TV, in-room VCRs, bar, babysitting, dry cleaning, laundry service, concierge, business services, parking (fee), some pets allowed, no-smoking floors* ⊟ *AE, D, DC, MC, V* ⦿⟊ *CP* Ⓜ *Subway: E, V to 5th Ave.*

$–$$$ ⊞ **The Hudson.** From the bower-draped lobby to the dark-wall rooms with their whiter-than-white furnishings, the Hudson is yet another extravaganza from the team of Ian Schrager and Philippe Starck. One thousand rooms are squeezed into 23 floors, some as small as 150 square feet, and service is at a minimum. Tight quarters are balanced by low (by Manhattan standards) rates, but if you're staying here, it's for the atmosphere, not the accommodations. Some bathrooms have see-through shower walls, and all have a supply of candles. Like a posh living room, the garden-lounge is one of the most coveted outdoor spaces in town. ✉ *356 W. 58th St., between 8th and 9th Aves., Midtown West 10019* ☎ *212/554–6000* 🖨 *212/554–6001* ⊕ *www.hudsonhotel.com* ✒ *1,000 rooms, 2 suites* ⟁ *Restaurant, room service, in-room safes, in-room data ports, Wi-Fi, health club, massage, bar, laundry service, concierge, business services, meeting rooms, parking (fee)* ⊟ *AE, D, DC, MC, V* Ⓜ *Subway: 1, A, B, C, D to 59th St./Columbus Circle.*

$–$$$ ⊞ **The Time Hotel.** This spot half a block from the din of Times Square tempers trendiness with a touch of humor. A ridiculously futuristic glass elevator—eggshells line the bottom of the shaft—transports guests to the second-floor lobby. In the adjoining bar, nature videos lighten up the low-slung, serious, grayscale furnishings. The smallish guest rooms, each themed on one of the primary colors—red, yellow, or blue—have mood lighting and even specific "color" aromas that create a unique, if contrived, hotel experience. ✉ *224 W. 49th St., between Broadway and 8th Ave., Midtown West 10019* ☎ *212/320–2900 or 877/846–3692* 🖨 *212/245–2305* ⊕ *www.thetimeny.com* ✒ *164 rooms, 29 suites* ⟁ *Restaurant, room service, in-room fax, in-room safes, minibars, refrigerators, cable TV with movies, in-room VCRs, gym, bar, dry cleaning, laundry service, concierge, business services, parking (fee), no-smoking floors* ⊟ *AE, D, DC, MC, V* Ⓜ *Subway: 1, C, E to 50th St.; R, W to 49th St.*

$$ ⊞ **The Blakely.** The cozy English clubhouse–like lobby sets the tone for this hotel, formerly the Gorham, with lots of maple and cherry paneling and wainscoting, large library chairs, and leather-bound books along the walls. Fully equipped kitchenettes and large work areas make the spacious rooms a bargain, and the dark woods and rich fabrics are stylish enough to make the hotel a favorite of Louis Vuitton employees.

19

Abboccato, the well-reviewed Italian restaurant, provides room service. The location across from City Center is a boon to arts lovers. ⊠ *136 W. 55th St., between 6th and 7th Aves., Midtown West 10019* ☎ *212/245–1800 or 800/735–0710* 🖷 *212/582–8332* ⊕ *www.blakelynewyork. com* ⇄ *57 rooms, 54 suites* ⚘ *Restaurant, room service, in-room safes, kitchenettes, microwaves, refrigerators, cable TV, in-room data ports, Wi-Fi, exercise equipment, gym, massage, dry cleaning, laundry service, concierge, business services, parking (fee), no-smoking rooms, no-smoking floors* ⊟ *AE, DC, MC, V* Ⓜ *Subway: N, Q, R, W to 57th St.*

$$ 🏨 **Casablanca.** This Morocco comes by way of Disney: mosaic tiles, framed Berber scarves and rugs, and a mural of a North African city. Rattan furniture, ceiling fans, and Moroccan-style wood shutters dress up the smallish and mysteriously tatty rooms, which have elaborately tiled bathrooms. In the spacious lounge with a fireplace, a piano, a 41-inch movie screen, and bookshelves stocked with Bogart-abilia, join guests for the popular nightly wine-and-cheese fest and free Continental breakfast in the morning. ⊠ *147 W. 43rd St., between 6th Ave. and Broadway, Midtown West 10036* ☎ *212/869–1212 or 888/922–7225* 🖷 *212/391–7585* ⊕ *www.casablancahotel.com* ⇄ *48 rooms, 5 suites* ⚘ *Restaurant, room service, in-room safes, minibars, refrigerators, cable TV, in-room VCRs, in-room data ports, lounge, piano, babysitting, dry cleaning, laundry service, business services, meeting rooms, parking (fee), no-smoking floors* ⊟ *AE, DC, MC, V* ❢⃝❙ *CP* Ⓜ *Subway: 1, 2, 3, 7, S, N, Q, R, W to 42nd St./Times Sq.*

$$ 🏨 **Dream Hotel.** A Kafkaesque dream by way of hotelier Vikram Chatwal, this Midtown scenester focuses more on style than comfort. The lobby oddly combines an enormous two-story cylindrical neon-lighted aquarium, an unsettling two-story photograph of a tattooed woman, and a copper sculpture of Catherine the Great. Step off the elevator onto your floor and you'll be met with a jarring neon photograph; rooms are almost as disquieting—stark white walls, black furniture, and light-box desks that glow from within. Stay here if you love things modern: plasma TVs, complimentary iPod use, a Deepak Chopra spa, and a velvet-rope rooftop bar scene. ⊠ *210 W. 55th St., at Broadway, Midtown West 10019* ☎ *212/247–2000 or 866/437–3266* 🖷 *212/974–0595* ⊕ *www.dreamny.com* ⇄ *208 rooms, 20 suites* ⚘ *Restaurant, room service, in-room safes, minibars, cable TV with movies, in-room data ports, exercise equipment, spa, 3 bars, dry cleaning, laundry service, concierge, meeting rooms, parking (fee), some pets allowed (fee)* ⊟ *AE, D, DC, MC, V* Ⓜ *Subway: N, Q, R, W to 57th St.*

$$ 🏨 **Flatotel.** Its name gives it away. This 46-story tower started life as British-built condominium apartments (flats), but has been transformed into a hotel full of spacious, minimalist rooms. At cocktail time, the contemporary leather-couch-filled lobby lounge is a hub of genteel carousing; later, diners sup at the Milan-style Moda, which spills outside in good weather. The beds are custom-designed with attached night-lights and anchored at their feet by built-in drawers, and fitted with goose-down duvets and luxe linens. Bathrooms have oversize marble Jacuzzi tubs. ⊠ *135 W. 52nd St., between 6th and 7th Aves., Midtown West 10019* ☎ *212/887–9400 or 800/352–8683* 🖷 *212/887–9442 for reservations,*

212/887–9795 for guests ⊕ www.flatotel.com ⇆ 210 rooms, 70 suites ♨ Restaurant, room service, in-room safes, kitchenettes, minibars, microwaves, refrigerators, cable TV, in-room broadband, exercise equipment, gym, bar, concierge ⊟ AE, DC, MC, V Ⓜ Subway: B, D, E to 7th Ave.; 1 to 50th St.; B, D, F, V to 47th–50th Sts./Rockefeller Center.

$$ Ⓗ **Hilton Times Square.** The Hilton Times Square sits atop a 335,000-square-foot retail and entertainment complex that includes a 25-theater movie megaplex and Madame Tussaud's Wax Museum. The building has a handsome Mondrian-inspired facade, but room decor is chain-hotel bland. Nonetheless, the rooms are comfortable and larger than at many chains, with amenities from in-room coffeemakers to CD players to bathrobes. The hotel is efficiently run and the staff is pleasant. Because all guest rooms are above the 21st floor, many afford excellent views of Times Square and midtown. Restaurant Above is off the "sky lobby" on the 21st floor. ⊠ *234 W. 42nd St., between 7th and 8th Aves., Midtown West 10036* ☎ *212/642–2500 or 800/445–8667* 🖷 *212/840–5516* ⊕ *www.hilton.com* ⇆ *444 rooms, 15 suites ♨ Restaurant, room service, in-room safes, minibars, cable TV with movies, in-room data ports, gym, bar, babysitting, laundry service, concierge, business services, meeting rooms, parking (fee), some pets allowed, no-smoking rooms, no-smoking floors* ⊟ *AE, D, DC, MC, V* Ⓜ *Subway: 1, 2, 3, 7, S, N, Q, R, W to 42nd St./Times Sq.*

$$ Ⓗ **Renaissance.** This link in the Marriott chain is a business hotel, but vacationers often take advantage of its low promotional rates and its location at the head of Times Square. For the businessperson, each spacious and plush room comes with a work desk, a duo of two-line speakerphones, call waiting, a fax, and a voice-mail system. For the diva, the marble bathrooms have deep soaking tubs and a princess phone. Elevators lead from street level to the third-floor art deco–style reception area. On the lobby floor are two bars and Foley's Restaurant & Bar, a restaurant with up-close views of Times Square. ⊠ *714 7th Ave., between W. 47th and W. 48th Sts., Midtown West 10036* ☎ *212/765–7676 or 800/628–5222* 🖷 *212/765–1962* ⊕ *www.renaissancehotels.com* ⇆ *300 rooms, 5 suites ♨ Restaurant, room service, in-room safes, minibars, cable TV with movies, in-room broadband, exercise equipment, gym, massage, 2 bars, babysitting, dry cleaning, laundry service, concierge, business services, meeting rooms, parking (fee), some pets allowed (fee), no-smoking floors* ⊟ *AE, D, DC, MC, V* Ⓜ *Subway: R, W to 49th St.; 1 to 50th St.*

$$ Ⓗ **The Westin New York at Times Square.** The Westin changed the skyline of midtown with this soaring skyscraper that subtly mimics the flow of the city—look for subway patterns in the carpets and the city reflected on the building's exterior. A thoughtful staff helps make the cavernous lobby and throngs of guests tolerable. Exceptionally large rooms are blissfully quiet and built to give you optimal views—especially the light-filled corner rooms. The much-noted Heavenly Bed and double showerheads are indeed praiseworthy, but for even more comfort, spa-floor rooms come with massage chairs, aromatherapy candles, and other pampering pleasures. ⊠ *270 W. 43rd St., at 8th Ave., Midtown West 10036* ☎ *212/201–2700 or 866/837–4183* 🖷 *212/201–2701* ⊕ *www.westinny.*

19

Lodging Alternatives

APARTMENT RENTALS

If you want a home base that's roomy enough for a family and comes with cooking facilities, consider a furnished rental. These can save you money, especially if you're traveling with a group. Home-exchange directories sometimes list rentals as well as exchanges.

International agents include: **Hideaways International** (✉ 767 Islington St., Portsmouth, NH 03801 ☎ 603/430-4433 or 800/843-4433 🖷 603/430-4444 ⊕ www.hideaways. com), annual membership $185. **Hometours International** (✉ 1108 Scottie La., Knoxville, TN 37919 ☎ 865/690-8484 or 866/367-4668 ⊕ thor.he.net/~hometour/).

Local agents include: **Abode Limited** (☏ Box 20022, New York, NY 10028 ☎ 800/835-8880 or 212/472-2000 ⊕ www.abodenyc.com) arranges rentals of furnished apartments. **Manhattan Getaways** (☏ Box 1994, New York, NY 10022 ☎ 212/956-2010 ⊕ www.manhattangetaways.com).

BED-AND-BREAKFASTS

Most bed-and-breakfasts in New York City are residential apartments. B&Bs booked through a service may be either hosted (you're the guest in someone's quarters) or unhosted (you have full use of someone's vacated apartment, including kitchen privileges). Reservation services include: **All Around the Town** (✉ 270 Lafayette St., Suite 804, New York, NY 10012 ☎ 212/334-2655 or 800/443-3800 🖷 212/675-6366 ⊕ www. newyorkcitybestbb.com). **Bed-and-Breakfast (and Books)** (✉ 35 W. 92nd St., Apt. 2C, between Central Park W and Columbus Ave., New York, NY 10025 ☎🖷 212/865-8740 please call

only weekdays 10 AM–5 PM). **Bed-and-Breakfast in Manhattan** (☏ Box 533, New York, NY 10150 ☎ 212/472-2528 🖷 212/988-9818). **Bed-and-Breakfast Network of New York** (✉ 134 W. 32nd St., Suite 602, between 6th and 7th Aves., New York, NY 10001 ☎ 212/645-8134 or 800/900-8134 ⊕ www. bedandbreakfastnetny.com). **City Lights Bed-and-Breakfast** (☏ Box 20355, Cherokee Station, New York, NY 10021 ☎ 212/737-7049 🖷 212/535-2755 ⊕ www.citylightsbedandbreakfast. com). **Manhattan Getaways** (☏ Box 1994, New York, NY 10101 ☎ 212/956-2010 ⊕ www.manhattangetaways. com). **Manhattan Stays** (☏ Box 20684, Cherokee Station, New York, NY 10021 ☎ 212/249-6255 🖷 212/265-3561 ⊕ www.manhattanstays.com). **New World Bed and Breakfast** (✉ 150 5th Ave., Suite 711, between 19th and 20th Sts., New York, NY 10011 ☎ 212/675-5600, 800/443-3800 in U.S. 🖷 212/675-6366). **New York Habitat** (✉ 307 7th Ave., Suite 306, between 27th and 28th Sts., New York, NY 10001 ☎ 212/647-9365 🖷 212/627-1416 ⊕ www.nyhabitat.com). **West Village Reservations** (☏ Village Station, Box 347, New York, NY 10014-0347 ☎ 212/614-3034 🖷 425/920-2384).

HOME EXCHANGES

If you would like to exchange your home for someone else's, join a home-exchange organization, which will send you its updated listings of available exchanges for a year and will include your own listing in at least one of them. It's up to you to make specific arrangements. Exchange clubs include: **HomeLink International** (☏ Box 47747, Tampa, FL 33647 ☎ 813/975-9825 or 800/638-3841 🖷 813/910-8144 ⊕ www.

homelink.org); $110 yearly for a listing, online access, and catalog; $70 without catalog. **Intervac U.S.** (✉ 30 Corte San Fernando, Tiburon, CA 94920 ☎ 800/756-4663 🖷 415/435-7440 ⊕ www.intervacus.com); $125 yearly for a listing, online access, and a catalog; $65 without catalog.

HOSTELS

In some 4,500 locations in more than 70 countries around the world, Hostelling International (HI), the umbrella group for a number of national youth-hostel associations, offers single-sex, dorm-style beds and, at many hostels, rooms for couples and family accommodations. Membership in any HI national hostel association, open to travelers of all ages, allows you to stay in HI-affiliated hostels at member rates; one-year membership is about $28 for adults (C$35 for a two-year minimum membership in Canada, £14 in the U.K., A$52 in Australia, and NZ$40 in New Zealand); hostels charge about $10–$30 per night. Members have priority if the hostel is full; they're also eligible for discounts around the world, even on rail and bus travel in some countries.

To contact the organizations: **Hostelling International–USA** (✉ 8401 Colesville Rd., Suite 600, Silver Spring, MD 20910 ☎ 301/495-1240 🖷 301/495-6697 ⊕ www.hiusa. org). **Hostelling International–Canada** (✉ 205 Catherine St., Suite 400, Ottawa, Ontario K2P 1C3 ☎ 613/237-7884 or 800/663-5777 🖷 613/237-7868 ⊕ www.hihostels.ca). **YHA England and Wales** (✉ Trevelyan House, Dimple Rd., Matlock, Derbyshire DE4 3YH, U.K. ☎ 0870/870-8808, 0870/770-8868, or 0162/959-2600 🖷 0870/770-6127 ⊕ www. yha.org.uk). **YHA Australia** (✉ 422 Kent St., Sydney, NSW 2001 ☎ 02/

9261-1111 🖷 02/9261-1969 ⊕ www.yha. com.au). **YHA New Zealand** (✉ Level 1, Moorhouse City, 166 Moorhouse Ave., Box 436, Christchurch ☎ 03/379-9970 or 0800/278-299 🖷 03/365-4476 ⊕ www.yha.org.nz).

HOTELS

All hotels listed have private bath unless otherwise noted.

🎫 Toll-Free Numbers **Best Western** ☎ 800/528-1234 ⊕ www. bestwestern.com. **Clarion** ☎ 800/424-6423 ⊕ www.choicehotels.com. **Days Inn** ☎ 800/325-2525 ⊕ www. daysinn.com. **Embassy Suites** ☎ 800/362-2779 ⊕ www. embassysuites.com. **Fairfield Inn** ☎ 800/228-2800 ⊕ www.marriott. com. **Four Seasons** ☎ 800/332-3442 ⊕ www.fourseasons.com. **Hilton** ☎ 800/445-8667 ⊕ www.hilton.com. **Holiday Inn** ☎ 800/465-4329 ⊕ www.ichotelsgroup.com. **Hyatt Hotels & Resorts** ☎ 800/233-1234 ⊕ www.hyatt.com. **Inter-Continental** ☎ 800/327-0200 ⊕ www. ichotelsgroup.com. **La Quinta** ☎ 800/531-5900 ⊕ www.lq.com. **Le Meridien** ☎ 800/543-4300 ⊕ www. lemeridien.com. **Marriott** ☎ 800/228-9290 ⊕ www.marriott.com. **Omni** ☎ 800/843-6664 ⊕ www. omnihotels.com. **Quality Inn** ☎ 800/424-6423 ⊕ www.choicehotels.com. **Radisson** ☎ 800/333-3333 ⊕ www. radisson.com. **Ramada** ☎ 800/228-2828, 800/854-7854 international reservations ⊕ www.ramada.com. **Renaissance Hotels & Resorts** ☎ 800/468-3571 ⊕ www. renaissancehotels.com/. **Ritz-Carlton** ☎ 800/241-3333 ⊕ www.ritzcarlton. com. **Sheraton** ☎ 800/325-3535 ⊕ www.starwood.com/sheraton. **Westin Hotels & Resorts** ☎ 800/228-3000 ⊕ www.starwood.com/ westin.

19

com ↪ *737 rooms, 126 suites* ☐ *Restaurant, café, room service, in-room fax, in-room safes, minibars, cable TV with movies, in-room data ports, Wi-Fi, gym, health club, spa, 2 bars, babysitting, dry cleaning, laundry service, concierge, business services, meeting rooms, parking (fee), some pets allowed, no-smoking rooms, no-smoking floors* ☰ *AE, D, DC, MC, V* Ⓜ *Subway: A, C, E to 42nd St./Times Sq.*

$–$$ ▦ **Ameritania Hotel.** Guests at this busy crash pad just off Broadway are divided pretty evenly: half come for business, half for pleasure. Dimly lighted hallways create a feeling of perpetual nighttime—an impression that lingers in the bedrooms, where black-metal furniture dominates. Rates may drop by as much as $100 a night off-season, depending on occupancy. ⊠ *230 W. 54th St., at Broadway, Midtown West 10019* ☎ *212/247–5000 or 888/664–6835* 🖷 *212/247–3316* ⊕ *www.nychotels.com/ameritania.html* ↪ *207 rooms, 12 suites* ☐ *Room service, some in-room safes, cable TV with movies, in-room data ports, bar, dry cleaning, laundry service, concierge, business services, parking (fee), no-smoking rooms* ☰ *AE, D, DC, MC, V* ❙❂❙ *CP* Ⓜ *Subway: B, D, E to 7th Ave.*

★ **$–$$** ▦ **Belvedere Hotel.** This affordable hotel has some fun with its art deco café and playful floor patterning, but the rooms are surprisingly conservative, with patterned bedspreads and curtains and traditional wooden headboards (an odd juxtaposition to the modern art prints on the walls). For the price, bathrooms and bedrooms are remarkably spacious with space enough for kitchenettes and two full beds if you need them (you can also request a queen- or king-size bed). A helpful desk staff and location convenient to theaters make this a great budget choice. ⊠ *319 W. 48th St., between 8th and 9th Aves., Midtown West 10036* ☎ *212/245–7000 or 888/468–3558* 🖷*212/245–4455* ⊕*www.belvederehotelnyc. com* ↪ *398 rooms, 2 suites* ☐ *Restaurant, café, in-room safes, kitchenettes, microwaves, refrigerators, cable TV with video games, in-room data ports, Wi-Fi, shop, dry cleaning, laundry facilities, laundry service, concierge, business services, parking (fee)* ☰ *AE, D, DC, MC, V* Ⓜ *Subway: C, E to 50th St.*

$–$$ ▦ **Broadway Inn.** In the heart of the theater district, this Midwestern-friendly B&B welcomes with a comfy brick-walled reception room with hump-backed sofa, bentwood chairs, fresh flowers, and stocked book shelves that encourage lingering. Impeccably clean neo-deco–style rooms with black-lacquer beds are basic, but cheerful. An extra $70 or $80 gets you a suite with an additional fold-out sofa bed, and a kitchenette hidden by closet doors. ⊠ *264 W. 46th St., between Broadway and 8th Ave., Midtown West 10036* ☎ *212/997–9200 or 800/826–6300* 🖷 *212/768–2807* ⊕ *www.broadwayinn.com* ↪ *28 rooms, 12 suites* ☐ *Some kitchenettes, some microwaves, refrigerators, cable TV, some in-room data ports, concierge, parking (fee), no-smoking rooms* ☰ *AE, D, DC, MC, V* ❙❂❙ *CP* Ⓜ *Subway: 1, 2, 3, 7, N, Q, R, S, W to 42nd St./Times Sq.*

★ **$–$$** ▦ **Hotel QT.** Giving budget a good name is this Times Square hotel by Andre Balazs, best known for the stylish Mercer Hotel. The unique lobby centers on a raised pool with peep-show-like windows that overlook the bar. Upstairs, rooms are modern, dorm-room in size, but have upscale hotel touches such as feather-pillow-topped mattresses, rain-head showers, and DVD players to accompany the flat-screen TVs. There's no work space, no bathtubs, and double rooms have bunk beds sprouting out of the wall; but you can't beat the price—rooms start at just $125, including Continental breakfast—and the location is as central as they come. ⊠ *125 W. 45th St., between 5th and 6th Aves., Midtown West 10036* ☎ *212/354–2323* 🖷 *212/302–8585* ⊕ *www.hotelqt.com* 🛏 *140 rooms* ⚏ *In-room safes, refrigerators, cable TV with movies, in-room DVD, in-room data ports, Wi-Fi, indoor pool, gym, sauna, steam room, bar* ▭ *AE, DC, MC, V* 🍴 *CP* Ⓜ *Subway: B, D, F, V to 42nd St.; 7 to 5th Ave.*

$–$$ 🏨 **Wellington Hotel.** This large, old-fashioned property's main advantages are reasonable prices and its proximity to Central Park and Carnegie Hall. The lobby has an aura of faded glamour, from the lighted-up red awning outside to the chandeliers and ornate artwork inside. The hotel appeals to families, groups, and those traveling on a budget. Rooms are small, baths are serviceable, and the staff is helpful. ⊠ *871 7th Ave., at W. 55th St., Midtown West 10019* ☎ *212/247–3900 or 800/652–1212* 🖷 *212/581–1719* ⊕ *www.wellingtonhotel.com* 🛏 *500 rooms, 100 suites* ⚏ *Restaurant, coffee shop, microwaves, cable TV with movies, in-room data ports, Wi-Fi, hair salon, bar, laundry facilities, laundry service, parking (fee), no-smoking floors* ▭ *AE, D, DC, MC, V* Ⓜ *Subway: N, Q, R, W to 57th St.*

¢–$$ 🏨 **Quality Hotel and Suites.** This small prewar hotel shares its block with a plethora of Brazilian restaurants and is near many theaters and Rockefeller Center. The peculiar lobby has a narrow corridor that snakes off around a corner and is decorated with some rather handsome art deco Bakelite lamps. The rooms are very plain, but most are well maintained and clean. This block is one of Midtown's most deserted at night, so travelers should be alert. ⊠ *59 W. 46th St., between 5th and 6th Aves., Midtown West 10036* ☎ *212/790–2710 or 800/567–7720* 🖷 *212/290–2760* ⊕ *www.applecorehotels.com* 🛏 *209 rooms* ⚏ *Cafeteria, in-room safes, cable TV with movies and video games, in-room data ports, hair salon, bar, business services, meeting rooms, parking (fee), no-smoking rooms* ▭ *AE, D, DC, MC, V* Ⓜ *Subway: B, D, F, V to 47th–50th Sts./Rockefeller Center.*

$ 🏨 **Hotel Edison.** This offbeat old hotel is a popular budget stop for tour groups from both the United States and abroad. The simple, serviceable guest rooms are clean and fresh, but the bathrooms tend to show their age. The loan-shark murder scene in *The Godfather* was shot in what is now Sofia's restaurant, and the pink-and-blue plaster Edison Café, known half jokingly as the Polish Tea Room, is a theater-crowd landmark consistently recognized as New York City's best coffee shop. ⊠ *228 W. 47th St., between Broadway and 8th Ave., Midtown West 10036* ☎ *212/840–5000 or 800/637–7070* 🖷 *212/596–6850* ⊕ *www. edisonhotelnyc.com* 🛏 *770 rooms, 30 suites* ⚏ *Restaurant, coffee shop, cable TV, Wi-Fi, gym, hair salon, 2 bars, piano, dry cleaning, business services, meeting rooms, airport shuttle, parking (fee), no-smoking rooms* ▭ *AE, D, DC, MC, V* Ⓜ *Subway: C, E to 50th St.*

¢–$ 🏨 **Portland Square Hotel.** You can't beat this theater district old-timer for value, given its clean, simple rooms that invite with flower-print bedspreads

19

and curtains. James Cagney once lived in the building, and—as the story goes—a few of his Radio City Rockette acquaintances lived upstairs. *Life* magazine used to have its offices here, and the original detailing evokes old New York. There are no no-smoking rooms, but if you check into one with a smoky scent, they'll move you to another. Rooms on the east wing have oversize bathrooms. ⊠ *132 W. 47th St., between 6th and 7th Aves., Midtown West 10036* ☎ *212/382–0600 or 800/388–8988* 🖷 *212/382–0684* ⊕ *www.portlandsquarehotel.com* 🖛 *142 rooms, 112 with bath* ⌂ *In-room safes, cable TV, gym, laundry facilities, business services* ⊟ *AE, MC, V* Ⓜ *Subway: R, W to 49th St.*

Midtown East

$$$$ 🏨 **The Drake.** Off Park Avenue in the center of corporate Manhattan, this Swissôtel property caters to business travelers with modern, comfortable rooms that are a cut above the average corporate variety. The deco-style accommodations are a welcome alternative to the traditional look of many hotels in this price category. The Q-56 restaurant is sleek and contemporary, and a branch of Fauchon—the first time this luxury food emporium ventured beyond Paris—has a shop and a lovely tearoom off the lobby. ⊠ *440 Park Ave., at E. 56th St., Midtown East 10022* ☎ *212/421–0900 or 800/372–5369* 🖷 *212/371–4190* ⊕ *www.swissotel. com* 🖛 *387 rooms, 109 suites* ⌂ *Restaurant, tea shop, room service, in-room fax, in-room safes, minibars, some refrigerators, cable TV, in-room data ports, gym, health club, spa, bar, babysitting, dry cleaning, laundry service, concierge, business services, meeting rooms, parking (fee), some pets allowed* ⊟ *AE, D, DC, MC, V* Ⓜ *Subway: 4, 5, 6, N, Q, R, W to 59th St./Lexington Ave.*

★ $$$$ 🏨 **Four Seasons.** Architect I. M. Pei designed this limestone-clad stepped spire amid the prime shops of 57th Street. Everything here comes in epic proportions—from the rooms averaging 600 square feet (and *starting* at $750) to the sky-high Grand Foyer, with French limestone pillars, marble, onyx, and acre upon acre of blond wood. Guest rooms can feel a bit cold if you don't like the clean minimalist style. They all have 10-foot-high ceilings, silk-covered walls, large plasma TVs, English sycamore walk-in closets, and blond-marble bathrooms with tubs that fill in 60 seconds. The lobby lounge with its massive marble fireplace is a civilized spot to have afternoon tea; L'Atelier del Joel Robuchon is the greatly anticipated first foray by the much lauded French chef in the United States. ⊠ *57 E. 57th St., between Park and Madison Aves., Midtown East 10022* ☎ *212/758–5700 or 800/487–3769* 🖷 *212/758–5711* ⊕ *www. fourseasons.com* 🖛 *300 rooms, 68 suites* ⌂ *Restaurant, room service, in-room fax, in-room safes, minibars, some microwaves, cable TV, in-room DVD, in-room broadband, gym, health club, spa, bar, lobby lounge, piano, babysitting, dry cleaning, laundry service, concierge, business services, meeting rooms, car rental, parking (fee), some pets allowed, no-smoking floors* ⊟ *AE, D, DC, MC, V* Ⓜ *Subway: 4, 5, 6, N, Q, R, W to 59th St./Lexington Ave.*

$$$$ 🏨 **New York Palace.** Connected mansions built in the 1880s by railroad baron Henry Villard create the base of this palatial hotel. The lobby,

CLOSE UP

Hotel Hibernation

FOR SOME TRAVELERS, a hotel is an ends to a mean, a place to rest their head after the real business of the day—either corporate or sightseeing—is done. But for more and more people, the hotel *is* the destination—the reason they've come to the city in the first place. From the New Yorker with an air-shaft view who wants a panorama of the Statue of Liberty; to the a couple who wants to escapte the winter cold with room service, eat a fine dinner, take in some shopping within an enclosed space, all without donning a coat to go outside; or a harried mom who wants to visit a spa and then return to her room still wearing her bathrobe and slippers, New York can be the perfect getaway.

Too cold to go outside? Check into one of the enormous rooms at **Mandarin Oriental** (⇨ Midtown West), gaze out at the sweeping vistas of icy Central Park, and then wander down to Asiate for sumptuous French dishes with a Japanese accent. Across from the restaurant and slightly to the left is MOBar, where a saketini is the drink of choice. The next morning, use the secret passageway on the third floor to access the Time Warner Center. You can take a tour of CNN, stock up on provisions at Whole Foods, buy a T-shirt at J Crew, and then stop by Jazz at Lincoln Center, which has performance space here, for tickets to a show. Still have some cash in your wallet? Book a table at Per Se, Masa, or Café Gray, all of which reap accolades from foodies. Then you can walk a few hundred yards back to your room with nary a hair blown out of place.

Want a change from the ordinary that won't break the bank? Check out **The Gershwin Hotel** (⇨ Murray Hill). Even though rooms here aren't luxe, they'll let you try a bit of bohemia on for size. Taste some tapas at the restaurant and lounge, then take in a poetry slam, live music, and a young vibe at the performance space off the lobby.

Looking for a healthful retreat? The **W New York** (⇨ Midtown East), on Lexington Avenue, has one of the most deluxe spas in the city, Bliss49, where you can spend a full day being pampered and pedicured; then head down to the health-oriented restaurant Heartbeat for a restorative treat.

How about somewhere to enjoy the summer weather? Head straight to the **Hotel Gansevoort** (⇨ Greenwich Village). The entire roof here has been turned into an enchanted outdoor space with a full-size heated swimming pool illuminated with colored lights and livened up with an underwater stereo system. At night there's a happening bar scene up high; at street level, wander through the lobby into scene-stealing Ono. Not only are the sushi and robitaki excellent, but the outdoor space here looks like South Beach's Delano hotel, with a dining room hovering over a reflecting pool and private lounge rooms with plasma TVs and curtains to shut out the crowds. Of course, if it's privacy you want, you could just hop the elevator back up to your room. How convenient!

19

with its sweeping staircases, golden chandeliers, and arched colonnades fit for royalty, is host to New American restaurant Istana. Standard rooms in the main section of the hotel are traditional in style and quite large, but a bit worn around the edges. Better options are rooms in the tower that vary between modern or classic, depending on the floor, and have more luxe decor and bathrooms, separate check-in, and more attentive service. Many rooms, including the 7,000-square-foot health club, have terrific views of St. Patrick's Cathedral. ☒ *455 Madison Ave., at E. 50th St., Midtown East 10022* ☎ *212/888–7000 or 800/697–2522* 🖷 *212/ 303–6000* ⊕ *www.newyorkpalace.com* ➘ *809 rooms, 88 suites* ⟐ *2 restaurants, room service, in-room fax, in-room safes, minibars, some refrigerators, cable TV with movies, in-room data ports, health club, spa, 2 bars, babysitting, dry cleaning, laundry service, concierge, business services, meeting rooms, some pets allowed, no-smoking rooms, no-smoking floors* ▭ *AE, D, DC, MC, V* Ⓜ *Subway: 6 to 51st St./Lexington Ave.; E, V to Lexington–3rd Aves./53rd St.*

$$$$ 🏨 **The Peninsula.** Step past the Beaux-Arts facade of this 1905 gem and into the luxurious lobby with original art nouveau accents. Guest rooms, many with sweeping views down 5th Avenue, have a modern sensibility. The high-tech amenities are excellent, from a bedside console that controls the lighting, sound, and thermostat for the room to a TV mounted over the tub for bath-time viewing (in all but standard rooms). Thoughtful service extends to the complimentary selection of bottled waters in each room to same-day laundry service. The rooftop health club, indoor pool, and seasonal open-air bar—which is something of a local hot spot—all have dazzling views of Midtown. ☒ *700 5th Ave., at E. 55th St., Midtown East 10019* ☎ *212/247–2200 or 800/262–9467* 🖷 *212/903–3943* ⊕ *www.peninsula.com* ➘ *185 rooms, 54 suites* ⟐ *2 restaurants, room service, in-room fax, in-room safes, minibars, cable TV with movies, in-room data ports, Wi-Fi, indoor pool, gym, health club, hair salon, spa, 2 bars, lobby lounge, lounge, babysitting, dry cleaning, laundry service, concierge, business services, meeting rooms, parking (fee), some pets allowed, no-smoking floors* ▭ *AE, D, DC, MC, V* Ⓜ *Subway: E, V to 5th Ave.*

★ **$$$$** 🏨 **The St. Regis.** A one-of-a-kind New York classic, this 5th Avenue Beaux-Arts landmark is a hive of activity in its unparalleled public spaces. The King Cole Bar is an institution in itself with its famous Maxfield Parrish mural. Guest rooms, all serviced by accommodating butlers, are straight out of the American Movie Channel, with high ceilings, crystal chandeliers, silk wall coverings, Louis XVI antiques, and world-class amenities such as Tiffany silver services. Marble bathrooms, with tubs, stall showers, and double sinks, are outstanding. ☒ *2 E. 55th St., at 5th Ave., Midtown East 10022* ☎ *212/753–4500 or 800/ 325–3589* 🖷 *212/787–3447* ⊕ *www.stregis.com* ➘ *222 rooms, 44 suites* ⟐ *Restaurant, room service, in-room fax, in-room safes, minibars, cable TV, in-room VCRs, in-room data ports, gym, health club, hair salon, massage, shops, babysitting, dry cleaning, laundry service, concierge, business services, meeting rooms, parking (fee), no-smoking rooms, no-smoking floors* ▭ *AE, D, DC, MC, V* Ⓜ *Subway: E, V to 5th Ave.*

$$$–$$$$ ⊞ **Waldorf-Astoria.** The lobby of this landmark 1931 art deco master-piece, full of murals, mosaics, and elaborate plaster ornamentation, features a grand piano once owned by Cole Porter and still played daily. Astoria-level rooms have the added advantages of great views, fax machines, and access to the Astoria lounge, where a lovely, free afternoon tea is served. The Bull and Bear Bar is a 1940s throwback complete with miniature soda bottles and no-nonsense barkeeps. Well known to U.S. presidents and other international luminaries, the ultra-exclusive Waldorf Towers (the 28th floor and above) has a separate entrance and management. ⊠ *301 Park Ave., between E. 49th and E. 50th Sts., Midtown East 10022* ☎ *212/355–3000 or 800/925–3673* 🖷 *212/872–7272* ⊕ *www.waldorfastoria.com* ➪ *1,176 rooms, 276 suites* ⌂ *4 restaurants, room service, in-room fax, some in-room safes, minibars, refrigerators, cable TV with movies, in-room broadband, gym, health club, hair salon, massage, 3 bars, piano, shops, babysitting, dry cleaning, laundry service, concierge, concierge floors, business services, meeting rooms, parking (fee), some pets allowed, no-smoking floors* ⊟ *AE, D, DC, MC, V* Ⓜ *Subway: 6 to 51st St./Lexington Ave.; E, V to Lexington–3rd Aves./53rd St.*

$$$$ ⊞ **W New York.** Window boxes filled with grass, bowls heaped with green apples, flowing curtains, and vast floor-to-ceiling windows that pour sunlight into the airy lobby all conjure up a calming outdoor vibe here. Quite a trick considering a hopping bar and a sunken sitting area flank the reception area. Although tiny, rooms are rich in natural materials, and soothe with elements such as featherbeds and slate-floor baths instead of the ubiquitous polished marble. Downstairs, Heartbeat Restaurant serves heart-healthy foods; the attached Whiskey Blue draws a young, hip, and moneyed crowd; and an uptown sibling of Bliss Spa draws legions of beauty devotees. ⊠ *541 Lexington Ave., between E. 49th and E. 50th Sts., Midtown East 10022* ☎ *212/755–1200 or 877/946–8357* 🖷 *212/319–8344* ⊕ *www.whotels.com* ➪ *629 rooms, 62 suites* ⌂ *Restaurant, snack bar, room service, in-room fax, in-room safes, minibars, cable TV, in-room broadband, health club, spa, bar, lobby lounge, dry cleaning, laundry facilities, laundry service, concierge, business services, meeting rooms, no-smoking floors* ⊟ *AE, D, DC, MC, V* Ⓜ *Subway: 6 to 51st St./Lexington Ave.; E, V to Lexington–3rd Aves./53rd St.*

$$–$$$$ ⊞ **Sherry-Netherland.** The marble-lined lobby of this grande dame wows with fine, hand-loomed carpets, crystal chandeliers, and wall friezes from the Vanderbilt mansion. White-gloved attendants man the elevators. Many floors of the hotel are private residences, and all hotel rooms are privately owned and individually decorated but adhere to the rigid standards of the hotel. The utterly luxurious suites have separate living and dining areas, crystal chandeliers, and serving pantries, and many have decorative fireplaces, antiques, and glorious marble baths. The cramped and stupendously expensive Harry Cipriani's provides room service (a liter of water costs about $20). Continental breakfast is complimentary for guests, and at lunch it's the best people-watching in town. ⊠ *781 5th Ave., at E. 59th St., Midtown East 10022* ☎ *212/355–2800 or 800/247–4377* 🖷 *212/319–4306* ⊕ *www.sherrynetherland.com* ➪ *30 rooms, 23 suites* ⌂ *Restaurant, room service, in-room fax, in-room safes,*

19

refrigerators, cable TV, in-room broadband, in-room VCRs, gym, hair salon, massage, bar, dry cleaning, laundry service, concierge, business services, meeting rooms, parking (fee) ⊟ *AE, D, DC, MC, V* ⦿ *CP* Ⓜ *Subway: N, R, Q, W to 5th Ave.*

$$$ ⊡ **Affinia Fifty.** This hotel has a distinctly businesslike mood, but it's also supremely comfortable for families or other leisure travelers. A top-to-bottom renovation modernized the spacious rooms, called suites here, all of which have a clean, modern design with oversize chairs and couches, kitchen facilities, and plenty of space to stretch out. And for the business travelers, the second-floor club lounge is devoted to complimentary business services, including snacks and beverages. There's no restaurant in the hotel, but a restaurant next door provides room service. ⊠ *155 E. 50th St., at 3rd Ave., Midtown East 10022* ☎ *212/751–5710 or 800/637–8483* 📠 *212/753–1468* ⊕ *www.affinia.com* ⥂ *56 rooms, 138 suites* ⌂ *Room service, in-room safes, kitchens, kitchenettes, microwaves, refrigerators, cable TV, in-room broadband, exercise equipment, gym, health club, dry cleaning, laundry facilities, laundry service, concierge, parking (fee), no-smoking floors* ⊟ *AE, D, DC, MC, V* Ⓜ *Subway: 6 to 51st St./Lexington Ave.; E, V to Lexington–3rd Aves./53rd St.*

$$$ ⊡ **The Alex.** The goal of the David Rockwell–designed Alex is to create a soothing environment for business travelers on long-term stays. Japanese-influenced rooms use unobtrusive sliding panels with nature prints to hide away the rooms' many gadgets. What remains is a clean, calm space where you can truly appreciate attentive details such as kitchenettes with Gaggenau range tops and SubZero refrigerators; nightstands that turn into leather desktops; and flat-screen bathroom TVs that you can watch from the impressively deep bathtubs. James Beard Foundation winner Marcus Samuelsson runs Asian-influenced Riingo restaurant, which also provides room service. ⊠ *205 E. 45th St., between 2nd and 3rd Aves., Midtown East 10017* ☎ *212/867–5100* 📠 *212/867–7878* ⊕ *www.thealexhotel.com* ⥂ *73 rooms, 130 suites* ⌂ *Restaurant, room service, some kitchens, minibars, cable TV, in-room DVD, in-room data ports, Wi-Fi, gym, spa, bar, concierge, business services* ⊟ *AE, MC, V* Ⓜ *Subway: 4, 5, 6, 7, S to 42nd St./Grand Central.*

$$$ ⊡ **Omni Berkshire Place.** Omni Berkshire's East Coast flagship hotel brings sophistication to the Omni name. Old-world maps hang in the reception area, which leads to a dramatic, two-story atrium lounge with a fireplace, an elaborately stained dark-wood floor, and a piano. The earth-tone spacious guest rooms have a contemporary simplicity as well as plush bedding, tasteful furnishings, spacious bathrooms, and Web TV. Kids receive their own welcome bag of treats. ⊠ *21 E. 52nd St., between 5th and Madison Aves., Midtown East 10022* ☎ *212/753–5800 or 800/843–6664* 📠 *212/754–5020* ⊕ *www.omnihotels.com* ⥂ *352 rooms, 44 suites* ⌂ *Restaurant, room service, in-room fax, in-room safes, minibars, cable TV with movies and video games, Wi-Fi, exercise equipment, health club, massage, bar, babysitting, dry cleaning, laundry facilities, laundry service, concierge, business services, meeting rooms, parking (fee), some pets allowed (fee), no-smoking floors* ⊟ *AE, D, DC, MC, V* Ⓜ *Subway: E, V to 5th Ave.*

$$$ 🏨 **The Regency.** Rough-hewn travertine punctuated by Regency-style furnishings, potted palms, and burnished gold sconces lines an understated lobby—the better to cloak heads of state and other VIP guests in modesty. The modern guest rooms have taupe-color silk wallpaper, velvet throw pillows, and polished Honduran mahogany, but the smallish bathrooms with their marble countertops are unspectacular. Goosedown duvets and ergonomic leather desk chairs reinforce the pleasingly modern feel. Feinstein's at the Regency hosts some of the hottest (and priciest) cabaret acts in town, and 540 Park has become a destination in its own right among restaurant-savvy locals. ✉ *540 Park Ave., at E. 61st St., Midtown East 10021* ☎ *212/759–4100 or 800/235–6397* 🖶 *212/826–5674* ⊕ *www.loewshotels.com* ⤳ *266 rooms, 86 suites* ♨ *Restaurant, room service, in-room fax, in-room safes, some kitchenettes, minibars, refrigerators, cable TV, in-room VCRs, in-room data ports, gym, hair salon, massage, sauna, bar, lobby lounge, cabaret, babysitting, dry cleaning, laundry service, concierge, business services, meeting rooms, parking (fee), some pets allowed, no-smoking floors* ▭ *AE, D, DC, MC, V* Ⓜ *Subway: 4, 5, 6, N, Q, R, W to 59th St./Lexington Ave.*

$$–$$$ 🏨 **Beekman Tower.** Three blocks north of the United Nations, this jazzy 1928 hotel is an art deco architectural landmark. Its swanky Top of the Towers lounge, a rooftop bar with live piano, is a superb place to take in the view of the East River and beyond; downstairs, the Zephyr Grill looks out on 1st Avenue. Suites, which range from studios to one-bedrooms, are all very spacious, and all have kitchens. Rooms are attractively decorated with chintz and dark-wood furniture, and all have separate sitting areas. The one-bedroom suites have dining tables as well. ✉ *3 Mitchell Pl., at 1st Ave. and E. 49th St., Midtown East 10017* ☎ *212/ 320–8018 or 800/637–8483* 🖶 *212/465–3697* ⊕ *www.affinia.com* ⤳ *174 suites* ♨ *2 restaurants, room service, in-room fax, in-room safes, kitchenettes, minibars, microwaves, cable TV, in-room data ports, Wi-Fi, exercise equipment, gym, 2 bars, lounge, piano bar, dry cleaning, laundry facilities, laundry service, concierge, business services, meeting rooms, parking (fee), no-smoking floors* ▭ *AE, D, DC, MC, V* Ⓜ *Subway: 6 to 51st St./Lexington Ave.; E, V to Lexington–3rd Aves./53rd St.*

$$–$$$ 🏨 **The Benjamin.** From the elegant marble-and-silver lobby with 30-foot ceilings and a sweeping staircase to the argon gas–filled windows that reduce street noises to near whispers, this place pleases in ways seen and unseen. Elegant rooms are done in warm beiges and golds, extensive in-room offices come with personalized business cards, and you can choose from more than a dozen pillow options for your plush bed. A small spa and clubby restaurant make it easy to relax here. Note that no rooms have two beds, so the clientele leans toward business travelers and couples. ✉ *125 E. 50th St., at Lexington Ave., Midtown East 10022* ☎ *212/715–2500 or 888/423–6526* 🖶 *212/715–2525* ⊕ *www. thebenjamin.com* ⤳ *109 rooms, 100 suites* ♨ *Restaurant, room service, in-room safes, kitchenettes, minibars, cable TV, in-room data ports, gym, health club, spa, bar, babysitting, dry cleaning, laundry service, concierge, concierge floors, business services, meeting rooms, parking*

19

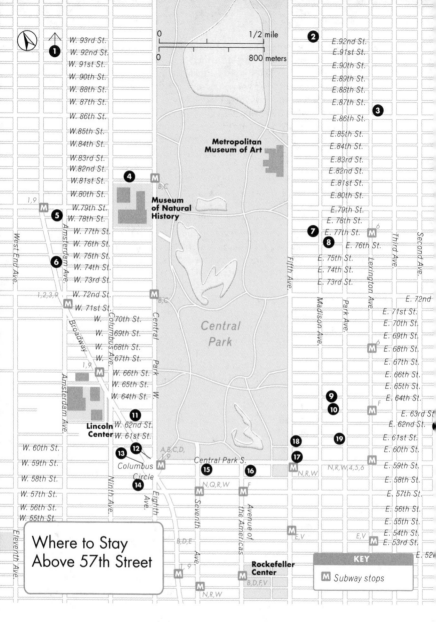

(fee) ⊟ *AE, D, DC, MC, V* Ⓜ *Subway: 6 to 51st St./Lexington Ave.; E, V to Lexington–3rd Aves./53rd St.*

$$–$$$ ⊡ **Crowne Plaza at the United Nations.** This 20-story building built in 1931 is in historic Tudor City, a stone's throw from the United Nations and Grand Central Terminal. Interior spaces are classic and unassuming, with marble floors, handmade carpets, and hardwood reproduction furniture upholstered in brocades and velvets. The traditional, well-kept rooms all come with CD players, irons and ironing boards, and coffeemakers. ⊠ *304 E. 42nd St., between 1st and 2nd Aves., Midtown East 10017* ☎ *212/986–8800 or 800/879–8836* 🖷 *212/297–3440* ⊕ *www. ichotelsgroup.com* ⇨ *300 rooms, 14 suites* ⌂ *Restaurant, room service, in-room safes, minibars, cable TV, in-room broadband, exercise equipment, gym, sauna, spa, bar, lounge, babysitting, dry cleaning, laundry service, concierge, business services, meeting rooms, parking (fee), some pets allowed (fee), no-smoking rooms* ⊟ *AE, D, DC, MC, V* Ⓜ *Subway: 4, 5, 6, 7, S to 42nd St./Grand Central.*

$$–$$$ ⊡ **The Dylan.** This 1903 Beaux Arts–style building with ornate plasterwork on its facade and a stunning marble staircase spiraling up its three floors once housed the Chemists Club. The 11-foot ceilings give the modern guest rooms a touch of grandeur, and the Carrara cut-marble bathrooms show the hotel's opulent intentions. Soaring columns and vaulted ceilings make the splendid Alchemy Suite—built in the 1930s to replicate a medieval laboratory—a Gothic confection. Guest service, however, doesn't seem to be a priority here, a fact that might be balanced by low Internet rates. ⊠ *52 E. 41st St., between Park and Madison Aves., Midtown East 10017* ☎ *212/338–0500* 🖷 *212/338–0569* ⊕ *www. dylanhotel.com* ⇨ *107 rooms, 2 suites* ⌂ *Restaurant, in-room safes, minibars, in-room data ports, gym, health club, bar, concierge, business services, meeting rooms* ⊟ *AE, D, DC, MC, V* Ⓜ *Subway: 4, 5, 6, 7, S to 42nd St./Grand Central.*

$$–$$$ ⊡ **Hotel Elysée.** Best known as the site of the Monkey Bar, a legendary watering hole, this intimate, Euro-style hotel has relatively affordable rates, given its location. All guests have access to the comfortable Club Room, where complimentary coffee, tea, and snacks are available all day. You can grab a breakfast pastry there in the morning and free wine and hors d'oeuvres on weeknights—a blessing, since room service is limited and there are no minibars in the guest rooms. Many of the old-world guest rooms have terraces. ⊠ *60 E. 54th St., between Madison and Park Aves., Midtown East 10022* ☎ *212/753–1066 or 800/535–9733* 🖷 *212/ 980–9278* ⊕ *www.elyseehotel.com* ⇨ *86 rooms, 15 suites* ⌂ *Restaurant, room service, in-room safes, some kitchenettes, microwaves, refrigerators, cable TV, in-room VCRs, in-room data ports, Wi-Fi, massage, bar, piano, babysitting, dry cleaning, laundry service, concierge, business services, meeting rooms, parking (fee), no-smoking floors* ⊟ *AE, D, DC, MC, V* ⁑⊙⁑ *CP* Ⓜ *Subway: E, V to 5th Ave.*

★ $$–$$$ ⊡ **Library Hotel.** Boutiquey and bookish, this handsome landmark brownstone (1900) gets its inspiration from the New York Public Library. Each of its 10 floors is dedicated to one of the 10 categories of the Dewey Decimal System; undersize modern rooms are stocked with art and books relevant to a subtopic such as erotica, astronomy, or bi-

19

ography—let your interests guide your room choice. The staff is incredibly hospitable and the whole property is old-leather-armchair comfortable, whether you're unwinding in front of the library fireplace, partaking of the complimentary wine and cheese or Continental breakfast, or relaxing in the roof garden. ⊠ *299 Madison Ave., at E. 41st St., Midtown East 10017* ☎ *212/983–4500 or 877/793–7323* 🖷 *212/499–9099* ⊕ *www.libraryhotel.com* 🛏 *60 rooms* ⌂ *Restaurant, room service, in-room safes, minibars, cable TV with movies, in-room VCRs, in-room data ports, massage, bar, lounges, babysitting, dry cleaning, laundry service, concierge, business services, meeting rooms, parking (fee), no-smoking floors* ▤ *AE, DC, MC, V* ⍩ *CP* Ⓜ *Subway: 4, 5, 6, 7, S to 42nd St./Grand Central.*

$$–$$$ ▦ **Millennium Hotel New York UN Plaza.** A name change and major renovation have modernized this sky-high tower near the United Nations. Rooms, which begin on the 28th floor, have breathtaking views, make generous use of warm woods and neutral tones, and have an array of up-to-the-minute telecommunications gadgets. The multilingual staff caters to a discerning clientele that includes heads of state. The views also dazzle from the elegant 27th-floor pool and health club, and the rooftop tennis court attracts name players. Service throughout the hotel is first-rate, and the business center is open until 11 PM. ⊠ *1 United Nations Plaza, at E. 44th St. and 1st Ave., Midtown East 10017* ☎ *212/758–1234 or 866/866–8086* 🖷 *212/702–5051* ⊕ *www.millenniumhotels.com* 🛏 *387 rooms, 40 suites* ⌂ *Restaurant, room service, in-room fax, in-room safes, some kitchens, minibars, cable TV with movies, in-room broadband, tennis court, indoor pool, health club, massage, bar, shop, babysitting, dry cleaning, laundry service, concierge, business services, meeting rooms, parking (fee), no-smoking floors* ▤ *AE, D, DC, MC, V* Ⓜ *Subway: 4, 5, 6, 7, S to 42nd St./Grand Central.*

★ $$ ▦ **Roger Smith.** The elusive Roger Smith lends his name to this colorful boutique hotel and adjacent gallery. Riotous murals cover the walls in Lily's, the café. The art-filled rooms are homey and comfortable, and some have stocked bookshelves and fireplaces. An eclectic mix of room service is provided by five local restaurants. Guests have access to the nearby New York Sports Club ($10 fee). Rates can drop by as much as $75 per night in winter and summer, so ask when booking. A complimentary Continental breakfast is included. ⊠ *501 Lexington Ave., between E. 47th and E. 48th Sts., Midtown East 10017* ☎ *212/755–1400 or 800/445–0277* 🖷 *212/758–4061* ⊕ *www.rogersmith.com* 🛏 *102 rooms, 28 suites* ⌂ *Restaurant, room service, some kitchenettes, refrigerators, cable TV with movies and video games, in-room data ports, Wi-Fi, massage, bar, babysitting, dry cleaning, laundry service, meeting rooms, parking (fee), some pets allowed, no-smoking floors* ▤ *AE, D, DC, MC, V* ⍩ *CP* Ⓜ *Subway: 6 to 51st St./Lexington Ave.; E, V to Lexington–3rd Aves./53rd St.*

$–$$ ▦ **The Fitzpatrick Manhattan Hotel.** This cozy hotel south of Bloomingdale's brings Irish charm to the New York hotel scene, which might explain why Irish citizens ranging from Gregory Peck to the Chieftains have all been guests. More than half of the units are suites, and all have golden draperies and carpets and traditional dark-wood furniture. Guests have free access to the Excelsior Athletic Club next door. Fitzer's, the pub-like bar at the heart of the hotel, is as welcoming as any in Dublin. ✉ 687 *Lexington Ave., at E. 57th St., Midtown East 10022* ☎ *212/355–0100 or 800/367–7701* 🖷 *212/355–1371* ⊕ *www.fitzpatrickhotels.com* 🛏 *40 rooms, 52 suites ⌂ Restaurant, room service, some in-room safes, some kitchenettes, minibars, some refrigerators, cable TV with movies and video games, in-room data ports, health club, massage, bar, pub, babysit-ting, dry cleaning, laundry service, concierge, business services, meet-ing rooms, airport shuttle, parking (fee), no-smoking rooms* ☰ *AE, D, DC, MC, V* Ⓜ *Subway: 4, 5, 6, N, Q, R, W to 59th St./Lexington Ave.*

$ 🏨 **The Bentley.** Although a budget-price hotel is certainly welcome in the often-pricey Bloomingdale's neighborhood, service complaints sometimes outweigh the low prices here. On the other hand, there are reasons to stay here, starting with the free cappuccino offered round-the-clock in the pocket-size lobby library. Rooms are relatively large compared to other hotels in the same price category. Sheets are Belgian, toiletries are boutiquey—the whole place is reminiscent of a small European hotel. Noise can sometimes be a problem on the lowest floors, so request a high floor, preferably with a view of the East River. The 21st-floor restaurant has wonderful river and city vistas. ✉ *500 E. 62nd St., at York Ave., Midtown East 10021* ☎ *212/644–6000 or 888/664–6835* 🖷 *212/207–4800* ⊕ *www.nychotels.com* 🛏 *200 rooms ⌂ Restaurant, room service, cable TV with movies, Wi-Fi, laundry service, no-smok-ing rooms* ☰ *AE, D, DC, MC, V* Ⓜ *Subway: 4, 5, 6, F, N, R, W to 59th St./Lexington Ave.*

¢–$ 🏨 **Pickwick Arms Hotel.** This no-frills but convenient East Side establish-ment is regularly booked solid by bargain hunters. Privations you en-dure to save a buck start and end with the lilliputian size of some rooms, all of which have cheap-looking furnishings; some doubles have bunk beds. However, some rooms look over the Manhattan skyline, and all are renovated on a regular basis. There's also a rooftop garden. ✉ *230 E. 51st St., between 2nd and 3rd Aves., Midtown East 10022* ☎ *212/ 355–0300 or 800/742–5945* 🖷 *212/755–5029* ⊕ *www.pickwickarms. com* 🛏 *360 rooms, 175 with bath ⌂ Café, some refrigerators, cable TV, in-room data ports, bar, airport shuttle, parking (fee)* ☰ *AE, DC, MC, V* Ⓜ *Subway: 6 to 51st St./Lexington Ave.; E, V to Lexington–3rd Aves./53rd St.*

¢–$ 🏨 **Vanderbilt YMCA.** Of the various Manhattan Ys that provide overnight accommodations, this one has the best facilities, including a full-scale fitness center and pools. Rooms are little more than dormitory-style cells, each with a bed (bunks in doubles), dresser, and TV; singles have desks. Only six rooms have phones and private baths (these cost extra), but communal showers and toilets are clean. The Turtle Bay neighborhood is safe and convenient; Grand Central Terminal and the United Nations are both a few blocks away. ✉ *224 E. 47th St., between 2nd and 3rd Aves., Midtown East 10017* ☎ *212/756–9600* 🖷 *212/752–0210* ⊕ *www. ymcanyc.org* 🛏 *375 rooms, 6 with bath ⌂ Restaurant, refrigerators, 2 indoor pools, gym, health club, massage, basketball, volleyball, laun-dry facilities, meeting rooms, airport shuttle; no phones in some rooms* ☰ *AE, MC, V* Ⓜ *Subway: 6 to 51st St.*

19

Upper East Side

★ $$$$ 🏨 **The Carlyle.** European tradition and Manhattan swank come together at New York's most lovable grand hotel. Everything about this Madison Avenue landmark suggests refinement, from rooms decorated with fine antique furniture and artfully framed Audubons and botanicals, to the first-rate service. Cabaret luminaries take turns holding court at the clubby Café Carlyle as well as Bemelmans Bar. Discreet whispers of change, such as the impeccable Thierry Despont–designed suite atop the hotel and the elegant new "C" logos on certain elevator doors, enrich the hotel's ambience, which to some still feels a bit stuffy and old-school. ⊠ *35 E. 76th St., between Madison and Park Aves., Upper East Side 10021* 🖥 *212/744–1600* ⊕ *www.thecarlyle.com* ➪ *122 rooms, 57 suites* ♿ *Restaurant, café, room service, in-room fax, in-room safes, some in-room hot tubs, kitchenettes, minibars, microwaves, cable TV, in-room DVD, in-room data ports, gym, health club, spa, bar, dry cleaning, laundry service, concierge, business services, meeting room, parking (fee), some pets allowed, no-smoking floors* ▭ *AE, DC, MC, V* Ⓜ *Subway: 6 to 77th St.*

$$$$ 🏨 **Hotel Plaza Athénée.** At this elegant French property in a building of a certain age, no two rooms share the same floor plan and all have ample space. Service is stellar and even the most modest rooms have sitting areas with inviting sofas and generous closet space. Handsomely furnished suites come with dining tables or dining rooms, and 12 suites have balconies. Rooms above the 12th floor have over-the-rooftops views. The Bar Seine is a romantic Moroccan fantasy, and the restaurant Arabelle serves world-class food. Ask about weekend packages, which can be much less expensive than the standard rates. ⊠ *37 E. 64th St., at Madison Ave., Upper East Side 10021* 🖥 *212/734–9100 or 800/447–8800* 🖥 *212/772–0958* ⊕ *www.plaza-athenee.com* ➪ *115 rooms, 35 suites* ♿ *Restaurant, room service, some in-room faxes, in-room safes, some kitchenettes, minibars, refrigerators, cable TV, in-room broadband, exercise equipment, gym, health club, massage, bar, lounge, babysitting, dry cleaning, laundry service, concierge, business services, meeting rooms, parking (fee), some pets allowed, no-smoking floors* ▭ *AE, D, DC, MC, V* Ⓜ *Subway: 6 to 68th St./Hunter College.*

FodorsChoice ★

$$$$ 🏨 **The Pierre.** The Pierre, once the jewel in the crown of the Four Seasons group, is now part of an Indian luxury chain called Taj. The Pierre's landmark building owes a lot to the Palace of Versailles, with chandeliers, murals depicting putti, and Corinthian columns in the Rotunda lounge. Chintz and dark wood adorn the grand and traditional guest rooms, whose gleaming black-and-white art deco bathrooms are spacious for New York. Although still a quintessential old New York place to stay, mutterings of rooms that need updating and more modern amenities make the exorbitant prices hard to justify. ⊠ *2 E. 61st St., between 5th and Madison Aves., Upper East Side 10021* 🖥 *212/838–8000 or 800/332–3442* 🖥 *212/758–1615* ⊕ *www.lhw.com/thepierre* ➪ *149 rooms, 52 suites* ♿ *2 restaurants, room service, in-room fax, in-room safes, minibars, cable TV, in-room broadband, exercise equipment, health club, hair salon, massage, bar, babysitting, dry cleaning,*

laundry service, concierge, business services, meeting rooms, travel services, parking (fee), some pets allowed, no-smoking floors = AE, D, DC, MC, V M *Subway: N, R, W to 5th Ave.*

★ **$$–$$$$** **The Mark.** A member of the Mandarin Oriental hotel group, the Mark, whose motto is "No jacket, no tie, no attitude," is refreshingly unpretentious considering its luxurious atmosphere. A petite art deco marble lobby leads into a clubby bar where even lone women travelers feel comfortable, and to the Mark's restaurant, where afternoon tea is served. Elegant bedrooms have English and Italian furnishings and prints and deep soaking tubs in the sleek marble bathrooms. Special touches here include hidden pantries with small kitchenettes in many of the rooms, a free shuttle to Wall Street, and complimentary cell phones. ⊠ *25 E. 77th St., at Madison Ave., Upper East Side 10021* ☎ *212/744–4300 or 800/843–6275* ☐ *212/472–5714* ⊕ *www.mandarinoriental.com* ⟿ *122 rooms, 54 suites* ⚐ *Restaurant, room service, in-room fax, in-room safes, some kitchenettes, minibars, cable TV, in-room VCRs, in-room broadband, exercise equipment, health club, massage, bar, babysitting, dry cleaning, laundry service, concierge, business services, meeting rooms, parking (fee), some pets allowed, no-smoking floors* = AE, D, DC, MC, V M *Subway: 6 to 77th St.*

$$$ **Hotel Wales.** Every effort has been made to retain the turn-of-the-20th-century mood of this 1901 Carnegie Hill landmark—from the cavernous lobby to the Pied Piper parlor, where vintage children's illustrations cover the walls. A complimentary European-style breakfast is served in the parlor; on a nice day head up to the rooftop terrace with your treats. Guest rooms are small, but they do have fine oak woodwork, and all are equipped with CD players. Most of the suites face Madison Avenue; unfortunately soundproofed windows are not de rigueur. The lovely Sarabeth's Restaurant, a local favorite for brunch, is in the hotel. ⊠ *1295 Madison Ave., between E. 92nd and E. 93rd Sts., Upper East Side 10128* ☎ *212/876–6000 or 877/847–4444* ☐ *212/860–7000* ⊕ *www.waleshotel.com* ⟿ *46 rooms, 41 suites* ⚐ *Restaurant, room service, in-room safes, some kitchenettes, minibars, cable TV with video games, in-room VCRs, Wi-Fi, gym, bar, babysitting, dry cleaning, laundry service, business services, parking (fee), some pets allowed, no-smoking floors* = AE, D, DC, MC, V ⦿ CP M *Subway: 6 to 96th St.*

$$$ **The Lowell.** This old-money refuge was built as an upscale apartment
Fodor's Choice hotel in the 1920s and still delivers genteel sophistication. Guest rooms
★ have all the civilized comforts of home, including stocked bookshelves, luxe bathrooms, and even umbrellas. Thirty-three of the suites have working fireplaces, and 11 have private terraces, the better for spying on posh neighboring abodes. A gym suite has its own fitness center, and a garden suite has two beautifully planted terraces. Most of the rooms have been redecorated in a more modern, streamlined style with less chintz and no patterns. The Pembroke Room serves a fine afternoon tea, and the Post House serves some of the best steaks in town. ⊠ *28 E. 63rd St., between Madison and Park Aves., Upper East Side 10021* ☎ *212/838–1400 or 800/221–4444* ☐ *212/319–4230* ⊕ *www.lhw.com/lowellhotel* ⟿ *23 rooms, 47 suites* ⚐ *2 restaurants, room service, in-room fax, in-room safes, kitchenettes, minibars, refrigerators, cable TV,*

19

in-room VCRs, in-room broadband, exercise equipment, health club, massage, bar, babysitting, dry cleaning, laundry service, concierge, business services, parking (fee), some pets allowed, ☰ *AE, D, DC, MC, V* Ⓜ *Subway: 4, 5, 6, N, R, W to 59th St./Lexington Ave.; F to 63rd St./Lexington Ave.*

$ 🏨 **The Franklin.** The Upper East Side's hippest, funkiest hotel has a pint-size lobby decorated with black granite, brushed steel, and cherrywood. Most rooms are also tiny (some measure 100 square feet), but what they lack in size they make up for in style: all have custom-built steel furniture, gauzy white canopies over the beds, cedar closets, and CD players. Added bonuses are the generous complimentary breakfast, fresh fruit in the evenings, and 24-hour cappuccino. ⊠ *164 E. 87th St., between Lexington and 3rd Aves., Upper East Side 10128* ☎ *212/369–1000 or 877/847–4444* 🖷 *212/894–5220* ⊕ *www.franklinhotel.com* ⇥ *50 rooms* ᗉ *In-room safes, cable TV, in-room VCRs, in-room data ports, Wi-Fi, lounge, library, dry cleaning, laundry service, no-smoking floors* ☰ *AE, DC, MC, V* ⑩ *CP* Ⓜ *Subway: 4, 5, 6 to 86th St.*

Upper West Side

$$$$ 🏨 **Trump International Hotel and Towers.** Rooms and suites in this expensive, showy hotel resemble mini-apartments: all have fully equipped kitchens with black-granite countertops, entertainment centers with stereos and CD players, and mini-telescopes, which you can use to gaze through the floor-to-ceiling windows, perhaps at the vast green expanse of Central Park that fronts the property. Creamy-beige marble bathrooms are equipped with Jacuzzis and Frette bathrobes, and slippers hang in the closets. Complimentary cellular phones and personalized stationery and business cards are also provided, just the tip of the exemplary service provided here. The restaurant, Jean-Georges, is one of the city's finest, and for a price a Jean-Georges's sous-chef will prepare a meal in your kitchenette. ⊠ *1 Central Park W, between W. 59th and W. 60th Sts., Upper West Side 10023* ☎ *212/299–1000 or 888/448–7867* 🖷 *212/299–1023* ⊕ *www.trumpintl.com* ⇥ *37 rooms, 130 suites* ᗉ *Restaurant, café, room service, in-room fax, in-room safes, in-room hot tubs, kitchenettes, minibars, microwaves, refrigerators, cable TV, in-room DVD/VCR, in-room data ports, indoor pool, gym, health club, spa, bar, babysitting, dry cleaning, laundry service, concierge, business services, meeting rooms, parking (fee), no-smoking rooms, no-smoking floors* ☰ *AE, D, DC, MC, V* Ⓜ *Subway: 1, A, B, C, D to 59th St./Columbus Circle.*

$$ 🏨 **Excelsior.** Directly across the street from the American Museum of Natural History, this well-kept spot rubs shoulders with fine prewar doorman apartment buildings (make sure to spring for a room with museum views). Fine traditional rooms come with amenities such as Web TV, a pants press, and an iron and ironing board. The second-floor breakfast room serves a good, if slightly pricey for the neighborhood, breakfast. The library lounge, with leather sofas, a cozy fireplace, and tables with built-in game boards, is an unexpected plus. On the minus side is a staff that seems to be too busy to focus on customer service. ⊠ *45 W. 81st St., between Central Park W and Columbus Ave.,*

Looking for a Scene?

The hottest trends, hippest bars, and coolest characters can be found in New York City's trendsetting hotels. Although most of the lounges and bars at these hipster hangouts require traversing a velvet-roped entrance, most extend automatic entry to guests of the hotel.

Ian Schrager started the concept of hotel as a see-and-be-seen place for local and global hipsters alike in the 1980s. His hotels are still at the forefront for this set, with the immense lobby lounge and secluded Vodka Room at the **Royalton** perennial favorites of the music and film industry, and the Hudson, with its greenery-draped lounge and cool outdoor bar, a must-visit for those in the know.

Down in SoHo, some of the chicest hotels in the city have rock-star-worthy scenes. Movie stars and their

hangers-on imbibe into the wee hours at cool Mercer Bar in the **Mercer Hotel. 60 Thompson**'s rooftop lounge is one of the hottest tickets in town on warm evenings; hotel guests get automatic entrance.

In Midtown, the trippy **Dream Hotel** has not only a rooftop bar that swings into action as soon as the weather warms, but also two other bars, not to mention a subterranean club that is rumored to be in the works. Hotel guests get priority entrance into all the trendy spots and a free drink coupon.

Hotel QT in Times Square has a bar that's adjacent to a lobby-level pool; you can see all the underwater action through voyeur windows above the bar. Just make sure to pay attention at the end of the evening, or you might be the hotel's next swimming sensation.

19

Upper West Side 10024 ☎ *212/362–9200 or 800/368–4575* 🖶 *212/721–2994* ⊕ *www.excelsiorhotelny.com* ⤴ *118 rooms, 80 suites* 🍴 *Restaurant, coffee shop, in-room fax, in-room safes, in-room data ports, Wi-Fi, gym, library, dry cleaning, laundry service, concierge, meeting rooms, some pets allowed, no-smoking floors* ☰ *AE, D, DC, MC, V* Ⓜ *Subway: B to 81st St.*

$$ 🏨 **The Lucerne.** The landmarked facade of this exquisite building has more pizzazz than the predictable guest rooms, with their requisite dark-wood reproduction furniture and chintz bedspreads. Health-conscious adults might like the gym on the top floor, with its city views, and children may be glued to the in-room Nintendo games. Service is the hotel's strong suit, and their popular restaurant Nice Matin is one of the better ones on the Upper West Side. The affluent residential neighborhood is filled with an impressive array of boutiques and gourmet food shops, and the American Museum of Natural History is a short walk away. ✉ *201 W. 79th St., at Amsterdam Ave., Upper West Side 10024* ☎ *212/875–1000 or 800/492–8122* 🖶 *212/721–1179* ⊕ *www.thelucernehotel. com* ⤴ *142 rooms, 42 suites* 🍴 *Restaurant, room service, some kitchenettes, some microwaves, some refrigerators, cable TV with movies and video games, in-room data ports, Web TV, Wi-Fi, gym, bar, lobby* *lounge, babysitting, dry cleaning, laundry service, concierge, business services, meeting rooms, parking (fee), no-smoking floors* ▭ *AE, D, DC, MC, V* Ⓜ *Subway: 1 to 79th St.*

★ **$–$$** 🏨 **Hotel Beacon.** The Upper West Side's best buy for the price is three blocks from Central Park and Lincoln Center, and footsteps from Zabar's gourmet bazaar. All of the generously sized rooms and suites include marble bathrooms, kitchenettes with coffeemakers, pots and pans, stoves, and ironing facilities. Closets are huge, and some of the bathrooms have Hollywood dressing room–style mirrors. High floors have views of Central Park, the Hudson River, or the midtown skyline; the staff here is especially friendly and helpful. ✉ *2130 Broadway, at W. 75th St., Upper West Side 10023* ☎ *212/787–1100 or 800/572–4969* 🖷 *212/787–8119* ⊕ *www.beaconhotel.com* ➷ *120 rooms, 110 suites* ⌂ *Café, in-room safes, kitchens, kitchenettes, microwaves, refrigerators, cable TV, babysitting, laundry facilities, business services, meeting rooms, parking (fee), no-smoking rooms* ▭ *AE, D, DC, MC, V* Ⓜ *Subway: 1, 2, 3 to 72nd St.*

¢–$ 🏨 **YMCA West Side.** Although the fitness center here is not quite as polished as the one at the Vanderbilt YMCA in Midtown East, you can't beat this Y for value, location, and atmosphere. Two blocks from Lincoln Center and a short jaunt from Central Park, it's housed in a building that looks like a Spanish cloister, with gargoyles adorning its arched neo-Byzantine entrance. Rooms are as tiny as jail cells; those with private bath cost extra. ✉ *5 W. 63rd St., at Central Park W, Upper West Side 10023* ☎ *212/875–4100 or 800/348–9622* 🖷 *212/875–1334* ⊕ *www.ymcanyc.org* ➷ *500 rooms, 33 with bath* ⌂ *Cafeteria, cable TV, 2 indoor pools, health club, massage, paddle tennis, racquetball, squash, laundry facilities, meeting rooms, airport shuttle; no room phones, no smoking* ▭ *AE, MC, V* Ⓜ *Subway: 1, A, B, C, D to 59th St./Columbus Circle.*

¢ 🏨 **Malibu Studios Hotel.** This youth-oriented budget crash pad could almost pass for a college dorm, especially given its proximity to Columbia University. Although it's farther north than you may care to venture, it's in a lively, safe neighborhood and the price is unheard-of for New York City. Double-occupancy rooms have private or shared baths; every room has a TV, CD player, and a desk with a writing lamp. For those truly on a student budget, hostel room beds are $29 per night. ✉ *2688 Broadway, between W. 102nd and W. 103rd Sts., Upper West Side 10025* ☎ *212/222–2954 or 800/647–2227* 🖷 *212/678–6842* ⊕ *www.malibuhotelnyc.com* ➷ *150 rooms, 100 with bath* ⌂ *Restaurant, room service, some cable TV, in-room data ports, dry cleaning, laundry service, business services, no-smoking rooms* ▭ *MC, V* Ⓜ *Subway: 1 to 103rd St.*

Brooklyn

$$ 🏨 **New York Marriott Brooklyn.** Don't discount staying in Brooklyn. What Manhattan hotel has room for an Olympic-length lap pool, an 1,100-car garage, and even a dedicated kosher kitchen? Large (if plain) guest rooms are enhanced by niceties such as 11-foot ceilings, massag-

ing showerheads, and rolling desks. Beautiful trompe l'oeil ceilings transform the multilevel foyer into a virtual open-air atrium. Major subway lines only a block away make for a mere 10-minute commute into Manhattan. Five-minute walks bring you to the Brooklyn Bridge's pedestrian path and the charming neighborhood of Brooklyn Heights. Marriott is preparing to add more than 250 rooms to this popular property. ☒ *333 Adams St., between Johnson and Willoughby Sts., Downtown Brooklyn 11201* ☎ *718/246–7000 or 800/843–4898* 🖷 *718/ 246–0563* ⊕ *www.marriott.com/nycbk* ⇋ *355 rooms, 21 suites* ⅋ *Restaurant, room service, in-room fax, in-room safes, minibars, cable TV, in-room data ports, indoor pool, health club, massage, bar, babysitting, dry cleaning, laundry service, concierge, business services, meeting rooms, airport shuttle, parking (fee), no-smoking floors* ▭ *AE, D, DC, MC, V* Ⓜ *Subway: 2, 3, 4, 5 to Borough Hall.*

SMART TRAVEL TIPS

There are planners and there are those who, excuse the pun, fly by the seat of their pants. We happily place ourselves among the planners. Our writers and editors try to anticipate all the issues you may face before and during any journey, and then they do their research. This section is the product of their efforts. Use it to get excited about your trip to New York City, to inform your travel planning, or to guide you on the road should the seat of your pants start to feel threadbare.

ADDRESSES

In Manhattan, the grid layout makes getting around easy. Avenues run north and south, with 5th Avenue dividing the east and west sides above 8th Street—the lower the address number on a street, the closer it is to 5th Avenue. The streets below 14th Street on the west side and 1st Street on the east side were settled before the grid system and follow no particular pattern.

To locate the cross street that corresponds to a numerical avenue address, or to find the avenue closest to a numerical street address, check the Web site below. (Cross streets for businesses are also listed in phone books.)

🚩 **Manhattan Address Locator** ⊕ www. manhattanaddress.com.

AIR TRAVEL

Schedules and fares for air service to New York vary from carrier to carrier and, sometimes, from airport to airport. For the best prices and for nonstop flights, consult several airlines. Generally, more international flights go in and out of Kennedy Airport, more domestic flights go in and out of LaGuardia Airport, and Newark Airport serves both domestic and international travelers.

FLYING TIMES

Some sample flying times are as follows: from Chicago (2½ hours), London (7 hours), Los Angeles (6 hours).

🚩 Major Airlines **American Airlines** ☎ 800/433-7300 ⊕ www.aa.com. **America West** ☎ 800/235-9292 or 480/693-6701 ⊕ www.americawest.com. **Continental Airlines** ☎ 800/523-3273 for U.S. and Mexico reservations, 800/231-0856 for international reservations ⊕ www.continental.com. **Delta Airlines** ☎ 800/221-1212 for U.S. reservations, 800/241-4141 for international reservations ⊕ www.delta.com. **jetBlue** ☎ 800/538-2583 ⊕ www.jetblue.com. **Midwest** ☎ 800/452-2022 ⊕ www.midwestairlines.com. **Northwest Airlines** ☎ 800/225-2525 for U.S. reservations, 800/447-4747 for international destinations ⊕ www.nwa.com. **Spirit Airlines** ☎ 800/772-7117 or 586/791-7300 ⊕ www.spiritair.com. **United Airlines** ☎ 800/864-8331 for U.S. reservations, 800/538-2929 for international reservations ⊕ www.united.com. **USAirways** ☎ 800/428-4322 for U.S. and Canada reservations, 800/622-1015 for international reservations ⊕ www.usairways.com.

CHECK-IN & BOARDING

Double-check your flight times, especially if you made your reservations far in advance. Airlines change their schedules, and alerts may not reach you. Always **bring a government-issued photo ID to the airport** (even when it's not required, a passport is best), and **arrive when you need to and not before.** Check in usually at least an hour before domestic flights and two to three hours for international flights. But many airlines have more stringent advance check-in requirements at some busy airports. The TSA estimates the waiting time for security at most major airports and publishes the information on its Web site. Note that if you aren't at the gate at least 10 minutes before your flight is scheduled to take off (sometimes earlier), you won't be allowed to board.

Don't stand in a line if you don't have to. Buy an e-ticket, check in at an electronic kiosk, or—even better—check in on your airline's Web site before you leave home. If you don't need to check luggage, you could bypass all but the security lines. These days, most domestic airline tickets are electronic; international tickets may be either electronic or paper.

You usually pay a surcharge (usually at least $25) to get a paper ticket, and its sole advantage is that it may be easier to endorse over to another airline if your flight is canceled and the airline with which you booked can't accommodate you on another flight. With an e-ticket, the only thing you receive is an e-mailed receipt citing your itinerary and reservation and ticket numbers. Be sure to carry this with you, as you'll need it to get past security. If you lose your receipt, though, you can simply print out another copy or ask the airline to do it for you at check-in.

Particularly during busy travel seasons and around holiday periods, if a flight is oversold, the gate agent will usually ask for volunteers and will offer some sort of compensation if you are willing to take a different flight. **Know your rights.** If you are bumped from a flight *involuntarily,* the airline must give you some kind of compensation if an alternate flight can't be found within one hour. If your flight is delayed because of something within the airline's control (so bad weather doesn't count), then the airline has a responsibility to get you to your destination on the same day, even if they have to book you on another airline and in an upgraded class if necessary. Read your airline's Contract of Carriage; it's usually buried somewhere on the airline's Web site.

Be prepared to quickly adjust your plans by programming a few numbers into your cell: your airline, an airport hotel or two, your destination hotel, your car service, and/or your travel agent. Bring snacks, water, and sufficient diversions, and you'll be covered if you get stuck in the airport, on the Tarmac, or even in the air during turbulence.

CUTTING COSTS

It's always good to **comparison shop.** Web sites (a.k.a. consolidators) and travel agents can have different arrangements with the airlines and offer different prices for exactly the same flight and day. Certain Web sites have tracking features that will e-mail you immediately when good deals are posted. Other people prefer to stick with one or two frequent-flier programs, racking up free trips and accumulating perks that can make trips easier. On some airlines, perks include a special reservations number, early boarding, access to upgrades, and more roomy economy-class seating.

Check early and often. Start looking for cheap fares up to a year in advance, and keep looking until you see something you can live with; you never know when a good deal may pop up. That said, **Jump on the good deals.** Waiting even a few minutes might mean paying more. For most people, saving money is more important than flexibility, so the more affordable nonrefundable tickets work. Just remember that you'll pay dearly (often as much as $100) if you must change your travel plans. Check on prices for departures at different times of the day and to and from alternate airports, and look for departures on Tuesday, Wednesday, and Thursday, typically the cheapest days to travel. Remember to **weigh your options,** though. A cheaper flight might have a long layover rather than being nonstop, or landing at a secondary airport might substantially increase your ground transportation costs.

Note that many airline Web sites—and most ads—show prices *without* taxes and surcharges. Don't buy until you know the full price. Government taxes add up quickly. Also **watch those ticketing fees.** Surcharges are usually added when you buy your ticket anywhere but on an airline's own Web site. (By the way, that includes on the phone—even if you call the airline directly—and for paper tickets regardless of how you book).

Online Consolidators **AirlineConsolidator.com** ⊕ www.airlineconsolidator.com; for international tickets. **Best Fares** ⊕ www.bestfares.com; $59.90 annual membership. **Cheap Tickets** ⊕ www.cheaptickets.com. **Expedia** ⊕ www.expedia.com. **Hotwire** ⊕ www.hotwire.com. **lastminute.com** ⊕ www.lastminute.com specializes in last-minute travel; the main site is for the U.K., but it has a link to a U.S. site. **Luxury Link** ⊕ www.luxurylink.com has auctions (surprisingly good deals) as well as offers at the high-end side of travel. **Orbitz** ⊕ www.orbitz.com. **Onetravel.com** ⊕ www.onetravel.com. **Priceline.com** ⊕ www.priceline.com. **Travelocity** ⊕ www.travelocity.com.

ENJOYING THE FLIGHT

Get the seat you want. Avoid those on the aisle directly across from the lavatories. Most frequent fliers say those are even worse than the seats that don't recline (e.g., those in the back row and those in front of a bulkhead). For more legroom, you can request emergency-aisle seats, but do so only if you're capable of moving the 35- to 60-pound airplane exit door—a Federal Aviation Administration requirement of passengers in these seats. Seats behind a bulkhead also offer more legroom, but they don't have under-seat storage. Often, you can pick a seat when you buy your ticket on an airline's Web site. But it's not always a guarantee, particularly if the airline changes the plane after you book your ticket; check back before you leave. SeatGuru.com has more information about specific seat configurations, which vary by aircraft.

Fewer airlines are providing free food for passengers in economy class. **Don't go hungry.** If you're scheduled to fly during mealtimes, verify if your airline offers anything to eat; even when it does, be prepared to pay. If you have dietary concerns, request special meals. These can be vegetarian, low-cholesterol, or kosher, for example. It's a good idea to pack some healthful snacks and a small (plastic) bottle of water in your carry-on bag.

Ask the airline about its children's menus, activities, and fares. On some lines infants and toddlers fly for free if they sit on a parent's lap, and older children fly for half price in their own seats. Also inquire about policies involving car seats; having one may limit where you can sit. While you're at it, ask about seat-belt extenders for car seats. And note that you can't count on a flight attendent to automatically produce an extender; you may have to inquire about it again when you board.

HOW TO COMPLAIN

If your baggage goes astray or your flight goes awry, complain right away. Most carriers require that you **file a claim immediately.** The Aviation Consumer Protection Division of the Department of Transportation publishes *Fly-Rights,* which discusses airlines and consumer issues and is available online. You can also find articles and information on mytravelrights.com, the Web site of the nonprofit Consumer Travel Rights Center.

Airline Complaints **Office of Aviation Enforcement and Proceedings** (Aviation Consumer Protection Division) ☎ 202/366-2220 ⊕ airconsumer.ost.

dot.gov. **Federal Aviation Administration Consumer Hotline** ☎ 866/835-5322 ⊕ www.faa.gov.

AIRPORTS

The major air gateways to New York City are LaGuardia Airport (LGA) and JFK International Airport (JFK) in the borough of Queens, and Newark Liberty International Airport (EWR) in New Jersey. Cab fares are generally higher to and from Newark, and LaGuardia is closer to Manhattan and easier to navigate than JFK. The AirTrain link between Newark Airport and Penn Station in Manhattan makes the journey in less than 30 minutes.

Long layovers don't have to be only about sitting around or shopping. These days they can be about burning off vacation calories. Check out www.airportgyms.com for lists of health clubs that are in or near many U.S. and Canadian airports.

🔀 Airlines & Airports **Airline and Airport Links. com** ⊕ www.airlineandairportlinks.com has links to many of the world's airlines and airports. **JFK International Airport** ☎ 718/244-4444 ⊕ www.panynj. gov. **LaGuardia Airport** ☎ 718/533-3400 ⊕ www. laguardiaairport.com. **Newark Liberty International Airport** ☎ 973/961-6000 or 888/397-4636 ⊕ www.newarkairport.com.

🔀 Airline Security Issues **Transportation Security Administration** ⊕ www.tsa.gov/public has answers for almost every question that might come up.

TRANSFERS BETWEEN AIRPORTS

Air-Ride provides detailed, up-to-the-minute recorded information on how to reach your destination from any of New York's airports. Note that if you arrive after midnight at any airport, you may wait a long time for a taxi. Consider calling a car service, as there is no shuttle service at that time.

🔀 **Air-Ride** ☎ 800/247-7433 (800/AIR-RIDE) ⊕ www.panynj.gov/aviation.html.

TRANSFERS—CAR SERVICES

Car services can be a great deal because the driver will often meet you on the concourse or in the baggage-claim area and help you with your luggage. The flat rates and tolls are often comparable to taxi fares, but some car services will charge for parking and waiting time at the airport.

To eliminate these expenses, other car services require that you telephone their dispatcher when you land so they can send the next available car to pick you up. New York City Taxi and Limousine Commission rules require that all car services be licensed and pick up riders only by prior arrangement; if possible, **call 24 hours in advance for reservations,** or at least a half day before your flight's departure. Drivers of nonlicensed vehicles ("gypsy cabs") often solicit fares outside the terminal in baggage-claim areas. Don't take them: even if you do have a safe ride you'll pay more than the going rate.

For phone numbers, see ⇨ Taxis & Car Services below.

TRANSFERS—TAXIS & SHUTTLES

Outside the baggage-claim area at each of New York's major airports are taxi stands where a uniformed dispatcher helps passengers find taxis (⇨ Taxis & Car Services). Cabs are not permitted to pick up fares anywhere else in the arrivals area, so if you want a taxi, take your place in line. Shuttle services generally pick up passengers from a designated spot along the curb.

New York Airport Service runs buses between JFK and LaGuardia airports, and buses from those airports to Grand Central Terminal, Port Authority Bus Terminal, Penn Station, Bryant Park, and hotels between 31st and 60th streets in Manhattan. Fares cost between $12 and $15. Buses operate from 6:15 AM to 11:10 PM from the airport; between 5 AM and 10 PM going to the airport.

SuperShuttle vans travel to and from Manhattan to JFK, LaGuardia, and Newark. These blue vans will stop at your home, office, or hotel. There are courtesy phones at the airports. For travel to the airport, the company recommends you make your requests 24 hours in advance. Fares range from $13 to $22 per person.

🔀 Shuttle Service **New York Airport Service** ☎ 718/875-8200 ⊕ www.nyairportservice.com. **SuperShuttle** ☎ 212/258-3826 ⊕ www. supershuttle.com.

TRANSFERS FROM JFK INTERNATIONAL AIRPORT

Taxis charge a flat fee of $45 plus tolls (which may be as much as $6) to Manhattan only, and take 35–60 minutes. Prices are roughly $16–$55 for trips to most other locations in New York City. You should also tip the driver.

AirTrain JFK links to the A subway line's Howard Beach station, and to Long Island Railroad's (LIRR) Jamaica Station, which is adjacent to the Sutphin Boulevard/Archer Avenue E/J/Z subway station, with connections to Manhattan. The light rail system runs 24 hours, leaving from the Howard Beach and the LIRR stations station every 4–8 minutes during peak times and every 12 minutes during low traffic times. From midtown Manhattan, the longest trip to JFK is via the A train, a trip of under an hour that costs $2 in subway fare in addition to $5 for the AirTrain. The quickest trip is with the Long Island Railroad (about 30 minutes), for a total cost of about $12. When traveling to the Howard Beach station, be sure to take the A train marked FAR ROCKAWAY or ROCKAWAY PARK, **not** LEFFERTS BOULEVARD.

🚇 **JFK Transfer Information AirTrain JFK** ⊕ www.airtrainjfk.com. **Long Island Railroad** Jamaica Station ⊠ 146 Archer Ave., at Sutphin Ave. ☎ 718/217–5477 ⊕ www.mta.info/lirr.

TRANSFERS FROM LAGUARDIA AIRPORT

Taxis cost $20–$30 plus tip and tolls (which may be as high as $6) to most destinations in New York City, and take at least 20–40 minutes.

For $2 you can ride the M-60 public bus (there are no luggage facilities on this bus) to 116th Street and Broadway, across from Columbia University on Manhattan's Upper West Side. From there, you can transfer to the No. 1 subway to Midtown. Alternatively, you can take Bus Q-48 to the Main Street subway station in Flushing, where you can transfer to the No. 7 train. Allow at least 90 minutes for the entire trip to Midtown.

TRANSFERS FROM NEWARK AIRPORT

Taxis to Manhattan cost $40–$65 plus tolls ($5) and take 20 to 45 minutes.

"Share and Save" group rates are available for up to four passengers between 8 AM and midnight—make arrangements with the airport's taxi dispatcher. If you're heading to the airport from Manhattan, a $15 surcharge applies to the normal taxi rates and the $5 toll.

AirTrain Newark is an elevated light rail system that connects to New Jersey Transit and Amtrak trains at the Newark Liberty International Airport Station. Total travel time to Penn Station in Manhattan is approximately 20 minutes and costs $14. AirTrain runs every three minutes from 5 AM to midnight and every 15 minutes from midnight to 5 AM.

Before heading to Manhattan, the AirTrain makes a stop at Newark's Penn Station. The five-minute ride here costs $7.50. From Newark Penn Station you can catch PATH trains, which run to Manhattan 24 hours a day. PATH trains run every 10 minutes on weekdays, every 15 to 30 minutes on weeknights and weekends. After stopping at Christopher Street, one line travels along 6th Avenue, making stops at West 9th Street, West 14th Street, West 23rd Street, and West 33rd Street. Other PATH trains connect Newark Penn Station with the World Trade Center site. PATH train fare is $1.50.

Olympia Trails buses leave for Grand Central Terminal and Penn Station in Manhattan about every 15 to 30 minutes until midnight. The trip takes roughly 45 minutes, and the fare is $12. Between the Port Authority or Grand Central Terminal and Newark, buses run every 20 to 30 minutes. The trip takes 55 to 65 minutes. Another route travels to downtown Manhattan. The fare is $13.

🚇 **Newark Airport Information AirTrain Newark** ☎ 888/397–4636 ⊕ www.airtrainnewark.com. **Olympia Trails** ☎ 212/964–6233 or 877/894–9155 ⊕ www.olympiabus.com. **PATH Trains** ☎ 800/234–7284 ⊕ www.pathrail.com.

BOAT & FERRY TRAVEL

The Staten Island Ferry runs across New York Harbor between Whitehall Street next to Battery Park in Lower Manhattan and St. George terminal in Staten Island. The free 25-minute ride gives you a view of the Financial District skyscrapers, the Statue of Liberty, and Ellis Island.

New York Water Taxi, in addition to serving commuters, shuttles tourists to the city's many waterfront attractions between the west and east sides and Lower Manhattan, the South Street Seaport, and Brooklyn's waterfront parks. The hop-on, hop-off ticket (good for two days) is $25 for adults.

FARES & SCHEDULES

Boat & Ferry Information **New York Water Taxi (NYWT)** ☎ 212/742-1969 ⊕ www.newyorkwatertaxi. com. **Staten Island Ferry** ⊕ www.siferry.com.

BUS TRAVEL TO & FROM NEW YORK CITY

Most long-haul and commuter bus lines feed into the Port Authority Bus Terminal, on 8th Avenue between West 40th and 42nd streets. You must purchase your ticket at a ticket counter, not from the bus driver, so give yourself enough time to wait in a line. Six bus lines, serving northern New Jersey and Rockland County, New York, make daily stops at the George Washington Bridge Bus Station from 5 AM to 1 AM. The station is connected to the 175th Street Station on the A line of the subway, which travels down the west side of Manhattan.

Bus Information **Adirondack, Pine Hill, and New York Trailways** ☎ 800/225-6815 ⊕ www. trailways.com. **Bonanza Bus Lines** ☎ 888/751-8800 ⊕ www.bonanzabus.com. **Greyhound Lines Inc.** ☎ 800/231-2222 ⊕ www.greyhound.com. **New Jersey Transit** ☎ 800/772-2222 ⊕ www.njtransit. com. **Peter Pan Trailways** ☎ 413/781-2900 or 800/237-8747 ⊕ www.peterpanbus.com. **Shortline** ☎ 800/631-8405 ⊕ www.shortlinebus.com. **Vermont Transit** ☎ 800/552-8737 ⊕ www. vermonttransit.com.

Bus Stations **George Washington Bridge Bus Station** ✉ 4211 Broadway, between 178th and 179th Sts., Washington Heights ☎ 800/221-9903 ⊕ www. panynj.gov. **Port Authority Bus Terminal** ✉ 625 8th Ave., at 42nd St., Midtown West ☎ 212/564-8484 ⊕ www.panynj.gov.

BUS TRAVEL WITHIN NEW YORK CITY

Most city buses follow easy-to-understand routes along the Manhattan street grid. Routes go up or down the north–south

avenues, or east and west on the major two-way crosstown streets: 96th, 86th, 79th, 72nd, 57th, 42nd, 34th, 23rd, and 14th. Most bus routes operate 24 hours, but service is infrequent late at night. Traffic jams can make rides maddeningly slow, especially along 5th Avenue in Midtown and the Upper East Side. Certain bus routes provide "Limited-Stop Service" during weekday rush hours, which saves travel time by stopping only at major cross streets and transfer points. A sign posted at the front of the bus indicates it has limited service; ask the driver whether the bus stops near where you want to go before boarding.

To find a bus stop, **look for a light-blue sign (green for a limited bus)** on a green pole; bus numbers and routes are listed, with the stop's name underneath.

FARES & SCHEDULES

Bus fare is the same as subway fare: $2. MetroCards (⇨ Public Transportation) allow you one free transfer between buses or from bus to subway; when using a token or cash, you can **ask the driver for a free transfer coupon,** good for one change to an intersecting route. Legal transfer points are listed on the back of the slip. Transfers generally have time limits of two hours. You cannot use the transfer to enter the subway system.

Route maps and schedules are posted at many bus stops in Manhattan and at major stops throughout the other boroughs. Each of the five boroughs of New York has a separate bus map; they're available from some station booths, but rarely on buses. The best places to obtain them are the MTA booth in the Times Square Information Center, or the information kiosks in Grand Central Terminal and Penn Station.

Bus Information **Metropolitan Transit Authority (MTA) Travel Information Line** ☎ 718/330-1234, 718/330-4847 for non-English speakers ⊕ www. mta.nyc.ny.us. **MTA Status information hotline** ☎ 718/243-7777, updated hourly.

PAYING

Pay your bus fare when you board, with exact change in coins (no pennies, and no change is given) or with a MetroCard.

CAR RENTAL

Request car seats and extras such as GPS when you book, and make sure that a confirmed reservation guarantees you a car. Agencies sometimes overbook, particularly for busy weekends and holiday periods. Rates are sometimes—but not always—better if you book in advance or reserve through a rental agency's Web site. There are other reasons to book ahead, though: for popular destinations, during busy times of the year, or to ensure that you get a certain type of car (vans, SUVs, exotic sports cars).

Rates in New York City are around $65–$100 day and $225–$300 a week for an economy car with air-conditioning, automatic transmission, and unlimited mileage. This includes the state tax on car rentals, which is 13.62%. Rental costs are lower just outside New York City, specifically in such places as Hoboken, New Jersey, and Yonkers, New York. The Yellow Pages are also filled with a profusion of local car-rental agencies, some renting secondhand vehicles. If you're traveling during a holiday period, make sure that a confirmed reservation guarantees you a car.

CUTTING COSTS

Really weigh your options. Find out if a credit card you carry or organization or frequent-renter program to which you belong has a discount program. And check that such discounts really are the best deal. You can often do better with special weekend or weekly rates offered by a rental agency. (And even if you only want to rent for five or six days, ask if you can get the weekly rate; it may very well be cheaper than the daily rate for that period of time.).

Price local car-rental companies as well as the majors. Also investigate wholesalers, which don't own fleets but rent in bulk from those that do and often offer better rates (note you must usually pay for such rentals before leaving home). Consider adding a car rental onto your air/hotel vacation package; the cost will often be cheaper than if you had rented the car separately on your own.

When traveling abroad, **look for guaranteed exchange rates,** which protect you against a falling dollar. With your rate locked in, you won't pay more, even if the price goes up in the local currency. (Note to self: Not the best thing if the dollar is surging rather than plunging.)

Beware of hidden charges. Those great rental rates may not be so great when you add in taxes, surcharges, cancellation penalties, taxes, drop-off charges (if you're planning to pick up the car in one city and leave it in another), and surchages (for being under or over a certain age, for additional drivers, or for driving over state or country borders or out of a specific radius from your point of rental).

Note that airport rental offices often add supplementary surcharges that you may avoid by renting from an agency whose office is just off airport property. Don't buy the tank of gas that's in the car when you rent it unless you plan to do a lot of driving. Avoid hefty refueling fees by filling the tank at a station well away from the rental agency (those nearby are often more expensive) just before you turn in the car.

🚗 **Major Agencies Alamo** ☎ 800/462-5266 ⊕ www.alamo.com. **Avis** ☎ 800/230-4898 ⊕ www.avis.com. **Budget** ☎ 800/527-0700 ⊕ www.budget.com. **Hertz** ☎ 800/654-3131 ⊕ www.hertz.com. **National Car Rental** ☎ 800/227-7368 ⊕ www.nationalcar.com.

INSURANCE

Everyone who rents a car wonders about whether the insurance that the rental companies offer is worth the expense. No one—not even us—has a simple answer. It all depends on how much regular insurance you have, how comfortable you are with risk, and whether or not money is an issue.

If you own a car and carry comprehensive car insurance for both collision and liability, your personal auto insurance will probably cover a rental, but read your policy's fine print to be sure. If you don't have auto insurance, then you should probably buy the collision- or loss-damage waiver (CDW or LDW) from the rental company. This eliminates your liability for damage to the car. Some credit cards offer CDW coverage, but it's usually supplemental to your own insurance and rarely covers SUVs, minivans, luxury models and the like. If your coverage is secondary, you may still be liable for loss-of-use costs from the car-rental company (again, read the fine print). But no credit-card insurance is valid unless you use that card for *all* transactions, from reserving to paying the final bill.

You may also be offered supplemental liability coverage; the car-rental company is required to carry a minimal level of liability coverage that covers all renters, but it's rarely enough to cover claims in a really serious accident if you're at fault. Your own auto insurance policy will protect you if you own a car; if you don't, you have to decide if you are willing to take the risk.

U.S. rental companies sell CDWs and LDWs for about $15 to $25 a day; supplemental liability is usually over $10 a day. The car-rental company may offer you all sorts of other policies, but they're rarely worth the cost. Personal accident insurance, which is basic hospitalization coverage, is an especially egregious rip-off if you already have health insurance.

Note that you can decline the insurance from the rental company and purchase it through a third-party provider such as Travel Guard (www.travelguard.com)— $9 per day for $35,000 of coverage. That's sometimes just under half the price of the CDW offered by some car-rental companies. Also, Diner's Club offers primary CDW coverage on all rentals reserved and paid for with the card. This means that Diner's Club's company—not your own car insurance—pays in case of an accident. It *doesn't* mean your car-insurance company won't raise your rates once it discovers you had an accident.

CAR TRAVEL
If you plan to drive into Manhattan, try to avoid the morning and evening rush hours (a problem at the crossings into Manhattan) and lunch hour. The deterioration of the bridges to Manhattan, especially those spanning the East River, mean repairs will be ongoing for the next few years. Listen to traffic reports on the radio (⇨ Media) before you set off, and don't be surprised if a bridge is partially or entirely closed.

Driving within Manhattan can be a nightmare of gridlocked streets, obnoxious drivers and bicyclists, and seemingly suicidal jaywalkers. Narrow and one-way streets are common, particularly downtown, and can make driving even more difficult. The most congested streets of the city lie between 14th and 59th streets and 3rd and 8th avenues.

GASOLINE
Fill up your tank when you have a chance—gas stations are few and far between in Manhattan. If you can, **fill up at stations outside the city,** where prices are anywhere from 10¢ to 50¢ cheaper per gallon. The average price of a gallon of regular unleaded gas is $2.50, at this writing. In Manhattan, you can refuel at stations along the West Side Highway and 11th Avenue south of West 57th Street and along East Houston Street. Some gas stations in New York require you to pump your own gas; others provide attendants. In New Jersey, the law requires that an attendant pump your gas.

PARKING
Free parking is difficult to find in Midtown, and violators may be towed away literally within minutes. All over town, parking lots charge exorbitant rates—as much as $23 for two hours (this includes an impressive sales tax of 18.625%). If you do drive, **use your car sparingly in Manhattan.** Instead, park it in a guarded parking garage for at least several hours; hourly rates decrease somewhat if a car is left for a significant amount of time. If you find a spot on the street, be sure to **check parking signs carefully.** Rules differ from block to block, and they're nearly all confusing.

ROAD CONDITIONS
New York City streets are in generally good condition, although there are enough potholes and bad patch jobs to make driving a little rough in some areas, as on Canal Street. Road and bridge repair seems to go on constantly, so you may encounter the occasional detour or a bottleneck where a three-lane street narrows to one lane. Heavy rains can cause street flooding in some areas, most notoriously

on the Franklin Delano Roosevelt Drive (known as the FDR and sometimes as East River Drive), where the heavy traffic can grind to a halt when lakes suddenly appear on the road. Traffic can be very heavy anywhere in the city at any time, made worse by the bad habits—double-parking, sudden lane changes, etc.—of some drivers. Many drivers don't slow down for yellow lights here—they speed up to make it through the intersection.

RULES OF THE ROAD

On city streets the speed limit is 30 mi per hour, unless otherwise posted. No right turns on red are allowed within city limits, unless otherwise posted. Be alert for one-way streets and "no left turn" intersections.

The law requires that front-seat passengers wear seat belts at all times. Children under 16 must wear seat belts in both the front and back seats. Always **strap children under age four into approved child-safety seats.** It is illegal to use a handheld cell phone while driving in New York State. Police will immediately seize the car of anyone arrested for DWI (driving while intoxicated) in New York City.

CHILDREN IN NEW YORK

For listings of children's events, consult *New York* magazine. The Friday *New York Times* "Weekend" section also includes children's activities. Other good sources on happenings for youngsters are the monthly magazines *New York Family* and *Big Apple Parent,* both available free at toy stores, children's museums, and other places around town where parents and children are found. The Web site goCityKids includes listings of what's going on. If you have access to cable television, check the local all-news channel New York 1, where you'll find a spot aired several times daily that covers current and noteworthy children's events. *Fodor's Around New York City with Kids* (available in bookstores everywhere) can help you plan your days together.

If you are renting a car, don't forget to arrange for a car seat when you reserve. For general advice about traveling with children, consult *Fodor's FYI: Travel with Your Baby* (available in bookstores everywhere).

◪ Publications & Web Sites **Big Apple Parent** ⊕ www.parentsknow.com. **goCityKids** ⊕ www.gocitykids.com.

BABYSITTING

The Baby Sitters' Guild will schedule sightseeing tours for a flat fee of $100. Regular babysitting rates are $20 an hour for one child and $25 for two and three children, plus a $4.50 transportation charge ($10 after midnight). More than 16 languages are spoken by staff members. Minimum booking is for four hours, and infants cost extra. Cash and travelers' checks are accepted.

◪ Agency **Baby Sitters' Guild** ☎ 212/682–0227 ⊕ www.babysittersguild.com ◷ Daily 9–9.

FLYING

Experts agree that it's a good idea to use safety seats aloft for children weighing less than 40 pounds. Airlines set their own policies: if you use a safety seat, U.S. carriers usually require that the child be ticketed, even if he or she is young enough to ride free, because the seats must be strapped into regular seats. And even if you pay the full adult fare for the seat, it may be worth it, especially on longer trips. Do **check your airline's policy about using safety seats during takeoff and landing.** Safety seats are not allowed everywhere in the plane, so get your seat assignments as early as possible.

When reserving, request children's meals or a freestanding bassinet (not available at all airlines) if you need them. But note that bulkhead seats, where you must sit to use the bassinet, may lack an overhead bin or storage space on the floor.

LODGING

Before you consider using a cot or fold-out couch for your child, ask just how large your hotel room is—New York City rooms tend to be small. Most hotels in New York allow children under a certain age to stay in their parents' room at no extra charge, but others charge for them as extra adults; be sure to find out the cutoff age for children's discounts.

PUBLIC TRANSPORTATION

Children shorter than 44 inches ride for free on MTA buses and subways. If you're pushing a stroller, don't struggle through a subway turnstile; **ask the station agent to buzz you through the gate** (the attendant will ask you to swipe your MetroCard through the turnstile nearest the gate). Keep a sharp eye on your young ones while on the subway. At some stations there is a gap between the train doors and the platform. During rush hour, crowds often try to push into spaces that look empty—but are actually occupied by a stroller. Unfortunately New York riders are not known to give up their seats for children, for someone carrying a child, or for much of anyone else.

SIGHTS & ATTRACTIONS

Places that are especially appealing to children are indicated by a rubber-duckie icon (🦆) in the margin.

COMPUTERS ON THE ROAD

The Web site JiWire allows you to find Wi-Fi hot spots in hotels, libraries, parks, and other locations throughout the city.

📶 JiWire ⊕ www.jiwire.com.

CONCIERGES

Good hotel concierges are invaluable—for arranging transportation, getting reservations at the hottest restaurant, and scoring tickets for a sold-out show or entree to an exclusive nightclub. They're in-the-know and well connected. That said, sometimes you have to take their advice with a grain of salt.

It's not uncommon for restaurants to ply concierges with free food and drink in exchange for steering diners their way. Indeed, European concierges often receive referral *fees*. Hotel chains usually have individual guidelines about what their concierges can accept. The best concierges, however, are above reproach. This is particularly true of those who belong to the prestigious international society of Les Clefs d'Or.

What can you expect of a concierge? At a typical tourist-class hotel, you can expect him or her to give you the basics: to show you something on a map, make a standard restaurant reservation (particularly if you don't speak the language), or help you book a tour or airport transportation. In Asia, concierges perform the vital service of writing out the name or address of your destination for you to give to a cab driver.

Savvy concierges at the finest hotels and resorts, though, can arrange for just about any good or service imaginable—and do so quickly. You should compensate them appropriately. A $10 tip is enough to show appreciation for a table at a hot restaurant. But the reward should really be much greater for tickets to that U2 concert that's been sold out for months or for those last-minute sixth-row-center seats for *The Lion King*.

CUSTOMS & DUTIES

You're always allowed to bring goods of a certain value back home without having to pay any duty or import tax. There's also a limit on the amount of tobacco and liquor you can bring back duty-free, and some countries have separate limits for perfumes; for exact figures, check with your customs department. The values of so-called "duty-free" goods are included in these amounts. When you shop abroad, save all your receipts, as customs inspectors may ask to see them as well as the items you purchased. If the total value of your goods is more than the duty-free limit, then you'll have to pay a tax (most often a flat percentage) on the value of everything beyond that limit.

DISABILITIES & ACCESSIBILITY

New York has come a long way in making life easier for people with disabilities. At most street corners, curb cuts allow wheelchairs to roll along unimpeded. Many restaurants, shops, and movie theaters with step-up entrances have wheelchair ramps. And though some New Yorkers may rush past those in need of assistance, you'll find plenty of people who are more than happy to help you get around.

Hospital Audiences maintains a Web site with information on the accessibility of many landmarks and attractions. A similar list, "Tourist and Cultural Information for the Disabled," is available from New York City's Web site. Big Apple Greeters has tours of New York City tailored to visitors' personal preferences. The Andrew Heiskell Braille and Talking Book Library houses an impressive collection of braille, large-print, and recorded books in a layout designed for people with vision impairments.

Local Resources **Andrew Heiskell Library** ✉ 40 W. 20th St., between 5th and 6th Aves., Flatiron District Ⓜ F or V to 23rd St. ☎ 212/206-5400 ⊕ www.talkingbooks.nypl.org. **Big Apple Greeters** ✉ 1 Centre St., Suite 2035, Lower Manhattan, New York, NY 10007 ☎ 212/669-2896 ⊕ www. bigapplegreeter.org. **Hospital Audiences** ☎ 212/575-7676 ⊕ www.hospaud.org. **New York City** ☎ 311 in New York City, 212/639-9675 (212/NEW-YORK) outside of New York ⊕ www.nyc.gov.

HOTEL RESERVATIONS

When discussing accessibility with an operator or reservations agent, ask hard questions. Are there any stairs, inside *or* out? Are there grab bars next to the toilet *and* in the shower/tub? How wide is the doorway to the room? To the bathroom? For the most extensive facilities meeting the latest legal specifications, opt for newer accommodations. If you reserve through a toll-free number, consider also calling the hotel's local number to confirm the information from the central reservations office. Get confirmation in writing when you can.

LODGING

Despite the Americans with Disabilities Act, the definition of accessibility seems to differ from hotel to hotel. Some properties may be accessible by ADA standards for people with mobility problems but not for people with hearing or vision impairments, for example.

If you have mobility problems, ask for the lowest floor on which accessible services are offered. If you have a hearing impairment, check whether the hotel has devices to alert you visually to the ring of the telephone, a knock at the door, and a fire/ emergency alarm. Some hotels provide these devices without charge. Discuss your needs with hotel personnel if this equipment isn't available, so that a staff member can personally alert you in the event of an emergency.

If you're bringing a guide dog, get authorization ahead of time and write down the name of the person with whom you spoke.

SIGHTS & ATTRACTIONS

Most public facilities in New York City, whether museums, parks, or theaters, are wheelchair-accessible. Some attractions have tours or programs for people with mobility, sight, or hearing impairments.

TRANSPORTATION

Other than at major subway exchanges, most stations are still all but impossible to navigate; people in wheelchairs should stick to public buses, most of which have wheelchair lifts and "kneelers" at the front to facilitate getting on and off. Bus drivers will provide assistance.

Reduced fares are available to all disabled passengers displaying a Medicare card. Visitors to the city are also eligible for the same Access-a-Ride program benefits as New York City residents. Drivers with disabilities may use windshield cards from their own state or Canadian province to park in designated handicapped spaces.

Complaints **Aviation Consumer Protection Division** (⇨ Air Travel) for airline-related problems. **Departmental Office of Civil Rights** ✉ For general inquiries, U.S. Department of Transportation, S-30, 400 7th St. SW, Room 10215, Washington, DC 20590 ☎ 202/366-4648 🖷 202/366-9371 ⊕ www.dot. gov/ost/docr/index.htm. **Disability Rights Section** ✉ NYAV, U.S. Department of Justice, Civil Rights Division, 950 Pennsylvania Ave. NW, Washington, DC 20530 ☎ ADA information line 202/514-0301, 800/514-0301, 202/514-0383 TTY, 800/514-0383 TTY ⊕ www.ada.gov. **U.S. Department of Transportation Hotline** ☎ For disability-related air-travel problems, 800/778-4838 or 800/455-9880 TTY.

TRAVEL AGENCIES

In the United States, the Americans with Disabilities Act requires that travel firms serve the needs of all travelers. Some agencies specialize in working with people with disabilities.

Travelers with Mobility Problems **Access Adventures/B. Roberts Travel** ✉ 206 Chestnut Ridge Rd., Scottsville, NY 14624 ☎ 585/889-9096

⊕ www.brobertstravel.com ✐ dltravel@prodigy.
net, run by a former physical-rehabilitation coun-
selor. **Accessible Vans of America** ⊠ 9 Spielman
Rd., Fairfield, NJ 07004 ☏ 877/282-8267, 888/282-
8267, 973/808-9709 reservations 🖷 973/808-9713
⊕ www.accessiblevans.com. **CareVacations** ⊠ No.
5, 5110-50 Ave., Leduc, Alberta, Canada, T9E 6V4
☏ 780/986-6404 or 877/478-7827 🖷 780/986-
8332 ⊕ www.carevacations.com, for group tours
and cruise vacations. **Flying Wheels Travel** ⊠ 143
W. Bridge St., Box 382, Owatonna, MN 55060
☏ 507/451-5005 🖷 507/451-1685 ⊕ www.
flyingwheelstravel.com.

🗗 Travelers with Developmental Disabilities **New
Directions** ⊠ 5276 Hollister Ave., Suite 207, Santa
Barbara, CA 93111 ☏ 805/967-2841 or 888/967-2841
🖷 805/964-7344 ⊕ www.newdirectionstravel.com.
Sprout ⊠ 893 Amsterdam Ave., New York, NY 10025
☏ 212/222-9575 or 888/222-9575 🖷 212/222-9768
⊕ www.gosprout.org.

EMERGENCIES

Dial 911 for police, fire, or ambulance services in an emergency (TTY is available
for persons with hearing impairments).

🗗 Hospitals **Bellevue** ⊠ 1st Ave. at E. 27th St.,
Gramercy ☏ 212/562-4141. **Beth Israel Medical
Center** ⊠ 1st Ave. at E. 16th St., Gramercy ☏ 212/
420-2000. **Lenox Hill Hospital** ⊠ 100 E. 77th St.,
between Lexington and Park Aves., Upper East Side
☏ 212/434-3030. **New York Downtown Hospital**
⊠ 170 William St., between Beekman and Spruce
Sts., Lower Manhattan ☏ 212/312-5000. **New York
Presbyterian Hospital** ⊠ 525 E. 68th St., at York
Ave., Upper East Side ☏ 212/746-5454. **NYU Medical Center** ⊠ 530 1st Ave., at E. 32nd St., Murray
Hill ☏ 212/263-7300. **St. Luke's-Roosevelt Hospital** ⊠ 10th Ave. at 59th St., Midtown West ☏ 212/
523-4000. **St. Vincent's Hospital** ⊠ 7th Ave. and
W. 12th St., Greenwich Village ☏ 212/604-7000.

🗗 Hotlines **LifeNet (counseling information and
referrals)** ☏ 800/543-3638. **Mental Health Crisis
Intervention Services** ☏ 212/219-5599. **Safe Horizon Crime Victims Hotline** ☏ 212/577-7700 or
800/621-4673 ⊕ www.safehorizon.org. **Sex Crimes
Report Line** ☏ 212/267-7273. **Terrorism** ☏ 888/
692-7233.

🗗 24-Hour Pharmacies **CVS** ⊠ 342 E. 23rd St.,
between 1st and 2nd Aves., Gramercy ☏ 212/505-
1555 ⊠ 630 Lexington Ave., at E. 53rd St., Midtown
East ☏ 917/369-8688 ⊕ www.cvs.com. **Rite-Aid**
⊠ 301 W. 50th St., at 8th Ave., Midtown West
☏ 212/247-8384 ⊕ www.riteaid.com.

GAY & LESBIAN TRAVEL

Attitudes toward same-sex couples are
very tolerant in Manhattan and many
parts of Brooklyn, perhaps less so in other
parts of the city. Chelsea, Greenwich Village, and Hell's Kitchen are the most
prominently gay neighborhoods, but gay
men and lesbians feel right at home almost
everywhere. The world's biggest gay-pride
parade takes place on 5th Avenue the last
Sunday in June.

PUBLICATIONS

For listings of gay events and places, check
out *HX, Next, New York Blade News,*
and the *Gay City News,* all distributed
free on the street and in many bars and
shops throughout Manhattan. Magazines
Paper and *Time Out New York* have a
gay-friendly take on what's happening in
the city.

🗗 Local Information **Gay & Lesbian Switchboard
of NY** ☏ 212/989-0999 or 888/843-4564 ⊕ www.
glnh.org. **Lesbian, Gay, Bisexual & Transgender
Community Center** ⊠ 208 W. 13th St., between 7th
and 8th Aves., Greenwich Village ☏ 212/620-7310
⊕ www.gaycenter.org.

🗗 Gay Publications **Gay City News** ⊕ www.
gaycitynews.com. *HX* ⊕ www.hx.com. **New York
Blade News** ⊕ www.nyblade.com. **Next** ⊕ www.
nextmagazine.net.

🗗 Gay- & Lesbian-Friendly Travel Agencies
Different Roads Travel ⊠ 8383 Wilshire Blvd.,
Suite 520, Beverly Hills, CA 90211 ☏ 323/651-5557
or 800/429-8747 (Ext. 14 for both) 🖷 323/651-5454.
Kennedy Travel ⊠ 130 W. 42nd St., Suite 401, New
York, NY 10036 ☏ 212/840-8659 or 800/237-7433
🖷 212/730-2269 ⊕ www.kennedytravel.com. **Now,
Voyager** ⊠ 4406 18th St., San Francisco, CA 94114
☏ 415/626-1169 or 800/255-6951 🖷 415/626-8626
⊕ www.nowvoyager.com. **Skylink Travel and Tour/
Flying Dutchmen Travel** ⊠ 1455 N. Dutton Ave.,
Suite A, Santa Rosa, CA 95401 ☏ 707/546-9888 or
800/225-5759 🖷 707/636-0951, serving lesbian
travelers.

GUIDEBOOKS

Plan well and you won't be sorry. Guidebooks are excellent tools—and you can
take them with you. You may want to
check out color-photo-illustrated *Fodor's
See It New York City* and pocket-size *New
York City's 25 Best,* with a large city map.

Flashmaps New York City is loaded with detailed theme maps. All are available at online retailers and bookstores everywhere.

INSURANCE

What kind of coverage do you honestly need? Do you even need trip insurance at all? Take a deep breath and read on.

We believe that comprehensive trip insurance is especially valuable if you're booking a very expensive or complicated trip (particularly to an isolated region) or if you're booking far in advance. Who knows what could happen six months down the road? But whether or not you get insurance has more to do with how comfortable you are assuming all that risk yourself.

Comprehensive travel policies typically cover trip cancellation and interruption, letting you cancel or cut your trip short because of a personal emergency, illness, or, in some cases, acts of terrorism in your destination. Such policies also cover evacuation and medical care. Some also cover you for trip delays because of bad weather or mechanical problems as well as for lost or delayed baggage. Another type of coverage to look for is financial default—that is, when your trip is disrupted because a tour operator, airline, or cruise line goes out of business. Generally you must buy this when you book your trip or shortly thereafter, and it's available to you only if your operator isn't on a list of excluded companies.

If you're going abroad, consider buying medical-only coverage at the very least. Neither Medicare nor some private insurers cover medical expenses anywhere outside of the United States besides Mexico and Canada (including time aboard a cruise ship, even if it leaves from a U.S. port). Medical-only policies typically reimburse you for medical care (excluding that related to preexisting conditions) and hospitalization abroad and provide for evacuation. You still have to pay the bills and await reimbursement from the insurer, though.

Expect comprehensive travel insurance policies to cost about 4% to 7% of the total price of your trip (it's more like 12% if you're over age 70). A medical-only pol-icy may or may not be cheaper than a comprehensive policy. Always read the fine print of your policy to make sure that you are covered for the risks that are of the most concern to you. Compare several policies to make sure you're getting the best price and range of coverage available.

Just as an aside: You know you can save a bundle on trips to warm-weather destinations by traveling in rainy season. But there's also a chance that a severe storm will disrupt your plans. The solution? Look for hotels and resorts that offer storm/hurricane guarantees. Although they rarely allow refunds, most guarantees do let you rebook later if a storm strikes.

🎵 Insurance Comparison Sites **Insure My Trip. com** ⊕ www.insuremytrip.com. **Square Mouth.com** ⊕ www.quotetravelinsurance.com.

🎵 Comprehensive Travel Insurers **Access America** ☎ 866/807-3982 ⊕ www.accessamerica.com. **CSA Travel Protection** ☎ 800/729-6021 ⊕ www. csatravelprotection.com. **HTH Worldwide** ☎ 610/ 254-8700 or 888/243-2358 ⊕ www.hthworldwide. com. **Travelex Insurance** ☎ 888/457-4602 ⊕ www.travelex-insurance.com. **Travel Guard International** ☎ 715/345-0505 or 800/826-4919 ⊕ www.travelguard.com. **Travel Insured International** ☎ 800/243-3174 ⊕ www.travelinsured.com.

🎵 Medical-Only Insurers **Wallach & Company** ☎ 800/237-6615 or 504/687-3166 ⊕ www.wallach. com. **International Medical Group** ☎ 800/628-4664 ⊕ www.imglobal.com. **International SOS** ☎ 215/942-8000 or 713/521-7611 ⊕ www. internationalsos.com.

FOR INTERNATIONAL TRAVELERS

CURRENCY

The dollar is the basic unit of U.S. currency. It has 100 cents. Coins are the penny (1¢); the nickel (5¢), dime (10¢), quarter (25¢), and half-dollar (50¢); and the very rare golden $1 coin and even rarer silver $1. Bills are denominated $1, $5, $10, $20, $50, and $100, all mostly green and identical in size; designs and background tints vary. You may come across a $2 bill, but the chances are slim.

CUSTOMS

🎵 U.S. Customs and Border Protection ⊕ www. cbp.gov.

DRIVING

Driving in the United States is on the right. Speed limits are posted in miles per hour along roads and highways (usually between 55 mph and 70 mph). Watch for lower limits in small towns and on back roads (usually 30 mph to 40 mph). Most states require front-seat passengers to wear seat belts; many states require children to sit in the backseat and to wear seat belts. In major cities, rush hour is between 7 and 10 AM; afternoon rush hour is between 4 and 7 PM. Expect heavy traffic. To encourage carpooling, some freeways have special lanes for so-called high-occupancy vehicles (HOV)—cars carrying more than one passenger, ordinarily marked with a diamond.

Highways are well paved. Interstate highways—limited-access, multilane highways whose numbers are prefixed by "I–"—are the fastest routes. Interstates with three-digit numbers encircle urban areas, which may have other limited-access expressways, freeways, and parkways as well. Tolls may be levied on limited-access highways. So-called U.S. highways and state highways are not necessarily limited-access but may have several lanes.

Gas stations are plentiful. Most stay open late (24 hours along large highways and in big cities), except in rural areas, where Sunday hours are limited and where you may drive long stretches without a refueling opportunity. Along larger highways, roadside stops with restrooms, fast-food restaurants, and sundries stores are well spaced. State police and tow trucks patrol major highways and lend assistance. If your car breaks down on an interstate, pull onto the shoulder and wait for help, or have your passengers wait while you walk to an emergency phone (available in most states). If you carry a cell phone, dial *55, noting your location on the small green roadside mileage markers.

ELECTRICITY

The U.S. standard is AC, 110 volts/60 cycles. Plugs have two flat pins set parallel to each other.

EMBASSIES

Australia ☎ 202/797-3000 ⊕ www.austemb. org. **United Kingdom** ☎ 202/588-7800 ⊕ www. britainusa.com. **Canada** ☎ 202/682-1740 ⊕ www. canadianembassy.org.

EMERGENCIES

For police, fire, or ambulance dial 911 (0 in rural areas).

HOLIDAYS

Major national holidays are New Year's Day (Jan. 1); Martin Luther King Day (3rd Mon. in Jan.); Presidents' Day (3rd Mon. in Feb.); Memorial Day (last Mon. in May); Independence Day (July 4); Labor Day (1st Mon. in Sept.); Columbus Day (2nd Mon. in Oct.); Thanksgiving Day (4th Thurs. in Nov.); Christmas Eve and Christmas Day (Dec. 24 and 25); and New Year's Eve (Dec. 31).

MAIL

You can buy stamps and aerograms and send letters and parcels in post offices. Stamp-dispensing machines can occasionally be found in airports, bus and train stations, office buildings, drugstores, and the like. U.S. mailboxes are stout, dark blue, steel bins at strategic locations in major cities; pickup schedules are posted inside the bin (pull down the handle to see them). Parcels more than 1 pound must be mailed at a post office or at a private mailing center.

Within the United States, a first-class letter weighing 1 ounce or less costs 39¢, and each additional ounce costs 24¢; postcards cost 24¢. A 1-ounce airmail letter to most countries costs 84¢, and an airmail postcard costs 75¢; to Canada and Mexico, a 1-ounce letter costs 63¢, a postcard 55¢. An aerogram—a single sheet of lightweight blue paper that folds into its own envelope, stamped for overseas airmail—costs 75¢ regardless of its destination.

To receive mail on the road, have it sent c/o General Delivery at your destination's main post office (use the correct five-digit ZIP code). You must pick up mail in person within 30 days and show a driver's license or passport.

▓ **DHL** ☎ 800/225-5345 ⊕ www.dhl.com. **Federal Express** ☎ 800/463-3339 ⊕ www.fedex.com. **Mail Boxes, Etc.** (The UPS Store) ⊕ www.mbe.com. **United States Postal Service** ⊕ www.usps.com.

PASSPORTS & VISAS

Visitor visas aren't necessary for citizens of Australia, Canada, or the United Kingdom, as well as for most citizens of European Union countries if you're coming for tourism and staying for fewer than 90 days. If you require a visa, the cost is $100 and, depending on where you live, the waiting time can be substantial. Apply for a visa at the U.S. consulate in your place of residence; look at the U.S. State Department's special Visa Web site for further information.

▓ Visa Information **Destination USA** ⊕ www.unitedstatesvisas.gov.

PHONES

All U.S. telephone numbers consist of a three-digit area code and a seven-digit local number. Within many local calling areas, you dial only the seven-digit number; in others, you must dial "1" first and then the area code. To call between area-code regions, dial "1" then all 10 digits; the same goes for calls to numbers prefixed by "800," "888," "866," and "877"—all toll-free. For calls to numbers preceded by "900" you must pay—usually dearly.

For international calls, dial "011" followed by the country code and the local number. For help, dial "0" and ask for an overseas operator. The country code is 61 for Australia, 64 for New Zealand, 44 for the United Kingdom. Calling Canada is the same as calling within the United States. Most phone books list country codes and U.S. area codes. The country code for the United States is 1.

For operator assistance, dial "0." To obtain someone's phone number, call directory assistance at 555–1212 or occasionally 411 (free at many public phones). You can reverse the charges on a long-distance call if you phone "collect"; dial "0" instead of "1" before the 10-digit number.

At pay phones, instructions often are posted. Usually you insert coins in a slot (usually 25¢–50¢ for local calls) and wait for a steady tone before dialing. When you call long-distance, the operator tells you how much to insert; prepaid phone cards, widely available in various denominations, can be used from any phone. Follow the directions to activate the card (there is usually an access number and then an activation code for the card), then dial your number.

The United States has several GSM (Global System for Mobile Communications) networks, so multiband mobile phones from most countries (except for Japan) work here. Unfortunately, it's almost impossible to buy a pay-as-you-go mobile SIM card in the U.S.—which allows you to avoid roaming charges—without a phone. That said, cell phones with pay-as-you-go plans are available for well under $100. The cheapest ones with decent national coverage are the GoPhone from Cingular and Virgin Mobile, which offers only pay-as-you-go service.

▓ Cell Phone Contacts **Cingular** ☎ 888/333-6651 ⊕ www.cingular.com. **Virgin Mobile** ☎ No phone ⊕ www.www.virginmobileusa.com.

INTERNET SERVICES

You can check your e-mail or surf the Internet at cafés, copy centers, and libraries. By far the most well equipped and probably most convenient is easyInternetCafé in Times Square, which has a staggering 650 computer terminals; it's open from 6 AM to 1 AM, seven days a week. The nearby Times Square Information Center (see Visitor Information) has free terminals for checking e-mail. In addition, many public entities and businesses, including public libraries and some McDonald's and Starbucks, now provide wireless Internet access. The organization NYCwireless keeps track of free Wi-Fi hot spots in the New York area.

▓ Internet Cafés **Cyber Café** ⊠ 250 W. 49th St., between 8th Ave. and Broadway, Midtown West ☎ 212/333-4109 ⊕ www.cyber-cafe.com. **easyInternetCafé** ⊠ 234 W. 42nd St., between 7th and 8th Aves., Midtown West ☎ 212/398-0724 ⊕ www.easyinternetcafe.com. **www.web2zone** ⊠ 54 Cooper Sq., East Village ☎ 212/614-7300 ⊕ www.web2zone.com.

Other Internet Locations **New York Public Library-Mid-Manhattan Library** ✉ 455 5th Ave., at E. 40th St., Midtown East ☎ 212/340-0833 ⊕ www.nypl.org. **NYCwireless** ⊕ www.nycwireless.net. **Times Square Information Center** ✉ 7th Ave. between 46th and 47th Sts., Midtown West ☎ 212/768-1560 ⊕ www.timessquarenyc.org ⊙ Daily 8–8.

LIMOUSINES

You can rent a chauffeur-driven car from one of many limousine services. Companies usually charge by the hour or a flat fee for sightseeing excursions.

Limousine Services **Carey Limousines** ☎ 212/599-1122 or 800/336-0646 ⊕ www.ecarey.com. **Concord Limousines, Inc.** ☎ 718/965-6100 ⊕ www.concordlimo.com. **London Towncars** ☎ 212/988-9700 or 800/221-4009 ⊕ www.londontowncars.com.

MAIL & SHIPPING

Most post offices are open weekdays 8 AM–5 PM or 8 AM–6 PM and Saturday from 9–4. There are dozens of branches in New York. The main post office on 8th Avenue is open daily 24 hours.

Post Offices **Grand Central Terminal** ✉ 450 Lexington Ave., between 44th and 45th Sts., Midtown East 10017 ☎ 800/275-8777 ⊕ www.usps.com. **J.A. Farley General Post Office** ✉ 8th Ave. at W. 33rd St., Midtown West 10001 ☎ 800/275-8777 ⊕ www.usps.com.

MEDIA

NEWSPAPERS & MAGAZINES

The major daily newspapers in New York are the *New York Times* and the *Wall Street Journal*, both broadsheets, and the *Daily News* and the *New York Post*, which are tabloids. The *Village Voice* and the *New York Press* are both free weeklies. Local magazines include the *New Yorker, New York,* and *Time Out New York*. All of these are widely available at newsstands and shops around town.

RADIO & TELEVISION

Some of the major radio stations include WBGO-FM (88.3; jazz), WBLS-FM (107.5; R&B), WFMU-FM (91.1; free-form music), WKTU-FM (103.5; urban), WPLJ (95.5; pop and rock), WQXR-FM (96.3; classical), and WXRK-FM (92.3; rock).

Talk stations include WNYC-AM (820; National Public Radio), WNYC-FM (93.9; NPR and classical), WNYE-FM (91.5), and WOR-AM (710). News stations include WABC-AM (770), WCBS-AM (880), and WINS-AM (1010).

The city has its own 24-hour cable TV news station, New York 1 (Channel 1), available through Time Warner Cable, with local and international news announcements around the clock. Weather forecasts are broadcast "on the ones" (1:01, 1:11, 1:21, etc.).

From 8 to 11 each evening, the public station WNYC (Channel 25) broadcasts a block of shows about local fashion, music, history, and events around town.

MONEY MATTERS

In New York, it's easy to get swept up in a debt-inducing cyclone of $60 per person dinners, $100 theater tickets, $20 nightclub covers, and $300 hotel rooms. But one of the good things about the city is that there's such a wide variety of options, you can spend in some areas and save in others. Within Manhattan, a cup of coffee can cost from 75¢ to $4, a pint of beer from $5 to $8, and a sandwich from $6 to $10. Generally, prices in the outer boroughs are lower than those in Manhattan.

The most generously bequeathed treasure of the city is the arts. The stated admission fee at the Metropolitan Museum of Art is a suggestion; those who can't afford it can donate a lesser amount and not be snubbed. Many other museums in town have special times during which admission is free. The Museum of Modern Art, for instance, is free on Friday 4–8. In summer a handful of free music, theater, and dance performances, as well as films (usually screened outdoors) fill the calendar each day.

Prices throughout this guide are given for adults. Substantially reduced fees are almost always available for children, students, and senior citizens. For information on taxes, *see* Taxes.

ATMS

Cash machines are abundant throughout all the boroughs and are found not only in banks but in many grocery stores, laundries, delis, and hotels. Many bank ATMs charge users a fee around $1.50, and the commercial ATMs in retail establishments may charge more. Be careful to remain at the ATM until you complete your transaction, which may require an extra step after receiving your money.

CREDIT CARDS

Throughout this guide, the following abbreviations are used: **AE,** American Express; **D,** Discover; **DC,** Diners Club; **MC,** MasterCard; and **V,** Visa.

It's a good idea to inform your credit card company before you travel, especially if you're going abroad and don't travel internationally very often. Otherwise, the credit-card company might put a hold on your card owing to unusual activity—not a good thing halfway through your trip. Record all your credit card numbers—as well as the phone numbers to call if your cards are lost or stolen—in a safe place so you're prepared should something go wrong. Both MasterCard and Visa have general numbers you can call (collect if you're abroad) if your card is lost, but you're better off calling the number of your issuing bank since MasterCard and Visa usually just transfer you to your bank; your bank's number is usually printed on your card.

🔢 Reporting Lost Cards **American Express** ☎ 800/992-3404 in U.S. or 336/393-1111 collect from abroad ⊕ www.americanexpress.com. **Diners Club** ☎ 800/234-6377 in U.S. or 303/799-1504 collect from abroad ⊕ www.dinersclub.com. **Discover** ☎ 800/347-2683 in U.S. or 801/902-3100 collect from abroad ⊕ www.discovercard.com. **MasterCard** ☎ 800/622-7747 in U.S. or 636/722-7111 collect from abroad ⊕ www.mastercard.com. **Visa** ☎ 800/847-2911 in U.S. or 410/581-9994 collect from abroad ⊕ www.visa.com.

TRAVELER'S CHECKS & CARDS

Some consider this the currency of the caveman, and it's true that fewer establishments accept traveler's checks these days. Nevertheless, they're a cheap and secure way to carry extra money, particularly on trips to urban areas. Both Citibank (under the Visa brand) and American Express issue traveler's checks in the United States, but Amex is better known and more widely accepted; you can also avoid hefty surcharges by cashing Amex checks at Amex offices. Whatever you do, keep track of all the serial numbers in case the checks are lost or stolen.

American Express now offers a stored-value card called a Travelers Cheque Card, which you can use wherever American Express credit cards are accepted, including ATMs. The card can carry a minimum of $300 and a maximum of $2,700, and it's a very safe way to carry your funds. Although you can get replacement funds in 24 hours if your card is lost or stolen, it doesn't really strike us as a very good deal. In addition to a high initial cost ($14.95 to set up the card, plus $5 each time you "reload"), you still have to pay a 2% fee for each purchase in a foreign currency (similar to that of any credit card). Further, each time you use the card in an ATM you pay a transaction fee of $2.50 on top of the 2% transaction fee for the conversion—add it all up and it can be considerably more than you would pay for simply using your own ATM card. Regular traveler's checks are just as secure and cost less.

🔢 **American Express** ☎ 888/412-6945 in the U.S., 801/945-9450 collect outside of the U.S. to add value or speak to customer service ⊕ www.americanexpress.com.

PACKING

Why do some people travel with a convoy of suitcases the size of large-screen TVs and yet never have a thing to wear? How do others pack a toaster-oven-size duffel with a week's worth of outfits *and* supplies for every possible contingency? We realize that packing is a matter of style—a very personal thing—but there's a lot to be said for traveling light. The tips in this section will help you win the battle of the bulging bag.

Make a list. In a recent Fodor's survey, 29% of respondents said they make lists (and often pack) at least a week before a trip. Lists can be used at least twice—once to pack and once to repack at the end of your trip. You'll also have a record of the contents of your suitcase, just in case it disappears in transit.

Think it through. What's the weather like? Is this a business trip or a cruise or resort vacation? Going abroad? In some places and/or sights, traditions of dress may be more or less conservative than you're used to. As your itinerary comes together, jot activities down and note possible outfits next to each (don't forget those shoes and accessories).

Edit your wardrobe. Plan to wear everything twice (better yet, thrice) and to do laundry along the way. Stick to one basic look—urban chic, sporty casual, etc. Build around one or two neutrals and an accent (e.g., black, white, and olive green). Women can freshen looks by changing scarves or jewelry. For a week's trip, you can look smashing with three bottoms, four or five tops, a sweater, and a jacket you can wear alone or over the sweater.

Be practical. Put comfortable shoes at the top of your list. (Did we need to tell you this?) Pack items that are lightweight, wrinkle resistant, compact, and washable. (Or this?) Try a simple wrinkling test: intentionally fold a piece of fabric between your fingers for a couple of minutes. If it refuses to crease, it will probably come out of your suitcase looking fresh. That said, if you stack and then roll your clothes when packing, they'll wrinkle less.

Check weight and size limitations. In the United States you may be charged extra for checked bags weighing more than 50 pounds. Abroad some airlines don't allow you to check bags weighing more than 60 to 70 pounds, or they charge outrageous fees for every pound your luggage is over. Carry-on size limitations can be stringent, too.

Be prepared to lug it yourself. If there's one thing that can turn a pack rat into a minimalist, it's a vacation spent lugging heavy bags over long distances. Unless you're on a guided tour or a cruise, select luggage that you can readily carry. Porters, like good butlers, are hard to find these days.

Lock it up. Several companies sell locks (about $10) approved by the Transportation Safety Administration that can be unlocked by all U.S. security personnel

should they decide to search your bags. Alternatively, you can use simple plastic cable ties, which are sold at hardware stores in bundles.

Tag it. Always put tags on your luggage with some kind of contact information; use your business address if you don't want people to know your home address. Put the same information (and a copy of your itinerary) inside your luggage, too.

Don't check valuables. On U.S. flights, airlines are liable for only about $2,800 per person for bags. On international flights, the liability limit is around $635 per bag. But just try collecting from the airline for items like computers, cameras, and jewelry. It isn't going to happen; they aren't covered. And though comprehensive travel policies may cover luggage, the liability limit is often a pittance. Your homeowners' policy may cover you sufficiently when you travel—or not. You're really better off stashing baubles and gizmos in your carryon—right near those prescription meds.

Report problems immediately. If your bags—or things in them—are damaged or go astray, file a written claim with your airline *before you leave the airport*. If the airline is at fault, it may give you money for essentials until your luggage arrives. Most lost bags are found within 48 hours, so alert the airline to your whereabouts for two or three days. If your bag was opened for security reasons in the United States and something is missing, file a claim with the TSA.

WHAT YOU'LL NEED IN NEW YORK CITY

In New York, a few restaurants still require men to wear jackets and ties. In general, New Yorkers tend to dress a bit more formally than their Midwest or West Coast counterparts for special events. Jeans and sneakers are acceptable for casual dining and sightseeing just about anywhere in the city. Always **bring sneakers or other flat-heeled walking shoes** for pounding the New York pavement.

In spring and fall, pack at least one warm jacket and sweater, since moderate daytime temperatures can drop after nightfall. Bring shorts for summer, which can be quite humid. You need a warm coat, hat, scarf, and gloves in winter; boots for often slushy streets are also a good idea.

PUBLIC TRANSPORTATION

When it comes to getting around New York, you have your pick of transportation in almost every neighborhood. The subway and bus networks are extensive, especially in Manhattan, although getting across town can take some extra maneuvering. If you're not pressed for time, take a public bus (⇨ Bus Travel Within New York City); they generally are slower than subways, but you can also see the city as you travel. Yellow cabs (⇨ Taxis & Car Services) are abundant, except during the evening rush hour, when many drivers' shifts change. Like a taxi ride, the subway (⇨ Subway Travel) is a true New York City experience; it's also often the quickest way to get around. But New York is really a walking town, and depending on the time of day and your destination, hoofing it could be the easiest and most enjoyable option.

During weekday rush hours (from 7:30 AM to 9:30 AM and 5 PM to 7 PM) **avoid the jammed midtown area,** both in the subways and on the streets—travel time on buses and taxis can easily double.

Subway and bus fares are $2, although reduced fares are available for senior citizens and people with disabilities during non-rush hours.

You pay for mass transit with a Metro-Card, a plastic card with a magnetic strip. After you swipe the card through a subway turnstile or insert it in a bus's card reader, the cost of the fare is automatically deducted. With the MetroCard, you can **transfer free** from bus to subway, subway to bus, or bus to bus. You must start with the MetroCard and use it again within two hours to complete your trip.

MetroCards are sold at all subway stations and at some stores—look for an "Authorized Sales Agent" sign. The MTA sells two kinds of MetroCards: unlimited-ride and pay-per-ride. Seven-day unlimited-ride MetroCards ($24) allow bus and subway travel for a week. If you will ride more than 13 times, this is the card to get.

The one-day unlimited-ride Fun Pass ($7) is good from the day of purchase through 3 AM the following day. It's sold only by neighborhood MetroCard merchants and MetroCard vending machines at stations (not through the station agent).

When you purchase a pay-per-ride card worth $10 or more, you get a 20% bonus—six rides for the price of five. Unlike unlimited-ride cards, pay-per-ride MetroCards can be shared between riders; unlimited-ride MetroCards can be used only once at the same station or bus route in an 18-minute period.

You can buy or add money to an existing MetroCard at a MetroCard vending machine, available at most subway station entrances (usually near the station booth). The machines accept major credit cards and ATM or debit cards. Many also accept cash, but note that the maximum amount of change they will return is $6.

🚩 Schedule & Route Information **Metropolitan Transit Authority (MTA) Travel Information Line** ☎ 718/330–1234, 718/596–8585 travelers with disabilities ⊕ www.mta.info.

RESTROOMS

Public restrooms in New York are few and far between; some are very clean, and some are filthy. Facilities in Penn Station and Grand Central Terminal are not only safe but fairly well maintained. Because of concerns about vandalism and other crime, restrooms in most subway stations have been largely sealed off. Two clean pay toilets (25¢) are at the adjacent Herald and Greeley squares on West 34th and West 32nd streets.

Head for midtown department stores, museums, or the lobbies of large hotels to find the cleanest bathrooms. Public atriums, such as those at the Citicorp Center and Trump Tower, also provide good public facilities, as do Bryant Park and the many Barnes & Noble bookstores and Starbucks coffee shops in the city. If you're in the area, the Times Square Information Center, on Broadway between 46th and 47th streets, can be a godsend.

Restaurants usually allow only their patrons to use their restrooms, but if you're dressed well and look as if you belong, you can often just sail right in. Be aware that cinemas, Broadway theaters, and concert halls have limited amenities, and there are often long lines before performances and during intermissions.

The Bathroom Diaries is a Web site that's flush with unsanitized info on restrooms the world over—each one located, reviewed, and rated.

⚑ Find a Loo **The Bathroom Diaries** ⊕ www.thebathroomdiaries.com

SAFETY

New York City is one of the safest large cities in the country. However, do not let yourself be lulled into a false sense of security. As in any large city, travelers in New York remain particularly easy marks for pickpockets and hustlers.

After 9/11, security was heightened throughout the city. Never leave any bags unattended, and expect to have yourself and your possessions inspected thoroughly in such places as airports, sports stadiums, museums, and city buildings.

Ignore the panhandlers on the streets and subways, people who offer to hail you a cab (they often appear at Penn Station, the Port Authority, and Grand Central), and limousine and gypsy cab drivers who (illegally) offer you a ride.

Keep jewelry out of sight on the street; better yet, **leave valuables at home.** Don't wear gold chains or gaudy jewelry, even if it's fake. Men should **carry their wallets in their front pants pocket** rather than in their back pockets. When in bars or restaurants, never hang your purse or bag on the back of a chair or put it underneath the table.

Avoid deserted blocks in unfamiliar neighborhoods. A brisk, purposeful pace helps deter trouble wherever you go.

The subway runs round-the-clock and is generally well trafficked until midnight (and until at least 2 AM on Friday and Saturday nights), and overall it is very safe. If you do take the subway at night, ride in the center car, with the conductor, and wait on the center of the platform or right in front

of the station agent. Watch out for unsavory characters lurking around the inside or outside of stations, particularly at night.

When waiting for a train, **stand far away from the edge of the subway platform,** especially when trains are entering or leaving the station. Once the train pulls into the station, **avoid empty cars.** While on the train don't engage in verbal exchanges with aggressive riders, who may accuse others of anything from pushing to taking up too much space. If a fellow passenger makes you nervous while on the train, trust your instincts and **change cars.** When disembarking, stick with the crowd until you reach the street.

Travelers Aid International helps crime victims, stranded travelers, and wayward children, and works closely with the police.

⚑ **Travelers Aid** ⊠ JFK International Airport, Terminal 6 ☎ 718/656–4870 ⊠ Newark International Airport, Terminal B ☎ 973/623–5052 ⊕ www.travelersaid.org.

LOCAL SCAMS

Someone who appears to have had an accident at the exit door of a bus may flee with your wallet or purse if you attempt to give aid. The individual who approaches you with a complicated story is probably playing a confidence game and hopes to get something from you. **Beware of people jostling you in crowds,** or someone tapping your shoulder from behind. Never play or place a bet on a sidewalk card game, shell game, or other guessing game—they are all rigged to get your cash, and they're illegal.

SENIOR-CITIZEN TRAVEL

The Metropolitan Transit Authority (MTA) offers lower fares for passengers 65 and over. Show your Medicare card to the bus driver or station agent, and for the standard fare ($2) you will be issued a MetroCard and a return-trip ticket.

⚑ **MTA Reduced Fare hotline** ☎ 718/243–4999 ⊕ www.mta.info.

SPORTS & THE OUTDOORS

The City of New York's Parks & Recreation division lists all of the recreational facilities and activities available through

New York's Parks Department. For information about athletic facilities in Manhattan as well as a calendar of sporting events, visit the Web site or pick up a copy of *MetroSports* at sporting-goods stores or health clubs. The sports section of *Time Out New York,* sold at most newsstands, lists upcoming events, times, dates, and ticket information.

🚩 *MetroSports* ⊕ www.metrosportsny.com. **Parks & Recreation division** ☎ 311 in New York City, 212/639-9675 or 212/NEW-YORK outside New York City ⊕ www.nyc.gov/parks.

BASEBALL

The subway will get you directly to stadiums of both New York–area major-league teams, but the *Yankee Clipper* cruises from Manhattan's East Side and from New Jersey to Yankee Stadium on game nights. The round-trip cost is $18. The regular baseball season runs from April through September.

The New York Mets play at Shea Stadium, at the next-to-last stop on the No. 7 train, in Queens. The New York Yankees, having won many a World Series in the 1990s and in 2000, are still licking their wounds after their 2004 curse-breaking loss to the Boston Red Sox. See them play at Yankee Stadium.

Founded in 2001, the minor-league Brooklyn Cyclones are named for Coney Island's famous wooden roller coaster. A feeder team for the New York Mets, the team plays its 38 home games at KeySpan Park, next to the boardwalk, with views of the Atlantic over the right-field wall and views of historic Astroland over the left-field wall. Most people make a day of it, with time at the beach and amusement rides before an evening game. Take the D, F, or Q subway to the end of the line, and walk one block to the right of the original Nathan's Famous hot dog stand.

For a fun, family-oriented experience, check out the Staten Island Yankees, one of New York's minor-league teams, which warms up many future New York Yankees players. The stadium, a five-minute walk from the Staten Island Ferry terminal, has magnificent panoramic views of Lower Manhattan and the Statue of Liberty.

🚩 **Brooklyn Cyclones** ✉ 1904 Surf Ave., at 19th St., Coney Island ☎ 718/449-8497 ⊕ www.brooklyncyclones.com Ⓜ Subway: D, F, Q to Stillwell Ave. **Shea Stadium** ✉ Roosevelt Ave. off Grand Central Pkwy., Flushing ☎ 718/507-8499 ⊕ www.mets.com Ⓜ Subway: 7 to Willets Pt./Shea Stadium. **Staten Island Yankees** ✉ Richmond County Bank Ballpark at St. George, Staten Island ☎ 718/720-9265 ⊕ www.siyanks.com. *Yankee Clipper* ☎ 800/533-3779 ⊕ www.nywaterway.com. **Yankee Stadium** ✉ 161st St. and River Ave., the Bronx ☎ 718/293-6000 Ⓜ Subway: B, D to 167th St., No. 4 to 161st St.-Yankee Stadium.

BASKETBALL

Watching pro basketball at Madison Square Garden is a legendary experience—if you can get a ticket. If the professional games are sold out, try to attend a college game where New York stalwarts Fordham, Hofstra, and St. John's compete against national top 25 teams during invitational tournaments. In addition to schedules for regular games, the Web site also provides listings of special basketball events, such as the Harlem Globetrotters.

The New York Knicks arouse intense hometown passions, which means tickets for home games at Madison Square Garden are hard to come by. The New Jersey Nets play at the Meadowlands in the Continental Airlines Arena but have plans to relocate and become the Brooklyn Nets. Tickets are generally easy to obtain. The men's basketball season runs from late October through April. The New York Liberty, a member of the Women's NBA, had its first season in 1997; some of the team's more high-profile players are already legendary. The season runs from Memorial Day weekend through August, with home games played at Madison Square Garden.

🚩 **Madison Square Garden** ⊕ www.thegarden.com. **New Jersey Nets** ☎ Box office 201/935-3900 or 800/765-6387 ⊕ www.nba.com/nets. **New York Knicks** ☎ 212/465-5867 ⊕ www.nyknicks.com. **New York Liberty** ☎ 877/962-2849 for tickets, 212/564-9622 fan hotline ⊕ www.wnba.com/liberty.

BICYCLING

Even in tiny apartments, many locals keep a bicycle for transportation—the intrepid ones swear it's the best (and fastest) way to get around—and for rides on glorious days. A sleek pack of dedicated racers zooms around Central Park at dawn and at dusk daily, and on weekends the parks swarm with recreational cyclists. Central Park has a 6-mi circular drive with a couple of decent climbs. It's closed to automobile traffic from 10 AM to 3 PM (except the southeast portion between 6th Avenue and East 72nd Street) and 7 PM to 10 PM on weekdays, and from 7 PM Friday to 6 AM Monday. On holidays it's closed to automobile traffic from 7 PM the night before until 6 AM the day after.

The bike lane along the Hudson River Park's esplanade parallels the waterfront from West 59th Street south to the esplanade of Battery Park City. The lane also heads north, connecting with the bike path in Riverside Park, the promenade between West 72nd and West 110th streets, and continuing all the way to the George Washington Bridge. From Battery Park it's a quick ride to the Wall Street area, which is deserted on weekends, and over to South Street and a bike lane along the East River.

The 3⅓-mi circular drive in Brooklyn's Prospect Park is closed to cars weekends year-round and from 9 AM to 5 PM and 7 PM to 10 PM weekdays. It has a long, gradual uphill that tops off near the Grand Army Plaza entrance.

🚲 Bike Rentals **Bicycle Rentals at Loeb Boathouse** ⊠ Midpark near E. 74th St., Central Park ☎ 212/517-2233. **Hub Station** ⊠ 517 Broome St., at Thompson St., SoHo ☎ 212/965-9334 Ⓜ Subway: A, C, E to Canal St. **Larry's & Jeff's Bicycles Plus** ⊠ 1690 2nd Ave., at E. 87th St., Upper East Side ☎ 212/722-2201 Ⓜ Subway: 4, 5, 6 to 86th St. **Pedal Pusher** ⊠ 1306 2nd Ave., between E. 68th and E. 69th Sts., Upper East Side ☎ 212/288-5592 Ⓜ Subway: 6 to 68th St.–Hunter College. **Toga Bike Shop** ⊠ 110 West End Ave., at W. 64th St., Upper West Side ☎ 212/799-9625 ⊕ www.togabikes.com Ⓜ Subway: 1, 9 to 66th St.

GROUP BIKE RIDES

For organized rides with other cyclists, call or e-mail before you come to New York. Bike New York runs a five-borough bike

ride in May. The Five Borough Bicycle Club organizes day and weekend rides. The New York Cycle Club sponsors weekend rides for every level of ability. Time's Up!, a nonprofit environmental group, leads free recreational rides at least twice a month for cyclists as well as skaters; the Central Park Moonlight Ride, departing from Columbus Circle at 10 PM the first Friday of every month, is a favorite. Transportation Alternatives lists group rides throughout the metropolitan area in its bimonthly e-mail newsletter.

🚲 **Bike New York** ⊠ 891 Amsterdam Ave., at W. 103rd St., Upper West Side ☎ 212/932-2453 ⊕ www.bikenewyork.org. **Five Borough Bicycle Club** ⊠ 891 Amsterdam Ave., at W. 103rd St., Upper West Side ☎ 212/932-2300 Ext. 115 ⊕ www.5bbc. org. **New York Cycle Club** 🖂 Box 20541, Columbus Circle Station, 10023 ☎ 212/828-5711 ⊕ www.nycc. org. **Time's Up!** ☎ 212/802-8222 ⊕ www.times-up. org. **Transportation Alternatives** ⊠ 127 W. 26th St., Suite 1002, Chelsea ☎ 212/629-8080 ⊕ www. transalt.org.

BOATING & KAYAKING

Central Park has rowboats (plus one Venetian gondola for glides in the moonlight) on the 18-acre Central Park Lake. Rent your rowboat at Loeb Boathouse, near East 74th Street, from March through October; gondola rides are available only during the summer.

In summer at the Downtown Boathouse you can take a sturdy kayak out for a paddle for free on weekends and weekday evenings. Beginners learn to paddle in the calmer embayment area closest to shore until they feel ready to venture farther out onto open water. More experienced kayakers can partake in the three-hour trips conducted every weekend and on holiday mornings. Sign-ups for these popular tours end at 8 AM. Due to high demand, names are entered into a lottery to see who gets to go out each morning. No reservations are taken in advance. **Manhattan Kayak Company** runs trips (these are not free) and gives lessons for all levels.

🚣 **Downtown Boathouse** ⊠ Pier 26, N. Moore St. and the Hudson River, TriBeCa ☎ 646/613-0740 daily status, 646/613-0375 information ⊕ www. downtownboathouse.org Ⓜ Subway: 1 to Franklin

St. or A, C, E to Canal St. for Pier 26. **Loeb Boathouse** ⊠ Midpark near E. 74th St., Central Park ☎ 212/517-2233 ⊕ www.centralparknyc.org. **Manhattan Kayak Company** ⊠ Chelsea Piers, Pier 63, W. 23rd St. and the Hudson River, Chelsea ☎ 212/924-1788 ⊕ www.manhattankayak.com Ⓜ Subway: C, E to 23rd St.

FOOTBALL

The football season runs from September through December. The enormously popular New York Giants play at Giants Stadium in the Meadowlands Sports Complex. Most seats for Giants games are sold on a season-ticket basis—and there's a very long waiting list for those. However, single tickets are occasionally available at the stadium box office. The New York Jets also play at Giants Stadium. Although Jets tickets are not as scarce as those for the Giants, most are snapped up by fans before the season opener.

🏈 **New York Giants** ☎ 201/935-8222 for tickets ⊕ www.giants.com. **New York Jets** ☎ 516/560-8200 for tickets, 516/560-8288 for fan club ⊕ www.newyorkjets.com.

ICE-SKATING

The outdoor rink in Rockefeller Center, open from October through early April, is much smaller in real life than it appears on TV and in movies. It's also very busy, so be prepared to wait—there are no advance ticket sales. Although it's also beautiful, especially when Rock Center's enormous Christmas tree towers above it, you pay for the privilege: adult rates including skates start at $17. If you're a self-conscious skater, note that there are usually huge crowds watching.

The city's outdoor rinks, open from roughly November through March, all have their own character. The beautifully situated Wollman Rink offers skating until long after dark beneath the lights of the city. Be prepared for daytime crowds on weekends. The Lasker Rink, at the north end of Central Park, is smaller and usually less crowded than Wollman Rink. Prospect Park's Kate Wollman Rink borders the lake, and has a picture-postcard setting. Chelsea Piers' Sky Rink has two

year-round indoor rinks overlooking the Hudson. Rentals are available at all rinks. The Pond at Bryant Park offers free skating, not including the cost of skate rental, from late October through January, from 8:30 AM to 10:30 PM.

🏈 **Bryant Park** ⊠ 6th Ave. between 40th and 42nd Sts., Midtown West ☎ 866/221-5157 ⊕ www.bryantpark.org Ⓜ Subway: B, D, F, V to 42nd St. **Kate Wollman Rink** ⊠ Ocean Ave. and Parkside Ave., Prospect Park, Brooklyn ☎ 718/287-6431 Ⓜ Subway: 2, 3 to Grand Army Plaza; B, Q to Prospect Park; F to 15th St./Prospect Park. **Lasker Rink** ⊠ Midpark near E. 106th St., Central Park ☎ 212/534-7639 ⊕ www.centralparknyc.org Ⓜ Subway: B, C to 103rd St. **Rockefeller Center** ⊠ 50th St. at 5th Ave., lower plaza, Midtown West ☎ 212/332-7654 ⊕ www.therinkatrockcenter.com Ⓜ Subway: B, D, F, V to 47th–50th Sts./Rockefeller Center; E, V to 5th Ave.–53rd St. **Sky Rink** ⊠ Pier 61, W. 23rd St. and the Hudson River, Chelsea ☎ 212/336-6100 ⊕ www.chelseapiers.com Ⓜ Subway: C, E to 23rd St. **Wollman Rink** ⊠ North of 6th Ave., between 62nd and 63rd Sts., north of park entrance, Central Park ☎ 212/439-6900 ⊕ www.wollmanskatingrink.com.

JOGGING

All kinds of New Yorkers jog, some with dogs or babies in tow, so you'll always have company on the regular jogging routes. What's not recommended is to set out on a lonely park path at dusk. Jog when and where everybody else does. On Manhattan streets, roughly 20 north–south blocks make a mile.

In Manhattan, Central Park is the busiest spot, specifically along the 1⅗-mi path circling the Jacqueline Kennedy Onassis Reservoir, where you jog in a counterclockwise direction. A runners' lane has been designated along the park roads. A good 1¾-mi route starts at Tavern on the Green along the West Drive, heads south around the bottom of the park to the East Drive, and circles back west on the 72nd Street park road to your starting point; the entire loop road is a hilly 6 mi. Riverside Park, along the Hudson River bank in Manhattan, is glorious at sunset. You can cover 4½ mi by running from West 72nd to 116th Street and back, and the Greenbelt trail extends 4 more miles north to the George Washington Bridge at 181st Street.

Other favorite Manhattan circuits are the Battery Park City esplanade (about 2 mi), which connects to the Hudson River Park (about 1½ mi), and the **East River Esplanade** (just over 3 mi from East 59th to East 125th streets). In Brooklyn try the Brooklyn Heights Promenade (⅓ mi), which faces the Manhattan skyline, or the loop in Prospect Park (3⅓ mi).

STUDENTS IN NEW YORK

New York is home to such major schools as Columbia University, New York University, Fordham University, and the City College of New York. With other colleges scattered throughout the five boroughs, as well as a huge population of public and private high-schoolers, it's no wonder the city is rife with student discounts. Wherever you go, especially museums, sightseeing attractions, and performances, identify yourself as a student up front and ask if a discount is available. However, **be prepared to show your ID** as proof of enrollment and/or age.

A great program for those between the ages of 13 and 18 (or anyone in middle or high school) is High 5 for the Arts. Tickets to all sorts of performances are sold for $5 online, and also at Ticketmaster outlets in the city, including at music stores such as HMV and Tower Records. Tickets are either for a single teen (Friday and weekends) or for a teen and his or her guest of any age (Monday–Thursday). Write or call to receive a free catalog of events, check it out online, or pick a catalog up at any New York public library or at High 5's offices. These $5 tickets cannot be bought over the phone or at the venue box offices. With the $5 museum pass or film-screening pass, a teen can bring a guest of any age to participating museums and movie theaters.

🎫 IDs & Services **High 5 for the Arts** ✉ 1 E. 53rd St., at 5th Ave., Midtown ☎ 212/445-8587 ⊕ www.highfivetix.org. **STA Travel** ✉ 10 Downing St., New York, NY 10014 ☎ 212/627-3111, 800/777-0112 24-hr service center 🖷 212/627-3387 ⊕ www.statravel.com. **Travel Cuts** ✉ 124 Macdougal St., New York, 10012 ☎ 212/674-2887 ⊕ www.travelcuts.com.

SUBWAY TRAVEL

The 714-mi subway system operates 24 hours a day and serves nearly all the places you're likely to visit. It's cheaper than a cab, and during the workweek it's often faster than either taxis or buses. The trains are clean, well lighted, and air-conditioned. Still, the New York subway is hardly problem-free. Many trains are crowded, and the older ones are noisy. Homeless people sometimes take refuge from the elements by riding the trains, and panhandlers head there for a captive audience. Although trains usually run frequently, especially during rush hours, you never know when some incident somewhere on the line may stall traffic. In addition, subway construction sometimes causes delays or limitation of service, especially on weekends.

Most subway entrances are at street corners and are marked by lampposts with an illuminated Metropolitan Transit Authority (MTA) logo or globe-shape green or red lights—green means the station is open 24 hours and red means the station closes at night (though colors don't always correspond to reality). Subway lines are designated by numbers and letters, such as the 3 line or the A line. Some lines run "express" and skip stops, and others are "locals" and make all stops. Each station entrance has a sign indicating the lines that run through the station. Some entrances are also marked "uptown only" or "downtown only." Before entering subway stations, **read the signs carefully.** One of the most frequent mistakes visitors make is taking the train in the wrong direction. Maps of the full subway system are posted in every train car and usually on the subway platform (though these are sometimes out-of-date). You can usually pick up free maps at station booths.

For the most up-to-date information on subway lines, call the MTA's Travel Information Center or visit its Web site. The Web site HopStop is a good source for figuring out the best line to take to reach your destination. Alternatively, ask a station agent.

FARES & TRANSFERS

Subway fare is the same as bus fare:
$2. You can transfer between subway lines
an unlimited number of times at any of the
numerous stations where lines intersect. If
you use a MetroCard (⇨ Public Transportation) to pay your fare, you can also
transfer to intersecting MTA bus routes
for free. Such transfers generally have
time limits of two hours.

PAYING

Pay your subway fare at the turnstile,
using a MetroCard bought at the station
booth or from a vending machine.

SMOKING

Smoking is not allowed on New York City
subways or in subway stations.

🚇 Subway Information **Hopstop** ⊕ www.hopstop.
com. **Metropolitan Transit Authority (MTA) Travel
Information Line** ☎ 718/330–1234, 718/330–4847
for non-English speakers ⊕ www.mta.info. **MTA
Lost Property Office** ☎ 212/712–4500. **MTA Status
information hotline** ☎ 718/243–7777, updated
hourly.

TAXES

The city charges tax on hotel rooms
(13.375%), rental cars (13.375%), and
parking in commercial lots or garages
(18.375%). An additional fee of $3.50 per
unit per day applies to hotel rooms.

SALES TAX

New York City's sales tax of 8.375% applies to almost everything you can buy retail, including restaurant meals.
Prescription drugs and nonprepared food
bought in grocery stores are tax exempt.

TAXIS & CAR SERVICES

There are several differences between taxis
(cabs) and car services, also known as livery cabs. For one thing, a taxi is yellow
and a car-service sedan is not. In addition,
taxis run on a meter, while car services
charge a flat fee. And by law, car services
are not allowed to pick up passengers unless you call for one first.

Taxis can be extremely difficult (if not impossible) to find in many parts of Brooklyn, Queens, the Bronx, and Staten Island.
As a result, you may have no choice but to
call a car service. Always **determine the fee**

beforehand when using a car service sedan;
a 10%–15% tip is customary above that.

Yellow cabs are in abundance almost
everywhere in Manhattan, cruising the
streets looking for fares. They are usually
easy to hail on the street or from a cab
stand in front of major hotels, though
finding one at rush hour or in the rain can
take some time. Even if you're stuck in a
downpour or at the airport, **do not accept
a ride from a gypsy cab.** If a cab is not
yellow and does not have a numbered
aqua-color plastic medallion riveted to the
hood, you could be putting yourself in
danger by getting into the car.

You can see if a taxi is available by checking its rooftop light; if the center panel is
lit and the side panels are dark, the driver
is ready to take passengers. Taxi fares cost
$2.50 for the first ⅕ mi, 40¢ for each ⅕ mi
thereafter, and 20¢ for each minute not in
motion. A $1 surcharge is added to rides
begun 4–8 PM and a 50¢ surcharge is
added between 8 PM and 6 AM.

One taxi can hold a maximum of four passengers (an additional passenger under the
age of seven is allowed if the child sits on
someone's lap). There is no charge for
extra passengers. You must pay any bridge
or tunnel tolls incurred during your trip (a
driver will usually pay the toll himself to
keep moving quickly, but that amount will
be added to the fare when the ride is over).
Taxi drivers expect a 15% to 20% tip.

To avoid unhappy taxi experiences, **try to
know where you want to go and how to
get there before you hail a cab.** A few cab
drivers are dishonest, and not all know the
city as well as they should. Direct your cab
driver by the cross streets of your destination (for instance, "5th Avenue and 42nd
Street"), rather than the numerical address,
which means little to many drivers. Also,
speak simply and clearly to make sure the
driver has heard you correctly—this will
save you time, money, and aggravation. A
quick call to your destination will give you
cross-street information, as will a glance at
a map marked with address numbers.
When you leave the cab, **remember to take
your receipt.** It includes the cab's medallion
number, which can help you track the cab-

bie down in the event that you lose your possessions in the cab.

🚗 Car Reservations **Carmel Car Service** ☎ 212/666-6666 or 800/922-7635 ⊕ www.carmelcarservice.com. **London Towncars** ☎ 212/988-9700 or 800/221-4009 ⊕ www.londontowncars.com. **Dial 7 Car Service** ☎ 212/777-7777 or 800/222-9888 ⊕ www.telavivlimo.com.

TIME

New York operates on eastern standard time. When it's noon in New York it's 9 AM in Los Angeles, 11 AM in Chicago, 5 PM in London, and 3 AM the following day in Sydney.

TIPPING

The customary tipping rate for taxi drivers is 15%–20%, with a minimum of $2; bellhops are usually given $2 per bag in luxury hotels, $1 per bag elsewhere. Hotel maids should be tipped $2 per day of your stay. A doorman who hails or helps you into a cab can be tipped $1–$2. You should also tip your hotel concierge for services rendered; the size of the tip depends on the difficulty of your request, as well as the quality of the concierge's work. For an ordinary dinner reservation or tour arrangements, $3–$5 should do; if the concierge scores seats at a popular restaurant or show or performs unusual services (getting your laptop repaired, finding a good pet-sitter, etc.), $10 or more is appropriate.

Waiters should be tipped 15%–20%, though at higher-end restaurants, a solid 20% is more the norm. Many restaurants add a gratuity to the bill for parties of six or more. Ask what the percentage is if the menu or bill doesn't state it. Tip $1 per drink you order at the bar, though if at an upscale establishment, those $15 martinis might warrant a $2 tip.

TOURS & PACKAGES

GUIDED TOURS

Guided tours are a good option when you don't want to do it all yourself. You travel along with a group (sometimes large, sometimes small), stay in pre-booked hotels, eat with your fellow travelers (sometimes included in the price of your tour, sometimes not), and follow a schedule. But not all guided tours are a "If This Is Tuesday, It Must Be Belgium" kind of experience. A knowledgable guide can take you places that you might never discover on your own, and you may be pushed to see more than you would have otherwise. Tours aren't for everyone, but they can be just the thing for trips to places where making travel arrangements is difficult or time-consuming (particularly when you don't speak the language). Whenever you book a guided tour, find out what's included and what isn't. A "land-only" tour includes all your travel (by bus, in most cases) in the destination, but not necessarily your flights to or even within it. Also, in most cases, prices in tour brochures don't include fees and taxes. And remember that you'll be expected to tip your guide (in cash) at the end of the tour.

VACATION PACKAGES

Packages *are not* guided tours. Packages combine airfare, accommodations, and perhaps a rental car or other extras (theater tickets, guided excursions, boat trips, reserved entry to popular museums, transit passes), but they let you do your own thing. During busy periods, packages may be your only option because flights and rooms may be otherwise sold out. Packages will definitely save you time. They can also save you money, particularly in peak seasons, but—and this is a really big "but"—you should price each part of the package separately to be sure. And be aware that prices advertised on Web sites and in newspapers rarely include service charges or taxes, which can up your costs by hundreds of dollars.

Note that local tourism boards can provide information about lesser-known and small-niche operators that sell packages to just a few destinations. And don't always assume that you can get the best deal by booking everything yourself. Some packages and cruises are sold only through travel agents.

Each year consumers are stranded or lose their money when packagers—even large ones with excellent reputations—go out of business. How can you protect yourself? First, always pay with a credit card; if you have a problem, your credit-card company may help you resolve it. Second, buy trip insurance that covers default. Third, choose a company that belongs to the United States Tour Operators Association, whose members must set aside funds ($1 million) to cover defaults. Finally choose a company that also participates in the Tour Operator Program of the American Society of Travel Agents (ASTA), which will act as mediator in any disputes. You can also check on the tour operator's reputation among travelers by posting an inquiry on one of the Fodors.com forums.

🖪 Organizations **American Society of Travel Agents (ASTA)** ☎ 703/739-2782 or 800/965-2782 24-hr hotline ⊕ www.astanet.com. **United States Tour Operators Association** (USTOA) ☎ 212/599-6599 ⊕ www.ustoa.com.

TRAIN TRAVEL

For information about traveling by subway within New York City, *see* Subway Travel.

Metro-North Commuter Railroad trains take passengers from Grand Central Terminal to points north of New York City, both in New York State and Connecticut. Amtrak trains from across the United States arrive at Penn Station. For trains from New York City to Long Island and New Jersey, take the Long Island Railroad and New Jersey Transit, respectively; both operate from Penn Station. The PATH trains offer service to Newark and Jersey City. All of these trains generally run on schedule, although occasional delays occur. Smoking is not permitted on any train.

🖪 Train Information **Amtrak** ☎ 800/872-7245 ⊕ www.amtrak.com. **Long Island Railroad** ☎ 718/217-5477 ⊕ www.mta.info/lirr. **Metro-North Commuter Railroad** ☎ 212/532-4900 ⊕ www.mta.info/mnr. **New Jersey Transit** ☎ 800/772-2222 ⊕ www.njtransit.com. **PATH** ☎ 800/234-7284 ⊕ www.pathrail.com.

🖪 Train Stations **Grand Central Terminal** ⊠ Park Ave. and E. 42nd St., Midtown East ☎ 212/340-2210 ⊕ www.grandcentralterminal.com. **Penn Station** ⊠ W. 31st to W. 33rd Sts., between 7th and 8th Aves., Midtown West ☎ 212/630-6401.

TRAVEL AGENTS

If you use an agent—brick-and-mortar or virtual—you'll pay a fee for the service. And know that the service you get from some online agents isn't comprehensive. For example Expedia or Travelocity don't search for prices on budget airlines like JetBlue, Southwest, or small foreign carriers. That said, some agents (online or not) *do* have access to fares that are difficult to find otherwise, and the savings can more than make up for any surcharge.

A knowledgeable brick-and-mortar travel agent can be a godsend if you're booking a cruise, a package trip that's not available to you directly, an air pass, or a complicated itinerary including several overseas flights. What's more, travel agents who specialize in a destination may have exclusive access to certain deals and insider information on things such as charter flights. Agents who specialize in types of travelers (senior citizens, gays and lesbians, naturists) or types of trips (cruises, luxury travel, safaris) can also be invaluable.

A top-notch agent planning your trip to Russia will make sure you get the correct visa application and complete it on time; the one booking your cruise may get you a cabin upgrade or arrange to have bottle of champagne chilling in your cabin when you embark. And complain about the surcharges all you like, but when things don't work out the way you'd hoped, it's nice to have an agent to put things right.

🖪 Agent Resources **American Society of Travel Agents** ☎ 703/739-2782 ⊕ www.travelsense.org.
🖪 Online Agents **Expedia** ⊕ www.expedia.com. **Onetravel.com** ⊕ www.onetravel.com. **Orbitz** ⊕ www.orbitz.com. **Priceline.com** ⊕ www.priceline.com. **Travelocity** ⊕ www.travelocity.com.

VISITOR INFORMATION

The Grand Central Partnership (a sort of civic Good Samaritans' group) has installed a number of information booths in and around Grand Central Terminal (there's one near Vanderbilt Ave. and E. 42nd St.). They're loaded with maps and helpful brochures on attractions throughout the city and they're staffed by friendly, knowledgeable, multilingual New Yorkers.

Contact NYC & Company for brochures, subway and bus maps, discount coupons to theaters and attractions, and multilingual information counselors. In addition to its main center near Times Square on 7th Avenue between 52nd and 53rd streets, the bureau also runs kiosks at the south tip of City Hall Park, in Chinatown at the intersection of Canal, Walker, and Baxter streets, and in Harlem at 163 West 125th Street, near Adam Clayton Powell Jr. Boulevard. The Downtown Alliance has information on the area encompassing City Hall south to Battery Park, and from the East River to West Street. For a free booklet listing New York City attractions and tour packages, contact the New York State Division of Tourism.

City Information **Brooklyn Information & Culture Inc. (BRIC)** ⊠ 647 Fulton St., 2nd fl., Brooklyn 11217 ☎ 718/855-7882 ⊕ www.brooklynx.org. **Downtown Alliance** ⊠ 120 Broadway, Suite 3340, between Pine and Thames Sts., Lower Manhattan 10271 ☎ 212/566-6700 ⊕ www.downtownny.com. **Grand Central Partnership** ⊕ www. grandcentralpartnership.org.

NYC & Company Convention & Visitors Bureau ⊠ 810 7th Ave., between W. 52nd and W. 53rd Sts., 3rd fl., Midtown West ☎ 212/484-1222 ⊕ www. nycvisit.com. **Times Square Information Center** ⊠ 1560 Broadway, between 46th and 47th Sts., Midtown West ☎ 212/768-1560 ⊕ www. timessquarenyc.org.

Statewide Information **New York State Division of Tourism** ☎ 518/474-4116 or 800/225-5697 ⊕ www.iloveny.com.

WEB SITES

We're really proud of our Web site: Fodors.com is a great place to begin any journey. Scan Travel Wire for suggested itineraries, travel deals, restaurant and hotel openings, and other up-to-the-minute info. Check out Booking to research prices and book plane tickets, hotel rooms, rental cars, and vacation packages. Head to Talk for on-the-ground pointers from travelers who frequent our message boards. You can also link to loads of other travel-related resources.

After your trip, be sure to rate the places you visited and share your experiences and travel tips with us and other Fodorites in Travel Ratings and Talk on www.fodors. com.

New York Citysearch supplies comprehensive, searchable events listings to help you find out what's going on around town. Check out Menupages for reasonably up-to-date, printable menus of over 4,500 Manhattan restaurants. The Official New York City Web site has plenty of links to agencies, services, and cultural activities. The cable channel New York 1's Web site is frequently updated with the city's breaking stories. To learn about the city in greater depth, go to the New York Public Library's site. The Gothamist blog is a good way to find out what New Yorkers are up to. The *New York Times* keeps online reviews of restaurants and current movies and theater, as well as music, dance, art listings, and show times. To get directions to New York destinations using the bus or subway, consult HopStop.

Web Addresses **Fodor's.com** ⊕ www.fodors. com. **Gothamist** ⊕ www.gothamist.com. **HopStop** ⊕ www.hopstop.com. **Menupages** ⊕ www. menupages.com. **New York Citysearch** ⊕ www. nycitysearch.com. **New York 1** ⊕ www.ny1.com. **New York Public Library** ⊕ www.nypl.org. *New York Times* ⊕ www.nytimes.com. **Official New York City Web site** ⊕ www.nyc.gov.

INDEX

PHOTO CREDITS

Logan/age fotostock. 212 (bottom), *Jerry L. Thompson*. 214-15, *Ken Ross/viestiphoto.com*. 216 (top left and right), *Ken Ross/viestiphoto.com*. 216 (bottom), *Dennis Finnin/AMNH*. 218, *Ken Ross/viestiphoto. com*. 219, *Dennis Finnin/AMNH*. 220, *Brooks Walker*. 221, *Renaud Visage/age fotostock*. 222 (top), *Renaud Visage/age fotostock*. 222 (center and bottom), *Metropolitan Museum of Art*. 224 (top), *Renaud Visage/age fotostock*. 224 (bottom), *Wild Bill Studio/Metropolitan Museum of Art*. 225, *Ken Ross/ viestiphoto.com*. 226 (top and bottom), *Metropolitan Museum of Art*. 227, *Ken Ross/viestiphoto.com*. 228, *Doug Scott/age fotostock*. 229, *Geoffrey Clements*. 230, *Ken Ross/viestiphoto.com*. **Chapter 15: The Performing Arts:** 253, *Carol Rosegg*. 254, *Joe Viesti/viestiphoto.com*. **Chapter 16: Nightlife:** 275, *Pictorial Press/Alamy*. 276, kriskat@afterglowpix.com. 282, *Lebrecht Music and Arts Photo Library/Alamy*. 283 (top and bottom), *Michael Belardo/Alamy*. 284 (top), kriskat@afterglowpix.com. 284 (bottom), *Gustavo Andrade/age fotostock*. 285 (top), *Carlos Davila/age fotostock*. 285 (bottom), *Happy Valley*. 286 (top), *Grant Winston*. 286 (bottom), *foodfolio/Alamy*. 287, *Café des Artistes*. 288, *Mike Faivre/Arlene's Grocery*. 289 (top), *Mike Faivre/Arlene's Grocery*. 289 (bottom left), *Nicole Fournier*. 289 (bottom right), *Ted Pink/Alamy*. **Chapter 17: Shopping:** 311, *Bruno Perousse/age fotostock*. 312, *Richard Levine/ Alamy*. 318, *Piero Ribelli*. 319 (left), *Piero Ribelli*. 319 (right), *Jonathan Adler*. 328 (top), *Yadid Levy/ Alamy*. 328 (bottom), *Sigerson Morrison*. 329, *Yadid Levy/Alamy*. 338 (top), *Piero Ribelli*. 338 (bottom), *Louis Vuitton*. 339, *Piero Ribelli*. 348-49, *Piero Ribelli*. 358 (top), *Piero Ribelli*. 358 (bottom), *Susan Rosenberg Jones*. 359, *Piero Ribelli*. 368 (top), *Las Venus*. 368 (bottom), *Sugar Sweet Sunshine Bakery*. 369 (top), *Frock*. 369 (bottom), *lowereastsideny.com*. **Chapter 18: Where to Eat:** 379, *Jeff Greenberg/age fotostock*. 380, *Ace Stock Limited/Alamy*. 382, *Alex Segre/Alamy*. 383, *Black Star/Alamy*. 391, *Lucia Pizzani*. 392, *Saxpix.com/age fotostock*. 393, *Ken Ross/viestiphoto.com*. 394 (top), *Union Square Hospitality Group*. 394 (bottom), *Bo Zaunders/viestiphoto.com*. **Chapter 19: Where to Stay:** 463, *Arcaid/Alamy*. 464, *On the Ave Hotel*. 466, *The Peninsula New York*.

NOTES

NOTES

NOTES

NOTES

NOTES

NOTES

ABOUT OUR WRITERS

New York native Lynne Arany is well-practiced in the art of uncovering the less-known gems in New York's cultural scene. Author of the *Little Museums* guidebook, contributor to the *New York Times,* and freelance travel writer and editor, she's covered areas from Scotland to the southwestern United States. But she most enjoys the serendipity of the search here at home.

Michelle Delio has lived in all five boroughs and now calls Manhattan home. She loved having a good reason to reacquaint herself with all of the city's most interesting spots—and discover new favorites—while researching and writing the Queens, Staten Island, Upper West Side, and Times Square/Midtown neighborhood profiles. Michelle is a regular contributor to *Fodors.com* and contributed to *Fodor's Guide to the Da Vinci Code.*

Melissa Klurman was happily able to indulge her passion for Frette sheets, plush robes, and deep soaking tubs while checking out the hotel scene for the Where to Stay chapter. A former Fodor's editor, Melissa is a freelance writer who has contributed to Fodor's *CityGuide New York* and *Up-Close New York* in addition to her other job as mom to two-year-old Aidan.

When not writing about her favorite cities, New York and Berlin, former Fodor's editor Christina Knight shares their quirks and histories as a professional tour guide. Why she can't kick the Big Apple: the grandeur of the New York Public Library (42nd Street), the disco Skate Circle in Central Park, and the view of the Empire State Building from DUMBO.

Nightlife updater, proud Brooklynite, and sometime rock musician Sara Marcus writes about music and culture for *Time Out New York* and the *Advocate,* all while working towards a master's degree in creative writing at Columbia University. After nearly four years of obsessive concert-going in the Big Apple, she's grateful that her travel-writing debut gives her the opportunity to tell the world what she really thinks about every music venue in the city.

Meryl Pearlstein uncovered the ghosts of the city for the architecture sights of the guide. New York is a popular topic in Meryl's articles in *New York Magazine, Boston Herald* and *Global Traveler,* and she energetically shares her city fever with in-depth looks at Central Park and Harlem. When not traveling to promote hotels, resorts or countries, Meryl explores the NYC arts and restaurant scene with her husband and two sons.

Shopping chapter updater Sandra Ramani is *likethis* with the city's store and spa scenes, having served as Shopping & Beauty Editor for both *Citysearch New York* and NewYorkMagazine.com. Now on the road a lot as a travel writer (outlets have included the *New York Daily News, Fodors.com, Travel + Leisure* and *The New York Times*) she still loves catching that first from-the-airport glimpse of her beloved Manhattan.

For more than five years, Tom Steele has covered the New York entertainment and restaurant scenes for *Fodor's New York City, Time Out New York,* and *Out* magazine. He lives in Manhattan.